MW00769173

Virtual Machine Design and Implementation in C/C++

Bill Blunden

Wordware Publishing, Inc.

Library of Congress Cataloging-in-Publication Data

Blunden, Bill
    Virtual machine design and implementation in C/C++ / by Bill Blunden.
       p. cm.
    Includes bibliographical references and index.
    ISBN 1-55622-903-8 (pbk.)
    1. Virtual computer systems.   2. C++ (Computer program language).   I. Title.

    QA76.9.V5 B59 2002
    005.4'3--dc21
                                      2002016755
                                        CIP

ISBN 1-55622-903-8

10 9 8 7 6 5 4 3 2 1
0202

All inquiries for volume purchases of this book should be addressed to Wordware Publishing, Inc., at the above address. Telephone inquiries may be made by calling:

(972) 423-0090

To my parents, who bought me a computer
in the sixth grade and encouraged me to study hard

To my nephew Theo, the life of the party

To Danny Solow and Art Obrock, who
told me the truth about life as a mathematician

To Art Bell, whose talk radio show helped
keep me awake while I wrote this book's final manuscript

About the Author

Bill Blunden has been obsessed with systems software since his first exposure to the DOS debug utility in 1983. His single-minded pursuit to discover what actually goes on under the hood has led him to program the 8259 interrupt controller and become an honorable member of the triple-fault club. After obtaining a BA in mathematical physics and an MS in operations research, Bill was unleashed upon the workplace. It was at an insurance company in the beautiful city of Cleveland, plying his skills as an actuary, that Bill first got into a fistfight with a cranky IBM mainframe. The scuffle was over a misguided COBOL program. Bloody but not beaten, Bill decided that groking software beat crunching numbers. This led Bill to a major ERP player in the Midwest, where he developed CASE tools in Java, performed technology research, and was assailed by various Control Data veterans. Having a quad-processor machine with 2 GB of RAM at his disposal, Bill was hard pressed to find any sort of reason to abandon his ivory tower. There were days when Bill used to disable paging and run on pure SDRAM. Nevertheless, the birth of his nephew forced him to make a pilgrimage out West to Silicon Valley. Currently on the peninsula, Bill survives rolling power blackouts and earthquakes, and is slowly recovering from his initial bout with COBOL.

Contents

Contents

Contents

Acknowledgments

Several people have contributed either directly or indirectly in the writing of this book. I would like to begin by thanking Jim Hill for giving me the opportunity to write this book. I have had several bad experiences with acquisition editors in the past whom I felt were less than honest. Jim has been straightforward and direct with me throughout the entire process and I truly appreciate it.

I would also like to thank Barry Brey, who agreed to be my technical reviewer, and as such has read through every single line of my book. I started e-mailing Barry several years ago with all sorts of obscure questions, and he has always done his best to answer them. Barry has written a multitude of books on the Intel 80x86 platform. He has been documenting and explaining the x86 processor since it arrived on the hardware scene. Because of his depth of knowledge, I knew that Barry's advice would be invaluable.

Finally, I would like to thank Paula Price and Wes Beckwith for doing a lot of grunt work and helping to coordinate everything so that the whole process ran smoothly. Thanks a lot, guys.

Introduction

"Eat flaming death, minicomputer mongrels!"
—IPM Thug

As a former physicist, I am painfully aware that doing any sort of ground-breaking experiment in an established field like particle physics typically requires the backing of a federal budget. Fortunately, this is not the case with computer science. For a couple hundred dollars, you can purchase a refurbished PC. For $50 more, you can buy a set of development tools and put yourself in business. You can actually do serious work on a cheap machine using readily available tools. This is exactly how I made the switch from mathematical physics to computer science in late 1994, when I salvaged an orphaned 80386 from a dumpster outside my apartment building. I had been in the process of filling out applications for various graduate programs in physics. After replacing its hard drive, I was able to revive the worn machine. Right then and there I decided to tear up my applications and study computer science. I consider the $200 that I spent for a hard drive to be one of the best investments I ever made.

In essence, computer science is still a very accessible field of study. It's extremely easy to sit down and play with different ideas and approaches. The personal computer is a superb laboratory. Naturally, I could not resist the urge to do a little empirical tinkering myself, particularly after devoting seven years of my life to physics, where state-of-the-art experimental equipment costs millions of dollars. This book is basically the published version of the journal that I have maintained for the past two years. The material included within these pages covers the design and implementation of the HEC run-time system.

The name HEC is borrowed from the "CPU Wars" comic strip, which depicts the struggle of employees at the Human Engineered Computer company (HEC) against a hostile takeover by the totalitarian thugs from Impossible to Purchase Machines (IPM). During the Reagan years of the 1980s, I was in high school. I completely missed two very pivotal decades of software history. I have never programmed with punch cards or entered commands at a teletype machine. I don't know any software engineers in my generation who have ever worked on a minicomputer. In fact, back in 1984 the only real business computer that I was able to get my hands on was an 8088 IBM PC. Christening my run-time system with the name *HEC* is my attempt to remind younger engineers of who preceded them and also to pay homage to the deep geeks who programmed in hex codes and paved the way for the Internet boom of the 1990s.

Anyone who developed software in the 1960s and 1970s probably understands that the fictitious corporate names HEC and IPM are thinly veiled references to Digital Equipment Corporation (DEC) and International Business Machines (IBM). In 1961 DEC introduced the PDP-1, and ushered in the age of minicomputers. Up until that point, computers were monolithic, expensive structures that were cloistered away in their own buildings and usually protected by a division of armed palace guards. Submitting a job to a mainframe was like visiting the Vatican to see the pope. At least a couple of older engineers have told me all sorts of horror stories about having to sign up for computer access at three o'clock in the morning.

The minicomputer changed all this. The minicomputer was smaller, much cheaper, and offered a convenient time-sharing environment. Rather than submit your punch cards to the exalted mainframe operators, you could log on to a minicomputer and avoid all the hassle of groveling and waiting. In contrast to the mainframe, minicomputers were friendly and accessible to the average developer. The popularity the minicomputer enjoyed probably gave IBM salespeople the willies.

 NOTE DEC was not the only company that stole IBM's thunder. In 1964, Control Data Corporation presented the CDC 6600 to the world. It was, hands down, the fastest and most powerful computer available at the time. It made IBM's top of the line look like a lightweight. This is not surprising, considering that the man who led the development was Seymour Cray. The CDC 6600 initially sold for $7 million, and Control Data would end up selling about 50 of them. I have been told that high-level execs at IBM were upset that Seymour had done such an effective job of outshining them. Supposedly, IBM put up a paper tiger and told the business world to wait for its supercomputer. Six months later, it became obvious that IBM had been bluffing in an attempt to rain on the 6600's parade.

One might even speculate that DEC's introduction of the minicomputer was partially responsible for the birth of the Unix operating system. In 1968, Ken Thompson, a researcher at Bell Labs, stumbled across a little-used DEC PDP-7 and decided it would be a neat platform for developing a game called *Space Travel*. Ken was a veteran of the MULTICS project. MULTICS (which stands for MULTIplexed Information and Computing Service) was a computer project which involved Bell Labs, General Electric, and MIT. The problem with MULTICS was that it attempted to provide operating system features which the hardware at the time was not really capable of supporting. Bell Labs dropped out of the project, leaving poor Ken with a lot of spare time on his hands. Although he had initially wanted to use the PDP-7 to implement *Space Travel*, Ken had been bitten by the operating system bug. The urge to build an operating system is not the kind of compulsion that ever goes away. Ken decided that he would scale back on the requirements of MULTICS and write a smaller version he could call his own. Shortly afterwards, Unix was born. The name Unix is a slightly modified version of the original, which was UNICS (UNIplexed Information and Computing Service). Windows people have been known to mockingly call it "eunuchs," probably because of the hobbled user interface.

It is now 2002 and DEC is, sadly, nothing more than a memory. After being swallowed up by Compaq in the late 1990s, the DEC brand name was gradually snuffed out.

Approach

The HEC run-time system, as described in this book, consists of an execution engine, a machine-level debugger, an assembler, and an assorted variety of other development tools. I built the HEC run-time system from scratch. During my journey, I was confronted with several architectural issues. The manner in which I addressed these issues ended up defining the programs I constructed. Rather than merely present you with a sequential blow-by-blow account of my implementation and then dump some source code in your lap, I thought it would be instructive to use a different methodology.

Professional mathematicians follow the standard operating procedure (SOP) of stating a proposition, providing a proof, and then offering an example. Most mathematics graduate students don't even have to think about it; they've seen it so many times that the proposition-proof-example approach is automatic. I decided to adopt a similar approach that allows me to explain architectural issues with equal rigor and consistency. The SOP which I formulated involves three fundamental steps:

1. Present a design problem and the necessary background.

2. Provide a solution.

3. Discuss alternatives and their relative merits.

I will spend the majority of Chapter 2 applying this methodology. I start each subject by providing an overview of fundamental concepts and theory. This sets the stage for an explanation of my decisions and enables the reader to understand the context in which I dealt with particular problems. In fact, I'm sure that some readers will scoff at some of my decisions unless they are familiar with the underlying constraints that resulted from my design goals.

Finally, every decision involves tradeoffs. If you implement a list data structure with an array, you sacrifice flexibility for access speed. If you implement a list data structure with a linked list, you sacrifice speed for the ability to increase the size of the list. There are rarely solutions that are optimal under every circumstance. This is a recurring theme in computer science which will rear its head several times in this book. As a result, I follow up each design decision with an analysis of how I benefited from a particular decision and what I sacrificed.

 NOTE This theme is not limited to the field of computer science. Any scenario where constraints and demands are placed on limited resources results in a collection of reciprocal tradeoffs.

Because a run-time system, by necessity, includes functionality that is normally assumed by the native operating system and hardware platform, the background material I cover has been gathered from a variety of sources. I have tried to make the book as complete and self-contained as possible. Readers who desire to investigate topics further may look into the references supplied at the end of each chapter.

Intended Use

This book is directed towards two groups of people:

- Systems engineers
- Students of computer science

Systems engineers will find this book useful because it offers them an alternative to the tyranny of computer hardware vendors. As hardware architecture becomes more complicated, engineers will be confronted with greater challenges in an effort to keep pace with Moore's Law. For example, current processors based on the Explicitly Parallel Instruction Computing (EPIC) scheme pose a much more daunting challenge to the compiler writer than the processors of the 1980s. To support features like instruction-level parallelism, much of the responsibility for managing efficient execution has been shifted from the processor to the shoulders of the systems engineer (whom I do not envy). Implementing predication to avoid mispredict penalties and generating code that uses speculation is an awful lot of work. In fact, it's enough to give any engineer a nosebleed.

To make matters worse, computer processors and their native instruction sets are temporal by nature. By the time a stable, efficient compiler has been released into production, and has gained acceptance as a standard tool, the engineers who designed it need to start reworking the back end to accommodate the latest advances in hardware. System software people, like me, are constantly in a race to play keep-up with the hardware folks, and it's a major pain.

There are alternatives to the gloomy prospect of continuously rewriting the back end of your development tools. Specifically, you have the option of targeting a virtual machine. Unlike a physical computer, a virtual machine is really just a specification. It is a collection of rules that can be implemented in any way that the software engineer deems fit. This effectively makes a virtual machine platform independent. A virtual machine can exist on any platform and be written in any computer language, as long as it obeys the rules of the specification. I constructed the HEC execution engine with this in mind. My primary goal was to create a stationary target that would save systems engineers from rewriting their development tools every two years. I also wanted to present a run-time system that would be straightforward and accessible to the average software engineer, much in the same way that DEC's PDP-11 was accessible to programmers in the 1970s.

Students who want to get a better understanding of how a computer functions without delving into the gory details of direct memory access or interval timers will also find this book useful. Regardless of which hardware platform a system is based on, the fundamental mechanism for executing programs is the same: Instructions are loaded from secondary storage into memory and then executed by the processor. This book invests a lot of effort into explaining this mechanism. The result is that the student is able to take this basic understanding and use it as a frame of reference when faced with a new system.

In addition, this book provides a solid explanation of assembly language programming. While developing software strictly in assembly language is a poor use of resources, an in-depth understanding of assembly-level programming offers certain insights into topics that cannot really be obtained in any other way. For example, sometimes the only way to discern the finer details of a compiler's optimizer is to examine what goes on in the basement, where the processor executes machine-encoded instructions.

"Pay no attention to that man behind the curtain...."
—Wizard of Oz

My own initial understanding of what Borland's Turbo C compiler did underneath the hood was very poor. I usually just wrote my code, invoked the compiler, closed my eyes, and crossed my fingers. When I felt it was safe, I would open my eyes and peruse the results. It was only after I started taking a look at Turbo C's assembly code listings that I was rewarded with a better grasp of what happened behind the scenes. This, in turn, allowed me to beat the compiler's optimizer at its own game on several occasions.

Prerequisites

This book assumes that you are fluent in the C and C++ programming languages. If you are not familiar with C and C++, and you have any sort of latent interest in systems engineering, I would encourage you to learn these languages as soon as you can. C is the language of choice for implementing system software. It is both a lightweight and versatile language which provides access to a number of low-level operations, but also abstracts the computer's operation enough to make porting easy.

C++ is an extension of C that allows more complicated problems to be addressed using what is known as the object-oriented paradigm. C++ is one of the three big object-oriented languages (Smalltalk, C++, and Java). I mention a couple of books at the end of this introduction which may be of use to those of you who do not speak C or C++.

Learning C, in particular, is a necessary rite of passage for anyone who wants to do systems engineering. The primary reason for this is that the Unix operating system has traditionally been implemented in C. The first version of Unix was implemented by Ken Thompson on a PDP-7 in assembler. After several thousand lines, any assembly program can become a real challenge to maintain. The fact that Ken was able to pull this off at all is a testimony to his fortitude as a programmer. Realizing that porting an operating system written in assembler was no fun, Ken joined heads with Dennis Ritchie and Brian Kernighan to create C. In 1973, the Unix kernel was rewritten in C for DEC's renowned PDP-11. If you think C is an anachronism that has been supplanted by more contemporary languages, think again. Take a look at the source code for the Linux operating system kernel; it's free, readily available all over the Internet, and almost entirely written in C.

Organization

This book examines both the philosophical motivation behind HEC's architecture and the actual implementation. In doing so, the design issues that presented themselves will be dissected and analyzed. I truly believe that a picture is worth a thousand words, so I included a diagram or illustration whenever I thought it was appropriate. Sections of source code are also present throughout the text.

This book is divided into three parts.

Part I — Overview The first two chapters lay the foundation for the rest of the book. Chapter 1 traces the historical development of computing technology and the requirements that this evolution has produced. In Chapter 1, I also present a set of design objectives that define the nature of HEC. In Chapter 2, I sketch out the basic facilities available to the HEC run-time system and the constraints that directed me towards certain solutions.

Part II — The HEC Virtual Machine In Chapters 3 and 4, I explain the operation of the HEC virtual machine and debugger. The HEC virtual machine is actually much less complicated than the HEC assembler, so these chapters are a good warm-up for later material. Chapter 3 covers the operation of the HEC virtual machine. Chapter 4 entails an exhaustive analysis of the debugger. The debugger is embedded within the virtual machine, so these two chapters are closely related.

Part III — HEC Assembly In the final four chapters, I introduce and discuss topics associated with the HEC assembler. I begin in Chapter 5 by investigating the HEC assembler itself. HEC's interface to the native operating system is provided by a set of interrupts. Chapter 6 is devoted to enumerating and describing these interrupts. The proper use of HEC's assembly language is explained in Chapter 7. Chapter 8 provides some thoughts on how object-oriented constructs can be implemented in terms of the HEC assembly language.

Companion CD-ROM

Software engineering is not a spectator sport. Eventually you will have to get your hands dirty. The extent to which you do so is up to you. For those of you who are content to target and use HEC, I have included a set of binaries on the companion CD-ROM. For those of you who want to muck about in the source code, I have included the source code to all the binaries.

I live in California and subsist on a limited, private research budget (i.e., my job). Thus, I did my initial implementation on Windows. I expect to hear gasps of dismay from the audience, and I can sympathize with them. However, I chose Windows primarily because I think it is easier to use than KDE or GNOME. The alternative would have been to purchase Sun hardware, which I can't afford. This does not mean that HEC is stuck on Windows. Porting the run-time system is fairly straightforward and discussed in Chapter 8.

Feedback

Nobody is perfect. However, that does not mean that one should not aspire to perfection. For the most part, learning through direct experience is the best way to obtain intimate knowledge of a subject. Hindsight is always 20/20, so the goal should be to implement enough code so that you gain hindsight.

There's an ancient Oriental game named "Go," which is so fraught with complexity that it takes years of careful study to become proficient. The primary advice to beginners is to "hurry up and lose." This is the same advice I would give to software engineers. Make plenty of mistakes while you're young. Most managers expect young software engineers to screw up anyway.

This is the advice that I tried to follow while constructing HEC. A couple of years ago, I dove into the implementation and corrected flaws after I recognized them. If asked to do it all over again, I know that there are a number of changes that I would make. Alas, eventually you have to pull the trigger and release your code.

If you discover an error in this book, please drop me a line and let me know. If I had money, I could offer an award like Don Knuth (pronounced Ka-Nooth). He places a bounty of $2.56 on each new error that is found in his books (32 cents for useful suggestions). He even goes to the extreme of suggesting that you fund your book purchase by ferreting out errors. Unfortunately, the high cost of living in California keeps me in a constant state of poverty (I don't know how Don does it). The best I can do is offer my thanks and perhaps mention your name in the next edition. You may send corrections, suggestions, and invective diatribes to me at:

Bill Blunden
c/o Wordware Publishing, Inc.
2320 Los Rios Blvd., Suite 200
Plano, Texas 75074

References

Andres, Charles. "CPU Wars." 1980: http://e-pix.com/CPUWARS/cpuwars.html.

This comic strip is an interesting dose of 1960s software culture. Anyone born after 1969 should read this strip, just to see what they missed while they were infants.

Intel. *IA-64 Architecture Software Developer's Manual, Volume 1: IA-64 Application Architecture*. Order Number 245317-001, January 2000. http://www.intel.com.

This is the first volume of a four-volume set on Intel's upcoming 64-bit processor. This volume, in particular, discusses some of the issues with regard to compiler design. After skimming through this volume, you'll understand why compiler design for IA-64 processors is such a complicated task.

Maxwell, Scott. *Linux Core Kernel Commentary.* The Coriolis Group, 1999. ISBN: 1576104699.

An in-depth look at the basic process management scheme implemented by Linux. It is also a very graphic example of how C is used to construct a production-quality operating system. This is definitely not something you can read in one sitting.

Ritchie, Dennis M. "The Development of the C Language." Association for Computing Machinery, Second History of Programming Languages conference, April 1993.

_____. "The Evolution of the Unix Time-sharing System." *AT&T Bell Laboratories Technical Journal* 63 No. 6 Part 2, October 1984. pp. 1577-93.

Schildt, Herbert. *C: The Complete Reference.* Osborne McGraw-Hill, 2000. ISBN: 0072121246.

This book is for people who have little or no programming experience and want to learn C. It's a fairly gentle introduction by an author who has a gift for explaining difficult concepts.

_____. *C++ from the Ground Up.* Osborne McGraw-Hill, 1994. ISBN: 0078819695.

This is the book you should read after reading Herbert's book on C.

van der Linden, Peter. *Expert C Programming: Deep C Secrets.* Prentice Hall, 1994. ISBN: 0131774298.

This is a truly great book. A lot of the things Peter discusses are subtle issues that separate the masters from the pedestrians.

Overview

History and Goals

Setting the Stage

In 1965, Gordon Moore predicted that every 18 to 24 months, the number of transistors that could be put on a chip would double. This observation evolved into a heuristic known as *Moore's Law.* Gordon's rule of thumb proved relatively accurate and serves as a basis for predictions about where transistor dimensions are headed.

 ASIDE   If the number of transistors in a given processor doubles every 18 months, this means that the linear dimensions of a transistor are cut in half every three years. In 1989, Intel came out with the 80486 chip, which had transistors that were on the scale of 1 micron (a human hair is about 100 microns wide). By crunching through the math (take a look at Figure 1-1), it becomes obvious that Moore's Law will hit a wall in under 40 years. This is because an electron needs a path at least three atoms wide. In a path less than three atoms wide, the laws of quantum mechanics take over. This means that electrons stop acting like particles and start acting like escaped convicts. Electrons do not like being confined. If you clamp down too hard on them, they rebel and tunnel through things, like Clint Eastwood in the movie *Alcatraz.* Given that IBM has recently discovered a way to use carbon nanotubes as semiconductors, we may be well on our way to manufacturing transistors which are several atoms wide. So, if I'm lucky, maybe I will get to see Moore's Law reach its limit before I'm senile.

Moore's Law

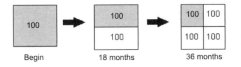

If the number of transistors in a CPU doubles every 18 months, then the linear length of a transistor is cut in half every 3 years.

1 micron = 10^{-6} meters = length of a bacterium
1 angstrom = 10^{-10} meters = .00001 microns = diameter of hydrogen atom

$N(t) = (0.5)^{t/3}$ = length of a transistor, in microns, (t) years after 1989
$N(36) = 0.0002$ microns = 2 angstroms wide in 2025

Figure 1-1

Hardware has not only gotten smaller, it has also gotten cheaper. With the emergence of cheap, sufficiently powerful computers, there has been a gradual move away from the centralized models provided by traditional mainframes towards distributed, network-based architectures.

In the 1950s such things were unheard of. The market for computers was assumed to be around…oh, I don't know…about six. Computers were huge, lumbering giants like something out of the movie *The Forbidden Planet*. Back then, when they performed a smoke test, it was literally a smoke test. The engineers turned the machine on and looked to see where the smoke was coming from.

The trend towards distributing processor workload actually began in 1961 when Digital Equipment Corporation (DEC) introduced the PDP-1. This event marks the start of the minicomputer revolution. Medium-sized companies that could not afford a mainframe bought *minicomputers*, which offered comparable performance on a smaller scale. Or, if a company that already owned a mainframe wanted to increase throughput without purchasing a larger mainframe, they would offload some of the mainframe's work to a departmental minicomputer. Regardless of how they were put to use, they were a small fraction of the cost of a room-sized computer and sold like crazy. The recurring theme that keeps rearing its head is one of *accessibility*.

This shift in processing, produced by offloading work to cheaper hardware, became even more pronounced after the IBM personal computer made its debut in 1981. The proliferation of personal computers (also known as *microcomputers*, or *PCs*), and resulting decrease in popularity of the minicomputer, is often referred to as the "attack of the killer microcomputers." The new battle cry was: "No one will survive the attack of the killer micros!"

I know an engineer who worked at Unisys back when mainframes still ruled the earth. He used to despise having to sign up for development time on his department's mainframe. Instead, he moved his source code onto an 8088 IBM PC and did as much work there as he could. The reason behind this was simple: Working on his own PC gave him a degree of control he did not have otherwise. The microcomputer empowered people. It gave them a small plot of RAM and a few kilobytes of disk storage they could call their own. This was a breath of fresh air to engineers who were used to surrendering all their control to a surly mainframe operator.

Using the PC as a server-side workhorse really didn't take off until 1996 when Microsoft came out with Windows NT 4.0. Before 1996, Intel's hardware didn't have enough muscle to handle server-side loads and Windows NT 3.51 was not mature as a product. Eventually, however, Intel and Microsoft were able to work together to come up with a primitive enterprise server. There were more sophisticated Unix variants that ran on the PC, like FreeBSD and Linux. The Berkeley people, unfortunately, did not have a marketing machine like Microsoft, and Linux had not yet gained much of a following. By early 1997, most of the Enterprise Resource Planning (ERP) vendors had either ported or had started porting their application suites to Windows NT. This was an irrefutable sign that NT was gaining attention as an alternative at the enterprise level.

ASIDE   DEC once again played an indirect part in the rise of the desktop computer. When Bill Gates wanted to begin development on Windows NT, he hired Dave Cutler who had done extensive work on operating system design at...you guessed it, DEC.

The latest incarnation of the Windows operating system, Windows XP, was released in October of 2001. There is a version that targets Intel's 64-bit Itanium processor. Itanium was supposed to be Intel's next big thing. Traditionally, the high-end server market has been dominated by the likes of Hewlett Packard, Sun Microsystems, and IBM. With its 32-bit processors, Intel was forced to eat with the kiddies. Itanium was touted as the vehicle that would allow Intel to move into the high-end server market and compete with the other 64-bit architectures. However, with Itanium's clock speed of 733 to 800 MHz and high price (starting at $1,177), I think that Itanium was doomed before it hit the market.

The close collaboration between Intel and Microsoft has come to be known as the Wintel conspiracy. The strongest motivator behind the adoption of Wintel-based servers by CIOs is the desire to minimize total cost of ownership. The trick is to take a large group of inexpensive Wintel servers (Intel servers running Windows) and allow them to cooperate so that the responsibility for a workload can be divided among the machines. This is called *clustering*. A collection of such servers is also known as a *cluster* or *server farm*.

Clustering is a relatively unsophisticated way to provide scalability and reliability. If a machine fails, for whatever reason, the other machines in the cluster can compensate while repairs are made. If data throughput starts to degrade, the problem can be addressed by adding more servers to the cluster. Because the Wintel machines used to build a server farm are comparatively cheaper than their mainframe counterparts, adding new nodes to the cluster is not seen as an impediment.

Figure 1-2 displays the server farm arrangement at E*trade, a well-known online bank. HTTP-based Internet traffic (i.e., a browser client somewhere on the Net) is filtered through a firewall and then hits a load balancer. Using a round-robin algorithm, the load balancer picks a web server to initiate a session with the client. Transactions initiated from the client execute their business logic on a set of application servers. Client transactions are completed when data is committed to an array of database servers. E*trade performs most of the clustering on hardware from Sun Microsystems, even though its actual portal to the stock market is provided by a mainframe.

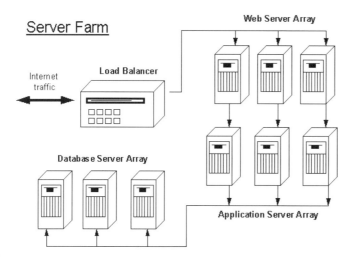

Figure 1-2

Mainframe pundits will argue that relying on mainframe technology is still a better solution. A single mainframe can do the work of several hundred commodity servers. Not only does this save on real estate, but it also saves on electricity. Over the course of a year, this kind of cost discrepancy can become conspicuous. Especially in California, which has suffered from a rash of power shortages and rolling blackouts.

Mainframes also tend to have a higher level of reliability and security at both the hardware and software level. This is both a function of the mindset of the mainframe architects and the technology they employ. When a mainframe crashes, it is treated like a major catastrophe by the manufacturer. Typically, a mainframe vendor will maintain an electronic link to every mainframe they sell, in an effort to provide monitoring services. Responding to a problem costs money and time. Hence, a lot more effort is spent on detecting software problems and recovering from them gracefully.

Traditionally, mainframes have also been the exclusive domain of an advanced technology known as *dynamic partitioning*, which allows system resources to be reallocated at run time to accommodate changing application workloads. This allows mainframes to sustain a higher level of performance for transaction and I/O-heavy operations. Dynamic partitioning is the type of intricate technology that puts mainframe operating systems on the same level as rocket science.

In general, mainframes are run in a highly managed and controlled environment, which is to say that the operator, not the program, decides what kind of resources a program will use (memory, processor allowance, etc.). A runaway program on a mainframe would never, ever, bring the entire machine down. Memory protection is strictly enforced and usually built into the hardware. In fact, some IBM mainframes are reported to have had uptimes in excess of 20 years! My Windows 2000 box, on the other hand, crashed last night while I was backing up files.

The idea of replacing a farm of servers with a mainframe has been labeled as *server consolidation*. It is also interesting to note that the term "mainframe" is no longer used.

Companies that manufacture mainframes have been calling their mainframes *enterprise servers*.

The punchline is that mainframes are not just big, fast machines. Clustering a bunch of low-budget servers together to get the equivalent processing power will still not get you mainframe performance. This is because mainframes are all about reliability and tightly managed execution, 24 hours a day, seven days a week, for years at a time. Microsoft has decided to appeal to the average consumer by investing a lot of effort in building an impressive user interface. They have paid for this decision by shipping an operating system that crashes far more frequently than a mainframe system.

Nevertheless, purchasing a mainframe is a <u>huge</u> investment. In a situation where a CIO has to get things done on a limited budget, being inexpensive is the great equalizer for the Wintel machine. You probably won't find many new organizations that can afford to make the down payment on a mainframe. It's far easier, cheaper, and faster to start off with a small cluster of inexpensive servers and increase the cluster's size as capacity demands grows.

As Wintel machines are cheap and readily available, the phenomenon of Wintel in the enterprise is very much a grass roots movement. By dominating the low end, Wintel has been able to slowly bootstrap itself into the enterprise scene. A Wintel box is a computer that almost anyone can afford. As a result, there is a whole generation of system admins who have been born and raised on Wintel. A college undergraduate who owns a couple of beat-up, secondhand Wintel boxes can hit the ground running in a business that is Windows-centric. This makes it easier for companies to fill positions because less training is required.

It's something that has happened many times before. Breakthroughs in manufacturing and technology lower the barriers to entry. Companies that could not afford the previous solutions flock to the new, cheaper alternatives. It doesn't matter if the technology is slightly inferior to more expensive options. What matters is that the performance provided by the cheaper technology is "good enough," and that it is accessible. See Figure 1-3 for a better look at this trend.

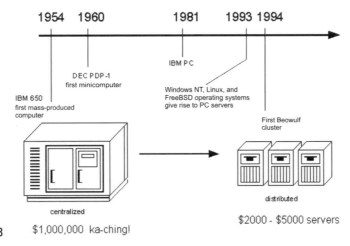

1954   1960   1981   1993 1994

DEC PDP-1
first minicomputer

IBM PC

Windows NT, Linux, and
FreeBSD operating systems
give rise to PC servers

IBM 650
first mass-produced
computer

First Beowulf
cluster

centralized

distributed

$2000 - $5000 servers

Figure 1-3 $1,000,000 ka-ching!

ASIDE The relationship between hardware and software has basically inverted itself from what it was back in the 1950s and 1960s. It used to be that a vendor sold you hardware and the software came along with the hardware at very little cost. In other words, the income from selling hardware subsidized the development of software. Today, just the opposite is true. Now, a vendor will deploy a business solution and then add hardware to the deal at little relative cost. Software is now subsidizing hardware. If you don't believe me, take a look at the cost of an MSDN subscription and compare it to the cost of a development machine.

There's another thing the mainframe people don't like to talk about. Using an off-the-shelf parts approach also offers protection against becoming dependent upon a single vendor. This is a notorious problem with commercial Unix vendors. Each vendor offers their own flavor of Unix, specially tailored for their own proprietary hardware. The system they offer strays from the standards just enough to lock the customer into a costly series of upgrades and investments. Deploying commodity hardware is a way to ensure that this doesn't happen. If one OEM fails to live up to standards, there are probably at least three other suppliers to take their place.

In the 1980s and early 1990s, the majority of new IT systems installed were Unix based. From the late 1990s on, Windows staked a claim on the corporate landscape. Again, this is primarily a matter of dollars and cents. Young companies and cash-strapped system admins often have to squeeze as much as they can out of their budgets. Windows appeals to this mindset. An incredible example of this is the Chicago Stock Exchange. It is based entirely on Windows. Not only did they implement a very contemporary clustering scheme, but they also deployed an object database and CORBA. It is truly a bleeding-edge architecture. I have to tip my hat to the CIO, Steve Randich, for successfully pulling off such an unorthodox stunt. It is vivid proof of concept for the clustering school of thought.

NOTE In all fairness I think I should also add that the Chicago Stock Exchange reboots their servers at the end of each day, a luxury that mainframes are not afforded and do not require. I suppose they do this to stifle memory leaks. Also, the system really only has to service about 150 clients, whereas a typical mainframe must be able to handle thousands. Finally, another fact that speaks volumes is that the lead software developer at the Chicago Stock Exchange decided not to use DCOM or SQL Server. One might interpret this decision as a statement on the stability of Microsoft's enterprise suite.

The explosion of mid-range Unix servers and Intel machines does not mean that mainframes are extinct. In fact, most businesses that do transaction-intensive computing still rely on mainframes. Banks, insurance companies, utilities, and government agencies all still execute core business operations with mainframes. This is one of the reasons why there will always be COBOL programmers. Take a look at Table 1-1 to see a comparison of the mainframe and cluster-based computing models.

Table 1-1

	Mainframe - Server Consolidation	Commodity Hardware - Clustering
Reliability	By design, fault prevention is the principal focus and ingrained in hardware and system software.	Through explicit redundancy, one machine blue-screens and others compensate.
Management	Centralized	Distributed
Scalability	Through dynamic partitioning and tightly coupled processors. Processor time and memory can be allocated dynamically at run time.	Can scale with finer granularity, one machine at a time, but with less management and control.
Dependence	Single vendor	Multiple vendors
Maturity	Established and tested	Relatively new

RANT If I were a CIO faced with a monster-sized load of mission-critical business transactions, my first inclination would be to think about deploying a mainframe. From an engineering standpoint, I think that high-end products like IBM's z900 machines are designed with an eye towards stability and raw throughput (something which, in the enterprise, I value more highly than a slick GUI).

As far as the enterprise is concerned, computers are used to do just that: compute.

Pretty multimedia boxes may impress the average Joe walking through a retail store, but they are of little use when it comes to handling a million transactions every hour. This is because the effort spent in developing an attractive GUI is usually invested at the expense of stability. The only thing that might dissuade me from following this path would be budgetary constraints. If I had very limited financial resources, I might decide to bite the bullet and go with Wintel.

The result of all this history is that corporate information systems have become an amalgam of different hardware platforms and operating systems. This is particularly true in large companies, which may have acquired other companies and have had to assimilate a number of disparate systems. I've worked in places where a business transaction may have to traverse through as many as five different platforms before completing.

NOTE The question of whether the mainframe or cluster-based computing model is better is irrelevant. What's important is that both models have become accepted and that this development has produced corporate information systems that are varied in nature.

The whole idea of a multiplatform IT system might run contrary to intuition. The promise of enterprise integration has, so far, turned out to be a myth sold by evangelists and salespeople out to make a buck. The CIOs that I've spoken with realize this and prefer to adopt a pet platform and stick with it. With smaller companies also opting for the low-cost alternative (i.e., Windows), it is no surprise that Microsoft currently owns about 40 percent of the server market. In spite of this trend, the inertia of legacy applications, outside influences, and availability constraints can foil a CIO's attempts to keep a company's computing landscape uniform.

The Need for a Virtual Machine

Faced with large, heterogeneous information systems and the accelerated rate of technological innovation, software engineers are beginning to rediscover the benefits of targeting virtual machines.

The name of the game in software development is return on investment. Companies want to invest money in software that will be useful long enough for the resources spent to be justified. Porting a software package from one platform to another is costly and, depending on the number of platforms supported, can prove to be a Sisyphean nightmare.

The worst-case scenario occurs when business logic is stranded on an aging system. Due to historical forces, a large base of code may end up on an obsolete platform that no one wants to deal with. The people who wrote the original code have either quit or been promoted and don't remember anything (sometimes intentionally). The source code has been transformed by time into an encrypted historical artifact that will require years of work by researchers to decipher. If the language and tools used to develop the initial code are linked to the original platform, porting may be out of the question. In pathological cases, the code may be so obscure and illegible that maintenance engineers are too scared to touch anything. I'm sure Y2K programmers are familiar with this type of imbroglio. The only recourse may be a complete rewrite and this is an extremely expensive alternative, fraught with all sorts of dangers and hidden costs. This is the kind of situation CIOs lose sleep over.

Using a virtual machine offers a degree of insurance against this kind of thing happening. When confronted with a new hardware platform or operating system, the only application that needs to be ported is the virtual machine itself. If a virtual machine is, say, 100,000 lines of code, you might think that actually porting the code is a bad investment. 100,000 lines of code is not a trivial porting job. However, let's say that the virtual machine runs an application suite that consists of 11 million lines of code. Suddenly, porting the virtual machine is not such a bad deal because the alternative would be to port the 11 million lines of application code. Don't think that this isn't realistic. I once visited an automobile insurance company that had around 30 million lines of application code.

For developers using a commercial run-time system that has already been ported to several platforms the savings are immediate and tangible. Sometimes the process of porting code that targets a virtual machine is as easy as copying the binaries.

Depreciating Assets

Like hardware, operating systems come and go. To add insult to injury, they tend to get bigger, slower, and more complicated.

The reason behind this is pretty simple. In order for software companies to make money on a consistent basis, they have to create a continuous stream of revenue. In a market that is already saturated, one way to do this is to release new versions of a product which have features that previously did not exist. It is not that you necessarily need these new features; some people are happy with what they bought back in 1995. Rather, these new features are an excuse that big software companies use to entice you to keep giving them your money. It's a racket, plain and simple. My advice would be to hang on to what you have as long as you can and try to ignore the marketing slogans.

Studying a subject like mathematics is generally a good investment. Not only will you meet lots of women and probably become a millionaire (I'm joking), but the foundations of the subject will never change. In math, you learn topics like geometry and algebra, and the resulting skills you gain are permanently applicable. Mathematics is the native tongue of the world around us. Quantitative patterns and relationships are everywhere. Becoming a skilled mathematician is like building a house on a solid, immovable foundation. The knowledge base that you build is good forever.

The opposite is true for commercial operating systems. Knowledge of a particular commercial operating system has a distinct half-life. After a few years, the skill set corresponding to a given platform decays until it is no longer useful or relevant. Try to find an employer who is interested in hiring an admin who knows how to operate a CDC 6600. If you find one such employer, it will probably be for a position at the Smithsonian Institution. Spending vast amounts of effort to master one platform is like investing in a rapidly depreciating asset. By the time you have attained any sort of proficiency, the next version has come out. If you identify with a particular platform, you may find yourself trying to resist change. It's very tempting to stay in familiar surroundings instead of having to start all over from scratch.

I can remember in 1990 when I felt like I had finally achieved guru status in DOS 3.3 and real-mode programming. It had taken years of relentlessly wading through technical manuals and reading every magazine article I could get my hands on. I was revered by my coworkers as a batch file master. In fact, I often mumbled DOS shell commands in my sleep. I was also very handy with Borland's Turbo C compiler and Tasm macro assembler. These tools were great, not only because they were simple, inexpensive, and straightforward, but also because they didn't try to push their religion on you. They were not out to sell you a component architecture or a design methodology. It was straight up ANSI C and I liked it that way.

At work I had written a serial port driver that allowed our 80386 boxes to talk to the company's mainframe. I was feeling like I could finally wrap my hands around everything and see the big picture. The PC domain was my kingdom and I was intimately familiar with every TSR and driver from the interrupt table to high memory. Two days after I proclaimed myself an expert to my supervisor, I found out about Windows 3.0. In fact, there was one IT guy who had gotten his hands on the early release and he took great pleasure in asking me questions I could not answer. To make matters worse, he liked to ask me these questions in front of my coworkers. My reputation had been put in jeopardy, and people began to whisper that I was behind the curve.

The gauntlet had been thrown down so I rushed into Windows 3.0. I spent a lot of my spare time on weekends learning about protected mode addressing and DOS-extenders. I rolled up my sleeves and bought Visual C++ 1.52 so that I could delve into the black art of writing VxDs. When integrated networking arrived via Windows for Workgroups in 1992, I was on it. After sufficient toiling and lost sleep, I regained my title as the departmental wizard. If someone had a problem setting up file sharing, they called on me — Mr. NetBEUI. For a couple of years I was riding high again. I thought I had the game licked.

However, while I was basking in my own glory, that same IT guy had secretly obtained a beta copy of Microsoft's next big thing. Its code name was Cairo and would soon be known to the rest of the world as Windows 95. Again, he started bringing up questions I couldn't answer.

Rather than face this onslaught of perpetual platform turnover, I wanted to be able to rely on a stationary target that would give me the ability to design software that would have a decent half-life. Computer technology is a raging ocean of change. I was looking for an island so I could avoid being tossed around every time something new came out.

One thing I observed was that there actually was a single, solitary constant that I could rely on: Every contemporary platform has an ANSI C or C++ compiler.

Rather than anchor a set of development tools to a particular hardware platform, why not base them on a specification? And why not construct a specification that can be easily implemented using ANSI C, which is universally available? Instead of relying on a native platform to execute my applications, I would use a virtual machine that could be easily ported when hardware transitions were forced on me.

Eureka! I felt like I had made a great discovery, until a few days later when it dawned on me that other people might have beaten me to it. Obviously, the idea of a virtual machine is nothing new. IBM has been doing it successfully for decades, and new companies like TransMeta have incorporated a virtual machine approach into their hardware. What makes my implementation different is a set of design goals, which ended up defining the fundamental characteristics of my virtual machine.

A Delicate Balance

I strongly believe that it's important to sit down before you begin a software project and create a list of fundamental design goals and requirements. Then, the trick is to faithfully stick to them. This is harder than it sounds. The urge to sacrifice your overall guidelines to address an immediate concern is very seductive.

My objective was to build a virtual machine that satisfied three criterion. In order of priority, these are:

1. Portability

2. Simplicity

3. Performance

Portability is the most important feature because being able to work with a uniform software interface, across multiple platforms, is the primary benefit of using a virtual machine. If you can't port a virtual machine, then you're stuck with a given platform, in which case you might as well use tools that compile to the native machine encoding.

Portability is also the most important priority in the sense that I had to make sacrifices in terms of simplicity and performance in order to achieve it. There is rarely a solution that is ever optimal under all conditions in software engineering.

If you've ever read any of the well-known journal articles on dynamic memory storage or process scheduling, you'll notice that the authors always qualify their conclusions with specific conditions. In other words, the results that an approach yields depend on the nature of the problem. Because of this, most decisions involve an implicit tradeoff of some sort.

The HEC run-time execution engine is about 10,000 lines of code. About 1,500 lines are platform specific. In order to maintain a modicum of portability, I was forced to pepper certain areas of code with preprocessor #ifdef directives. Naturally, this hurts readability and makes maintenance a little more complicated. I succeeded in isolating most of the platform-specific code in two source files. Nevertheless, there are portions of the code where I sacrificed simplicity for portability.

One way of boosting performance would be to make heavy use of assembly code. However, using an assembler does not necessarily guarantee faster program execution. In order to be able to justify using an assembler, the programmer has to have an intimate knowledge of both the assembly code a compiler generates and the kind of optimizations it performs. The goal is to be able to write faster assembly code than the compiler can. This requires a certain amount of vigilance and skill because, in most cases, the optimizer in a C compiler can do a better job than the average programmer.

Another problem with using assembly language is that it ties your code to the hardware you're working on. To port the code to new hardware, you'll need to rewrite every single line of assembly code. This can turn out to be much more work than you think. Again, in the effort to maintain a certain degree of portability, I opted out of low-level, high-performance assembly coding and wrote everything in ANSI C.

While I was a graduate student, I learned a dirty little secret about how to get research published. If a professor makes a discovery that can be explained in simple terms, he will go to great lengths and use any number of obfuscation techniques to make the discovery look more complicated than it really is. This is more of a sociological phenomenon than anything else. The train of thought behind this is that if an idea is simple, then it must not be very revolutionary or clever. People who referee journal submissions are more likely to be impressed by an explanation that wraps around itself into a vast Gordian knot.

This may work for professors who want tenure, but it sure doesn't work for software engineers. In his Turing Award lecture, "On Building Systems that will Fail," one of the conclusions Fernando Corbató makes is that sticking to a simple design is necessary for avoiding project failure. You should listen to this man. Corbató is a voice of experience and one of the founding fathers of modern system design. He led the project to build MULTICS back in the 1960s.

MULTICS was one of those ambitious Tower of Babel projects that attempted to reach for the heavens. MULTICS was designed to be a multiuser system that implemented paging, shared memory multiprocessing, and dynamic reconfiguration. This is especially impressive when one considers that the hardware available at the time wasn't really up to the task. Corbató was forced to stare the dragon of complexity straight in the eyes and he learned some very expensive lessons.

To me, simplicity has priority over performance by virtue of my desire to make the code maintainable. A year from now, I would like to be able to modify my code without having to call in a team of archaeologists. Code that is optimized for performance can become very brittle and resistant to change. Developers writing high-performance C code will often use all sorts of misleading and confusing conventions, like bitwise shifting to divide by 2. What is produced is usually illegible by anyone but the original developer, and given enough time even the original developer may forget what he had done and why he had done it. In an extreme case, a programmer who has created a mess and is too scared to clean it up may opt to quit and go work somewhere else. I've heard people refer to this as "the final solution" or "calling in for air support and pulling out."

I knew that if I tried to be everything to everyone, I probably wouldn't do anything very efficiently. The desktop has already pretty much been conquered by Microsoft and Internet Explorer. Also, attempting to create a GUI-intensive run-time system seemed like a poor investment of a tremendous amount of effort. Not to mention that including GUI code would hurt portability. I'd much rather follow the approach of a mainframe engineer and concern myself with creating a solution that focused on fault tolerance and stability. Because of this, I decided that the HEC run-time system would eschew a GUI API and be aimed at executing application logic on the server side.

Finally, another reason for keeping a simple design has to do with individual creativity. In order for programmers to exercise the creative side of their brain, they have to feel like they have a complete understanding of what they're dealing with. In other words, they should be able to keep the overall design completely in main memory. Being creative requires the ability to experiment with different ideas, and this necessitates an intimate understanding of the ideas. Without a solid understanding, the chance to do any sort of innovation is stifled.

I worked at a company that has a code base of 16 million lines. The code base is old enough and big enough that there is no one who really understands how everything works. There are a couple old veterans in each department who know a certain portion, but that's it. If an engineer is lucky, maybe one of the old hands will pass on some knowledge verbally. Being a software engineer in this company is more like belonging to a guild during the Renaissance. It's a classic big ball of mud scenario. No one understands anyone else's area of specialty and source code has evolved into a large amorphous mess.

Back in the 1980s an executive VP at this company concluded that in-source comments were slowing down compile time (from a day to two days) and had them all removed. The company now owns 16 million lines of K&R C source code which have zero documentation. This may have made a very small group of people happy, seeing as how they now had a monopoly on useful information. New hires, however, faced a 90 degree learning curve.

In a situation like this, creativity does not exist. In fact, new engineers consider it a victory if they can understand what a single 5,000-line program does. This is dangerous because in order to survive, a company has to be able to listen and respond to the demands of their customers. What are the odds that this company's system will be able to innovate enough to compete in the future? Very slim in my opinion. Unless they perform some serious research, I'd give them a couple more years of survival.

With all that said, I tried to squeeze every ounce of performance out of the run-time system that I could under the constraints that I did not adversely impact portability or design simplicity.

Arguments Against a Virtual Machine

There are several arguments against using a virtual machine, the primary one being performance. One might argue that because a compiled language, like C, is executed using the native machine encoding, it will run faster. This is not necessarily true.

In 1996 I was discussing the merits of Java's portability with a coworker. The company had decided to rewrite its user interface and the entire business had split into two camps: C++ evangelists and Java fanatics.

Given that Java was still hot off the press, it didn't yet have mature GUI components and its enterprise facilities were nonexistent. To make matters worse, the C++ sect was showing off an elaborate IDE and other sophisticated development tools. The Java developers, on the other hand, only had the command-line tools of the JDK. This kind of distinction doesn't make much difference to experienced developers. It did, unfortunately, make a big impression on the executive officers.

One Achilles heel of C++ was its lack of portability across the platforms the company deployed on. When I mentioned the fact that Java did not have this problem, there was this one developer from the C++ crowd who would stand up and yell out: "Oh, yeah, Java ...write once, runs like crap everywhere!"

I knew he was wrong, but, hey, this was a religious war and he was merely spreading disinformation and spouting off propaganda. In the end, upper management gave in to the slick sales pitch of the C++ proponents. The Java people, however, did get the last laugh: The C++ project failed miserably, for a variety of reasons, and the vice presidents who initially shunned us came running back to us and begged us to rescue their jobs after wasting 29 man-years and millions of dollars.

Native C++ code is not necessarily faster than bytecode executed by a virtual machine. The truth is that the majority of execution time is spent in run-time libraries and kernel-mode interrupt handlers. The only time native code would actually execute faster is when you are dealing with an isolated unit of code that stands completely by itself and does not invoke a user library or system call.

An example of this would be a program that encrypts data. Encryption is a computationally intensive process that involves a large number of fundamental arithmetic and bitwise operations. Calls made to the operating system constitute a minority of the work done. Most of the time is spent twiddling bits and exercising the processor's most primitive facilities. In this case, C++ would probably be faster.

If you want to push the envelope for virtual machine performance, most virtual machines have facilities to convert the virtual machine's bytecode to native. There are any number of mechanisms. A program's bytecode can be converted to the native machine encoding at compile time using a bytecode-to-native compiler. Or, bytecode instructions can be converted to native at run time using a just-in-time (JIT) compiler. An even more sophisticated approach is to have the run-time system monitor which bytecode is executed the most frequently, and then have the most frequently executed bytecode instructions converted to native at run time. This is what is known as an adaptive form of JIT compiling. Some people would argue that this is all a moot point because the portability achieved by targeting a virtual machine can often more than compensate for any perceived loss in performance.

Looking Ahead

When Moore's Law succumbs to the laws of physics, the hardware engineers will no longer be able to have their cake and eat it too. They will not be able to make transistors any smaller. As a result, the only way to increase the number of transistors on a chip will be to increase the size of the chip itself. That's right, computers will have to start getting larger!

In an effort to keep processors at a manageable size, the software algorithms that use the hardware will have to become more efficient. Thus, part of the responsibility for constructing fast programs will be passed back to the theoreticians and their whiteboards.

There is a tendency among commercial software engineers to solve a performance problem by throwing more hardware at it. It is a common solution because the results are immediate and it expedites time to market. Within the next 50 years, it may actually become more cost effective to invest in developing better software instead of relying on faster machines. Suddenly it will be worth an engineer's time to sit down and think about efficient solutions instead of hacking out a kludge.

The end of Moore's Law may provide enough impetus for a major paradigm shift in computer science as researchers are forced to look for better algorithms.

By the time Moore's Law has exhausted itself, computer processors may also be as sophisticated and powerful as the human brain. This will allow computers to address and solve problems which have, in the past, only been contemplated by humans. However, this kind of computing power also provides ample opportunity for misuse. Lest you forget, the development of other technological innovations, like atomic energy and radar, were first put to use, on a large scale, as instruments of war.

Computers in the future could be designed to accurately model and forecast human behavior. If recursive optimization algorithms allowed a computer to beat a chess grand master, imagine what several generations of advancement will produce. Human behavior might very well be distilled into an elaborate decision matrix. Given a couple hundred thousand personality input parameters, a computer could take a particular person and determine how he or she will behave in a given situation. If you can predict how someone is going to behave under certain circumstances, then you can effectively control their behavior, or at least preempt it. Imagine how a government could use this kind of tool to repress its citizens by instituting behavior modification on a national scale. As computing technology becomes more powerful and more ubiquitous, several ethical questions will no doubt rise to the surface and demand attention.

Lessons Learned

There are a few things I've learned during the implementation phase of my project that I'd like to share with you before we move to the next chapter.

First, I'd like to point out that there is no panacea for sloppy code that has been poorly written in an effort to get a product out the door. Rushing to meet a deadline and relying on the quality assurance (QA) people to do the rest is a recipe for disaster.

The only way to produce bulletproof software is to do it the slow, gradual, painful way. Anyone who tells you otherwise has an agenda or is trying to sell you snake oil. This means that after constructing each individual module of code, you need to barrage it with test cases. Throw everything at that code but the kitchen sink. The goal is to try and find that one obscure combination of application data and program state you didn't prepare for. One trick I like to use is to imagine that I'm a lawyer preparing a binding contract. Assume that at every point in this contract, some other opposing lawyer is going to try and find a loophole so that the agreement can be invalidated. I write every line of source code with the intention of foiling some imagined adversary who's going to try to bamboozle me. It's a cumulative process; each time you add more functionality to your application you need to test. This is not the QA's responsibility either, it's the developer's.

There are a couple of engineering techniques I use that can make the process easier. First, build your own test modules and use them to verify that your code works after you have made any significant changes. If you're using an object-oriented language, this is as easy as adding another method to the class that you're working on. I understand that creating a test module can be difficult, especially when the component you're working on interacts with several other complicated modules. This means that you're going to have to invest the time to recreate the environment in which your component functions. This may seem like a lot of work, but it's time well spent because it allows you to isolate your code from the rest of the system and tinker with it.

Another thing you can do is insert debugging statements into your code that print run-time information to standard output. One problem with this technique is that debugging statements can take a toll on performance. A program that pipes several lines of data to the screen before committing a transaction wastes valuable processor cycles. One way to eliminate the overhead is to simply comment out the debugging statements before sending the program into production. This is a questionable solution because when the developers discover a bug and need to turn debugging back on, they'll have to go through and manually activate each individual debugging statement. If the application in question consists of 150,000 lines of code, manually un-commenting debug statements is not an elegant solution.

If you're using a language like C, which has a preprocessor, you're in luck. I find that using macro-based debug statements is a nice compromise. You can activate them on a file-wide or program-wide basis simply by defining a macro. Likewise, you can strip them out completely by leaving the macro undefined.

For example:

```
#define DEBUG          1

#ifdef DEBUG
#define     DEBUG_PRINT(arg);      printf(arg);
#else
#define     DEBUG_PRINT(arg);
#endif
```

NOTE   These techniques may sound stupidly simple. However, to borrow a line from Murphy, if it's simple and it works, then it's not stupid. Another thing I should point out is that these techniques are intended to be applied during development. QA engineers have their own universe of testing methodologies and strategies, which I won't even try to delve into.

The process of testing during development may also require that a certain amount of temporary scaffolding be written around the partially constructed application. Think of this like you would think of scaffolding set up around a building under construction. Scaffolding provides a temporary testing environment. It allows the developer to move around and add features without having to rely on the paths of execution that will be there when the application goes into production. When the application is done, the scaffolding naturally falls away and you can pass things on to the QA people.

Some engineers might think that writing all this throwaway code is a waste of effort, particularly if they are under a tight schedule. The investment in time, however, is well spent. I'd rather spend a little extra time during development and write a moderate amount of throwaway code than get called at 3 A.M. by an angry system admin whose server has crashed because of my software, and then be forced to dissect a core dump.

Once you've integrated all the modules of your program, and you feel like you have a finished product, you should stop and take a moment to remind yourself of something. Don't think about adding new features. Don't even think about optimizing the code to speed things up. Go back to your source code and fix it. I guarantee you, there's something that's broken that you haven't taken into account. Pretend you're Sherlock Holmes and go find it. Only when you're spending several days searching without finding a problem should you feel secure enough to allow the QA people to take a look.

This mindset runs in direct opposition to that of the marketing employee. This is particularly true in a startup company where the primary objective of every manager is to get product out the door. Marketing people don't want to hear: "slow, gradual, painful." Marketing people want to hear: "Next week." I have a special dark corner of my heart reserved for people in sales, primarily because they spend a good portion of their days trying to manipulate potential customers by telling them half-truths. Not only that, but most of them are unaware of what is involved in developing software. I don't know how many times some salesperson has put me in a difficult position because he made an unrealistic promise to a customer about when the next release of a product was due.

As a software developer, you can take steps to protect yourself. One thing you should realize is that all the software projects that you work on may end up being "code red" emergencies. In these cases, you should realize that management is merely crying wolf. Their proclamation that the sky is falling is just a technique they use to get you to work faster.

Another evil that may be attributed to marketing people is feature creep. In order to distinguish their product from the competitors, a salesperson will often take liberties with the product description. A few days later, said salesperson will appear in your cube to break the news about the features you have only three days to implement. Again, you can protect yourself. When a project begins, get the requirements signed by the head of marketing. When the salesperson shows up in your cube and attempts to coerce you, shove the requirements in his face and tell him to take a hike.

The only alternative to pedantic testing is to ship software that is "good enough." I hate this idea. I hate it because it attempts to legitimize the practice of shipping software that contains bugs that the developers know about and could fix. Instead of fixing the bugs, they decide to ship it, and that is unacceptable. Once shipping significantly faulty software becomes the status quo, where does it stop? It effectively lowers the bar for the entire industry.

Fortunately, free enterprise, to an extent, takes care of this problem. If company A slips up and sells a lemon, then company B can step up to the plate and offer something better. This normally causes company A to institute sufficient quality controls so that company B does not have the opportunity to offer its services. The only case where shipping "good enough" software allows a company to stay in business is when that company has a captive audience.

The bad news is that it's easy to become a captive audience. Consulting firms have been known to burn clients this way. Once a client has hired a consulting firm and started shelling out cash, it is basically at the mercy of the consulting firm. To make matters worse, the name of the game for consultants is billable hours. If things head south, the consultants may decide to keep their mouths shut and their heads low while the meter runs. In this scenario they may very well freeze their code, declare victory, and then get the heck out of town. By the time the client realizes that the system he was promised doesn't function properly, the consultants are already on the airplane to their next victim. Naturally the client has the option of litigation, but most of the damage has already been done: Time and money have been invested that will never show a return.

The lesson I have learned from this is that people cannot discover the truth about developing robust software because the truth is not always something people want to accept. In a way, it's similar to physical fitness. There is no easy way to become physically fit other than to sacrifice, be rigidly disciplined, and be consistent. There is a whole industry of magic pills and diets which has been built up around appealing to naive people who think that they can sidestep the necessary hard work. I think software is the same way. Robust software is best constructed through a lot of careful planning, gradual software development, constant vigilance with regard to isolating errors, and frequent testing. The only way is the painful way.

References

Brooks, Frederick. *The Mythical Man-Month*. Addison-Wesley: 1995. ISBN: 0201835959.

This reprint contains extra material, like Brooks' famous "No Silver Bullet" essay. Brooks touches on some interesting points with respect to creativity being a necessary ingredient in great designs. This book is nothing short of the canon of modern software engineering.

Buyya, Rajkumar. *High Performance Cluster Computing: Volume 1 Architectures and Systems*. Prentice Hall: 1999. ISBN: 0130137847.

A solid, though somewhat theoretical, look at design issues for clustered systems and contemporary implementations.

Corbató, Fernando. "On Building Systems that will Fail." *Communications of the ACM*, 34(9): 72-81, September 1991.

This is Corbató's Turing Award lecture on building robust computer systems.

Halfhill, Tom. "Crash-Proof Computing." *BYTE*, April 1998.

This is a very enlightening article on what, besides size and processing power, exactly distinguishes a mainframe from a PC.

Kurzweil, Ray. *The Age of Spiritual Machines: When Computers Exceed Human Intelligence*. Penguin Paperback, 2000. ISBN: 0140282025.

Microsoft, http://www.howstevedidit.com.

This link will take you to a web site that includes an in-depth look at how the Chicago Stock Exchange runs its entire operation on commodity hardware and Windows NT. This case study is a graphic example of cluster computing.

Stross, Randall. *The Microsoft Way*. Addison-Wesley, 1996. ISBN: 0201409496.

Recounts the development of Microsoft before the Internet explosion. This book focuses on internal issues like how Microsoft hires new employees and develops new products. Stross seems to emphasize that Microsoft's success is not just a matter of luck.

Basic Execution Environment

Overview

This chapter discusses the basic resources the HEC run-time environment has at its disposal and how it manages them. Determining how HEC would handle its resources entailed making far-reaching architectural decisions. Because of this, I made it a point to do some research on the issues of memory management, process management, and processor operation. In this chapter, I share a few of my findings with you and then explain how they influenced HEC's design.

ASIDE It may seem like I am wading through an awful lot of irrelevant theory. This is, however, a necessary evil. Just like learning algebra, trigonometry, and calculus before you jump into differential equations, covering the fundamentals is a prerequisite to understanding certain decisions that I made about HEC's makeup.

In fact, some of the choices that I make will seem arbitrary unless you can understand the context in which I make them. The somewhat dry topics I present in this chapter provide an underlying foundation for the rest of this book. So don't doze off!

Notation Conventions

Numeric literals in this text are represented using the standard conventions of the C programming language. Decimal literals always begin with a decimal digit in the range from 1 to 9. Hexadecimal literals begin with a 0-x prefix (0x or 0X). Octal literals begin with 0.

314159	Decimal numeric literal
0xA5	Hexadecimal numeric literal
0644	Octal numeric literal

NOTE Some people may view octal literals as a thing of the past. It really depends mostly on your own experience. Engineers who muck about in Windows probably think that octal is some type of historical oddity. Octal constants are, however, used all over the place in Unix to define file access rights, application permissions, and other system-related attributes. As one of my co-workers, Gene Dagostino, once said: "Sometimes, it just depends on where you are coming from."

A *bit* is defined as a single binary digit that is either 0 or 1. A *byte* is a series of eight bits. A long time ago in a galaxy far, far away the size of a byte varied from one hardware platform to the next. But almost everyone, with the exception of maybe Donald Knuth (who is stuck in the 1960s with his hypothetical MIX machine), treats a byte as a collection of eight bits. A whole hierarchy of units can be defined in terms of the byte.

1 byte	8 bits
1 word	2 bytes (*bytes*, not bits)
1 double word	4 bytes
1 quad word	8 bytes
1 paragraph	16 bytes
1 kilobyte (1 KB)	1024 bytes
1 megabyte (1 MB)	1024 KB = 1,048,576 bytes
1 gigabyte (1 GB)	1024 MB = 1,073,741,824 bytes
1 terabyte (1 TB)	1024 GB = 1,099,511,627,776 bytes

Bits within a byte will be displayed in this book from right to left, starting with the least significant bit on the right side. For an example, see Figure 2-1.

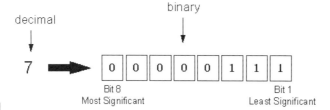

Figure 2-1

Veterans of the hardware wars that took place in the turbulent 1960s tend to get a nostalgic, faraway look in their eyes when they recall the 16 KB core memory that their fabled supercomputers used to have (like the CDC 6600). Back when memory was implemented using circular magnets, 16 KB of memory required the same space as a deluxe model refrigerator. Engineers who have worked on such machines have been known to say things like: "It was quite an impressive machine in its day…sigh."

NOTE   Let this be a lesson to you. Don't get too attached to hardware; there's always something faster and more powerful around the corner. Today's supercomputer is tomorrow's workstation. It is wiser to attach yourself to an idea. Take the quicksort algorithm, for example. It was discovered by C.A.R. Hoare in 1962 and is still used today as an in-place sorting mechanism. Good ideas live on; hardware is temporal and fleeting. C.A.R. Hoare is like Dijkstra; he tends to pop up everywhere in computer science.

Run-time Systems and Virtual Machines

A *run-time system* is an environment in which computer programs execute. A run-time system provides everything a program needs in order to run. For example, a run-time system is responsible for allocating memory for an application, loading the application into the allocated memory, and facilitating the execution of the program's instructions. If the program requests services from the underlying operating system through the invocation of system calls, the run-time system is in charge of handling those service requests. For instance, if an application wants to perform file I/O, the run-time system must offer a mechanism to communicate with the disk controller and provide read/write access.

There are different kinds of run-time systems. One way to classify run-time systems is to categorize them based on how they execute a program's instructions. For programs whose instructions use the processor's native machine encoding, the run-time system consists of a tightly knit collaboration between the computer's processor and the operating system. The processor provides a mechanism for executing program instructions. The CPU does nothing more than fetch instructions from memory, which are encoded as numeric values, and perform the actions corresponding to those instructions. The operating system implements the policy side of a computer's native run-time system. The CPU may execute instructions, but the operating system decides how, when, and where things happen. Think of the operating system as a fixed set of rules the CPU has to obey during the course of instruction execution.

Thus, for programs written in native machine instructions, the computer itself is the run-time system. Program instructions are executed at the machine level, by the physical CPU, and the operating system manages how the execution occurs. This type of run-time system involves a mixture of hardware and software.

Programs whose instructions are not directly executed by the physical processor require a run-time system that consists entirely of software. In such a case, the program's instructions are executed by a *virtual machine*. A virtual machine is a software program that acts like a computer. It fetches and executes instructions just like a normal processor. The difference is that the processing of those instructions happens at the software level instead of the hardware level. A virtual machine also usually contains facilities to manage the path of execution and to offer an interface to services normally provided by the native operating system.

A virtual machine is defined by a specification. A virtual machine is not a particular software implementation, but rather a set of rules. These rules form a contract that the engineer, who builds an instantiation of the virtual machine, must honor. A virtual machine can be implemented in any programming language on any hardware platform, as long as it obeys the specification. You could create a version of the HEC virtual machine on an OS/390 using APL if you really wanted to. This is what makes the idea of a virtual machine so powerful. You can run HEC executables, without recompilation, anywhere there is a run-time system that obeys the specification.

 NOTE Virtual machines are run-time systems, but not all run-time systems are virtual machines.

Memory Management

Memory provides a way to store information. A computer's storage facilities may be classified according to how quickly the processor can access stored data. Specifically, memory can be broken up into five broad categories. Ranked from fastest to slowest access speed, they are:

- Processor registers
- Processor cache
- Random access memory
- Local disk-based storage
- Data stored over a network connection

A processor's registers are small storage slots (usually 16 to 128 bits in length) located within the processor itself. Some processors also have a larger built-in area, called a *cache*, where up to several hundred kilobytes of data can be stored. Because both the registers and the cache are located within the processor, the processor can most quickly access data in the registers and cache. The amount of storage provided by the registers and cache, however, is strictly limited due to size constraints. As a result, most of the data a processor works with during program execution is stored in random access memory.

NOTE As our ability to miniaturize transistors nears the three-atom limit, more memory and peripheral functionality will be placed within the processor itself. This could potentially lead to an entire computer being placed within a single chip — a system on a chip.

Random access memory holds the middle ground in the memory hierarchy. It is usually provided by a set of chips that share real estate with the processor on the motherboard. Random access memory is slower but more plentiful than the resources on the processor. It is, however, much faster than disk-based or network-based storage. Because disk- and network-based storage involve much longer access times than random access memory, they are primarily used only when random access memory has been exhausted. Disk and network storage are also used to persist data so that it remains even after the computer is powered down.

NOTE In the remainder of the book, when the term "memory" is used, I will be referring to random access memory.

The question of what memory is has been answered. Now we will look at how memory is used. There are three levels at which memory can be managed by a computer:

- Machine level
- Operating system level
- Application level

Machine-Level Management

At the machine level, memory consists of a collection of cells that are read and written to by the processor. A memory cell is a transistor-based electrical component that exists in two possible states. By mapping the digits 1 and 0 to these two states, we can represent the state of a memory cell using a bit.

Memory cells can be grouped together to form bytes such that memory can be viewed as a contiguous series of bytes. Each byte in the series is assigned a nonnegative sequence integer, starting with 0. Figure 2-2 illustrates this approach. The sequence number assigned to a byte is referred to as the *address* of the byte. This is analogous to the way houses on a block are assigned addresses.

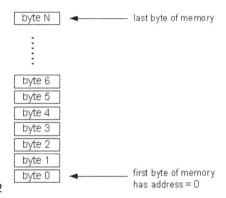

Figure 2-2

The processor accesses and manipulates memory using buses. A bus is nothing more than a collection of related wires that connect the processor to the subsystems of the computer (see Figure 2-3). To interact with memory, the processor uses three buses: the control bus, the address bus, and the data bus. The control bus is used to indicate whether the processor wants to read from memory or write to memory. The address bus is used to specify the address of the byte in memory to manipulate. The data bus is used to ferry data back and forth between the processor and memory.

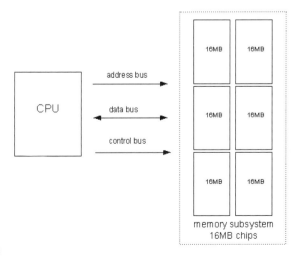

Figure 2-3

The number of wires in an address bus determines the maximum number of bytes that a processor can address. This is known as the memory address space (MAS) of the processor. Each address bus wire corresponds to a bit in the address value. For example, if a processor's address bus has 32 lines, an address is specified by 32 bits such that the processor can address 2^{32} bytes, or 4 GB.

To read a byte, the following steps are performed:

1. The processor places the address of the byte to read on the address bus.

2. The processor sends the read signal to memory using the control bus.

3. Memory sends the byte at the specified address on the data bus.

To write a byte, the following steps are performed:

1. The processor places the address of the byte to be written on the address bus.

2. The processor sends the write signal to memory using the control bus.

3. The processor sends the byte to be written to memory on the data bus.

The above steps are somewhat simplified versions of what really occurs. Specifically, the processor usually reads and writes several bytes at a time. For example, most Intel chips currently read and write data in four-byte clumps (which is why they are often referred to as 32-bit chips). The processor will refer to a 32-bit packet of data using the address of the byte that has the smallest address.

In general, a processor executes instructions in memory by starting at a given address and sequentially moving upwards towards a higher address, such that execution flows from a lower address to a higher address (see Figure 2-4).

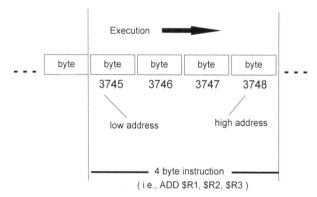

Figure 2-4

Memory is not just used to store program instructions. It is also used to store data. When a data value only requires a single byte, we can refer to the data value using its address. If a data value consists of multiple bytes, the address of the lowest byte of the value is used to reference the value as a whole. Figure 2-5 illustrates this point.

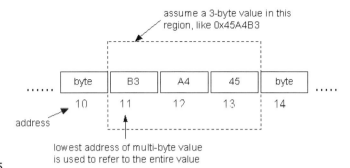

Figure 2-5

There are two different ways to store multibyte data values in memory: *big-endian* and *little-endian*. The big-endian convention dictates that the most significant byte of a value has the lowest address in memory. The little-endian convention is just the opposite — the least significant byte of a value must have the lowest address in memory (Figure 2-5 uses the little-endian format).

Here's an example. Let's say you have the multibyte value 0xABCDEF12 sitting somewhere in memory (for example, starting at address 24). The big- and little-endian representations of this value are displayed in Figure 2-6.

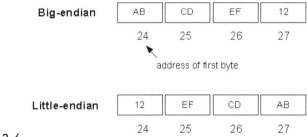

Figure 2-6

The storage method used will vary according to the hardware platform you're on. For example, the Intel family of 32-bit processors is a little-endian platform. If you own a PC that uses an Intel processor, you can prove this to yourself with the following program:

```c
#include<stdio.h>

void main(int argc, char *argv[])
{
    unsigned long value = 0xABCDEF12;
    unsigned char *arr;
    arr = (unsigned char *)&value;
    printf("%X %X %X %X\n",arr[0],arr[1],arr[2],arr[3]);
    return;
}
```

If you are on an Intel-based platform, this program should print out: 12 EF CD AB

NOTE   Arrays in C are always indexed from low address to high address. Thus, the first element of the array (i.e., arr[0]) also has the lowest address. The reason behind this is that arr[3] is the same as arr+3. This means that the index is really an offset from the first element of the array.

 ASIDE   Endianness is a major issue in terms of porting code from one platform to the next. For the sake of keeping HEC applications uniform, I arbitrarily decided that all multibyte values will be stored in a HEC executable file using the big-endian format. It is up to the HEC run-time system to convert these values to the native format at run time. If the native format is big-endian, the run-time doesn't have to do anything. If the native format, however, is little-endian, the run-time system will have to do a quick conversion. The specifics of this conversion are covered in Chapter 3.

 NOTE   Data represented using the big-endian method is said to be in *network order*. This is because network protocols like TCP/IP require certain pieces of information to be sent across a network in big-endian format.

Operating System Level

Instead of viewing memory in terms of component subsystems and bus interfaces, operating systems have the luxury of an abstracted view of memory, where memory consists of a series of contiguous bytes. Each byte has its own unique integer address starting with 0. The byte whose address is 0 is said to be at the bottom of memory.

An operating system is really just a complicated program that governs the execution of other programs and handles requests that those other programs might make for machine resources. Operating systems have a lot of responsibility when it comes to administrating the internal operation of a computer. Think of an operating system like a den mother who is presiding over a whole troop of Cub Scouts. If a certain amount of discipline is not occasionally applied, chaos will ensue.

Rather than treat memory as one big amorphous blob of bytes, and face almost certain application failures and memory shortages, there are two mechanisms an operating system can apply to manage memory effectively: *segmentation* and *paging*.

Computers usually have less memory than their memory address space allows. For example, the typical 32-bit Intel processor can address 4 GB of memory, but unless you've got a lot of cash to burn on RAM chips you'll probably have only a fraction of this. Most people are satisfied with 128 MB of memory. Disk storage is much cheaper and much more plentiful than memory. Because of this, disk storage is often used to simulate memory and increase the effective addressable memory. This is what paging is all about.

When paging is used by an operating system, the addressable memory space artificially increases such that it becomes a *virtual address space*. The address of a byte in the new, larger virtual memory space no longer matches what the processor places on the address bus. Translations must be made so that physical memory and virtual memory remain consistently mapped to each other.

Paging is implemented by dividing virtual memory (memory that resides in the virtual address space) into fixed-size "pages" of storage space (on the Intel platform, the page size is usually 4,096 bytes). If an operating system detects that it is running out of physical memory, it has the option of moving page size chunks of memory to disk (see Figure 2-7).

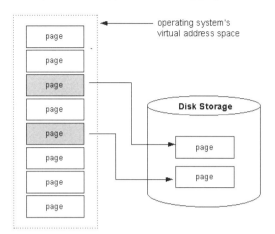

Figure 2-7

Modern implementation of paging requires the integration of processor and operating system facilities. Neither the operating system nor the processor can do it all alone; they both have to work together closely. The operating system is responsible for setting up the necessary data structures in memory to allow the chip to perform bookkeeping operations. The processor expects these data structures to be there, so the operating system has to create them according to a set specification. The specifics of paging are hardware dependent. Most vendors will provide descriptions in their product documentation.

ASIDE   The current family of 32-bit Intel processors can page memory to disk in three different sizes: 4,096 KB, 2 MB, and 4 MB. There is a system register named CR4 (control register 4). The fourth and fifth bits of this register are flags (PSE and PAE) that can be set in certain combinations to facilitate different page sizes, although, to be honest, I have no idea why anyone would want to use 4 MB memory pages. I prefer to buy a lot of RAM and then turn paging off entirely.

The hardware/software cooperation involved in paging is all done in the name of performance. Paging to disk storage is such an I/O-intensive operation that the only way to maintain an acceptable degree of efficiency is to push the work down as close to the processor as possible. Even then, that might not be enough. I've been told that hardware-based paging can incur a 10 percent performance overhead on Microsoft Windows. This is probably one reason why Windows allows you to disable paging.

Segmentation is a way to institute protection. The goal of segmentation is to isolate programs in memory so that they cannot interfere with one another or with the operating system. Operating systems like DOS do not provide any protection at all. A malicious program can very easily take over a computer running DOS and reformat your hard drive.

Segmentation is established by dividing a program up into regions of memory called *segments*. A program will always consist of at least one segment and larger programs will have several (see Figure 2-8). Each of an application's segments can be classified so that the operating system can define specific security policies with regard to certain segments. For example, segments of memory containing program instructions can be classified as read only, so that other segments cannot overwrite a program's instructions and alter its behavior.

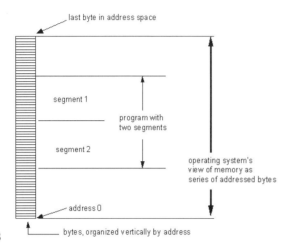

Figure 2-8

 ASIDE Some paging schemes, like the one Intel processors use, allow pages of memory to be classified in a manner similar to the way in which memory segments are classified. A page of memory can be specified as belonging to a particular process, having a certain privilege level, etc. This means that paging can be used to augment the segmentation mechanism, or even replace it completely.

Because memory is referenced by programs so frequently, segmentation is normally implemented at the hardware level so that run-time checks can be performed quickly. There are, however, a couple of ways that protection may be instituted without relying on hardware. There are two purely software-based mechanisms I stumbled across in my research: *sandboxing* and *proof-carrying code*.

Initial research on sandboxing was done in an effort to speed up interprocess communication. Researchers (Wahbe et. al.) took the address space allocated to a program and artificially divided it into two subspaces and a small common space. The small common space was used to allow the two subprograms to communicate. Traditionally, interprocess communication involves using operating system services. Using operating system services, however, results in a certain amount of overhead because the program has to stop and wait for the operating system to respond to its requests. The initial goal of this research was to find a way to speed up IPC, but in the process they also discovered a software-based protection mechanism.

The researchers found a way to divide a single memory segment into sections whose barriers were entirely enforced by software checks, which can be performed at run time. Using a DEC Alpha 400, the researchers determined that the additional run-time checks incurred an additional overhead of 4 percent when compared to a traditional IPC approach.

The idea of proof-carrying code (PCC) is to use specially modified development tools that will compile applications to a special format. The resulting executable is encoded in such a way that the run-time system can verify that the application obeys a certain security model. This is an interesting alternative to sandboxing because the proof verification occurs once when the application is loaded into memory, as opposed to a continuous series of run-time checks.

The bytecode verification facilities provided by Java are an example of this approach. Safety constructs are embedded in the language itself to facilitate protection without the need to rely on hardware. This is particularly important for Java because the language requires a degree of platform independence.

There are problems with proof-carrying code. The first one is performance. If a large application is loaded into memory, there is the potential for a considerable time lag before execution begins. I worked for a bank that had this problem. The application server they used was written completely in Java and consisted of thousands of individual class files. When the server restarted, usually after a crash of some sort, there would often be noticeable time lags as objects were dynamically loaded into memory. To address this issue, they merely forced all the objects to load into memory when the Java virtual machine was invoked. This, in turn, forced verification to be performed before the system actually went back into production.

Another problem with proof-carrying code is that there is no mechanism to verify that the verifier itself is functioning correctly. This is like a police department that has no internal affairs division. The verifier might be corrupt and allow malicious code to execute.

Application Level

As stated earlier, an operating system allocates memory on behalf of an application and then divides this memory into one or more segments. There are several different types of segments an application makes use of (see Figure 2-9). These types are:

- Text segment
- Data segment
- Stack segment
- Heap

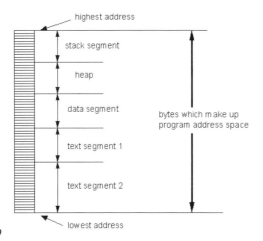

Figure 2-9

Depending on the size of a program and the particular settings used with the compiler that built the application, there may potentially be several segments of each type. Furthermore, the arrangement of the segments in memory can also vary (there may be a data segment between two text segments, or two consecutive data segments followed by a text segment, etc.).

The important thing to remember is that every program has two basic elements: instructions and data. What distinguishes different approaches to memory management at the application level is how the instructions and data of a program are divided up and organized. They are, however, all variations of the same theme.

Text segments are used to store program instructions. If you prefer to be unconventional, and you know how to program in assembly language, you can use an unconditional jump statement to store data in a text segment. Using a text segment to store data, however, is usually done when a program has only a single segment, and thus everything (instructions and data) has to be in the same place. Normally, however, the text segment stores processor instructions and that's it.

The data segment is used to store global data that is allocated at compile time. Storage space in the data segment is static — it does not grow or shrink without making an explicit system call. References to storage areas in the data segment are good for the entire life of a program. At any point during the execution of a program, a variable can refer to storage in the data segment and be guaranteed that the address referenced represents a legitimate value.

The stack segment is used at run time as a kind of temporary scratch pad. The processor will use the stack to allocate temporary storage for function arguments, local variables, and function return values. What allows the stack to be effective is the fact that stack memory allocations typically follow a pattern. When a function is invoked, all the memory for the arguments, return value, and local variables is allocated on the stack. When the function returns, all this memory is freed. This regularity is what makes the stack useful.

The heap, depending on the run-time system involved, will not always be an official segment. Rather, it is often a clump of bytes that sits between other segments as a kind of purgatory. The heap is used to dynamically allocate memory at run time, like the stack.

The difference between the heap and the stack is that the pattern of allocation and deallocation in the heap is much more irregular than that in the stack. If this doesn't make sense, don't worry. Both the stack and the heap will be examined more carefully later on.

The degree of sophistication of a memory management scheme often is a function of the programming language being used. Early languages like COBOL and FORTRAN were fairly primitive. COBOL, in particular, provided only for static storage allocation in data segments. COBOL does not implement recursion, and thus has no use for a stack. Take a look at Table 2-1 for a brief comparison of various languages and their memory management facilities.

Table 2-1

Language	Data Segment	Stack Segment	Heap
COBOL-85	yes	no	no
ANSI C	yes	yes	manual recycling
Java	no	yes	garbage collection

Both Java and C have heaps. The difference between the two languages is that Java has services that automatically recycle allocated memory. In C, the user is responsible for freeing allocated memory when it is no longer needed. The Java virtual machine is a stack-based execution engine, so it does not have the equivalent of a data segment.

Let's take a deeper look at the data segment, stack segment, and heap. The best way to do this is to look at a concrete example. Take the following program as a short case study:

```c
#include<stdio.h>
#include<stdlib.h>

int *array;          ◄─────────────────── data segment used here

int main(int argc, char *argv[])
{
    int size=0;      ◄─────────────── stack used here
    int i;

array = (int*)malloc(argc*sizeof(int));  ◄─────── heap used here

    if(argc<2) { return(0); }

    for(i=1;i<argc;i++)
    {
        array[i]=atoi(argv[i]);
        printf("%d\n",array[i]);
    }

    free(array);
    return(0);
}
```

The data segment is like a footlocker. You have a fixed amount of space, and you know what you are going to put in it and where you are going to put it (usually ahead of time). Global variables are stored in the data segment because they exist for the life span of the application and need to be placed somewhere static. In the above listing, the pointer variable named `array` will have its value stored in the data segment. On the Intel platform, four bytes would be allocated for `array` in the data segment (because an address for x86 CPUs is 32 bits in length). You can see this by looking at the assembly listing:

```
_DATA     SEGMENT
COMM      _array:DWORD
_DATA     ENDS
```

A stack, in the study of data structures, is a last-in-first-out (LIFO) list. Just like a stack of cafeteria trays, items are added and removed from the same point. This means that the last item placed on a stack will also be the first item to be removed.

Inserting an item into a stack is known as a push operation. Removing an item from the stack is known as a pop operation. The location where stack items are pushed and popped is known as the top-of-stack (TOS) (see Figure 2-10).

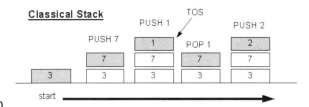

Figure 2-10

The primary feature of a stack is its ability to create a way for actions to be done, and then undone. For example, most text editors have a menu item for canceling the last action you've taken. This is done by pushing text editor actions onto a stack. If you want to cancel an action, you just pop the last action off the stack and invert it. A web browser's Back button is another example of how stacks are used to do, and then undo, an action.

The implementation of a stack in a computer differs slightly from the classical data structure. Instead of growing upwards as items are added, stacks in memory begin at the end of the stack segment and grow downwards as new items are pushed on, such that the TOS always has the lowest address. This is illustrated in Figure 2-11, where the end stack segment ends at address 1011.

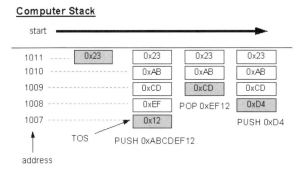

Figure 2-11

NOTE   Part of the reason for this is that computers reference a multibyte data value using the address of the byte with the smallest address. In order to make referencing items on the stack simple, the stack grows towards a lower address such that the address of the TOS is also the address of an actual data item.

C programs, like the previous one, use the stack to allocate temporary storage. This includes things like local variables, function parameters, and function return values. Such variables come into existence when a function is invoked and are dissolved when it returns. This is right in line with the ability of a stack to do and then undo something.

The heap is a region of memory that is basically up for grabs. Unlike the stack, the heap does not have the regularity provided by the push/pop operations. This makes management of the heap a little more flexible, but also potentially much more complicated.

The layout of the heap in a program's address space is often a function of the operating system and the tools used to develop the program. For example, Figure 2-12 displays the differences between the heaps used by programs compiled to the ELF and COFF executable file formats.

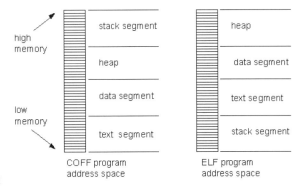

Figure 2-12

Dynamic Memory Management

The process of directing the allocation and recycling of memory from the heap is known as *dynamic memory management* (DMM). There are a couple of ways to implement dynamic memory management. One approach is known as *explicit memory management* (EMM). In explicit memory management, memory is allocated from the heap and then recycled manually (programmatically in the source code). The program listing in the previous section uses explicit memory management. The program allocates an array of integers using a call to `malloc()` and then explicitly gives those bytes back to the heap with a call to the `free()` function.

The other approach is known as *automatic memory management* (AMM), or *garbage collection*. The Java programming language implements automatic memory management. Unlike explicit memory management, the run-time system takes care of recycling allocated storage that isn't needed anymore. Both explicit memory management and automatic memory management involve explicit allocation of memory; the difference between the two methods is how they deal with memory that isn't needed anymore and must be discarded back into the heap.

 ASIDE   How does a run-time system know when a variable's storage isn't needed anymore? Most implementations of garbage collection will only free the storage allocated to an object when the last reference (i.e., pointer) to the object has reached the end of its scope visibility in the program. How and when the recycling part occurs, specifically, is up to the garbage collection scheme.

Regardless of whether explicit or automatic techniques are implemented, all heap management schemes face a few common issues and potential pitfalls:

- Internal fragmentation
- External fragmentation
- Location-based latency

Internal fragmentation occurs when memory is wasted because a request for memory resulted in the allocation of a block of memory that was much too big, relative to the request size. For example, let's say you request 128 bytes of storage and the run-time system gives you a block of 512 bytes. Most of the memory you've been allocated will never be used. Management schemes that allocate fixed-sized memory blocks can run into this problem.

External fragmentation occurs when a series of memory requests leave several free blocks of available memory, none of which are large enough to service a typical request.

Latency problems can occur if two data values are stored far apart from one another in memory. The farther apart two values are in memory, the longer it takes for the processor to perform operations that involve those values. In an extreme case, one value may be so far away that it gets paged out to disk and requires a disk I/O operation to bring it back into the ball game.

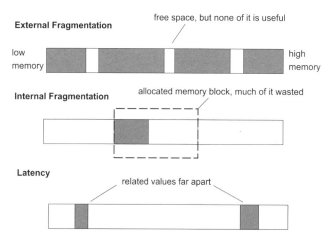

Figure 2-13

Explicit memory management tends to be faster than garbage collection. Explicit memory management shifts responsibility onto the shoulders of the developer with regard to keeping track of allocated memory. The result of this is that the algorithms implemented by the run-time systems are simpler and involve less bookkeeping. This is both a blessing and a curse. Explicit memory management allows programs to be smaller because the compiler does not have to emit any extra instructions or data to handle garbage collection. In addition, explicit memory management also gives the programmer a better idea of what's actually going on behind the curtain.

The curse of this extra complexity is that it can lead to mistakes (this is an understatement). If a dynamically allocated variable leaves its scope before being recycled, the memory cannot be recycled and the program will gradually drain away memory until the computer halts. This is known as a *memory leak*, and is an insidious problem to try to correct (the author is a voice of experience in this matter). If a dynamically allocated variable is recycled before it goes out of scope, the variable will become an invalid reference and potentially crash the program (or produce incorrect results, which is even worse). The invalid reference in this kind of situation is known as a *dangling pointer*.

Garbage collection, on the other hand, takes care of all the details of memory recycling. This allows the programmer to focus on domain-specific problem solving. This makes sense because an analyst who is writing a purchase-order system already has enough complexity to deal with just trying to get the logic of the purchase-order application to function. Having to manage low-level details like memory only makes the job more difficult.

Psychologists have claimed that the average human can only keep track of about seven things at any point in time. By forcing the developer to keep track of memory recycling, the number of things the developer has to juggle increases. Garbage collection is a solution to this problem.

Table 2-2 summarizes the costs and benefits of explicit and automatic memory management.

Table 2-2

	Explicit Memory Management	Automatic Memory Management
Benefits	size (smaller)	stay focused on domain issues
	speed (quicker)	
	control (can see under the hood)	
Costs	complexity, bookkeeping	larger memory footprint
	memory leaks	comparable performance
	dangling pointers	

Garbage collection advocates claim that the energy committed to dealing with memory leaks and dangling pointers would be better spent on building a garbage collection mechanism. This is a very powerful argument if the performance hit from garbage collection isn't noticeable.

This is a big "if." Early garbage collection implementations were notoriously slow, sometimes accounting for almost 50 percent of execution time. Not to mention that explicit memory management proponents will argue that the emergence of tools that detect memory leaks have eliminated traditional problems. Thus, performance is a key issue.

 RANT During my research I came across a number of journal articles in which the authors claimed that the performance of their garbage collection approach was comparable to that provided by manual memory managers. Comparable? How do you define comparable? The word "comparable" cannot be directly quantified. For all I know, some professor (who needs to publish articles to obtain tenure) is taking creative liberties to show his algorithm in a favorable light so that the journal editors will print his findings. Not that this is a bad thing; the business world is even worse.

Much of the previous discussion may seem like a lot of arm waving. To get a better idea of what the potential tradeoffs are, it helps to look at concrete examples. Let's start by looking at how garbage collection has been used in practice.

Garbage collection was entirely theoretical until 1959, when Dan Edwards implemented the first garbage collection facilities. It just so happened that Dan was involved with John McCarthy in the development of the LISP programming language. LISP, which was intended for algebraic List Processing, started off as a notational concept which evolved into a computer language. When compared to other programming languages that existed during its development, LISP was way ahead of its time.

There were, however, significant problems with LISP's performance and this was probably the price that LISP paid for its advanced features. The garbage collection schemes in early implementations of LISP were notoriously slow. One response to this problem was to push basic operations down to the hardware level. There were companies that attempted to follow this route, like Symbolics, which sold LISP machines. LISP machines were manufactured in the 1970s and 1980s. The idea, unfortunately, never really caught on. In the mid-1990s, Symbolics went bankrupt.

There are three basic classical algorithms for garbage collection:

- Reference counting
- Mark-sweep
- Copying collection

There are also a couple of more recent approaches like:

- Generational garbage collection
- Conservative garbage collection

Which is the best? The answer to this is: <u>There is no best approach</u>. The performance of a particular garbage collection algorithm depends upon the behavior of the program the algorithm is servicing, the hardware platform the empirical data is being collected on, and subtle variations in the implementation of the recycling algorithm. There are an infinite number of potential test cases, each with its own unique behavior. This makes it difficult to come up with a conclusion that isn't inherently statistical.

Rather than try to analyze the best algorithm, it's probably more productive to look at one that is readily available on the Internet. The Boehm-Demers-Weiser (BDW) collector is what is known as a conservative garbage collector. It is available for download at http://www.hpl.hp.com/personal/Hans_Boehm/gc.

The BDW collector is a convenient, add-on replacement for C's `malloc()` and `free()` functions. No special behavior is required from your C compiler. All of the collector's functionality is provided by an extension API. The BDW collector also doubles as a nifty leak detector.

The BDW garbage collector is not a small implementation. I do not have space to explain its inner workings (that could take a whole book). Interested readers will find sufficient documentation at Boehm's web site. What I'm really concerned with is the performance of the BDW collector. The following two articles take a good look at the BDW collector. The first, a 1992 paper by Benjamin Zorn, demonstrates that the BDW collector is, on the average, about 20 percent slower than the fastest explicit memory manager in each experimental trial. The second, published by Detlefs et. al. in 1993, indicates that the BDW collector is, on the average, about 27 percent slower than the fastest explicit memory manager in each experimental trial.

NOTE   Now we know what "comparable" means. A garbage collector that performs comparably to explicit memory management will be, on the average, about 20 to 30 percent slower.

Explicit memory management is as densely populated with algorithms as garbage collection. There are five basic approaches to explicit memory management.

- Table-driven algorithms
- Sequential fit
- Buddy systems
- Segregated storage
- Sub-allocation

Table-driven algorithms break memory into a set number of fixed-size blocks. These blocks are then indexed using some type of abstract data structure. For example, a bit map could be used to keep track of which blocks are free and which have been allocated. The problem with this approach is that a bit map, depending on the memory block size, can take up a lot of space. In addition, searching for a series of free memory blocks could require searching the entire bit map, and this hurts performance.

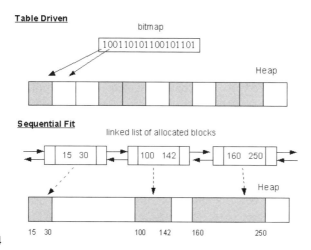

Figure 2-14

Sequential fit algorithms allow memory to be allocated in different sizes. This approach keeps track of the allocated and free areas of the heap using linked lists of some sort. Because the list data structures are only concerned with where the memory blocks begin and end, there is less potential overhead in terms of data structure size and search time.

Sequential fit memory management can be broken down according to how it allocates free blocks of memory. There are three basic subcategories:

■ First fit — Allocates the first free block large enough to handle the memory request

■ Best fit — Allocates the block whose size is closest to the amount requested

■ Worst fit — Allocates the largest block (which often yields a large free sub-block)

Buddy systems are an approach that attempt to speed up the merging of free memory zones when allocated memory is freed. Unfortunately, using a buddy system algorithm for explicit memory management can lead to internal fragmentation. When I found this out, I stopped researching this topic.

The segregated storage technique involves breaking the heap up into zones and applying a different memory management scheme to each zone. This has proven to be very effective in situations where memory requests tend to follow certain patterns. For example, if you know that you will have several files open for the life span of a program, you can allocate memory for them in a zone that is intended for long-term storage. Likewise, variables that will exist for only a few function calls can be allocated in a zone that is tailored for short-lived storage.

Sub-allocators attempt to solve the memory allocation problem by allocating a large chunk of memory from the underlying run-time system and then managing it alone. In other words, your program takes complete responsibility for allocating and recycling memory from its own private stockpile, without any help from the run-time system. This is a good technique to use when you know, ahead of time, what kind of allocation requests are going to be made. In other words, you should use a sub-allocator when you can constrain the problem at hand. It may entail a lot of extra complexity, but you can dramatically improve performance. In his 1990 book on C compiler design, Allen Holub makes excellent use of sub-allocators to speed up his compiler implementation.

Again, you might ask which of these algorithms yields the best performance. Again, the answer is: There isn't a best approach. The efficiency of an explicit memory manager is a function of the requests that it services. The spectrum of program behavior that exists in production environments is so broad that there does not seem to be any fundamental class of requests to cater to. To survive in the wild, an explicit memory manager must be flexible and have the capacity to respond to several different types of requests.

 ASIDE   In the end, using explicit or automatic memory management is a religious question. Deciding to use explicit or automatic methods reflects the fundamental beliefs, values, and priorities of the developer. As I've stated before, there are no perfect solutions. Every approach involves making some sort of concession. Explicit memory management offers speed and control at the expense of complexity. Manual memory management forsakes performance in order to restrain complexity. You'll see what my preferences are in the next section.

A summary of memory management is depicted in Figure 2-15.

memory management overview

```
                       ┌─ what ──── RAM, disk storage
        ── machine level ─┤
                       └─ how ───── CPU, bus interfaces

                       ┌─ what ──── memory address space
        operating      ─┤           ┌── segmentation
        system level    └─ how ─────┤
                                    └── paging

                       ┌─ what ──── ┌── static memory ( data segment )
                                    └── dynamic memory ( stack, heap )
        ── program level ─┤
                          └─ how ───┌── compiler policies ( data segment, stack )
                                    └── dynamic management ( heap )
                                        ├── issues ( fragmentation, locality, speed )
                                        ├── explicit memory management
                                        └── automatic memory management
```

Figure 2-15

HEC Memory Management

To allow HEC binaries to execute on different hardware platforms without needing to recompile, I arbitrarily decided that numeric values in HEC executable files should all be encoded using the big-endian format. If a given platform is little-endian, then it is the responsibility of the HEC run-time to perform the necessary conversions before any program instructions are decoded and run. The intended result is that numeric values will be able to morph to their native format during the virtual machine's boot phase. This is discussed at length in Chapter 3.

If you recall, one of the principal design goals for HEC was portability. As a result, I knew that I would have to implement memory protection completely in software. There was no way I was going to be able to use native segmentation facilities without anchoring myself to a hardware platform. I was encouraged by the results of my research on sandboxing and proof-carrying code and I implemented limited forms of each in HEC.

When the HEC run-time is invoked, it allocates memory from the native operating system to construct an artificial address space for a single application. This address space has exactly three segments: a text segment, a heap segment, and a stack segment (see Figure 2-16).

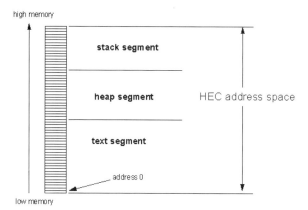

Figure 2-16

The HEC address space starts at 0 and extends to the end of the stack segment. The size of the text segment is fixed at compile time, but the stack and heap are adjustable. The HEC virtual machine has command-line options that allow the size of the stack and heap to be set to nonnegative values. This means that although we know the first address is 0, we will not know what the last address is until the virtual machine actually starts up.

Run-time checks are instituted such that memory references beyond the stack segment or below the text segment are not allowed. The run time also checks to make sure that the stack does not overflow into the heap or underflow into the forbidden zone at the top of the address space. This is how protection is instituted in HEC. The primary goal is to protect the run-time system and the native operating system from a runaway HEC program.

Another thing I do to safeguard the native platform is to fix the amount of memory available to the address space. Once the text, stack, and heap have been allocated, that's it. In Unix parlance, there is no `sbrk()` function. The program doesn't get any more memory. This prevents a HEC application from draining memory away from the native machine and causing a crash.

It also allows for resource planning. If you know you need to run 20 HEC virtual machines, where each run time uses 5 MB of memory, you know in advance that you'll need a machine with 100 MB of RAM. Note that this scenario assumes that enough benchmarking has been done to safely assume that each virtual machine can subsist on 5 MB of memory for sustained periods in a production environment.

When the HEC virtual machine initially loads a program into memory, it does a one-time check to make sure that the program's binary encoded instructions (i.e., the program's bytecode) are legitimate. This one-time check is known as bytecode *verification*. For example, the HEC virtual machine checks to see that instruction operands have the correct values, and also checks to make sure that address literals aren't out of bounds and that all instruction opcodes are valid.

Virtual memory is a disk I/O-intensive facility. The only way to obtain satisfactory performance is to push the basic operations down to the hardware. For the sake of portability and performance I decided not to implement any kind of paging. If I had decided to implement paging in HEC, I would have had to do it entirely in software (to keep it portable), and the performance hit would have been tremendous.

You might notice that there is no data segment in the HEC address space. In order to simplify the process of bytecode verification, I decided that the text segment should consist only of instructions and include no data. This allows the verifier to serially work its way up HEC's text segment and do its thing quickly. If you want to be sneaky, you could get around my requirement by using an unconditional jump statement, followed by a whole load of dummy instructions. However, I don't recommend this. Instead, global data is allocated on the stack when a program begins to execute. Thus, the stack is used both for static global data and dynamic local storage.

To eliminate some of the dangers that arise from memory latency, I decided that the HEC run-time will be loaded into physical memory, if at all possible. Before HEC actually sets up its address space, it makes a call to see how much physical memory its host computer has free. If insufficient physical memory is available, the HEC virtual machine will not start.

The final and most complicated issue I faced was managing the heap. After reading a number of journal articles (some of which I have already made reference to), I decided to use an explicit memory management scheme. I am sure a number of computer science people will be, in the words of Jackie Chiles, "shocked and chagrined." Nevertheless, I had my reasons. I justify my adoption of explicit memory management with the following arguments.

Argument One:

I think that most garbage collection implementations assume a multithreaded environment where there will be plenty of CPU cycles off the critical path. This allows the garbage collector to supposedly do its thing in the background while the rest of the program chugs merrily along. For reasons I will explain later in this chapter, HEC is not a multithreaded environment. Any garbage collection that would need to be done would have to be performed on the critical path of execution.

Argument Two:

Recall my design goals (portability, simplicity, performance). Conservative garbage collectors like the BDW collector are not simple or immediately portable. I do not like the comparable performance exhibited by garbage collectors in general. By nature, garbage collection requires the run-time system to do a lot of extra work to keep track of allocated memory. This extra work translates into extra instructions, which are often redundant and unnecessary, and this translates into degraded performance.

Argument Three:

My own professional experience has left me biased. I spent several years working for an ERP company whose primary competitive advantage was performance. ERP companies, in general, have to survive in a very small market and compete against giants like SAP, PeopleSoft, and Oracle. In this type of cutthroat environment, where customers require high-volume OLTP business applications, every little bit of performance counts. I've known engineers who are willing to jump through all sorts of syntactic hoops to make something execute faster without increasing the memory footprint. I remember looking though parts of the transaction manager where function calls had been replaced by labels and goto statements in an effort to eliminate the overhead of building an activation record. I also recall a VP who fined engineers for performing unecessary disk I/O. It goes without saying that garbage collection was out of the question. Memory leaks, when they developed, could be located and eliminated using commercial tools designed expressly for that purpose.

Having precluded garbage collection, I was confronted with choosing an explicit memory management algorithm. As I stated earlier, there seems to be no optimal solution in the general case. This may just be a side effect of the undeveloped nature of computer science as a discipline. How long did it take physics to develop quantum field theory? A few thousand years? In a couple of hundred years, maybe a breakthrough will occur and the problem of efficient memory allocation will be resolved. For the time being, we are left stumbling around in the dark. I suppose the most I could hope for would be an approach that would be flexible enough to service most requests, and simple enough for me to maintain.

The problem of explicit memory management has been tackled before in the past 50 years. I took a look at existing solutions to see what production-level products utilized. I did this with the hope that the engineers who built the product had done some research of their own, so that their implementation would encapsulate some of their knowledge.

I looked under the hood of RxDOS, a real-time, multitasking clone of Microsoft's original DOS operating system. I also looked at a couple of publicly available implementations of C's malloc() function. What I found was that most of them, in addition to RxDOS, use some variation of sequential fit.

I understand that DOS is not considered an "interesting" platform by most people. And I am sure there will be Unix people who simply turn their noses up and smirk. But it is a simple and straightforward operating system, and I was able to borrow a few ideas.

I found something interesting while I was experimenting with DOS 6.22. Take a look at the following program.

```
#include<stdio.h>
#include<stdlib.h>

void main(int argc, char *argv[])
{
    int i;
```

```
unsigned char *ucptr;
for(i=0;i<10;i++)
{
    ucptr = malloc(128);
    printf("allocated address=%Fp\n",ucptr);
}
return;
}
```

Besides creating a small memory leak (because I do not explicitly free the allocated memory), this program produces the following output:

```
allocated address=02EC:1802
allocated address=02EC:1A86
allocated address=02EC:1B08
allocated address=02EC:1B8A
allocated address=02EC:1C0C
allocated address=02EC:1C8E
allocated address=02EC:1D10
allocated address=02EC:1D92
allocated address=02EC:1E14
allocated address=02EC:1E96
```

This program allocates 128 bytes at a time. Every single one of the calls to `malloc()`, with the exception of the first, allocates 130 bytes. There's an extra two bytes attached to each allocated block of memory. This leads me to suspect that DOS's `malloc()` function is using part of the heap memory itself to help manage the list of free and allocated memory blocks.

There are a few contemporary segregated storage algorithms that try to optimize performance by exploiting patterns and regularities that sometimes occur. I did not, however, want to base the performance of my allocator on behavior that is stochastic. I wanted to use a design that would handle several different types of memory requests equally well. A survey of dynamic memory allocation by Wilson et. al., in 1995, found that, "If all else fails, relying on best fit and first fit usually won't be a disaster."

Development time was also a factor. This is true in the case of all commercial products. I could not afford to spend six months developing an explicit memory manager. Especially when it was such a small part of what I was building. I wanted to remain focused and spend time on core functionality.

As a result of all this digging around, I decided to use an explicit memory management technique based on the sequential fit algorithm. My solution uses a first-fit approach to allocating new blocks, and uses the heap space itself for sequential fit data structures. The specific details of this scheme are provided in Chapter 6.

Machine Design

Central processors can be implemented as register-based or stack-based machines. A register-based processor, like Intel's Pentium, has eight 32-bit registers it uses to perform basic computation. A stack-based processor, like the Harris semiconductor RTX 32P, has two on-chip stacks to perform basic operations.

Stack-based processors tend to be popular for use in embedded systems because they support smaller programs and work well in situations where resources are limited. A stack-based processor instruction like IADD pops two integers off the stack, adds them, and then pushes the sum of the two values back onto the stack. The IADD instruction possesses a memory footprint that is much smaller than the register-based version, which looks like:

```
ADD  $R1, $R2, $R3
```

This instruction takes the sum of $R3 and $R2 and places their sum in $R1. The stack-based IADD instruction requires only a single byte. The register-based ADD instruction requires at least four bytes. A typical program may have thousands of such instructions, such that a program compiled for a stack-based machine may be several times smaller than the same program compiled for a register-based machine.

Performing a function call is also much more efficient on a stack-based machine. This is because the function arguments are already on the stack. On a register-based machine, arguments must be collected and placed on the stack manually, and this takes more work.

Context switches are less expensive on stack-based computers. A register-based computer has to manually save the state of all of its registers during a context switch. On RISC architectures, where there are a proliferation of registers, context switching can be a memory-intensive operation. Stack-based machines do not have this problem. Stack-based computers can keep a stack for each process and perform a context switch merely by changing stacks.

You may be wondering why stack-based machines haven't taken over the landscape of computer architecture. The reason they haven't is that register-based processors have one big advantage: They are fast. Registers lie within the CPU itself, and any manipulation involving values held in the registers can be accomplished very quickly. Intel's new 64-bit processor, Itanium, has hundreds of on-chip registers in an effort to keep as much program execution on the chip as possible. Stack-based processors, on the other hand, almost always have their on-chip stacks spill out into memory. The consequence of this is that performing basic stack-oriented operations requires the processor to fetch data from memory. This slows the execution speed of a stack-based processor significantly.

The argument that register-based processors lend themselves to larger executables is not as big an issue as it was in the 1970s. Today, memory is relatively cheap compared to what it was in the 1970s. I can remember, in the early 1990s, that having 16 MB of memory on an Intel 80486 box pretty much gave you "workstation" status in the eyes of your peers, as opposed to just being a desktop computer.

Another thing that I have heard from hardware people is that register-based processors are easier to debug because the execution of instructions is more transparent. Remember, with the stack-based IADD instruction, you lose the original operands when the instruction completes. With a register-based processor, you at least can take a look at what you added together to double-check that the sum is correct. Not to mention that if a stack-based processor's stack pointer gets corrupted somehow, everything else is invalidated with it.

Table 2-3

	Stack-Based Processor	Register-Based Processor
Benefits	smaller memory footprint	basic operations are fast
	faster function calls	(overall performance is better)
	faster context switches	execution more transparent
Costs	basic operations are slow	memory-intensive context switches
		work-intensive function calls

The bottom line in the marketplace is performance. Hardware companies have invested billions of dollars to keep pace with Moore's Law and stay ahead of their competitors. In an environment like this, the chip design that provides the fastest execution is the one that will survive. Darwin's ideas are playing themselves out in the chip industry. Register-based processors have thrived and stack-based processors have perished.

HEC Machine Design

The discussion of stack-based versus register-based processor designs provided in the previous section really only applies to actual hardware implementation. A virtual machine is constructed completely out of software, so more than a few of the previous tradeoffs are irrelevant. My final solution is a mixture of the two extremes.

In the beginning, I knew I was going to be working somewhat in the dark. I didn't know whether my implementation of a certain numeric operation was going to work or not. I decided that it would make life much easier for me to adopt a register-based design. I sacrificed a smaller memory footprint for the sake of getting a better idea of what the virtual machine was doing.

At the same time, I liked the way that stack-based processors handle function calls, facilitate recursion, and support expeditious context switches. Because of this, I gave the HEC virtual machine a stack to use. The stack segment, which is the topmost segment in HEC's address space, is used to support some of these features.

I also think that my prolonged exposure to the x86 instruction set also had an influence. We are often the culmination of our own experiences. 8088 Assembler was the first programming language that I learned, probably because Microsoft's debug utility came with every DOS machine and I had access to debug before I could scrounge enough money together to buy a compiler. I distinctly remember using debug's "A" command to assemble small programs. I was the first kid on my block to use hexadecimal.

Finally, I knew that there were several other stack-based virtual machines, like Forth's stack-based execution engine, Pascal's P-code interpreter, and the Java virtual machine. Rather than tread over a well-defined path, I thought it would be fun to try something different.

I decided to make HEC's registers 64 bits wide, which reflects my earlier decision to go with a 64-bit address space. While this may be slightly awkward on a 32-bit platform, and even more so on a 16-bit computer, I was looking ahead when I made the decision. Within the next couple of years, Intel will start to mass produce 64-bit processors. This will effectively commoditize a technology which, in the past, has been the domain of expensive Unix machines and mainframes. When this happens, porting HEC to take advantage of this new technology will be easy.

The HEC virtual machine has 42 64-bit registers and 10 32-bit registers (see Figure 2-17). The registers are broken down as follows:

- Five segment registers ($BE, $HS, $HE, $SS, $TOP)

- Three pointers ($IP, $SP, $FP)

- Twenty-four general-purpose integer registers ($R1–$R24)

- Ten double-precision IEEE 754 floating-point registers ($D1–$D10)

- Ten single-precision IEEE 754 floating-point registers ($F1–$F10)

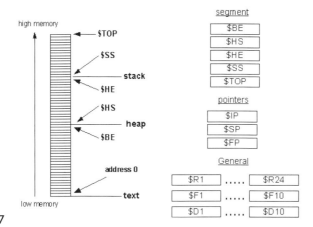

Figure 2-17

The segment registers are initialized when the virtual machine is invoked. The segment registers are used to delimit the different segments of the address space. These registers can be modified, but I suggest that you treat them like read only, or at least save their values if you are going to modify them. The text segment always starts at address 0 and ends at the address stored in $BE (bytecode end). The heap segment starts and ends at the addresses stored in $HS and $HE (heap start and heap end). The stack segment starts and ends at the addresses stored in $SS and $TOP (stack start and the top of the memory partition).

While the virtual machine runs, the $IP register stores the address of the first byte of the next instruction to be executed. The $SP register stores the address of the current top of the stack. When function calls are made, the $FP register is used to define the *procedure frame* (also known as the *activation record*), which is temporarily allocated on the stack in the event of a function call.

When the HEC virtual machine starts up, $IP is set to 0, $SP stores the same value as $TOP, and $FP is 0.

The remaining registers are used for general computation. The 64-bit registers $R1 through $R24 are meant to store integer values. The 32-bit registers $F1 through $F10 are meant to store single-precision IEEE 754 floating-point values. The 64-bit registers $D1 through $D10 are meant to store double-precision IEEE 754 floating-point values.

Task Management

During my research on task management, I had read a lot about processes but had a hard time actually finding a clear definition of what a process was. Some documentation called a process a "unit of work." What does that mean? I'm a physicist by training and when I see this definition, I think of something like:

$$W = \mathbf{F} \bullet \mathbf{d} = Fd\cos\theta$$

Hey! What is the magnitude of the force? Over what distance is the force being applied? Defining a term using a previously undefined term is not very enlightening. It only left me wondering what the author meant by the term "work." This kind of definition is ambiguous at best.

As a physicist, I was instructed to solve a problem by describing the solution in terms of known quantities or concepts. In a similar way, I am going to define a process in terms of concrete physical entities I've already introduced.

A *path of execution* is a series of machine instructions executed sequentially. These instructions do not necessarily have to be contiguous in memory, but rather merely executed one after another such that the execution of one instruction leads to the execution of the next instruction (i.e., a JMP instruction might move the instruction pointer to an ADD instruction several kilobytes away).

A computer's *machine state* is a combination of the values the processor stores in its on-chip resources (i.e., registers, on-chip stack, on-chip cache) and the contents of the memory it accesses.

A *process*, or *task*, is a path of execution and the associated machine state the path of execution produces. The hardware state that is associated with a particular task is known as the task *context*.

One excellent analogy I found was in Andrew Tanenbaum's book on Minix. He likened a program to a cake recipe, in that it is merely a set of instructions. Then he equated a process to the actions consisting of collecting the ingredients, reading the recipe, and baking the cake. A program is a static entity, defined by a set of binary commands. A process is the execution of those commands and the results they produce.

The early computers of the 1950s executed only a single task at a time. Modern computers can allow several tasks to share machine resources using a technique known as *multitasking*. Multitasking allows tasks to share the processor by dispatching a single task to execute for an amount of time and keeping all the other tasks suspended. The motivation behind multitasking was to make optimal use of the processor. While one process is waiting for input, another process can be executed to prevent the CPU from having to wait along with the other process.

It is convenient to divide the topic of process management into mechanism and policy. The *mechanism* portion of process management explains the basic operation of how a task is dispatched, executed, and suspended. The *policy* portion of process management explains how the mechanism can be applied to decide when the current executing task should be suspended and which of the remaining tasks should be dispatched.

The mechanism behind process management is interrupt driven. A processor receives signals from other low-level components like I/O devices and the hardware clock. These signals take the form of interrupts. As the exact nature of an interrupt varies from one hardware platform to the next, suffice it to say that an *interrupt* is a machine-level message that is transmitted to the CPU from other hardware subsystems.

The hardware clock is particularly important for multitasking. On the IBM PC, there is the I8253/8254 programmable interval timer. The timer generates an interrupt for each tick of the computer's clock, which occurs over known time intervals. The process of suspending a task in order to execute another task is called a *context switch*. Every time a timer interrupt is received by the processor, the operating system has the opportunity to apply a given policy and decide if it is time to perform a context switch.

The *kernel* of an operating system is the component that administrates context switches and schedules tasks for execution. The name "kernel" is meant to imply that this part of the operating system is the core element (which it is).

Information about processes is, by necessity, maintained by the operating system. Most operating systems maintain a process table, which usually consists of a heavily nested set of data structures. The process table is a small database of information which records, among other things, the state of each process. A process may be in one of three states: executing, suspended, or blocking (see Figure 2-18).

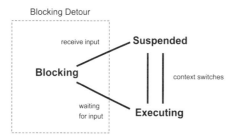

Figure 2-18

A process in the executing state is currently having its instructions executed by the processor. The operating system may, according to some policy, decide to suspend the process via a context switch and force the process into the suspended state. Another alternative is that an executing process might require input of some sort and will <u>voluntarily</u> suspend itself and enter the blocking state. For example, a call to C's `scanf()` function will cause a process to block until the user types in some text and presses the Enter key. Once a process is in the blocking state, if it receives the input it was waiting for it will enter into the suspended state.

Each hardware platform has its own special way of supporting multitasking. I won't even try to go into the specific details (trust me, that would take a couple chapters in and of itself). Instead, I'm going to give you a general overview of the basic ideas that apply to most platforms.

Operating systems normally initiate a context switch by securing the machine state information of the current executing process and storing it either in the process table itself or in a well-known spot of memory that the process table can index. Once the machine state of the currently executing process is acquired, the operating system will officially change the state of the process to "suspended" by modifying the state field of the task's entry in the process table. Next, the operating system will apply its process management policy and decide which process to dispatch. When it has picked a process to dispatch, it will change the chosen task's state field in the process table to "executing," load the task's machine state, and proceed with execution of the chosen process. This is illustrated in Figure 2-19.

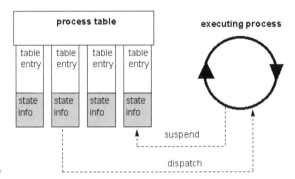

Figure 2-19

I've described how a context switch is performed. Now we need to look at the policy side of process management. Specifically, we need to look into different ways of deciding when a context switch is performed and which suspended process should be dispatched.

There are basically two times when a context switch can be performed. In the case of *cooperative multitasking*, a process will voluntarily yield when it sees fit. This demands a certain amount of discipline on behalf of the engineer who writes the program because the program itself is entirely responsible for yielding. If the program is designed incorrectly, the program may not yield at all and all the other processes will starve. Not a pretty thought.

In the case of *preemptive multitasking*, the operating system decides when a process should make a context switch. Most contemporary operating systems manage multiple tasks preemptively to give the illusion that all of the tasks are executing simultaneously. This is done by rapidly switching from executing one task to the next.

Deciding which process to dispatch during a context switch is a matter of *process scheduling*. There are hundreds of possible scheduling algorithms. For example, in the round-robin scheduling approach, each process is given a set quantum of time in which to execute. The scheduler continually cycles sequentially through the process table and allows each process to run for the same amount of time. When one process is suspended, the next task in the process table gets its turn.

ASIDE With respect to the round-robin approach, a clever trick that can be used involves ending early the time slice of a process that is waiting for I/O. This can radically improve performance in a situation where there is a user entering data at a console, because in such a case there may be several seconds when the user's process is waiting for input.

You could modify the round-robin scheme by introducing the concept of *priority*, which is to say that some processes are more important than others and should get more CPU cycles. One way of implementing this is to dispatch processes that have a higher relative priority. When the scheduler suspends the current process, it looks at the process table and dispatches the task with the highest priority. If there are several tasks that have a high priority level, then a policy needs to be implemented to decide which high priority process is dispatched. The combinations of different scheduling algorithms are endless.

A summary of task management is provided in Figure 2-20.

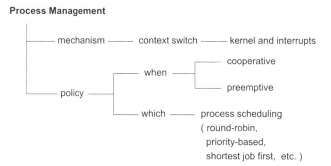

Figure 2-20

Threads

A *thread*, or *lightweight process*, is a path of execution that is confined to the address space of a particular task. A thread can have its own private machine state, but it can also alter the machine state belonging to the task to which it is confined.

Normally, a task consists of a single thread, where the machine state of the thread is the same as the machine state of the process. However, a task can be partitioned up into multiple threads where each thread has its own private stack, memory storage, and execution instructions. In this case, the task is said to be *multithreaded*.

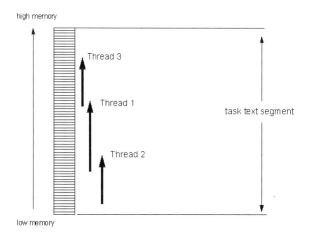

Figure 2-21

Threads are often called lightweight processes because they are somewhat like little miniature tasks. There are, however, some significant differences (see Table 2-4).

Table 2-4

	Threads	Tasks
Segmentation	no	yes
Single owner	yes (task)	no (tasks are spawned by different users)
Scheduled	yes	yes
Machine state	private and common	single set of state parameters

 NOTE Memory segmentation is not applied at the thread level, so threads have access to each other's resources. There is no hardware-based protection instituted at the thread level, like there is for processes.

Because threads are confined to, and share, the address space of a process, they have access to the global data of the process. This includes things like open file handles, subprocesses, and variables in the task's data segment. The fact that threads in a process can share process resources is a double-edged sword. On one hand, it allows the threads to communicate. Threads often use global process memory like a post office where messages can be delivered and received. On the other hand, if two threads in a process are sharing a common resource, the possibility exists that the two threads will try to modify the resource at the same time and the resource will be corrupted. This requires that common task resources be *synchronized*, such that only one thread at a time can access the resource. There are several different techniques used to provide synchronization, but I will not go into them here. Instead, I would recommend that you take a look at Tanenbaum's book, which is listed in the reference section.

There are two ways to provide the mechanism for managing multiple threads. Threads can be implemented using an API extension that runs entirely in user-space, or they can be implemented in the operating system kernel. Threads managed strictly in user-space offer better performance because system calls to the kernel are eliminated. In addition, threads managed in user-space allow customized scheduling algorithms to be used.

The problem with threads managed in user-space is that the kernel knows nothing of them. The kernel still thinks it is only dealing with a single-threaded process. The result of this is that when a thread in a process makes a call to a function like `scanf()`, the thread will have to block for input. The kernel sees that the process is waiting for input and blocks the process as a whole. This causes all the threads to be suspended until the one thread that made the `scanf()` call gets its data. To be honest, this one gotcha pretty much negates any of the benefits of using threads at all.

Managing threads using the kernel does get around the blocking problem at the expense of increasing the amount of work the kernel has to do. This is because the process table not only has to keep track of tasks, but it now also has to keep track of the threads within a task. Naturally, giving the kernel more work to do slows down execution speed.

Threads are like tasks with regard to policy. Threads can be preemptively or coopera-tively scheduled in much the same way that tasks are. In fact, if a computer has multiple processors, each thread can be scheduled to execute on its own processor.

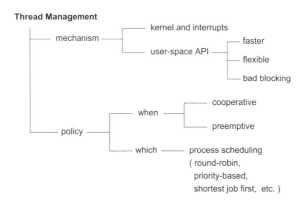

Figure 2-22

HEC Task Management

The HEC run-time executes as a single process. In order to simulate multitasking I would have to make HEC a multithreaded process.

Unfortunately, threading implementations vary from one operating system to the next. For example, let us assume there is a process consisting of two threads that print out the digits 1 through 5. On a platform that uses preemptive time-slicing to schedule threads, the two threads would create the following output stream:

Thread A	1
Thread B	1
Thread A	2
Thread A	3
Thread B	2
Thread B	3
Thread A	4
Thread B	4
Thread A	5
Thread B	5

On a platform that uses a cooperative, priority-based thread scheduling approach, the two threads would create the following output stream:

Thread A	1
Thread A	2
Thread A	3
Thread A	4
Thread A	5

Thread B	1
Thread B	2
Thread B	3
Thread B	4
Thread B	5

As you can see, there is no way I could achieve any sort of uniform behavior and still maintain a portable code base. The only way I could guarantee consistent operation would be if I implemented the simulated multitasking completely in HEC, without any help from the underlying system.

The problem with implementing everything entirely in HEC is the same one threads have that run strictly in user-space. When one of the simulated tasks makes a system call that blocks, all of the simulated tasks will be suspended because the HEC process as a whole will block.

The bottom line is that I really didn't feel like I had a good way to implement multitasking at the virtual machine level. If I used native threading, I would sacrifice portability. This is a major problem because portability was my primary design goal. If I did everything within the context of HEC, I would lose most of the benefits of multitasking because of blocking. The only decision that seemed to make sense was to abandon simulated multitasking and design the HEC virtual machine to execute as a single-threaded task.

Input/Output

In my opinion, this is the most difficult part of operating system design. This is one reason why authors of texts on operating systems, with the exception of Andrew Tanenbaum, shy away from this area. You will find plenty of material on task scheduling and memory management because these are relatively straightforward topics. When the time comes to explain the subtleties of a production-quality file system, you will find the details sadly lacking. This is somewhat of a disservice because many system engineers consider the file system to be second only to the kernel in terms of overall importance.

Communicating with external devices has always been a bit of a secret art, particularly at the operating system level where there is nothing between your source code and the devices but the bare metal. At this murky, machine-level depth every hardware vendor has its own rules with regard to talking to the outside world. Each platform is its own little microcosm of chip sets, technical jargon, and I/O assembler commands.

Take the 80x86 Intel platform as an example. There are two instructions that can be used to read and write data to external devices in register-sized chunks: IN and OUT.

The IN instruction reads data from an I/O port. The OUT instruction writes data to an I/O port. An I/O port is a numeric value that is mapped to a specific device or a component of a specific device. Port numbers range from 0 to 65,535. Table 2-5 displays the mapping of a couple of port values to hardware components.

Table 2-5

Port	Device
0x60	8255 8-bit register (PA), stores keyboard scan code when key is pressed
0x61	8255 8-bit register (PB), interface to speaker and acknowledges keypress
0x20	master 8259 8-bit interrupt command register
0x21	master 8259 8-bit interrupt mask register
0xA0	slave 8259 8-bit interrupt command register
0xA1	slave 8259 8-bit interrupt mask register

You're probably asking yourself: "What the heck is the 8255?"

The 8255 programmable peripheral interface (PPI) acts as a liaison to the keyboard. The Intel processor does not directly communicate with I/O devices. Instead, it uses intermediary controllers like the 8255 PPI to do most of the grunt work. When a key is pressed, its scan code gets stored in an 8-bit register of the 8255, named PA. The 8255 has another 8-bit register, named PB, which can be used to acknowledge a keypress by setting and then clearing its highest-order bit. The PB register can also be used to fiddle with your PC's speaker.

The IN instruction can read data from a device in three sizes. It can read a single byte, a word, or a double word. It stores the data it reads in a register. The amount of data it reads from a device is determined by the size of the register specified in the IN command. The IN command can use the 8-bit AL register, the 16-bit AX register, or the 32-bit EAX register. In all three cases, the port number is specified by the 16-bit DX register. For example:

```
IN AX,DX
```

This command reads 16 bits of data from the port specified by the DX register. The OUT instruction is very much like the IN instruction with the exception that it sends data instead of reading it. For example:

```
OUT DX,EAX
```

This writes 32 bits of data to the port specified by the DX register.

NOTE   If you want to read and write data to external devices in larger blocks, you can use the INS and OUTS instructions (as in in-string and out-string).

But the problem really does not end with IN and OUT. Using IN and OUT lets you, the programmer, send data to a device via the processor. In order for devices to be able to get their messages back to the processor, you must configure the 8259 programmable interrupt controller (PIC). The 8259 PIC is a middleman that allows hardware-generated interrupts to get the attention of the processor. The most common setup involves two 8259 PICs arranged in a master-slave configuration such that the processor can interact with 15 different devices.

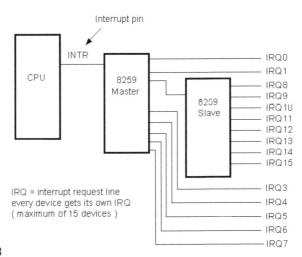

Figure 2-23

The 8259 PIC must be programmed by sending it a sequence of 8-bit commands, called *initialization command words*. This is where the OUT instruction comes in handy because you have to use OUT to get the command words to the 8259. Specifically, the OUT instruction sends initialization command words to the interrupt command register (ICR) and to the interrupt mask register (IMR) of the 8259. Both the master and slave 8259 are programmed this way. The details of bit assignments within the command words themselves are irrelevant; I'm merely trying to show you how complicated system-level I/O really is.

Normally, the 8259 is programmed by the computer BIOS when the machine starts up, and is then reprogrammed by the operating system to provide customized behavior. It's such a sensitive operation that you probably wouldn't want to do it after the operating system has booted, and most operating systems will rebel if you try to.

In general, the 8259 PIC can be a royal pain to program (the author is a voice of experience). Programmable I/O hardware is very unforgiving. If you do a single thing wrong, you get a one-way ticket on the triple-fault express (i.e., your machine restarts). I found out the hard way that you often need to follow an OUT command to the 8259 with a couple of dummy NOP instructions in order to give the 8259 enough time to digest the last command.

RANT This is the type of thing that really drove me to think about building a virtual machine. Setting up the I/O hardware on a computer involves hundreds of little specific settings. It took me the better part of a year to get a minimal, home-brewed operating system up and running. I didn't implement paging or segmentation, and the command interpreter was a part of the kernel. Several times I had to buy schematics and specifications from hardware manufacturers. I even had to hunker down and do some disassembly. When I realized that the half-life of the information that I had spent so long gathering was about 18 months, I knew that the effort of playing keep-up would require full-time devotion, and I didn't have that kind of time to invest.

HEC I/O

It is obvious from the previous section that I/O operations are extremely machine specific. This led me to base most of HEC's I/O facilities on the functions found in C's `stdio.h` header file. Not only does this insulate me from the hardware, but it also gives me a high degree of portability.

The argument could be made that I sacrificed a lot of speed by relying on the standard C API. To an extent, this argument is correct. I could have achieved better performance by using system calls, which are far more primitive and often provide no buffering or extra formatting. Standard C functions are built upon the system call layer, and the extra features that they offer take their toll on execution speed. The problem with using system calls is that they are different for each operating system. By implementing HEC's I/O using system calls, I would be sacrificing portability. So I decided against this approach.

The one place where I did have to tailor the HEC virtual machine to its native platform was networking. It just so happens that Microsoft's Win32 networking code deviates enough from the standard Berkeley sockets API that I had to bite the bullet and go native. Traditionally, Microsoft has always favored competition to cooperation, so I was not very surprised.

References

Brey, Barry. *Intel Microprocessors*. Prentice Hall, 1999. ISBN: 0139954082.

This complete treatment covers the entire family of Intel CPUs. Barry's book is what you want to have on hand late at night, when there's no one around to answer your questions.

Burgess, Richard. *Develop Your Own 32-bit Operating System*. Sams Publishing, 1995. ISBN: 0672306557.

Richard Burgess is a one-man army. Not only did he build his own operating system, but he built all the development tools to go with it. After reading this book, you will appreciate the amount of work that goes into implementing an OS. You'll also see how much of his code will have to be rewritten when Intel comes out with its 64-bit chip. Ouch.

Detlefs, David, Al Dosser, and Benjamin Zorn. "Memory Allocation Costs in Large C and C++ Programs." University of Colorado at Boulder, 1993. Technical Report CU-CS-665-93.

This article is a study that examines the performance of garbage collectors.

Duntemann, Jeff. *Assembly Language Step-by-Step*. John Wiley and Sons, 1992. ISBN: 0471578142.

Jeff Duntemann is a geek's geek (my type of guy). He gives an unusually clear explanation of how memory is managed in the PC.

Holub, Allen. *Compiler Design in C*. Prentice Hall, 1990. ISBN: 0131550454.

Holub is one of those authors with a bent towards optimizing performance. In this book, he covers a whole smorgasbord of techniques and tricks that will speed up a compiler.

Jones, Robert and Rafael Lins. *Garbage Collection: Algorithms for Automatic Dynamic Memory Management*. John Wiley & Sons, 1996. ISBN: 0471941484.

This book is the distillation of hundreds of research journal articles. I highly recommend it for anyone who wants to implement garbage collection.

Koopman, Phillip. *Stack Computers: The New Wave*. Ellis Horwood Ltd., 1989. ISBN: 0745804187.

Unfortunately, Phillip was wrong about stack computers being the next wave. The book is, however, an interesting read.

Loshin, David. *Efficient Memory Programming*. McGraw-Hill, 1999. ISBN: 0070388687.

Necula, George C. and Peter Lee. "Proof-Carrying Code." Carnegie Mellon University, 1996. Memorandum CMU-CS-FOX-96-03.

Pate, Steve. *UNIX Internals — A Practical Approach*. Addison-Wesley, 1996. ISBN: 020187721X.

This book is a rigorous treatment of SCO Unix.

Podanoffsky, Michael. *Dissecting DOS*. Addison-Wesley, 1995. ISBN: 020162687X.

A real-time multitasking version of DOS, written entirely in assembler.

Sedgewick, Robert. *Algorithms in C, 3rd ed.* Addison-Wesley, 1998. ISBN: 0201314525.

Although some people tout Knuth's books, I find having to wade through MIX assembler both tedious, inefficient, and annoying. This book explains concepts using snippets of C code that are lucid and easy to digest.

Tanenbaum, Andrew. *Operating Systems: Design and Implementation*. Prentice Hall, 1997. ISBN: 0136386776.

People don't often realize that it was Minix that led to the development of Linux. I don't think people give Andrew enough credit. His ideas on modularity are very contemporary.

Wahbe, Robert, Steven Lucco, Thomas E. Anderson, and Susan L. Graham. "Efficient Software-Based Fault Isolation." Symposium on Operating System Principles, 1993.

This article is an in-depth look at the sandboxing technique of software-based segmentation.

Wilson, Paul R., Mark S. Johnstone, Michael Neely, and David Boles. "Dynamic Storage Allocation: A Survey and Critical Review." *Proc. 1995, Int'l. Workshop on Memory Management*, 1995. Springer Verlag.

Van Gilluwe, Frank. *The Undocumented PC: A Programmer's Guide to I/O, CPUs, and Fixed Memory Areas*. Addison-Wesley, 1996. ISBN: 0201479508.

> An exhaustive look at the hardware interface of desktop PCs. When I was interested in programming the 8259 interrupt controller, this was the book I referenced. One of the reasons I designed HEC was to escape having to deal with the topics this book explains.

Zorn, Benjamin. "The Measured Cost of Conservative Garbage Collection." University of Colorado at Boulder, 1992. Technical Report CU-CS-573-92.

## Part II

The HEC Virtual Machine

Virtual Machine Implementation

Overview

The HEC virtual machine is merely a program which, when invoked properly at the command line, executes instructions stored in a *bytecode executable*. The bytecode executable is a binary file whose name is provided on the command line when the HEC virtual machine is invoked. For example, let us assume that there is a bytecode executable named `myfile.RUN`. The virtual machine command line would look something like:

```
C:\apps\hec> hecvm  myfile.RUN
```

The bytecode executable consists primarily of byte-sized machine instructions (i.e., bytecode) which can be understood by the HEC virtual machine. The virtual machine loads the bytecode file from secondary storage (i.e., a disk drive), stores the file's machine instructions into its own fabricated address space, and then executes them. This scheme of events is somewhat similar to the way in which an operating system's program loader normally operates.

The life span of the HEC virtual machine can be divided into five stages (see Figure 3-1). The organization of these stages is very simple — they occur serially. The HEC virtual machine's first stage is entered when it is invoked at the command line.

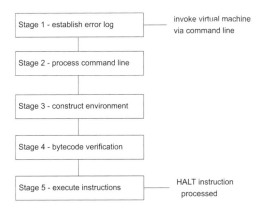

Figure 3-1

The virtual machine begins by setting up a log file to record errors. This allows run-time problems to be recorded in a straightforward, XML-based format. Once the error log has been created, the HEC virtual machine occupies itself by processing the arguments supplied on its command line. The HEC run-time uses its command-line options (or lack thereof) to initiate the third stage, which involves setting up an execution environment. Actions performed during the third stage include initializing virtual machine registers, constructing an artificial address space, and reading the bytecode executable into this artificial address space.

Once an execution environment has been established, bytecode verification can proceed. Bytecode verification is the fourth stage. The HEC run-time system starts by translating big-endian numeric values, loaded from the bytecode executable into memory, to the native machine format. The virtual machine then checks to make sure that the elements of every bytecode instruction are legitimate. The verifier looks at the instruction opcode to make sure that it corresponds to an actual instruction, and it also looks at the instruction operands. After all the bytecode instructions have passed through the verifier, execution may begin.

Execution is the last stage. The virtual machine sets the $IP register to 0 and begins executing the instruction located at the very bottom of memory. The virtual machine will continue to execute bytecode instructions until the HALT instruction is processed or until a fatal error occurs.

In terms of implementation, the HEC virtual machine consists of 24 source files. From my own experience with enterprise-scale software projects, I think that this is an easily manageable number of files. The virtual machine's source code has been written in such a way that these files can be classified according to the stages of the virtual machine's life cycle (see Figure 3-2).

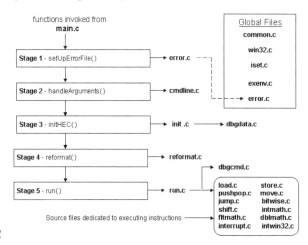

Figure 3-2

Keep Figure 3-2 in the back of your mind as you read on. This is a very important diagram. In fact, there have been times in the past when I was maintaining someone else's project that I wished I had been given such a diagram. A picture is worth a thousand words and such is the case with Figure 3-2.

NOTE Of the 24 source files, there are five files that are global to all stages (common.c, win32.c, iset.c, exenv.c, and error.c), but these files are an exception to the rule.

As with most C programs, the basic operation of the HEC virtual machine is directed by the main() function, which is supplied in a file named main.c (big surprise). From this function, all of the five stages are launched and managed. By looking at the body of the main() function, you can get a preliminary idea of how the virtual machine's life cycle is implemented.

```c
void main(int argc, char *argv[])
{
    struct CmdLine cl;

    /*1) establishing error log */

    DBG_MAINO("1) establishing error log\n");
    setUpErrorFile();

    /*2) handle command line arguments, set computer switches*/

    DBG_MAINO("2) invoking handleArguments()\n");
    cl = handleArguments(argc,argv);
    if(cl.ok==FALSE)
    {
        FATAL_ERROR1("main(): errors during handleArguments()\n");
    }

    /*3) init execution environment and load bytecode */

    DBG_MAINO("3) invoking initHEC()\n");
    RAM = NULL;
    if(initHEC(cl)==FALSE)
    {
        FATAL_ERROR1("main(): errors during initHEC()\n");
    }

    /*4) re-format numeric operands to native and verify */

    DBG_MAINO("4) invoking reformat()\n");
    if(reformat()==FALSE)
    {
        FATAL_ERROR1("main(): errors during reformat()\n");
    }

    /*5) begin execution*/

    DBG_MAINO("5) invoking run()\n");

    run(cl.debug);
```

```
    /*6) safe-shutdown*/

    DBG_MAIN0("6) HEC VM shutting down via HALT instruction\n");
    shutDown(SHUTDOWN_OK);
    return;

}/*end main*/
```

The error log is established by calling the `setUpErrorFile()` function in `error.c`. Command-line processing is facilitated by the `handleArguments()` function in `cmdline.c`. The virtual machine's execution environment is set up using the `initHEC()` routine in `init.c` (which subsequently invokes functions in `dbgdata.c`). Bytecode verification is performed using the `reformat()` function in `reformat.c`. The remainder of the source code files support instruction execution (`run.c`, `dbgcmd.c`, `load.c`, `store.c`, etc.).

The basic approach of this chapter will be to trace the execution of `main()` from beginning to end. At each stage, we will follow the path of execution, which branches off from `main()`, and scrutinize the actions that are performed.

 NOTE In the following sections, I include copious amounts of source code. I do this in an attempt to save you from having to constantly reference a separate source listing. I list all the relevant source code in the section in which it is being discussed. There's nothing more annoying than having to constantly flip to the end of a book or to an external printout. I remember one book on operating system design that required me to use at least five bookmarks in order to follow an explanation. Eventually, the number of bookmarks needed grew to the extent that I was forced to improvise with pens and rulers until the book's binding gave way under the pressure.

Global Elements

As stated earlier, there are five global source files which are used throughout the virtual machine's life cycle:

- `common.c` — Frequently used macro definitions
- `win32.c` — Microsoft Windows-specific code
- `iset.c` — Instruction set definitions
- `exenv.c` — Execution environment components
- `error.c` — Error handling code

common.c

The source file `common.c` is used to map integer values to the macros TRUE and FALSE. With respect to Boolean values, in the C programming language, the integer value of 0 always represents false. The value for true, however, tends to vary from one standard library implementation to the next. The ANSI standard only requires that the value for true be a nonzero integer literal. I use the TRUE and FALSE Boolean macros frequently, so I want to guarantee that I know exactly what integer values they correspond to.

```
#define TRUE  1
#define FALSE 0
```

`common.c` also defines a couple of shutdown codes which the virtual machine returns to the command shell when it exits. These exit values allow the command shell to determine if the virtual machine has died of unnatural causes or if the virtual machine has terminated normally via the HALT instruction.

```
#define SHUTDOWN_OK        0
#define SHUTDOWN_ERROR     1
```

win32.c

The `win32.c` source file contains definitions and functions that are platform dependent. For example, the HEC virtual machine deals with signed and unsigned data types that are one, two, four, and eight bytes in size. Different compilers will map different atomic data types, in the C programming language, to a value of a given size. For example, an old C compiler which targets Microsoft DOS will treat the integer data type (i.e., `int`) as a 16-bit value. A compiler that targets Windows 2000, however, will treat the integer data type as a 32-bit value. To deal with this inconsistency, I define my own data types in `win32.c`. The "S" prefix indicates a signed value and a "U" prefix indicates an unsigned value. The digit following the prefix determines the number of bytes in the data type.

```
#define S1    signed char
#define S2    signed short
#define S4    signed long
#define S8    signed __int64

#define U1    unsigned char
#define U2    unsigned short
#define U4    unsigned long
#define U8    unsigned __int64
```

Thanks to the IEEE 754-1985 standard, the C float and double data types have a more consistent implementation across different platforms. The IEEE 754 standard is a specification that describes how floating-point values should be represented on the binary level. Most C compiler designers have the good sense to treat variables of type float as single-precision IEEE 754 floating-point values. Likewise, most C compilers also treat variables of type double as double-precision IEEE 754 floating-point values. One of the primary characteristics that distinguishes single-precision values from double-precision values is that single-precision floats require only four bytes of storage and double-precision floats require eight bytes of storage. I define the following macros to help remind you of this difference:

```
#define F4    float
#define F8    double
```

In addition to different, atomic, data type assignments, different compiler vendors also supply their own input/output format descriptors for certain data types (this is particularly true when it comes to values which are 64 bits in size). Again, I deal with this issue by defining my own input/output mechanisms in `win32.c`.

```
#define PRINT_UREG(rstr,reg)    printf("%-6s=%-21I64u",rstr,reg)
#define PRINT_SREG(rstr,reg)    printf("%-6s=%-21I64d",rstr,reg)
#define PRINT_FREG(rstr,reg)    printf("%-6s=%g",rstr,(F4)reg)
#define PRINT_DREG(rstr,reg)    printf("%-6s=%g",rstr,(F8)reg)

#define pU1(arg)                printf("%u",arg)
#define pU2(arg)                printf("%hu",arg)
#define pU4(arg)                printf("%lu",arg)
#define pU8(arg)                printf("%I64lu",arg)

#define pS1(arg)                printf("%d",arg)
#define pS2(arg)                printf("%hd",arg)
#define pS4(arg)                printf("%ld",arg)
#define pS8(arg)                printf("%I64d",arg)

#define rU8(arg)                scanf("%I64lu",arg)

#define fpU8(ptr,arg)           fprintf(ptr,"%I64lu",arg)
#define fpS8(ptr,arg)           fprintf(ptr,"%I64d",arg)
```

Numeric values, in HEC bytecode executables, are stored using the big-endian format. This was an arbitrary decision that I made to ensure that bytecode executables are consistent and platform neutral. The Windows operating system, running on Intel hardware, performs numeric operations on values in the little-endian format. This means that I have to provide facilities to convert big-endian numbers to little-endian. The `win32.c` source file has a number of functions to support big-to-little endian conversion. In fact, the bulk of code in `win32.c` is spent on providing this functionality. The conversion functions are:

```
void checkEndian();

U2 bytecodeToWord(U1 bytes[]);
U4 bytecodeToDWord(U1 bytes[]);
U8 bytecodeToQWord(U1 bytes[]);
F4 bytecodeToFloat(U1 bytes[]);
F8 bytecodeToDouble(U1 bytes[]);

void wordToBytecode(U2 word, U1 arr[]);
void dwordToBytecode(U4 dword, U1 arr[]);
void qwordToBytecode(U8 qword, U1 arr[]);
void floatToBytecode(F4 flt, U1 arr[]);
void doubleToBytecode(F8 dbl, U1 arr[]);
```

If you're not sure if the platform you're working on is big-endian or little-endian, then you should use the `checkEndian()` function to find out. The `checkEndian()` routine really has no practical use with respect to the normal day-to-day operation of the virtual machine. I wrote `checkEndian()` for the sole purpose of confirming that Intel was little-endian.

NOTE In general, if you have read something about the behavior of a particular operating system or hardware platform, there's nothing better than writing some code on your own to test what you've been told. On several occasions, I have been faced with documentation that was incorrect. When in doubt, check it out yourself.

```c
void checkEndian()
{
    int i=0xDEED1234;
    int j;
    unsigned char *buff;

    printf("value = %lx\n",i);
    buff = (unsigned char*)&i;
    if(buff[0]==0x34)
    {
        printf("machine is LITTLE endian - LOWER order bytes come first");
    }
    else
    {
        printf("machine is BIG endian - HIGHER order bytes come first");
    }

    printf("\nhere are the 4 bytes\n");
    for(j=0;j<4;j++){ printf(" byte [%d]=%x ",j,buff[j]); }
    printf("\n");
    return;

}/*end checkEndian*/
```

On the Intel platform, running Microsoft Windows, I obtained the following results using `checkEndian()`:

```
value = 0xDEED1234
machine is LITTLE endian - LOWER order bytes come first
here are the 4 bytes
[0]=0x34 [1]=0x12 [2]=0xED [3]=0xDE
```

The remaining functions convert between big-endian and little-endian. The `bytecodeToXXXX()` functions are intended to take a big-endian value, represented as a series of bytes, and spit out a little-endian value. The `XXXXToBytecode()` functions are intended to take a little-endian value and convert it into an array of big-endian bytes.

```c
U2 bytecodeToWord(U1 bytes[])
{
    U2 word;
    U1 *buffer;

    buffer = (U1*)&word;
    buffer[0] = bytes[1];
    buffer[1] = bytes[0];

    return(word);
```

```
}/*end bytecodeToWord*/

U4 bytecodeToDWord(U1 bytes[])
{
    U4 dword;
    U1 *buffer;

    buffer = (U1*)&dword;
    buffer[0] = bytes[3];
    buffer[1] = bytes[2];
    buffer[2] = bytes[1];
    buffer[3] = bytes[0];

    return(dword);

}/*end bytecodeToDWord*/

U8 bytecodeToQWord(U1 bytes[])
{
    U8 qword;
    U1 *buffer;

    buffer = (U1*)&qword;
    buffer[0] = bytes[7];
    buffer[1] = bytes[6];
    buffer[2] = bytes[5];
    buffer[3] = bytes[4];
    buffer[4] = bytes[3];
    buffer[5] = bytes[2];
    buffer[6] = bytes[1];
    buffer[7] = bytes[0];

    return(qword);

}/*end bytecodeToQWord*/

F4 bytecodeToFloat(U1 bytes[])
{
    F4 flt;
    U1 *buffer;

    buffer = (U1*)&flt;
    buffer[0] = bytes[3];
    buffer[1] = bytes[2];
    buffer[2] = bytes[1];
    buffer[3] = bytes[0];

    return(flt);

}/*end bytecodeToFloat*/

F8 bytecodeToDouble(U1 bytes[])
{
    F8 dbl;
```

```c
    U1 *buffer;

    buffer = (U1*)&dbl;
    buffer[0] = bytes[7];
    buffer[1] = bytes[6];
    buffer[2] = bytes[5];
    buffer[3] = bytes[4];
    buffer[4] = bytes[3];
    buffer[5] = bytes[2];
    buffer[6] = bytes[1];
    buffer[7] = bytes[0];

    return(dbl);

}/*end bytecodeToDouble*/

void wordToBytecode(U2 word, U1 arr[])
{
    U1 *buffer;

    buffer = (U1*)&word;
    arr[0] = buffer[1];
    arr[1] = buffer[0];

    return;

}/*end wordToBytecode*/

void dwordToBytecode(U4 dword, U1 arr[])
{
    U1 *buffer;

    buffer = (U1*)&dword;
    arr[0] = buffer[3];
    arr[1] = buffer[2];
    arr[2] = buffer[1];
    arr[3] = buffer[0];

    return;

}/*end dwordToBytecode*/

void qwordToBytecode(U8 qword, U1 arr[])
{
    U1 *buffer;

    buffer = (U1*)&qword;
    arr[0] = buffer[7];
    arr[1] = buffer[6];
    arr[2] = buffer[5];
    arr[3] = buffer[4];
    arr[4] = buffer[3];
    arr[5] = buffer[2];
    arr[6] = buffer[1];
```

```
        arr[7] = buffer[0];

        return;

}/*end qwordToBytecode*/

void floatToBytecode(F4 flt, U1 arr[])
{
    U1 *buffer;

    buffer = (U1*)&flt;
    arr[0] = buffer[3];
    arr[1] = buffer[2];
    arr[2] = buffer[1];
    arr[3] = buffer[0];

    return;

}/*end floatToBytecode*/

void doubleToBytecode(F8 dbl, U1 arr[])
{
    U1 *buffer;

    buffer = (U1*)&dbl;
    arr[0] = buffer[7];
    arr[1] = buffer[6];
    arr[2] = buffer[5];
    arr[3] = buffer[4];
    arr[4] = buffer[3];
    arr[5] = buffer[2];
    arr[6] = buffer[1];
    arr[7] = buffer[0];

    return;

}/*end doubleToBytecode*/
```

ASIDE　In all C compiler implementations, function calls incur a certain amount of overhead. Invoking a function normally entails pushing values on the stack, transferring program execution to a distant location in memory, and then finally popping values off the stack. One way to avoid this overhead is to use a macro. This gives you the benefit of function call notation without the corresponding performance cost.

With the ample cache memory that most processors have today, a macro can sometimes run several times faster than a function. A function entails jumping to a distant location in memory, and this can force the processor to dump and then reload the cache. Macros, on the other hand, are all in-line.

There is, however, a catch (rarely in computer science can you have your cake and eat it too; there are always tradeoffs). The catch is that because the macro substitutes its associated code whenever it is applied, the size of the compiled executable will be much larger than if functions were used. During the early days, this was a big deal because 16 KB of memory was considered to be an expensive plot of real estate and every byte counted.

This is one of the fundamental tradeoffs you will see again and again: size versus speed. You can make a program faster by using a more sophisticated algorithm, which caters to the peculiarities of a given problem. This results in a larger binary because optimized algorithms have more instructions than simple ones (i.e., quicksort has more instructions than bubble sort). Likewise, you can make a program faster by eschewing program control jumps in favor of implementing redundant blocks of instructions. Both techniques speed up program execution at the expense of the size of the program's executable.

During the verification stage, speed is of the essence. I am more than willing to sacrifice executable size for efficiency's sake. Instead of relying on functions to do the big-endian to little-endian conversion, I use the following set of macros:

```
#define FORMAT_WORD(arr,start){  fb[0]=arr[start+1];\
                                 fb[1]=arr[start];\
                                 arr[start]=fb[0];\
                                 arr[start+1]=fb[1]; }

#define FORMAT_DWORD(arr,start){ fb[0]=arr[start+3];\
                                 fb[1]=arr[start+2];\
                                 fb[2]=arr[start+1];\
                                 fb[3]=arr[start];\
                                 arr[start]=fb[0];\
                                 arr[start+1]=fb[1];\
                                 arr[start+2]=fb[2];\
                                 arr[start+3]=fb[3]; }

#define FORMAT_QWORD(arr,start){ fb[0]=arr[start+7];\
                                 fb[1]=arr[start+6];\
                                 fb[2]=arr[start+5];\
                                 fb[3]=arr[start+4];\
                                 fb[4]=arr[start+3];\
                                 fb[5]=arr[start+2];\
                                 fb[6]=arr[start+1];\
                                 fb[7]=arr[start];\
                                 arr[start]=fb[0];\
                                 arr[start+1]=fb[1];\
                                 arr[start+2]=fb[2];\
                                 arr[start+3]=fb[3];\
                                 arr[start+4]=fb[4];\
                                 arr[start+5]=fb[5];\
                                 arr[start+6]=fb[6];\
                                 arr[start+7]=fb[7]; }
```

These macros use a common eight-byte buffer to perform the change in format:

```
U1 fb[8];
```

In practice, we feed these macros an array of bytes and an index that indicates where the big-endian value begins. For example:

```
U1 array[] = { 0xAB, 0xCD, 0x12, 0x34 };

/* to reverse the order of bytes in this double word */
FORMAT_DWORD(array,0);
```

One thing you might want to note is how I avoided using a for loop in the conversion macros. The conversion macros are used several times during the verification stage, so it's in my best interest to make them as fast as possible. Specifically, I used an optimization technique known as *loop unrolling*. Instead of using a for loop to automate the execution of a particular statement, I manually perform each iteration of the statement. This cuts down on the unnecessary comparison and increment operations which exist in for loops.

The `win32.c` source file also has a couple of miscellaneous functions that are used to help the HEC run-time system set up its execution environment. Both functions make use of Windows-specific system calls.

```
U4 getAvailableMemory();
U4 getFileSize(char *name);
```

The `getAvailableMemory()` routine returns the number of bytes of free physical memory. Note that I'm talking about memory that is available from the RAM chips, not the 4 GB virtual address space that Windows uses. I'm interested in physical memory because that's where I would like to place the HEC run-time system. By avoiding the use of virtual memory, my goal is to minimize the memory-based latency that the virtual machine will encounter. If I invoke the virtual machine when the operating system is low on physical memory, I run the risk of having different portions of the virtual machine being stored in separate pages on the hard drive. This could lead to all sorts of performance problems because running the virtual machine could require frequent disk I/O operations.

```
#include<windows.h>

U4 getAvailableMemory()
{
    U4 free;
    MEMORYSTATUS mem_status;
    mem_status.dwLength = sizeof(MEMORYSTATUS);
    free = 0;
    GlobalMemoryStatus(&mem_status);
    free = mem_status.dwAvailPhys;
    return(free);

}/*end getAvailableMemory*/
```

RANT   In a way, virtual memory is a relic from earlier days when physical memory was much more expensive than disk storage. Today, the cost-to-byte ratio between the two options is not as substantial. Purchasing a gigabyte of memory is not out of reach for the average consumer. In fact, there have been times when I have decided to turn off paging on a computer in order to boost performance. Some operating systems institute mandatory paging, even when only a small portion of memory is actually in use. Disk I/O is one of the most expensive operations a computer can perform, even if it is managed at the machine level by the bowels of an operating system. I have been told by some hardware engineers that paging on Windows introduces a performance penalty of 10 percent. I'd rather pay a little extra and buy 512 MB of RAM than be stuck with the overhead of paging.

The getFileSize() function is used to determine the size of a bytecode executable before it is loaded. This is done in an effort to ensure that the HEC run-time system does not try to load a bytecode executable that is too big for physical memory. Like getAvailableMemory(), this function uses the Windows API to do most of the dirty work.

```
U4 getFileSize(char *name)
{
    U4 size;
    S1 ret;
    WIN32_FILE_ATTRIBUTE_DATA fdata;

    size=0;
    ret = GetFileAttributesEx(name,GetFileExInfoStandard,&fdata);
    size = fdata.nFileSizeLow;

    if(ret > 0){ return(size); }
    else{ return(0); }

}/*end getFileSize*/
```

You might remember that the HEC virtual machine uses a 64-bit address space. The getAvailableMemory() and getFileSize() functions return 32-bit values. This is a foible of Windows that we have to live with. The fact that Windows is currently a 32-bit operating system places a ceiling on what we can do, meaning that we cannot work with more than 4 GB of memory. (Windows reserves a significant portion of the 4 GB for the operating system, so we actually have less than that.) On enterprise-scale platforms, like AIX or IRIX, we would actually be able to request memory on the scale of 64 bits.

iset.c

Bytecode executable files are composed primarily of bytecode instructions. Technically speaking, a bytecode executable has several other components (which we will look at in the next chapter), but the chief payload of a bytecode file is bytecode instructions.

Bytecode instructions consist of a single opcode and zero or more operands. An opcode is a single byte that defines what an instruction will do. The operands specify the data the instruction will process. Note that a single operand may be several bytes long, but the opcode is always a single byte in length. HEC's virtual machine instructions have been designed such that the opcode completely specifies both the number of operands and the form the operands will take (i.e., register or literal constant). See Figure 3-3 for an illustration of this.

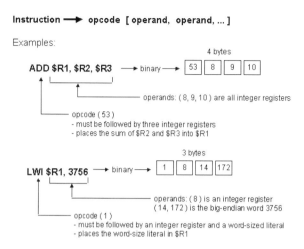

Figure 3-3

The `iset.c` file stores the mapping of instruction opcodes to their integer equivalents. The HEC virtual machine recognizes 73 different opcodes, ranging from 0 to 72. Don't feel like you have to understand what each opcode does. What is important for now is to remember that `iset.c` is where the opcode-integer mappings are located.

```
/* DATA TRANSFER ---------------------------------------------------*/

#define LBI          0    /* load byte immediate */
#define LWI          1    /* load word immediate */
#define LDI          2    /* load double word immediate */
#define LQI          3    /* load quad word immediate */
#define LF1I         4    /* load single-precision float immediate */
#define LF2I         5    /* load double-precision float immediate */

#define LAD          6    /* load address direct */
#define LAI          7    /* load address indirect */

#define LB           8    /* load byte */
#define LW           9    /* load word */
#define LD          10    /* load double word */
#define LQ          11    /* load quad word */
#define LF1         12    /* load single-precision float */
#define LF2         13    /* load double-precision float */

#define SB          14    /* store byte */
#define SW          15    /* store word */
#define SD          16    /* store double word */
#define SQ          17    /* store quad word */
#define SF1         18    /* store single-precision float */
#define SF2         19    /* store double-precision float */

#define PUSHB       20    /* push byte on stack */
#define PUSHW       21    /* push word on stack */
#define PUSHD       22    /* push double word on stack */
#define PUSHQ       23    /* push quad word on stack */
#define PUSHF1      24    /* push single-precision float on stack */
```

```
#define PUSHF2        25   /* push double-precision float on stack */

#define POPB          26   /* pop byte off stack */
#define POPW          27   /* pop word off stack */
#define POPD          28   /* pop double word off stack */
#define POPQ          29   /* pop quad word off stack */
#define POPF1         30   /* pop single-precision float off stack */
#define POPF2         31   /* pop double-precision float off stack */

#define MOV           32   /* move an integer value */
#define MOVF          33   /* move a single-precision float value */
#define MOVD          34   /* move a double-precision float value */

/* PROGRAM FLOW CONTROL-----------------------------------------*/

#define JMP           35   /* unconditional jump */
#define JE            36   /* jump if equal */
#define JNE           37   /* jump if not equal */
#define SLT           38   /* set if less than */
#define INT           39   /* perform interrupt */
#define DI            40   /* disable interrupts */
#define EI            41   /* enable interrupts */
#define HALT          42   /* stop the virtual machine */
#define NOP           43   /* dummy operation, NOP = No OPeration */

/* BITWISE ------------------------------------------------------*/

#define AND           44   /* bitwise AND */
#define OR            45   /* bitwise OR */
#define XOR           46   /* bitwise XOR */
#define NOT           47   /* bitwise NOT */
#define BT            48   /* bitwise test */
#define BS            49   /* bitwise set */

/* SHIFT --------------------------------------------------------*/

#define SRA           50   /* shift arithmetic right */
#define SRL           51   /* shift logical right */
#define SL            52   /* shift left */

/* INTEGER ARITHMETIC -------------------------------------------*/

#define ADD           53   /* integer addition */
#define SUB           54   /* integer subtraction */
#define MULT          55   /* integer multiplication */
#define DIV           56   /* integer division */

/* CONVERSION ---------------------------------------------------*/

#define CAST_IF       57   /* convert a single-precision float to an integer */
#define CAST_ID       58   /* convert a double-precision float to an integer */
#define CAST_FI       59   /* convert an integer to a single-precision float */
#define CAST_FD       60   /* double-precision float to a single-precision */
#define CAST_DI       61   /* convert an integer to a double-precision float */
```

```
        #define CAST_DF    62    /* single-precision float to a double-precision */

        /* FLOATING-POINT MATH ------------------------------------------*/

        #define FADD       63    /* single-precision float addition */
        #define FSUB       64    /* single-precision float subtraction */
        #define FMULT      65    /* single-precision float multiplication */
        #define FDIV       66    /* single-precision float division */
        #define FSLT       67    /* single-precision float set if less then */

        #define DADD       68    /* double-precision float addition */
        #define DSUB       69    /* double-precision float subtraction */
        #define DMULT      70    /* double-precision float multiplication */
        #define DDIV       71    /* double-precision float division */
        #define DSLT       72    /* double-precision float set if less then */

        #define BAD        -1    /* not an instruction */

        char *I_Set[73] =
        {
            "LBI","LWI","LDI","LQI","LF1I","LF2I",
            "LAD","LAI",
            "LB","LW","LD","LQ","LF1","LF2",
            "SB","SW","SD","SQ","SF1","SF2",
            "PUSHB","PUSHW","PUSHD","PUSHQ","PUSHF1","PUSHF2",
            "POPB","POPW","POPD","POPQ","POPF1","POPF2",
            "MOV","MOVF","MOVD",
            "JMP","JE","JNE","SLT","INT","DI","EI","HALT","NOP",
            "AND","OR","XOR","NOT","BT","BS",
            "SRA","SRL","SL",
            "ADD","SUB","MULT","DIV",
            "CAST_IF","CAST_ID","CAST_FI","CAST_FD","CAST_DI","CAST_DF",
            "FADD","FSUB","FMULT","FDIV","FSLT",
            "DADD","DSUB","DMULT","DDIV","DSLT"
        };
```

The I_Set pointer array can be used to obtain a string representation of instruction opcodes. By plugging in the instruction opcode as an index into the array, you can get a string version of the opcode. For example, the following code prints "AND" to the screen:

```
        printf("%s\n",I_Set[AND]);
```

exenv.c

The basic execution environment which the HEC virtual machine has at its disposal consists of a memory address space and a collection of 52 registers (see Figure 3-4). The memory address space is a contiguous series of bytes that is dedicated as storage space for a single process. The memory address space is broken into three segments: a text segment, a heap, and a stack. There are eight registers used to delimit these three segments ($BE, $HS, $HE, $SS, $TOP) and serve as address pointers ($IP, $SP, $FP). There are 24 general purpose integer registers ($R1 through $R24), 10 general purpose single-precision floating-point registers ($F1 through $F10), and 10 general purpose double-precision floating-point registers ($D1 through $D10).

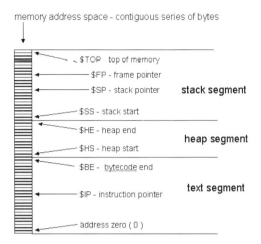

memory address space - contiguous series of bytes

$TOP   top of memory
$FP - frame pointer
$SP - stack pointer   **stack segment**
$SS - stack start
$HE - heap end
                           heap segment
$HS - heap start
$BE - bytecode end
                           text segment
$IP - instruction pointer
address zero (0)

Figure 3-4

Naturally, the constituents of the execution environment must correspond to data structures in the C programming language. Because the number of registers is fixed and the size of the address space (at run time) is also fixed, I decided to use array-based lists to implement the virtual machine's resources. The HEC virtual machine's address space is nothing more than an array of unsigned bytes. The integer registers of the virtual machine are implemented by an array of 64-bit integer variables. Likewise, the single- and double-precision floating-point registers of the virtual machine are represented by arrays of single- and double-precision floating-point variables. Individual registers are referenced using macros that specify an index into the associated array. The exenv.c source file contains all of these definitions.

```
U1 *RAM;       /* memory address space pointer, malloc to an array at startup */

U8 R[32];      /* integer registers */

#define $IP         0      /* address of next instruction to execute */
#define $SP         1      /* address of most recent value pushed on stack */
#define $FP         2      /* stack frame pointer */
#define $BE         3      /* address of last byte of bytecode section */

#define $HS         4      /* address of first (lowest) byte of heap */
#define $HE         5      /* address of last (highest) byte used by heap */

#define $SS         6      /* address of bottom of stack (lowest) */
#define $TOP        7      /* address of top-of-stack (highest)*/

/* General purpose registers */

#define $R1         8
#define $R2         9
#define $R3         10
#define $R4         11
```

```
#define $R5          12
#define $R6          13
#define $R7          14
#define $R8          15
#define $R9          16
#define $R10         17
#define $R11         18
#define $R12         19
#define $R13         20
#define $R14         21
#define $R15         22
#define $R16         23
#define $R17         24
#define $R18         25
#define $R19         26
#define $R20         27
#define $R21         28
#define $R22         29
#define $R23         30
#define $R24         31


/* to get the string version of a register, use R_STR[$IP]="$IP" */

char *R_STR[] =
{
    "$IP","$SP","$FP","$BE","$HS","$HE","$SS","$TOP",
    "$R1","$R2","$R3","$R4","$R5","$R6","$R7","$R8","$R9","$R10",
    "$R11","$R12","$R13","$R14","$R15","$R16","$R17","$R18","$R19","$R20",
    "$R21","$R22","$R23","$R24"
};

F4 Rf[10];
char *Rf_STR[]={"$F1","$F2","$F3","$F4","$F5","$F6","$F7","$F8","$F9","$F10"};

#define $F1           0
#define $F2           1
#define $F3           2
#define $F4           3
#define $F5           4
#define $F6           5
#define $F7           6
#define $F8           7
#define $F9           8
#define $F10          9


F8 Rd[10];
char *Rd_STR[]={"$D1","$D2","$D3","$D4","$D5","$D6","$D7","$D8","$D9","$D10"};

#define $D1           0
#define $D2           1
#define $D3           2
#define $D4           3
#define $D5           4
#define $D6           5
```

```
#define $D7        6
#define $D8        7
#define $D9        8
#define $D10       9
```

To support diagnostic features, the exenv.c source file also has several functions that print out the contents of memory and the registers:

```
void printMemorySection(U8 address,U8 bytes);
void printAllRAM();
void printBasicRegisters();
void printGeneralRegisters();
void printFloatRegisters();
void printDoubleRegisters();
```

These six functions all build upon the base output functionality provided in win32.c.

```
void printMemorySection(U8 address,U8 bytes)
{
    U8 index;
    for(index=address;index<address+bytes;index++)
    {
        if(index > R[$TOP])
        {
            printf("printMemorySection(): address ");
            pU8(index);
            printf(" out of bounds\n");
        }
        else
        {
            PRINT_MEM(index);printf("\n");
        }
    }
    return;

}/*end printMemorySection*/

void printAllRAM()
{
    U8 index;
    for(index=0;index<(U8)R[$TOP];index++)
    {
        PRINT_MEM(index);printf("\n");
    }
    return;

}/*end printAllRAM*/

void printBasicRegisters()
{
    printf("BASIC REGISTERS----------------------\n");
    PRINT_UREG(R_STR[$IP],R[$IP]); printf(" ");
    PRINT_UREG(R_STR[$SP],R[$SP]); printf("\n");
    PRINT_UREG(R_STR[$FP],R[$FP]); printf(" ");
    PRINT_UREG(R_STR[$BE],R[$BE]); printf("\n");
```

```
        PRINT_UREG(R_STR[$HS],R[$HS]); printf(" ");
        PRINT_UREG(R_STR[$HE],R[$HE]); printf("\n");
        PRINT_UREG(R_STR[$SS],R[$SS]); printf(" ");
        PRINT_UREG(R_STR[$TOP],R[$TOP]); printf("\n");
        printf("---------------------------------------\n");
        return;

}/*end printBasicRegisters*/

void printGeneralRegisters()
{
        printf("GENERAL REGISTERS----------------------\n");
        PRINT_SREG(R_STR[$R1],R[$R1]); printf(" ");
        PRINT_SREG(R_STR[$R2],R[$R2]); printf("\n");
        PRINT_SREG(R_STR[$R3],R[$R3]); printf(" ");
        PRINT_SREG(R_STR[$R4],R[$R4]); printf("\n");
        PRINT_SREG(R_STR[$R5],R[$R5]); printf(" ");
        PRINT_SREG(R_STR[$R6],R[$R6]); printf("\n");
        PRINT_SREG(R_STR[$R7],R[$R7]); printf(" ");
        PRINT_SREG(R_STR[$R8],R[$R8]); printf("\n");
        PRINT_SREG(R_STR[$R9],R[$R9]); printf(" ");
        PRINT_SREG(R_STR[$R10],R[$R10]); printf("\n");
        PRINT_SREG(R_STR[$R11],R[$R11]); printf(" ");
        PRINT_SREG(R_STR[$R12],R[$R12]); printf("\n");
        PRINT_SREG(R_STR[$R13],R[$R13]); printf(" ");
        PRINT_SREG(R_STR[$R14],R[$R14]); printf("\n");
        PRINT_SREG(R_STR[$R15],R[$R15]); printf(" ");
        PRINT_SREG(R_STR[$R16],R[$R16]); printf("\n");
        PRINT_SREG(R_STR[$R17],R[$R17]); printf(" ");
        PRINT_SREG(R_STR[$R18],R[$R18]); printf("\n");
        PRINT_SREG(R_STR[$R19],R[$R19]); printf(" ");
        PRINT_SREG(R_STR[$R20],R[$R20]); printf("\n");
        PRINT_SREG(R_STR[$R21],R[$R21]); printf(" ");
        PRINT_SREG(R_STR[$R22],R[$R22]); printf("\n");
        PRINT_SREG(R_STR[$R23],R[$R23]); printf(" ");
        PRINT_SREG(R_STR[$R24],R[$R24]); printf("\n");
        printf("---------------------------------------\n");
        return;

}/*end printGeneralRegisters*/

void printFloatRegisters()
{
        printf("FLOAT REGISTERS------------------------\n");
        PRINT_FREG(Rf_STR[$F1],Rf[$F1]); printf(" ");
        PRINT_FREG(Rf_STR[$F2],Rf[$F2]); printf("\n");
        PRINT_FREG(Rf_STR[$F3],Rf[$F3]); printf(" ");
        PRINT_FREG(Rf_STR[$F4],Rf[$F4]); printf("\n");
        PRINT_FREG(Rf_STR[$F5],Rf[$F5]); printf(" ");
        PRINT_FREG(Rf_STR[$F6],Rf[$F6]); printf("\n");
        PRINT_FREG(Rf_STR[$F7],Rf[$F7]); printf(" ");
        PRINT_FREG(Rf_STR[$F8],Rf[$F8]); printf("\n");
        PRINT_FREG(Rf_STR[$F9],Rf[$F9]); printf(" ");
        PRINT_FREG(Rf_STR[$F10],Rf[$F10]); printf("\n");
```

```
        printf("---------------------------------------\n");
        return;

}/*end printFloatRegisters*/

void printDoubleRegisters()
{
        printf("DOUBLE REGISTERS----------------------\n");
        PRINT_DREG(Rd_STR[$D1],Rd[$D1]); printf(" ");
        PRINT_DREG(Rd_STR[$D2],Rd[$D2]); printf("\n");
        PRINT_DREG(Rd_STR[$D3],Rd[$D3]); printf(" ");
        PRINT_DREG(Rd_STR[$D4],Rd[$D4]); printf("\n");
        PRINT_DREG(Rd_STR[$D5],Rd[$D5]); printf(" ");
        PRINT_DREG(Rd_STR[$D6],Rd[$D6]); printf("\n");
        PRINT_DREG(Rd_STR[$D7],Rd[$D7]); printf(" ");
        PRINT_DREG(Rd_STR[$D8],Rd[$D8]); printf("\n");
        PRINT_DREG(Rd_STR[$D9],Rd[$D9]); printf(" ");
        PRINT_DREG(Rd_STR[$D10],Rd[$D10]); printf("\n");
        printf("---------------------------------------\n");
        return;

}/*end printDoubleRegisters*/
```

Again, note how I use loop unrolling in the register display functions to avoid the overhead of unnecessary comparison and increment operations.

error.c

When it comes to handling errors, there are basically two types of engineers. One group of engineers favors an accelerated release cycle at the expense of stability. The other group of engineers is willing to sacrifice development speed for the sake of building a robust product. In all fairness, most engineers usually do not have control over their deadlines, so this distinction is somewhat artificial. However, I have actually looked through production code where some negligent developer left something like:

```
try{  dbptr = openDataBase("/usr/bin/dbserver","admin:password"); }
catch(int i){ /*this will never happen*/ }
```

The potential exception is not even handled because the engineer writing the code thought that it would never happen! This engineer must have been under one heck of a deadline.

In the case of the HEC virtual machine, I had complete control over the development schedule and decided to invest time and effort into handling errors. The error.c source file contains error handling facilities. My error handling scheme allows both fatal and non-fatal errors to occur. In both cases, a message will be printed to the console and persisted in an error log file. The difference between error messages sent to the console and error messages written to the error log has to do with the amount of information emitted. The error log file is intended to record extended error messages, whereas the console messages are fairly terse. The error log messages are also formatted using XML, whereas the console messages are not.

Most of the virtual machine's error messages are generated by calling one of the following macros located in `error.c`:

```
#define FATAL_ERROR();       shutDown(SHUTDOWN_ERROR);

#define FATAL_ERROR1(str); printf(str);\
                           xmlBegin();fprintf(errPtr,str);xmlEnd();\
                           shutDown(SHUTDOWN_ERROR);

#define ERROR_LVL1(str);     FATAL_ERROR1(str);

#define ERROR0_LVL2(str);    printf(str);\
                             xmlBegin();fprintf(errPtr,str);xmlEnd();

#define ERROR1_LVL2(str,arg1);    printf(str,arg1);\
                                  xmlBegin();fprintf(errPtr,str,arg1);xmlEnd();

#define ERROR2_LVL2(str,arg1,arg2);    printf(str,arg1,arg2);\
                                       xmlBegin();fprintf(errPtr,str,arg1,arg2);xmlEnd();
```

Notice the following snippet of code:

```
xmlBegin();fprintf(errPtr,str);xmlEnd();
```

This snippet of code is responsible for generating an entry in the error log file. The file pointer named `errPtr` is the handle to the error log file. The `errPtr` variable is initialized in `setUpErrorFile()`, which is also defined in `error.c`. Because the facilities for tracking errors must be established as soon as possible, the `setUpErrorFile()` routine is the first function invoked from `main()`.

```
void setUpErrorFile()
{
    time_t now;
    struct tm local_time;
    char digits[16];

    int retval;

    now = time(NULL);
    local_time = *(localtime(&now));

    strcpy(errFileName,"VM_ERROR_");

    sprintf(digits,"%u",(local_time.tm_mon+1));
    strcat(errFileName,digits);
    strcat(errFileName,"_");

    sprintf(digits,"%u",local_time.tm_mday);
    strcat(errFileName,digits);
    strcat(errFileName,"_");

    sprintf(digits,"%lu",(local_time.tm_year+1900));
    strcat(errFileName,digits);
    strcat(errFileName,"_");
```

```
        sprintf(digits,"%u",local_time.tm_hour);
        strcat(errFileName,digits);
        strcat(errFileName,"_");

        sprintf(digits,"%u",local_time.tm_min);
        strcat(errFileName,digits);
        strcat(errFileName,"_");

        sprintf(digits,"%u",local_time.tm_sec);
        strcat(errFileName,digits);

        strcat(errFileName,".XML");

        if((errPtr=fopen(errFileName,"wb"))==NULL)
        {
              printf("setUpErrorFile(): error opening %s\n",errFileName);
              FATAL_ERROR();
        }

        retval = fprintf(errPtr,"<ERRORS>\r\n");
        if(retval < 0)
        {
              printf("setUpErrorFile(): ");
              printf("error writing to %s\n",errFileName);
              FATAL_ERROR();
        }

        return;

}/*end setUpErrorFile*/
```

By looking at the previous code, you will see that the name of the error log will always have the form:

```
VM_ERROR_month_day_year_hour_minute_second.XML
```

For example:

```
VM_ERROR_6_1_2001_18_57_54.XML
```

One reason I do this is so the HEC virtual machine does not erase its old error logs. The HEC virtual machine always opens the error log in the "wb" mode. This means that it will erase an error log of the same name if it already exists. If, for some reason, the machine crashes and is subsequently restarted, this naming scheme saves the old error log from being unintentionally destroyed.

Another reason I use this naming scheme is to help organize log files for easy reference. If all the log messages were appended to a single file (i.e., VM_ERROR.XML), searching for a particular error could require a lot of work.

There are a couple of problems with this naming scheme that I can discern. First, the naming convention can lead to a proliferation of log files. The HEC virtual machine only knows how to create error log files; it does not keep track of the old ones or limit the size of the current error log file. This means it is the administrator's responsibility to occasionally clean up old error logs and keep track of disk usage. I have had experiences in the past where I was working on a Unix machine that ran out of disk space. Only after doing some emergency cleanup, and taking a careful look at the file system, did the problem become obvious — the application logs were 500 MB in size.

 NOTE If you are not familiar with XML (Extensible Markup Language), then you need to take a look at one of the books I mention in the reference section. I use XML to format the error log, so part of the following discussion may not make much sense if you are not XML savvy.

The error log is an XML document. Every XML document must have what is known as a root element. In setUpErrorFile(), I open the log file for writing and then write the first half of the root element (i.e., <ERRORS>) to the log file. The final half of the root element (i.e., </ERRORS>) is written to the error log by the shutDown() function, directly before I close the error log and exit the virtual machine. This guarantees that the closing tag of the root element is the last thing written to the error log (which is necessary in order for the error log to be a well-formed XML document).

```
void shutDown(U1 code)
{
    if(RAM != NULL){ free(RAM); }
    else{  printf("shutDown(): no RAM[] allocated\n"); }

    if(errPtr!=NULL)
    {
        int retval;
        retval = fprintf(errPtr,"</ERRORS>");
        if(retval < 0)
        {
            printf("shutDown(): ");
            printf("error writing </ERROR> to %s\n",errFileName);
        }
        if(fclose(errPtr))
        {
            printf("shutDown(): error closing %s\n",errFileName);
        }
    }

    exit(code);

}/*end shutDown*/
```

The shutDown() function provides a single point of exit for the HEC virtual machine, which is to say that the HEC virtual machine cannot normally exit without invoking shutDown(). This provides a way for me to ensure that all of HEC's dynamically allocated resources are cleaned up and that all the open files are closed.

We now understand how the error log is created and closed, and we also know how the document's root element is constructed. The error messages that lie within the root element are written to the error log by the xmlBegin(), xmlEnd(), and fprintf() functions.

The functions `xmlBegin()` and `xmlEnd()` generate the prefix and the suffix of the error message. Note how the `xmlBegin()` function embeds the current time in the error message.

```
void xmlBegin()
{
    char str1[]="<Message>\r\n\t";
    char str2[]="<time>\r\n\t%s\r\t</time>\r\n\t<content>\r\n\t";
    time_t now;
    int retval;

    now = time(NULL);
    retval = fprintf(errPtr,str1);
    if(retval < 0)
    {
        printf("xmlBegin(): ");
        printf("error writing to %s\n",errFileName);
        return;
    }

    retval = fprintf(errPtr,str2,ctime(&now));
    if(retval < 0)
    {
        printf("xmlBegin(): ");
        printf("error writing to %s\n",errFileName);
    }
    return;

}/*end xmlBegin*/

void xmlEnd()
{
    int retval;

    retval = fprintf(errPtr,"\r\t</content>\r\n</Message>\r\n");
    if(retval < 0)
    {
        printf("xmlEnd(): ");
        printf("error writing to %s\n",errFileName);
    }
    return;

}/*end xmlEnd*/
```

The content of the message (which is the most important part) is written to the error log with one or more calls to the `fprintf()` function. This must always occur between the `xmlBegin()` and `xmlEnd()` calls.

The end result of all this is to generate log file entries that have the form displayed in Figure 3-5.

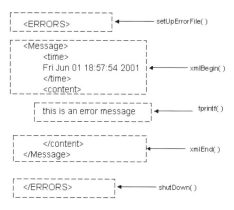

Figure 3-5

If I really had wanted to go all the way (or been extraordinarily bored over the weekend), I could have built a small, self-contained ISAM database to persist error messages. I did not, however, think that this approach was warranted. It is my intention that the HEC virtual machine be reliable enough that a database is not needed to record its errors. For most purposes, an XML-formatted log file, whose entries are time-indexed, seems to be sufficient.

In Figure 3-6, I have included a summary of the source files discussed in this section and their relevant contents organized by category.

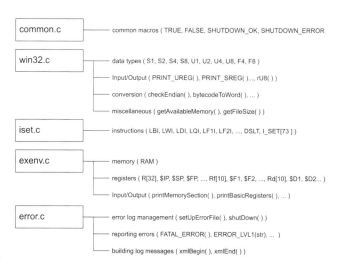

Figure 3-6

Command-Line Invocation

The HEC virtual machine is run by invoking it at the command line. Figure 3-7 displays the command-line usage of the HEC virtual machine.

Command-line usage

HECVM [options] file.RUN   [arguments]

example:
```
C:\apps\HEC\VM> HECVM -s=500 -d test.RUN billb passwd
```

HECVM - name of the HEC virtual machine program

options:
  -h=XXX   set virtual machine heap to XXX kilobytes
  -s=XXX   set virtual machine stack to XXX kilobytes
  -d   start the virtual machine in debugging mode
  -?   display command-line usage

file.RUN - the bytecode executable to be loaded and run

arguments - command-line arguments passed to executable

Figure 3-7

There are a couple of things to remember when invoking the HEC virtual machine. First, the bytecode executable supplied on the command line must have the .RUN file name extension. This extension should be entirely in capital letters. The virtual machine will not accept a lowercase file extension (i.e., .run) or a mixture of cases (i.e., .RuN).

The executable name can be preceded by one or more virtual machine options. Virtual machine options modify the operation of the HEC virtual machine. All of these options begin with a dash. In order to separate the name of the bytecode executable from virtual machine options, the bytecode filename cannot begin with a dash. Also, virtual machine options should contain no white spaces. That is, there should be no white space between the dash, the option letter, and anything that follows the letter (like an equal sign). For example:

  −s=640

is a valid command-line option. There is no white space between any of the characters in the option. If there is white space in a command-line option (i.e., `-s  = 178`), the virtual machine will complain and then refuse to start. I instituted this convention to speed up command-line processing.

Finally, command-line arguments following the name of the bytecode executable will be passed on to the executable itself. These command-line arguments can be anything; it is up to the executable to do something with them. The only caveat is that the HEC virtual machine will only pass a maximum of 32 arguments to the executable. If you need to pass more than 32 arguments to your program, you should use a configuration file (in which case you need only one program argument, i.e., the name of the configuration file).

NOTE   If you take a close look at Figure 3-7, you might notice that all of the virtual machine options are a single character long. I did this for the sake of performance. Having to only look for a single character saves me the overhead of having to constantly use the `strcmp()` routine.

Debugging Code

Implementing source code statements that print debug messages to the console is an old tactic. Probably as least as old as the console display. It is a practice that allows you to see what is going on inside a program as it executes. This kind of information can be invaluable in terms of tracking down bugs (especially if you're too lazy to crank up a debugger or don't have access to one). The problem with using debug statements is that they consume processor cycles and take up space in the binary. For example, let's say you've got something like:

```
if(debug)
{
        printf("state of the machine is %lu\n",state.value);
}
```

Even if the debug variable is 0 (i.e., false), the process still has to check the value of the debug variable at run time, to see if it is true or false. The If statement will have its expression evaluated even if it is guaranteed to be false. This kind of unnecessary run-time checking can slow down an application, especially when there are thousands of such debug statements.

In addition, a customer may figure out a way to turn on debugging and see things that will only confuse him (and possibly make existing problems worse). I've heard stories from Fortune 100 CIOs who have bought ERP software from a large European vendor. They discovered a switch that floods the console with messages in German!

To deal with this problem, I decided to implement debugging code using preprocessor macros. This way, I can strip out debugging statements when I want to build the production version of the HEC virtual machine. Consider the debugging statements in main.c:

```
#define DBG_MAIN          1

#ifdef DBG_MAIN
#define DBG_MAIN0(str)            printf("main(): "); printf(str);
#define DBG_MAIN1(str,arg1)       printf("main(): "); printf(str,arg1);
#define DBG_MAIN2(str,arg1,arg2) printf("main(): "); printf(str,arg1,arg2);
#else
#define DBG_MAIN0(str)
#define DBG_MAIN1(str,arg1)
#define DBG_MAIN2(str,arg1,arg2)
#endif
```

If DBG_MAIN is defined, these debugging macros will resolve to printf() function calls. If I decide to comment out the DBG_MAIN definition, the debugging macros will resolve to empty space and will not appear in the final binary.

To keep things flexible, I give each module of code its own set of debugging macros. This way I can toggle debugging on a per-module basis.

Handling Configuration Options

Command-line processing is the second stage of the HEC virtual machine's life cycle. It is initiated in `main.c` directly after the error log is established:

```
struct CmdLine cl;

/*1) establishing error log */

DBG_MAIN0("1) establishing error log\n");
setUpErrorFile();

/*2) handle command-line arguments, set computer switches*/

DBG_MAIN0("2) invoking handleArguments()\n");
cl = handleArguments(argc,argv);
if(cl.ok==FALSE)
{
    FATAL_ERROR1("main(): errors during handleArguments()\n");
}
```

The majority of command-line processing work is performed by the `handle-Arguments()` function, which resides in the `cmdline.c` source file. This function populates and returns a `CmdLine` structure, which stores a distillation of all the command-line information.

```
struct CmdLine
{
    char *binaryFile;      /* name of the bytecode file to execute */
    U8 heapRequest;        /* RAM to allocate for heap in KB*/
    U8 stackRequest;       /* RAM to allocate for stack in KB*/
    U1 debug;              /* if TRUE, start in debug mode */
    U1 ok;                 /* TRUE or FALSE*/
};
```

Arguments passed to the bytecode program are stored in a global structure named `ProgramArgs`:

```
#define MAX_PROGRAM_ARGS    32
struct ProgramArgs
{
    char *args[MAX_PROGRAM_ARGS];    /* program arguments */
    U1 nArgs;                        /* number of arguments */
};
struct ProgramArgs programArgs;
```

Before we dive into the implementation of the `handleArguments()` function, there are a number of lesser functions and macros that `handleArguments()` uses that must be introduced. For example, in a manner similar to `main.c`, the `cmdline.c` source file has its own set of debugging macros:

```
#ifdef DBG_CMDLINE
#define DBG_CMDLINE0(str)                printf("handleArguments(): "); printf(str);
```

```
#define DBG_CMDLINE1(str,arg1)          printf("handleArguments(): ");\
                                        printf(str,arg1);
#define DBG_CMDLINE2(str,arg1,arg2)     printf("handleArguments(): ");\
                                        printf(str,arg1,arg2);
#else
#define DBG_CMDLINE0(str)
#define DBG_CMDLINE1(str,arg1)
#define DBG_CMDLINE2(str,arg1,arg2)
#endif
```

If an incorrect command line is used to invoke the virtual machine, the handle-
Arguments() function will invoke the printUsage() function, which prints a usage
summary to the console:

```
void printUsage()
{

    printf("\n\tHECVM [options] file.RUN [arguments]\n\n");

    printf("\tvirtual machine options:\n\n");

    printf("\t-h=XXXX\tmemory to allocate for heap in KB\n");
    printf("\t-s=XXXX\tmemory to allocate for stack in KB\n");
    printf("\t-d\tenable debug mode\n");
    printf("\t-?\tprint help\n\n");

    printf("\tthere are no spaces in the -h and -s options!\n\n");
    return;

}/*end printUsage*/
```

There are also several smaller helper functions that generate various error messages in the
event of a bad command line:

```
void badHeapSize(char *str)
{
    ERROR1_LVL2("badHeapSize(): bad heap request (%s)\n",str);
    ERROR0_LVL2("badHeapSize(): require positive integer\n");
    return;

}/*end badHeapSize*/

void badHeapOption()
{
    ERROR0_LVL2("badHeapOption(): incorrect \'-h\' switch\n");
    return;

}/*end badHeapOption*/

void badStackSize(char *str)
{
    ERROR1_LVL2("badStackSize(): bad stack request (%s)\n",str);
    ERROR0_LVL2("badStackSize(): require positive integer\n");
    return;
```

```
}/*end badStackSize*/

void badStackOption()
{
    ERROR0_LVL2("badStackOption(): incorrect \'-s\' switch\n");
    return;

}/*end badStackOption*/

void badOptionChar(char ch)
{
    ERROR1_LVL2("badOptionChar(): \'-%c\' is invalid\n",ch);
    return;

}/*end badOptionChar*/
```

In the event that the size of the heap and stack are not explicitly set at the command line, they will both be set to their default values:

```
#define DEF_HEAP          64    /* default heap = 64KB = 65,536 bytes */
#define DEF_STACK         64    /* default stack = 64KB = 65,536 bytes */
```

Now that we've covered the prerequisites, we are ready to take a look at the handle-Arguments() function. Remember, the primary goal of handleArguments() is to parse the command line and persist command-line information into a CmdLine structure. It may be a good idea to look back at Figure 3-7 and keep it in mind as you look at the following listing.

 NOTE The handleArguments() function also populates an Application-MetaData structure. However, this is used for debugging and will be discussed in the next chapter.

```
struct CmdLine handleArguments(int argc, char *argv[])
{
    struct CmdLine cmdline;
    int i;
    int name_length;

    /* set default values */

    cmdline.binaryFile = NULL;
    cmdline.heapRequest = DEF_HEAP;
    cmdline.stackRequest = DEF_STACK;
    cmdline.debug = FALSE;
    cmdline.ok = TRUE;

    programArgs.nArgs = 0;

    /* handle case when only 1 argument (name of executable) */

    if(argc==1)
    {
        ERROR0_LVL2("handleArguments(): no arguments\n");
```

```c
            printUsage();
            cmdline.ok = FALSE;
            return(cmdline);
}

/* handle virtual machine options */
/*
        -h=XXX, -s=XXX, -d, -?
        argv[i][0]= '-'
        argv[i][1]= letter
        argv[i][2]= '='
        argv[i][3]= number
*/

i=1;
while(argv[i][0]=='-')
{
        switch(argv[i][1])
        {
            case 'h':
            case 'H':
            {
                    if(argv[i][2]=='=')
                    {
                        char *stop;
                        S4 temp;
                        temp = strtol(&argv[i][3], &stop, 10);
                        if(temp<=0)
                        {
                            badHeapSize(argv[i]);
                            printUsage();
                            cmdline.ok = FALSE;
                            return(cmdline);
                        }
                        cmdline.heapRequest = (U8)temp;
                        DBG_CMDLINE0("heap size set\n");
                    }
                    else
                    {
                        badHeapOption();
                        printUsage();
                        cmdline.ok = FALSE;
                        return(cmdline);
                    }
            }break;
            case 's':
            case 'S':
            {
                    if(argv[i][2]=='=')
                    {
                        char *stop;
                        S4 temp;
```

```
                                temp = strtol(&argv[i][3], &stop, 10);
                                if(temp<=0)
                                {
                                        badStackSize(argv[i]);
                                        printUsage();
                                        cmdline.ok = FALSE;
                                        return(cmdline);
                                }
                                cmdline.stackRequest = (U8)temp;
                                DBG_CMDLINE0("stack size set\n");
                        }
                        else
                        {
                                badStackOption();
                                printUsage();
                                cmdline.ok = FALSE;
                                return(cmdline);
                        }
                }break;
                case 'd':
                case 'D':
                {
                        cmdline.debug = TRUE;
                        DBG_CMDLINE0("debug switch toggled\n");

                }break;
                case '?':
                {
                        printUsage();
                        cmdline.ok = FALSE;
                        return(cmdline);

                }break;
                default:
                {
                        badOptionChar(argv[i][1]);
                        printUsage();
                        cmdline.ok = FALSE;
                        return(cmdline);
                }
        }/*end switch*/

        i++;
        if(i==argc)
        {
                ERROR0_LVL2("handleArguments(): executable missing\n");
                printUsage();
                cmdline.ok = FALSE;
                return(cmdline);
        }

}/*end While loop */
```

```
/* set filename, check for .RUN extension */

name_length = strlen(argv[i]);

if(name_length<4)
{
    ERROR0_LVL2("handleArguments(): no .RUN suffix\n");
    printUsage();
    cmdline.ok = FALSE;
    return(cmdline);
}

if((argv[i][name_length-4]=='.')&&
   (argv[i][name_length-3]=='R')&&
   (argv[i][name_length-2]=='U')&&
   (argv[i][name_length-1]=='N'))
{
    cmdline.binaryFile = argv[i];
    appMetaData.fileName = argv[i];
    i++;
}
else
{
    ERROR0_LVL2("handleArguments(): missing .RUN suffix\n");
    printUsage();
    cmdline.ok = FALSE;
    return(cmdline);
}

/* collect program arguments */

while(i<argc)
{
    if(programArgs.nArgs<MAX_PROGRAM_ARGS)
    {
        programArgs.args[programArgs.nArgs]=argv[i];
        programArgs.nArgs++;
    }
    i++;
}

/* summarize command line */

DBG_CMDLINE0("Command line summary--------------------\n\n");

DBG_CMDLINE1("\theapRequest=%lu KB\n",cmdline.heapRequest);
DBG_CMDLINE1("\tstackRequest=%lu KB\n",cmdline.stackRequest);
if(cmdline.debug == TRUE)
{
    DBG_CMDLINE0("\tdebugging enabled\n\n");
}
else
{
    DBG_CMDLINE0("\tdebugging mode OFF\n\n");
```

```
        }

        DBG_CMDLINE1("\tfile to load=%s\n\n",cmdline.binaryFile);

        for(i=0;i<programArgs.nArgs;i++)
        {
                DBG_CMDLINE2("arg[%d]=%s\n",i,programArgs.args[i]);
        }
        return(cmdline);

}/*end handleArguments*/
```

If the command line is acceptable, the field named `ok` in the `CmdLine` structure will be set to TRUE and the data in the `CmdLine` structure will be used to set up the HEC virtual machine's environment. Otherwise, the virtual machine will complain and shut down.

Setting Up the Environment

Once the `CmdLine` structure has been populated with data, we can start setting up the virtual machine's run-time environment. As in the previous stage, everything begins in the `main.c` source file. To help illuminate things, I'll include the preceding code that initiates command-line processing.

```
/*2) handle command-line arguments, set computer switches*/

DBG_MAIN0("2) invoking handleArguments()\n");
cl = handleArguments(argc,argv);
if(cl.ok==FALSE)
{
        FATAL_ERROR1("main(): errors during handleArguments()\n");
}

/*3) init execution environment and load bytecode */

DBG_MAIN0("3) invoking initHEC()\n");
RAM = NULL;
if(initHEC(cl)==FALSE)
{
        FATAL_ERROR1("main(): errors during initHEC()\n");
}
```

The `CmdLine` structure returned by `handleArguments()` is fed as an argument to the `initHEC()` function. The `initHEC()` function, whose implementation is located in the `init.c` source file, uses the information in the `CmdLine` structure to set up the execution environment.

Before you look at the source code for `initHEC()`, it will probably help to examine a flow diagram of the actions this function performs (see Figure 3-8).

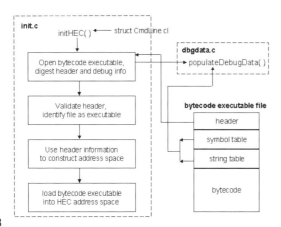

Figure 3-8

The HEC virtual machine starts by opening the bytecode executable and reading in the file's header and debug information. A bytecode file is not just a set of bytecode instructions. Bytecode executables have four distinct sections. Every HEC executable has a header, a symbol table, a string table, and a bytecode section (in that order). The header is a mere 26 bytes long and contains four contiguous fields of information:

- 16-bit magic number

- 64-bit value specifying size (in bytes) of the symbol table

- 64-bit value specifying size (in bytes) of the string table

- 64-bit value specifying size (in bytes) of the bytecode section

The symbol table and string table are used by the debugger and are described in the next chapter. With regard to debugging, the initHEC() function invokes the populate-DebugData() function from the dbgdata.c source file to process the symbol and string tables. That is all you need to know for the time being. What we are interested in right now is the magic number and the size of the bytecode section.

Once the initHEC() routine has digested the header and extracted the necessary information, it validates the magic number and bytecode size. The magic number must be 0xDEED; otherwise the virtual machine thinks that the file is not a bytecode executable and the virtual machine will shut down. If the size of the bytecode section is 0, the virtual machine will assume that there are no instructions to execute and will also shut down.

If header verification is a success (i.e., the magic number is 0xDEED and the bytecode size is nonzero), the virtual machine will use the header information, in conjunction with command-line settings, to set up the virtual machine's address space. The HEC virtual machine's address space consists of a text segment, a heap segment, and a stack segment.

The size of the text segment is specified by the size of the executable file's bytecode section. The size of the stack and heap are either set via the command line or set to their default values (64 KB). The initHEC() function adds the size of the executable file's bytecode section to the amount of memory requested for the heap and the stack. If this sum is greater than the amount of free physical memory (memory available from the motherboard's memory chips), the virtual machine will shut down. Otherwise, an array of unsigned bytes equal to the sum will be allocated, and the address of the first byte will be assigned to the RAM pointer declared in `exenv.c` (see Figure 3-9).

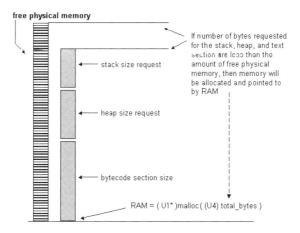

free physical memory

If number of bytes requested for the stack, heap, and text section are less than the amount of free physical memory, then memory will be allocated and pointed to by RAM

stack size request

heap size request

bytecode section size

RAM = (U1*)malloc((U4) total_bytes)

Figure 3-9

Once the address space has been allocated, the registers that delimit the various segments (i.e., $BE, $HS, $HE, $SS, $TOP) can be initialized to the appropriate values (see Figure 3-4). In addition, the $IP and $FP registers are set to address 0, and the $SP register is set to the same value as that stored in $TOP.

The only thing left to do is to load the bytecode executable file's bytecode section into the text section of the virtual machine's address space. When this is all complete, `initHEC()` is done with its job and the virtual machine's execution path returns to `main()` to begin the next stage.

```
U1 initHEC(struct CmdLine cl)
{
    U8 fileSize;                /* size of bytecode file in bytes */
    FILE *fptr;                 /* pointer to open file */

    struct HeaderRec hr;        /* header read from file*/

    U8 bytecodeStart;           /* byte offsets into executable file*/
    U8 bytecodeEnd;

    U8 exec_bytes;              /* bytes in bytecode section of RAM[] */
    U8 total_bytes;             /* total bytes allocated for RAM[] */
    U8 free_bytes;              /* available physical RAM */

    U8 index;                   /* index into file*/
    U8 i;                       /* index into RAM[]*/
    int read_byte;

    /*1) open executable and read header and debug data */

    fileSize = getFileSize(cl.binaryFile);

    if(fileSize == 0)
```

```
{
     ERROR0_LVL2("initHEC(): executable has zero size\n");
     return(FALSE);
}

if((fptr=fopen(cl.binaryFile,"rb"))== NULL)
{
     ERROR1_LVL2("initHEC(): cannot open %s\n",cl.binaryFile);
     return(FALSE);
}

DBG_INIT0("populate symbol table---------------------\n");
populateDebugData(&hr,&debugData,fptr);
PRINT_SYM_TBL();
DBG_INIT0("end symbol table population----------------\n");

DBG_INIT0("finished reading header and symbol table\n");
DBG_INIT1("magic number=%X\n",hr.magic);
DBG_INIT1("symbol table size=%lu\n",hr.szSymTbl);
DBG_INIT1("string table size=%lu\n",hr.szStrTbl);
DBG_INIT1("bytecode table size=%lu\n",hr.szByteCode);

/*2) validate header data */

if(hr.magic!=(U2)APPLICATION)
{
     ERROR0_LVL2("initHEC(): file not HEC executable\n");
     FCLOSE(fptr);
     return(FALSE);
}

if(hr.szByteCode==0)
{
     ERROR1_LVL2("initHEC(): no bytecode in %s\n",cl.binaryFile);
     FCLOSE(fptr);
     return(FALSE);
}

/*3) user header data to allocate RAM and init registers*/

bytecodeStart = SIZE_HEADER + hr.szSymTbl + hr.szStrTbl;
bytecodeEnd = (bytecodeStart+hr.szByteCode)-1;

DBG_INIT1("bytecodeStart in file=%lu\n",bytecodeStart);
DBG_INIT1("bytecodeEnd in file=%lu\n",bytecodeEnd);

exec_bytes = (bytecodeEnd - bytecodeStart) + 1;

total_bytes = exec_bytes+
                   (cl.heapRequest*1024)+
                   (cl.stackRequest*1024);

free_bytes = getAvailableMemory();
```

```
if(total_bytes > free_bytes)
{
     ERRORO_LVL2("initHEC(): not enough memory to init runtime\n");
     FCLOSE(fptr);
     return(FALSE);
}

DBG_INIT1("available physical RAM= %lu\n", free_bytes);
DBG_INIT1("file size= %lu\n", fileSize);
DBG_INIT1("size of bytecode in file= %lu\n", exec_bytes);
DBG_INIT1("heap bytes= %lu\n", cl.heapRequest*1024);
DBG_INIT1("stack bytes= %lu\n", cl.stackRequest*1024);
DBG_INIT1("total required bytes= %lu\n", total_bytes);

/* we're legal, so can allocate RAM  */

printf("allocating %lu bytes\n",total_bytes);

/* U4 size limit is imposed here!!!! */

RAM = (U1*)malloc((U4)total_bytes);

/*
     now set up registers

     memory layout:  [0 -> $BE] [$HS -> $HE] [$SS -> $TOP]
*/

DBG_INIT0("setting up registers\n");

R[$IP]=0;
R[$SP]=total_bytes-1;
R[$FP]=0;
R[$BE]=exec_bytes-1;

R[$HS]=exec_bytes;
R[$HE]=exec_bytes+(cl.heapRequest*1024)-1;

R[$SS]=exec_bytes+(cl.heapRequest*1024);
R[$TOP]=total_bytes-1;

appMetaData.fileSize = fileSize;
appMetaData.szSymTbl=hr.szSymTbl;
appMetaData.szStrTbl=hr.szStrTbl;
appMetaData.szByteCode=hr.szByteCode;
appMetaData.bCodeFileStart=bytecodeStart;
appMetaData.bCodeFileEnd=bytecodeEnd;
appMetaData.heapSize = cl.heapRequest*1024;
appMetaData.stackSize= cl.stackRequest*1024;
appMetaData.ram = total_bytes;

/*4) load bytecode into RAM[] */
```

```
/*load bytecode into RAM*/

rewind(fptr);     /* rewind to start of file */

/*
note: fseek starts index at zero, so our scheme is correct
note: (U4) cast, limits us to 4GB file
*/

if(fseek(fptr,(U4)bytecodeStart,SEEK_SET))
{
     ERROR0_LVL2("initHEC(): could not find bytecode start\n");
     return(FALSE);
}

i=0;
for(index=bytecodeStart;index<=bytecodeEnd;index++)
{
     read_byte = fgetc(fptr);
     if(read_byte==EOF)
     {
          ERROR0_LVL2("initHEC(): error reading bytecode file\n");
          FCLOSE(fptr);
          return(FALSE);
     }
     RAM[i]=(U1)read_byte;
     i++;
}

FCLOSE(fptr);
return(TRUE);

}/*end initHEC*/
```

Verification

During the verification stage, the virtual machine checks each instruction to make sure that:

- The instruction has a legal opcode
- Register operands reference actual registers
- Address literals are within range
- Instructions do not end prematurely
- Big-endian values are converted to the processor's numeric format

The whole point of the verification stage is to perform a certain amount of fault detection before execution begins. This way, instead of having to perform checks repeatedly at run time, we can get away with doing them once during startup and save the virtual machine from having to do a lot of extra work.

Bytecode verification checks are performed by the following set of helper functions in `reformat.c`:

```
void badIntReg(U1 arg, U8 currentbyte);
void badFltReg(U1 arg, U8 currentbyte);
void badDblReg(U1 arg, U8 currentbyte);
void checkAddress(U1 *arr, U8 cb);
void checkCurrentByte(U8 cb, U8 end);
void checkEndCurrentByte(U8 cb, U8 end);
```

All of these helper functions print a brief message to the console if something is awry (via ERROR macros defined in `error.c`) and then record extended information to the error log.

The functions `badIntReg()`, `badFltReg()`, and `badDblReg()` all check to make sure that register operands are legal. Register operands appear in bytecode instructions as individual bytes whose values correspond to the macro definitions in `exenv.c`. For example, a register operand that was meant to represent $D3 would appear in bytecode as a single byte and this byte would store the value 0x02.

In the following function definitions, the `arg` parameter is expected to contain the bytecode operand value of the register being checked, and the `currentbyte` parameter holds the address of this bytecode operand.

```
void badIntReg(U1 arg, U8 currentbyte)
{
    if(arg>$R24)
    {
        ERROR1_LVL2("badIntReg(): (%d) not integer register\n",arg);

        xmlBegin();
        fprintf(errPtr,"badIntReg(): bad register at address ");
        fpU8(errPtr,currentbyte);
        fprintf(errPtr,"\n");
        xmlEnd();

        FATAL_ERROR();
    }
    return;

}/*end badIntReg*/

void badFltReg(U1 arg, U8 currentbyte)
{
    if(arg>$F10)
    {
        ERROR1_LVL2("badFltReg(): (%d) not float register\n",arg);

        xmlBegin();
        fprintf(errPtr,"badFltReg(): bad register at address ");
        fpU8(errPtr,currentbyte);
        fprintf(errPtr,"\n");
        xmlEnd();
```

```
                        FATAL_ERROR();
            }
        return;

}/*end badFltReg*/

void badDblReg(U1 arg, U8 currentbyte)
{
    if(arg>$D10)
    {
            ERROR1_LVL2("badDblReg(): (%d) not double register\n",arg);

            xmlBegin();
            fprintf(errPtr,"badDblReg(): bad register at address ");
            fpU8(errPtr,currentbyte);
            fprintf(errPtr,"\n");
            xmlEnd();

            FATAL_ERROR();
    }
    return;

}/*end badDblReg*/
```

The checkAddress() function makes sure that bytecode address literals do not reference memory beyond the end of the address space.

```
void checkAddress(U1 *arr, U8 cb)
{
    U8* addr;
    addr = (U8*)&arr[cb];
    if(*addr > R[$TOP])
    {
            ERROR0_LVL2("checkAddress(): address out of bounds\n");

            xmlBegin();
            fprintf(errPtr,"checkAddress(): invalid address literal ");
            fpU8(errPtr,*addr);
            fprintf(errPtr," at memory location ");
            fpU8(errPtr,cb);
            fprintf(errPtr,"\n");
            xmlEnd();

            FATAL_ERROR();
    }
    return;

}/*end checkAddress*/
```

The last thing that the verifier has to safeguard against is incomplete instructions. Specifically, it is possible for the text segment to end before an instruction does. In other words, there could be an instruction that does not have all of its necessary operands. The checkCurrentByte() and checkEndCurrentByte() functions are used to test for this scenario.

```
void checkCurrentByte(U8 cb, U8 end)
{
    if(cb>=end)
    {
        ERROR0_LVL2("checkCurrentByte(): incomplete instruction\n");

        xmlBegin();
        fprintf(errPtr,"checkCurrentByte(): ");
        fprintf(errPtr,"incomplete instruction at address ");
        fpU8(errPtr,cb);
        fprintf(errPtr,"\n");
        xmlEnd();

        FATAL_ERROR();
    }
    return;

}/*end checkCurrentByte*/


/*
last byte of an instruction is allowed to be at end of bytecode, so
use checkEndCurrentByte
*/

void checkEndCurrentByte(U8 cb, U8 end)
{
    if(cb>end)
    {
        ERROR0_LVL2("checkEndCurrentByte(): incomplete instruction\n");

        xmlBegin();
        fprintf(errPtr,"checkEndCurrentByte(): ");
        fprintf(errPtr,"incomplete instruction at address ");
        fpU8(errPtr,cb);
        fprintf(errPtr,"\n");
        xmlEnd();

        FATAL_ERROR();
    }
    return;

}/*end checkEndCurrentByte*/
```

In order to get a better understanding of what the virtual machine's verifier has to do for a particular instruction, it is necessary to take a preliminary look at the virtual machine's instruction set. This way you can see why certain instructions are subject to a particular set of verification operations. Table 3-1 presents a summary of the HEC virtual machine's instruction set.

Table 3-1

Instruction	Opcode	Meaning	Encoding
LBI $R, byte	0	Store byte constant in $R (think "load byte immediate")	BBB
LWI $R, word	1	Store word constant in $R	BBW
LDI $R, dword	2	Store dword constant in $R	BBD
LQI $R, qword	3	Store qword constant in $R	BBQ
LF1I $F, float	4	Store float constant in $F	BBD
LF2I $D, double	5	Store double constant in $D	BBQ
LAD $R, address	6	Store address constant in $R (direct addressing)	BBQ
LAI $R1, $R2, qword	7	Store sum of qword and $R2 in $R1 (indirect addressing)	BBBQ
LB $R1, $R2	8	Take byte at address in $R2 and store in $R1	BBB
LW $R1, $R2	9	Take word at address in $R2 and store in $R1	BBB
LD $R1, $R2	10	Take dword at address in $R2 and store in $R1	BBB
LQ $R1, $R2	11	Take qword at address in $R2 and store in $R1	BBB
LF1 $F, $R2	12	Take float at address in $R2 and store in $F	BBB
LF2 $D, $R2	13	Take double at address in $R2 and store in $D	BBB
SB $R1, $R2	14	Place byte in $R1 at the address in $R2	BBB
SW $R1, $R2	15	Place word in $R1 at the address in $R2	BBB
SD $R1, $R2	16	Place dword in $R1 at the address in $R2	BBB
SQ $R1, $R2	17	Place qword in $R1 at the address in $R2	BBB
SF1 $F, $R2	18	Place float in $F at the address in $R2	BBB
SF2 $D, $R2	19	Place double in $D at the address in $R2	BBB
PUSHB $R	20	Push byte in $R on stack	BB
PUSHW $R	21	Push word in $R on stack	BB
PUSHD $R	22	Push dword in $R on stack	BB
PUSHQ $R	23	Push qword in $R on stack	BB
PUSHF1 $F	24	Push float in $F on stack	BB
PUSHF2 $D	25	Push double in $D on stack	BB
POPB $R	26	Pop byte off stack and place in $R	BB
POPW $R	27	Pop word off stack and place in $R	BB
POPD $R	28	Pop dword off stack and place in $R	BB
POPQ $R	29	Pop qword off stack and place in $R	BB
POPF1 $F	30	Pop float off stack and place in $F	BB
POPF2 $D	31	Pop double off stack and place in $D	BB
MOV $R1, $R2	32	Copy contents of $R2 into $R1	BBB
MOVF $F1, $F2	33	Copy contents of $F2 into $F1	BBB
MOVD $D1, $D2	34	Copy contents of $D2 into $D1	BBB

Instruction	Opcode	Meaning	Encoding
JMP $R	35	Jump to the address in $R	BB
JE $R1, $R2, $R3	36	Jump to the address in $R3 if $R1 equals $R2	BBBB
JNE $R1, $R2, $R3	37	Jump to the address in $R3 if $R1 does not equal $R2	BBBB
SLT $R1, $R2, $R3	38	Set $R1 to 1 if $R2 is less than $R3, otherwise set $R1 to 0	BBBB
INT byte	39	Execute interrupt specified by byte constant	BB
DI	40	Disable interrupt processing	B
EI	41	Enable interrupt processing	B
HALT	42	Shut down the virtual machine	B
NOP	43	Does nothing (no operation)	B
AND $R1, $R2, $R3	44	Set $R1 to the bitwise AND of $R2 and $R3	BBBB
OR $R1, $R2, $R3	45	Set $R1 to the bitwise OR of $R2 and $R3	BBBB
XOR $R1, $R2, $R3	46	Set $R1 to the bitwise XOR of $R2 and $R3	BBBB
NOT $R1, $R2	47	Set $R1 to the bitwise NOT of $R2	BBB
BT $R1, $R2, $R3	48	Set $R1 to 1 if the $R3rd bit in $R2 is on, otherwise set $R1 to 0	BBBB
BS $R1, $R2	49	Set the $R2nd bit in $R1	BBB
SRA $R1, $R2, $R3	50	$R1 = $R2 shifted $R3 bits right, sign bit enters left	BBBB
SRL $R1, $R2, $R3	51	$R1 = $R2 shifted $R3 bits right, zero enters left	BBBB
SL $R1, $R2, $R3	52	$R1 = $R2 shifted $R3 bits left, zero enters right	BBBB
ADD $R1, $R2, $R3	53	$R1 = $R2 + $R3	BBBB
SUB $R1, $R2, $R3	54	$R1 = $R2 – $R3	BBBB
MULT $R1, $R2, $R3	55	$R1 = $R2 * $R3	BBBB
DIV $R1, $R2, $R3, $R4	56	$R1 = $R2 / $R3 and $R2 = $R3 % $R4	BBBB
CAST_IF $R, $F	57	Cast a float in $F to an integer in $R	BBB
CAST_ID $R, $D	58	Cast a double in $D to an integer in $R	BBB
CAST_FI $F, $R	59	Cast an integer in $R to a float in $F	BBB
CAST_FD $F, $D	60	Cast a double in $D to a float in $F	BBB
CAST_DI $D, $R	61	Cast an integer in $R to a double in $D	BBB
CAST_DF $D, $F	62	Cast a float in $F to a double in $D	BBB
FADD $F1, $F2, $F3	63	$F1 = $F2 + $F3	BBBB
FSUB $F1, $F2, $F3	64	$F1 = $F2 – $F3	BBBB
FMULT $F1, $F2, $F3	65	$F1 = $F2 * $F3	BBBB
FDIV $F1, $F2, $F3	66	$F1 = $F2 / $F3	BBBB
FSLT $F1, $F2, $F3	67	Set $F1 to 1 if $F2 is less than $F3, otherwise set $F1 to 0	BBBB
DADD $D1, $D2, $D3	68	$D1 = $D2 + $D3	BBBB

Instruction	Opcode	Meaning	Encoding
DSUB $D1, $D2, $D3	69	$D1 = $D2 – $D3	BBBB
DMULT $D1, $D2, $D3	70	$D1 = $D2 * $D3	BBBB
DDIV $D1, $D2, $D3	71	$D1 = $D2 / $D3	BBBB
DSLT $D1, $D2, $D3	72	Set $D1 to 1 if $D2 is less than $D3, otherwise set $D1 to 0	BBBB

NOTE In Table 3-1 the symbol $R is supposed to represent a generic integer-valued register. For example, $R could be $R12, $IP, $FP, or any other integer-valued register. Likewise, the $F and $D symbols are meant to represent single-precision and double-precision floating-point valued registers.

The information in the Encoding column in the table is used to give you an idea of the form an instruction takes in bytecode. The following scheme is applied:

- B = byte
- W = word
- D = double word
- Q = quad word

For example, an instruction with an encoding of BBBD requires seven bytes. Instruction opcodes are always a byte long and are always located at the beginning of an instruction. Thus, we know that the BBBD encoded instruction has an opcode (B) and three operands (BBD). The three operands consist of a byte, followed by another byte, and ending with a double word.

The act of verification is performed by the reformat() function, which is invoked from main() after the virtual machine's environment has been established. The reformat() function is defined in the reformat.c source file.

```
/*3) init execution environment and load bytecode */

DBG_MAIN0("3) invoking initHEC()\n");
RAM = NULL;
if(initHEC(cl)==FALSE)
{
     FATAL_ERROR1("main(): errors during initHEC()\n");
}

/*4) reformat numeric operands to native and verify */

DBG_MAIN0("4) invoking reformat()\n");
if(reformat()==FALSE)
{
     FATAL_ERROR1("main(): errors during reformat()\n");
}
```

The verification process begins at address 0 and continues until the beginning of the heap segment is reached. Each time the verifier has finished validating an instruction, it expects the next byte in memory to either be an instruction opcode or the end of the text segment.

This verification technique does not allow the text segment to be used for data storage. In other words, a requirement that verification imposes is that the text segment consists only of instructions. You could be sneaky and get around this constraint using a JMP instruction followed by a series of NOP instructions. However, I do not recommend this approach.

 NOTE One of the subtasks of the `reformat()` function is to apply the FORMAT_WORD, FORMAT_DWORD, and FORMAT_QWORD macros (which I presented earlier in this chapter) to switch big-endian values to the format used by the native hardware platform. This accounts for the name of the source file (`reformat.c`) and the function's name. Initially, I wrote `reformat()` to do only big-endian-to-native adjustments. As construction progressed, I added more and more additional functionality into `reformat()` until the majority of work was directed towards bytecode verification instead of reformatting. Even I couldn't escape scope creep completely.

Now that I have covered the basics of verification, you should be able to understand what `reformat()` is doing.

```
U1 reformat()
{
    U8 current_byte;
    U8 stop;

    current_byte = 0;
    stop = R[$HS];

    DBG_FMT0("initiating reformat\n\n");
    DBG_FMT_PU8("starting at address->",current_byte);
    DBG_FMT_PU8("stop address->",stop);

    while(current_byte < stop)
    {
        switch(RAM[current_byte])
        {
            case LBI:   /* LBI $r1, byte_constant BBB */
            {
                DBG_FMT1("opcode %s\n",I_Set[RAM[current_byte]]);
                current_byte++;
                checkCurrentByte(current_byte,stop);

                badIntReg(RAM[current_byte],current_byte);
                DBG_FMT1("operand %s\n",R_STR[RAM[current_byte]]);
                current_byte++;
                checkCurrentByte(current_byte,stop);

                DBG_FMT1("byte %d\n\n",(S1)RAM[current_byte]);
                current_byte = current_byte++;
                checkEndCurrentByte(current_byte,stop);

            }break;
            case LWI:   /* LWI $r1, word_constant BBW */
            {
```

```
                        DBG_FMT1("opcode %s\n",I_Set[RAM[current_byte]]);
                        current_byte++;
                        checkCurrentByte(current_byte,stop);

                        badIntReg(RAM[current_byte],current_byte);
                        DBG_FMT1("operand %s\n",R_STR[RAM[current_byte]]);
                        current_byte++;
                        checkCurrentByte(current_byte,stop);

                        FORMAT_WORD(RAM,current_byte);
                        DBG_FMT1("word %hd\n\n",*((S2 *)&RAM[current_byte]));
                        current_byte = current_byte+2;
                        checkEndCurrentByte(current_byte,stop);

                }break;
                case LDI:    /* LDI $r1, dword_constant BBD */
                {
                        DBG_FMT1("opcode %s\n",I_Set[RAM[current_byte]]);
                        current_byte++;
                        checkCurrentByte(current_byte,stop);

                        badIntReg(RAM[current_byte],current_byte);
                        DBG_FMT1("operand %s\n",R_STR[RAM[current_byte]]);
                        current_byte++;
                        checkCurrentByte(current_byte,stop);

                        FORMAT_DWORD(RAM,current_byte);
                        DBG_FMT1("dword %ld\n\n",*((S4*)&RAM[current_byte]));
                        current_byte = current_byte+4;
                        checkEndCurrentByte(current_byte,stop);

                }break;
                case LQI:    /* LQI $r1, qword_constant  BBQ*/
                {
                        DBG_FMT1("opcode %s\n",I_Set[RAM[current_byte]]);
                        current_byte++;
                        checkCurrentByte(current_byte,stop);

                        badIntReg(RAM[current_byte],current_byte);
                        DBG_FMT1("operand %s\n",R_STR[RAM[current_byte]]);
                        current_byte++;
                        checkCurrentByte(current_byte,stop);

                        FORMAT_QWORD(RAM,current_byte);
                        DBG_FMT_PS8("qword ",*((S8 *)&RAM[current_byte]));
                        current_byte = current_byte+8;
                        checkEndCurrentByte(current_byte,stop);

                }break;
                case LF1I: /* LF1I $f1, float_constant  BBD */
                {
                        DBG_FMT1("opcode %s\n",I_Set[RAM[current_byte]]);
                        current_byte++;
```

```
        checkCurrentByte(current_byte,stop);

        badFltReg(RAM[current_byte],current_byte);
        DBG_FMT1("operand %s\n",Rf_STR[RAM[current_byte]]);
        current_byte++;
        checkCurrentByte(current_byte,stop);

        FORMAT_DWORD(RAM,current_byte);
        DBG_FMT1("float %g\n\n",*((F4 *)&RAM[current_byte]));
        current_byte = current_byte+4;
        checkEndCurrentByte(current_byte,stop);

}break;
case LF2I:  /* LQI $d1, double_constant  BBQ*/
{
        DBG_FMT1("opcode %s\n",I_Set[RAM[current_byte]]);
        current_byte++;
        checkCurrentByte(current_byte,stop);

        badDblReg(RAM[current_byte],current_byte);
        DBG_FMT1("operand %s\n",Rd_STR[RAM[current_byte]]);
        current_byte++;
        checkCurrentByte(current_byte,stop);

        FORMAT_QWORD(RAM,current_byte);
        DBG_FMT1("float %g\n\n",*((F8 *)&RAM[current_byte]));
        current_byte = current_byte+8;
        checkEndCurrentByte(current_byte,stop);

}break;
case LAD:   /* LAD $r1, address = BBQ */
{
        DBG_FMT1("opcode %s\n",I_Set[RAM[current_byte]]);
        current_byte++;
        checkCurrentByte(current_byte,stop);

        badIntReg(RAM[current_byte],current_byte);
        DBG_FMT1("operand %s\n",R_STR[RAM[current_byte]]);
        current_byte++;
        checkCurrentByte(current_byte,stop);

        FORMAT_QWORD(RAM,current_byte);
        checkAddress(RAM,current_byte);
        DBG_FMT_PU8("address ",*((U8 *)&RAM[current_byte]));
        current_byte = current_byte+8;
        checkEndCurrentByte(current_byte,stop);

}break;
case LAI:   /* LAI $r1, $r2, qword      BBBQ*/
{
        DBG_FMT1("opcode %s\n",I_Set[RAM[current_byte]]);
        current_byte++;
        checkCurrentByte(current_byte,stop);
```

```
                    badIntReg(RAM[current_byte],current_byte);
                    DBG_FMT1("operand %s\n",R_STR[RAM[current_byte]]);
                    current_byte++;
                    checkCurrentByte(current_byte,stop);

                    badIntReg(RAM[current_byte],current_byte);
                    DBG_FMT1("operand %s\n",R_STR[RAM[current_byte]]);
                    current_byte++;
                    checkCurrentByte(current_byte,stop);

                    FORMAT_QWORD(RAM,current_byte);
                    DBG_FMT_PS8("qword ",*((S8 *)&RAM[current_byte]));
                    current_byte = current_byte+8;
                    checkEndCurrentByte(current_byte,stop);

                }break;
                case LB:    /* LB $r1,$r2    BBB */
                case LW:
                case LD:
                case LQ:
                case SB:    /* SB $r1,$r2    BBB*/
                case SW:
                case SD:
                case SQ:
                {
                    DBG_FMT1("opcode %s\n",I_Set[RAM[current_byte]]);
                    current_byte++;
                    checkCurrentByte(current_byte,stop);

                    badIntReg(RAM[current_byte],current_byte);
                    DBG_FMT1("operand %s\n",R_STR[RAM[current_byte]]);
                    current_byte++;
                    checkCurrentByte(current_byte,stop);

                    badIntReg(RAM[current_byte],current_byte);
                    DBG_FMT1("operand %s\n\n",R_STR[RAM[current_byte]]);
                    current_byte++;
                    checkEndCurrentByte(current_byte,stop);

                }break;
                case LF1:   /* LF1  $f1, $r1   BBB */
                case SF1:
                {
                    DBG_FMT1("opcode %s\n",I_Set[RAM[current_byte]]);
                    current_byte++;
                    checkCurrentByte(current_byte,stop);

                    badFltReg(RAM[current_byte],current_byte);
                    DBG_FMT1("operand %s\n",Rf_STR[RAM[current_byte]]);
                    current_byte++;
                    checkCurrentByte(current_byte,stop);

                    badIntReg(RAM[current_byte],current_byte);
                    DBG_FMT1("operand %s\n\n",R_STR[RAM[current_byte]]);
```

```
                    current_byte++;
                    checkEndCurrentByte(current_byte,stop);

            }break;
            case LF2:   /*  LF2  $d1, $r1   BBB */
            case SF2:
            {
                    DBG_FMT1("opcode %s\n",I_Set[RAM[current_byte]]);
                    current_byte++;
                    checkCurrentByte(current_byte,stop);

                    badDblReg(RAM[current_byte],current_byte);
                    DBG_FMT1("operand %s\n",Rd_STR[RAM[current_byte]]);
                    current_byte++;
                    checkCurrentByte(current_byte,stop);

                    badIntReg(RAM[current_byte],current_byte);
                    DBG_FMT1("operand %s\n\n",R_STR[RAM[current_byte]]);
                    current_byte++;
                    checkEndCurrentByte(current_byte,stop);

            }break;
            case PUSHB:       /* PUSHB $r1   BB */
            case PUSHW:
            case PUSHD:
            case PUSHQ:
            case POPB:        /* POPB $r1    BB*/
            case POPW:
            case POPD:
            case POPQ:
            case JMP:         /* JMP $r1  BB*/
            {
                    DBG_FMT1("opcode %s\n",I_Set[RAM[current_byte]]);
                    current_byte++;
                    checkCurrentByte(current_byte,stop);

                    badIntReg(RAM[current_byte],current_byte);
                    DBG_FMT1("operand %s\n\n",R_STR[RAM[current_byte]]);
                    current_byte++;
                    checkEndCurrentByte(current_byte,stop);

            }break;
            case PUSHF1: /* PUSHF1 $f */
            case POPF1:
            {
                    DBG_FMT1("opcode %s\n",I_Set[RAM[current_byte]]);
                    current_byte++;
                    checkCurrentByte(current_byte,stop);

                    badFltReg(RAM[current_byte],current_byte);
                    DBG_FMT1("operand %s\n\n",Rf_STR[RAM[current_byte]]);
                    current_byte++;
                    checkEndCurrentByte(current_byte,stop);
```

```
}break;
case PUSHF2:        /* PUSHF2 $d */
case POPF2:
{
     DBG_FMT1("opcode %s\n",I_Set[RAM[current_byte]]);
     current_byte++;
     checkCurrentByte(current_byte,stop);

     badDblReg(RAM[current_byte],current_byte);
     DBG_FMT1("operand %s\n\n",Rd_STR[RAM[current_byte]]);
     current_byte++;
     checkEndCurrentByte(current_byte,stop);

}break;
case MOVF:          /* MOVF $f1, $f2 */
{
     DBG_FMT1("opcode %s\n",I_Set[RAM[current_byte]]);
     current_byte++;
     checkCurrentByte(current_byte,stop);

     badFltReg(RAM[current_byte],current_byte);
     DBG_FMT1("operand %s\n",Rf_STR[RAM[current_byte]]);
     current_byte++;
     checkCurrentByte(current_byte,stop);

     badFltReg(RAM[current_byte],current_byte);
     DBG_FMT1("operand %s\n\n",Rf_STR[RAM[current_byte]]);
     current_byte++;
     checkEndCurrentByte(current_byte,stop);

}break;
case MOVD:          /* MOVF $d1, $d2 */
{
     DBG_FMT1("opcode %s\n",I_Set[RAM[current_byte]]);
     current_byte++;
     checkCurrentByte(current_byte,stop);

     badDblReg(RAM[current_byte],current_byte);
     DBG_FMT1("operand %s\n",Rd_STR[RAM[current_byte]]);
     current_byte++;
     checkCurrentByte(current_byte,stop);

     badDblReg(RAM[current_byte],current_byte);
     DBG_FMT1("operand %s\n\n",Rd_STR[RAM[current_byte]]);
     current_byte++;
     checkEndCurrentByte(current_byte,stop);

}break;
case MOV:           /* MOV $r1, $r2    BBB */
case NOT:
case BS:
{
     DBG_FMT1("opcode %s\n",I_Set[RAM[current_byte]]);
     current_byte++;
```

```
                    checkCurrentByte(current_byte,stop);

                    badIntReg(RAM[current_byte],current_byte);
                    DBG_FMT1("operand %s\n",R_STR[RAM[current_byte]]);
                    current_byte++;
                    checkCurrentByte(current_byte,stop);

                    badIntReg(RAM[current_byte],current_byte);
                    DBG_FMT1("operand %s\n\n",R_STR[RAM[current_byte]]);
                    current_byte++;
                    checkEndCurrentByte(current_byte,stop);

}break;
case JE:          /*JE $r1, $r2, $r3  BBBB */
case JNE:
case SLT:
case AND:         /*AND $r1, $r2, $r3  BBBB*/
case OR:
case XOR:
case BT:
case SRA:         /*SRA  $r1, $r2, $r3  BBBB */
case SRL:
case SL:
case ADD:         /* ADD $r1, $r2, $r3  BBBB*/
case SUB:
case MULT:
{
                    DBG_FMT1("opcode %s\n",I_Set[RAM[current_byte]]);
                    current_byte++;
                    checkCurrentByte(current_byte,stop);

                    badIntReg(RAM[current_byte],current_byte);
                    DBG_FMT1("operand %s\n",R_STR[RAM[current_byte]]);
                    current_byte++;
                    checkCurrentByte(current_byte,stop);

                    badIntReg(RAM[current_byte],current_byte);
                    DBG_FMT1("operand %s\n",R_STR[RAM[current_byte]]);
                    current_byte++;
                    checkCurrentByte(current_byte,stop);

                    badIntReg(RAM[current_byte],current_byte);
                    DBG_FMT1("operand %s\n\n",R_STR[RAM[current_byte]]);
                    current_byte++;
                    checkEndCurrentByte(current_byte,stop);

}break;
case INT:         /* INT #vector    BB */
{
                    DBG_FMT1("opcode %s\n",I_Set[RAM[current_byte]]);
                    current_byte++;
                    checkCurrentByte(current_byte,stop);

                    DBG_FMT1("vector %d\n\n",RAM[current_byte]);
```

```
                              current_byte++;
                              checkEndCurrentByte(current_byte,stop);

                     }break;
                     case EI:           /* EI      B */
                     case DI:
                     case HALT:
                     case NOP:
                     {
                              DBG_FMT1("opcode %s\n\n",I_Set[RAM[current_byte]]);
                              current_byte++;
                              checkEndCurrentByte(current_byte,stop);

                     }break;
                     case DIV:          /* DIV $r1, $r2, $r3, $r4 */
                     {
                              DBG_FMT1("opcode %s\n",I_Set[RAM[current_byte]]);
                              current_byte++;
                              checkCurrentByte(current_byte,stop);

                              badIntReg(RAM[current_byte],current_byte);
                              DBG_FMT1("operand %s\n",R_STR[RAM[current_byte]]);
                              current_byte++;
                              checkCurrentByte(current_byte,stop);

                              badIntReg(RAM[current_byte],current_byte);
                              DBG_FMT1("operand %s\n",R_STR[RAM[current_byte]]);
                              current_byte++;
                              checkCurrentByte(current_byte,stop);

                              badIntReg(RAM[current_byte],current_byte);
                              DBG_FMT1("operand %s\n",R_STR[RAM[current_byte]]);
                              current_byte++;
                              checkCurrentByte(current_byte,stop);

                              badIntReg(RAM[current_byte],current_byte);
                              DBG_FMT1("operand %s\n\n",R_STR[RAM[current_byte]]);
                              current_byte++;
                              checkEndCurrentByte(current_byte,stop);

                     }break;
                     case CAST_IF:      /* CAST_IF  $r, $f */
                     {
                              DBG_FMT1("opcode %s\n",I_Set[RAM[current_byte]]);
                              current_byte++;
                              checkCurrentByte(current_byte,stop);

                              badIntReg(RAM[current_byte],current_byte);
                              DBG_FMT1("operand %s\n",R_STR[RAM[current_byte]]);
                              current_byte++;
                              checkCurrentByte(current_byte,stop);

                              badFltReg(RAM[current_byte],current_byte);
                              DBG_FMT1("operand %s\n\n",Rf_STR[RAM[current_byte]]);
```

```
        current_byte++;
        checkEndCurrentByte(current_byte,stop);

}break;
case CAST_ID:    /* CAST_ID  $r, $d */
{
        DBG_FMT1("opcode %s\n",I_Set[RAM[current_byte]]);
        current_byte++;
        checkCurrentByte(current_byte,stop);

        badIntReg(RAM[current_byte],current_byte);
        DBG_FMT1("operand %s\n",R_STR[RAM[current_byte]]);
        current_byte++;
        checkCurrentByte(current_byte,stop);

        badDblReg(RAM[current_byte],current_byte);
        DBG_FMT1("operand %s\n\n",Rd_STR[RAM[current_byte]]);
        current_byte++;
        checkEndCurrentByte(current_byte,stop);

}break;
case CAST_FI:    /* CAST_FI  $f, $r */
{
        DBG_FMT1("opcode %s\n",I_Set[RAM[current_byte]]);
        current_byte++;
        checkCurrentByte(current_byte,stop);

        badFltReg(RAM[current_byte],current_byte);
        DBG_FMT1("operand %s\n",Rf_STR[RAM[current_byte]]);
        current_byte++;
        checkCurrentByte(current_byte,stop);

        badIntReg(RAM[current_byte],current_byte);
        DBG_FMT1("operand %s\n\n",R_STR[RAM[current_byte]]);
        current_byte++;
        checkEndCurrentByte(current_byte,stop);

}break;
case CAST_FD:    /* CAST_FD  $f, $d */
{
        DBG_FMT1("opcode %s\n",I_Set[RAM[current_byte]]);
        current_byte++;
        checkCurrentByte(current_byte,stop);

        badFltReg(RAM[current_byte],current_byte);
        DBG_FMT1("operand %s\n",Rf_STR[RAM[current_byte]]);
        current_byte++;
        checkCurrentByte(current_byte,stop);

        badDblReg(RAM[current_byte],current_byte);
        DBG_FMT1("operand %s\n\n",Rd_STR[RAM[current_byte]]);
        current_byte++;
        checkEndCurrentByte(current_byte,stop);
```

```
}break;
case CAST_DI:     /* CAST_DI  $d, $r */
{
     DBG_FMT1("opcode %s\n",I_Set[RAM[current_byte]]);
     current_byte++;
     checkCurrentByte(current_byte,stop);

     badDblReg(RAM[current_byte],current_byte);
     DBG_FMT1("operand %s\n",Rd_STR[RAM[current_byte]]);
     current_byte++;
     checkCurrentByte(current_byte,stop);

     badIntReg(RAM[current_byte],current_byte);
     DBG_FMT1("operand %s\n\n",R_STR[RAM[current_byte]]);
     current_byte++;
     checkEndCurrentByte(current_byte,stop);

}break;
case CAST_DF:     /* CAST_DF  $d, $f */
{
     DBG_FMT1("opcode %s\n",I_Set[RAM[current_byte]]);
     current_byte++;
     checkCurrentByte(current_byte,stop);

     badDblReg(RAM[current_byte],current_byte);
     DBG_FMT1("operand %s\n",Rd_STR[RAM[current_byte]]);
     current_byte++;
     checkCurrentByte(current_byte,stop);

     badFltReg(RAM[current_byte],current_byte);
     DBG_FMT1("operand %s\n\n",Rf_STR[RAM[current_byte]]);
     current_byte++;
     checkEndCurrentByte(current_byte,stop);

}break;
case FADD:        /* FADD $f1, $f2, $f3    BBBB */
case FSUB:
case FMULT:
case FDIV:
case FSLT:
{
     DBG_FMT1("opcode %s\n",I_Set[RAM[current_byte]]);
     current_byte++;
     checkCurrentByte(current_byte,stop);

     badFltReg(RAM[current_byte],current_byte);
     DBG_FMT1("operand %s\n",Rf_STR[RAM[current_byte]]);
     current_byte++;
     checkCurrentByte(current_byte,stop);

     badFltReg(RAM[current_byte],current_byte);
     DBG_FMT1("operand %s\n",Rf_STR[RAM[current_byte]]);
     current_byte++;
```

```
                    checkCurrentByte(current_byte,stop);

                    badFltReg(RAM[current_byte],current_byte);
                    DBG_FMT1("operand %s\n\n",Rf_STR[RAM[current_byte]]);
                    current_byte++;
                    checkEndCurrentByte(current_byte,stop);

            }break;
            case DADD:          /* DADD $d1, $d2, $d3    BBBB */
            case DSUB:
            case DMULT:
            case DDIV:
            case DSLT:
            {
                    DBG_FMT1("opcode %s\n",I_Set[RAM[current_byte]]);
                    current_byte++;
                    checkCurrentByte(current_byte,stop);

                    badDblReg(RAM[current_byte],current_byte);
                    DBG_FMT1("operand %s\n",Rd_STR[RAM[current_byte]]);
                    current_byte++;
                    checkCurrentByte(current_byte,stop);

                    badDblReg(RAM[current_byte],current_byte);
                    DBG_FMT1("operand %s\n",Rd_STR[RAM[current_byte]]);
                    current_byte++;
                    checkCurrentByte(current_byte,stop);

                    badDblReg(RAM[current_byte],current_byte);
                    DBG_FMT1("operand %s\n\n",Rd_STR[RAM[current_byte]]);
                    current_byte++;
                    checkEndCurrentByte(current_byte,stop);

            }break;
            default:
            {
                    ERROR1_LVL2("reformat(): bad opcode %d\n",
                                RAM[current_byte]);
                    return(FALSE);
            }

        }/*end switch*/

    }/*end while*/

    DBG_FMT0("reformatting complete\n");

    return(TRUE);

}/*end reformat*/
```

You might notice that several instructions are often grouped together under a common verification check. This reflects the fact that different instructions often have the same encoding format.

Instruction Execution

OK, now we get to the really interesting part. The virtual machine has done all the necessary setup work and is ready to begin executing instructions. Program control returns to main() after the verification stage is complete, and the run() function is invoked from within main().

```
/*4) reformat numeric operands to native and verify */

DBG_MAIN0("4) invoking reformat()\n");
if(reformat()==FALSE)
{
      FATAL_ERROR1("main(): errors during reformat()\n");
}

/*5) begin execution*/

DBG_MAIN0("5) invoking run()\n");
run(cl.debug);

/*6) safe shutdown*/

DBG_MAIN0("6) HEC VM shutting down via HALT instruction\n");
shutDown(SHUTDOWN_OK);
return;
```

The run() function will cause bytecode instructions to be executed. Bytecode execution begins at address 0, in the virtual machine's synthetic address space, and continues on until either the HALT instruction is processed or until a fatal error occurs (see Figure 3-10). The HALT instruction causes program control to return from run(), back to main(), and perform a "safe" shutdown.

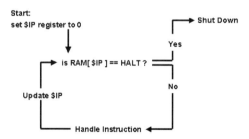

Figure 3-10

The run() function is defined in the run.c source file. It is relatively straightforward. It looks at the byte in the text segment that is currently pointed to by $IP. The virtual machine assumes that $IP points to an opcode, so it compares the value of the current byte against all the instruction opcodes. If a match is found, the instruction corresponding to the opcode will be "executed" by the HEC virtual machine. Otherwise, the virtual machine will generate a fatal error and die. Such is the life of the execution engine.

NOTE There is a bit of the HEC debugger's code in `run()`. A detailed look at the debugger, however, has been relegated to the next chapter. So, for now, I will conveniently be ignoring the debugging code. You can cooperate by suspending your disbelief and pretending that it is not there. Please temporarily dismiss variables and functions that contain the word "debug" or "dbg" as you read through the following code.

```
void run(U1 dbg)
{
    U2 tick;
    U8 start_debug_instr;

    tick=0;
    debug = dbg;   /*set global from dbgcmd.c*/

    interruptOn=TRUE;

    DBG_RUN0("initiating bytecode execution\n");

    while(RAM[ R[$IP] ] != HALT)
    {
        if(debug==TRUE){ readDbgCmd(); }
        start_debug_instr = (U8)R[$IP];

        switch(RAM[ R[$IP] ])
        {
            case LBI:{ HANDLE_LBI(); }break;
            case LWI:{ HANDLE_LWI(); }break;
            case LDI:{ HANDLE_LDI(); }break;
            case LQI:{ HANDLE_LQI(); }break;
            case LF1I:{ HANDLE_LF1I(); }break;
            case LF2I:{ HANDLE_LF2I(); }break;

            case LAD:{ HANDLE_LAD(); }break;
            case LAI:{ HANDLE_LAI(); }break;

            case LB:{ HANDLE_LB(); }break;
            case LW:{ HANDLE_LW(); }break;
            case LD:{ HANDLE_LD(); }break;
            case LQ:{ HANDLE_LQ(); }break;
            case LF1:{ HANDLE_LF1(); }break;
            case LF2:{ HANDLE_LF2(); }break;

            case SB:{ HANDLE_SB(); }break;
            case SW:{ HANDLE_SW(); }break;
            case SD:{ HANDLE_SD(); }break;
            case SQ:{ HANDLE_SQ(); }break;
            case SF1:{ HANDLE_SF1(); }break;
            case SF2:{ HANDLE_SF2(); }break;
```

```
case PUSHB:{ HANDLE_PUSHB(); }break;
case PUSHW:{ HANDLE_PUSHW(); }break;
case PUSHD:{ HANDLE_PUSHD(); }break;
case PUSHQ:{ HANDLE_PUSHQ(); }break;
case PUSHF1:{ HANDLE_PUSHF1(); }break;
case PUSHF2:{ HANDLE_PUSHF2(); }break;

case POPB:{ HANDLE_POPB(); }break;
case POPW:{ HANDLE_POPW(); }break;
case POPD:{ HANDLE_POPD(); }break;
case POPQ:{ HANDLE_POPQ(); }break;
case POPF1:{ HANDLE_POPF1(); }break;
case POPF2:{ HANDLE_POPF2(); }break;

case MOV:{ HANDLE_MOV(); }break;
case MOVF:{ HANDLE_MOVF(); }break;
case MOVD:{ HANDLE_MOVD(); }break;

case JMP:{ HANDLE_JMP(); }break;
case JE:{ HANDLE_JE(); }break;
case JNE:{ HANDLE_JNE(); }break;
case SLT:{ HANDLE_SLT(); }break;
case INT:{ HANDLE_INT(); }break;
case DI:{ HANDLE_DI(); }break;
case EI:{ HANDLE_EI(); }break;
case NOP:{ HANDLE_NOP(); }break;

case AND:{ HANDLE_AND(); }break;
case OR:{ HANDLE_OR(); }break;
case XOR:{ HANDLE_XOR(); }break;
case NOT:{ HANDLE_NOT(); }break;
case BT:{ handleBT(); }break;
case BS:{ handleBS(); }break;

case SRA:{ HANDLE_SRA(); }break;
case SRL:{ HANDLE_SRL(); }break;
case SL:{ HANDLE_SL(); }break;

case ADD:{ HANDLE_ADD(); }break;
case SUB:{ HANDLE_SUB(); }break;
case MULT:{ HANDLE_MULT(); }break;
case DIV:{ HANDLE_DIV(); }break;

case CAST_IF:{ HANDLE_CAST_IF(); }break;
case CAST_ID:{ HANDLE_CAST_ID(); }break;
case CAST_FI:{ HANDLE_CAST_FI(); }break;
case CAST_FD:{ HANDLE_CAST_FD(); }break;
case CAST_DI:{ HANDLE_CAST_DI(); }break;
case CAST_DF:{ HANDLE_CAST_DF(); }break;

case FADD:{ HANDLE_FADD(); }break;
case FSUB:{ HANDLE_FSUB(); }break;
case FMULT:{ HANDLE_FMULT(); }break;
case FDIV:{ HANDLE_FDIV(); }break;
```

```
            case FSLT:{ HANDLE_FSLT(); }break;

            case DADD:{ HANDLE_DADD(); }break;
            case DSUB:{ HANDLE_DSUB(); }break;
            case DMULT:{ HANDLE_DMULT(); }break;
            case DDIV:{ HANDLE_DDIV(); }break;
            case DSLT:{ HANDLE_DSLT(); }break;

            default:
            {
                xmlBegin();
                fprintf(errPtr,"run(): ");
                fprintf(errPtr,"bad instruction (%d) ",RAM[R[$IP]]);
                fprintf(errPtr,"at address = ");
                fpU8(errPtr,(U8)R[$IP]);
                fprintf(errPtr,"\n");
                xmlEnd();

                ERROR_LVL1("run(): fatal error\n");

            }break;

        }/*end switch*/

        if(debug==TRUE){ printDbgInstr(start_debug_instr); }

        tick++;
        if(tick==65535){ tick = 0; }

    }/*end while*/

    if(debug==TRUE){ readDbgCmd(); }
    DBG_RUN0("HALT instruction executed\n");
    return;

}/*end run*/
```

 NOTE   You might have noticed the variable named `tick`. The `tick` variable is incremented every time an instruction is executed until it rolls over to 0 at 65,535. If you suspect that `tick` does not have a real use, you are partially correct. I defined `tick` with the intention of making the HEC run-time into a multitasking environment. I planned on implementing a round-robin scheduling scheme that allocated each running process a quantum of ticks. Due to blocking problems, which I discuss at length in Chapter 2, I had to abandon this train of thought. The `tick` variable is an artifact of this failed attempt that I have preserved, perhaps for future use of some kind.

Execution of the individual instructions is performed by the `HANDLE_XXX()` macros that appear in the previous listing (I will refer to these macros as *instruction handlers*). The virtual machine's instruction handlers are grouped together into a collection of 12 source files:

- `load.c`
- `store.c`
- `pushpop.c`
- `move.c`
- `jump.c`
- `bitwise.c`
- `shift.c`
- `intmath.c`
- `fltmath.c`
- `dblmath.c`
- `interupt.c`
- `intwin32.c`

By now you have a fairly complete understanding of how the HEC virtual machine functions. The only thing left to do is to delve into the details of how the virtual machine actually executes its instruction set. Hence, the game plan from here on out will be to examine these 12 files in sequential order.

I've had extensive experience with the Intel x86 instruction set. I've also played around with MIPS assembler. The exposure I had to these instruction sets definitely had an impact with regard to the final form the HEC virtual machine instruction set has taken. I tried to keep the instruction set as small as possible and still provide as much functionality as I could.

ASIDE One thing you will notice is the somewhat obfuscated nature of my instruction handlers. However, I am not trying to frustrate you. I have solid reasons for using terse coding conventions.

There have been times in the past where I have gone to great lengths to write a particularly efficient snippet of optimized code. More often than not, I would come back to the snippet of code several months later, look at it, and think: "Hey, who's the $%*# son of a $#%&* who wrote this piece of ... oh, it was me."

This is the tradeoff you are often forced to make to optimize your code. In terms of implementing the virtual machine instructions, I decided to sacrifice readability for performance. A typical program may cause a specific instruction to be executed a hundred thousand times, so I cut corners whenever I had the chance. This resulted in some rather obfuscated statements. In fact, I was tempted to submit portions of the HEC virtual machine to the International Obfuscated C Code Contest (http://www.ioccc.org/).

The following code is a simple illustration of the savings that can be achieved by keeping the evaluation of an expression entirely in-line.

```
void main()
{
```

```
    int w=2, x, y, z;

    /* observe complicated expression, 18 Intel machine instructions */

    w = ((w+225*w)+w)/((((w+1)*(w+1))+(1+w*w))*w);
    printf("%d\n",w);

    /* simplify, but hurt performance (5 extra machine instructions)*/

    w=2;
    x = (w+225*w)+w; y = (w+1)*(w+1); z = (1+w*w); w = x/((y+z)*w);
    printf("%d\n",w);
}
```

On the Intel hardware platform, using Visual C++, the first version of the expression:

```
    w = ((w+225*w)+w)/((((w+1)*(w+1))+(1+w*w))*w);
```

translates into 18 assembler instructions:

```
    mov   eax, DWORD PTR _w$[ebp]
    imul  eax, 225
    mov   ecx, DWORD PTR _w$[ebp]
    add   ecx, eax
    add   ecx, DWORD PTR _w$[ebp]
    mov   edx, DWORD PTR _w$[ebp]
    add   edx, 1
    mov   eax, DWORD PTR _w$[ebp]
    add   eax, 1
    imul  edx, eax
    mov   eax, DWORD PTR _w$[ebp]
    imul  eax, DWORD PTR _w$[ebp]
    lea   esi, DWORD PTR [edx+eax+1]
    imul  esi, DWORD PTR _w$[ebp]
    mov   eax, ecx
    cdq
    idiv  esi
    mov   DWORD PTR _w$[ebp], eax
```

The simplified form of the expression:

```
    x = (w+225*w)+w; y = (w+1)*(w+1); z = (1+w*w); w = x/((y+z)*w);
```

translates into 23 assembler instructions:

```
    mov   edx, DWORD PTR _w$[ebp]
    imul  edx, 225
    mov   eax, DWORD PTR _w$[ebp]
    add   eax, edx
    add   eax, DWORD PTR _w$[ebp]
    mov   DWORD PTR _x$[ebp], eax
    mov   ecx, DWORD PTR _w$[ebp]
    add   ecx, 1
    mov   edx, DWORD PTR _w$[ebp]
    add   edx, 1
    imul  ecx, edx
    mov   DWORD PTR _y$[ebp], ecx
    mov   eax, DWORD PTR _w$[ebp]
```

```
imul    eax, DWORD PTR _w$[ebp]
add     eax, 1
mov     DWORD PTR _z$[ebp], eax
mov     ecx, DWORD PTR _y$[ebp]
add     ecx, DWORD PTR _z$[ebp]
imul    ecx, DWORD PTR _w$[ebp]
mov     eax, DWORD PTR _x$[ebp]
cdq
idiv    ecx
mov     DWORD PTR _w$[ebp], eax
```

Using the condensed form eliminates a whole set of unnecessary assignment operations. The HEC virtual machine's instruction handlers are the most frequently executed code in the program. (I verified this with a profiling tool.) Thus, it made sense to squeeze every drop of performance out of the code that I could. This means using macros to eliminate function call overhead and compacting expressions.

My only hope is that my decision does not come back to haunt me when I need to perform modifications.

load.c

The HEC virtual machine has a number of instructions that transfer an immediate constant or data from memory into a register. These instructions have their implementations located in the load.c file. Table 3-2 summarizes the instruction handlers implemented in load.c.

Table 3-2

Instruction	Opcode	Meaning	Encoding
LBI $R, byte	0	Store byte constant into $R	BBB
LWI $R, word	1	Store word constant into $R	BBW
LDI $R, dword	2	Store dword constant into $R	BBD
LQI $R, qword	3	Store qword constant into $R	BBQ
LF1I $F, float	4	Store float constant into $F	BBD
LF2I $D, double	5	Store double constant into $D	BBQ
LAD $R, address	6	Store address constant into $R	BBQ
LAI $R1, $R2, qword	7	Store sum of qword and $R2 in $R1	BBBQ
LB $R1, $R2	8	Take byte at address in $R2 and store in $R1	BBB
LW $R1, $R2	9	Take word at address in $R2 and store in $R1	BBB
LD $R1, $R2	10	Take dword at address in $R2 and store in $R1	BBB
LQ $R1, $R2	11	Take qword at address in $R2 and store in $R1	BBB
LF1 $F, $R2	12	Take float at address in $R2 and store in $F	BBB
LF2 $D, $R2	13	Take double at address in $R2 and store in $D	BBB

There are three basic classes of load instructions. The first class places an immediate value into a register (LBI, LWI, LDI, etc.). The second class places a memory address into a register (LAD, LAI). The third class of load instructions places a value at a particular address in memory into a register (LB, LW, LD, etc.).

LBI translates roughly into "load byte immediate," which is to say that the instruction takes a byte-sized constant (more formally, an immediate byte-sized operand) and loads it into a specified register. If you look at Table 3-2, you'll see that this instruction is comprised of three bytes: an opcode, a register operand, and an immediate byte operand. Figure 3-11 illustrates how we can use the definition of the LBI instruction, in Table 3-2, to derive the LBI instruction handler.

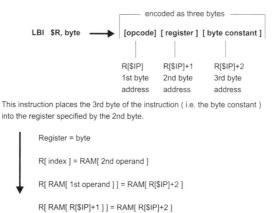

Figure 3-11

When I was trying to figure out how to implement the instruction handler, the thought process I went through is very similar to that in Figure 3-11. I would start from first principles and then work my way to a final expression. Although I will admit that I did have a number of false starts.

The definition of the other load-immediate instructions are similar to that of LBI. Once you catch on to how I derived HANDLE_LBI, the rest should be easy.

```
#define HANDLE_LBI();   DBG_RUN0("Optimized HANDLE_LBI\n"); \
                        R[RAM[R[$IP]+1]]=(S1)RAM[R[$IP]+2];\
                        R[$IP]=R[$IP]+3;

#define HANDLE_LWI();   DBG_RUN0("Optimized HANDLE_LWI\n"); \
                        R[RAM[R[$IP]+1]]=(S2)*((S2*)&RAM[R[$IP]+2]);\
                        R[$IP]=R[$IP]+4;

#define HANDLE_LDI();   DBG_RUN0("Optimized HANDLE_LDI\n"); \
                        R[RAM[R[$IP]+1]]=(S4)*((S4*)&RAM[R[$IP]+2]);\
                        R[$IP]=R[$IP]+6;

#define HANDLE_LQI();   DBG_RUN0("Optimized HANDLE_LQI\n"); \
                        R[RAM[R[$IP]+1]]=(S8)*((S8*)&RAM[R[$IP]+2]);\
                        R[$IP]=R[$IP]+10;

#define HANDLE_LF1I();  DBG_RUN0("Optimized HANDLE_LF1I\n"); \
                        Rf[RAM[R[$IP]+1]]=(F4)*((F4*)&RAM[R[$IP]+2]);\
```

```
                            R[$IP]=R[$IP]+6;

    #define HANDLE_LF2I(); DBG_RUN0("Optimized HANDLE_LF2I\n"); \
                           Rd[RAM[R[$IP]+1]]=(F8)*((F8*)&RAM[R[$IP]+2]);\
                           R[$IP]=R[$IP]+10;
```

Integer values, as viewed by the HEC virtual machine, are all signed. This explains the proliferation of cast operations in the previous source code.

NOTE If values consisting of one, two, four, and eight bytes are interpreted as signed values, they have the following numeric ranges:

- byte   −128 to 127
- word   −32,768 to 32,767
- double word   −2,147,483,648 to 2,147,483,647
- quad word   −9,223,372,036,854,775,808 to
                        9,223,372,036,854,775,807

Like the other modules in the virtual machine, the instruction handler module has its own set of debug macros to help display what's going on:

```
#ifdef DBG_RUN
#define DBG_RUN0(str);          printf("run(): "); printf(str);
#define DBG_RUN1(str,arg1);     printf("run(): "); printf(str,arg1);
#else
#define DBG_RUN0(str);
#define DBG_RUN1(str,arg1);
#endif
```

The LAD instruction is used to "load address directly." This means that we are explicitly providing an address literal, as the second operand, to load into an integer register. Figure 3-12 shows how I derived the handler that implements this instruction.

Figure 3-12

```
                        ┌── encoded as 10 bytes ──┐
LAD  $R, address  ────► [opcode] [ register ] [ 64-bit constant ]

                        R[$IP]    R[$IP]+1   R[$IP]+2
                        1st byte  2nd byte   address of 1st
                        address   address    byte of constant
This instruction takes the address, specified by the 2nd operand, and stores
it in the register specified by the 1st operand.

       Register = address constant

       R[ index ] = (U8)*((U8*) address of 1st byte of 64-bit constant )

       R[ RAM[ 1st operand ] ] = (U8)*((U8*)&RAM[ 3rd instruction byte ])

       R[ RAM[R[$IP]+1] ] = (U8)*((U8*)&RAM[R[$IP]+2])
```

The final product looks like:

```
#define HANDLE_LAD();   DBG_RUNO("Optimized HANDLE_LAD\n"); \
                        R[RAM[R[$IP]+1]]=(U8)*((U8*)&RAM[R[$IP]+2]);\
                        badAddress(R[RAM[R[$IP]+1]],R[$IP]);\
                        R[$IP]=R[$IP]+10;
```

When I said that the HEC virtual machine treats all integers as signed values, it was a lie (sort of). The HEC virtual machine treats address integers as unsigned values. Thus, unlike the LBI instruction, LAD treats addresses like unsigned integers.

Note how I check for a bad address. This is a run-time check that is performed every time the LAD instruction is executed. I decided to take the performance hit for the sake of protecting the virtual machine's address space from a runaway pointer. The badAddress() method is defined in reformat.c:

```
void badAddress(U8 arg, U8 currentbyte)
{
    if(arg>R[$TOP])
    {
        ERRORO_LVL2("badAddress(): invalid address literal\n");

        xmlBegin();
        fprintf(errPtr,"badAddress(): invalid address literal ");
        fpU8(errPtr,arg);
        fprintf(errPtr," at memory location ");
        fpU8(errPtr,currentbyte);
        fprintf(errPtr,"\n");
        xmlEnd();

        FATAL_ERROR();
    }
    return;

}/*end badAddress*/
```

The LAI instruction stands for "load address indirect." When an address is referenced indirectly, it means that we are not explicitly providing an address (as with LAD). Instead, we create an address indirectly by adding an offset value to a base address. In the case of the LAI instruction, the base address is assumed to be in the register specified by the second operand (see Table 3-2). The offset value is a quad word literal which is supplied as the third operand of the instruction. The address is computed by adding the quad word literal to the contents of the integer register containing the base address. The resulting value is stored in the register specified by the first operand.

```
#define HANDLE_LAI();   DBG_RUNO("Optimized HANDLE_LAI\n"); \
                        R[RAM[R[$IP]+1]]=(R[RAM[R[$IP]+2]])+((S8)*((S8*)&RAM[R[$IP]+3]));\
                        badAddress(R[RAM[R[$IP]+1]],R[$IP]);\
                        R[$IP]=R[$IP]+11;
```

There is a minor caveat to this instruction. The offset value is a signed value. The base address the register holds is an unsigned address. This allows us to use negative offsets when the situation warrants it. However, it also effectively limits the range of values that the offset can take.

The presence of the LAD and LAI instructions means that the HEC virtual machine has basically two different addressing modes: direct and indirect. Unlike the Intel platform, which has roughly a dozen different addressing modes, I decided to keep things simple and stay in line with my underlying design goals.

The LB instruction (i.e., load byte) takes a byte in the virtual machine's address space and loads it into a register. Because the second operand specifies a register, which contains an address, the derivation of the instruction is a little more involved (see Figure 3-13).

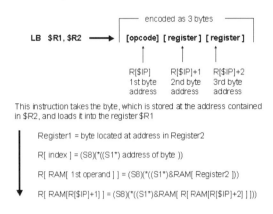

Figure 3-13

Once you've got a grasp of how the LB instruction is implemented, the rest of the related instructions are easy to understand.

```
#define HANDLE_LB();  DBG_RUNO("Optimized HANDLE_LB\n");\
                      badAddress(R[RAM[R[$IP]+2]],R[$IP]); \
                      R[RAM[R[$IP]+1]] = (S8)(*((S1*)&RAM[R[RAM[R[$IP]+2]]])); \
                      R[$IP]=R[$IP]+3;

#define HANDLE_LW();  DBG_RUNO("Optimized HANDLE_LW\n");\
                      badAddress(R[RAM[R[$IP]+2]],R[$IP]); \
                      R[RAM[R[$IP]+1]] =(S8)(*((S2*)&RAM[(U8)R[RAM[R[$IP]+2]]]));\
                      R[$IP]=R[$IP]+3;

#define HANDLE_LD();  DBG_RUNO("Optimized HANDLE_LD\n");\
                      badAddress(R[RAM[R[$IP]+2]],R[$IP]); \
                      R[RAM[R[$IP]+1]] =(S8)(*((S4*)&RAM[(U8)R[RAM[R[$IP]+2]]]));\
                      R[$IP]=R[$IP]+3;

#define HANDLE_LQ();  DBG_RUNO("Optimized HANDLE_LQ\n");\
                      badAddress(R[RAM[R[$IP]+2]],R[$IP]); \
                      R[RAM[R[$IP]+1]] =(S8)(*((S8*)&RAM[(U8)R[RAM[R[$IP]+2]]]));\
                      R[$IP]=R[$IP]+3;

#define HANDLE_LF1(); DBG_RUNO("Optimized HANDLE_LF1\n");\
                      badAddress(R[RAM[R[$IP]+2]],R[$IP]); \
                      Rf[RAM[R[$IP]+1]] = *((F4*)&RAM[(U8)R[RAM[R[$IP]+2]]]); \
                      R[$IP]=R[$IP]+3;
#define HANDLE_LF2(); DBG_RUNO("Optimized HANDLE_LF2\n");\
                      badAddress(R[RAM[R[$IP]+2]],R[$IP]); \
```

```
Rd[RAM[R[$IP]+1]] = *((F8*)&RAM[(U8)R[RAM[R[$IP]+2]]]); \
R[$IP]=R[$IP]+3;
```

store.c

The store.c file contains the implementation of the virtual machine's store instructions. These instructions take a value in a register and store it at an address in the virtual machine's memory space. Table 3-3 summarizes the instruction handlers implemented in store.c.

Table 3-3

Instruction	Opcode	Meaning	Encoding
SB $R1, $R2	14	Place byte in $R1 at address in $R2	BBB
SW $R1, $R2	15	Place word in $R1 at address in $R2	BBB
SD $R1, $R2	16	Place dword in $R1 at address in $R2	BBB
SQ $R1, $R2	17	Place qword in $R1 at address in $R2	BBB
SF1 $F, $R2	18	Place float in $F at address in $R2	BBB
SF2 $D, $R2	19	Place double in $D at address in $R2	BBB

Because these instructions store a value at a location in the virtual machine's address space, they are a little more involved than the load instructions. Figure 3-14 illustrates how I derived the implementation of the SB ("store byte") instruction.

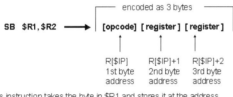

Figure 3-14

```
#define HANDLE_SB();    DBG_RUNO("Optimized HANDLE_SB\n"); \
                        badAddress(R[RAM[R[$IP]+2]],R[$IP]);\
                        RAM[R[RAM[R[$IP]+2]]] = (S1)R[RAM[R[$IP]+1]];\
                        R[$IP] = R[$IP]+3;\

#define HANDLE_SW();    DBG_RUNO("Optimized HANDLE_SW\n");\
                        badAddress(R[RAM[R[$IP]+2]],R[$IP]);\
                        *((S2*)&RAM[R[RAM[R[$IP]+2]]]) = (S2)R[RAM[R[$IP]+1]];\
                        R[$IP] = R[$IP]+3;

#define HANDLE_SD();    DBG_RUNO("Optimized HANDLE_SD\n");\
                        badAddress(R[RAM[R[$IP]+2]],R[$IP]);\
```

```
                              *((S4*)&RAM[R[RAM[R[$IP]+2]]]) = (S4)R[RAM[R[$IP]+1]];\
                              R[$IP] = R[$IP]+3;

#define HANDLE_SQ();    DBG_RUNO("Optimized HANDLE_SQ\n");\
                        badAddress(R[RAM[R[$IP]+2]],R[$IP]);\
                        *((S8*)&RAM[R[RAM[R[$IP]+2]]]) = (S8)R[RAM[R[$IP]+1]];\
                        R[$IP] = R[$IP]+3;

#define HANDLE_SF1();   DBG_RUNO("Optimized HANDLE_SF1\n");\
                        badAddress(R[RAM[R[$IP]+2]],R[$IP]);\
                        *((F4*)&RAM[R[RAM[R[$IP]+2]]]) = Rf[RAM[R[$IP]+1]];\
                        R[$IP] = R[$IP]+3;

#define HANDLE_SF2();   DBG_RUNO("Optimized HANDLE_SF2\n");\
                        badAddress(R[RAM[R[$IP]+2]],R[$IP]);\
                        *((F8*)&RAM[R[RAM[R[$IP]+2]]]) = Rd[RAM[R[$IP]+1]];\
                        R[$IP] = R[$IP]+3;
```

pushpop.c

The pushpop.c source file contains the implementation of the various push and pop instructions, which are used to manipulate the stack. Table 3-4 summarizes the instruction handlers implemented in pushpop.c.

Table 3-4

Instruction	Opcode	Meaning	Encoding
PUSHB $R	20	Push byte in $R on stack	BB
PUSHW $R	21	Push word in $R on stack	BB
PUSHD $R	22	Push dword in $R on stack	BB
PUSHQ $R	23	Push qword in $R on stack	BB
PUSHF1 $F	24	Push float in $F on stack	BB
PUSHF2 $D	25	Push double in $D on stack	BB
POPB $R	26	Pop byte off stack and place in $R	BB
POPW $R	27	Pop word off stack and place in $R	BB
POPD $R	28	Pop dword off stack and place in $R	BB
POPQ $R	29	Pop qword off stack and place in $R	BB
POPF1 $F	30	Pop float off stack and place in $F	BB
POPF2 $D	31	Pop double off stack and place in $D	BB

The push instructions decrement the stack pointer ($SP) and then place a value on the stack. The lowest-order byte of the value placed on the stack will be located at the stack pointer's ($SP) new value. Figure 3-15 illustrates how I derived the implementation of the PUSHB ("push byte") instruction.

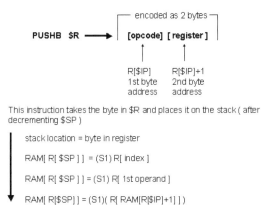

Figure 3-15

Once you have a feeling for how I implemented PUSHB, understanding how the other PUSH instructions are implemented is straightforward.

```
#define HANDLE_PUSHB();   DBG_RUNO("Optimized HANDLE_PUSHB\n");\
                          R[$SP]= R[$SP]-1; badStack(R[$SP],R[$IP]); \
                          RAM[R[$SP]] = (S1)(R[RAM[R[$IP]+1]]);\
                          R[$IP]=R[$IP]+2;

#define HANDLE_PUSHW();   DBG_RUNO("Optimized HANDLE_PUSHW\n");\
                          R[$SP]= R[$SP]-2; badStack(R[$SP],R[$IP]); \
                          *((S2*)&RAM[R[$SP]]) = (S2)(R[RAM[R[$IP]+1]]);\
                          R[$IP]=R[$IP]+2;

#define HANDLE_PUSHD();   DBG_RUNO("Optimized HANDLE_PUSHD\n");\
                          R[$SP]= R[$SP]-4; badStack(R[$SP],R[$IP]); \
                          *((S4*)&RAM[R[$SP]]) = (S4)(R[RAM[R[$IP]+1]]);\
                          R[$IP]=R[$IP]+2;

#define HANDLE_PUSHQ();   DBG_RUNO("Optimized HANDLE_PUSHQ\n");\
                          R[$SP]= R[$SP]-8; badStack(R[$SP],R[$IP]); \
                          *((S8*)&RAM[R[$SP]]) = (S8)(R[RAM[R[$IP]+1]]);\
                          R[$IP]=R[$IP]+2;

#define HANDLE_PUSHF1();  DBG_RUNO("Optimized HANDLE_PUSHF1\n");\
                          R[$SP]= R[$SP]-4; badStack(R[$SP],R[$IP]); \
                          *((F4*)&RAM[R[$SP]]) = Rf[RAM[R[$IP]+1]];\
                          R[$IP]=R[$IP]+2;

#define HANDLE_PUSHF2();  DBG_RUNO("Optimized HANDLE_PUSHF2\n");\
                          R[$SP]= R[$SP]-8; badStack(R[$SP],R[$IP]); \
                          *((F8*)&RAM[R[$SP]]) = Rd[RAM[R[$IP]+1]];\
                          R[$IP]=R[$IP]+2;
```

The PUSH instructions do run-time checking to make sure that the stack does not overflow or underflow. This checking is performed by the badStack() routine, which is defined in the reformat.c source file. As with the LAD and LAI instructions, I decided to take the performance hit that would result from stack checking to offer a degree of memory protection.

```
void badStack(U8 arg, U8 currentbyte)
{
    if(arg<=R[$HE])
    {
        ERROR0_LVL2("badStack(): stack overflow into heap\n");

        xmlBegin();
        fprintf(errPtr,"badStack(): ");
        fpU8(errPtr,arg);
        fprintf(errPtr," stack overflow into heap ");
        fprintf(errPtr,"at address ");
        fpU8(errPtr,currentbyte);
        fprintf(errPtr,"\n");
        xmlEnd();

        FATAL_ERROR();
    }
    else if(arg>R[$TOP])
    {
        ERROR0_LVL2("badStack(): stack underflow beyond $TOP\n");

        xmlBegin();
        fprintf(errPtr,"badStack(): ");
        fpU8(errPtr,arg);
        fprintf(errPtr," stack underflow beyond $TOP ");
        fprintf(errPtr,"at address ");
        fpU8(errPtr,currentbyte);
        fprintf(errPtr,"\n");
        xmlEnd();

        FATAL_ERROR();
    }
    return;

}/*end badStack*/
```

The POPB instruction takes the byte stored at the memory location pointed to by $SP and stores it in a register. POPB then increments the stack pointer to reflect this fact. Figure 3-16 illustrates how I derived the implementation of the POPB ("pop byte") instruction.

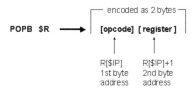

encoded as 2 bytes

POPB $R ⟶ [opcode] [register]

R[$IP]   R[$IP]+1
1st byte 2nd byte
address   address

This instruction takes the byte on the top of the stack and places it in $R

register = byte on top of stack

R[index] = (S8)*((S1) address of the top of the stack)

R[operand] = (S8)*((S1*)&RAM[R[$SP]])

R[RAM[R[$IP]+1]] = (S8)*((S1*)&RAM[R[$SP]])

Figure 3-16

Once you have a feeling for how I implemented POPB, understanding how the other pop instructions are implemented is easy.

```
#define  HANDLE_POPB();   DBG_RUNO("Optimized HANDLE_POPB\n");\
                          R[RAM[R[$IP]+1]]=(S8)*((S1*)&RAM[R[$SP]]);\
                          R[$SP]=R[$SP]+1;\
                          badStack(R[$SP],R[$IP]);R[$IP] = R[$IP]+2;

#define  HANDLE_POPW();   DBG_RUNO("Optimized HANDLE_POPW\n");\
                          R[RAM[R[$IP]+1]]=(S8)*((S2*)&RAM[R[$SP]]);\
                          R[$SP]=R[$SP]+2;\
                          badStack(R[$SP],R[$IP]);R[$IP] = R[$IP]+2;

#define  HANDLE_POPD();   DBG_RUNO("Optimized HANDLE_POPD\n");\
                          R[RAM[R[$IP]+1]]=(S8)*((S4*)&RAM[R[$SP]]);\
                          R[$SP]=R[$SP]+4;\
                          badStack(R[$SP],R[$IP]);R[$IP] = R[$IP]+2;

#define  HANDLE_POPQ();   DBG_RUNO("Optimized HANDLE_POPQ\n");\
                          R[RAM[R[$IP]+1]]=(S8)*((S8*)&RAM[R[$SP]]);\
                          R[$SP]=R[$SP]+8;\
                          badStack(R[$SP],R[$IP]);R[$IP] = R[$IP]+2;

#define  HANDLE_POPF1();  DBG_RUNO("Optimized HANDLE_POPF1\n");\
                          Rf[RAM[R[$IP]+1]]=(F4)*((F4*)&RAM[R[$SP]]);\
                          R[$SP]=R[$SP]+4;\
                          badStack(R[$SP],R[$IP]);R[$IP] = R[$IP]+2;

#define  HANDLE_POPF2();  DBG_RUNO("Optimized HANDLE_POPF2\n");\
                          Rd[RAM[R[$IP]+1]]=(F8)*((F8*)&RAM[R[$SP]]);\
                          R[$SP]=R[$SP]+8;\
                          badStack(R[$SP],R[$IP]);R[$IP] = R[$IP]+2;
```

move.c

The move.c file contains the implementation of three move instructions that copy data from one register into another. Table 3-5 summarizes the instruction handlers implemented in move.c.

Table 3-5

Instruction	Opcode	Meaning	Encoding
MOV $R1, $R2	32	Copy contents of $R2 into $R1	BBB
MOVF $F1, $F2	33	Copy contents of $F2 into $F1	BBB
MOVD $D1, $D2	34	Copy contents of $D2 into $D1	BBB

The implementation of these three instructions is relatively clear.

```
#define HANDLE_MOV();    DBG_RUN0("Optimized HANDLE_MOV\n"); \
                         R[RAM[R[$IP]+1]]=R[RAM[R[$IP]+2]]; \
                         R[$IP] = R[$IP]+3;

#define HANDLE_MOVF();   DBG_RUN0("Optimized HANDLE_MOVF\n"); \
                         Rf[RAM[R[$IP]+1]]=Rf[RAM[R[$IP]+2]]; \
                         R[$IP] = R[$IP]+3;

#define HANDLE_MOVD();   DBG_RUN0("Optimized HANDLE_MOVD\n"); \
                         Rd[RAM[R[$IP]+1]]=Rd[RAM[R[$IP]+2]]; \
                         R[$IP] = R[$IP]+3;
```

jump.c

The jump.c file contains the implementation of instructions that can be used to control the flow of program execution. Table 3-6 summarizes the instruction handlers implemented in jump.c.

Table 3-6

Instruction	Opcode	Meaning	Encoding
JMP $R	35	Jump to the address in $R	BB
JE $R1, $R2, $R3	36	Jump to address in $R3 if $R1==$R2	BBBB
JNE $R1, $R2, $R3	37	Jump to address in $R3 if $R1!=$R2	BBBB
SLT $R1, $R2, $R3	38	Set $R1=1 if $R2 < $R3, else $R1=0	BBBB
INT byte	39	Execute interrupt specified by byte	BB
DI	40	Disable interrupt processing	B
EI	41	Enable interrupt processing	B
HALT	42	Shut down the virtual machine	B
NOP	43	Does nothing (no operation)	B

The JMP instruction is used to perform an unconditional jump to a new address. The JMP instruction is pretty simple. It takes the $IP register and changes it to the value stored in its register operand:

```
#define HANDLE_JMP();    DBG_RUN0("Optimized HANDLE_JMP\n"); \
                         badAddress(R[RAM[R[$IP]+1]],R[$IP]);\
```

```
                            R[$IP] = R[RAM[R[$IP]+1]];
```

The JE and JNE instructions are used to perform conditional jumps. Both instructions compare the contents of their first and second register operands. The JE instruction ("jump if equal") will jump to the address stored in the third register operand if the first and second register operands are equal. The JNE instruction ("jump if not equal") will jump to the address stored in the third register operand if the first and second register operands are not equal.

```
#define HANDLE_JE();    DBG_RUN0("Optimized HANDLE_JE\n"); \
                        if(R[RAM[R[$IP]+1]]==R[RAM[R[$IP]+2]])\
                        {\
                            badAddress(R[RAM[R[$IP]+3]],R[$IP]);\
                            R[$IP] = R[RAM[R[$IP]+3]];\
                        }\
                        else{ R[$IP]=R[$IP]+4; }


#define HANDLE_JNE();   DBG_RUN0("Optimized HANDLE_JNE\n"); \
                        if(R[RAM[R[$IP]+1]]!=R[RAM[R[$IP]+2]])\
                        {\
                            badAddress(R[RAM[R[$IP]+3]],R[$IP]);\
                            R[$IP] = R[RAM[R[$IP]+3]];\
                        }\
                        else{ R[$IP]=R[$IP]+4; }
```

The SLT instruction stands for "set if less than." It compares the second and third register operands. If the value stored in the second register operand is less than that in the third, then the first register operand will be set to 1. Otherwise, the first register operand is set to 0. This is a useful instruction for compiler writers who wish to implement a selection statement.

```
#define HANDLE_SLT();   DBG_RUN0("Optimized HANDLE_SLT\n"); \
                        if(R[RAM[R[$IP]+2]]<R[RAM[R[$IP]+3]])\
                        {\
                            R[RAM[R[$IP]+1]] = (U8)0x1;\
                        }else{ R[RAM[R[$IP]+1]] = (U8)0; }\
                        R[$IP]=R[$IP]+4;
```

The INT instruction executes an interrupt. The byte operand in this instruction is known as an *interrupt vector*. Interrupt routines are indexed by a vector number. To perform a certain interrupt routine, its vector number must be provided as the operand in the INT instruction. In the case of the HEC virtual machine, the interrupt vector is fed as an argument to the handleInt() function. The handleInt() function is defined in interupt.c.

```
#define HANDLE_INT();   DBG_RUN0("Optimized HANDLE_INT\n"); \
                        handleInt((U1)RAM[R[$IP]+1]); \
                        R[$IP]=R[$IP]+2;
```

The DI and EI instructions disable and enable interrupt processing. The interruptOn flag is defined in interupt.c. It is a byte-sized flag that can be toggled to prevent the virtual machine from servicing interrupts. Initially, I declared the interruptOn flag in order to implement synchronization, back when I was planning on making HEC a multitasking virtual machine. Given that HEC runs as a single-threaded process, the DI and EI instructions are somewhat anachronistic. Nevertheless, I kept them as instructions because I thought they might be useful somehow.

```
#define HANDLE_DI();    DBG_RUNO("Optimized HANDLE_DI\n"); \
                        interruptOn=FALSE; \
                        R[$IP]=R[$IP]+1;

#define HANDLE_EI();    DBG_RUNO("Optimized HANDLE_EI\n"); \
                        interruptOn=TRUE; \
                        R[$IP]=R[$IP]+1;
```

The HALT instruction does not have an implementation. This is because it is really just a flag which tells the virtual machine that it can shut down.

The NOP instruction does nothing more than increment the instruction pointer:

```
#define HANDLE_NOP();   DBG_RUNO("Optimized HANDLE_NOP\n"); \
                        R[$IP]=R[$IP]+1;
```

bitwise.c

The bitwise.c file contains the implementation of instructions that can be used to perform bitwise operations. Table 3-7 summarizes the instruction handlers implemented in bitwise.c.

Table 3-7

Instruction	Opcode	Meaning	Encoding
AND $R1, $R2, $R3	44	Set $R1 to the bitwise AND of $R2 and $R3	BBBB
OR $R1, $R2, $R3	45	Set $R1 to the bitwise OR of $R2 and $R3	BBBB
XOR $R1, $R2, $R3	46	Set $R1 to the bitwise XOR of $R2 and $R3	BBBB
NOT $R1, $R2	47	Set $R1 to the bitwise NOT of $R2	BBB
BT $R1, $R2, $R3	48	Set $R1 to 1 if the $R3rd bit in $R2 is on, otherwise set $R1 to 0	BBBB
BS $R1, $R2	49	Set the $R2nd bit in $R1	BBB

The implementation of the AND, OR, XOR, and NOT instructions is simple.

```
#define HANDLE_AND();   DBG_RUNO("Optimized HANDLE_AND\n"); \
                        R[RAM[R[$IP]+1]] = R[RAM[R[$IP]+2]] & R[RAM[R[$IP]+3]];\
                        R[$IP]=R[$IP]+4;

#define HANDLE_OR();    DBG_RUNO("Optimized HANDLE_OR\n"); \
                        R[RAM[R[$IP]+1]] = R[RAM[R[$IP]+2]] | R[RAM[R[$IP]+3]];\
                        R[$IP]=R[$IP]+4;

#define HANDLE_XOR();   DBG_RUNO("Optimized HANDLE_XOR\n"); \
                        R[RAM[R[$IP]+1]] = R[RAM[R[$IP]+2]] ^ R[RAM[R[$IP]+3]];\
                        R[$IP]=R[$IP]+4;

#define HANDLE_NOT();   DBG_RUNO("Optimized HANDLE_NOT\n"); \
                        R[RAM[R[$IP]+1]] = ~R[RAM[R[$IP]+2]];\
                        R[$IP]=R[$IP]+3;
```

The BT and BS instructions ("bit test" and "bit set") are a little more complicated. In fact, because of this, I decided to implement these instructions using functions instead of just macros. This means that both the BT and BS functions incur a small amount of additional overhead when they are called.

The BT instruction tests to see if a bit is on in a particular quad word. Specifically, it takes the quad word stored in the second register operand and looks at the bit, in the quad word, specified by the third register operand. If this bit is on, the first register operand is set to 1. Otherwise, the first register operand is cleared to 0.

```
void handleBT()
{
    int index;
    U8 mask;
    U8 bit; /* 0-63 */

    DBG_RUN0("handleBT\n");
    bit = R[RAM[R[$IP]+3]];
    if(bit > 63)
    {
        ERROR0_LVL2("handleBT(): bit index is out of range\n");
        bit = 63;
    }
    mask = (U8)0x1;
    for(index=0;index<bit;index++)
    {
        mask = mask*2;
    }
    mask = R[RAM[R[$IP]+2]] & mask;
    if(mask > 0){ R[RAM[R[$IP]+1]] = 0x1; }
    else{ R[RAM[R[$IP]+1]] = 0x0; }
    R[$IP]=R[$IP]+4;
    return;

}/*end handleBT*/
```

 NOTE A bit is said to be "set" when its value is 1 and "cleared" when its value is 0.

The BS instruction is used to set a bit in a particular quad word. Specifically, it takes the quad word in the first register operand and sets the bit, in the quad word, specified by the value in the second register operand.

```
void handleBS()
{
    int index;
    U8 mask;
    U8 bit; /* 0-63 */

    DBG_RUN0("handleBS\n");
    bit = R[RAM[R[$IP]+2]];
    if(bit > 63)
    {
        ERROR0_LVL2("handleBS(): bit index is out of range\n");
```

```
            bit = 63;
        }
        mask = (U8)0x1;
        for(index=0;index<bit;index++)
        {
            mask = mask*2;
        }
        R[RAM[R[$IP]+1]] = R[RAM[R[$IP]+1]] | mask;
        R[$IP]=R[$IP]+3;
        return;

    }/*end handleBS*/
```

On a final note, I think the `handleBT()` and `handleBS()` functions could probably be optimized and then rewritten as macros. This is on my list of things to do. During development, I was more interested in making sure that these instructions actually worked.

shift.c

The `shift.c` file contains the implementation of instructions that can be used to perform bitwise shifting operations. Table 3-8 summarizes the instruction handlers implemented in `shift.c`.

Table 3-8

Instruction	Opcode	Meaning	Encoding
SRA $R1, $R2, $R3	50	$R1 = $R2 shifted $R3 bits right, sign bit enters left	BBBB
SRL $R1, $R2, $R3	51	$R1 = $R2 shifted $R3 bits right, zero enters left	BBBB
SL $R1, $R2, $R3	52	$R1 = $R2 shifted $R3 bits left, zero enters right	BBBB

The SRA instruction ("shift right arithmetic") takes the second register operand and shifts its contents to the right. The number of bits shifted is determined by the third register operand. The shifting is arithmetic, such that the sign bit of the value being shifted enters in on the left as bits are shifted right. The resulting value is placed in the first register operand.

 NOTE What's a sign bit? For those of you who do not know about the "two's complement" convention for representing signed binary integers, here is what you need to know: According to the two's complement convention, the highest-order bit of a binary number is used to denote the sign of the number's value. This highest-order bit is known as the *sign bit*. If the sign bit is 1, the binary value represents a negative value. If the sign bit is 0, the binary value represents a nonnegative value. I mention a book in the reference section for this chapter that offers a more detailed explanation of the two's complement binary notation.

The SRL instruction ("shift right logical") takes the second register operand and shifts its contents to the right. The number of bits shifted is determined by the third register operand. The shifting is logical, so the 0 bit enters in on the left as bits are shifted right. The resulting value is placed in the first register operand.

The SL instruction ("shift left") takes the second register operand and shifts its contents to the left. The number of bits shifted is determined by the third register operand. The 0 bit enters on the right as bits are shifted left. The resulting value is placed in the first register operand.

These instructions are illustrated in Figure 3-17.

Figure 3-17

Following are the instruction implementations:

```
#define HANDLE_SRA(); DBG_RUNO("Optimized HANDLE_SRA\n"); \
                      R[RAM[R[$IP]+1]] = ((S8)R[RAM[R[$IP]+2]]) >>
                          ((S8)R[RAM[R[$IP]+3]]);\
                      R[$IP]=R[$IP]+4;

#define HANDLE_SRL(); DBG_RUNO("Optimized HANDLE_SRL\n"); \
                      R[RAM[R[$IP]+1]] = R[RAM[R[$IP]+2]] >> R[RAM[R[$IP]+3]];\
                      R[$IP]=R[$IP]+4;

#define HANDLE_SL();  DBG_RUNO("Optimized HANDLE_SL\n"); \
                      R[RAM[R[$IP]+1]] = R[RAM[R[$IP]+2]] << R[RAM[R[$IP]+3]];\
                      R[$IP]=R[$IP]+4;
```

intmath.c

The intmath.c source file contains the implementation of instructions that can be used to perform integer arithmetic. Table 3-9 summarizes the instruction handlers implemented in intmath.c.

Table 3-9

Instruction	Opcode	Meaning	Encoding
ADD $R1, $R2, $R3	53	$R1 = $R2 + $R3	BBBB
SUB $R1, $R2, $R3	54	$R1 = $R2 – $R3	BBBB
MULT $R1, $R2, $R3	55	$R1 = $R2 * $R3	BBBB
DIV $R1, $R2, $R3, $R4	56	$R1 = $R3 / $R4 and $R2 = $R3 % $R4	BBBBB

The implementation of these instructions does not require a lot of explanation. However, I should probably mention a couple of things. First, no errors are thrown when values overflow. The only operation that tries to detect an error is division, which tests for cases where an attempt is being made to divide by zero. If an instruction attempts to divide by zero, the virtual machine places 0xFFFFFFFFFFFFFFFF in the first register operand of the division instruction.

Also, remember that all integer values (with the exception of memory addresses) are treated as signed integer values by the HEC virtual machine. This fact is reflected by the proliferation of cast operations in the following source code.

```
#define HANDLE_ADD(); DBG_RUNO("Optimized HANDLE_ADD\n"); \
                      R[RAM[R[$IP]+1]] = ((S8)R[RAM[R[$IP]+2]]) +
                          ((S8)R[RAM[R[$IP]+3]]);\
                      R[$IP]=R[$IP]+4;

#define HANDLE_SUB();  DBG_RUNO("Optimized HANDLE_SUB\n"); \
                      R[RAM[R[$IP]+1]] = ((S8)R[RAM[R[$IP]+2]]) -
                          ((S8)R[RAM[R[$IP]+3]]);\
                      R[$IP]=R[$IP]+4;

#define HANDLE_MULT(); DBG_RUNO("Optimized HANDLE_MULT\n"); \
                      R[RAM[R[$IP]+1]] = ((S8)R[RAM[R[$IP]+2]]) *
                          ((S8)R[RAM[R[$IP]+3]]);\
                      R[$IP]=R[$IP]+4;

#define HANDLE_DIV();  DBG_RUNO("Optimized HANDLE_DIV\n"); \
                      if(R[RAM[R[$IP]+4]]==0){ \
                      ERRORO_LVL2("Divide by zero!\n");\
                      R[RAM[R[$IP]+1]]=R[RAM[R[$IP]+2]]=0xFFFFFFFFFFFFFFFF; }\
                      else{ R[RAM[R[$IP]+1]] = ((S8)R[RAM[R[$IP]+3]]) /
                          ((S8)R[RAM[R[$IP]+4]]);\
                      R[RAM[R[$IP]+2]] = ((S8)R[RAM[R[$IP]+3]]) %
                          ((S8)R[RAM[R[$IP]+4]]);}\
                      R[$IP]=R[$IP]+5;
```

fltmath.c

The `fltmath.c` source file contains the implementation of instructions that can be used to perform arithmetic on single-precision floating-point values. The `fltmath.c` source file also contains definitions for instructions that are used for casting values to different data types. Table 3-10 summarizes the instruction handlers implemented in `fltmath.c`.

Table 3-10

Instruction	Opcode	Meaning	Encoding
CAST_IF $R, $F	57	Cast the float in $F to an integer in $R	BBB
CAST_ID $R, $D	58	Cast the double in $D to an integer in $R	BBB
CAST_FI $F, $R	59	Cast the integer in $R to a float in $F	BBB
CAST_FD $F, $D	60	Cast the double in $D to a float in $F	BBB
CAST_DI $D, $R	61	Cast the integer in $R to a double in $D	BBB
CAST_DF $D, $F	62	Cast the float in $F to a double in $D	BBB
FADD $F1, $F2, $F3	63	$F1 = $F2 + $F3	BBBB
FSUB $F1, $F2, $F3	64	$F1 = $F2 − $F3	BBBB
FMULT $F1, $F2, $F3	65	$F1 = $F2 * $F3	BBBB
FDIV $F1, $F2, $F3	66	$F1 = $F2 / $F3	BBBB
FSLT $F1, $F2, $F3	67	$F1 = 1 if $F2 < $F3, else $F1 = 0	BBBB

The cast instructions basically use C's casting facilities to take the contents of one type of register and translate those contents into a form that can be stored in a register of a different type.

```
#define HANDLE_CAST_IF();    DBG_RUNO("Optimized CAST_IF\n"); \
                             R[RAM[R[$IP]+1]] = (S8)Rf[RAM[R[$IP]+2]]; \
                             R[$IP] - R[$IP]+3;

#define HANDLE_CAST_ID();    DBG_RUNO("Optimized CAST_ID\n"); \
                             R[RAM[R[$IP]+1]] = (S8)Rd[RAM[R[$IP]+2]]; \
                             R[$IP] = R[$IP]+3;

#define HANDLE_CAST_FI();    DBG_RUNO("Optimized CAST_FI\n"); \
                             Rf[RAM[R[$IP]+1]] = (F4)((S8)R[RAM[R[$IP]+2]]); \
                             R[$IP] = R[$IP]+3;

#define HANDLE_CAST_FD();    DBG_RUNO("Optimized CAST_FD\n"); \
                             Rf[RAM[R[$IP]+1]] = (F4)Rd[RAM[R[$IP]+2]]; \
                             R[$IP] = R[$IP]+3;

#define HANDLE_CAST_DI();    DBG_RUNO("Optimized CAST_DI\n"); \
                             Rd[RAM[R[$IP]+1]] = (F8)((S8)R[RAM[R[$IP]+2]]); \
                             R[$IP] = R[$IP]+3;

#define HANDLE_CAST_DF();    DBG_RUNO("Optimized CAST_DF\n"); \
                             Rd[RAM[R[$IP]+1]] = (F8)Rf[RAM[R[$IP]+2]]; \
                             R[$IP] = R[$IP]+3;
```

The implementation of the single-precision, floating-point arithmetic instructions is very similar to that of their integer counterparts.

```
#define HANDLE_FADD();    DBG_RUNO("Optimized HANDLE_FADD\n"); \
                          Rf[RAM[R[$IP]+1]] = Rf[RAM[R[$IP]+2]]+Rf[RAM[R[$IP]+3]];\
                          R[$IP]=R[$IP]+4;

#define HANDLE_FSUB();    DBG_RUNO("Optimized HANDLE_FSUB\n"); \
                          Rf[RAM[R[$IP]+1]] = Rf[RAM[R[$IP]+2]]-Rf[RAM[R[$IP]+3]];\
                          R[$IP]=R[$IP]+4;

#define HANDLE_FMULT();   DBG_RUNO("Optimized HANDLE_FMULT\n"); \
                          Rf[RAM[R[$IP]+1]] = Rf[RAM[R[$IP]+2]]*Rf[RAM[R[$IP]+3]];\
                          R[$IP]=R[$IP]+4;

#define HANDLE_FDIV();    DBG_RUNO("Optimized HANDLE_FDIV\n"); \
                          Rf[RAM[R[$IP]+1]] = Rf[RAM[R[$IP]+2]]/Rf[RAM[R[$IP]+3]];\
                          R[$IP]=R[$IP]+4;

#define HANDLE_FSLT();    DBG_RUNO("Optimized HANDLE_FSLT\n");\
                          if(Rf[RAM[R[$IP]+2]] < Rf[RAM[R[$IP]+3]]){ Rf[RAM[R[$IP]+1]]
                                = 1.0; }\
                          else{ Rf[RAM[R[$IP]+1]] = 0.0; }\
                          R[$IP]=R[$IP]+4;
```

dblmath.c

The dblmath.c source file contains the implementation of instructions that can be used to perform arithmetic on double-precision, floating-point values. Table 3-11 summarizes the instruction handlers implemented in dblmath.c.

Table 3-11

Instruction	Opcode	Meaning	Encoding
DADD $D1, $D2, $D3	68	$D1 = $D2 + $D3	BBBB
DSUB $D1, $D2, $D3	69	$D1 = $D2 – $D3	BBBB
DMULT $D1, $D2, $D3	70	$D1 = $D2 * $D3	BBBB
DDIV $D1, $D2, $D3	71	$D1 = $D2 / $D3	BBBB
DSLT $D1, $D2, $D3	72	$D1 = 1 if $D2 < $D3, else $D1 = 0	BBBB

Like the code in fltmath.c, the implementation of these instructions is very similar to that of their integer counterparts.

```
#define HANDLE_DADD()  DBG_RUNO("Optimized HANDLE_DADD\n"); \
                       Rd[RAM[R[$IP]+1]] = Rd[RAM[R[$IP]+2]]+Rd[RAM[R[$IP]+3]];\
                       R[$IP]=R[$IP]+4;

#define HANDLE_DSUB()  DBG_RUNO("Optimized HANDLE_DSUB\n"); \
                       Rd[RAM[R[$IP]+1]] = Rd[RAM[R[$IP]+2]]–Rd[RAM[R[$IP]+3]];\
                       R[$IP]=R[$IP]+4;

#define HANDLE_DMULT() DBG_RUNO("Optimized HANDLE_DMULT\n"); \
                       Rd[RAM[R[$IP]+1]] = Rd[RAM[R[$IP]+2]]*Rd[RAM[R[$IP]+3]];\
                       R[$IP]=R[$IP]+4;

#define HANDLE_DDIV()  DBG_RUNO("Optimized HANDLE_DDIV\n"); \
                       Rd[RAM[R[$IP]+1]] = Rd[RAM[R[$IP]+2]]/Rd[RAM[R[$IP]+3]];\
                       R[$IP]=R[$IP]+4;

#define HANDLE_DSLT()  DBG_RUNO("Optimized HANDLE_DSLT\n");\
                       if(Rd[RAM[R[$IP]+2]] < Rd[RAM[R[$IP]+3]]){ Rd[RAM[R[$IP]+1]] =
                           1.0; }\
                       else{ Rd[RAM[R[$IP]+1]] = 0.0; }\
                       R[$IP]=R[$IP]+4;
```

interupt.c

Recall that the HANDLE_INT() macro defined in jump.c processes INT instructions and results in the invocation of the handleInt() function. The whole purpose of the interupt.c source file is to implement this function. The handleInt() routine accepts an integer argument (the interrupt vector), which is supposed to be an index to one of the virtual machine's many interrupt service routines. A large switch statement in handleInt() is used to redirect the virtual machine's execution path to the appropriate service routine.

```
U1 interruptOn;

void handleInt(U1 byte)
{
    DBG_RUN1("handleInt(): received vector (%u)\n",byte);

    if(interruptOn==FALSE)
    {
        DBG_RUN0("handleInt(); interrupts are disabled\n");

        return;
    }

    switch(byte)
    {
        case 0:
        {
            DBG_RUN0("handleInt(): handling vector 0\n");
            handlefileIO();
        }break;
        case 1:
        {
            DBG_RUN0("handleInt(): handling vector 1\n");
            handleFileManagement();
        }break;
        case 2:
        {
            DBG_RUN0("handleInt(): handling vector 2\n");
            handleProcessManagement();

        }break;
        case 3:
        {
            DBG_RUN0("handleInt(): handling vector 3\n");
            debug = TRUE;
        }break;
        case 4:
        {
            DBG_RUN0("handleInt(): handling vector 4\n");
            handleTimeDateCall();

        }break;
        case 5:
        {
            DBG_RUN0("handleInt(): handling vector 5\n");
            handleCommandLine();

        }break;
        case 6:
        {
            DBG_RUN0("handleInt(): handling vector 6\n");
            handleMemoryStatus();
```

```
        }break;
        case 7:
        {
              DBG_RUN0("handleInt(): handling vector 7\n");
              handleAllocCall();

        }break;
        case 8:
        {
              DBG_RUN0("handleInt(): handling vector 8\n");
              handleMathCall();

        }break;
        case 9:
        {
              DBG_RUN0("handleInt(): handling vector 9\n");
              handleNativeCall();

        }break;
        case 10:
        {
              DBG_RUN0("handleInt(): handling vector 10\n");
              handleIPC();

        }break;
        default:
        {
              DBG_RUN1("handleInt(): vector not handled (%u)\n",byte);
        }
    }

    return;

}/*end handleInt*/
```

After perusing this file, you'll notice a couple of things. First, most of the interrupt vector values (11 to 255) are not handled. This is intentional. I want the virtual machine to have a lot of extra room. This will give me the ability to grow and modify the virtual machine's interrupt services in the future. The vectors that are actually handled require a secondary index value to be specified in $R1. This allows functions like handlefileIO() to service several different requests that all fall under the same general category.

Finally, you should notice that only one of the interrupt handlers is implemented within interupt.c (i.e., INT 3). The only components in interupt.c are the declaration of the interruptOn variable and the definition of the handleInt() function. This is because interrupt service routines can often be very system dependent. In order to localize system-dependent code away from the core source base, I placed all the interrupt definitions in a separate source file (i.e., intwin32.c for Windows, intlinux.c for Linux, intaix.c for AIX, etc.).

intwin32.c

This source file contains the definitions of the HEC virtual machine's interrupt service routines. This file will be discussed at length later in the book.

Review

Portability, simplicity, and performance. I tried to balance these three requirements in my design of the HEC virtual machine. To satisfy the need of keeping the virtual machine portable, I isolated platform-specific code in `win32.c` and `intwin32.c`. To port the virtual machine to another platform, all you would have to do is replace these two files. I also think I have kept the operation of the virtual machine as simple as I could. In fact, I'm not sure how much simpler I could have designed HEC's virtual machine. Obviously there is a certain degree of tension between the need to keep things simple and the desire to make components fast. Outside of the instruction handlers, which I knew would be executed frequently, I used a very basic scheme in an effort to ease future modification and revisiting. Those of you who curse me for my obfuscated instruction implementations probably also know that I did not leave performance completely out of the picture.

Like any carpenter or sculptor, it's always very gratifying to sit down when you're done and appreciate a finished piece of work. You have paid your dues and can now take a look at the virtual machine's "big picture" (see Figure 3-18).

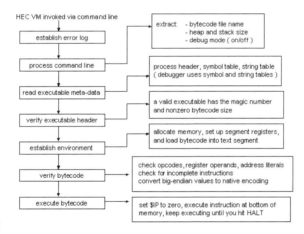

Figure 3-18

References

IEEE Std 754-1985. *IEEE Standard for Binary Floating-Point Arithmetic*. Institute of Electrical and Electronics Engineers, Inc., 1985.

This document was reaffirmed by ANSI on May 21, 1991.

ISO/IEC 9899:1999(E). *Programming Languages - C*. American National Standards Institute, 2000.

When people talk about ANSI C, this is what they are talking about. This document is the final word on what is and what isn't ANSI C.

Parhami, Behrooz. *Computer Arithmetic: Algorithms and Hardware Designs*. Oxford University Press, 1999. ISBN: 0195125835.

This text provides an exhaustive discussion of number representation. I would recommend this book to readers who need to understand the two's complement technique for representing signed integer values.

St. Laurent, Simon and Robert J. Biggar. *Inside XML DTDs: Scientific and Technical*. McGraw-Hill, 1999. ISBN: 007134621X.

The title of this book is slightly misleading, but I really liked this book's coverage of XML DTDs.

W3C. "Extensible Markup Language (XML) 1.0 Recommendation" 2nd ed., http://www.w3c.org/TR/REC-xml.

This is the formal specification for XML.

The HEC Debugger

Overview

This chapter explains the design, implementation, and usage of the HEC debugger. For those of you who do not know what a debugger is, I will begin with a definition.

A *debugger* is a development tool that allows the path of execution of a program to be temporarily paused such that the machine state of the process may be inspected and modified. Recall that I defined the terms "path of execution" and "machine state" in Chapter 2.

I like to think of a debugger as a utility that allows you to execute a program in a controlled environment. The debugger gives you a special kind of laboratory, where you can run and examine a program to see exactly what it is doing when it executes. For example, at a certain point along a program's path of execution, you may decide to freeze everything and take a look at the registers, or peek at a region of memory to verify the value of a given variable.

There are some subtle program bugs that can only be captured and studied in this kind of environment. I have known some engineers who, after weeks of analysis and inserting `printf()` statements, could not find the source of a fatal program error. They were literally in a state of denial. They blamed the fatal errors on flaws in the operating system, or the development tools, or even EMF interference. Only after breaking down and using a debugger did the truth come to light. Sometimes a terminal exception is as simple as incorrectly casting a pointer variable (I am a voice of experience on this).

Debugging tools are what separate computer scientists from physical scientists. One of the discoveries quantum physicists made in the 1920s was that, on the quantum scale (i.e., the subatomic scale), it is impossible for observers to separate themselves from the events they are measuring. In other words, the very act of observation can influence the outcome of an experiment. The observer, in effect, becomes a part of the experiment. This is an inescapable fact of life on the subatomic level. Fortunately, computer scientists are not burdened with this paradox. A debugger allows a developer to take a neutral frame of reference and observe program execution without becoming a part of it.

In some cases, a debugger is a weapon of last resort. Large corporations, which foster the development and maintenance of monolithic business applications, often end up with millions of lines of convoluted spaghetti code. In a scenario like this, the only way to determine what is really going on inside the black box is to fire up a debugger and trace the path of execution. Indeed, in the hands of a seasoned maintenance developer, a debugger can prove to be a formidable instrument.

There are two basic types of debuggers:

■ Machine-level debuggers

■ Source-level debuggers

These two debugger species are distinguished based on the *granularity of instructions* which they manage.

A machine-level debugger works with instructions that consist of low-level, binary encoded machine instructions. This puts you down in the basement, where you can observe the most fundamental operations of the computer. Machine-level debuggers are the last line of defense and are typically reserved for looking at programs that are already in production.

Source-level debuggers work with instructions that consist of high-level, programming language statements. With a source-level debugger, you can trace a program's execution from the frame of reference of a particular programming language. In general, a source-level debugger is easier to work with than a machine-level debugger because it abstracts away a lot of machine-level detail.

The HEC debugger is a machine-level debugger. I did this because I wanted to provide debugging facilities without biasing the HEC virtual machine towards a specific programming language. Not to mention that I did not have a high-level language compiler constructed for HEC at the time I was implementing the virtual machine. The HEC debugger is a low-level utility which allows the basic operation of the virtual machine to be inspected. During the implementation of the virtual machine, the HEC debugger was used primarily as a way for me to check my own work.

This does not mean that a source-level debugger could not be built for HEC. In the near future, I plan to implement one. Think of the machine-level debugger as a layer of scaffolding that permits the construction of more elaborate tools and provides a final layer of defense against application errors in a production deployment.

Debugging Techniques

All debuggers use two basic mechanisms to provide basic debugging functionality:

■ Breakpoints

■ Single-step execution

Breakpoints

A *breakpoint* is a special type of machine instruction that is injected into a program's text segment. This insertion can be done at run time, by placing breakpoints into the memory image of a process, or it can be done at compile time such that breakpoints exist in the executable file. Either way, a breakpoint causes the processor to pause a task's execution and yield program control to the debugger, so that the user may inspect or modify the machine state of the task being debugged.

Different debuggers offer different ways for a user to view the machine state of a task. Some debuggers provide only a simple (but effective) command-line interface. Other debuggers are integrated into slick GUI environments. To be honest, I lean towards the GUI debuggers because they are capable of presenting and maintaining more machine state information. The only thing that bothers me about GUI debuggers is the amount of time they take to load. When I initiate a debugging session in a GUI environment, the 10-second overhead gives me the impression that I just made a huge commitment. It's like getting engaged or signing a mortgage. Or it could just be that I'm an old fogey.

Single-Step Execution

Single-step execution is a mode of processor execution in which the processor will execute a single statement and then yield program control to the debugger. Single-step execution is used by debuggers in order to trace the path of execution one instruction at a time.

Typically, a user will set a breakpoint near a region of code in which is or she is interested. When the path of execution encounters this breakpoint and program control is given to the debugger, the user will then single-step through the code in question to see what's going on. This is kind of like using a VCR. You can fast forward to the part of the movie that you want to watch. Then, you can inch forward, frame by frame, to delineate every little detail of your favorite scene.

Debugging Techniques on Intel

The Intel hardware platform has facilities specifically dedicated to providing breakpoints and single-step execution. In particular, the Intel platform uses two interrupts to support these debugging features.

- INT 3 implements breakpoints.
- INT 1 supports single-step execution.

The INT 3 instruction is used to create a breakpoint. When program execution encounters the INT 3 instruction, the running process freezes and the interrupt service routine (ISR) for INT 3 is run. This ISR could do anything, but most debuggers use it as an opportunity to give the user the chance to examine and modify the machine state of the frozen process. For example, when a program being executed under the supervision of a command-line debugger (like `debug`) hits an INT 3 instruction, the debugger will display a command prompt so that the user can enter commands and have a look around.

The INT 1 instruction is used to respond to single-step execution. Intel processors have a 32-bit EFLAGS register which is treated as a collection of 32 flag bits. There is a flag bit named TF (trap flag) which is the ninth bit in the 32-bit register (bit 8 if you index starting at 0). When TF is set (i.e., when its value is 1), the processor will go into single-step mode. In single-step mode, the INT 1 interrupt is executed automatically after every instruction. This gives the debugger the ability to trace through a program in slow motion. After each instruction, the INT 1 interrupt forces control to be returned to the debugger.

There is nothing special about these interrupts. INT 1 and INT 3 merely reference slots in the interrupt vector table, like other interrupts. Invoked in the absence of a debugger (or some other tool which volunteers to handle these two interrupts), INT 1 and INT 3 don't do that much in real mode. Protected mode is a different story. I've often zapped my command prompt window when randomly executing INT 3 and INT 1 in protected mode. You can verify this for yourself by writing a ten-line assembly program that executes INT 3 and INT 1. It is the responsibility of the debugger to harness these interrupts and supply the necessary handlers.

Intel Interrupts

The previous section might leave you scratching your head if you're not familiar with the Intel platform. What's all this talk about interrupts? If you're new to the Intel 80x86 family of processors, this section provides some background information. If you've already been exposed to Intel real-mode programming, you should skip to the next section.

In Chapter 2, I defined an interrupt as a machine-level message that is transmitted to the CPU from other hardware subsystems. This definition was intentionally abstract. Now, however, I am focusing on the Intel hardware platform and will need to offer you a few more specific details.

Interrupts can be generated by hardware subsystems, but they can also be generated by software. The interrupts used for debugging on the Intel platform are software generated. For the duration of this section, I will be concentrating on software-generated interrupts. To keep things simple, I will also limit the discussion to real-mode processor operation.

Real-mode operation means that the processor is functioning with no memory protection, no virtual memory, and a 20-bit address space. In other words, the processor is supporting an operating system like DOS. It is a very primitive, bare-bones mode of operation. Modern, 32-bit operating systems like Windows XP switch the processor into protected mode at boot time, which enables advanced features like memory protection, paging, and privilege levels.

To understand software interrupts in real mode, you'll need to become familiar with two basic components of the real-mode execution environment. Specifically, you'll need to learn about how addresses are composed and be familiar with the registers the processor uses. The synopsis I'm about to provide is terse, to say the least, and I've supplied a few references at the end of the chapter if you need to fill in any blanks.

Real-Mode Addressing

In real mode's 20-bit address space, the address of a byte in memory is specified by a pair of 16-bit values known as the *segment address* and *offset address*. The memory address of a given byte is formed by taking the 16-bit segment address, multiplying it by 16 (i.e., 0x10), and then adding the result to the offset address.

NOTE By multiplying the 16-bit segment address by 0x10, we are producing a 20-bit value. For example, assume we have a 16-bit segment address of 0x1A00. When we multiply this value by 0x10, we get 0x1A000, which is 20 bits in size. This is a sneaky way of storing a 20-bit value in a 16-bit register. We basically assume that the segment address has an extra hexadecimal zero stuck on the end. This convention allows the processor to address memory using a 20-bit value, when all it has at its disposal is 16-bit registers.

The segment address and offset address represent concrete elements in memory. They are not just two abstract numbers. Given that a processor in real mode has a 20-bit address space, the processor can address 1 MB of memory. Thus, the real-mode memory space can be divided into 16 contiguous 64 KB segments. A segment address specifies a particular 64 KB segment of memory. To locate a specific byte within a segment, the 16-bit offset address is used. An offset address of 0 specifies the first byte in a segment, an offset address of 1 specifies the second byte in a segment, and so on. The fact that a 16-bit offset can specify 65,536 bytes is what limits real-mode memory segments to 64 KB.

For example, given a segment address of 0x1345 and an offset address of 0x3456, the memory address of the byte we are working with is 0x168A6:

$$0x1345 * 0x10 = 0x13450$$
$$+ \underline{0x03456}$$
$$0x168A6 = \text{physical address } 92{,}326$$

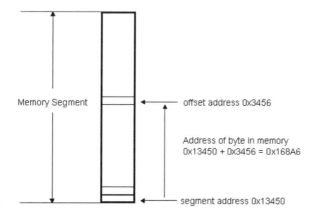

Figure 4-1

One thing to keep in mind is that real-mode addresses correspond to actual physical addresses (i.e., the value the processor places on the address line when accessing the memory chips). Also, real-mode segments do not have any protection mechanisms. A rampant program can ravage the entire memory space if it wants to.

Real-Mode Registers

In real mode, an Intel processor has eight general purpose integer registers, four segment registers, an instruction pointer, and a flags register (which is just a 16-bit, truncated version of EFLAGS). All of the registers are 16 bits in length. These registers and their usage are detailed in Figure 4-2.

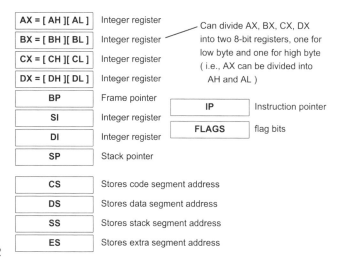

Figure 4-2

The AX, BX, CX, and DX registers can be referred to in terms of their 8-bit subregisters. For example, the lower-order byte of AX can be referenced as AL, and the higher-order byte can be accessed via AH.

The segment registers are used to store the segment portion of a physical address. The pointer registers, like SP and IP, hold offset addresses. Processor instructions always have their segment address specified by the CS register and their offset address specified by the IP register. The IP register tracks the offset of the current instruction byte as the path of execution moves through a code segment. The value in CS, on the other hand, tends to remain fairly static.

Real-Mode Interrupt Handling

Real-mode software interrupts can be enabled and disabled by toggling the tenth bit (bit 9 if you index starting at 0) in the EFLAGS register. This bit is known as IF (interrupt flag).

The IF bit can be toggled using two instructions. The STI instruction sets IF so that all interrupts can be recognized and serviced by the processor. The CLI instruction clears IF, causing (most) interrupts to be ignored.

Software interrupts are produced when the INT instruction is executed. The INT instruction expects a single, immediate, byte-sized operand, called an *interrupt vector*. For example, the instruction INT 12 processes interrupt vector 12.

The interrupt vector can assume any value in the range from 0 to 255. The interrupt vector is really an index into a table of double words called the *interrupt vector table* (IVT). Given that there are 256 possible vector values, this table is 1,024 bytes long. The interrupt vector table starts at the bottom of the processor's address space, such that it occupies the first kilobyte of memory. Each double word entry in the table contains the segment and offset address of an ISR. The offset address is stored in the first word, and the segment address is stored in the following word. Figure 4-3 displays what the interrupt vector table looks like.

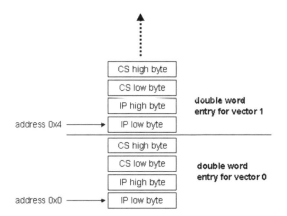

Figure 4-3

I like to think of the interrupt vector table as a kind of phone book for ISRs. When the processor encounters an INT instruction, it looks up the corresponding ISR in the IVT using the interrupt vector. Once it finds the ISR's address, it transfers the path of execution to the ISR and lets the ISR do whatever it needs to do. It might help if I describe this sequence of events in terms of a series of steps. Specifically, when an interrupt instruction is executed, the processor takes the following steps:

1. Pushes the FLAGS register on the stack.

2. Pushes the CS register on the stack.

3. Pushes the IP register on the stack (points to instruction following interrupt).

4. Clears IF and TF.

5. Locates IVT entry corresponding to the supplied vector.

6. Loads the IVT segment and offset address into CS and IP.

This effectively causes program control to jump to the ISR. The body of an ISR can do anything you want it to. There are, however, a few things you may want to keep in mind. First, for the sake of returning the processor back to a "sane" state, the first instruction you'll want to place in an ISR is the STI instruction. This allows the processor to wake up and recognize interrupts again. Also, to return from an ISR you'll need to use the IRET instruction. The IRET instruction basically reverses the steps above so that program execution can continue to the instruction following the interrupt. Specifically, the IRET instruction performs the following steps:

1. Pops the 16-bit value on the top of the stack into IP.

2. Pops the 16-bit value on the top of the stack into CS.

3. Pops the 16-bit value on the top of the stack into FLAGS.

Dosdbg

To get a better understanding of how debugging facilities actually work with regard to the 80x86 family of Intel processors, I built a crude approximation of a debugger named dosdbg. What I've constructed is by no means a fully functional debugging tool. Rather, it is an illustration of the kind of techniques that are used by debuggers to provide basic debugging services. The dosdbg program will give you an introductory look at breakpoints and single-step execution on the Intel platform.

The implementation of dosdbg has a significant amount of assembler, so I think it would be a good idea to provide an overview of what happens when dosdbg runs. Figure 4-4 displays a flowchart of what happens when dosdbg is invoked.

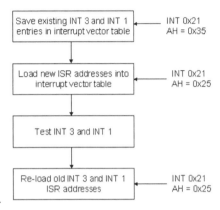

Figure 4-4

The dosdbg program begins by saving the old interrupt vector table entries for INT 3 and INT 1. These initial entries aren't really useful for anything, it's just that it is good programming etiquette to return the machine to its original state when we're done. This can be done using an ISR provided by DOS via INT 0x21. This service is applied in the following manner:

■ Before INT 0x21 is executed, we need to populate AH and AL:

  AH = DOS function specifier = 0x35

  AL = interrupt vector

■ After INT 0x21 has been executed, we will have values in ES and BX:

  ES = segment address of the ISR

  BX = offset address of the ISR

After saving the old interrupt table entries for INT 3 and INT 1, we need to replace them with new entries. This is a way for a program to offer temporary ISRs. Again, we turn to DOS interrupt INT 0x21. This time we use function 0x25, which is applied in the following manner:

■ Before we execute INT 0x21, we populate AH, AL, DS, and DX:

  AH = DOS function specifier = 0x25

  AL = interrupt vector

  DS = segment address to place in vector table

  DX = offset address to place in vector table

One important thing to note is that the DS register must be saved before the 0x25 function is applied. This is because DS points to the data segment of the program and if DS is not restored to its original state, the program will crash in a big way. I save the value of DS by temporarily pushing it on the stack before I execute 0x25.

Once the address information for the temporary ISRs have been loaded, dosdbg gives the user the opportunity to apply them by executing a series of test instructions. In a way, dosdbg is an introspective program in that it really does nothing more than debug itself. When dosdbg is done with its test instructions, the old interrupt table entries for INT 3 and INT 1 are restored and the program ends.

The ISRs which I use to implement INT 3 and INT 1 are defined within main(). I keep them out of the normal flow of traffic by jumping over their implementations with a GOTO statement. Also, I use a label at the beginning of each ISR implementation in order to refer to their addresses. These labels (int1: and int3:) come in very handy when I have to store the addresses of my ISR implementations in the interrupt vector table.

The basic scheme of events within both ISRs is displayed in Figure 4-5.

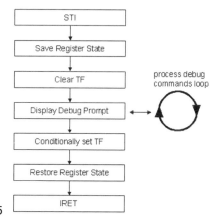

Figure 4-5

The first instruction executed is STI. Recall that the INT instruction clears IF, so we need to re-enable interrupts within the body of the ISR. Next, I save the current state of the registers, because the operation of the ISR itself changes them. After that, I clear the TF bit in the FLAGS value that has been popped onto the stack.

Clearing TF involves setting the ninth bit of the FLAGS register to 0. The FLAGS register does not like being manipulated directly. Instead, TF is cleared by operating on the FLAGS value that has been pushed on the stack by the interrupt instruction. By bitwise ANDing this value with 65,279 (1111111011111111 in binary), TF can be cleared.

Once TF has been cleared, dosdbg presents the user with a command prompt which allows several single-letter commands to be invoked. These commands are implemented within the procCmd() function. Table 4-1 is a cursory summary of dosdbg commands.

Table 4-1

Command	Description
a	Prints the address of the INT1_STR string
d	Dumps the register contents to the screen
i	Increments the AX register

Command	Description
m	Displays a 16-byte region of memory
q	Quits the debugger and continues execution
t	Traces (single-step) through the next execution

Once the debugger's command loop has been exited, the ISR checks to see if TF should be set. If TF needs to be set, the ISR will bitwise OR the FLAGS value on the stack with 256 (100000000 in binary). Finally, the ISR will restore the register values that were saved earlier and execute an IRET instruction.

NOTE You may be wondering why single-stepping does not affect the code in the ISRs. In other words, why doesn't the debugger itself single-step once TF is set? The answer to this lies in the nature of the INT instruction and the way in which TF is set in the ISR. If you recall from the earlier discussion of interrupts, the INT instruction pushes the FLAGS register on the stack and then clears TF directly (something we cannot do programmatically). This allows the ISR to execute normally, and yet still allows single-step mode to persist when the ISR returns. Also, the code modifies TF using the FLAGS value that has been pushed on the stack. The means that the TF change does not take effect until the ISR has returned and the FLAGS value is popped off the stack.

After the previous discussion, you should be ready to take a look at the source code:

```c
#include<stdio.h>

/*global variables--------------------------------------------------*/

char INT1_STR[]="->SINGLE-STEP<-\n";
char INT3_STR[]="->BREAKPOINT<-\n";

unsigned short rCS,rSS,rDS;
short rAX,rBX,rCX,rDX;
unsigned short rIP;

unsigned char traceOn=0;

/*prototypes--------------------------------------------------------*/

void procCmd(int *lptr);

/*definitions-------------------------------------------------------*/

void main()
{
    unsigned short oldInt1Seg;
    unsigned short oldInt1Offset;
    unsigned short oldInt3Seg;
    unsigned short oldInt3Offset;

    goto past_interrupts;
```

```
/* Handle INT 1 -----------------------------------------------*/

int1:
__asm
{
    STI
    MOV rCS,CS
    MOV rSS,SS
    MOV rDS,DS
    MOV rAX,AX
    MOV rBX,BX
    MOV rCX,CX
    MOV rDX,DX

    POP CX
    MOV rIP,CX
    POP DX
    POP AX
    AND AX,65279
    PUSH AX
    PUSH DX
    PUSH CX
}

printf("%s",INT1_STR);
printf("next instruction at IP=%u\n",rIP);
{
    int loop = 1;

    while(loop)
    {
        procCmd(&loop);
    }
}

if(traceOn)
{
    __asm
    {
        POP CX
        POP DX
        POP AX
        OR AX,256
        PUSH AX
        PUSH DX
        PUSH CX
    }
}

__asm
{
    MOV AX,rAX
    MOV BX,rBX
    MOV CX,rCX
```

```
        MOV DX,rDX
        IRET
}

/* Handle INT 3 ---------------------------------------------*/

int3:
__asm
{
        STI
        MOV rCS,CS
        MOV rSS,SS
        MOV rDS,DS
        MOV rAX,AX
        MOV rBX,BX
        MOV rCX,CX
        MOV rDX,DX

        POP CX
        POP DX
        POP AX
        AND AX,65279
        PUSH AX
        PUSH DX
        PUSH CX
}

printf("%s",INT3_STR);
{
        int loop = 1;

        while(loop)
        {
                procCmd(&loop);
        }
}

if(traceOn)
{
        __asm
        {
                POP CX
                POP DX
                POP AX
                OR AX,256
                PUSH AX
                PUSH DX
                PUSH CX
        }
}

__asm
{
        MOV AX,rAX
```

```
        MOV BX,rBX
        MOV CX,rCX
        MOV DX,rDX
        IRET
}

/* Execution path begins here -------------------------------*/

past_interrupts:

printf("Save old interrupts SEG:OFF\n");

__asm
{
        MOV AH,0x35
        MOV AL,0x1
        INT 0x21
        MOV oldInt1Seg,ES
        MOV oldInt1Offset,BX

        MOV AH,0x35
        MOV AL,0x3
        INT 0x21
        MOV oldInt3Seg,ES
        MOV oldInt3Offset,BX
}

printf("Load new interrupts SEG:OFF\n");

__asm
{
        MOV AH,0x25
        MOV AL,0x1
        PUSH DS
        MOV CX,CS
        MOV DS,CX
        MOV DX,OFFSET int1
        INT 0x21
        POP DS

        MOV AH,0x25
        MOV AL,0x3
        PUSH DS
        MOV CX,CS
        MOV DS,CX
        MOV DX,OFFSET int3
        INT 0x21
        POP DS
}

/* actually do something here to provoke debugger -------------*/

__asm
{
```

```
        INT 3

        MOV DX,20
        INC DX
        NOP
        MOV DX,3501
        MOV DX,72
        DEC DX
}

printf("Re-loading old interrupts SEG:OFF\n");

__asm
{
        PUSH DS
        MOV AH,0x25
        MOV AL,0x1
        MOV DS,oldInt1Seg
        MOV DX,oldInt1Offset
        INT 0x21
        POP DS

        PUSH DS
        MOV AH,0x25
        MOV AL,0x3
        MOV DS,oldInt3Seg
        MOV DX,oldInt3Offset
        INT 0x21
        POP DS
}
    return;
}/*end main*/

void procCmd(int *lptr)
{
    char ch;

    traceOn=0;

    printf("dbg>");
    scanf("%c",&ch);
    fflush(stdin);

    switch(ch)
    {
        case 'a':
        {
            printf("INT1_STR address=%u\n",INT1_STR);
        }break;
        case 'd':
        {
            printf("CS=%u\n",rCS);
            printf("SS=%u\n",rSS);
            printf("DS=%u\n",rDS);
```

```
                    printf("AX=%d\n",rAX);
                    printf("BX=%d\n",rBX);
                    printf("CX=%d\n",rCX);
                    printf("DX=%d\n",rDX);
            }break;
            case 'i':
            {
                    rAX++;
                    printf("AX=%d\n",rAX);
            }break;
            case 'm':
            {
                    int i;
                    unsigned long address;
                    unsigned long limit = rCS+65535;
                    unsigned char *sptr;
                    printf("memory address>");
                    scanf("%lu",&address);
                    fflush(stdin);
                    sptr = (unsigned char*)address;
                    printf("address=%u\n",sptr);
                    if(address > limit)
                    {
                            printf("address is beyond .COM segment\n");
                    }
                    else
                    {
                            for(i=0;i<16;i++)
                            {
                                    if((sptr[i]>0x20)&&(sptr[i]<0x7F))
                                    {
                                            printf("byte[%lu]=%c\n",address+i,sptr[i]);
                                    }
                                    else
                                    {
                                            printf("byte[%lu]=%X\n",address+i,sptr[i]);
                                    }
                            }
                    }
            }break;
            case 'q':
            {
                    *lptr=0;
            }break;
            case 't':
            {
                    traceOn=1;
                    printf("trace flag set\n");
                    *lptr=0;
            }break;
            default:
            {
                    printf("not valid command\n");
            }
```

```
        }
    return;
}/*end procCmd*/
```

 NOTE   I implemented `dosdbg` to run as a `.COM` executable. I apologize for using such a dated file format, but it was a necessary evil in this case. Contemporary versions of Windows do not allow direct access to the computer's hardware and system data structures. In addition, using a `.COM` file format simplified address bookkeeping because `.COM` programs must occupy a single 64 KB segment of memory.

You can build `.COM` binaries with Borland's 4.5 C++ compiler or Microsoft's Visual C++ 1.52. I've noticed that Borland is still selling its 4.5 C++ compiler. If you have access to the Internet, Borland has an online museum where it is giving away old versions of Turbo C, which can also be used to build `.COM` executables.

However, do not assume that this shackles `dosdbg` to DOS. I've run `dosdbg` on several versions of Windows (NT, 2000, ME) under the auspices of the Virtual DOS Machine interface (VDM). The VDM is a simulation of a computer running DOS. The difference between a computer running DOS 6.22 and the VDM is that the DOS virtual environment is merely an approximation of the real thing. It accesses the hardware through the Win32 system call interface like everything else (so a lot of things aren't really happening, …they just seem to be). This explains why the majority of DOS applications do not work within the VDM. The VDM supplies only limited backwards compatibility. Most of this is not really important, anyway. My primary goal was to provide a concise illustration of how debugging works on the 80x86 family of Intel processors.

The books I reference for this chapter show you how to do this type of manipulation using either assembler exclusively or Windows function calls exclusively (which are sometimes even more painful than assembler). I decided to take a different route and implement everything using a mixture of C and assembler. I think this makes the program easier to read and understand without giving up essential hardware details. The source code for `dosdbg` is included on the CD-ROM.

As far as I can tell, there are no other books that explain this subject in the same manner that I did. Thus, I was a pioneer and I took a lot of arrows. I had to dust off my real-mode programming skills, which I haven't used in a couple of years.

What you should be able to see from all this is that debugging can be laden with complexity and subtle details. Writing a fully featured debugger can be like arguing your own existence with someone who has a doctorate in philosophy. There may be times where you think you've proven that it is not possible to build a debugger. Once more, this whole discussion has been presented in the context of real-mode processor operation, which is relatively simple. I bet you can guess how nasty things get when you have to debug in protected mode.

Debugger construction is somewhat of a secret art, although I hope I have shed some light on it. Fortunately, for me, I was able to embed the HEC debugger within the HEC virtual machine proper. This allowed me to effectively sidestep most of the complexity that arises from having to debug native machine instructions. In the remaining portion of this chapter, I devote a lot of effort to explaining how the HEC debugger works and the manner in which I implemented it. But first, a bit of fun…

Monkey Business

> "Whatever Nature has in store for mankind, unpleasant as it may be,
> men must accept, for ignorance is never better than knowledge."
> — Enrico Fermi

Do you remember what I said earlier about the primary benefit of using a debugger? I said that it allows a computer scientist to assume a neutral frame of reference and observe a program's path of execution without actually being a part of the execution. In addition to being the greatest strength of a debugger, it is also the greatest weakness.

There are black hat engineers out there who spend their time inventing ways to defeat program debuggers. It is an insidious practice. One can only guess what their motives are (perhaps job security?). The underlying strategy behind these techniques is to undermine the ability of the debugger to stand apart from the events which constitute program execution. The idea is to create a program that recognizes that a debugger is present and takes certain actions as a result.

Most authors would rather keep your head in the sand, with the justification that they are only interested in discussing constructive development practices. I beg to differ. Like Enrico Fermi, I would favor awareness and understanding over ignorance. By explaining these techniques to you, I'm giving you the ability to recognize them when they are being used against you.

Stack Smashing

There are some debuggers that use the stack of the program they are inspecting as their own stack. In this case, you can defeat the debugger by using a stack that is big enough only for the program. Specifically, your program needs to set the stack pointer to the last byte of a region of memory in the code segment. The region of memory in question effectively becomes a new stack. The region of memory should be just large enough to handle ordinary program requests.

When the debugger loads and starts the program, it will need a lot more space than your modified stack can offer it. As a result, the stack will overflow into instructions in the code segment and the debugger will be looking at garbage. Following is an example I constructed using Intel assembler.

```
.386
mycode SEGMENT USE16
ASSUME CS:mycode,DS:mycode,SS:mycode,ES:mycode
ORG 100H
entry:
PUSH DS
MOV AH,0H
PUSH AX

JMP pastvars
string          DB "smash the stack"
endchar         DB '$'
originalstack   DW ?
```

```
pastvars:

MOV [originalstack],SP
MOV SP,OFFSET newstack

MOV AH,09H
LEA DX,string
INT 21H

MOV SP,[originalstack]
RETF
DB 30 dup ('T')
newstack:
DB 1
mycode ENDS
END entry
```

This technique will take a little experimentation to determine what the "minimal" size of the stack needs to be. In the previous program, I found that this was somewhere between 25 and 30 bytes.

The DOS debug utility does not use the stack of the program it is analyzing, so don't expect any fireworks. Other debuggers, like Borland's Turbo Debugger and Microsoft's CodeView debugger, are also protected from this tactic. This technique only works when the debugger uses the program's stack.

 NOTE The HEC debugger is immune to this tactic because it is a part of the run-time environment and does not use the program's stack segment.

Multithreaded Mayhem

Debuggers often have a hard time dealing with multithreaded applications. Some debuggers cannot tell which threads are blocking and which are capable of executing. Others have difficulty pausing execution on a thread level of granularity; they place breakpoints that are activated by whichever thread happens to execute them. Furthermore, the use of threads exposes a program to a whole species of thread-indigenous pitfalls. Multithreaded applications that are poorly designed can create paths of execution that result in deadlock and data corruption. If these types of problems exist, tracking them down with a debugger can prove to be a daunting task, even if the debugger functions perfectly.

The basic message here: threads, lots of threads, have threads generate their own children threads and grandchildren threads. If you're working on a recently released operating system, this technique is even more effective because there are probably still a lot of thread management bugs lurking around in the depths of the kernel. This is the price that is paid for buying software produced by a company that ships its product when it is "good enough."

NOTE The HEC debugger does not suffer from these flaws because the HEC virtual machine, in the interest of portability and consistent behavior, executes as a single thread.

Self-Modifying Programs

This is probably my favorite tactic. The idea of a program that can alter itself at run time has cropped up in a number of different areas, including computer viruses and artificial intelligence. Recall that a debugger places breakpoints in the instruction stream of a program. One tactic involves searching your text segment for these breakpoints. If your operating system allows for read-write text segments, you can remove them. Or, rather than simply disposing of the breakpoints, you might consider moving them around. Better yet, you can send the debugger on a wild goose chase. If your program finds a breakpoint in its memory image, you can redirect the path of execution to a distant function that computes Pi to a billion decimal places. This ought to keep the user busy for a few hours...

All of these techniques rely upon your program's ability to ferret out breakpoints in its text segment. The following program is intended to give you an idea of how an application might scan itself at run time.

```c
#include<stdio.h>

unsigned char flag=0;

void alert(unsigned char *ptr);

void main()
{
    int i;
    unsigned char breakpoint = 0xCC;
    unsigned char *sptr;        /*start*/
    unsigned char *eptr;        /*end*/
    unsigned char *cptr;        /*current*/
start:
    __asm
    {
        LEA EAX,start
        MOV sptr,EAX
        LEA EAX,end
        MOV eptr,EAX
    }

    cptr = sptr;
    while(cptr<eptr)
    {
        if(*cptr==breakpoint)
        {
            alert(cptr);
        }
        cptr++;
    }
```

```
    /* bulk of code between start and end labels */

    printf("do some work...\n");
    i++;

end:
    if(flag){ printf("breakpoints found\n"); }
    else{ printf("no breakpoints\n"); }
    return;
}/*end main*/

void alert(unsigned char *ptr)
{
    printf("a break point exists!\n");
    printf("address %1X\n",ptr);
    flag=1;
    return;
}
```

On the Intel platform, the breakpoint instruction INT 3 shows up in memory as 0xCC. Notice how I use assembly code to assign addresses to the pointers that mark the beginning and end of the code to be scanned. Also, I had to use a variable to represent the 0xCC breakpoint value because if I had used a macro, the breakpoint value would have shown up in the text segment and the program would have mistakenly caught it.

I built the source code above with the latest version of Visual Studio. If you crank up Visual Studio (or C++Builder) and place a breakpoint somewhere between the start and end labels, you'll see that the scanning code detects them. The only caveat of this technique is that the scope of labels is function based. This means that you'll have to place labels in, and scan, each individual function you want to check for breakpoints. You could probably create some sort of macro to cut down on redundant work.

A similar trick involves having your program hook into the debugging interrupts and provide its own ISRs for INT 3 and INT 1. You could have these routines print out fake error messages that direct the user's attention elsewhere.

```
Fatal Error: Windows incorrect version
```

If you want to create some real fireworks on the Intel platform and send the debugger into hyperspace, zero out the INT 3 and INT 1 entries in the interrupt vector table. This gives the ISRs in charge of INT 3 and INT 1 an address of 0, which is strictly *verboten*. The following code shows how this could be done with respect to dosdbg.

```
    /* load zero ISR addresses */

    _asm
    {
        MOV AH,0x25
        MOV AL,0x1
        PUSH DS
        MOV CX,0x0
        MOV DS,CX
        MOV DX,0
        INT 0x21
```

```
        POP DS

        MOV AH,0x25
        MOV AL,0x3
        PUSH DS
        MOV CX,0x0
        MOV DS,CX
        MOV DX,0
        INT 0x21
        POP DS
    }
```

Mixed Memory Models

Some operating systems support different memory models. But some memory models are more equal than others. Certain memory models are supported for the sake of legacy applications, or to allow special types of programs to interface with hardware. Rarely are development tools, like debuggers, perfectly suited to deal with every memory model that a platform supports. Most debuggers are engineered to work with a specific memory model and perhaps have limited support for others. This is an Achilles heel of which you can take advantage.

This is particularly true when it comes to Wintel. The plethora of different Wintel memory models have traditionally been divided into 16-bit and 32-bit varieties. When Intel finally comes out with a 64-bit chip that outperforms their current 32-bit processor, we'll have three different varieties (naturally, this will only exacerbate things). The documentation I have looked over seems to indicate that Microsoft would prefer that you take your old 16-bit code and port it to the 32-bit environment. Can you guess why?

It is actually possible to mix 16-bit Microsoft code and 32-bit code using a technique called *thunking*. Thunking comes in three flavors: *universal thunking*, *flat thunking*, and *generic thunking*. Universal thunking allows applications running under Windows 3.1 (i.e., Win32s) to load and call a 16-bit DLL. Flat thunking allows 16-bit and 32-bit DLLs to talk to each other on Windows 95. Generic thunking can be used on Windows 95 or Windows NT to allow a 16-bit application to load and call a 32-bit DLL.

Of the three techniques, generic thunking is probably the simplest. Generic thunking is implemented by a special API that is an extension of the traditional DLL API. For example, instead of calling `LoadLibrary()`, a generic thunking application calls `LoadLibraryEx32W()`. The technique of flat thunking, on the other hand, is probably the most convoluted.

There's not much lucid documentation on flat thunking. I assume Microsoft has kept the technology obscure in an effort to encourage you to port your code instead of thunking. Flat thunking in particular is an elaborate, multistage process. It requires the creation of a special script, which is compiled into assembler code by a special tool called a *thunk compiler* (it used to be part of the Windows SDK). The assembler that is generated must be transformed into both 16-bit and 32-bit object files by Microsoft's MASM assembler. The 16-bit object file must be linked with the 16-bit DLL and the 32-bit object file must be linked with the 32-bit DLL. If you make last-minute changes to your 16-bit code, you have to rewrite your thunk script and repeat the entire procedure. There are a couple of other additional contortions that must be performed, but I think you get the general idea. Flat thunking is not for the timid developer.

When it comes to debugging programs that have been built using thunking, the Microsoft documentation states that debugging is "difficult not only because the mechanism itself is complex, but also because the necessary debugging tools are difficult to master." Complicated?…Difficult to master?…It almost sounds like they're talking about DCOM. From the standpoint of a person who wants to foil a Microsoft debugger, things just keep getting better and better.

I've tried to run code that thunks on Windows 2000 with no success. The thunking application completely froze my machine and I was forced to reboot. This, in and of itself, is a testimony to the flimsy level of memory protection that Windows offers. It appears that only a certain number of older platforms support thunking (the rest just crash and burn). The basic premise of this technique, however, is still applicable: When faced with an operating system that supports different memory models, you can frustrate a debugger either by using an extremely old memory model or by mixing memory models together.

 NOTE   For those readers who do not know what DCOM is, DCOM stands for "Distributed Component Object Model." It was Microsoft's answer to CORBA, which is to say that it provided an infrastructure for objects separated on a network to interact. The primary benefit of using DCOM is that all of the necessary supporting services are bundled with the Windows operating system (big surprise there). In other words, there is no ORB to purchase and license. As it turned out, DCOM was so complicated to work with that it never took off. Never mind the fact that they couldn't get it to work on anything other than 80x86 hardware. The marketing people at Microsoft, sensing the lack of success, buried DCOM with a flurry of new acronyms, like ATL and COM+. These "new" technologies were really just revisions of existing technology. ATL and COM+ attempted to compensate for the complexity that working with development tools like DCOM had created to begin with. In my opinion, Microsoft's success to date with any object technology has been limited.

 NOTE   The HEC virtual machine uses a single, relatively simple, memory model. This prevents the mixed memory model tactic from being used against the HEC debugger.

Assorted Fun and Games

There are other unorthodox ways to fool a debugger. For example, you could build a small tool to fiddle with the debug information which is stored in the executable. There are several variations of this technique. Specifically, the development tools themselves could be subverted to generate erroneous debug records. This tactic is more insidious on a subtle level, where only small (but crucial) modifications are instituted. The best lie always has an element of truth. This allows those using the debugger to believe that they are still dealing with legitimate data. Otherwise, they'll suspect something is wrong and possibly refresh the tainted binary.

HEC File Format

On the most basic level, a program consists of two elements: data storage and machine instructions. Any program can be decomposed and understood as the realization of these two atomic components. Most programming languages, however, prefer to offer the developer a syntax that allows a program to be viewed in abstract terms, such that the developer is left blithely unaware of the details of machine operation.

For example, data storage items (i.e., variables) are typically assigned a data type and an arbitrary name. This allows a variable to be referenced using a designation that has significance to the programmer. It also allows the development tools to enforce certain behavioral constraints on the storage item.

Programming languages also allow instructions to be grouped together to form a kind of hierarchy. A set of one or more contiguous instructions can form a statement. Related statements can be used to build a block of code. Sequential blocks of code are then used to create functions. This is similar to the manner in which letters form words, which are then merged together to form sentences, which are then used to build paragraphs.

As with variables, programming languages almost always provide a way for users to refer to functions using a name. The alternative would be for the programmer to refer to functions by their address, but this is much more complicated and error prone. Some programming languages even allow the address of a particular instruction within a function to be named using labels.

 NOTE There are several terms used to refer to a function, including *procedure*, *routine*, *module*, *method*, and *member*. The nomenclature used often reflects the background and alignment of the speaker. I've already used a couple of these terms interchangeably. The COBOL programming language, which is notorious for its self-evident grammar, uses the term *paragraph* to refer to a function. The fundamental idea is the same in all cases: The entity being referenced is an aggregation of contiguous machine instructions that syntactically bound and can be referred to using a single name.

The name given to a variable, function, or label is known as an *identifier*. When a program is translated from source code into an executable file, the identifiers are stripped from the source code and replaced by their corresponding addresses. This is a necessity, seeing as how processors (physical or otherwise) access and modify memory by specifying an address.

In order for a debugger to resolve memory addresses at run time to their associated identifiers in the source code, the identifier-to-address mappings must be recorded in a database that the debugger can query. Some development environments store this information in its own special file. For the sake of keeping things simple, I decided to place all the metadata on a program's identifiers within the bytecode executable itself. This requires that HEC executables be partitioned into different sections.

HEC bytecode executables have four primary sections:

■ Header section

■ Symbol table

■ String table

■ Bytecode section

The makeup of these sections is decomposed in Figure 4-6.

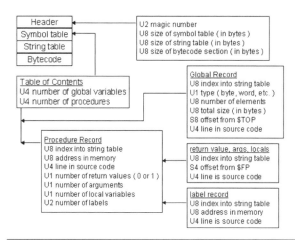

Figure 4-6

 NOTE   Remember, all numeric values stored in a HEC bytecode executable are persisted in the big-endian format.

Header Section

The header section serves two purposes. It serves to both identify the file as an executable and to specify the size of the file's different sections. The header is 26 bytes long and consists of four consecutive fields. The first field, which is a word in size, stores the magic number (i.e., 0xDEED) that indicates to the virtual machine that the file is a bytecode executable. The following three fields are all quad words and specify the size of the symbol table, the string table, and the bytecode section (in that order).

 NOTE   If the size of the symbol table and string table are 0, the virtual machine will not attempt to extract debug metadata from the executable.

Symbol Table

The symbol table is a series of multibyte records that store metadata on the identifiers of a program. The symbol table starts with a table of contents. The table of contents is eight bytes long and consists of two double words. The first double word specifies the number of global variable records in the symbol table. The second double word specifies the number of procedure records in the symbol table.

What follows the table of contents is a series of global variable records and then a series of procedure records. Each procedure record will have its own private entourage of subrecords, which follow directly after the procedure record, to describe elements specific to the procedure (like arguments and local variables). This means that the space allocated for a particular procedure in the symbol table will vary from one procedure to the next. Figure 4-7 is an example of how records would be organized in a typical symbol table.

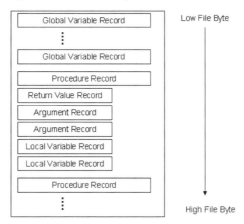

Figure 4-7

Global variable records are 37 bytes in size. They consist of six fields. The first field, a double word, is an index into the string table, where the actual text for the variable's identifier is located. The second, which is a single byte in size, specifies the data type of the global variable (i.e., byte, word, double word, quad word). If the global variable in question is an array, the third field, a quad word, stores the number of elements in the array. The total number of bytes that constitute the global variable can be determined by multiplying the third field by the second field. If you're too lazy to perform this operation, you are in luck because the fourth field of the record stores this value.

HEC bytecode executables do not have a data segment to store global variables. This requires global variable storage to be allocated on the stack when program execution begins. The fifth field in a global variable's record, a quad word, indicates the location of the variable's first byte on the stack. The value stored in this field is a negative offset relative to $TOP. The last field, a double word, specifies the line in the corresponding assembler source file where the global variable is defined.

The symbol table's collection of global variable records is followed by zero or more procedure records. Procedure records are 25 bytes in size and each one is normally followed by a train of related subrecords. As with global variable records, the first field in a procedure record is a quad word that specifies an index into the string table. The address of the procedure in memory is given by the second field, which is a quad word. The third field is a double word that indicates the line in the corresponding assembler source file where the procedure is defined. The last four fields determine the number of subrecords that will immediately follow the procedure record. These fields specify the number of return values, arguments, local variables, and labels used by the procedure (in that order). Each of these procedure-specific elements has its own record in the symbol table. For example, if a procedure has no return value, three arguments, ten local variables, and five labels, the procedure record will be followed by 18 subrecords (three subrecords for the arguments, ten subrecords for the local variables, and five subrecords for the labels).

The size of the last four fields in a procedure record also places an implicit constraint on the number of arguments, local variables, and labels a function can have. For example, the number of local variables is determined by a byte-sized field. This means that, at most, a function can have 255 local variables. This didn't seem like too much of a problem for me, given that even the hardiest functions I've worked with usually have included less than 100 local variables. The number of return values a function has is either one or zero, so this really doesn't apply to the return value field.

The format for a return value, argument, and local variable record is the same for all three of these procedure-specific elements. The record format is 16 bytes in length and consists of three fields. The first field is an index to the string table. The second field is an offset value that is added to $FP to obtain the memory address of the item. Return values, arguments, and local variables are allocated as part of a function's stack frame and $FP serves as a reference point with regard to the stack frame in memory. The last field specifies the line in the assembler source file in which the item appears.

The format for procedure label records is slightly different. The difference lies in the label record's second field, which specifies the address of the byte in memory the label represents, instead of being an offset from $FP.

String Table

The string table is nothing more than a contiguous series of null-terminated strings. Each identifier in a program will have its text stored in this table. Using a string table is a way to minimize redundant storage. If a string table is not used, it is more than likely that the same string of text would be stored in several different places. A string table allows a string to be stored in one place and one place only.

Bytecode Section

The bytecode section contains the bytecode instructions which the virtual machine will load into its address space and execute. The primary payload of a bytecode executable is located in this section. An executable file can have an empty symbol table and string table, but the bytecode section must always be a nonzero number of bytes in size.

Modes of Operation

The Intel family of 32-bit processors has several modes of operation, including real mode, protected mode, system management mode, and virtual 8086 mode. Depending on the mode in which a processor operates, it will treat memory, data, and instructions in a particular manner.

Rather than force you to contend with half a dozen different modes of operation, I decided to adhere to a simple approach and allow the HEC virtual machine to operate in two distinct modes. (Remember, one of my underlying goals was simplicity.) These two modes are production mode and debug mode.

In debug mode, a variable named `debug` (defined in `dbgdata.c`), is set to true. When the virtual machine is placed into debug mode, the next bytecode instruction will be executed and then the virtual machine will pause. The virtual machine will present the user with a command prompt so that debugging commands can be entered. Debug mode offers the user a bare-bones environment where it is possible to peek under the hood and see what's going on.

There are two ways to place the HEC virtual machine in debug mode:

- Command-line option

- Breakpoint

The first way is to use the `-d` command-line option when invoking the virtual machine. This causes the virtual machine to begin execution in debug mode. The virtual machine will execute the first instruction of the bytecode executable and then display a debug command prompt. The other way to place the virtual machine into debug mode is to place a breakpoint (i.e., the INT 3 instruction) in the bytecode executable.

Production mode is how the HEC virtual machine was meant to run normally. In production mode, the virtual machine executes instructions, without pausing, until the HALT instruction is executed. In production mode, the `debug` variable is set to false.

Implementation Overview

The HEC debugger is a part of the virtual machine. This actually makes life much easier for me because this approach gives me immediate access to machine state information and better control over machine execution. The implementation of the debugger requires the cooperation of six source files and rears its head in three of the five stages of the virtual machine's life cycle. The organization of these files is displayed in Figure 4-8.

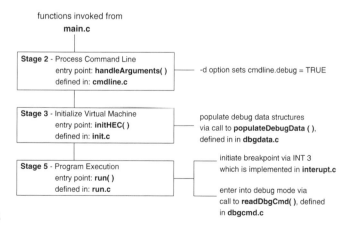

Figure 4-8

Debugger related code initially shows up in the `cmdline.c` source file, which handles the command-line option to start the debugger in debug mode. During the initialization phase, the `populateDebugData()` function defined in `dbgdata.c` is invoked in the `init.c` source file. This causes debug metadata, located in the executable, to be read into virtual machine data structures. During virtual machine execution, which is managed by code in the `run.c` source file, there are hooks to enter into debug mode. These hooks call functions defined in `dbgcmd.c`. Finally, the implementation of breakpoints is provided in `interupt.c`.

Command-Line Processing

Recall command-line processing as initiated in `main.c`:

```
/*2) handle command line arguments, set computer switches */

DBG_MAIN0("2) invoking handleArguments()\n");
cl = handleArguments(argc,argv);
if(cl.ok==FALSE)
{
    FATAL_ERROR1("main(): errors during handleArguments()\n");
}
```

The `CmdLine` structure returned from `handleArguments()` has a field named `debug` which can cause the virtual machine to start in debug mode. If you look at the code in `cmdline.c`, you'll see that the `-d` command-line option sets the `CmdLine` structure's `debug` field to true. This is significant because the `CmdLine` structure is passed as an argument to the `run()` function:

```
/*5) begin execution*/

DBG_MAIN0("5) invoking run()\n");
run(cl.debug);
```

The debug field in the `CmdLine` structure is used to determine if the virtual machine should be placed in debug mode.

Storing Debug Metadata

Once the command line has been processed, the virtual machine will use the options on the command line (or the lack thereof) to initialize the virtual machine's run-time environment.

```
/*3) init execution environment and load bytecode */

DBG_MAIN0("3) invoking initHEC()\n");
RAM = NULL;
if(initHEC(cl)==FALSE)
{
    FATAL_ERROR1("main(): errors during initHEC()\n");
}
```

The bulk of the work is done by the initHEC() function, which is invoked from main.c. The initHEC() function is defined in the init.c source file. One of the first things that initHEC() does is process the debug information stored in the bytecode executable.

```
DBG_INIT0("populate symbol table--------------------\n");
populateDebugData(&hr,&debugData,fptr);
PRINT_SYM_TBL();
DBG_INIT0("end symbol table population--------------\n");
```

The populateDebugData() function processes the header, symbol table, and string table. The information this function digests is then placed in a tree-like hierarchy of structures. The rudiments of this hierarchy are displayed in Figure 4-9.

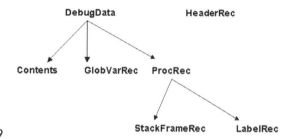

Figure 4-9

All told, there are about seven different structures. Of these seven, HeaderRec, which is used to store the executable's header information, is the only one that stands alone. The HeaderRec structure, produced within populateDebugData(), is used by the invoking code in initHEC() to set up the virtual machine's environment. The rest of the structures are used by the debugger when the virtual machine is in debug mode.

The root of the debugger's metadata tree is a DebugData structure. It is the starting point for all queries concerning application symbol metadata.

```
struct DebugData
{
    struct Contents contents;
    struct GlobVarRec *gvRec;
    struct ProcRec *pRec;
    U1 *strTbl;
};
struct DebugData debugData;
```

The DebugData structure has four members: contents, gvRec, pRec, and strTbl. The contents member is a structure of type Contents. The Contents structure stores the table of contents, which is the first eight bytes of the executable's symbol table.

```
struct Contents
{
    U4 nGlobVarRec;        /* number of global variable records in symbol table*/
    U4 nProcRec;           /* number of procedure records in symbol table*/
};
```

The information stored in `contents` is used to allocate an array of `GlobVarRec` and `ProcRec` structures, which are pointed to by the `gvRec` and `pRec` members of `DebugData`.

```
struct GlobVarRec
{
    U8 text;        /* index to StrTbl of where identifier begins*/
    U1 dType;       /* SZ_BYTE, SZ_WORD, SZ_DWORD, SZ_QWORD */
    U8 len;         /* # elements if array */
    U8 size;        /* total byte size */
    S8 offset;      /* offset below $TOP, address(g) = $TOP - offset*/
    U4 line;        /* source code line containing declaration */
};

struct ProcRec
{
    U8 text;        /* index to StrTbl of where identifier begins */
    U8 address;     /* address of procedure */
    U4 line;        /* source code line containing declaration */
    struct StackFrameRec ret;
    U1 nRet;        /* 0 = void return, 1 = returns a value*/
    struct StackFrameRec *arg;
    U1 nArg;
    struct StackFrameRec *local;
    U1 nLocal;
    struct LabelRec *label;
    U2 nLabel;
};
```

The `ProcRec` structure has members that use the `StackFrameRec` structure to represent return values, arguments, and local variables. It also has a member that uses the `LabelRec` structure to store information on the labels within a procedure.

```
struct StackFrameRec
{
    U8 text;        /* index to StrTbl of where identifier begins */
    S4 fpOffset;    /* +n or -n from $FP */
    U4 line;        /* source code line containing declaration */
};

struct LabelRec
{
    U8 text;        /* index to StrTbl of where identifier begins */
    U8 address;     /* address of label*/
    U4 line;        /* source code line containing declaration */
};
```

The actual process of reading in the bytecode executable's header, symbol table, and string table is performed by the following collection of functions:

```
struct HeaderRec readHeaderRec(FILE *fptr);
struct Contents readContents(FILE* fptr);
struct GlobVarRec readGlobVarRec(FILE *fptr);
struct ProcRec readProcRec(FILE *fptr);
```

```
struct StackFrameRec readStackFrameRec(FILE *fptr);
struct LabelRec readLabelRec(FILE *fptr);
```

The invocation of these functions is managed from populateDebugData().

```
void populateDebugData(struct HeaderRec *hptr,
                       struct DebugData *ptr,
                       FILE *fptr)
{
    U8 i;
    U4 np;
    U4 ng;

    /*1) read header, skip population if zero sizes */

    (*hptr) = readHeaderRec(fptr);

    if(((*hptr).szSymTbl==0)&&((*hptr).szStrTbl==0))
    {
        (*ptr).contents.nGlobVarRec = 0;
        (*ptr).contents.nProcRec = 0;
        return;
    }

    /*2) read table of contents, info on number of globs and procs */

    (*ptr).contents = readContents(fptr);
    ng = ((*ptr).contents).nGlobVarRec;
    np = ((*ptr).contents).nProcRec;

    /*3) based on contents info, allocate globs and procs */

    (*ptr).gvRec = (struct GlobVarRec*)malloc(sizeof(struct GlobVarRec)*ng);

    if((*ptr).gvRec==NULL)
    {
        FCLOSE(fptr);
        FATAL_ERROR1("error allocating global variable records\n");
    }

    (*ptr).pRec = (struct ProcRec*)malloc(sizeof(struct ProcRec)*np);

    if((*ptr).pRec==NULL)
    {
        FCLOSE(fptr);
        FATAL_ERROR1("could not allocate space for procedure records\n");
    }

    /*4) read in globvar recs following contents */

    for(i=0;i<ng;i++)
    {
        (*ptr).gvRec[i]= readGlobVarRec(fptr);
    }
```

```
                 /*5) read in procs which follow globvars */

                 for(i=0;i<np;i++)
                 {
                      (*ptr).pRec[i]= readProcRec(fptr);
                 }

                 /*6) allocate and populate string table (follows symbol table)
                   note: native limit via malloc(size_t)
                 */

                 (*ptr).strTbl = (U1*)malloc((size_t)(*hptr).szStrTbl);

                 if((*ptr).strTbl==NULL)
                 {
                      FCLOSE(fptr);
                      FATAL_ERROR1("could not allocate space for string table\n");
                 }

                 for(i=0;i<(*hptr).szStrTbl;i++)
                 {
                      (*ptr).strTbl[i] = (U1)fgetc(fptr);
                 }
                 return;

        }/*end populateDebugData*/
```

The first thing that populateDebugData does is read the bytecode executable's header. To do this, it invokes the readHeaderRec() function.

```
        struct HeaderRec readHeaderRec(FILE *fptr)
        {
             struct HeaderRec hr;
             int i;
             i = fread(debugbytes,sizeof(U1),SIZE_HEADER,fptr);
             if(i<SIZE_HEADER)
             {
                  FCLOSE(fptr);
                  FATAL_ERROR1("error reading header record\n");
             }

             if((debugbytes[0]==0xDE)&&(debugbytes[1]==0xED))
             {
                  hr.magic = 0xDEED;
             }
             else
             {
                  hr.magic = 0xBAD;
             }

             hr.szSymTbl = bytecodeToQWord(&(debugbytes[2]));
             hr.szStrTbl = bytecodeToQWord(&(debugbytes[10]));
             hr.szByteCode = bytecodeToQWord(&(debugbytes[18]));
```

```
        return(hr);

}/*end readHeaderRec*/
```

 NOTE It is possible to create a bytecode executable that does not have a symbol table and string table. This can be accomplished by creating a header section whose symbol table size field and string table size field are 0. If you look at populate-DebugData(), you'll see that the function does any early return and skips the rest of the processing if these header fields are 0. Constructing a bytecode executable that lacks a symbol table and string table can be done for the sake of saving file space, or to prevent a third party from peeking at your application.

PopulateDebugData() is pretty much done with the header after readHeader-Rec() returns. The header will be used in initHEC() to validate the executable and set up the address space of the virtual machine. Once the header is read, populate-DebugData() reads the table of contents from the symbol table of the executable. The table of contents is processed by calling the readContents() function.

```
struct Contents readContents(FILE* fptr)
{
    struct Contents ct;
    int i;
    i = fread(debugbytes,sizeof(U1),8,fptr);
    if(i<8)
    {
        FCLOSE(fptr);
        FATAL_ERROR1("error reading contents record\n");
    }

    ct.nGlobVarRec = bytecodeToDWord(&(debugbytes[0]));
    ct.nProcRec = bytecodeToDWord(&(debugbytes[4]));

    return(ct);

}/*end readContents*/
```

The whole purpose of the table of contents is to indicate how many global variable records and procedure records there are in the symbol table section. This is important to have because we have to use malloc() to allocate storage for these records in the Debug-Data structure, and in order to do this we need to know how much storage we should allocate.

Once storage for global variables and procedure records has been allocated, the global variable records are read in from the symbol table using the readGlobVarRec() function.

```
struct GlobVarRec readGlobVarRec(FILE *fptr)
{
    struct GlobVarRec gr;
    int i;
    i = fread(debugbytes,sizeof(U1),SIZE_GLOBREC,fptr);
    if(i<SIZE_GLOBREC)
```

```
        {
            FCLOSE(fptr);
            FATAL_ERROR1("error reading global record\n");
        }
        gr.text = bytecodeToQWord(&(debugbytes[0]));
        gr.dType = debugbytes[8];
        gr.len = bytecodeToQWord(&(debugbytes[9]));
        gr.size = bytecodeToQWord(&(debugbytes[17]));
        gr.offset = bytecodeToQWord(&(debugbytes[25]));
        gr.line = bytecodeToDWord(&(debugbytes[33]));

        return(gr);

}/*end readGlobVarRec*/
```

After `populateDebugData()` has processed the global variable records, it reads the procedure records using the `readProcRec()` function.

```
struct ProcRec readProcRec(FILE *fptr)
{
        struct ProcRec pr;
        int i;
        i = fread(debugbytes,sizeof(U1),SIZE_PROCREC,fptr);
        if(i<SIZE_PROCREC)
        {
            FCLOSE(fptr);
            FATAL_ERROR1("error reading procedure record\n");
        }

        pr.text = bytecodeToQWord(&(debugbytes[0]));
        pr.address = bytecodeToQWord(&(debugbytes[8]));
        pr.line = bytecodeToDWord(&(debugbytes[16]));
        pr.nRet = debugbytes[20];
        pr.nArg = debugbytes[21];
        pr.nLocal = debugbytes[22];
        pr.nLabel = bytecodeToWord(&(debugbytes[23]));

        pr.arg = (struct StackFrameRec *)malloc(pr.nArg*sizeof(struct StackFrameRec));
        pr.local= (struct StackFrameRec *)malloc(pr.nLocal*sizeof(struct StackFrameRec));
        pr.label= (struct LabelRec *)malloc(pr.nLabel*sizeof(struct LabelRec));

        if(pr.arg==NULL)
        {
            FCLOSE(fptr);
            FATAL_ERROR1("could not allocate procedure-argument records\n");
        }
        if(pr.local==NULL)
        {
            FCLOSE(fptr);
            FATAL_ERROR1("could not allocate procedure-local records\n");
        }
        if(pr.label==NULL)
        {
            FCLOSE(fptr);
```

```
                          FATAL_ERROR1("could not allocate procedure-label records\n");
            }

            if(pr.nRet)
            {
                      pr.ret = readStackFrameRec(fptr);
            }
            for(i=0;i<pr.nArg;i++)
            {
                      pr.arg[i]= readStackFrameRec(fptr);
            }
            for(i=0;i<pr.nLocal;i++)
            {
                      pr.local[i]= readStackFrameRec(fptr);
            }
            for(i=0;i<pr.nLabel;i++)
            {
                      pr.label[i]= readLabelRec(fptr);
            }

            return(pr);

}/*end readProcRec*/
```

As I've described earlier, each procedure record in the symbol table is followed by its own private entourage of return value, argument, local variable, and label records. The `readProcRec()` function invokes the `readStackFrameRec()` function to process return value, local variable, and argument records. This is because all of these records have the same basic form. The `readLabelRec()` function is used to read label records.

```
struct StackFrameRec readStackFrameRec(FILE *fptr)
{
      struct StackFrameRec sfr;
      int i;
      i = fread(debugbytes,sizeof(U1),SIZE_RETREC,fptr);
      if(i<SIZE_RETREC)
      {
            FCLOSE(fptr);
            FATAL_ERROR1("error reading stackframe record\n");
      }

      sfr.text = bytecodeToQWord(&(debugbytes[0]));
      sfr.fpOffset = bytecodeToDWord(&(debugbytes[8]));
      sfr.line = bytecodeToDWord(&(debugbytes[12]));

      return(sfr);

}/*end readStackFramerec*/

struct LabelRec readLabelRec(FILE *fptr)
{
      struct LabelRec lr;
      int i;
      i = fread(debugbytes,sizeof(U1),SIZE_LBLREC,fptr);
```

```
        if(i<SIZE_LBLREC)
        {
              FCLOSE(fptr);
              FATAL_ERROR1("error reading label record\n");
        }

        lr.text = bytecodeToQWord(&(debugbytes[0]));
        lr.address = bytecodeToQWord(&(debugbytes[8]));
        lr.line = bytecodeToDWord(&(debugbytes[16]));

        return(lr);

}/*end readLabelRec*/
```

Once the `readProcRec()` function has returned to `populateDebugData()`, the `populateDebugData()` function reads in the string table from the bytecode executable. This is the last step of the journey with regard to extracting debug information from the bytecode executable.

In `dbgdata.c`, I've also included a collection of functions that will allow you to examine the data structures that are populated. I used these functions to check my work while I was constructing this part of the HEC run-time. If the DBG_INIT macro is defined in the `init.c` source file, then the PRINT_SYM_TBL macro, used in `init.c`, resolves to:

```
        #define PRINT_SYM_TBL();              printDebugData(&debugData);
```

The invocation of `printDebugData()`, in turn, leads to the following functions being called:

```
void printDebugData(struct DebugData *ptr);
void printProcRec(struct ProcRec *pptr, struct DebugData *ptr);
void printStackFrameRec(struct StackFrameRec *sptr, struct DebugData *ptr);
void printLabelRec(struct LabelRec *lptr, struct DebugData *ptr);
```

As with `populateDebugData()`, all the related subtasks that need to be performed branch off from a single routine, which in this case is the `printDebugData()` function. The basic game plan consists of traversing the data structure tree built by `populateDebugData()`.

```
void printDebugData(struct DebugData *ptr)
{
        U8 i;

        for(i=0;i<((*ptr).contents).nGlobVarRec;i++)
        {
              printf("GLOBVAR "); pU8(i); printf("\n");
              printf("\tid=%s\n",&((*ptr).strTbl[(*ptr).gvRec[i].text]));
              printf("\ttype=%s",globSz[(*ptr).gvRec[i].dType]);
              printf("\tlen="); pU8((*ptr).gvRec[i].len); printf("\n");
              printf("\tsize="); pU8((*ptr).gvRec[i].size); printf("\n");
              printf("\toffset="); pS8((*ptr).gvRec[i].offset); printf("\n");
              printf("\tline="); pU4((*ptr).gvRec[i].line); printf("\n\n");
        }
```

```c
        for(i=0;i<((*ptr).contents).nProcRec;i++)
        {
            printf("PROC "); pU8(i); printf("\n");
            printProcRec(&((*ptr).pRec[i]),ptr);
        }

        return;

}/*end printDebugData*/

void printProcRec(struct ProcRec *pptr, struct DebugData *ptr)
{
    U4 i;

    printf("\tid=%s\n",&((*ptr).strTbl[(*pptr).text]));
    printf("\taddress="); pU8((*pptr).address); printf("\n");
    printf("\tline="); pU4((*pptr).line); printf("\n");
    if((*pptr).nRet)
    {
        printf("\tRET\n");
        printStackFrameRec(&((*pptr).ret), ptr);
    }
    for(i=0;i<(*pptr).nArg;i++)
    {
        printf("\tARG->"); pU4(i); printf("\n");
        printStackFrameRec(&((*pptr).arg[i]), ptr);
    }
    for(i=0;i<(*pptr).nLocal;i++)
    {
        printf("\tLOCAL->"); pU4(i); printf("\n");
        printStackFrameRec(&((*pptr).local[i]), ptr);
    }
    for(i=0;i<(*pptr).nLabel;i++)
    {
        printf("\tLABEL->"); pU4(i); printf("\n");
        printLabelRec(&((*pptr).label[i]), ptr);
    }
    return;

}/*end printProcRec*/

void printStackFrameRec(struct StackFrameRec *sptr, struct DebugData *ptr)
{
    printf("\t\tid=%s\n",&((*ptr).strTbl[(*sptr).text]));
    printf("\t\tfpOffset="); pS4((*sptr).fpOffset); printf("\n");
    printf("\t\tline="); pU4((*sptr).line); printf("\n");
    return;

}/*end printStackFrameRec*/

void printLabelRec(struct LabelRec *lptr, struct DebugData *ptr)
{
    printf("\t\tid=%s\n",&((*ptr).strTbl[(*lptr).text]));
    printf("\t\taddress="); pU8((*lptr).address); printf("\n");
```

```
    printf("\t\tline="); pU4((*lptr).line); printf("\n");
    return;

}/*end printLabelRec*/
```

 NOTE   There's one scenario that I haven't planned for: What if the header section or symbol table section of the bytecode executable is corrupt? In the current release of the HEC virtual machine, you are out of luck. The HEC virtual machine assumes that the assembler has done its job correctly. This places a lot of trust in the assembler and also leaves the HEC virtual machine open to malicious bytecode. A corrupt symbol table is not a huge problem. The worst thing that could happen is that the symbol information a debugger produces is incorrect. A corrupt header is a much bigger problem because you could end up executing instructions which are actually part of the string table or symbol table, and this could lead to some rather spectacular crashes.

The Problem with Structures

There is one important point about my implementation that I would like to mention. The average engineer would be tempted to implement symbol table records as structures and then persist them to a file by writing the structures themselves to the file in binary mode.

Take the following example, where I populate a structure, write the structure to a file, and then read it from the file:

```
#include<stdio.h>

struct MyStruct
{
    char ch;
    short si;
    int i;
    unsigned long uli;
    float f;
};

struct MyStruct write;
struct MyStruct read;

void main()
{
    int ret;
    FILE *fptr;

    if((fptr = fopen("myfile.bin","wb"))==NULL)
    {
        printf("could not open file for writing\n");
    }

    write.ch='a';
    write.si=-5;
    write.i=123456;
```

```
        write.uli=(unsigned long)754887987;
        write.f=-1.2e+4;

        printf("sizeof(MyStruct)=%d\n",sizeof(struct MyStruct));

        ret = fwrite(&write,sizeof(struct MyStruct),1,fptr);
        if(ret<1){ printf("error writing\n"); return; }

        if(fclose(fptr)){ printf("error closing file\n"); return; }

        if((fptr = fopen("myfile.bin","rb"))==NULL)
        {
            printf("could not open file for reading\n");
        }

        ret = fread(&read,sizeof(struct MyStruct),1,fptr);
        if(ret<1){ printf("error reading\n"); return; }

        printf("read.ch=%c\n",read.ch);
        printf("read.si=%d\n",read.si);
        printf("read.i=%d\n",read.i);
        printf("read.uli=%lu\n",read.uli);
        printf("read.f=%f\n",read.f);

        fclose(fptr);
        return;
}
```

This technique is conceptually tidy because it reinforces the idea that a record is a collection of related fields. However, there is a big problem with this approach. It is a problem that I am aware of only because a senior architect at an ERP company pointed it out to me. The structure-related flaw I'm about to discuss innocently appeared in the core middleware of the aforementioned ERP company back in the 1980s. It has haunted the company for the past 15 years and caused them all sorts of untold grief. By the time they discovered the flaw, it was too late: The flaw had become an established part of the code base and was everywhere. As a result, the company had to invest effort in working around the problem instead of eliminating it.

The problem with reading and writing structures to a file is that the byte size a structure assumes can vary from one hardware platform to the next. Specifically, the value returned by the `sizeof()` operator in the previous example will return a different value depending on the hardware platform. This is primarily due to the fact that processors have different memory alignment constraints with regard to data types.

For example, a four-byte integer, on some platforms, must begin at an address that is a multiple of four. Another way of saying this is that the four-byte integer must begin on a byte boundary that is a multiple of four. On other platforms, a four-byte integer can begin at any address.

Take, for example, the following structure:

```
struct Record
{
```

```
    int i;
    char ch;
};
```

On a platform where integers are four bytes long and must begin on a byte boundary that is a multiple of four, the Record structure will take up eight bytes (four bytes for the integer, a byte for the character, and three bytes of padding). If you have an array of such structures, this guarantees that the integer member of each structure element in the array will begin at an address that is a multiple of four. See Figure 4-10 for an illustration of this.

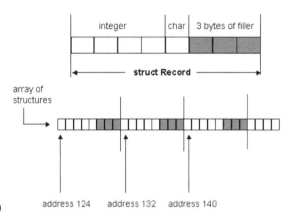

Figure 4-10

The end result of this is that using structures to directly construct an executable's symbol table would tie the executable to the platform on which it was built.

If you'll recall, portability is my primary concern. I avoided the structure size pitfall by writing and reading the symbol table on a field-by-field level of granularity. If you take a second look at readHeaderRec(), readContents(), readGlobVarRec(), etc., you will see how I did this.

Processing Debug Commands

As stated earlier, the CmdLine structure passed to the run() function will determine if the HEC virtual machine starts in debug mode or not. If you take a look at the run() function defined in run.c, you will see that if debug is set to true, a call to readDbgCmd() will be performed. The readDbgCmd() function is defined in the dbgcmd.c source file. This routine is what places the HEC machine into debug mode. The following code provides a brief sketch of what this function does.

```
void readDbgCmd()
{
    int size;

    printf("\n");

    while(1)
    {
```

```
                    printf("debug>");
                    scanf("%s",debugLine);

                    size = strlen(debugLine);
                    if(size>=MAX_DBG_CHARS)
                    {
                          ERRORO_LVL2("error: input command out of bounds");
                    }

                    switch(debugLine[0])
                    {
                          case command_char :
                          {
                                // handle command
                          }break;
                          .
                          .
                          .
                          default:{ BAD_CMD(); }

                    }/*end switch*/

                    if(fflush(stdin)){ ERRORO_LVL2("error: flushing STDIN\n"); }

              }/*end while*/

              return;

       }/*end readDbgCmd*/
```

As you can see, `readDbgCmd()` displays a debug command prompt and then accepts debugger commands. The command string scanned in enters a lengthy switch statement, which I have not entirely fleshed out. Each debugger command has an associated case block inside of this switch statement. What I'm going to do for the remainder of this section is present each command, show you its corresponding case block, and then discuss implementation-specific details.

? - Help

This command prints a brief list of debugger commands to the console.

```
       case '?':
       {
             if(debugLine[1]=='\0'){ printHelp(); }
             else{ BAD_CMD(); }

       }break;
```

Specifically, this command makes use of the `printHelp()` function.

```
 void printHelp()
 {
     printf("\nHEng debug mode help\n");
     printf("--------------------\n");
```

```
printf("?\ndisplay this help screen\n\n");
printf("d start stop\ndump memory in the range [start, stop]\n\n");
printf("f\ndisplay executable file information\n\n");
printf("l string\nquery meta-data for a program identifier\n\n");
printf("p\nquery current procedure\n\n");
printf("q\nexit debug mode and return to production mode\n\n");
printf("ri\ndisplay integer registers\n\n");
printf("rf\ndisplay float registers\n\n");
printf("rd\ndisplay double registers\n\n");
printf("s start stop string\nsearch memory range [start, stop]\n\n");
printf("t\ntrace through next instruction\n\n");
return;

}/*end printHelp*/
```

Q - Quit

The quit command toggles the virtual machine out of debug mode, exits the debugger, and then turns control back to run().

```
case 'q':
case 'Q':
{
        if(debugLine[1]=='\0')
        {
                toggleDebugging(DEBUG_OFF);
                return;
        }
        else{ BAD_CMD(); }

}break;
```

To get the virtual machine out of debug mode, the quit command uses the toggle-Debugging() function.

```
void toggleDebugging(int state)
{
    if(state==DEBUG_ON){ debug = TRUE; }
    else if(state==DEBUG_OFF){ debug = FALSE; }
    else
    {
        ERROR0_LVL2("invalid state change request\n");
        debug = TRUE;
    }
    return;

}/*end toggleDebugging*/
```

F - Executable Information

This gives a summary of general status information that the virtual machine has collected. Most of this information concerns the bytecode file (hence the command letter "F," as in File).

```
case 'f':
case 'F':
{
    if(debugLine[1]=='\0'){ printAppData(); }
    else{ BAD_CMD(); }
}break;
```

This command makes use of the `printAppData()` function.

```
void printAppData()
{
    printf("\nEXECUTABLE FILE---------------------\n");
    printf("file name->%s\n",appMetaData.fileName);
    printf("file size->"); pU8(appMetaData.fileSize);
    printf("\nfile symbol table size->"); pU8(appMetaData.szSymTbl);
    printf("\nfile string table size->"); pU8(appMetaData.szStrTbl);
    printf("\nfile bytecode size->"); pU8(appMetaData.szByteCode);
    printf("\nbytecode offset begin in file->")
            pU8(appMetaData.bCodeFileStart);
    printf("\nbytecode offset end in file->"); pU8(appMetaData.bCodeFileEnd);
    printf("\n\nMEMORY LAYOUT-----------------------\n");
    printf("heap allocated->"); pU8(appMetaData.heapSize);
    printf("\nstack allocated->"); pU8(appMetaData.stackSize);
    printf("\ntotal ram->"); pU8(appMetaData.ram);
    printf("\n\n");
    return;

}/*end printFileData*/
```

The `printAppData()` function basically displays the contents of the `AppMetaData` structure we encountered earlier. The `AppMetaData` structure has its fields populated both in `cmdline.c` and `init.c`.

D Start Stop - Dump Memory

The dump memory command is used to display the bytes that constitute a specified range of memory.

```
case 'd':
case 'D':
{
    if(debugLine[1]=='\0')
    {
        struct DbgRange rng;
        rng.ok=VALID_RANGE;
        rng = parseRangeStr();
        if(rng.ok!=BAD_RANGE)
        {
            dumpRamRng(rng.start,rng.stop);
        }
    }
    else{ BAD_CMD(); }

}break;
```

To read in the start and end values of the memory range, the dump memory command calls the `parseRangeStr()` function. The `parseRangeStr()` function returns a `DbgRange` structure that contains the values for the start and end of the range.

```
struct DbgRange
{
    U8 start;
    U8 stop;
    int ok;
};
```

The `parseRangeStr()` function also does some bound checking to ensure that the range of memory addresses is valid.

```
struct DbgRange parseRangeStr()
{
    struct DbgRange rng;
    int ret;

    ret = rU8(&rng.start);
    if((ret==EOF)||(ret==0))
    {
        printf("bad start range\n");
        rng.ok=BAD_RANGE;
        return(rng);
    }

    ret = rU8(&rng.stop);
    if((ret==EOF)||(ret==0))
    {
        printf("bad end range\n");
        rng.ok=BAD_RANGE;
        return(rng);
    }

    if((rng.start<0)||(rng.stop<0))
    {
        printf("negative range values not allowed\n");
        rng.ok=BAD_RANGE;
        return(rng);
    }
    else if(rng.start > rng.stop)
    {
        printf(" (start > stop) not allowed\n");
        rng.ok=BAD_RANGE;
        return(rng);
    }

    if(rng.start > R[$TOP])
    {
        printf("range start value is greater than $TOP\n");
        rng.ok=BAD_RANGE;
        return(rng);
    }
```

```
        if(rng.stop > R[$TOP])
        {
            printf("range stop value is greater than $TOP\n");
            rng.ok=BAD_RANGE;
            return(rng);
        }

        return(rng);

}/*end parseRangeStr*/
```

To perform the job of actually displaying the memory bytes, the dump memory command invokes the dumpRamRng() function.

```
void dumpRamRng(U8 strt, U8 stp)
{
    U8 i;
    U8 j;
    j=0;
    printf("\n");
    for(i=strt;i<=stp;i++)
    {
        PRINT_MEM(i); printf("\t");
        if((RAM[i]>32)&&(RAM[i]<127))
        {
            printf("ASCII=%c ",RAM[i]);
        }
        else
        {
            switch(RAM[i])
            {
                case ' ':{ printf("ASCII=<SP>"); }break;
                case '\n':{ printf("ASCII=<TAB>");}break;
                case '\r':{ printf("ASCII=<CR>");}break;
                case '\t':{ printf("ASCII=<NL>");}break;
                default:{ printf("control char(%lu)",RAM[i]); }
            }
        }
        printf("\n");
        j++;
    }
    printf("\n");
    return;

}/*end dumpRamRng*/
```

Note how dumpRamRng() prints the numeric value of the byte (an unsigned value in the range 0 to 255) and then also prints out its ASCII equivalent, if it is in the necessary range.

S Start Stop String - Search for String

The search command searches a specified range of memory for a given string.

```
        case 'S':
        case 's':
```

```
        {
            if(debugLine[1]=='\0'){ searchForStr(); }
            else{ BAD_CMD(); }
        }break;
```

The search command invokes the `searchForStr()` function to perform the search.

```
void searchForStr()
{
    int ret;
    struct DbgRange rng;
    U8 i;
    U4 size;
    U1 found;

    found = FALSE;

    rng.ok = VALID_RANGE;
    rng = parseRangeStr();
    if(rng.ok==BAD_RANGE){ return; }

    ret = scanf("%s",debugLine);
    if((ret==EOF)||(ret==0))
    {
        printf("bad search string entered\n");
        return;
    }

    /* search rng.start->rng.stop for debugLine */

    size = strlen(debugLine);
    if(size==0)
    {
        printf("bad search string entered\n");
        return;
    }

    for(i=rng.start;i<=rng.stop;i++)
    {
        if(RAM[i]==debugLine[0])
        {
            ret = cmpRAMStr(debugLine,&RAM[i],size);
            if(ret==TRUE)
            {
                printf("Match-> address=");
                pU8(i);
                printf("\n");
                found = TRUE;
            }
        }
    }

    if(found==FALSE)
    {
        printf("no such string in memory range ");
```

```
                    pU8(rng.start);
                    printf("->");
                    pU8(rng.stop);
                    printf("\n");
            }
            return;

    }/*end searchForStr*/
```

The searchForStr() function calls parseRangeStr() to read in the range of memory to scan and also uses a function named cmpRAMStr() to check for matches.

```
U1 cmpRAMStr(U1 *ptr1, U1 *ptr2, U4 len)
{
    U4 i;
    for(i=0;i<len;i++)
    {
            if(ptr1[i]!=ptr2[i]){ return(FALSE);}
    }
    return(TRUE);

}/*end cmpRAMStr*/
```

L String - Symbol Lookup

This command searches the debugger's data structures to find an identifier that matches the string specified on the debugger command line. The symbol lookup command begins by invoking the getIdentifierMetaData() function.

```
    case 'L':
    case 'l':
    {
            if(debugLine[1]=='\0'){ getIdentifierMetaData(); }
            else{ BAD_CMD(); }
    }break;
```

Then, the real fun begins. The getIdentifierMetaData() function starts by looking for global variables and procedures whose names might match the specified string. If that doesn't work, symbols that are local to the current procedure will be examined.

```
void getIdentifierMetaData()
{
    int ret;
    S8 proc_ind;

    ret = scanf("%s",debugLine);
    if((ret==EOF)||(ret==0))
    {
            printf("bad identifier entered\n");
            return;
    }

    /* look through globals */

    ret = searchForGlobal(debugLine);
```

```
        if(ret==TRUE){ return; }

        /* if not in globals get current proc */

        proc_ind = showCurrentProc(FALSE);
        if(proc_ind==-1)
        {
            printf("symbol not global, currently outside all procedures\n");
            return;
        }

        ret = matchProcName(debugLine,(U4)proc_ind);
        if(ret==TRUE){ return; }

        /* if not proc name, look for ret, args, locals, and labels */

        ret = searchCurrentProc(debugLine,(U4)proc_ind);
        if(ret==TRUE){ return; }

        printf("could not resolve symbol\n");

        return;

}/*end getIdentifierMetaData*/
```

The `searchForGlobal()` function is invoked by `getIdentifierMetaData()`
in order to check to see if the identifier under scrutiny is a global variable.

```
U1 searchForGlobal(char *str)
{
    U4 i;
    U8 j;
    U8 addr;
    char *temp;

    for(i=0;i<debugData.contents.nGlobVarRec;i++)
    {
        temp = &(debugData.strTbl[debugData.gvRec[i].text]);
        if(strcmp(str,temp)==0)
        {
            printf("global variable->%s\n",str);
            printf("type->%s\n",globSz[debugData.gvRec[i].dType]);
            printf("length->");
            pU8(debugData.gvRec[i].len); printf("\n");
            printf("total size->");
            pU8(debugData.gvRec[i].size); printf("\n");
            printf("line->");
            pU4(debugData.gvRec[i].line); printf("\n");
            printf("values:\n");
            addr = R[$TOP] - debugData.gvRec[i].offset;
            for(j=0;j<debugData.gvRec[i].size;j++)
            {
                printf("\t"); pU8(j+1); printf(") address-> ");
                pU8(addr+j);
```

```
                    printf(" value->%u\n",RAM[addr+j]);
                }
                return(TRUE);
            }
        }
        return(FALSE);

}/*end searchForGlobal*/
```

If the identifier in question is not a global variable, getIdentifierMetaData()
then checks to see if the identifier is the name of a procedure. To perform this check, the
matchProcName() function is invoked.

```
U1 matchProcName(char *str, U4 ind)
{
    char *procname;
    procname = &debugData.strTbl[debugData.pRec[ind].text];
    if(strcmp(str,procname)==0)
    {
        printf("function->%s\n",str);
        printf("address->");
        pU8(debugData.pRec[ind].address); printf("\n");
        printf("line="); pU4(debugData.pRec[ind].line); printf("\n");
        return(TRUE);
    }
    return(FALSE);

}/*end searchForProc*/
```

If the identifier, supplied as an argument to the symbol lookup command, is neither a
global variable nor a procedure, the getIdentifierMetaData() function will look
at the list of symbols defined within the scope of the current executing procedure. Specifically, the searchCurrentProc() function will be called in an effort to determine
if the identifier is the name of a return value, argument, local variable, or label.

```
U1 searchCurrentProc(char *str, U4 ind)
{
    U4 i;
    char *temp;
    U8 addr;
    U1 narg;
    U1 nloc;
    U2 nlbl;
    narg = debugData.pRec[ind].nArg;
    nloc = debugData.pRec[ind].nLocal;
    nlbl = debugData.pRec[ind].nLabel;

    if(debugData.pRec[ind].nRet==1)
    {
        temp = &(debugData.strTbl[debugData.pRec[ind].ret.text]);
        if(strcmp(str,temp)==0)
        {
            printf("return value->%s\n",str);
            printf("address->");
```

```
                      addr = R[$FP]+debugData.pRec[ind].ret.fpOffset;
                      pU8(addr);
                      printf("\n");
                      return(TRUE);
                 }
            }
            for(i=0;i<narg;i++)
            {
                 temp = &(debugData.strTbl[debugData.pRec[ind].arg[i].text]);
                 if(strcmp(str,temp)==0)
                 {
                      printf("procedure argument->%s\n",str);
                      printf("address->");
                      addr = R[$FP]+debugData.pRec[ind].arg[i].fpOffset;
                      pU8(addr);
                      printf("\n");
                      return(TRUE);
                 }
            }
            for(i=0;i<nloc;i++)
            {
                 temp = &(debugData.strTbl[debugData.pRec[ind].local[i].text]);
                 if(strcmp(str,temp)==0)
                 {
                      printf("local storage->%s\n",str);
                      printf("address->");
                      addr = R[$FP]+debugData.pRec[ind].local[i].fpOffset;
                      pU8(addr);
                      printf("\n");
                      return(TRUE);
                 }
            }
            for(i=0;i<nlbl;i++)
            {
                 temp = &(debugData.strTbl[debugData.pRec[ind].label[i].text]);
                 if(strcmp(str,temp)==0)
                 {
                      printf("label->%s\n",str);
                      printf("address->");
                      pU8(debugData.pRec[ind].label[i].address);
                      printf("\n");
                      return(TRUE);
                 }
            }
            return(FALSE);

}/*end searchCurrentProc*/
```

P - Procedure Display

This command displays the name of the current procedure being executed by the bytecode
program in memory.

```
        case 'P':
        case 'p':
        {
            if(debugLine[1]=='\0'){ showCurrentProc(TRUE); }
            else{ BAD_CMD(); }
        }break;
```

The procedure display command relies on the `showCurrentProc()` function to do all the work. The basic idea behind `showCurrentProc()` is to take the current address and then look through the debugger's data structures to find a procedure that has the current address in its range.

```
S8 showCurrentProc(U1 display)
{
    U4 i;
    U4 nprocs;
    nprocs = debugData.contents.nProcRec;
    for(i=0;i<nprocs;i++)
    {
        if(((U8)R[$IP]) > debugData.pRec[nprocs-1].address)
        {
            if(display==TRUE)
            {
                printf("current proc->%s\n",
                &(debugData.strTbl[debugData.pRec[nprocs-1].text]));
                printf("address->");
                pU8(debugData.pRec[nprocs-1].address);
                printf("\n");
                printf("line->"); pU4(debugData.pRec[nprocs-1].line);
                printf("\n");
            }
            return(nprocs-1);
        }
        else if((debugData.pRec[i].address <= ((U8)R[$IP]))&&
                (debugData.pRec[i+1].address > ((U8)R[$IP])))
        {
            if(display==TRUE)
            {
                printf("current proc->%s\n",
                &(debugData.strTbl[debugData.pRec[i].text]));
                printf("address->");
                pU8(debugData.pRec[i].address);
                printf("\n");
                printf("line->"); pU4(debugData.pRec[i].line);
                printf("\n");
            }
            return(i);
        }
    }
    printf("could not find current function\n");
    return(-1);

}/*end showCurrentProc*/
```

RX - Register Display (Ri, Rf, Rd)

This series of three commands displays the contents of the registers. The Ri command displays all the integer-valued registers. The Rf command displays all the single-precision floating-point registers. The Rd command displays all the double-precision floating-point registers. These three commands invoke functions that are defined in exenv.c.

```
case 'R':
case 'r':
{
        if((debugLine[1]=='i')&&(debugLine[2]=='\0'))
        {
            printBasicRegisters();
            printGeneralRegisters();
        }
        else if((debugLine[1]=='f')&&(debugLine[2]=='\0'))
        {
            printFloatRegisters();
        }
        else if((debugLine[1]=='d')&&(debugLine[2]=='\0'))
        {
            printDoubleRegisters();
        }
        else{ BAD_CMD(); }

}break;
```

T - Trace

The trace command causes the next bytecode instruction to be executed and then transfers program control back to the debugger.

```
case 'T':
case 't':
{
        if(debugLine[1]=='\0'){ return; }
        else{ BAD_CMD(); }
}break;
```

Every time an instruction gets executed when the virtual machine is in debug mode, the virtual machine will (from within the body of the run() function) invoke print-DbgInstr(). The printDbgInstr() function is responsible for printing the instruction that was most recently executed by the virtual machine. Both the disassembled, human-readable version of the instruction and its binary equivalent are displayed.

Also, because the $IP register is updated during the course of an instruction's execution, the original value of $IP is saved in a variable named start_debug_instr. If you take a look at the run() function, you will notice this variable. This variable is what gets passed as an argument to printDbgInstr() when it is called.

```
void printDbgInstr(U8 addr)
{
    /*display in assembler and in binary*/
```

```
U8 current_byte; /*lookahead from addr*/
U1 raw[11];      /*buffer to hold binary representation*/

current_byte = addr;

printf("address->"); pU8(addr); printf("\n");

switch(RAM[current_byte])
{
    case LBI:  /* LBI $r1, byte constant  BBB */
    {
        printf("%s ",I_Set[RAM[current_byte]]);
        raw[0] = RAM[current_byte];
        current_byte++;

        printf("%s ",R_STR[RAM[current_byte]]);
        raw[1] = RAM[current_byte];
        current_byte++;

        printf("%d\n",(S1)RAM[current_byte]);
        raw[2] = RAM[current_byte];

        printRawBytes(raw,3);

    }break;
    case LWI:  /* LWI $r1, word constant  BBW */
    {
        S2 *si;

        printf("%s ",I_Set[RAM[current_byte]]);
        raw[0] = RAM[current_byte];
        current_byte++;

        printf(" %s ",R_STR[RAM[current_byte]]);
        raw[1] = RAM[current_byte];
        current_byte++;

        raw[2] = RAM[current_byte];
        current_byte++;
        raw[3] = RAM[current_byte];

        si = ((S2*)(&RAM[current_byte-1]));
        pS2(*si); printf("\n");

        printRawBytes(raw,4);

    }break;
    case LDI:  /* LDI $r1, dword constant  BBD */
    {
        S4 *li;

        printf("%s ",I_Set[RAM[current_byte]]);
```

```
                        raw[0] = RAM[current_byte];
                        current_byte++;

                        printf("%s ",R_STR[RAM[current_byte]]);
                        raw[1] = RAM[current_byte];
                        current_byte++;

                        raw[2] = RAM[current_byte];
                        current_byte++;
                        raw[3] = RAM[current_byte];
                        current_byte++;
                        raw[4] = RAM[current_byte];
                        current_byte++;
                        raw[5] = RAM[current_byte];

                        li = (S4 *)&RAM[current_byte-3];
                        pS4(*li); printf("\n");

                        printRawBytes(raw,6);

                }break;
                case LQI:   /* LQI $r1, qword constant  BBQ*/
                {
                        printf("%s ",I_Set[RAM[current_byte]]);
                        raw[0] = RAM[current_byte];
                        current_byte++;

                        printf("%s ",R_STR[RAM[current_byte]]);
                        raw[1] = RAM[current_byte];
                        current_byte++;

                        raw[2] = RAM[current_byte];
                        current_byte++;
                        raw[3] = RAM[current_byte];
                        current_byte++;
                        raw[4] = RAM[current_byte];
                        current_byte++;
                        raw[5] = RAM[current_byte];
                        current_byte++;
                        raw[6] = RAM[current_byte];
                        current_byte++;
                        raw[7] = RAM[current_byte];
                        current_byte++;
                        raw[8] = RAM[current_byte];
                        current_byte++;
                        raw[9] = RAM[current_byte];

                        pS8(*((S8 *)&RAM[current_byte-7]));
                        printf("\n");
                        printRawBytes(raw,10);

                }break;
                case LF1I:  /* LF1I $f, float */
                {
```

```
                F4 *fi;

                printf("%s ",I_Set[RAM[current_byte]]);
                raw[0] = RAM[current_byte];
                current_byte++;

                printf("%s ",Rf_STR[RAM[current_byte]]);
                raw[1] = RAM[current_byte];
                current_byte++;

                raw[2] = RAM[current_byte];
                current_byte++;
                raw[3] = RAM[current_byte];
                current_byte++;
                raw[4] = RAM[current_byte];
                current_byte++;
                raw[5] = RAM[current_byte];

                fi = (F4 *)&RAM[current_byte-3];
                printf("%g\n",*fi);

                printRawBytes(raw,6);

        }break;
        case LF2I:  /* LF2I $d, double */
        {
                F8 *di;

                printf("%s ",I_Set[RAM[current_byte]]);
                raw[0] = RAM[current_byte];
                current_byte++;

                printf("%s ",Rd_STR[RAM[current_byte]]);
                raw[1] = RAM[current_byte];
                current_byte++;

                raw[2] = RAM[current_byte];
                current_byte++;
                raw[3] = RAM[current_byte];
                current_byte++;
                raw[4] = RAM[current_byte];
                current_byte++;
                raw[5] = RAM[current_byte];
                current_byte++;
                raw[6] = RAM[current_byte];
                current_byte++;
                raw[7] = RAM[current_byte];
                current_byte++;
                raw[8] = RAM[current_byte];
                current_byte++;
                raw[9] = RAM[current_byte];

                di = (F8 *)&RAM[current_byte-7];
```

```
                printf("%g\n",*di);

                printRawBytes(raw,10);

        }break;
        case LAD:   /* LAD $r1, address = BBQ */
        {
                printf("%s ",I_Set[RAM[current_byte]]);
                raw[0] = RAM[current_byte];
                current_byte++;

                printf("%s ",R_STR[RAM[current_byte]]);
                raw[1] = RAM[current_byte];
                current_byte++;

                raw[2] = RAM[current_byte];
                current_byte++;
                raw[3] = RAM[current_byte];
                current_byte++;
                raw[4] = RAM[current_byte];
                current_byte++;
                raw[5] = RAM[current_byte];
                current_byte++;
                raw[6] = RAM[current_byte];
                current_byte++;
                raw[7] = RAM[current_byte];
                current_byte++;
                raw[8] = RAM[current_byte];
                current_byte++;
                raw[9] = RAM[current_byte];

                pU8(*((U8 *)&RAM[current_byte-7]));
                printf("\n");
                printRawBytes(raw,10);

        }break;
        case LAI:   /* LAI $r1, $r2, qword       BBBQ*/
        {
                printf("%s ",I_Set[RAM[current_byte]]);
                raw[0] = RAM[current_byte];
                current_byte++;

                printf("%s ",R_STR[RAM[current_byte]]);
                raw[1] = RAM[current_byte];
                current_byte++;

                printf("%s ",R_STR[RAM[current_byte]]);
                raw[2] = RAM[current_byte];
                current_byte++;

                raw[3] = RAM[current_byte];
                current_byte++;
                raw[4] = RAM[current_byte];
                current_byte++;
```

```
                            raw[5] = RAM[current_byte];
                            current_byte++;
                            raw[6] = RAM[current_byte];
                            current_byte++;
                            raw[7] = RAM[current_byte];
                            current_byte++;
                            raw[8] = RAM[current_byte];
                            current_byte++;
                            raw[9] = RAM[current_byte];
                            current_byte++;
                            raw[10] = RAM[current_byte];

                            pS8(*((S8 *)&RAM[current_byte-7]));
                            printf("\n");
                            printRawBytes(raw,11);

                    }break;
                    case LB:    /* LB $r1,$r2     BBB */
                    case LW:
                    case LD:
                    case LQ:
                    case SB:    /* SB $r1,$r2     BBB*/
                    case SW:
                    case SD:
                    case SQ:
                    case MOV:   /* MOV $r1, $r2     BBB */
                    {
                            printf("%s ",I_Set[RAM[current_byte]]);
                            raw[0] = RAM[current_byte];
                            current_byte++;

                            printf("%s ",R_STR[RAM[current_byte]]);
                            raw[1] = RAM[current_byte];
                            current_byte++;

                            printf("%s\n",R_STR[RAM[current_byte]]);
                            raw[2] = RAM[current_byte];

                            printRawBytes(raw,3);

                    }break;
                    case LF1:   /* LF1  $f, $r */
                    case SF1:
                    {
                            printf("%s ",I_Set[RAM[current_byte]]);
                            raw[0] = RAM[current_byte];
                            current_byte++;

                            printf("%s ",Rf_STR[RAM[current_byte]]);
                            raw[1] = RAM[current_byte];
                            current_byte++;

                            printf("%s\n",R_STR[RAM[current_byte]]);
```

```c
            raw[2] = RAM[current_byte];

            printRawBytes(raw,3);

    }break;
    case LF2:   /* LF2  $d, $r */
    case SF2:
    {
            printf("%s ",I_Set[RAM[current_byte]]);
            raw[0] = RAM[current_byte];
            current_byte++;

            printf("%s ",Rd_STR[RAM[current_byte]]);
            raw[1] = RAM[current_byte];
            current_byte++;

            printf("%s\n",R_STR[RAM[current_byte]]);
            raw[2] = RAM[current_byte];
            printRawBytes(raw,3);

    }break;
    case MOVF: /*MOVF  $f1, $f2*/
    {
            printf("%s ",I_Set[RAM[current_byte]]);
            raw[0] = RAM[current_byte];
            current_byte++;

            printf("%s ",Rf_STR[RAM[current_byte]]);
            raw[1] = RAM[current_byte];
            current_byte++;

            printf("%s\n",Rf_STR[RAM[current_byte]]);
            raw[2] = RAM[current_byte];

            printRawBytes(raw,3);

    }break;
    case MOVD: /*MOVD  $d1, $d2*/
    {
            printf("%s ",I_Set[RAM[current_byte]]);
            raw[0] = RAM[current_byte];
            current_byte++;

            printf("%s ",Rd_STR[RAM[current_byte]]);
            raw[1] = RAM[current_byte];
            current_byte++;

            printf("%s\n",Rd_STR[RAM[current_byte]]);
            raw[2] = RAM[current_byte];

            printRawBytes(raw,3);

    }break;
    case PUSHB: /* PUSHB $r1  BB */
```

```
case PUSHW:
case PUSHD:
case PUSHQ:
case POPB:
case POPW:
case POPD:
case POPQ:
{
     printf("%s ",I_Set[RAM[current_byte]]);
     raw[0] = RAM[current_byte];
     current_byte++;

     printf("%s\n",R_STR[RAM[current_byte]]);
     raw[1] = RAM[current_byte];

     printRawBytes(raw,2);

}break;
case PUSHF1:      /* PUSHF1 $f */
case POPF1:
{
     printf("%s ",I_Set[RAM[current_byte]]);
     raw[0] = RAM[current_byte];
     current_byte++;

     printf("%s\n",Rf_STR[RAM[current_byte]]);
     raw[1] = RAM[current_byte];

     printRawBytes(raw,2);

}break;
case PUSHF2:      /* PUSHF2 $d */
case POPF2:
{
     printf("%s ",I_Set[RAM[current_byte]]);
     raw[0] = RAM[current_byte];
     current_byte++;

     printf("%s\n",Rd_STR[RAM[current_byte]]);
     raw[1] = RAM[current_byte];

     printRawBytes(raw,2);

}break;
case JMP:   /* JMP $r1 */
{
     printf("%s ",I_Set[RAM[current_byte]]);
     raw[0] = RAM[current_byte];
     current_byte++;

     printf("%s\n",R_STR[RAM[current_byte]]);
     raw[1] = RAM[current_byte];
```

```
                                printRawBytes(raw,2);

                }break;
                case JE:    /*JE $r1, $r2, $r3 BBBB */
                case JNE:
                case SLT:
                case AND:    /* AND $r1, $r2, $r3 */
                case OR:
                case XOR:
                case BT:
                case SRA:   /*SRA   $r1, $r2, $r3    BBBB */
                case SRL:
                case SL:
                case ADD: /* ADD $r1, $r2, $r3   */
                case SUB:
                case MULT:
                {
                        printf("%s ",I_Set[RAM[current_byte]]);
                        raw[0] = RAM[current_byte];
                        current_byte++;

                        printf("%s ",R_STR[RAM[current_byte]]);
                        raw[1] = RAM[current_byte];
                        current_byte++;

                        printf("%s ",R_STR[RAM[current_byte]]);
                        raw[2] = RAM[current_byte];
                        current_byte++;

                        printf("%s\n",R_STR[RAM[current_byte]]);
                        raw[3] = RAM[current_byte];

                        printRawBytes(raw,4);

                }break;
                case INT: /* INT #vector      BB */
                {
                        printf("%s ",I_Set[RAM[current_byte]]);
                        raw[0] = RAM[current_byte];
                        current_byte++;

                        printf("%u\n",RAM[current_byte]);
                        raw[1] = RAM[current_byte];

                        printRawBytes(raw,2);

                }break;
                case EI:          /* EI      B */
                case DI:
                case HALT:
                case NOP:
                {
                        printf("%s\n",I_Set[RAM[current_byte]]);
```

```
                raw[0] = RAM[current_byte];

                printRawBytes(raw,1);

    }break;
    case NOT:  /* NOT $r1, $r2 */
    case DS:
    {
                printf("%s ",I_Set[RAM[current_byte]]);
                raw[0] = RAM[current_byte];
                current_byte++;

                printf("%s ",R_STR[RAM[current_byte]]);
                raw[1] = RAM[current_byte];
                current_byte++;

                printf("%s\n",R_STR[RAM[current_byte]]);
                raw[2] = RAM[current_byte];
                printRawBytes(raw,3);

    }break;
    case DIV:  /* DIV $r1, $r2, $r3, $r4 */
    {
                printf("%s ",I_Set[RAM[current_byte]]);
                raw[0] = RAM[current_byte];
                current_byte++;

                printf("%s ",R_STR[RAM[current_byte]]);
                raw[1] = RAM[current_byte];
                current_byte++;

                printf("%s ",R_STR[RAM[current_byte]]);
                raw[2] = RAM[current_byte];
                current_byte++;

                printf("%s ",R_STR[RAM[current_byte]]);
                raw[3] = RAM[current_byte];
                current_byte++;

                printf("%s\n",R_STR[RAM[current_byte]]);
                raw[4] = RAM[current_byte];

                printRawBytes(raw,5);

    }break;
    case CAST_IF: /* CAST_IF $r, $f  BBB*/
    {
                printf("%s ",I_Set[RAM[current_byte]]);
                raw[0] = RAM[current_byte];
                current_byte++;

                printf("%s ",R_STR[RAM[current_byte]]);
                raw[1] = RAM[current_byte];
```

```
                    current_byte++;

                    printf("%s\n",Rf_STR[RAM[current_byte]]);
                    raw[2] = RAM[current_byte];

                    printRawBytes(raw,3);

            }break;
            case CAST_ID: /* CAST_ID $r, $d  BBB*/
            {
                    printf("%s ",I_Set[RAM[current_byte]]);
                    raw[0] = RAM[current_byte];
                    current_byte++;

                    printf("%s ",R_STR[RAM[current_byte]]);
                    raw[1] = RAM[current_byte];
                    current_byte++;

                    printf("%s\n",Rd_STR[RAM[current_byte]]);
                    raw[2] = RAM[current_byte];

                    printRawBytes(raw,3);

            }break;
            case CAST_FI: /* CAST_FI $f, $r  BBB*/
            {
                    printf("%s ",I_Set[RAM[current_byte]]);
                    raw[0] = RAM[current_byte];
                    current_byte++;

                    printf("%s ",Rf_STR[RAM[current_byte]]);
                    raw[1] = RAM[current_byte];
                    current_byte++;

                    printf("%s\n",R_STR[RAM[current_byte]]);
                    raw[2] = RAM[current_byte];

                    printRawBytes(raw,3);

            }break;
            case CAST_FD: /* CAST_FD $f, $d  BBB*/
            {
                    printf("%s ",I_Set[RAM[current_byte]]);
                    raw[0] = RAM[current_byte];
                    current_byte++;

                    printf("%s ",Rf_STR[RAM[current_byte]]);
                    raw[1] = RAM[current_byte];
                    current_byte++;

                    printf("%s\n",Rd_STR[RAM[current_byte]]);
                    raw[2] = RAM[current_byte];
```

```
                    printRawBytes(raw,3);

        }break;
        case CAST_DI: /* CAST_DI $d, $r  BBB*/
        {
             printf("%s ",I_Set[RAM[current_byte]]);
             raw[0] - RAM[current_byte];
             current_byte++;

             printf("%s ",Rd_STR[RAM[current_byte]]);
             raw[1] = RAM[current_byte];
             current_byte++;

             printf("%s\n",R_STR[RAM[current_byte]]);
             raw[2] = RAM[current_byte];

             printRawBytes(raw,3);

        }break;
        case CAST_DF: /* CAST_DF $d, $f  BBB*/
        {
             printf("%s ",I_Set[RAM[current_byte]]);
             raw[0] = RAM[current_byte];
             current_byte++;

             printf("%s ",Rd_STR[RAM[current_byte]]);
             raw[1] = RAM[current_byte];
             current_byte++;

             printf("%s\n",Rf_STR[RAM[current_byte]]);
             raw[2] = RAM[current_byte];

             printRawBytes(raw,3);

        }break;
        case FADD: /* FADD $f1, $f2, $f3    BBBB */
        case FSUB:
        case FMULT:
        case FDIV:
        case FSLT:
        {
             printf("%s ",I_Set[RAM[current_byte]]);
             raw[0] - RAM[current_byte];
             current_byte++;

             printf("%s ",Rf_STR[RAM[current_byte]]);
             raw[1] = RAM[current_byte];
             current_byte++;

             printf("%s ",Rf_STR[RAM[current_byte]]);
             raw[2] = RAM[current_byte];
             current_byte++;

             printf("%s\n",Rf_STR[RAM[current_byte]]);
```

```
                            raw[3] = RAM[current_byte];

                            printRawBytes(raw,4);

                }break;
                case DADD: /* DADD $d1, $d2, $d3    BBBB */
                case DSUB:
                case DMULT:
                case DDIV:
                case DSLT:
                {
                            printf("%s ",I_Set[RAM[current_byte]]);
                            raw[0] = RAM[current_byte];
                            current_byte++;

                            printf("%s ",Rd_STR[RAM[current_byte]]);
                            raw[1] = RAM[current_byte];
                            current_byte++;

                            printf("%s ",Rd_STR[RAM[current_byte]]);
                            raw[2] = RAM[current_byte];
                            current_byte++;

                            printf("%s\n",Rd_STR[RAM[current_byte]]);
                            raw[3] = RAM[current_byte];

                            printRawBytes(raw,4);

                }break;
                default:
                {
                            printf("instruction (%u), not handled\n",RAM[current_byte]);
                }
        }

        printBasicRegisters();
        return;

}/*end void printDbgInstr*/
```

Future Considerations

I am more than aware that the HEC debugger is a pretty rough implementation and has its limitations. In the next version of the HEC debugger, I am thinking of implementing a number of improvements. This section discusses a few of the potential features for the next release.

Faster Algorithms

The data structures the HEC debugger uses are simple array-based lists. The debugger uses arrays instead of linked lists because bytecode executables contain length information in their symbol tables. There are, however, performance issues with the array-based lists that the debugger uses. For example, none of the elements in the lists are sorted. This means that the debugger may have to traverse an entire list to find a particular symbol.

Initially, I thought that this would not be a major problem. The debugger involves a lot of run-time interaction with the user and I assumed that the user's "think time" would overshadow any shortcomings with respect to performance. In other words, a debugger is more of an OLAP (online analytic processing) application. Most compilers and assemblers are OLTP (online transaction processing) type applications, where the name of the game is throughput speed. OLAP programs, on the other hand, require user input at run time and this allows less emphasis to be placed on performance. A user making simple queries at the command line usually cannot tell the difference between a query that takes 1 millisecond and one that takes 100 milliseconds.

Nevertheless, with larger applications the time needed to search unsorted lists will increase linearly. The time lag produced from traversing a entire list could become noticeable (to an embarrassing degree). In the future I will probably not only implement sorted lists so that more efficient searching algorithms can be applied, but also complement the array lists with a hash table data structure of some sort.

O(n) Notation

In the previous discussion I mentioned that certain algorithms are more efficient than others. It would be nice if the performance of an algorithm could be quantified somehow, to save me from having to rely on arm-waving explanations. As it turns out, computer scientists have a convention for quantitatively describing the general performance of an algorithm. This convention is known as big-Oh notation.

Assume **R** is the set of real numbers and **N** is the set of natural numbers.

Given two functions $y = f(n)$ and $y = g(n)$ where $n \in \mathbf{N}$ and $y \in \mathbf{R}$

$f(n)$ is $O(g(n))$ if $\exists\ k \in \mathbf{R}$, $k > 0$ and $m \in \mathbf{N}$, $m \geq 1$ such that $f(n) \leq kg(n)\ \forall\ n \geq m$

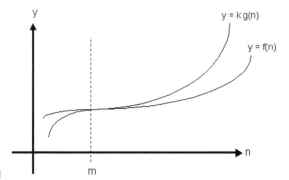

Figure 4-11

For those of you who have never had to wade through Schur's lemma, I will translate the previous hieroglyphs.

In English: Given two functions $y = f(n)$ and $y = g(n)$ which map nonnegative integers to real numbers, $f(n)$ is said to be order $g(n)$ (i.e., $O(g(n))$) if there exists a positive real constant k and a positive integer constant m, such that $f(n)$ is less than or equal to the product of k and $g(n)$ for all integer values greater than or equal to m.

In other words, f(n) behaves asymptotically like g(n).

NOTE O(g(n)) represents a whole class of mathematical functions, not just a single function.

People often refer to O(g(n)) as the *asymptotic cost* (or *growth rate*) of an algorithm. In practice, O(g(n)) is typically used to represent one of two things:

■ Running time

■ Storage space requirements

The independent variable n is context sensitive. For example, if O(g(n)) represents the number of operations needed to sort a list, the n variable represents the number of items to be sorted. Or, if O(g(n)) represents the number of operations needed to search a list, the n variable represents the size of the list to be searched. In general, you can see the n variable as a general indicator of a problem's size.

NOTE An *arm-waving explanation* is a proposition which has not been established using precise mathematical statements. Mathematical statements have the benefit of being completely unambiguous: They are either true or false. An arm-waving explanation tends to eschew logical rigor entirely in favor of arguments that appeal to intuition. Such reasoning is at best dubious, not only because intuition can often be incorrect but also because intuitive arguments are ambiguous. For example, people who argue that the world is flat tend to rely on arm-waving explanations.

ASIDE Some engineers may argue that big-Oh notation is a waste of time. They might say: "Just time the algorithms to see which is fastest." Timing the performance of an algorithm is a useful technique for determining which algorithm is the most efficient. But only under a specific set of circumstances.

   If someone asked you how well an algorithm performs, and you said, "About 5 milliseconds," this wouldn't really answer their question because you didn't tell them under what conditions the algorithm was being applied. Remember, algorithms are sensitive to:

■ The distribution of data on which they operate

■ The hardware that is executing the algorithm's instructions

■ The implementation of the algorithm

To give a truly accurate answer, you would have to say: "About 5 milliseconds, on a Pentium III, using Aho's implementation, with data that follows a beta distribution possessing the following parameters … "

   You can see how tedious it would be to refer to the efficiency of an algorithm using nothing but a time measurement. This would also make it difficult, if not impossible, to agree on a common metric.

   The bottom line is that big-Oh notation is a way to refer to the general performance of an algorithm. It provides a way to classify algorithms without having to include half a dozen context-sensitive qualifiers.

Dynamic Patching

The HEC debugger is a read-only instrument. It's like the one-way mirror cops use when they interrogate a suspect. The HEC debugger will only allow you to observe the state of the virtual machine; it will not allow you to modify anything. This probably reflects my own experience with, and past use of, command-line debuggers on Unix. Debuggers are generally used to hunt down bugs by a person who has access to the source code of the program being debugged. When a bug is uncovered, usually the developer will modify the source code, rebuild the executable, and then test to see if the error persists.

There may be times when it is useful to change a value in memory during the debugging session. In other words, rather than go back to the source code and institute a change, it may be more expedient to directly modify the machine state and see if a bug can be resolved. The only problem with this approach is that it might not illuminate the true origin of a bug. The fix you make during a debugging session might only offer you short-term relief. Nevertheless, in the future I am going to consider adding memory editing facilities to the HEC debugger.

Dynamic Breakpoints

The HEC debugger currently requires the user to manually place an INT 3 instruction in the source code to insert a breakpoint. Also, INT 3 breakpoints are unconditional. When the virtual machine encounters INT 3 it will pause the path of execution every time.

In the next version of the HEC debugger, I may include facilities which support dynamic breakpoints. Dynamic breakpoints can be set, modified, and removed at run time while the virtual machine mode is in debug mode. They are also capable of conditional activation. Dynamic breakpoints can be set to execute only under a certain set of conditions. For example, a dynamic breakpoint may activate when a program variable has achieved a specified value or when a Boolean expression evaluates to true. This allows the debugger to watch for particular types of program exceptions.

Session Logging

The HEC debugger, as it is currently implemented, is only capable of reporting on the most recent state of the virtual machine. In other words, if you display the registers, the values you see will be their present values. This can make things difficult if you want to track certain variables and registers. There have been times during the development of the HEC virtual machine where I have had to keep a paper and pencil by my computer in order to follow the evolution of a given region of memory.

I plan to address this problem in the next version of the HEC debugger by implementing session logging. This will allow the debugger to clone and redirect console output to a log file, so that the details of a debugging session can be reviewed.

Program Frequency Counts

In addition to session logging, which is intended to offer a post mortem summary of a debugging session, it would also be useful to have access to summary data at run time while the HEC debugger is running. Program frequency counting is one way of offering this type of service. Program frequency counting keeps track of the number of times that an identifier is referenced in a program so that the trajectory of the program's execution path can be verified.

For example, you might have a variable that is accessed every single time a program transaction is committed. By examining the number of times that this variable has appeared in the path of execution, you can infer the number of transactions that have been committed.

Symbolic Debugger

When I built the HEC debugger, all I had to work with was the virtual machine itself. I did not have a compiler at my disposal, or even an assembler. For the most part, I was working in the dark and was focused almost exclusively on getting the virtual machine to function correctly.

Thus, it makes sense that building a symbolic debugger was not high on my list of things to do. I did, however, need to look under the hood while the engine was running, so to speak. Thus, I constructed the HEC debugger to be a machine-level debugger that offers a fairly clear view of what the HEC virtual machine is doing. Even though it is a machine debugger, the HEC debugger proved to be an effective tool. During the initial stages of construction, before I had the debugger functioning, I stumbled around blindly for the most part.

I also did not want to bias the HEC virtual machine towards a particular language. I've heard this type of complaint from CORBA developers who ridiculed the Java virtual machine because it is an ice cream parlor that only serves a single flavor. In other words, to make use of the Java virtual machine's advanced features, like RMI and object serialization, you have to program everything in Java. This is a bigger constraint than the people at Javasoft would like you to think.

An engineer has to use different tools for different problems. If a language like Java attempts to be everything to everyone, it will really be good at nothing. Try not to be caught up in the irrational exuberance of the Java marketing folks at Sun.

When I target the HEC virtual machine with a high-level programming language, I will probably implement a full-fledged symbolic debugger. This may entail modifications to the virtual machine, but I'm hoping I can rely entirely on external APIs. Time will tell.

Taking HEC for a Test Drive

Eventually, you have to get your hands dirty. There is no substitute for direct experience. When I was building the HEC virtual machine, I did not have a functioning assembler handy. In fact, I implemented the HEC assembler only after I was sure that the virtual machine functioned correctly. You are currently in a similar position. You have gained an understanding of the virtual machine, but you have not been exposed to any development tools. So how did I test the virtual machine?

The answer is: I built several bytecode executables by hand. Yes, that's right, I built the first series of programs byte by byte. It was an ugly job, but someone had to do it. It wasn't, however, a complete waste of time because it did give me a much deeper understanding of how instructions are encoded from the virtual machine's point of view. This insight turned out to be invaluable when I was implementing the assembler.

Rather than make you sit on your hands until the assembler is discussed, I am going to show you how to build a bytecode executable the hard way, so that you can take the virtual machine for a spin around the block.

The following program builds such a test application. I simply populate an array of bytes and write it to disk. I decided to keep things simple and preclude debug information from my handcrafted bytecode executable. This is accomplished by zeroing out certain fields in the executable's header section. While I wrote this program, I found myself referencing `iset.c` and `exenv.c` frequently. In fact, in order to make things easier, I included `win32.c`, `iset.c`, and `exenv.c` so that I could use their macro definitions.

The following program is included on the CD-ROM in a file named `rawbin.c`. The purpose of this program is basically to showcase the different bytecode instructions. I would recommend starting the virtual machine in debug mode and tracing through each instruction. At certain points you'll probably want to dump regions of memory to verify that the load/store and push/pop instructions are working properly.

```c
#include<stdio.h>
#include<win32.c>
#include<iset.c>
#include<exenv.c>

void main(int argc, char *argv[])
{
    FILE *fptr;
    U2 i;
    U1 buffer[1024];

    fptr = fopen("rawbin.RUN","wb");
    if(fptr==NULL){ printf("cannot open file\n"); }

    /*
        Recall the header section elements
            U2 magic
            U8 szSymTbl
            U8 szStrTbl
           +U8 szByteCode
            --------------
            26 bytes total

        We will exclude symbol table info, so the
        szSymTbl and szStrTbl will be zeroed

        if add commands, will need to modify
```

```
        i) szByteCode field in header = last_index-25
        ii) i loop range in for loop [0,last_index]

*/

/*start header-------------------------------------------------*/

/* magic number */
buffer[0]=0xDE; buffer[1]=0xED;

/* szSymTbl */
buffer[2]=0; buffer[3]=0; buffer[4]=0; buffer[5]=0;
buffer[6]=0; buffer[7]=0; buffer[8]=0; buffer[9]=0;

/* szStrTbl */
buffer[10]=0; buffer[11]=0; buffer[12]=0; buffer[13]=0;
buffer[14]=0; buffer[15]=0; buffer[16]=0; buffer[17]=0;

/* szByteCode */
buffer[18]=0; buffer[19]=0; buffer[20]=0; buffer[21]=0;
buffer[22]=0; buffer[23]=0; buffer[24]=1; buffer[25]=58;

/*end header---------------------------------------------------*/

/*bytecode ----------------------------------------------------*/

/*LBI $R1, −25*/
butter[26]=LBI;buffer[27]=$R1;buffer[28]=−25;

/*LWI $R2, −150*/
buffer[29]=LWI;buffer[30]=$R2;buffer[31]=255;buffer[32]=106;

/*LDI $R3, 10,234,768 */
buffer[33]=LDI;buffer[34]=$R3;
buffer[35]=0;buffer[36]=156;buffer[37]=43;buffer[38]=144;

/*LQI $R5, -2,147,483,649  */
buffer[39]=LQI;buffer[40]=$R5;
buffer[41]=255;buffer[42]=255;buffer[43]=255;buffer[44]=255;
buffer[45]=127;buffer[46]=255;buffer[47]=255;buffer[48]=255;

/*LF1I $F1, 23.45e4 */
buffer[49]=LF1I;buffer[50]=$F1;
buffer[51]=72;buffer[52]=101;buffer[53]=1;buffer[54]=0;

/*LF2I $D1, −100.2e−4*/
buffer[55]=LF2I;buffer[56]=$D1;
buffer[57]=191;buffer[58]=132;buffer[59]=133;buffer[60]=93;
buffer[61]=162;buffer[62]=114;buffer[63]=134;buffer[64]=47;

/*CAST_IF $R7, $F1*/
```

```
buffer[65]=CAST_IF;buffer[66]=$R7;buffer[67]=$F1;

/*CAST_ID $R8, $D1*/
buffer[68]=CAST_ID;buffer[69]=$R8;buffer[70]=$D1;

/*CAST_FI $F2, $R1*/
buffer[71]=CAST_FI;buffer[72]=$F2;buffer[73]=$R1;

/*CAST_FD $F3, $D1*/
buffer[74]=CAST_FD;buffer[75]=$F3;buffer[76]=$D1;

/*CAST_DI $D2, $R5*/
buffer[77]=CAST_DI;buffer[78]=$D2;buffer[79]=$R5;

/*CAST_DF $D3, $F1*/
buffer[80]=CAST_DF;buffer[81]=$D3;buffer[82]=$F1;

/*LAD $R9,400*/
buffer[83]=LAD;buffer[84]=$R9;
buffer[85]=0;buffer[86]=0;buffer[87]=0;buffer[88]=0;
buffer[89]=0;buffer[90]=0;buffer[91]=1;buffer[92]=144;

/*LAI $R10,$R9,20*/
buffer[93]=LAI;buffer[94]=$R10;buffer[95]=$R9;
buffer[96]=0;buffer[97]=0;buffer[98]=0;buffer[99]=0;
buffer[100]=0;buffer[101]=0;buffer[102]=0;buffer[103]=20;

/*SB $R3,$R9*/
buffer[104]=SB;buffer[105]=$R3;buffer[106]=$R9;

/*SW $R3,$R9*/
buffer[107]=SW;buffer[108]=$R3;buffer[109]=$R9;

/*SD $R3,$R9*/
buffer[110]=SD;buffer[111]=$R3;buffer[112]=$R9;

/*SQ $R3,$R9*/
buffer[113]=SQ;buffer[114]=$R3;buffer[115]=$R9;

/*SF1 $F1,$R9*/
buffer[116]=SF1;buffer[117]=$F1;buffer[118]=$R9;

/*SF2 $D1,$R9*/
buffer[119]=SF2;buffer[120]=$D1;buffer[121]=$R9;

/*LB $R1,$R9*/
buffer[122]=LB;buffer[123]=$R1;buffer[124]=$R9;

/*LW $R1,$R9*/
buffer[125]=LW;buffer[126]=$R1;buffer[127]=$R9;

/*LD $R1,$R9*/
buffer[128]=LD;buffer[129]=$R1;buffer[130]=$R9;
```

```
/*LQ $R1,$R9*/
buffer[131]=LQ;buffer[132]=$R1;buffer[133]=$R9;

/*LF1 $F2,$R9*/
buffer[134]=LF1;buffer[135]=$F2;buffer[136]=$R9;

/*LF2 $D2,$R9*/
buffer[137]=LF2;buffer[138]=$D2;buffer[139]=$R9;

/*PUSHB $R1*/
buffer[140]=PUSHB;buffer[141]=$R1;

/*PUSHW $R2*/
buffer[142]=PUSHW;buffer[143]=$R2;

/*PUSHD $R3*/
buffer[144]=PUSHD;buffer[145]=$R3;

/*PUSHQ $R4*/
buffer[146]=PUSHQ;buffer[147]=$R4;

/*PUSHF1 $F1*/
buffer[148]=PUSHF1;buffer[149]=$F1;

/*PUSHF2 $D1*/
buffer[150]=PUSHF2;buffer[151]=$D1;

/*POPB $R1^/
buffer[152]=POPB;buffer[153]=$R1;

/*POPW $R1*/
buffer[154]=POPW;buffer[155]=$R1;

/*POPD $R1*/
buffer[156]=POPD;buffer[157]=$R1;

/*POPQ $R1*/
buffer[158]=POPQ;buffer[159]=$R1;

/*POPF1 $F2*/
buffer[160]=POPF1;buffer[161]=$F2;

/*POPF2 $D2*/
buffer[162]=POPF2;buffer[163]=$D2;

/*MOV $R3,$R4*/
buffer[164]=MOV;buffer[165]=$R3;buffer[166]=$R4;

/*MOVF $F3,$F1*/
buffer[167]=MOVF;buffer[168]=$F3;buffer[169]=$F1;

/*MOVD $D3,$D1*/
buffer[170]=MOVD;buffer[171]=$D3;buffer[172]=$D1;
```

```
/*LWI $R1,*/
buffer[173]=LWI;buffer[174]=$R1;
buffer[175]=0;buffer[176]=155; //181-26=155

/*JMP $R1 */
buffer[177]=JMP;buffer[178]=$R1;

/*NOP NOP NOP*/
buffer[179]=NOP;buffer[180]=NOP;

/*LBI $R1,10*/
buffer[181]=LBI;buffer[182]=$R1;buffer[183]=10;

/*LBI $R2,10*/
buffer[184]=LBI;buffer[185]=$R2;buffer[186]=10;

/*LWI $R3,170*/
buffer[187]=LWI;buffer[188]=$R3;
buffer[189]=0;buffer[190]=170; //196-26=170

/*JE $R1, $R2, $R3 */
buffer[191]=JE;buffer[192]=$R1;buffer[193]=$R2;buffer[194]=$R3;

/*NOP NOP NOP*/
buffer[195]=NOP;

/*JNE $R1, $R2, $R3 */
buffer[196]=JNE;buffer[197]=$R1;buffer[198]=$R2;buffer[199]=$R3;

/*SLT $R1,$R2,$R3*/
buffer[200]=SLT;buffer[201]=$R1;buffer[202]=$R2;buffer[203]=$R3;

/*LBI $R1,2*/
buffer[204]=LBI;buffer[205]=$R1;buffer[206]=2;

/*LBI $R2,8*/
buffer[207]=LBI;buffer[208]=$R2;buffer[209]=8;

/*LBI $R3,4*/
buffer[210]=LBI;buffer[211]=$R3;buffer[212]=4;

/*AND $R3,$R1,$R2*/
buffer[213]=AND;buffer[214]=$R3;buffer[215]=$R1;buffer[216]=$R2;

/*OR  $R3,$R1,$R2*/
buffer[217]=OR;buffer[218]=$R3;buffer[219]=$R1;buffer[220]=$R2;

/*XOR $R3,$R1,$R2*/
buffer[221]=XOR;buffer[222]=$R3;buffer[223]=$R1;buffer[224]=$R2;

/*BT $R1,$R2,$R3*/
buffer[225]=BT;buffer[226]=$R1;buffer[227]=$R2;buffer[228]=$R3;

/*BS $R1,$R2*/
```

```
buffer[229]=BS;buffer[230]=$R1;buffer[231]=$R2;

/*SRA $R1,$R2,$R3*/
buffer[232]=SRA;buffer[233]=$R1;buffer[234]=$R2;buffer[235]=$R3;

/*SRL $R1,$R2,$R3*/
buffer[236]=SRL;buffer[237]=$R1;buffer[238]=$R2;buffer[239]=$R3;

/*SL $R1,$R2,$R3*/
buffer[240]=SL;buffer[241]=$R1;buffer[242]=$R2;buffer[243]=$R3;

/*LBI $R2,-8*/
buffer[244]=LBI;buffer[245]=$R2;buffer[246]=-8;

/*LBI $R3,4*/
buffer[247]=LBI;buffer[248]=$R3;buffer[249]=4;

/*ADD $R4,$R2,$R3*/
buffer[250]=ADD;buffer[251]=$R4;buffer[252]=$R2;buffer[253]=$R3;

/*SUB $R4,$R2,$R3*/
buffer[254]=SUB;buffer[255]=$R4;buffer[256]=$R2;buffer[257]=$R3;

/*MULT $R4,$R2,$R3*/
buffer[258]=MULT;buffer[259]=$R4;buffer[260]=$R2;buffer[261]=$R3;

/*DIV $R1,$R4,$R2,$R3*/
buffer[262]=DIV;buffer[263]=$R1;buffer[264]=$R4;buffer[265]=$R2;
buffer[266]=$R3;

/*LF1I $F2,-8.0e2*/
buffer[267]=LF1I;buffer[268]=$F2;
buffer[269]=196;buffer[270]=72;buffer[271]=0;buffer[272]=0;

/*LF1I $F3,1.2e2*/
buffer[273]=LF1I;buffer[274]=$F3;
buffer[275]=66;buffer[276]=240;buffer[277]=0;buffer[278]=0;

/*FADD $F4,$F2,$F3*/
buffer[279]=FADD;buffer[280]=$F4;buffer[281]=$F2;buffer[282]=$F3;

/*FSUB $F4,$F2,$F3*/
buffer[283]=FSUB;buffer[284]=$F4;buffer[285]=$F2;buffer[286]=$F3;

/*FMULT $F4,$F2,$F3*/
buffer[287]=FMULT;buffer[288]=$F4;buffer[289]=$F2;buffer[290]=$F3;

/*FDIV $F4,$F2,$F3*/
buffer[291]=FDIV;buffer[292]=$F4;buffer[293]=$F2;buffer[294]=$F3;

/*FSLT $F4,$F2,$F3*/
buffer[295]=FSLT;buffer[296]=$F4;buffer[297]=$F2;buffer[298]=$F3;

/*LF2I $D2,-8.0e2*/
```

```
buffer[299]=LF2I;buffer[300]=$D2;
buffer[301]=192;buffer[302]=137;buffer[303]=0;buffer[304]=0;
buffer[305]=0;buffer[306]=0;buffer[307]=0;buffer[308]=0;

/*LF2I $D3,1.2e2*/
buffer[309]=LF2I;buffer[310]=$D3;
buffer[311]=64;buffer[312]=94;buffer[313]=0;buffer[314]=0;
buffer[315]=0;buffer[316]=0;buffer[317]=0;buffer[318]=0;

/*DADD $D4,$D2,$D3*/
buffer[319]=DADD;buffer[320]=$D4;buffer[321]=$D2;buffer[322]=$D3;

/*DSUB $D4,$D2,$D3*/
buffer[323]=DSUB;buffer[324]=$D4;buffer[325]=$D2;buffer[326]=$D3;

/*DMULT $D4,$D2,$D3*/
buffer[327]=DMULT;buffer[328]=$D4;buffer[329]=$D2;buffer[330]=$D3;

/*DDIV $D4,$D2,$D3*/
buffer[331]=DDIV;buffer[332]=$D4;buffer[333]=$D2;buffer[334]=$D3;

/*DSLT $D4,$D2,$D3*/
buffer[335]=DSLT;buffer[336]=$D4;buffer[337]=$D2;buffer[338]=$D3;

buffer[339]=HALT;

for(i=0;i<340;i++){ fputc(buffer[i],fptr); }

if(fclose(fptr)){ printf("cannot close test executable\n"); }
return;

}/*end main*/
```

References

There is not a lot of material available on the theory of debugging. The dark art of building a debugger is not what I would call a mainstream topic. In fact, I have had an easier time finding books on graph theory. If you feel like the background I have provided doesn't answer one of your questions, I would recommend you take a look at one of the following books.

Aho, Alfred V., Ravi Sethi, and Jeffrey D. Ullman. *Compilers: Principles, Techniques, and Tools.* Addison-Wesley, 1988. ISBN: 0201100886.

Almost every student of computer science has at one point taken a look at the "Dragon Book." In fact, I can't pick up this book without thinking of my graduate school days at Case Western Reserve University in Cleveland. This book is a true classic. It has withstood the test of time and still covers a lot of relevant subjects. This includes, fortunately, debugger theory.

Chebotko, Igor, et al. *Master Class Assembly Language.* Wrox Press, 1995. ISBN: 1874416346.

This book has a few interesting bits. Unfortunately, it also comes across as a collection of hastily covered topics that are seemingly grouped together at random. This is probably because there are over a dozen contributing authors. Another disappointing feature of this book is that there are a large number of examples that do not function correctly.

Microsoft Developers Network Library, Microsoft Corporation, 2001

Microsoft distributes a collection of CDs known as the MSDN library. Updates are provided every quarter. This collection of CDs is the digital motherlode of everything that Microsoft publishes. The only problem is that older documentation tends to be excluded. This puts people maintaining legacy applications at a distinct disadvantage.

Microsoft MASM Programmer's Guide. Microsoft Corporation, 1992. Document No. DB35747-1292.

This manual is actually a fairly lucid exposition on Intel assembler. The material is presented in such a way, however, that you really need to be familiar with Intel assembler before you start reading. This book is not for beginners. In addition, the author skimps on protected mode programming. Considering that most of Microsoft's applications run in protected mode, I find this to be completely negligent.

Rollins, Dan. *IBM-PC 8088 MACRO Assembler Programming*. MacMillan, 1985. ISBN: 0024032107.

This book is the first computer science related book I ever bought. I had to save several weeks worth of lawn-mowing funds to purchase it. An oldie but a goodie.

Rosenberg, Jonathan B. *How Debuggers Work: Algorithms, Data Structures, and Architecture*. John Wiley, 1996. ISBN: 0471149667.

Simply amazing. This is probably the only book completely devoted to discussing debuggers. It is a short but insightful read. This book is worth the investment to purchase, even if you're just going to use it as a reference. If you can't find the answer to a question here, then you're probably in for some heavy-duty research.

Solow, Daniel. *How To Read and Do Proofs*. John Wiley, 1990. ISBN: 0471510041.

In the last part of this chapter, I offer a mathematical definition of $O(g(n))$. If you did not understand the obscure notation I use but you'd like to be able to, this book is an excellent place to begin. Danny's book assumes no previous exposure and is a unique exposition on how to construct mathematical proofs.

www.phrack.org

Before there was hacking, there was phone phreaking. This site is one of the oldest and best known places to get hard-core, and suppressed, technical information. This site is a historical compendium of gray hat and black hat research. If you need in-depth coverage of "Things to do in Cisco-Land When You're Dead," or need to build an industrial strength Windows "root kit," this is the place to go.

HEC Assembly

Part III

225

Assembler Implementation

Overview

In the last chapter, I showed you how to build a bytecode executable manually. If you had the requisite patience, photographic memory, and organizational skills, you could probably build all your bytecode executables this way. However, most software engineers, including myself, would become lost in the thousands of little details that are necessary to keep in mind.

An alternative to building bytecode executables by hand does exist. Specifically, it is possible to represent a bytecode executable in terms of assembly language. Assembly language is a low-level programming language. To get a better understanding of what this means, you need to be familiar with some preliminary definitions.

A *programming language* is a system of symbols used to precisely represent a program. Programming languages are defined in terms of their *syntax* (the language's symbols and the rules governing those symbols' usage) and *semantics* (the meaning the symbols convey).

Like mathematical statements, the symbolic statements of a given programming language are unambiguous. However, unlike mathematical statements, programming language statements do not necessarily always resolve to true or false.

The syntax of a language can be defined formally using a collection of rules known as a *context-free grammar*. Most grammars present their rules using a notation known as *Backus-Naur form* (BNF). Most books on compiler theory present an in-depth explanation of BNF. This includes Pat Terry's book, which I mention in the reference section.

The semantics of a language are a little more complicated to describe using logically precise notation. I find it more productive to describe a language's semantics by offering examples accompanied by informal descriptions. This is the approach followed by most programming language tutorials.

Assembly language is a programming language that directly maps symbolic mnemonics to machine instructions. This mapping results in a nearly one-to-one correspondence between machine instructions and mnemonics.

For example, look at the following machine instructions:

```
0x02 0x0A 0x90 0x2B 0x9C 0x00 0x3B 0x01 0x08 0x11 0x0A 0x10
```

These machine instructions can be broken up and mapped directly to assembly code:

```
LDI     $R3,  10234768    [0x02][0x0A][0x90 0x2B 0x9C 0x00]
CAST_FI $F2,  $R1         [0x3B][0x01][0x08]
SQ      $R3,  $R9         [0x11][0x0A][0x10]
```

Assembly language also incorporates the use of *macro directives*. Macro directives are symbols that can be used as a shorthand for representing memory addresses, numeric constants, or a series of related machine instructions. Assembly language's usage of macro directives is similar to that of the C programming language.

NOTE   One thing I had a hard time understanding when I began my journey into assembly language was the difference between assembly language instructions and macro directives. Assembly language instructions are converted directly into machine instructions. Macro directives are not. Think of a macro directive as a special command that is directed at and processed by the assembler. This will become clearer later on when we delve deeper into the HEC assembly language.

Typically, an assembly language source file is translated, or *assembled*, into a bytecode executable by a development tool known as an *assembler*. The assembler absolves the programmer of having to keep track of various memory addresses, offsets, and other bookkeeping duties.

A language can be classified with regard to the degree to which it abstracts itself from a processor's machine instructions. Low-level languages, like assembly, are characterized by a fairly direct correspondence to machine instructions. A single statement in assembly language typically specifies a single machine instruction. High-level languages, like APL, are far more removed from the details of machine operation. A single statement in APL can easily translate into 50, or even 1,000, machine instructions. Mid-level languages, like C, provide facilities that offer access to both high-level and low-level operations. For the time being, we are stuck in the basement with assembly language. Later in this book I will discuss the implementation of development tools that target a high-level language.

Currently, you have an understanding of the HEC virtual machine and debugger. It's time to move on to the next piece of the puzzle. In this chapter, the design, implementation, and usage of the HEC assembler (HASM) are discussed. These three system software components (virtual machine, debugger, assembler) provide the structural foundation that allows for the construction of more sophisticated and powerful development tools. Investing the necessary time now to learn how the plumbing works will pay off later.

Although the duties an assembler performs are simple, the data structures the assembler uses to do its job are tolerably sophisticated. Because of this, I begin this chapter with a brief review of elementary data structures. This is followed by a divide-and-conquer look at the internals of the assembler. Like the HEC virtual machine, the assembler's path of execution can be decomposed into a set of sequential stages. This internal organization lends itself to the kind of approach I use to discuss the assembler's operation.

NOTE The HEC virtual machine is fairly straightforward in its operation and, by its nature, requires that a large number of its program elements possess global visibility. Because of this, I decided to implement the virtual machine in C. The HEC assembler, believe it or not, is much more complicated than the virtual machine. I initially wrote the assembler in C, but found that it was too difficult to maintain. Because of this, I decided to refactor HASM using C++. I was, however, very careful to only use a certain subset of C++ language features. For example, I eschewed C++ I/O mechanisms in favor of relying on C's standard I/O library (which I think is much more direct and efficient). I also intentionally avoided C++ language features, like operator overloading, which I believe make source code harder to read. Finally, I resisted the temptation to declare everything as an object. There are different tools required for different jobs, and I believe that C-based structure data types still have their place.

NOTE *Refactoring* is an approach to modifying source code through the use of a special set of techniques, which aims to make the source code easier to maintain, extend, and use. The first version of HASM, even though it functioned perfectly, was an unbelievable mess. There was no encapsulation, there were global variables all over the place, and I couldn't understand parts of my own code. The only option was to refactor. I needed to impose a semblance of order on my source code. Refactoring is a gradual, somewhat recursive process, much in the same way that gold is refined. After making one successful round of improvements, other potential areas for change often present themselves. So far, I have renovated HASM twice. Each time, my code has achieved greater structural integrity and readability. If I didn't have to eat or sleep, I probably would have refactored a third and fourth time.

NOTE I christened the HEC assembler with the name HASM in the tradition of other well-known assemblers like NASM, TASM, and MASM. NASM, in particular, is a free Intel assembler available on the Internet. I discovered NASM a couple of years ago while I was reading a Linux HOW-TO on assembly language. When I was doing my initial research on assembler implementation, having access to NASM's source code was very educational, and I would recommend taking a look yourself if you have the time.

Data Structure Briefing

The following is a review of elementary data structures.

HASM Assembler Algorithms

An assembler is basically a tool that takes an assembly language source file and translates it into a bytecode executable. Naturally, in order to process the assembly language source file, it must read from the file and digest what it reads. This leads us to the definition of a pass.

A *pass* is a single reading of the source file(s) by a development tool from beginning to end.

Most development tools perform several passes, although in the interest of speed it is often desirable to keep the number of passes to a minimum. This is due to the overhead associated with disk I/O.

HASM is a variation of a two-pass assembler. It reads in the assembly language source file twice. It uses the first pass for the purpose of address resolution and involves the utilization of the following algorithm:

First Pass (Address Resolution)

1. Obtain the next identifier.

2. Determine the address of the identifier.

3. Place this information in storage for the second pass (assuming that the identifier is not already in storage).

4. Goto step 1.

The second pass is used to generate bytecode by taking advantage of the address information collected during the first pass. The second pass involves the employment of the following algorithm:

Second Pass (Code Generation)

1. Obtain the next instruction.

2. Check to see if the instruction involves an identifier.
   2a. If it does not, goto step 3.
   2b. If it does, retrieve the identifier's address from storage.
   2c. Replace the identifier with its address.

3. Translate the instruction to bytecode.

4. Goto step 1.

It is obvious that the assembler does a lot of storing and retrieving of symbol information. What we need to do now is to sketch out the basic operation of the symbol storage mechanism in an effort to move a step closer towards a feasible implementation.

As it turns out, the management of symbol information required by the previous algorithms can be modeled in terms of abstract data types.

Abstract Data Types

An *abstract data type* (ADT) is a specification for a data storage entity which defines:

- The nature of the data items stored (i.e., the data's *type*)

- A set of operations that can be performed on the stored data items, where each operation is defined solely in terms of its input and output parameters

NOTE The collection of operations exposed by an ADT is also known as the abstract data type's *interface*.

Rigorous ADT specifications also include what are known as *preconditions* and *axioms*. Some ADT operations require certain circumstances in order to be performed. These necessary requirements are known as preconditions. Axioms are precise, mathematical definitions of an ADT's operations. In the interest of time, I have adopted a more informal approach, and will avoid discussing preconditions and axioms.

Because it is a specification, an ADT does not indicate how it should be implemented. This leaves room for creativity and ingenuity on behalf of the developer. Also, the operations an ADT defines are supposed to be the only access mechanism to the data being stored. This is done in the interest of keeping discussion of an ADT away from implementation issues.

A *data structure* is a concrete implementation of an ADT using the basic syntactic tools of a given programming language.

Normally, a given ADT will have at least two or three well-known data structure implementations. Some ADTs have hundreds. The implementation of efficient data structures is still an active area of research in computer science.

There are a variety of ADTs that populate textbooks on data structures and algorithms, such as sets, vectors, lists, sequences, queues, deques, stacks, trees, priority queues, graphs, and dictionaries.

The ADTs we are interested in are the ones that will help the assembler store and manage symbol information. There happen to be three ADTs that are useful to this end: vectors, trees, and dictionaries.

For the remainder of this section, I will examine each of these three ADTs closely. In particular I will:

- Provide an ADT specification.

- Describe how the ADT is used by the assembler.

- Discuss the corresponding data structure I used in HASM.

 NOTE Performance is a major issue for the data structures that I use to implement the list, tree, and dictionary ADTs. Remember, an assembler is a species of program belonging to the OLTP family of applications. The name of the game with OLTP applications is throughput speed. Likewise, we desire the operation of the assembler to be as fast as possible.

Vector ADT

A *vector* is a finite series of linearly arranged data items. These items tend to all have the same data type (i.e., they are all integers, or all strings, etc.), but this is not a necessary feature. The vector ADT exposes the following interface:

Table 5-1

Operation	Description
getElement(i)	Return element at index i
setElement(E, i)	Set element at index i to E
deleteElment(i)	Delete the element at index i
size()	Return the number of elements in the vector

The vector ADT shows up everywhere in HASM's internals. For example, the string table, used by HASM to centralize identifier text, is one big vector. Also, the symbol table, which is the repository of identifier metadata, is essentially a series of heavily nested vectors. Vectors play a core role in the normal operation of the assembler.

The two traditional data structures in C used to implement the vector ADT are arrays and linked lists. Neither of these is what I would call a perfect solution. Rather, it's more an issue of using the right tool for the right job. Table 5-2 summarizes the drawbacks and benefits of the array and linked list.

Table 5-2

Feature	Array	Linked List
Access speed	Fast, via memory offset	Slow, must traverse links
Insert/delete	Slow, must shift elements	Fast, reassign pointers
Memory used	Minimal, contiguous	Overhead of pointers
Size	Set at definition	Dynamic

An *array* is a contiguous series of items in memory. As a result of this, obtaining a specific element is as easy as specifying an index. The index resolves to a memory offset from the first element of the array, so access is quick. Quantitatively, the access speed for array elements is $O(1)$.

The only problem is that arrays have a fixed size. Also, if you want to insert or delete an element into an array at a certain position, you may have to shift several values. This means that the time needed to insert an array value can be $O(N)$, because we may need to shift all of the N array values.

Linked lists lie at the other end of the spectrum. The linked list data structure consists of a series of linked nodes, which are rarely contiguous in memory. This means that in order to access a certain element, you may have to traverse the entire data structure to find it, and access speed is $O(N)$. On the other hand, inserting new elements and deleting them is as easy as reassigning a couple of pointer values, such that the time required for these operations is $O(2)$.

Rather than position myself at one of the two extremes, I decided to make a compromise between the two. This compromise is known as an extendable array.

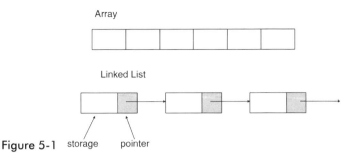

Figure 5-1   storage   pointer

Extendable Arrays

The primary benefit of the linked list data structure is its ability to grow dynamically. The primary benefit of the array data structure is its quick access speed. The extendable array data structure offers both of these advantages. An *extendable array* uses an array as its storage mechanism. However, it also keeps track of the capacity of the array and the number of elements currently occupied. When the extendable array runs out of space, it allocates a larger array and then copies over the currently occupied cells to the larger array. The old array is deallocated after the new, larger array has been assimilated.

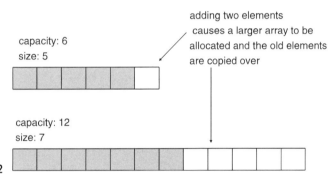

Figure 5-2

My implementation is primitive, but it does the trick. Once you've read through it, you will easily be able to recognize the various incarnations of extendable arrays in the HASM source code (which is really the whole point of all this).

An extendable array can be declared as follows:

```
class List
{
    int LIST_INIT;
    int LIST_INC;

    public:
    int *ptr;   /*pointer to start of list*/
    int nCells; /*current capacity*/
    int iNext;  /*next free space*/
```

```
    List(int init,int inc);
    ~List();
    void addToList(int val);
    void printList();
};
```

There will, no doubt, be C++ pedants in the audience who will complain that I have exposed too many internal data members as public. To an extent, this is true. Guilty as charged. For the most part, however, the HASM source code will only call addToList() and then access vector members directly through the ptr variable.

The extendable array declaration has the following member function implementations:

```
List::List(int init,int inc)
{
    LIST_INIT=init;
    LIST_INC=inc;
    ptr = (int*)malloc(LIST_INIT*sizeof(int));
    if(ptr==NULL)
    {
        printf("List(): cannot allocate memory\n");
        exit(1);
    }
    iNext = 0;
    nCells = LIST_INIT;
    return;

}/*end constructor*/

List::~List()
{
    free(ptr);
    return;

}/*end destructor*/

void List::addToList(int val)
{
    int i;
    int *temp_ptr;

    /*
    if nCell=n will have valid indices 0,...,n-1
    thus, if index=n we are out of bounds
    */

    if(iNext >= nCells)
    {
        temp_ptr = (int*)malloc((nCells+LIST_INC)*sizeof(int));
        if(temp_ptr==NULL)
        {
            printf("List.addToList(): cannot allocate more memory\n");
            exit(1);
        }
```

```
            else
            {
                printf("List.addToList(): not enough room for %d\n",val);
                printf("List.addToList(): allocating %d more\n",LIST_INC);
                for(i=0;i<nCells;i++){ temp_ptr[i] = ptr[i]; }
                free(ptr);
                ptr = temp_ptr;
                nCells = nCells+LIST_INC;
            }
        }

    ptr[iNext]=val;
    iNext++;
    return;

}/*end addToList*/

void List::printList()
{
    int i;

    printf("list capacity =%d\n",nCells);
    printf("next index    =%d\n",iNext);

    for(i=0;i<iNext;i++)
    {
        printf("%d) %d\n",i,ptr[i]);
    }
    return;

}/*printList*/
```

To give you an idea of how this class is used in practice, I've included the following driver. All of this source code is in the `list.cpp` file on the companion CD-ROM.

```
void main()
{

    List list(4,4);

    list.addToList(4);
    list.addToList(-5);
    list.addToList(1);
    list.addToList(11);

    list.addToList(7);
    list.addToList(8);
    list.addToList(-12);
    list.addToList(122);

    list.addToList(4);
    list.addToList(5);
    list.addToList(5);
    list.addToList(-101);
```

```
        list.addToList(3);

        list.printList();

        printf("list[2]=%d\n",list.ptr[2]);

        return;

    }/*end main*/
```

Tree ADT

A *tree* is a finite series of data items that have been arranged hierarchically. In a tree ADT, these data items are called *nodes*. Each node in a tree has one or more children nodes and a single parent node. The only exception to this rule is the *root* node, which does not have a parent. This is an apt term, seeing as how a tree can be viewed such that all the nodes seem to branch out from the root node. The *descendents* of a node are all the children nodes, and all of the children's children, and all of those children's children, and so forth. (This is not a rigorous definition, but I think you get the idea.)

A node is *external* if it has no children. An external node is also known as a *leaf*. A node that has one or more children is known as an *internal* node. A *subtree* of a given tree is a smaller tree consisting of a non-root node and all of its descendents.

An example tree is displayed in Figure 5-3.

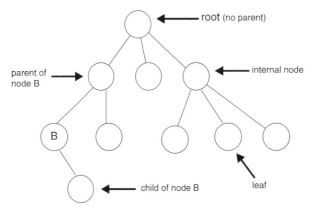

Figure 5-3

The tree ADT exposes the following interface:

Table 5-3

Operation	Description
getRoot()	Returns the root of the tree
getParent(N)	Returns the parent of node N
getChildren(N)	Returns the children of node N
isNodeInternal(N)	Returns true if node N is internal
isNodeExternal(N)	Returns true if node N is external
isRoot(N)	Returns true if node N is the root

The tree ADT is used by HASM to help manage the indexing of assembly language identifiers. When HASM wants to query the symbol table to see if a certain identifier has been declared, it will look up the identifier in the index. This is like looking up a name in the phone book to find its address. Indexing identifiers is primarily the job of the dictionary ADT that HASM implements. However, the dictionary uses a tree data structure, in a secondary role, to help it do its job. The purpose the tree ADT has in the operation of HASM will become clearer later on when we look at the dictionary ADT.

There are a number of data structures used to implement the tree ADT. Some data structures, such as AVL trees and splay trees, guarantee a certain level of performance at the expense of complexity. I decided to opt for the simple approach and implement the tree ADT using the binary search tree data structure.

Binary Search Trees

A *binary search tree* (BST) is a tree data structure that obeys the following rules:

- Internal nodes can have at most two children.
- Each node is assigned a key, which is a value that identifies the node.
- A left child's key is less than its parent's key.
- A right child's key is greater than or equal to its parent's key.

A simple BST is displayed in Figure 5-4.

This binary tree is formed by inserting the following values
in the given order {10, 8, 9, 15, 5, 11, 19, 7}

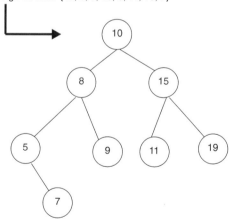

Figure 5-4

Like an extendable array, a BST is a compromise between an array and a linked list. Specifically, a BST has faster inserts than an array and quicker access than a linked list. There is one problem with BSTs: The form a BST takes is dependent upon the order in which the tree elements are added.

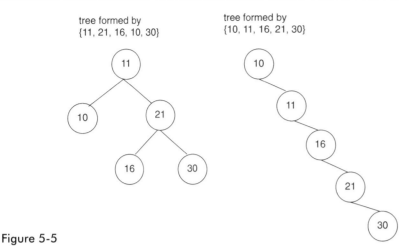

tree formed by
{11, 21, 16, 10, 30}

tree formed by
{10, 11, 16, 21, 30}

Figure 5-5

As you can see, if the tree elements are added in strictly increasing or decreasing order, we will end up with something that is essentially a linked list. This makes searching the BST as inefficient as searching a linked list. In quantitative terms, searching a linked list takes an amount of work, O(N). This means that a linked list of N items may require that we search the entire list in order to find a particular element.

Tree data structures like AVL trees, splay trees, and red-black trees use complicated algorithms to guarantee that this kind of thing doesn't happen. In general, searching one of these data structures would require an effort of O(log(N)), where N is the number of nodes in the tree.

I decided to stick with the rudimentary BST because it's easy to implement and debug. The performance for searches and inserts can range from O(log(N)) to O(N). Thus, there is no guarantee that we will not end up with a linked list. Nevertheless, I suspected that the data stored in my BSTs would be random enough that I wouldn't have to worry about my BSTs degenerating into linked lists.

To *traverse* a tree is to visit, or access, every node in the tree.

What distinguishes one tree traversal from the next is the order in which a tree's nodes are visited. There are three well-known ways for traversing a BST:

■ Preorder traversal

■ Inorder traversal

■ Postorder traversal

All three algorithms assume that the traversal starts at the root node of the BST.

The preorder traversal technique obeys the following algorithm:

1. Perform the "visit" action on the current node.

2. Traverse the left subtree, if it exists, in preorder.

3. Traverse the right subtree, if it exists, in preorder.

If we perform a preorder traversal of the tree in Figure 5-4, we obtain these values: { 10, 8, 5, 7, 9, 15, 11, 19 }.

The inorder traversal technique obeys the following algorithm:

1. Traverse the left subtree, if it exists, in inorder.

2. Perform the "visit" action on the current node.

3. Traverse the right subtree, if it exists, in inorder.

If we perform an inorder traversal of the tree in Figure 5-4, we obtain these values: { 5, 7, 8, 9, 10, 11, 15, 19 }. One useful feature with respect to an inorder traversal of a BST is that it produces a sorted list. I use a variation of the inorder traversal algorithm to print out the binary tree I've implemented in this section.

The postorder traversal technique obeys the following algorithm:

1. Traverse the left subtree, if it exists, in inorder.

2. Traverse the right subtree, if it exists, in inorder.

3. Perform the "visit" action on the current node.

If we perform a postorder traversal of the tree in Figure 5-4, we obtain these values: { 7, 5, 9, 8, 11, 19, 15, 10 }.

The BST I use in HASM has the following declaration:

```
struct BiNode
{
    int value;
    struct BiNode *left;
    struct BiNode *right;
};

class BinarySearchTree
{
    public:
    struct BiNode *root_ptr;

    void insertNode(struct BiNode **link, int val);

    struct BiNode* findNode(struct BiNode *link, int val);

    struct BiNode* deleteSmallestNode(struct BiNode **link);
    void deleteNode(struct BiNode **link, int val);
    void deleteAll(struct BiNode **link);

    void printTree(struct BiNode *link, int level);
    int getHeight(struct BiNode *link);

};
```

The operations that HASM uses frequently are insertNode() and findNode(). Everything else is window dressing. For example, I don't really have a pressing need to delete BST nodes or calculate the height of a BST.

NOTE In general, HASM builds up an elaborate series of data structures in memory to manage symbol data. Being the pedant that I am, I invested the effort to provide a way for the assembler to decompose and free everything. Naturally, some engineers might roll their eyes at me. In a sense, doing this kind of explicit freeing is a waste of effort. When the HASM is done with its job and dies, all that memory is going to the same place anyway. It's far easier, not to mention faster, to just let the HASM application finish executing and allow the operating system to reclaim everything in one fell swoop.

As you look at the implementation of the BST I provide, it helps if you keep the BST properties in your head while you read. Repeat them to yourself like a mantra, and eventually they will sink in.

The BST member functions have the following implementations:

```
/*
    given struct Binode **link
    link  = address of a variable which holds the address of the node
    *link = address of the node
    **link  = node
*/

void BinarySearchTree::insertNode(struct BiNode **link, int val)
{
    if(*link==NULL)
    {
        (*link) = (struct BiNode*)malloc(sizeof(struct BiNode));
        (*(*link)).value = val;
        (*(*link)).left = NULL;
        (*(*link)).right = NULL;
        printf("insertNode(): inserting %d\n",val);
    }
    else if(val < (*(*link)).value)
    {
        printf("insertNode(): moving left\n",val);
        insertNode(&((*(*link)).left),val);
    }
    else
    {
        printf("insertNode(): moving right\n",val);
        insertNode(&((*(*link)).right),val);
    }
    return;

}/*end insertNode*/

struct BiNode* BinarySearchTree::findNode(struct BiNode *link, int val)
{
    if(link==NULL)
    {
        return(NULL);
    }
    else if((*link).value == val)
```

```
        {
            return(link);
        }
        else if(val >= (*link).value)
        {
            return(findNode((*link).right,val));
        }
        else
        {
            return(findNode((*link).left,val));
        }

}/*end findNode*/

struct BiNode* BinarySearchTree::deleteSmallestNode(struct BiNode **link)
{
    if((*(*link)).left != NULL)
    {
        return(deleteSmallestNode(&((*(*link)).left)));
    }
    else
    {
        struct BiNode *temp;
        temp = *link;
        (*link) = (*(*link)).right;
        return(temp);
    }

}/*end deleteSmallestNode*/

void BinarySearchTree::deleteNode(struct BiNode **link, int val)
{
    if((*link)==NULL)
    {
        printf("deleteNode(): %d does not exist\n",val);
        return;
    }

    if(val < (*(*link)).value)
    {
        deleteNode(&((*(*link)).left),val);
    }
    else if(val > (*(*link)).value)
    {
        deleteNode(&((*(*link)).right),val);
    }
    else
    {
        /*
        have equality
        3 cases
            i) node has no children (just delete it)
            ii) node has one child
            (set parent of current node
```

```
                            to child of current node, delete current node)
                        iii) node has two children/subtrees

                        In the third case, get smallest/leftmost node in right
                        subtree of current node. Then delete the leftmost node
                        and place its value in the current node
                        (allows us to retain binary tree properties)
            */

            struct BiNode *temp;
            temp = *link;

            if((*(*link)).right==NULL)
            {
                (*link) = (*(*link)).left;
            }
            else if((*(*link)).left==NULL)
            {
                (*link) = (*(*link)).right;
            }
            else
            {
                temp = deleteSmallestNode(&((*(*link)).right));
                (*(*link)).value = (*temp).value;
            }

            printf("deleteNode(): freeing %d\n",val);
            tree(temp);

    }
    return;

}/*end deleteNode*/

void BinarySearchTree::deleteAll(struct BiNode **link)
{
    if((*link)==NULL)
    {
        return;
    }
    deleteAll(&((*(*link)).left));
    deleteAll(&((*(*link)).right));

    printf("deleteAll(): freeing %d\n",(*(*link)).value);
    free((*link));
    *link=NULL;
    return;

}/*end deleteAll*/

void BinarySearchTree::printTree(struct BiNode *link, int level)
{
    int i;
    if(link==NULL)
```

```
        {
            return;
        }

        printTree((*link).right,level+1);

        for(i=0;i<level;i++){ printf("-"); }
        printf("(%d)\n",(*link).value);

        printTree((*link).left,level+1);
        return;

    }/*end printTree*/

    int BinarySearchTree::getHeight(struct BiNode *link)
    {
        int u;
        int v;

        if(link==NULL){ return(-1); }

        u = getHeight((*link).left);
        v = getHeight((*link).right);

        if(u > v){ return(u+1); }
        else{ return(v+1); }

    }/*end getHeight*/
```

To give you an idea of how this class is used in practice, I've included the following driver.
All of this source code is in the `tree.cpp` file on the companion CD-ROM.

```
    void main()
    {
        BinarySearchTree bst;
        bst.root_ptr=NULL;

        bst.insertNode(&(bst.root_ptr),15);
        bst.insertNode(&(bst.root_ptr),20);
        bst.insertNode(&(bst.root_ptr),7);
        bst.insertNode(&(bst.root_ptr),17);
        bst.insertNode(&(bst.root_ptr),25);
        bst.insertNode(&(bst.root_ptr),2);
        bst.insertNode(&(bst.root_ptr),30);
        bst.insertNode(&(bst.root_ptr),1);
        bst.insertNode(&(bst.root_ptr),7);

        printf("height=%d\n",bst.getHeight(bst.root_ptr));
        bst.printTree(bst.root_ptr,0);

        bst.deleteNode(&(bst.root_ptr),20);
        printf("height=%d\n",bst.getHeight(bst.root_ptr));
        bst.printTree(bst.root_ptr,0);
```

```
    bst.deleteNode(&(bst.root_ptr),2);
    printf("height=%d\n",bst.getHeight(bst.root_ptr));
    bst.printTree(bst.root_ptr,0);

    bst.deleteNode(&(bst.root_ptr),13);
    printf("height=%d\n",bst.getHeight(bst.root_ptr));
    bst.printTree(bst.root_ptr,0);

    if((bst.findNode(bst.root_ptr,17))!=NULL){ printf("found 17\n"); }
    else{ printf("could NOT find 17\n"); }

    if((bst.findNode(bst.root_ptr,8))!=NULL){ printf("found 8\n"); }
    else{ printf("could NOT find 8\n"); }

    bst.deleteAll(&(bst.root_ptr));
    printf("height=%d\n",bst.getHeight(bst.root_ptr));
    bst.printTree(bst.root_ptr,0);

    return;

}/*end main*/
```

Dictionary ADT

A dictionary is a finite series of key-record pairs. A *record* is some piece of information. It can be anything from a single variable to an aggregation of object data types. A *key* is an identifier that is associated with a record and serves to identify that record. A key can be a part of its record or completely separate from the record. Typically, the key is much smaller than the record with which it is associated. If each record in a dictionary has a unique key, then that key is called the record's *primary key*. Otherwise, a key is known as a *secondary key*.

A dictionary basically spells out a way to manage records through the use of their keys. The dictionary ADT exposes the following interface:

Table 5-4

Operation	Description
getRecords()	Returns the set of all records
getKeys()	Returns the set of all keys
getSize()	Returns the number of key-record pairs
isEmpty()	Returns true if the dictionary is empty
getRecords(K)	Returns the records associated with key K
insertRecord(R, K)	Inserts a new key-record pair
deleteRecords(K)	Deletes the records associated with key K

The HASM assembler needs to keep track of program identifiers in order to resolve memory addresses while it is translating a source file. I could have built HASM so that identifiers were indexed alphabetically using their string text. If I wanted to know if a certain identifier had been declared in a program, I would have to traverse the index of strings and use the C strcmp() function repeatedly to see if the given identifier was in the index. This is a lot of unnecessary work. Comparing strings in C/C++ can be a processor-intensive operation, especially if the strings are long.

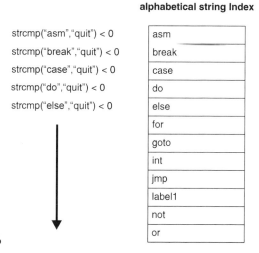

Figure 5-6

A better solution would be to associate an integer value with the string text of each identifier. This way, I could check to see if a string existed in the index by comparing numeric values instead of comparing strings. Comparing two numbers is far quicker than comparing strings. This was actually the final solution that I decided upon. Formally, this number-based indexing data structure is known as a hash table.

Hash Tables

A *hash table* is an array of N slots, numbered 0 to (N–1). A mapping, known as a *hash function* h(K), takes a record's key value K and maps it to an integer in the range [0, N–1]. In this way, a record can be assigned a slot in the hash table.

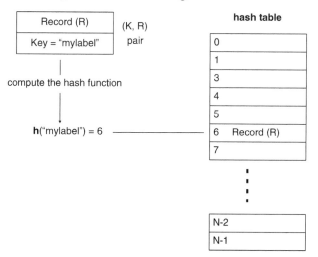

Figure 5-7

To see if a particular record has been assigned a slot in the hash table, we compute the hash value of its key h(K) and then look at the hash table slot corresponding to the integer value returned by the hash function h(K).

There may be instances in which the hash function assigns two different keys to the same hash table slot. This is known as a *collision*. An algorithm that implements *perfect hashing* does not allow collisions to occur. Even if a hash function leads to collisions, we would hope it would produce a distribution of hash values that are evenly distributed among the available hash slots, such that the number of collisions is kept to a minimum. A hash function that uniformly distributes key values among hash tables slots is known as a *good hash function*.

Most hash table implementations are not perfect. Instead, they rely upon what is known as a *collision resolution policy*.

The collision resolution policy known as *open addressing* attempts to take a record that has collided and store it somewhere else in the hash table. This is usually done by taking the first hash function result h1(K) and using it to perform a secondary hash function computation h2(h1(K)) in hopes that the second hash function value will resolve to a slot in the hash table that is empty. If the second hash function result resolves to a hash table slot that is already occupied, a third hash function h3(h2(h1(K))) will be applied, and so on. The goal of open addressing is to keep on hashing until you obtain an empty hash table slot.

In my opinion, the performance of open addressing begins to degrade when the hash table starts to fill up because several hash function computations may have to be performed in order to place a record in the hash table. It's like trying to find an empty room in a hotel that only has a few vacancies by randomly checking rooms until you find an empty one. Also, open addressing limits the number of records that can be hashed to a finite number.

The collision resolution policy I rely on is known as *separate chaining*. In separate chaining, records that have collided are stored outside the hash table in an external data structure.

This is where the BST comes into play!

I treat each hash table slot as the root of its own BST. When a collision occurs, I just add the new record to the slot's binary tree. BST entries are inserted using the record value as a key value for the BST. (In other words, the record value of the original key-record pair is treated like a key by the BST.) Unlike open addressing, separate chaining avoids having to perform additional hashes and also allows for an arbitrary number of records.

The basic idea behind all this is illustrated in Figure 5-8.

 NOTE One thing to keep in mind: In HASM's implementation, the hash table record-key pair really only consists of a record. In other words, the key is also the record. This is because HASM uses a hash table to index identifiers. The identifier is both the key that is fed to the hash function and the record that gets stored in the hash slot. This should become clearer once you look at the implementation.

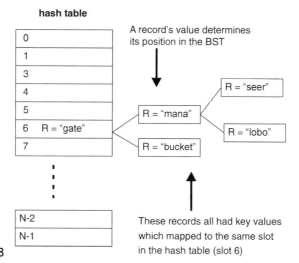

Figure 5-8

I think you're ready to look at some source code. Following is the declaration of the basic type of hash table data structure that HASM uses:

```
struct HashTbl
{
    unsigned char empty;            /*indicates if entry is used or not*/
    char str[32];                   /*string payload*/
    struct HashTbl *left;
    struct HashTbl *right;
};

#define PRIME 5

class HashTable
{
    struct HashTbl hashTbl[PRIME];     /*the hash table itself*/

    int hashpjw(char *s);

    /*binary tree routines needed for collision resolution*/

    struct HashTbl* findNode(struct HashTbl* link, char *val);
    void insertNode(struct HashTbl** link, char *val);
    void printTree(struct HashTbl* link, int level);
    void deleteAll(struct HashTbl **link);

    public:
    HashTable();
    ~HashTable();
    struct HashTbl* queryHashTbl(char *str);
    void addHashTblEntry(char *val);
    void printHashTbl();
};
```

The addHashTblEntry() and queryHashTbl() functions are the primary entry points. Both of these functions use a well-known hash function, named hashpjw, to generate key values. The hashpjw function is spoken highly of by people like Alfred Aho and Allen Holub in terms of its ability to uniformly distribute keys to hash table slots. I decided to take Alfred Aho's word and use hashpjw to perform day-to-day hashing operations.

Most of the private member functions take care of collision resolution. Specifically, they manage the BST that belongs to each hash table slot. You may recognize them from the BST implementation that I provided earlier.

```
HashTable::HashTable()
{
    int i;
    for(i=0;i<PRIME;i++)
    {
        hashTbl[i].empty = TRUE;
        hashTbl[i].str[0]='\0';
    }
    return;

}/*end constructor*/

HashTable::~HashTable()
{
    int i;
    for(i=0;i<PRIME;i++)
    {
        deleteAll(&(hashTbl[i].left));
        deleteAll(&(hashTbl[i].right));
    }
    return;

}/*end destructor*/

/*
if symbol exists in hash table, we get a pointer to the node
if a symbol does not exist in the hash table, we get NULL
*/

struct HashTbl* HashTable::queryHashTbl(char *str)
{
    int hash;

    hash = hashpjw(str);

    if(hashTbl[hash].empty==TRUE)
    {
        return(NULL);
    }

    return(findNode(&(hashTbl[hash]), str));
```

```
}/*end queryHashTbl*/

void HashTable::addHashTblEntry(char *val)
{
    struct HashTbl *ptr;
    int hash;

    hash = hashpjw(val);

    printf("HashTable.addHashTblEntry(): hash(%s)=%d\n",val,hash);

    if(hashTbl[hash].empty==TRUE)
    {
        hashTbl[hash].empty=FALSE;
        strcpy(hashTbl[hash].str,val);
        hashTbl[hash].left = NULL;
        hashTbl[hash].right = NULL;
        return;
    }

    ptr = &hashTbl[hash];
    insertNode(&ptr, val);
    return;

}/*end addHashTblEntry*/

void HashTable::printHashTbl()
{
    int i;
    for(i=0;i<PRIME;i++)
    {
        if(hashTbl[i].empty == FALSE)
        {
            printf("--Hash Slot (%d)--\n",i);
            printTree(&(hashTbl[i]), 0);
            printf("\n");
        }
    }
    printf("\n");
    return;

}/*end printHashTbl*/

int HashTable::hashpjw(char *s)
{
    unsigned char * p;
    unsigned h = 0, g;

    for (p = ((unsigned char*)s); *p != '\0'; p = p + 1)
    {
        h = (h < 4) + (*p);
        if (g = (h & 0xf0000000))
        {
```

```
                    h = h ^ (g > 24);
                    h = h ^ g;
                }
        }

        return h % PRIME;

}/*end hashpjw*/

struct HashTbl* HashTable::findNode(struct HashTbl* link, char *val)
{
    if(link==NULL)
    {
        return(NULL);
    }
    else if(strcmp(val,(*link).str)==0)
    {
        return(link);
    }
    else if(strcmp(val,(*link).str)>0)
    {
        return(findNode((*link).right,val));
    }
    else
    {
        return(findNode((*link).left,val));
    }

}/*end findNode*/


void HashTable::insertNode(struct HashTbl** link, char *val)
{
    if((*link) == NULL)
    {
        (*link) = (struct HashTbl*)malloc(sizeof(struct HashTbl));
         (*(*link)).empty = FALSE;
         strcpy((*(*link)).str,val);
        (*(*link)).left         = NULL;
        (*(*link)).right    = NULL;
    }
    else if(strcmp(val,(*(*link)).str) == 0)
    {
        printf("HashTable.insertNode(): redundant identifier %s\n",val);
        return;
    }
    else if(strcmp(val,(*(*link)).str) < 0)
    {
        insertNode(&((*(*link)).left) , val);
    }
    else
    {
        insertNode(&((*(*link)).right) ,val);
    }
```

```
        return;

}/*end insertNode*/

/*
print tree by giving root to node and zero as args
*/

void HashTable::printTree(struct HashTbl* link, int level)
{
    int i;
    if(link==NULL)
    {
        return;
    }

    printTree((*link).right,level+1);

    for(i=0;i<level;i++){ printf("-"); }
    printf("identifier =%s\n",(*link).str);

    printTree((*link).left,level+1);

    return;

}/*end printTree*/

void HashTable::deleteAll(struct HashTbl **link)
{
    if((*link)==NULL)
    {
        return;
    }
    deleteAll(&((*(*link)).left));
    deleteAll(&((*(*link)).right));

    printf("HashTable.deleteAll(): freeing %s\n",(*(*link)).str);
    free((*link));
    *link=NULL;
    return;

}/*end deleteAll*/

/*
Do not have routines to delete hash table entries
Take unnecessary time to perform demolition of the symbol table,
string table, and hash table. Effort spent taking them apart and
freeing them is wasted. Quicker and easier to let the assembler
complete and let the operating system reclaim everything.
*/

void main()
{
    char str[32];
```

```
        HashTable ht;

        ht.addHashTblEntry("register");
        ht.addHashTblEntry("asm");
        ht.addHashTblEntry("union");
        ht.addHashTblEntry("goto");
        ht.addHashTblEntry("do");
        ht.addHashTblEntry("public");
        ht.addHashTblEntry("extern");
        ht.addHashTblEntry("main");
        ht.addHashTblEntry("break");
        ht.addHashTblEntry("this");
        ht.addHashTblEntry("float");
        ht.addHashTblEntry("if");
        ht.addHashTblEntry("void");
        ht.addHashTblEntry("new");
        ht.addHashTblEntry("case");
        ht.addHashTblEntry("sizeof");

        ht.addHashTblEntry("goto"); /*attempt redefinition*/

        ht.printHashTbl();

        strcpy(str,"float");
        if((ht.queryHashTbl(str))!=NULL){ printf("found %s\n",str); }
        else{ printf("did NOT find %s\n",str); }

        strcpy(str,"tax_audit");
        if((ht.queryHashTbl(str))!=NULL){ printf("found %s\n",str); }
        else{ printf("did NOT find %s\n",str); }

        strcpy(str,"extern");
        if((ht.queryHashTbl(str))!=NULL){ printf("found %s\n",str); }
        else{ printf("did NOT find %s\n",str); }

        strcpy(str,"technobabble");
        if((ht.queryHashTbl(str))!=NULL){ printf("found %s\n",str); }
        else{ printf("did NOT find %s\n",str); }


        return;

    }/*end main*/
```

Summary

It might seem like you just waded through a whole truckload of superfluous theory. Nevertheless, I am not trying to waste your time. I had good reasons for starting this chapter with a theoretical review. I followed this approach so that it is easier to read the assembler's source code. The three data structures I have described and implemented are pivotal components of the assembler's engine. By introducing these data structures early on, I'm hoping that you can focus on the actions the assembler performs instead of being bogged down with data structure specifics.

For example, extendable arrays are ubiquitous in the symbol table and string table. By recognizing and understanding these data structures early on, you can focus on what the symbol table and string table are used for, instead of trying to figure out how they operate. In other words, it helps to know German before you read Nietzsche. Likewise, before you read the assembler's source, you need to speak data structures. A summary of this section's discussions and findings is provided in Table 5-5.

Table 5-5

ADT	Data Structure	HASM-specific Use
Vector	Extendable array	String table and symbol table lists
Tree	Binary search tree	Separate chaining, collision resolution
Dictionary	Hash table	Indexing program identifiers

If you remember, earlier in this chapter I presented you with a very primitive version of the basic algorithms the assembler uses to translate an assembly language program into a bytecode executable. Given the previous data structures I have discussed, I think we are ready to recast these algorithms in terms of these data structures.

First Pass (Address Resolution)

1. Obtain the next identifier.

2. Determine the address of the identifier.

3. Place this information in storage for the second pass (assuming that the identifier is not already in storage).
   3a. Store the identifier's text in the string table list.
   3b. Store the identifier's metadata in the symbol table list.
   3c. Add the identifier to the hash table index.
4. Goto step 1.

Second Pass (Code Generation)

1. Obtain the next instruction.

2. Check to see if the instruction involves an identifier.
   2a. If it does not, goto step 3.
   2b. If it does, look up the identifier in the hash table.
   2c. Use hash table information to index the symbol table.
   2d. Get the identifier's address from its symbol table entry.
   2e. Replace the identifier with its address.
3. Translate the instruction to bytecode.

4. Goto step 1.

Command-Line Usage

The HASM assembler has a very simple command line: It expects a single assembly file-name and then a series of one or more options.

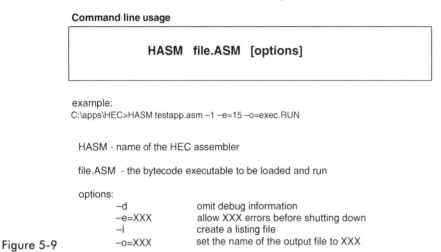

Command line usage

> **HASM   file.ASM   [options]**

example:
C:\apps\HEC>HASM testapp.asm −1 −e=15 −o=exec.RUN

HASM - name of the HEC assembler

file.ASM - the bytecode executable to be loaded and run

options:
−d	omit debug information
−e=XXX	allow XXX errors before shutting down
−l	create a listing file
−o=XXX	set the name of the output file to XXX

Figure 5-9

There are a few things to keep in mind with regard to the HASM command line. First, if you used the −o option to set the name of the output file, the name must end with the .RUN extension. Also, the −o and −e options do not tolerate whitespace. Both of the options must be completely defined without whitespace (i.e., −e = 15 is invalid; you should use −e=15 instead).

The development cycle of the HASM assembler involves processing a single assembly language file and producing up to three different output files. If HASM completes without error, it will generate a bytecode executable (which has a .RUN extension) and an intermediate file (which has a .TMP extension). If the listing flag is set on the HASM command line, a listing file is also created by HASM as an output file. The listing file has an .LST extension.

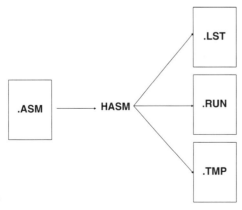

Figure 5-10

Implementation

The process of translating an assembly language source file into a bytecode executable can be dissected into four steps:

1. Process the command-line arguments.

2. Perform the first pass of the source file.

3. Perform the second pass of the source file.

4. Build the bytecode executable.

The fun begins when a user invokes HASM at the command line. Assuming that the command line is valid, it is processed in order to configure the basic operation of the assembler. During the first pass, the source file whose name was supplied on the command line is scanned for symbol definitions (global variable identifiers, procedure names, procedure argument identifiers, etc.). These definitions are used to populate a small, in-memory database that I will refer to as the *symbol repository*. The symbol repository is a collection of classes and data structures that serve to record metadata on the source file symbols.

The second pass scans the source file yet again. However, instead of scanning the source file for symbol definitions, this time the source file is scanned for assembly language instructions. If the assembler encounters an instruction that includes an identifier, it queries the symbol repository in order to replace the identifier with its corresponding address. The second pass takes the source file's instructions and places them all in an intermediate file. This intermediate file has the .TMP file extension. If the assembler's listing flag was set as a command-line option, the second pass will also generate a listing file.

From a source code perspective, there are nine fundamental classes involved in the translation process. Figure 5-11 displays how these classes can be organized with regard to the previous four steps.

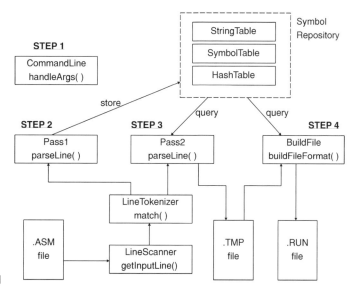

Figure 5-11

Command-line arguments are processed by the CommandLine class. The CommandLine class has a method named handleArgs(), which digests and assimilates the command line.

Once CommandLine is done with its job, the symbol repository is initialized so that symbol metadata can be stored. The symbol repository is comprised of three fundamental classes: the StringTable class, the SymbolTable class, and the HashTable class. The hash table, represented by the HashTable class, serves as an index to information stored in the string table and symbol table. Of the three repository components, the SymbolTable class is the most elaborate. It uses four secondary structures to do its job (GlobalVariable, Procedure, StackFrame, and Label). We will go into much greater detail on this topic later.

The first pass is performed through the tightly knit cooperation of several classes. The LineScanner class applies its getInputLine() member function to decompose the source file into a series of text lines. These lines are fed to the Pass1 class, through its parseLine() function, where it uses the LineTokenizer class to break up the text line to look for symbol definitions. Every time the Pass1 class hits a symbol definition, it stores the symbol identifier and its related metadata in the symbol repository. This is the essence of the first pass. The Pass1 class looks for symbols and populates the symbol repository.

The second pass takes advantage of the work done by the first pass. Again, the LineScanner class is used to obtain lines of text from the source file. These lines of text are fed to the Pass2 class via its parseLine() member function. This time, the Pass2 class uses the LineTokenizer class to extract bytecode instructions from the text that the LineScanner class provides. At this phase of the game, everything must be converted to a number. The assembly language instructions, parsed by the Pass2 class, are transformed into their bytecode equivalents. If the Pass2 class hits an instruction including an identifier, it will query the symbol repository to resolve the identifier to its address. During this operation, the Pass2 class saves the transformed instructions to an intermediate file and maybe also produces a listing file. The Pass2 class is the workhorse of the assembler.

When Pass2 has completed its mission, the BuildFile class takes over. The BuildFile class creates the final product: the bytecode executable. If you remember from the discussion of the virtual machine, a bytecode executable is much more than just bytecode instructions. There's also a lot of special formatting information included. The BuildFile class creates the file's header, symbol table, and string table sections. It uses the symbol repository to do this. When it is done building the first three sections of the bytecode executable, it constructs the bytecode sections of the file by appending the contents of the intermediate file generated during the second pass.

For the sake of organization, I isolated each class in its own source file. I also tried to make the name of each source file similar to the name of the class it contains.

```
BuildFile        bldfile.cpp
CommandLine      cmdline.cpp
GlobalVariable   globvar.cpp
HashTable        hashtbl.cpp
Label            label.cpp
```

```
LineScanner  lnscan.cpp
LineTokenizer  linetok.cpp
Pass1  pass1.cpp
Pass2  pass2.cpp
Procedure  proc.cpp
StackFrame  sframe.cpp
StringTable  strthl.cpp
SymbolTable  symtbl.cpp
```

Four of these files (`globvar.cpp`, `label.cpp`, `proc.cpp`, and `sframe.cpp`) contain structure definitions instead of full-blown class definitions. In other words, `GlobalVariable`, `Label`, `Procedure`, and `StackFrame` are structures, not classes. Nevertheless, I thought it would help to fend off chaos by placing them in their own files.

There are five global files that I borrowed from the virtual machine:

- `common.c`
- `error.c`
- `exenv.c`
- `iset.c`
- `win32.c`

As with the virtual machine, the `main()` function is responsible for staging and managing all five stages of the assembler's execution. The `main()` function is located in a file named `main.cpp`. Taking a preliminary look at its contents will give you a better idea of how the assembler classes are interrelated.

```
/*++++++++++++++++++++++++++++++++++++++++++++++++++++++++++++++++++++++++
+                                                                        +
+ main.cpp - this is the boot-strap file                                 +
+                                                                        +
++++++++++++++++++++++++++++++++++++++++++++++++++++++++++++++++++++++++*/


/*++++++++++++++++++++++++++++++++++++++++++++++++++++++++++++++++++++++++
+ ANSI includes                                                          +
++++++++++++++++++++++++++++++++++++++++++++++++++++++++++++++++++++++++*/

#include<stdio.h>
#include<stdlib.h>
#include<string.h>


/*++++++++++++++++++++++++++++++++++++++++++++++++++++++++++++++++++++++++
+ virtual machine includes                                               +
++++++++++++++++++++++++++++++++++++++++++++++++++++++++++++++++++++++++*/

#define WINDOWS_32

#ifdef WINDOWS_32
#include<win32.c>
#endif
```

```
#include<iset.c>
#include<exenv.c>


/*++++++++++++++++++++++++++++++++++++++++++++++++++++++++++++++++++++++
+ prototypes                                                          +
++++++++++++++++++++++++++++++++++++++++++++++++++++++++++++++++++++++*/

void main(int argc, char *argv[]);
void shutDown(U1 code);


/*++++++++++++++++++++++++++++++++++++++++++++++++++++++++++++++++++++++
+ assembler components                                                +
++++++++++++++++++++++++++++++++++++++++++++++++++++++++++++++++++++++*/

#include<common.c>
#include<error.c>
#include<cmdline.cpp>
#include<lnscan.cpp>
#include<strtbl.cpp>
#include<globvar.cpp>
#include<sframe.cpp>
#include<label.cpp>
#include<proc.cpp>
#include<symtbl.cpp>
#include<hashtbl.cpp>
#include<linetok.cpp>
#include<pass1.cpp>
#include<pass2.cpp>
#include<bldfile.cpp>


/*++++++++++++++++++++++++++++++++++++++++++++++++++++++++++++++++++++++
+ macros                                                              +
++++++++++++++++++++++++++++++++++++++++++++++++++++++++++++++++++++++*/

/*#define MAIN_DEBUG         1*/

#ifdef  MAIN_DEBUG
#define MAIN_DEBUG0(arg);               printf("main(): ");printf(arg);
#define MAIN_DEBUG1(arg1,arg2);         printf("main(): ");printf(arg1,arg2);
#define MAIN_DEBUG2(arg1,arg2,arg3);    printf("main(): ");\
                                        printf(arg1,arg2,arg3);
#else
#define MAIN_DEBUG0(arg);
#define MAIN_DEBUG1(arg1,arg2);
#define MAIN_DEBUG2(arg1,arg2,arg3);
#endif

/*++++++++++++++++++++++++++++++++++++++++++++++++++++++++++++++++++++++
+ function definitions                                                +
++++++++++++++++++++++++++++++++++++++++++++++++++++++++++++++++++++++*/

void main(int argc, char *argv[])
{
    CommandLine cmdLine(&maxErrors);
```

```
nErrors = 0;

/*1) handle command line arguments */

MAIN_DEBUG0("handling arguments\n");

if((cmdLine.handleArgs(argc,argv))==FALSE)
{
    FATAL_ERROR();
}

/*2) PASS1 -  scan, parse, populate symbol table*/

MAIN_DEBUG0("initiating first pass\n");

StringTable strTbl;
HashTable hashTbl(&strTbl);
SymbolTable symTbl(&strTbl);

struct Line line;
{
    Pass1 pass1(&strTbl,&symTbl,&hashTbl);
    LineScanner scanner(&cmdLine);
    line = scanner.getInputLine();
    while(line.end!=TRUE)
    {
        pass1.parseLine(&line);
        line = scanner.getInputLine();
    }
    pass1.parseLine(&line);
}

/*if errors exist, shut down before generate anything*/

if(nErrors > 0)
{
    printf("%d Error(s) during first pass\n",nErrors);
    printf("build failed\n");
    FATAL_ERROR();
}

/*3) PASS2 - create bytecode temp file and listing file */

MAIN_DEBUG0("initiating second pass\n");
{
    Pass2 pass2(&cmdLine,&strTbl,&symTbl,&hashTbl);
    LineScanner scanner(&cmdLine);
    line = scanner.getInputLine();
    while(line.end!=TRUE)
    {
        pass2.parseLine(&line);
        line = scanner.getInputLine();
    }
    pass2.parseLine(&line);
```

```
                    if(cmdLine.listing==TRUE){ pass2.generateSymbolSummary(); }
            }
        MAIN_DEBUG1("%lu bytes written to tempfile\n",pass2.bytePosPass2);


        /*if errors exist after 2nd pass, shut down */

        if(nErrors > 0)
        {
            printf("main(): %d Error(s) during second pass\n",nErrors);
            printf("main(): build failed\n");
            FATAL_ERROR();
        }

        /*4) build compilation unit */

        MAIN_DEBUG0("building bytecode executable\n");
        {
            BuildFile bldfile(&cmdLine,&strTbl, &symTbl);
            bldfile.buildFileFormat();
        }

        /*5) safe-shutdown */

        printf("main(): exiting with (%d) errors\n",nErrors);
        shutDown(SHUTDOWN_OK);
        return;

}/*end main*/


void shutDown(U1 code)
{
    exit(code);

}/*end shutDown*/
```

Global Elements

From our discussion of the virtual machine, you may recall that there were five files which were intended to have elements that were visible to the entire program (common.c, error.c, exenv.c, iset.c, and win32.c). I found it necessary to also make these files a part of the assembler. I also needed to modify a few of the files. For example, in common.c, I added the following macros:

```
#define KILOBYTE      1024
#define BUFFER_SIZE   4*KILOBYTE
```

Much of what the assembler does is related to reading from and writing to files. In an attempt to keep the assembler moving along, buffers are utilized to minimize disk I/O. Rather than reading and writing every individual byte to disk, it saves time to place them in a buffer. This way, data is transported to and from the disk in large chunks. I use the `BUFFER_SIZE` macro to standardize buffer sizes across the assembler's components.

 NOTE Both the operating system and the C standard I/O library calls implement their own buffering. The operating system buffers low-level, direct access calls to the disk hardware. The C standard library buffers on top of this. This means that there's already a lot of copying going on between external buffers before anything reaches the assembler. I could have partially gotten around this problem by using low-level Win32 calls that do not buffer. Taking this route, however, would have hurt portability, so I decided against it.

I also did a major overhaul of the `error.c` file:

```
int maxErrors;        /*maximum # errors before shutdown, default = 10 */
int nErrors;          /*keep track of number of errors*/

#define ERROR0(str);              printf("error: ");\
                                  printf(str); incErrors();

#define ERROR1(str,arg1);         printf("error: ");\
                                  printf(str,arg1); incErrors();

#define ERROR2(str,arg1,arg2);    printf("error: ");\
                                  printf(str,arg1,arg2); incErrors();

#define ERROR3(str,arg1,arg2,arg3);   printf("error: ");\
                                  printf(str,arg1,arg2,arg3); incErrors();

#define FATAL_ERROR();            printf("shutting
down\n");shutDown(SHUTDOWN_ERROR);

void incErrors()
{
    nErrors++;
    if(nErrors >= maxErrors)
    {
        printf("incErrors(): hit max. errors ->(%d)\n",maxErrors);
        FATAL_ERROR();
    }
    return;

}/*end incErrrors*/
```

In the virtual machine's implementation, I had errors written to an XML-formatted error log. When an assembler runs, usually the user is right there at the console and can view error messages as they occur. Because of this, I didn't see any point in persisting error messages to a file.

NOTE One alternative way to record and manage errors is by using an *error stack*. When an error occurs, its details are recorded in an error structure of some sort and then popped onto a stack. Error stacks are useful for applications that cannot simply emit messages to the console, such as HASM. A program module can perform its duties and then return an error stack pointer to the invoking function. If the stack is not empty, the invoking function can examine the stack's error messages and take the appropriate action. I thought about using an error stack with HASM, but it seemed so much more efficient just to pipe everything to the console.

I also wanted the assembler to be robust. A production assembler should be able to continue if it encounters a syntax error. In fact, it should be capable of detecting and reporting several errors before shutting down. On the other hand, I don't want the user to have to deal with so many error messages that they start scrolling out of view. This is particularly frustrating on a platform that doesn't have a console for buffering its output.

To allow HASM to report errors, but not report too many, I allow the user to specify the number of errors the assembler will report before it exits. This value is specified on the HASM command line (i.e., the `-e=XXX` option). This option sets the value of the `maxErrors` variable. As errors occur, the `nErrors` variable is incremented from 0. When the `nErrors` variable hits the value stored in `maxErrors`, the assembler will shut down. If the `-e` option is not explicitly set on the command line, `maxErrors` is set to its default value of 10.

I made one change to `win32.c`. Specifically, I added a function that converts a string to a 64-bit integer. There is no equivalent function in the C standard library, so I had to bite the bullet and wrap a native call.

```
U8 stringToU8(char *str)
{
    return(_atoi64(str));

}/*end stringToU8*/
```

Handling Configuration Options

The first thing the HASM assembler does is process the command line and set configuration variables that influence the rest of the translation process. As with every stage in HASM, the fun begins in `main.cpp`.

```
CommandLine cmdLine(&maxErrors);
struct Line line;
nErrors = 0;

/*1) handle command line arguments */

MAIN_DEBUG0("handling arguments\n");
```

```
if((cmdLine.handleArgs(argc,argv))==FALSE)
{
      FATAL_ERROR();
}
```

The entire process of command-line processing is managed by the CommandLine class. This class is declared and defined in cmdline.cpp. The CommandLine class is instantiated in main() as an object named cmdLine. Once the cmdLine object has done its duty, the rest of the assembler will access command-line settings through its public member variables.

Like several other modules, the CommandLine class uses debugging macros. These debugging facilities are implemented as macros so that they can be stripped out in the release version.

```
#define CMD_LINE_DEBUG            1

#ifdef  CMD_LINE_DEBUG
#define CMD_LINE_DEBUG0(arg);                    printf("handleArgs(): ");printf(arg);
#define CMD_LINE_DEBUG1(arg1,arg2);              printf("handleArgs(): ");printf(arg1,arg2);
#define CMD_LINE_DEBUG2(arg1,arg2,arg3);         printf("handleArgs():
                                                    ");printf(arg1,arg2,arg3);
#else
#define CMD_LINE_DEBUG0(arg);
#define CMD_LINE_DEBUG1(arg1,arg2);
#define CMD_LINE_DEBUG2(arg1,arg2);
#endif
```

There's another macro in cmdline.cpp which is used to define the maximum size of filenames:

```
#define FNAME_SIZE   255         /*maximum size of file name*/
```

The declaration of the CommandLine class is dominated by global member variables, which are used to persist settings entered on the command line. I didn't see any point in defining set and get wrapper methods, so I just left them exposed.

```
class CommandLine
{
    /* file extensions */

    char IN_EXT[5];  /*source*/
    char TMP_EXT[5]; /*intermediate*/
    char LST_EXT[5]; /*listing*/
    char OUT_EXT[5]; /*executable*/

    char nullName[FNAME_SIZE];   /*default name of file*/

    void addFileSuffix(char *out, char *in, char *ext);
    void printUsage();

    public:
    char inputFile[FNAME_SIZE]; /*source file*/
    char listFile[FNAME_SIZE];  /*listing file*/
    char tempFile[FNAME_SIZE];  /*temporary bytecode*/
```

```
        char outputFile[FNAME_SIZE]; /*compilation unit*/

        U1 omitDebugData;              /*TRUE if omit debug data*/
        U1 listing;                    /*TRUE if desire a listing*/
        int *maxErrors;                /*maximum number of errors*/


        CommandLine(int *merros);
        U1 handleArgs(int argc,char *arg[]);

    };
```

The CommandLine class has a constructor that does some preliminary housekeeping and initialization. The constructor is passed a pointer to the global maxErrors variable defined in error.c. This allows the CommandLine class to be completely self contained.

```
    CommandLine::CommandLine(int *merrors)
    {
        strcpy(IN_EXT,".ASM");
        strcpy(TMP_EXT,".TMP");
        strcpy(LST_EXT,".LST");
        strcpy(OUT_EXT,".RUN");

        strcpy(nullName,"UN-NAMED");

        inputFile[0]='\0';
        listFile[0]-'\0';
        tempFile[0]='\0';
        outputFile[0]='\0';

        omitDebugData = FALSE;
        listing = FALSE;
        maxErrors = merrors;
        *maxErrors = 10;

        return;

    }/*end CommandLine*/
```

If an invalid command line is entered, the printUsage() function is called. This member function displays a summary of proper command-line usage.

```
    void CommandLine::printUsage()
    {
        printf("\nHASM file.ASM [options]\n\n");
        printf("\tOptions:\n\n");

        printf("\t-d\n\t\tomit debug information\n");
        printf("\t-e=XXX\n\t\tnumber of errors to report\n");
        printf("\t-l\n\t\tproduce a listing file\n");
        printf("\t-o=XXX\n\t\tname of output file (compilation unit)\n");
```

```
        printf("\n\tthere are no spaces between option characters\n\n");
        return;

}/*end printUsage*/
```

The construction of output filenames (for the listing file, bytecode executable, etc.) from command-line information requires some file extension acrobatics. To append a particular file extension to a given filename, the CommandLine class uses a member function named addFileSuffix():

```
void CommandLine::addFileSuffix(char *out, char *in, char *ext)
{
    char *cptr;
    int index;

    if((out==NULL)||(in==NULL)||(ext==NULL))
    {
        ERRORO("addFileSuffixe(): null pointer args\n");
        FATAL_ERROR();
    }

    cptr = strrchr(in,'.');

    /*if no extension, then just add suffix*/

    if(cptr==NULL)
    {
        strcpy(out,in);
        strcat(out,ext);
    }

    /*otherwise, copy until we hit '.' and then add suffx*/

    else
    {
        index =0;
        while((in[index]!='.')&&(index<FNAME_SIZE-4))
        {
            out[index]=in[index];
            index++;
        }
        out[index]='\0';
        strncat(out,ext,4);
    }
    return;

}/*end addFileSuffix*/
```

The majority of the command-line processing work is performed by the handleArgs() member function:

```
U1 CommandLine::handleArgs(int argc,char *argv[])
{
    int i;
```

```
/* no arguments */

if(argc==1)
{
    CMD_LINE_DEBUG0("No Arguments\n");
    printUsage();
    return(FALSE);
}

/* get input file name "filename.RUN" */

if(argv[1][0]!='-')
{
    int len;
    strncpy(inputFile,argv[1],FNAME_SIZE);
    inputFile[FNAME_SIZE-1]='\0';
    len = strlen(inputFile);

    if(len<4)
    {
        ERROR0("handleArgs(): expecting .ASM file\n");
        return(FALSE);
    }

    if(!((inputFile[len-4]=='.')&&
        ((inputFile[len-3]=='A')||(inputFile[len-3]=='a'))&&
        ((inputFile[len-2]=='S')||(inputFile[len-2]=='s'))&&
        ((inputFile[len-1]=='M')||(inputFile[len-1]=='m'))))
    {
        ERROR0("handleArgs(): expecting .ASM file\n");
        return(FALSE);
    }
}
else
{
    printUsage();
    return(FALSE);
}

/* process options */

for(i=2;i<argc;i++)
{
    if(argv[i][0]=='-')
    {
        switch(argv[i][1])
        {
            case 'd':
            case 'D':
            {
                omitDebugData=TRUE;

                if(argv[i][2]!='\0')
                {
```

```
                                ERRORO("handleArgs(): bad \'-d\'\n");
                                printUsage();
                                return(FALSE);
                        }

                        CMD_LINE_DEBUGO("omitDebugData is TRUE\n");

                }break;
                case 'e':
                case 'E':
                {
                        char intstr[32];

                        if(argv[i][2]=='=')
                        {
                                strcpy(intstr, &argv[i][3]);
                                *maxErrors = atoi(intstr);
                                *maxErrors = abs(*maxErrors);
                        }
                        else
                        {
                                ERRORO("handleArgs(): bad \'-e\'\n");
                                printUsage();
                                return(FALSE);
                        }

                        CMD_LINE_DEBUGO("number of errors set\n");

                }break;
                case 'l':
                case 'L':
                {
                        listing = TRUE;

                        if(argv[i][2]!='\0')
                        {
                                ERRORO("handleArgs(): bad \'-l\'\n");
                                printUsage();
                                return(FALSE);
                        }

                        CMD_LINE_DEBUGO("ListFile set to TRUE\n");

                }break;
                case 'o':
                case 'O':
                {
                        /* output file must look like (file.RUN) */

                        if(argv[i][2]=='=')
                        {
                                int len;

                                strncpy(outputFile,
```

```
                                        &argv[i][3],
                                        FNAME_SIZE);
                            outputFile[FNAME_SIZE-1]='\0';
                            len = strlen(outputFile);

                            if(len<4)
                            {
                            ERROR0("handleArgs(): bad -o=file\n");
                                    return(FALSE);
                            }

                            if(!((outputFile[len-4]=='.')&&
                            (outputFile[len-3]=='R')&&
                            (outputFile[len-2]=='U')&&
                            (outputFile[len-1]=='N')))
                            {
                            ERROR0("handleArgs(): bad -o=file\n");
                                    return(FALSE);
                            }

                            CMD_LINE_DEBUG0("output file set\n");
                    }
                    else
                    {
                            ERROR0("handleArgs(): bad \'-o\'\n");
                            printUsage();
                            return(FALSE);
                    }

            }break;
            default:
            {
                    ERROR1("handleArgs(): %s bad option\n",
                                    argv[i]);
                    printUsage();
                    return(FALSE);
            }

        }/*end-switch*/

    }/*end if*/
    /*not an option, does not begin with dash*/
    else
    {
            printUsage();
            return(FALSE);
    }

}/*end for-loop*/

if(outputFile[0]=='\0')
{
    addFileSuffix(outputFile,inputFile,OUT_EXT);
}
```

```
            addFileSuffix(tempFile,outputFile,TMP_EXT);
            addFileSuffix(listFile,outputFile,LST_EXT);

            CMD_LINE_DEBUG0("Command line summary\n");
            CMD_LINE_DEBUG1("\tfile to load=%s\n",inputFile);
            CMD_LINE_DEBUG1("\toutput file=%s\n",outputFile);
            CMD_LINE_DEBUG1("\ttemp file=%s\n",tempFile);
            CMD_LINE_DEBUG1("\tlist file=%s\n",listFile);
            CMD_LINE_DEBUG1("\terrors to report=%d\n",*maxErrors);

            if(listing == TRUE)
            {
                CMD_LINE_DEBUG0("\tlisting is ON\n");
            }
            else
            {
                CMD_LINE_DEBUG0("\tlisting is OFF\n");
            }

            if(omitDebugData == TRUE)
            {
                CMD_LINE_DEBUG0("\tomitting debug data\n\n");
            }
            else
            {
                CMD_LINE_DEBUG0("\tdebug data included\n\n");
            }

            return(TRUE);

        }/*end handleArguments*/
```

Pass 1 – Populate the Symbol Table

Overview

Once the command-line arguments have been swallowed and digested, we're ready to make the first pass over the source file. The core actions taken by the assembler during the first pass are summed up by the following snippet of code from `main.cpp`:

```
        /*2) PASS1 - scan, parse, populate symbol table*/

        MAIN_DEBUG0("initiating first pass\n");

        StringTable strTbl;
        HashTable hashTbl(&strTbl);
        SymbolTable symTbl(&strTbl);

        struct Line line;
        {
            Pass1 pass1(&strTbl,&symTbl,&hashTbl);
            LineScanner scanner(&cmdLine);
```

```
            line = scanner.getInputLine();
            while(line.end!=TRUE)
            {
                    pass1.parseLine(&line);
                    line = scanner.getInputLine();
            }
            pass1.parseLine(&line);
    }

    /*if errors exist, shutdown before generate anything*/

    if(nErrors > 0)
    {
            printf("%d Error(s) during first pass\n",nErrors);
            printf("build failed\n");
            FATAL_ERROR();
    }
```

First the symbol repository (`StringTable`, `SymbolTable`, and `HashTable`) is initialized. Next, the `LineScanner` object reads in lines of text from the source file and passes them to the `Pass1` object, which searches through them looking for symbol definitions. When `Pass1` finds a symbol definition, it stores the symbol and its corresponding metadata in the symbol repository. What we need to do now is to look at this process under a microscope. Let's start with the `LineScanner`.

LineScanner

The `LineScanner` class has the `CommandLine` class fed to its constructor. This gives the `LineScanner` access to necessary information, like the name of the source file to be scanned. The `LineScanner`'s job is to break the source file up into lines of text, store them in a `Line` structure, and then return the populated `Line` structure when its `getInputLine()` member function is invoked.

The `Line` structure is pretty simple:

```
struct Line
{
    char src[LINE_SIZE]; /*single line of assembler code*/
    unsigned long line;  /*line number*/
    char *fName;         /*file reading assembly code from*/
    unsigned char end;   /*(TRUE|FALSE), indicates we've hit EOF*/
};
```

When the `LineScanner` has reached the last line of the source file, it will set the `Line` structure's `end` field to true.

The internal operation of the `LineScanner` class is also fairly direct. The `LineScanner` has an internal buffer where it keeps bytes from the source file. When `getInputLine()` is called, `LineScanner` relies on repeated calls to `getInputChar()` to get the next line of text from the internal buffer. If the buffer is exhausted, a function named `fillInputBuffer()` is called to replenish the supply of bytes. The relationship of these functions is illustrated in Figure 5-12.

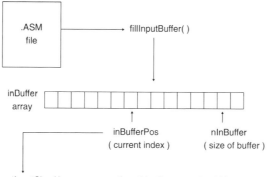

Figure 5-12

Given the previous discussion, you should be able to understand the implementation of the `LineScanner` class.

```
class LineScanner
{
    FILE *iFptr;                /*pointer to assembly code file*/
    char iFname[FNAME_SIZE];    /*name of assembly code file*/
    char inBuffer[BUFFER_SIZE]; /*buffer for input from assembly file*/
    int  nInBuffer;             /*number of bytes in inBuffer*/
    int  inBufferPos;           /*index into inBuffer: 0 -> nInBuffer-1 */
    unsigned long inLine;       /*current line in file*/

    void fillInputBuffer();
    char getInputChar();
    void prep(char ch, char *str);

    public:
    LineScanner(CommandLine *cl_obj);
    ~LineScanner();

    struct Line getInputLine();
    void printScannedLine(struct Line *lptr);

    void test();
};

LineScanner::LineScanner(CommandLine *cl_obj)
{
    if(((*cl_obj).inputFile==NULL)||(strlen((*cl_obj).inputFile)==0))
    {
        INPUT_SCAN_DEBUG0("LineScanner(): file name empty\n");
        strcpy(iFname,(*cl_obj).nullName);
    }
    else
    {
        strncpy(iFname,(*cl_obj).inputFile,FNAME_SIZE);
        iFname[FNAME_SIZE-1]='\0';
        INPUT_SCAN_DEBUG1("LineScanner(): opened %s\n",iFname);
    }
```

```
        iFptr = fopen(iFname,"rb");
        if(iFptr==NULL)
        {
                printf("LineScanner::LineScanner(): could not open %s\n",iFname);
                exit(SHUTDOWN_ERROR);
        }
        inLine = 1;
        fillInputBuffer();
        return;

}/*end constructor*/

LineScanner::~LineScanner()
{
        if(iFptr!=NULL)
        {
                if(fclose(iFptr))
                {
                        printf("LineScanner::~LineScanner(): ");
                        printf("could not close %s\n",iFname);
                }
        }
        else
        {
                INPUT_SCAN_DEBUG0("~LineScanner(): null file pointer\n");
        }

        INPUT_SCAN_DEBUG0("~LineScanner(): closed file\n");

        return;

}/*end destructor*/

void LineScanner::fillInputBuffer()
{
        int nbytes;

        nbytes=0;
        nbytes = fread(inBuffer,sizeof(char),BUFFER_SIZE,iFptr);

        /*if nbytes is less than BUFFER_SIZE, have hit EOF or have an error*/

        if(nbytes<BUFFER_SIZE)
        {
                if(feof(iFptr)==0)
                {
                        printf("LineScanner::fillInputBuffer(): ");
                        printf("error reading from %s\n",iFname);
                        exit(SHUTDOWN_ERROR);
                }
                else
                {
                        /*add a byte to buffer size and set it to IN_END*/
```

```
                        nInBuffer = nbytes+1;
                        inBuffer[nInBuffer-1] = IN_END;
                INPUT_SCAN_DEBUG0("fillInputBuffer(): hit EOF filling buffer\n");
                }
        }
        else
        {
                nInBuffer = BUFFER_SIZE;
        }

        INPUT_SCAN_DEBUG1("fillInputBuffer(): read %d bytes\n",nInBuffer);

        inBufferPos = -1;   /*init for first call to getInputChar()*/
        return;

}/*end fillInputBuffer*/

char LineScanner::getInputChar()
{
        //char str[4];

        inBufferPos++;

        /*
        if read entire buffer (0-(nInBuffer-1))
        and are at the char following the end (nInBuffer)
        then fill in a new one
        */

        if(inBufferPos == nInBuffer)
        {
        INPUT_SCAN_DEBUG0("getInputBufferChar(): hit end, filling buffer\n");
                fillInputBuffer();
                inBufferPos++;   /*fillInputBuffer set to -1*/
        }

        /*if at very last char of buffer, look at last char for EOF flag*/

        if(inBufferPos == nInBuffer-1)
        {
                if(inBuffer[inBufferPos]==IN_END)
                {
                        INPUT_SCAN_DEBUG0("getInputBufferChar():hit EOF\n");
                        /*make sure always stay at end, if call again*/
                        inBufferPos--;
                        return(IN_END);
                }
        }

        //prep(inBuffer[inBufferPos],str)
        //INPUT_SCAN_DEBUG1("getInputBufferChar():read %s\n",str);
```

```c
        return(inBuffer[inBufferPos]);

}/*end getInputChar*/

/* prepares a character to be printed to screen */

void LineScanner::prep(char ch,char* str)
{
    switch(ch)
    {
        case '\n':
        {
            strcpy(str,"NL");
            return;
        }
        case '\r':
        {
            strcpy(str,"CR");
            return;
        }
        case '\t':
        {
            strcpy(str,"TAB");
            return;
        }
        case ' ':
        {
            strcpy(str,"SP");
            return;
        }
    }
    str[0]=ch;
    str[1]='\0';
    return;

}/*end prep*/

struct Line LineScanner::getInputLine()
{
    struct Line line;
    char ch;
    int i;

    i=0;
    line.end = FALSE;
    line.fName = iFname;

    /*get first non-whitespace character*/

    ch = getInputChar();

    while((ch=='\n')||(ch=='\r'))
    {
            if(ch=='\n'){ inLine++; }
```

```
                    ch = getInputChar();
            }

            /*keep reading until hit end of line, file, or buffer*/

            while((ch!='\n')&&(ch!=IN_END)&&(i<LINE_SIZE-1))
            {
                    if(ch=='\r'){ ch = getInputChar(); }
                    else
                    {
                            line.src[i]=ch;
                            ch = getInputChar();
                            i++;
                    }
            }

            if(ch==IN_END){ line.end = TRUE; }

            line.src[i]='\0';
            line.line = inLine;
            inLine++;
            INPUT_SCAN_DEBUG1("getInputLine(): scanned %s\n",line.src);
            return(line);

    }/*end getInputLine*/

    void LineScanner::printScannedLine(struct Line *lptr)
    {
            printf("file=%s ",(*lptr).fName);
            printf("line=%lu ",(*lptr).line);
            printf("text=%s\n",(*lptr).src);
            return;

    }/*end printScannedLine*/
```

LineScanner feeds its results to the Pass1 object, which then masticates the lines in search of symbol definitions (like variable and procedure names). However, the Pass1 object does not do the dirty work of breaking up the line of text itself. Instead, it passes the Line structure to its henchman, the LineTokenizer class.

LineTokenizer

The LineTokenizer class takes a single line of text and breaks it up into tokens. A *token* is a sequence of characters that represents an atomic language element. For example, the LBI assembly language instruction is a token. The process of breaking up a source file into a series of tokens is known as *lexical analysis*. The components of a development tool that perform lexical analysis are referred to, in aggregate, as the *lexical analyzer*. In the case of the HASM assembler, the lexical analyzer is manifested by the combined efforts of the LineScanner class and the LineTokenizer class. The LineScanner decomposes the source file into lines of text, and the LineTokenizer breaks those lines up even further into tokens. Some books often refer to a lexical analyzer as a *scanner* or *tokenizer*. In the context of my class hierarchy, I have used synonyms to name different parts of the lexical analysis process, even if it was merely to remind myself that the two classes have related functionality.

The `LineTokenizer` class has the following declaration:

```
class LineTokenizer
{
    char tokenBuffer[LINE_SIZE];      /*whole line of assembler text*/
    int ntChars;                      /*number chars + null char */
    int itChars;                      /*index into buffer*/
    struct Line *lineptr;             /*ptr to Line fed to constructor*/

    /*called by process---- functions*/
    char getNextLineChar();
    void goBackOneChar();
    char skipLineWhiteSpace();

    /*called by getNextLineToken*/
    void processRegister(struct Token *tptr);
    void processCharConst(struct Token *tptr);
    void processIdentifier(struct Token *tptr, char ch);
    void processNumConst(struct Token *tptr, char ch);

    public:
    LineTokenizer(struct Line *ln);

    /*called by match*/
    struct Token getNextLineToken();

    U1 match(struct Token *tptr, int ttype); /* big one */
    void printToken(struct Token *tptr);
};
```

As you can see, there are four public member functions. The really vital member function is the `getNextLineToken()` function. When invoked, this function returns the next token in the line of text fed to the class via its constructor. The `getNextLineToken()` function returns a `Token` structure that completely describes the token:

```
struct Token
{
    char text[ID_SIZE];
    char *fName;      /*file reading assembly code from*/
    U4 line;          /* line number in source file */
    U1 type;          /* type of token */
    S8 val;           /* register bytecode val, char val, integer const */
    F8 fval;          /* floating-pt val */
};
```

The big question is: How does `LineTokenizer`'s `getNextLineToken()` function work? The algorithm is fairly simple, though several books on compiler theory will often use lexical analysis as an opportunity to venture into topics like finite automata. The basic algorithm the `LineTokenizer` uses performs the following steps:

1. Skip tab or space characters until a token character is encountered.

2. Use this first character to determine the token type.

3. Keep reading characters until a character is encountered that does not belong to the token type

The `LineTokenizer` recognizes eight basic types of tokens:

- Integer registers (i.e., $R17)
- Float registers (i.e., $F3)
- Double registers (i.e., $D8)
- Character constants (i.e., `'s'`)
- Identifiers (i.e., instructions like PUSHB, function names)
- Integer constants (i.e., 437)
- Floating-point constants (i.e., 2.37e-10)
- Commas

In the `linetok.cpp` source code, I use the following macros to specify the type of a token:

```
#define TOK_IDENTIFIER    0
#define TOK_INT_REG       1
#define TOK_FLT_REG       2
#define TOK_DBL_REG       3
#define TOK_CHAR_CONST    4
#define TOK_INT_CONST     5
#define TOK_FLT_CONST     6
#define TOK_COMMA         7
#define TOK_NO_MORE       8
#define TOK_BAD           9
```

These macros are used to populate the type field of the `Token` structure. To obtain a string representation of these types, a type-indexed string array is used.

```
char *TokStr[] = {    "TOK_IDENTIFIER",
                      "TOK_INT_REG",
                      "TOK_FLT_REG",
                      "TOK_DBL_REG",
                      "TOK_CHAR_CONST",
                      "TOK_INT_CONST",
                      "TOK_FLT_CONST",
                      "TOK_COMMA",
                      "TOK_NO_MORE",
                      "TOK_BAD"};
```

I have defined token types such that the first character of a token determines its basic type. For example, register tokens all begin with a dollar sign. Character constants begin with a single quote. Identifier tokens begin with a letter, an underscore, a period, a question mark, or an @ symbol. Numeric constant tokens begin with a digit.

Another thing the algorithm implies is that each token type has a specific set of characters that can be used to generate a valid token after the first character has been specified.

A series of flow diagrams are provided in Figures 5-13 and 5-14 to demonstrate how certain tokens are produced and which characters may be used.

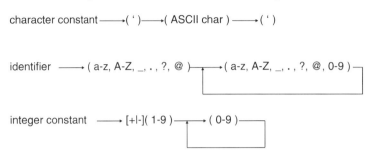

Figure 5-13

A character constant token begins with an opening single quote, followed by an ASCII character and a closing single quote. The ASCII character must be a printable character whose decimal value in the ASCII collating sequence is in the range 32 to 126.

An identifier token begins with a letter, an underscore, a period, a question mark, or an @ symbol. The first character may then be followed by one or more characters of the same class, and also by one or more decimal digits. Identifier tokens can be up to 255 characters in length. This size limit is established by the ID_SIZE macro in linetok.cpp:

```
#define ID_SIZE 256        /* max. chars in identifier */
```

An integer constant token can begin with a decimal digit ranging from 1 to 9. The first character can be followed by decimal digits ranging from 0 to 9. The first digit can be prefixed with a unary sign character.

A floating-point constant token is a little more complicated. A floating-point token consists of a string with one of the following three forms:

```
[+|−] NZ [digits] (e|E) [+|−] digits          (i.e., 622e–8)
[+|−] NZ [digits] .digits [ (e|E) [+|−] digits ]   (i.e., −1.34)
[+|−]  0.digits [ (e|E) [+|−] digits ]        (i.e., 0.41e+11)
```

Elements in brackets are optional. Elements in parentheses are mandatory. The vertical bar represents the logical OR operator. The "NZ" element represents a single decimal digit in the range from 1 through 9 (nonzero). The "digits" element represents a series of one or more decimal digits that range from 0 through 9. We can also represent these possible combinations using a flow diagram.

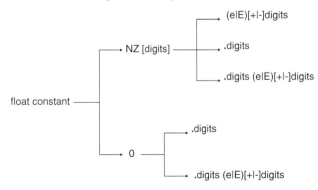

Figure 5-14

To implement its algorithm, the `getNextLineToken()` function ends up invoking several secondary, private member functions of `LineTokenizer`. Depending on the token type, a different combination of private functions will be called and a different execution path will result. A summary of the paths of execution that are taken to generate a token and populate its fields is displayed in Figure 5-15.

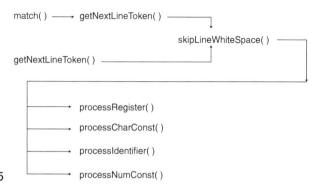

Figure 5-15

Almost every secondary function makes calls to `getNextLineChar()` and `goBackOneChar()` in order to extract a token from the `Line` structure's text. These two functions are nested away deep in the bowels of `LineTokenizer`.

Like other components in the assembler, the `LineTokenizer`'s source file has debugging macros:

```
#define LINE_TOK_DEBUG            1

#ifdef LINE_TOK_DEBUG
#define LINE_TOK_DEBUG0(arg);                 printf(arg);
#define LINE_TOK_DEBUG1(arg1,arg2);           printf(arg1,arg2);
#define LINE_TOK_DEBUG2(arg1,arg2,arg3);      printf(arg1,arg2,arg3);
#else
#define LINE_TOK_DEBUG0(arg);
#define LINE_TOK_DEBUG1(arg1,arg2);
#define LINE_TOK_DEBUG2(arg1,arg2,arg3);
#endif
```

The constructor of the `LineTokenizer` class accepts a `Line` structure as an argument and uses it to initialize the buffer the class will use to extract tokens from.

```
LineTokenizer::LineTokenizer(struct Line *ln)
{
    lineptr = ln;
    strcpy(tokenBuffer,(*ln).src);
    ntChars = strlen(tokenBuffer)+1; /*include null char*/
    itChars = -1;
    return;

}/*end constructor*/
```

Now let's take a look at the source code implementation of the `LineTokenizer`'s functions. The best way to read this code is to follow the execution paths detailed in Figure

5-15. Start with match() and continue from there to the peripheral functions. The match() function is invoked frequently by the Pass1 and Pass2 objects. It is used to verify that the next token in the Line structure is of a certain type.

```
U1 LineTokenizer::match(struct Token *tptr, int ttype)
{
    (*tptr) = getNextLineToken();
    if((*tptr).type!=ttype)
    {
        ERROR5("%s:(%lu) expecting %s, not %s in\"%s\"\n",
                    (*tptr).fName,
                    (*tptr).line,
                    TokStr[ttype],
                    TokStr[(*tptr).type],
                    (*tptr).text);
        return(FALSE);
    }

    return(TRUE);

}/*end match*/
```

As you can see, the match() function ends up calling getNextLineToken():

```
#define EOL            '\0'

/*
    Gameplan:

    i) skip white space (space or tab)
    ii) look at first char (determines tok type)
                $ = register ($R_, $F_, $D_)
                ' = char constant ('a')
                a-z, A-Z, @, _, ?, . = identifier
                0-9, +, - = numeric constant
                , = comma
                '\0' = end of string
    iii) keep reading until
                -hit end of line
                -reach char not belonging to tok type
    iv) populate token attributes and return
*/

struct Token LineTokenizer::getNextLineToken()
{
    struct Token token;
    char current;

    /* still need to set text,type,val/fval*/

    token.line = (*lineptr).line;
    token.fName = (*lineptr).fName;
    token.val  = 0;
    token.fval = 0.0;
```

```
        current = skipLineWhiteSpace();

        if(current=='$'){ processRegister(&token); }

        else if(current=='\''){ processCharConst(&token); }

        else if(((current>='a')&&(current<='z'))||
                ((current>='A')&&(current<='Z'))||
                 (current=='@')||
                 (current=='_')||
                 (current=='?')||
                 (current=='.')){ processIdentifier(&token,current); }

        else if(((current>='0')&&(current<='9'))||
                (current=='-')||
                (current=='+')){ processNumConst(&token,current); }

        else if(current==',')
        {
            token.text[0]=current;
            token.text[1]='\0';
            token.type = TOK_COMMA;
        }
        else if(current==EOL)
        {
            strcpy(token.text,"EOL");
            token.type = TOK_NO_MORE;
        }
        else
        {
            token.text[0]=current;
            token.text[1]='\0';
            token.type = TOK_BAD;
        }

        return(token);

}/*end getNextLineToken*/
```

The `getNextLineToken()` function always calls the `skipLineWhiteSpace()` function and then, depending on the token type, might invoke one of four secondary functions.

```
char LineTokenizer::skipLineWhiteSpace()
{
    char ch;
    ch=getNextLineChar();
    while((ch==' ')||(ch=='\t'))
    {
        ch=getNextLineChar();
    }
    return(ch);
```

```
}/*end skipLineWhiteSpace*/

void LineTokenizer::processRegister(struct Token *tptr)
{
    char current;
    current = getNextLineChar();

    switch(current)
    {
        /*INT_REGISTER----------------------------------------*/
        case 'R':
        case 'r':
        {
            current = getNextLineChar();

            switch(current)
            {
                case '1': /* $R1- */
                {
                    char peek = getNextLineChar();

                    switch(peek)
                    {
                        case '0':
                        {
                            strcpy((*tptr).text,"$R10");
                            (*tptr).type = TOK_INT_REG;
                            (*tptr).val = $R10;
                        }break;
                        case '1':
                        {
                            strcpy((*tptr).text,"$R11");
                            (*tptr).type = TOK_INT_REG;
                            (*tptr).val = $R11;
                        }break;
                        case '2':
                        {
                            strcpy((*tptr).text,"$R12");
                            (*tptr).type = TOK_INT_REG;
                            (*tptr).val = $R12;
                        }break;
                        case '3':
                        {
                            strcpy((*tptr).text,"$R13");
                            (*tptr).type = TOK_INT_REG;
                            (*tptr).val = $R13;
                        }break;
                        case '4':
                        {
                            strcpy((*tptr).text,"$R14");
                            (*tptr).type = TOK_INT_REG;
                            (*tptr).val = $R14;
                        }break;
                        case '5':
```

```c
                              {
                                   strcpy((*tptr).text,"$R15");
                                   (*tptr).type = TOK_INT_REG;
                                   (*tptr).val = $R15;
                              }break;
                              case '6':
                              {
                                   strcpy((*tptr).text,"$R16");
                                   (*tptr).type = TOK_INT_REG;
                                   (*tptr).val = $R16;
                              }break;
                              case '7':
                              {
                                   strcpy((*tptr).text,"$R17");
                                   (*tptr).type = TOK_INT_REG;
                                   (*tptr).val = $R17;
                              }break;
                              case '8':
                              {
                                   strcpy((*tptr).text,"$R18");
                                   (*tptr).type = TOK_INT_REG;
                                   (*tptr).val = $R18;
                              }break;
                              case '9':
                              {
                                   strcpy((*tptr).text,"$R19");
                                   (*tptr).type = TOK_INT_REG;
                                   (*tptr).val = $R19;
                              }break;
                              default:
                              {
                                   strcpy((*tptr).text,"$R1");
                                   (*tptr).type = TOK_INT_REG;
                                   (*tptr).val = $R1;
                                   goBackOneChar();
                              }
                         }/*end of $R1 sub-switch*/
                    }break;
                    case '2': /* $R2- */
                    {
                         char peek = getNextLineChar();

                         switch(peek)
                         {
                              case '0':
                              {
                                   strcpy((*tptr).text,"$R20");
                                   (*tptr).type = TOK_INT_REG;
                                   (*tptr).val = $R20;
                              }break;
                              case '1':
                              {
                                   strcpy((*tptr).text,"$R21");
                                   (*tptr).type = TOK_INT_REG;
```

```
                                             (*tptr).val = $R21;
                            }break;
                            case '2':
                            {
                                    strcpy((*tptr).text,"$R22");
                                    (*tptr).type = TOK_INT_REG;
                                    (*tptr).val = $R22;
                            }break;
                            case '3':
                            {
                                    strcpy((*tptr).text,"$R23");
                                    (*tptr).type = TOK_INT_REG;
                                    (*tptr).val = $R23;
                            }break;
                            case '4':
                            {
                                    strcpy((*tptr).text,"$R24");
                                    (*tptr).type = TOK_INT_REG;
                                    (*tptr).val = $R24;
                            }break;
                            default:
                            {
                                    strcpy((*tptr).text,"$R2");
                                    (*tptr).type = TOK_INT_REG;
                                    (*tptr).val = $R2;
                                    goBackOneChar();
                            }
                    }/*end of $R2 sub-switch*/
            }break;
            case '3':
            {
                    strcpy((*tptr).text,"$R3");
                    (*tptr).type = TOK_INT_REG;
                    (*tptr).val = $R3;
            }break;
            case '4':
            {
                    strcpy((*tptr).text,"$R4");
                    (*tptr).type = TOK_INT_REG;
                    (*tptr).val = $R4;
            }break;
            case '5':
            {
                    strcpy((*tptr).text,"$R5");
                    (*tptr).type = TOK_INT_REG;
                    (*tptr).val = $R5;
            }break;
            case '6':
            {
                    strcpy((*tptr).text,"$R6");
                    (*tptr).type = TOK_INT_REG;
                    (*tptr).val = $R6;
            }break;
            case '7':
```

```
                         {
                             strcpy((*tptr).text,"$R7");
                             (*tptr).type = TOK_INT_REG;
                             (*tptr).val = $R7;
                         }break;
                         case '8':
                         {
                             strcpy((*tptr).text,"$R8");
                             (*tptr).type = TOK_INT_REG;
                             (*tptr).val = $R8;
                         }break;
                         case '9':
                         {
                             strcpy((*tptr).text,"$R9");
                             (*tptr).type = TOK_INT_REG;
                             (*tptr).val = $R9;
                         }break;
                         default: /*does not start with 0-9*/
                         {
                             (*tptr).text[0]='$';
                             (*tptr).text[1]='R';
                             (*tptr).text[2]=current;
                             (*tptr).text[3]='\0';
                             (*tptr).type = TOK_BAD;
                         }
                 }/*end $R switch*/
        }break;
        /*FLT_REGISTER-----------------------------------------*/
        case 'F':
        case 'f':
        {
             current = getNextLineChar();

             switch(current)
             {
                 case '1':
                 {
                     current = getNextLineChar();

                     if(current=='0')
                     {
                         strcpy((*tptr).text,"$F10");
                         (*tptr).type = TOK_FLT_REG;
                         (*tptr).val = $F10;
                     }
                     else
                     {
                         strcpy((*tptr).text,"$F1");
                         (*tptr).type = TOK_FLT_REG;
                         (*tptr).val = $F1;
                         goBackOneChar();
                     }
                 }break;
                 case '2':
```

```
                        {
                            strcpy((*tptr).text,"$F2");
                            (*tptr).type = TOK_FLT_REG;
                            (*tptr).val = $F2;
                        }break;
                        case '3':
                        {
                            strcpy((*tptr).text,"$F3");
                            (*tptr).type = TOK_FLT_REG;
                            (*tptr).val = $F3;
                        }break;
                        case '4':
                        {
                            strcpy((*tptr).text,"$F4");
                            (*tptr).type = TOK_FLT_REG;
                            (*tptr).val = $F4;
                        }break;
                        case '5':
                        {
                            strcpy((*tptr).text,"$F5");
                            (*tptr).type = TOK_FLT_REG;
                            (*tptr).val = $F5;
                        }break;
                        case '6':
                        {
                            strcpy((*tptr).text,"$F6");
                            (*tptr).type = TOK_FLT_REG;
                            (*tptr).val = $F6;
                        }break;
                        case '7':
                        {
                            strcpy((*tptr).text,"$F7");
                            (*tptr).type = TOK_FLT_REG;
                            (*tptr).val = $F7;
                        }break;
                        case '8':
                        {
                            strcpy((*tptr).text,"$F8");
                            (*tptr).type = TOK_FLT_REG;
                            (*tptr).val = $F8;
                        }break;
                        case '9':
                        {
                            strcpy((*tptr).text,"$F9");
                            (*tptr).type = TOK_FLT_REG;
                            (*tptr).val = $F9;
                        }break;
                        case 'P':
                        case 'p':
                        {
                            strcpy((*tptr).text,"$FP");
                            (*tptr).type = TOK_INT_REG;
                            (*tptr).val = $FP;
                        }break;
```

```
                         default: /* not 0-9*/
                         {
                                 (*tptr).text[0]='$';
                                 (*tptr).text[1]='F';
                                 (*tptr).text[2]=current;
                                 (*tptr).text[3]='\0';
                                 (*tptr).type = TOK_BAD;
                         }
                  }/*end of $F switch*/
          }break;
          /*DBL_REGISTER----------------------------------------*/
          case 'D':
          case 'd':
          {
                  current = getNextLineChar();

                  switch(current)
                  {
                         case '1':
                         {
                                 current = getNextLineChar();

                                 if(current=='0')
                                 {
                                     strcpy((*tptr).text,"$D10");
                                     (*tptr).type = TOK_DBL_REG;
                                     (*tptr).val = $D10;
                                 }
                                 else
                                 {
                                     strcpy((*tptr).text,"$D1");
                                     (*tptr).type = TOK_DBL_REG;
                                     (*tptr).val = $D1;
                                     goBackOneChar();
                                 }
                         }break;
                         case '2':
                         {
                                 strcpy((*tptr).text,"$D2");
                                 (*tptr).type = TOK_DBL_REG;
                                 (*tptr).val = $D2;
                         }break;
                         case '3':
                         {
                                 strcpy((*tptr).text,"$D3");
                                 (*tptr).type = TOK_DBL_REG;
                                 (*tptr).val = $D3;
                         }break;
                         case '4':
                         {
                                 strcpy((*tptr).text,"$D4");
                                 (*tptr).type = TOK_DBL_REG;
                                 (*tptr).val = $D4;
                         }break;
```

```
                                case '5':
                                {
                                     strcpy((*tptr).text,"$D5");
                                     (*tptr).type = TOK_DBL_REG;
                                     (*tptr).val = $D5;
                                }break;
                                case '6':
                                {
                                     strcpy((*tptr).text,"$D6");
                                     (*tptr).type = TOK_DBL_REG;
                                     (*tptr).val = $D6;
                                }break;
                                case '7':
                                {
                                     strcpy((*tptr).text,"$D7");
                                     (*tptr).type = TOK_DBL_REG;
                                     (*tptr).val = $D7;
                                }break;
                                case '8':
                                {
                                     strcpy((*tptr).text,"$D8");
                                     (*tptr).type = TOK_DBL_REG;
                                     (*tptr).val = $D8;
                                }break;
                                case '9':
                                {
                                     strcpy((*tptr).text,"$D9");
                                     (*tptr).type = TOK_DBL_REG;
                                     (*tptr).val = $D9;
                                }break;
                                default: /* not 0-9*/
                                {
                                     (*tptr).text[0]='$';
                                     (*tptr).text[1]='D';
                                     (*tptr).text[2]=current;
                                     (*tptr).text[3]='\0';
                                     (*tptr).type = TOK_BAD;
                                }
                           }/*end of $D switch*/

                 }break;
                 /*end case D*/
                 case 'I':
                 case 'i':
                 {
                      current = getNextLineChar();
                      if((current=='P')||(current=='p'))
                      {
                           strcpy((*tptr).text,"$IP");
                           (*tptr).type = TOK_INT_REG;
                           (*tptr).val = $IP;
                      }
                      else
                      {
```

```
                        (*tptr).text[0]='$';
                        (*tptr).text[1]='I';
                        (*tptr).text[2]=current;
                        (*tptr).text[3]='\0';
                        (*tptr).type = TOK_BAD;
                }

        }break;
        case 'B':
        case 'b':
        {
                current = getNextLineChar();
                if((current=='E')||(current=='e'))
                {
                        strcpy((*tptr).text,"$BE");
                        (*tptr).type = TOK_INT_REG;
                        (*tptr).val = $BE;
                }
                else
                {
                        (*tptr).text[0]='$';
                        (*tptr).text[1]='B';
                        (*tptr).text[2]=current;
                        (*tptr).text[3]='\0';
                        (*tptr).type = TOK_BAD;
                }

        }break;
        case 'S':
        case 's':
        {
                current = getNextLineChar();
                if((current=='P')||(current=='p'))
                {
                        strcpy((*tptr).text,"$SP");
                        (*tptr).type = TOK_INT_REG;
                        (*tptr).val = $SP;
                }
                else if((current=='S')||(current=='s'))
                {
                        strcpy((*tptr).text,"$SS");
                        (*tptr).type = TOK_INT_REG;
                        (*tptr).val = $SS;
                }
                else
                {
                        (*tptr).text[0]='$';
                        (*tptr).text[1]='S';
                        (*tptr).text[2]=current;
                        (*tptr).text[3]='\0';
                        (*tptr).type = TOK_BAD;
                }

        }break;
```

```
case 'H':
case 'h':
{
    current = getNextLineChar();
    if((current=='S')||(current=='s'))
    {
        strcpy((*tptr).text,"$HS");
        (*tptr).type = TOK_INT_REG;
        (*tptr).val = $HS;
    }
    else if((current=='E')||(current=='e'))
    {
        strcpy((*tptr).text,"$HE");
        (*tptr).type = TOK_INT_REG;
        (*tptr).val = $HE;
    }
    else
    {
        (*tptr).text[0]='$';
        (*tptr).text[1]='H';
        (*tptr).text[2]=current;
        (*tptr).text[3]='\0';
        (*tptr).type = TOK_BAD;
    }

}break;
case 'T':
case 't':
{
    current = getNextLineChar();
    if((current=='o')||(current=='O'))
    {
        current = getNextLineChar();
        if((current=='P')||(current=='p'))
        {
            strcpy((*tptr).text,"$TOP");
            (*tptr).type = TOK_INT_REG;
            (*tptr).val = $TOP;
        }
        else
        {
            (*tptr).text[0]='$';
            (*tptr).text[1]='T';
            (*tptr).text[2]='O';
            (*tptr).text[3]=current;
            (*tptr).text[4]='\0';
            (*tptr).type = TOK_BAD;
        }
    }
    else
    {
        (*tptr).text[0]='$';
        (*tptr).text[1]='T';
        (*tptr).text[2]=current;
```

```
                                (*tptr).text[3]='\0';
                                (*tptr).type = TOK_BAD;
                        }

                }break;
                /*NOT $R_,$F_,$D_, or $IP, $SP, $FP, $BE, $HS, $HE, $SS, $TOP*/
                default:
                {
                        (*tptr).text[0]='$';
                        (*tptr).text[1]=current;
                        (*tptr).text[2]='\0';
                        (*tptr).type = TOK_BAD;
                }
        }/*end switch*/

        return;

}/*end processRegister*/

void LineTokenizer::processCharConst(struct Token *tptr)
{
        char current;
        char ch;
        ch = current = getNextLineChar();
        if((current>=32)&&(current<=126))
        {
                (*tptr).text[0]=current;
                (*tptr).text[1]='\0';
                (*tptr).val=current;
                (*tptr).type = TOK_CHAR_CONST;
                current = getNextLineChar();
                if(current!='\'')
                {
                        (*tptr).text[0]='\'';
                        (*tptr).text[1]=ch;
                        (*tptr).text[2]=current;
                        (*tptr).text[3]='\0';
                        (*tptr).type = TOK_BAD;
                }
        }
        else
        {
                        (*tptr).text[0]='\'';
                        (*tptr).text[1]=current;
                        (*tptr).text[2]='\0';
                        (*tptr).type = TOK_BAD;
        }
        return;

}/*end processCharConstant*/

void LineTokenizer::processIdentifier(struct Token *tptr, char ch)
{
        int i;
```

```
        char current;

        i=0;
        (*tptr).text[i]=ch;
        current = getNextLineChar();
        while(((current>='a')&&(current<='z'))||
                ((current>='A')&&(current<='Z'))||
                ((current>='0')&&(current<='9'))||
                (current=='@')||
                (current=='_')||
                (current=='?')||
                (current=='.'))
        {
                i++;
                (*tptr).text[i]=current;
                current = getNextLineChar();
        }
        i++;
        (*tptr).text[i]='\0';
        (*tptr).type=TOK_IDENTIFIER;
        goBackOneChar();
        return;

}/*end processIdentifier*/

void LineTokenizer::processNumConst(struct Token *tptr, char ch)
{
        int i;
        char current;

        i=0;
        current = ch;

        if((current=='+')||(current=='-'))
        {
                (*tptr).text[i]=current;
                i++;
                current = getNextLineChar();
        }

        /* float/integer starts with 0-9 */

        if((current>='0')&&(current<='9'))
        {
                /* if 0 is first digit, must be followed by decimal place*/

                if(current=='0')
                {
                        current = getNextLineChar();
                        if(current =='.')
                        {
                                current = '0';
                                goBackOneChar();
                        }
```

```
        else
        {
            (*tptr).text[i]=current;
            (*tptr).text[i+1]='\0';
            (*tptr).type = TOK_INT_CONST;
            return;
        }
}

while((current>='0')&&(current<='9'))
{
    (*tptr).text[i]=current;
    i++;
    current = getNextLineChar();
}

/* digits end in decimal point*/

if(current=='.')
{
    (*tptr).text[i]='.';
    i++;
    current = getNextLineChar();

    if((current>='0')&&(current<='9'))
    {
        while((current>='0')&&(current<='9'))
        {
            (*tptr).text[i]=current;
            i++;
            current = getNextLineChar();
        }
    }
    else /* no digits following decimal point, required */
    {
        (*tptr).text[i]='\0';
        (*tptr).type = TOK_BAD;
        goBackOneChar();
        return;
    }

    if((current=='e')||(current=='E'))
    {
        (*tptr).text[i]=current;
        i++;
        current = getNextLineChar();

        if((current=='+')||(current=='-'))
        {
            (*tptr).text[i]=current;
            i++;
            current = getNextLineChar();
        }
```

```
                              if((current>='0')&&(current<='9'))
                              {
                                   while((current>='0')&&(current<='9'))
                                   {
                                        (*tptr).text[i]=current;
                                        i++;
                                        current = getNextLineChar();
                                   }

                                   (*tptr).text[i]='\0';
                                   (*tptr).type=TOK_FLT_CONST;
                                   (*tptr).fval = atof((*tptr).text);
                                   goBackOneChar();
                                   return;
                              }
                              else /*no digits after +/- */
                              {
                                   (*tptr).text[i]='\0';
                                   (*tptr).type = TOK_BAD;
                                   goBackOneChar();
                                   return;
                              }

                    }
                    else /*no e/E following .digits */
                    {
                         (*tptr).text[i]='\0';
                         (*tptr).type=TOK_FLT_CONST;
                         (*tptr).fval = atof((*tptr).text);
                         goBackOneChar();
                         return;

                    }
          }

          /*digits end in e/E potential float*/

          else if((current=='e')||(current=='E'))
          {
               (*tptr).text[i]=current;
               i++;
               current = getNextLineChar();

               if((current=='+')||(current=='-'))
               {
                    (*tptr).text[i]=current;
                    i++;
                    current = getNextLineChar();
               }

               if((current>='0')&&(current<='9'))
               {
                    while((current>='0')&&(current<='9'))
                    {
                         (*tptr).text[i]=current;
```

```
                                    i++;
                                    current = getNextLineChar();
                            }

                            (*tptr).text[i]='\0';
                            (*tptr).type=TOK_FLT_CONST;
                            (*tptr).fval = atof((*tptr).text);
                            goBackOneChar();
                            return;
                    }
                    else /*no digits after +/- */
                    {
                            (*tptr).text[i]='\0';
                            (*tptr).type = TOK_BAD;
                            goBackOneChar();
                            return;
                    }
            }

            /*digits do not end in decimal point or e/E, have integer*/

            else
            {
                    (*tptr).text[i]='\0';
                    (*tptr).type = TOK_INT_CONST;
                    (*tptr).val = stringToU8((*tptr).text);
                    goBackOneChar();
                    return;
            }
    }

    /*does start with 0-9  after +/- */

    else
    {
            (*tptr).text[0]='\0';
            (*tptr).type = TOK_BAD;
            goBackOneChar();
    }
    return;

}/*end processNumConstant*/
```

Finally, `LineTokenizer` also has a couple of low-level functions that pop up all over the place in the four secondary functions:

```
char LineTokenizer::getNextLineChar()
{
    itChars++; /* can be in range 0,1, ..., (ntChars-1)*/

    if(itChars>=ntChars-1)
    {
            return(EOL);
    }
```

```
              return(tokenBuffer[itChars]);

   }/*end getNextLineChar*/

   void LineTokenizer::goBackOneChar()
   {
       if(itChars >= 0){ itChars--; }
       return;

   }/*end goBackOneChar*/
```

As an afterthought, I implemented a function that would print out information about a token:

```
   void LineTokenizer::printToken(struct Token *tptr)
   {
       printf("TOK-> file=%s line=%d type=%s ",
                   (*tptr).fName,
                   (*tptr).line,
                   TokStr[(*tptr).type]);
       switch((*tptr).type)
       {
            case TOK_IDENTIFIER:
            {
                printf("text=%s\n",(*tptr).text);
            }break;
            case TOK_INT_REG:
            {
                printf("text=%s val=%d\n",(*tptr).text,(*tptr).val);
            }break;
            case TOK_FLT_REG:
            {
                printf("text=%s val=%d\n",(*tptr).text,(*tptr).val);
            }break;
            case TOK_DBL_REG:
            {
                printf("text=%s val=%d\n",(*tptr).text,(*tptr).val);
            }break;
            case TOK_CHAR_CONST:
            {
                printf("text=%s\n",(*tptr).text);
            }break;
            case TOK_INT_CONST:
            {
                printf("text=%s val=",(*tptr).text);
                pS8((*tptr).val);
                printf("\n");
            }break;
            case TOK_FLT_CONST:
            {
                printf("text=%s fval=%g\n",(*tptr).text,(*tptr).fval);
            }break;
            case TOK_COMMA:
            {
```

```
                                    printf("text=%s\n",(*tptr).text);
                         }break;
                         case TOK_NO_MORE:
                         {
                                printf("text=%s\n",(*tptr).text);
                         }break;
                         case TOK_BAD:
                         {
                                printf("text=%s\n",(*tptr).text);
                         }break;
                 }
                 return;

}/*end printToken*/
```

Pass1

The `Pass1` object parses the source file for symbol definitions. Its class has the following
declaration:

```
class Pass1
{
        StringTable *strTbl;              /*pointers to symbol repository structures*/
        SymbolTable *symTbl;
        HashTable *hashTbl;

        U4 currentProcPass1;             /*index into symTbl of current procedure*/
        U8 bytePosPass1;                 /*current index of bytecode being generated*/
        U8 globalTotal;                  /*current total size of globals*/

        void  processDirective(struct Token *tptr, LineTokenizer *ptr);
        void  processGDirective(struct Token *tptr, LineTokenizer *ptr);
        void  processPDirective(struct Token *tptr, LineTokenizer *ptr);

        void  processInstruction(struct Token *tptr);

        public:
        Pass1(StringTable *st, SymbolTable *syt, HashTable *ht);
        void parseLine(struct Line *line);
};
```

The `Pass1` class only exposes two public functions. It has a public constructor and a public `parseLine()` function. When the `Pass1` object encounters a symbol definition, it
stores all the information about the symbol in the symbol repository. Because of this, the
constructor has parameters that allow the `Pass1` object to access the three members of the
symbol repository.

```
#define OUTSIDE_PROC_PASS1 -1

Pass1::Pass1(StringTable *st, SymbolTable *syt, HashTable *ht)
{
    strTbl = st;
    symTbl = syt;
    hashTbl = ht;
```

```
        currentProcPass1 = OUTSIDE_PROC_PASS1;
        bytePosPass1 = 0;
        globalTotal = 0;
        return;

    }/*end constructor*/
```

The `OUTSIDE_PROC_PASS1` macro is used to ensure that assembler procedures are not nested inside of each other. Just like C, the HEC assembly language does not allow procedures to be defined within one another.

Before we dive into its implementation, take a look at Figure 5-16, which displays the paths of execution that branch off from `parseLine()`.

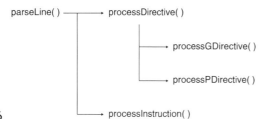

Figure 5-16

The `parseLine()` public member function of the `Pass1` class takes the `Line` structure passed to it by the `LineScanner` object in `main.cpp` and uses a `LineTokenizer` object to help it find symbol definitions.

```
void Pass1::parseLine(struct Line *line)
{
    struct Token token;

    /*
    line can be
        i) a directive (starts with a period, i.e., .IP)
        ii) an instruction (opcode operand(s))
        iii) a comment (starts with #)
    */

    LineTokenizer toker(line);
    token = toker.getNextLineToken();
    switch(token.text[0])
    {
        case '.':{ processDirective(&token,&toker); }break;
        case '#':{ /*comment, ignore line*/ }break;
        default:{ processInstruction(&token); }
    }
    return;

}/*end parseLine*/
```

In the HEC assembly language, symbols are always defined using a directive. There are ten directives available. All directives begin with a period, followed by the letter "G" or the letter "P."

- ■ .GB   Defines a global variable (byte size)
- ■ .GW   Defines a global variable (word size)
- ■ .GD   Defines a global variable (double word size)
- ■ .GQ   Defines a global variable (quad word size)
- ■ .PB   Marks the beginning of a procedure
- ■ .PE   Marks the end of a procedure
- ■ .PR   Defines a procedure return value
- ■ .PA   Defines a procedure argument
- ■ .PV   Defines a procedure local variable
- ■ .PL   Defines a procedure label

 NOTE   I'm only going to provide a cursory discussion of directives in this chapter. Later in this book I will reintroduce directives and look at them in depth.

The `parseLine()` function processes both directives (via `ProcessDirective()`) and instructions (via `processInstruction()`). The `Pass1` class, however, really doesn't generate anything when it encounters an instruction. It only processes instructions to keep track of the current address, so that when we encounter a procedure definition or a label, we will know which address it represents.

The `processDirective()` private member function delegates the work involved in processing directives to two different functions. One function, `processGDirective()` is used to parse global variable directives (start with a .G). The other function, `processPDirective()`, is used to parse procedure-related directives (start with a .P).

```
void  Pass1::processDirective(struct Token *tptr, LineTokenizer *ptr)
{
    if((*tptr).type==TOK_IDENTIFIER)
    {
        switch((*tptr).text[1])
        {
            case 'G':{ processGDirective(tptr,ptr); }break;
            case 'P':{ processPDirective(tptr,ptr); }break;
            default:
            {
                ERROR2("Pass1::processDirective(): %s not directive,
                        line %lu\n",(*tptr).text,(*tptr).line);
            }
        }
    }
    else
    {
        ERROR2("Pass1::processDirective(): %s not directive,
                line %lu\n",(*tptr).text,(*tptr).line);
    }
    return;
```

```
}/*end processDirective*/
```

All global variable directives have the following form:

```
.GB   identifier   [ integer ]
```

The B suffix on the .G directive indicates that this global variable is byte-sized. The identifier, which represents the global variable, follows directly after the .G directive. If the global variable is an array, the number of elements is provided after the identifier.

```
void  Pass1::processGDirective(struct Token *tptr, LineTokenizer *ptr)
{
    struct Token t;
    struct HashTbl *hptr; /*returned from hash table*/
    U1 bret;

    /*global variable metadata*/
    char id[ID_SIZE];
    U1 dtype;
    U8 length;
    U8 size;
    U8 offset;
    U4 line;

    switch((*tptr).text[2]) /*.GB identifier  [ integer ]*/
    {
        /*third char, text[2], gives datatype*/

        case 'B':{ dtype = SZ_BYTE; }break;
        case 'W':{ dtype = SZ_WORD; }break;
        case 'D':{ dtype = SZ_DWORD; }break;
        case 'Q':{ dtype = SZ_QWORD; }break;
        default:
        {
            ERROR2("Pass1::processGDirective(): line %d,
            invalid global data type (%s)\n",(*tptr).line,(*tptr).text);
            return;
        }
    }

    /*set some defaults*/

    length = 1;
    size = dtype*length;
    offset = 0;
    line = (*tptr).line;

    bret = (*ptr).match(&t,TOK_IDENTIFIER);
    if(bret!=TRUE)
    {
        ERROR1("Pass1::processGDirective(): line %d,
                global missing identifier\n",(*tptr).line);
        return;
    }
```

```
strcpy(id,t.text);

/*
the [integer] modifiers is optional
so we cannot use match() because there are 2 correct ways

i)   .GX identifier integer EOL
ii)  .GX identifier EOL
*/

t = (*ptr).getNextLineToken();

/* .GX identifier integer EOL */

if(t.type==TOK_INT_CONST)
{
    length = (U8)t.val;
    size = dtype*length;

    globalTotal = globalTotal + size;
    offset = globalTotal;

    bret = (*ptr).match(&t,TOK_NO_MORE);
    if(bret==FALSE)
    {
        ERROR1("Pass1::processGDirective(): line %d,
                bad global declaration\n",(*tptr).line);
        return;
    }
}

/*.GX identifier EOL*/

else if(t.type==TOK_NO_MORE)
{
    size = dtype;
    globalTotal = globalTotal + size;
    offset = globalTotal;
}

/*.GX identifer XXXX */

else
{
    ERROR1("Pass1::processGDirective(): line %d,
            bad global declaration\n",(*tptr).line);
    return;
}

/*if evade all errors, add .GB entry*/

PASS1_DEBUG0("Pass1::processGDirective(): adding .GX to symbol table\n");
hptr =  (*hashTbl).queryHashTbl(id);
if(hptr!=NULL)
```

```
        {
                ERROR2("Pass1::processGDirective(): line %d,
                                %s re-defined\n",line,id);
                return;
        }
        else
        {
                struct GlobalVariable gv;
                gv.text = (*strTbl).iStr;
                gv.dType = dtype;
                gv.len = length;
                gv.size = size;
                gv.offset = offset;
                gv.line= line;
                (*strTbl).addStrTbl(id);
                (*symTbl).addGlobVar(&gv);
                (*hashTbl).addHashTblEntry(id,gv.text,GLOBAL_VAR,
                                        ((*symTbl).iGlobVar-1),0,line);
        }
        return;

}/*end processGDirective*/
```

The last few lines of processGDirective() are crucial because this is where we actually add the global variable to the symbol repository. Everything up to this point has been staging for this event. We start by adding the text of the identifier to the string table. Then, a GlobalVariable structure is populated and added to the symbol table. Finally, we add the global variable to the hash table. We will discuss the particulars of the symbol repository later in this section.

Procedure-related directives have the following form:

```
.PB     identifier
.PR     identifier  +integer
.PA     identifier  +integer
.PV     identifier  -integer
.PL     identifier
.PE
```

Return values, arguments, and local variables are all followed by an integer offset that specifies their position in the procedure's activation record. This value ends up being added to the value in the $FP register to produce an indirect address. The process-PDirective() function spends most of its effort on parsing these expressions. When a valid one has been completely parsed, the corresponding symbol is placed in the symbol repository.

```
void  Pass1::processPDirective(struct Token *tptr, LineTokenizer *ptr)
{
    struct Token t;
    U1 bret;

    if(strcmp((*tptr).text,".PB")==0)   /*.PB identifier EOL*/
    {
            char id[ID_SIZE];
```

```
U8 address;
U4 line;
struct HashTbl *hptr;

/*set some defaults*/
address = 0;
line  = 0;

bret = (*ptr).match(&t,TOK_IDENTIFIER);
if(bret!=TRUE)
{
      ERROR1("Pass1::processPDirective(): line %lu,
                  bad directive\n",(*tptr).line);
      return;
}

strcpy(id,t.text);
line = t.line;
address = bytePosPass1;

bret = (*ptr).match(&t,TOK_NO_MORE);
if(bret==FALSE)
{
      ERROR1("Pass1::processPDirective(): line %lu,
                  bad directive\n",(*tptr).line);
      return;
}

hptr =  (*hashTbl).queryHashTbl(id);

if(hptr!=NULL)
{
      ERROR2("Pass1::processPDirective(): line %d,
                  %s re-definition\n",line,id);
      return;
}
else if(currentProcPass1!=OUTSIDE_PROC_PASS1)
{
      ERROR2("Pass1::processPDirective(): line %d,
                  %s, cannot nest procedures\n",line,id);
      return;
}
else
{
      struct Procedure p;
      p.text = (*strTbl).iStr;
      p.address = address;
      p.line= line;
      (*strTbl).addStrTbl(id);
      (*symTbl).addProc(&p);
      (*hashTbl).addHashTblEntry(id,p.text,
                      PROC,((*symTbl).iProc-1),0,line);
      currentProcPass1 = (*symTbl).iProc-1;
}
```

```
}/*end .PB*/
else if(strcmp((*tptr).text,".PR")==0)   /*.PR identifier +n     */
{
    char name[ID_SIZE];
    S4 offset;
    U4 line;
    struct HashTbl *hptr;

    line = (*tptr).line;

    bret = (*ptr).match(&t,TOK_IDENTIFIER);
    if(bret!=TRUE)
    {
        ERROR1("Pass1::processPDirective(): line %lu,
                bad directive\n",(*tptr).line);
        return;
    }

    strcpy(name,t.text);

    bret = (*ptr).match(&t,TOK_INT_CONST);
    if(bret!=TRUE)
    {
        ERROR1("Pass1::processPDirective(): line %lu,
                bad directive\n",(*tptr).line);
        return;
    }

    offset = (S4)t.val;

    bret = (*ptr).match(&t,TOK_NO_MORE);
    if(bret!=TRUE)
    {
        ERROR1("Pass1::processPDirective(): line %lu,
                bad directive\n",(*tptr).line);
        return;
    }

    hptr =  (*hashTbl).queryHashTbl(name);
    if(hptr!=NULL)
    {
        ERROR2("processPDirective(): line %d,
                %s re-defined\n",line,name);
        return;
    }
    else
    {
        struct StackFrame sf;
        sf.text = (*strTbl).iStr;
        sf.fpOffset = offset;
        sf.line = line;
        (*strTbl).addStrTbl(name);
        (*symTbl).setProcRetHL(&sf);
        (*hashTbl).addHashTblEntry(name,sf.text,
```

```
                              PROC_RET,((*symTbl).iProc-1),0,line);
            }

}/*end .PR*/
else if(strcmp((*tptr).text,".PA")==0)   /*.PA identifier +n*/
{
        char name[ID_SIZE];
        S4 offset,
        U4 line;
        struct HashTbl *hptr;

        bret = (*ptr).match(&t,TOK_IDENTIFIER);
        if(bret!=TRUE)
        {
                ERROR1("Pass1::processPDirective(): line %lu,
                        bad directive\n",(*tptr).line);
                return;
        }

        strcpy(name,t.text);
        line = t.line;

        bret = (*ptr).match(&t,TOK_INT_CONST);
        if(bret!=TRUE)
        {
                ERROR1("Pass1::processPDirective(): line %lu,
                        bad directive\n",(*tptr).line);
                return;

        }

        offset = (S4)t.val;

        bret = (*ptr).match(&t,TOK_NO_MORE);
        if(bret!=TRUE)
        {
                ERROR1("Pass1::processPDirective(): line %lu,
                        bad directive\n",(*tptr).line);
                return;
        }

        hptr =  (*hashTbl).queryHashTbl(name);
        if(hptr!=NULL)
        {
                ERROR2("processPDirective(): line %d,
                        %s re-defined\n",line,name);
                return;
        }

        struct StackFrame sf;
        sf.text = (*strTbl).iStr;
        sf.fpOffset = offset;
        sf.line = line;
        (*strTbl).addStrTbl(name);
```

```
                    (*symTbl).addProcArgHL(&sf);
                    (*hashTbl).addHashTblEntry(name,
                                                sf.text,
                                                PROC_ARG,
                                                ((*symTbl).iProc-1),
                                                (((*symTbl).proc[(*symTbl).iProc-1]).iArg-1),
                                                    line);

        }/*end .PA*/
        else if(strcmp((*tptr).text,".PV")==0)    /*.PV identifier -n*/
        {
                char name[ID_SIZE];
                S4 offset;
                U4 line;
                struct HashTbl *hptr;

                line = (*tptr).line;

                bret = (*ptr).match(&t,TOK_IDENTIFIER);
                if(bret!=TRUE)
                {
                        ERROR1("Pass1::processPDirective(): line %lu,
                                    bad directive\n",(*tptr).line);
                        return;
                }

                strcpy(name,t.text);

                bret = (*ptr).match(&t,TOK_INT_CONST);
                if(bret!=TRUE)
                {
                        ERROR1("Pass1::processPDirective(): line %lu,
                                    bad directive\n",(*tptr).line);
                        return;
                }

                offset = (S4)t.val;

                bret = (*ptr).match(&t,TOK_NO_MORE);
                if(bret!=TRUE)
                {
                        ERROR1("Pass1::processPDirective(): line %lu,
                                    bad directive\n",(*tptr).line);
                        return;
                }

                hptr =  (*hashTbl).queryHashTbl(name);
                if(hptr!=NULL)
                {
                        ERROR2("processPDirective(): line %d,
                                    %s re-defined\n",line,name);
                        return;
                }
```

```
                      struct StackFrame sf;
                      sf.text = (*strTbl).iStr;
                      sf.fpOffset = (S4)offset;
                      sf.line = line;
                      (*strTbl).addStrTbl(name);
                      (*symTbl).addProcLocHL(&sf);
                      (*hashTbl).addHashTblEntry(name,
                                              sf.text,
                                              PROC_LOC,
                                              ((*symTbl).iProc-1),
                                              (((*symTbl).proc[(*symTbl).iProc-1]).iLocal-1),
                                                  line);

}/*end .PV*/
else if(strcmp((*tptr).text,".PL")==0)   /*.PL identifier*/
{
        char name[ID_SIZE];
        U8 address;
        U4 line;
        struct HashTbl *hptr;

        line = (*tptr).line;
        bret = (*ptr).match(&t,TOK_IDENTIFIER);
        if(bret!=TRUE)
        {
              ERROR1("Pass1::processPDirective(): line %lu,
                          bad directive\n",(*tptr).line);
              return;

        }

        strcpy(name,t.text);
        address = bytePosPass1;

        bret = (*ptr).match(&t,TOK_NO_MORE);
        if(bret!=TRUE)
        {
              ERROR1("Pass1::processPDirective(): line %lu,
                          bad directive\n",(*tptr).line);
              return;

        }

        hptr =  (*hashTbl).queryHashTbl(name);
        if(hptr!=NULL)
        {
              ERROR2("processPDirective(): line %d,
                          %s re-defined\n",line,name);
              return;
        }

        struct Label lb;
        lb.text = (*strTbl).iStr;
        lb.address = address;
```

```
                         lb.line = line;
                         (*strTbl).addStrTbl(name);
                         (*symTbl).addProcLblHL(&lb);
                         (*hashTbl).addHashTblEntry(name,
                                                   lb.text,
                                                   PROC_LBL,
                                                   ((*symTbl).iProc-1),
                                                   (((*symTbl).proc[(*symTbl).iProc-1]).iLabel-1),
                                                        line);

        }/*end .PL*/
        else if(strcmp((*tptr).text,".PE")==0)/*.PE*/
        {
                bret = (*ptr).match(&t,TOK_NO_MORE);
                if(bret==TRUE)
                {
                        /*
                        cannot define code outside of a procedure
                        */
                        currentProcPass1 = OUTSIDE_PROC_PASS1;
                }
                else
                {
                        ERROR1("Pass1::processPDirective(): line %lu,
                                bad directive\n",(*tptr).line);
                        return;
                }

        }/*end .PE*/
        else
        {
                ERROR1("Pass1::processPDirective(): line %lu,
                                bad directive\n",(*tptr).line);
        }
        return;

}/*end processPDirective*/
```

As I stated earlier, the processInstruction() function really only keeps track of
the current address so that we can assign valid address values to functions and labels. To
this end, the processInstruction() function updates the bytePosPass1 private
variable, which stores the address of the next byte in the executable HASM is going to
generate.

```
void Pass1::processInstruction(struct Token *tptr)
{
    if((*tptr).type!=TOK_IDENTIFIER)
    {
            ERROR1("Pass1::processInstruction(): %s not a valid opcode\n",
                        (*tptr).text);
            return;
    }

    switch((*tptr).text[0])
```

```
                    {
                case 'A':
                {
                    if(strcmp((*tptr).text,"ADD")==0)
                    { bytePosPass1 = bytePosPass1 + 4;}
                    else if(strcmp((*tptr).text,"AND")==0)
                    { bytePosPass1 = bytePosPass1 + 4;}
                    else
                    {
                        ERROR2("Pass1::processInstruction(): line %d,
                        invalid opcode (%s)\n",(*tptr).line,(*tptr).text);
                        return;
                    }
                }break;
                case 'B':
                {
                    if(strcmp((*tptr).text,"BS")==0)
                    { bytePosPass1 = bytePosPass1 + 3;}
                    else if(strcmp((*tptr).text,"BT")==0)
                    { bytePosPass1 = bytePosPass1 + 4;}
                    else
                    {
                        ERROR2("Pass1::processInstruction(): line %d,
                        invalid opcode (%s)\n",(*tptr).line,(*tptr).text);
                        return;
                    }
                }break;
                case 'C':
                {
                    if(strcmp((*tptr).text,"CAST_IF")==0)
                    { bytePosPass1 = bytePosPass1 + 3;}
                    else if(strcmp((*tptr).text,"CAST_ID")==0)
                    { bytePosPass1 = bytePosPass1 + 3;}
                    else if(strcmp((*tptr).text,"CAST_FI")==0)
                    { bytePosPass1 = bytePosPass1 + 3;}
                    else if(strcmp((*tptr).text,"CAST_FD")==0)
                    { bytePosPass1 = bytePosPass1 + 3;}
                    else if(strcmp((*tptr).text,"CAST_DI")==0)
                    { bytePosPass1 = bytePosPass1 + 3;}
                    else if(strcmp((*tptr).text,"CAST_DF")==0)
                    { bytePosPass1 = bytePosPass1 + 3;}
                    else
                    {
                        ERROR2("Pass1::processInstruction(): line %d,
                        invalid opcode (%s)\n",(*tptr).line,(*tptr).text);
                        return;
                    }
                }break;
                case 'D':
                {
                    if(strcmp((*tptr).text,"DIV")==0)
                    { bytePosPass1 = bytePosPass1 + 5;}
                    else if(strcmp((*tptr).text,"DI")==0)
                    { bytePosPass1 = bytePosPass1 + 1;}
```

```
                else if(strcmp((*tptr).text,"DADD")==0)
                { bytePosPass1 = bytePosPass1 + 4;}
                else if(strcmp((*tptr).text,"DSUB")==0)
                { bytePosPass1 = bytePosPass1 + 4;}
                else if(strcmp((*tptr).text,"DMULT")==0)
                { bytePosPass1 = bytePosPass1 + 4;}
                else if(strcmp((*tptr).text,"DDIV")==0)
                { bytePosPass1 = bytePosPass1 + 4;}
                else if(strcmp((*tptr).text,"DSLT")==0)
                { bytePosPass1 = bytePosPass1 + 4;}
                else
                {
                     ERROR2("Pass1::processInstruction(): line %d,
                     invalid opcode (%s)\n",(*tptr).line,(*tptr).text);
                     return;
                }
        }break;
        case 'E':
        {
             if(strcmp((*tptr).text,"EI")==0)
             { bytePosPass1 = bytePosPass1 + 1;}
             else
             {
                     ERROR2("Pass1::processInstruction(): line %d,
                     invalid opcode (%s)\n",(*tptr).line,(*tptr).text);
                     return;
             }
        }break;
        case 'F':
        {
             if(strcmp((*tptr).text,"FADD")==0)
             { bytePosPass1 = bytePosPass1 + 4;}
             else if(strcmp((*tptr).text,"FSUB")==0)
             { bytePosPass1 = bytePosPass1 + 4;}
             else if(strcmp((*tptr).text,"FMULT")==0)
             { bytePosPass1 = bytePosPass1 + 4;}
             else if(strcmp((*tptr).text,"FDIV")==0)
             { bytePosPass1 = bytePosPass1 + 4;}
             else if(strcmp((*tptr).text,"FSLT")==0)
             { bytePosPass1 = bytePosPass1 + 4;}
             else
             {
                     ERROR2("Pass1::processInstruction(): line %d,
                     invalid opcode (%s)\n",(*tptr).line,(*tptr).text);
                     return;
             }
        }break;
        case 'H':
        {
             if(strcmp((*tptr).text,"HALT")==0)
             { bytePosPass1 = bytePosPass1 + 1;}
             else
             {
                     ERROR2("Pass1::processInstruction(): line %d,
```

```
                            invalid opcode (%s)\n",(*tptr).line,(*tptr).text);
                            return;
                    }
            }break;
            case 'I':
            {
                    if(strcmp((*tptr).text,"INT")==0)
                    { bytePosPass1 = bytePosPass1 + 2;}
                    else
                    {
                            ERROR2("Pass1::processInstruction(): line %d,
                            invalid opcode (%s)\n",(*tptr).line,(*tptr).text);
                            return;
                    }
            }break;
            case 'J':
            {
                    if(strcmp((*tptr).text,"JMP")==0)
                    { bytePosPass1 = bytePosPass1 + 2;}
                    else if(strcmp((*tptr).text,"JE")==0)
                    { bytePosPass1 = bytePosPass1 + 4;}
                    else if(strcmp((*tptr).text,"JNE")==0)
                    { bytePosPass1 = bytePosPass1 + 4;}
                    else
                    {
                            ERROR2("Pass1::processInstruction(): line %d,
                            invalid opcode (%s)\n",(*tptr).line,(*tptr).text);
                            return;
                    }
            }break;
            case 'L':
            {
                    if(strcmp((*tptr).text,"LBI")==0)
                    { bytePosPass1 = bytePosPass1 + 3;}
                    else if(strcmp((*tptr).text,"LWI")==0)
                    { bytePosPass1 = bytePosPass1 + 4;}
                    else if(strcmp((*tptr).text,"LDI")==0)
                    { bytePosPass1 = bytePosPass1 + 6;}
                    else if(strcmp((*tptr).text,"LQI")==0)
                    { bytePosPass1 = bytePosPass1 + 10;}
                    else if(strcmp((*tptr).text,"LF1I")==0)
                    { bytePosPass1 = bytePosPass1 + 6;}
                    else if(strcmp((*tptr).text,"LF2I")==0)
                    { bytePosPass1 - bytePosPass1 + 10;}
                    else if(strcmp((*tptr).text,"LB")==0)
                    { bytePosPass1 = bytePosPass1 + 3;}
                    else if(strcmp((*tptr).text,"LW")==0)
                    { bytePosPass1 = bytePosPass1 + 3;}
                    else if(strcmp((*tptr).text,"LD")==0)
                    { bytePosPass1 = bytePosPass1 + 3;}
                    else if(strcmp((*tptr).text,"LQ")==0)
                    { bytePosPass1 = bytePosPass1 + 3;}
                    else if(strcmp((*tptr).text,"LF1")==0)
                    { bytePosPass1 = bytePosPass1 + 3;}
```

```
                    else if(strcmp((*tptr).text,"LF2")==0)
                    { bytePosPass1 = bytePosPass1 + 3;}
                    else if(strcmp((*tptr).text,"LAD")==0)
                    { bytePosPass1 = bytePosPass1 + 10;}
                    else if(strcmp((*tptr).text,"LAI")==0)
                    { bytePosPass1 = bytePosPass1 + 11;}
                    else
                    {
                         ERROR2("Pass1::processInstruction(): line %d,
                         invalid opcode (%s)\n",(*tptr).line,(*tptr).text);
                         return;
                    }
             }break;
             case 'M':
             {
                    if(strcmp((*tptr).text,"MOV")==0)
                    { bytePosPass1 = bytePosPass1 + 3;}
                    else if(strcmp((*tptr).text,"MOVF")==0)
                    { bytePosPass1 = bytePosPass1 + 3;}
                    else if(strcmp((*tptr).text,"MOVD")==0)
                    { bytePosPass1 = bytePosPass1 + 3;}
                    else if(strcmp((*tptr).text,"MULT")==0)
                    { bytePosPass1 = bytePosPass1 + 4;}
                    else
                    {
                         ERROR2("Pass1::processInstruction(): line %d,
                         invalid opcode (%s)\n",(*tptr).line,(*tptr).text);
                         return;
                    }
             }break;
             case 'N':
             {
                    if(strcmp((*tptr).text,"NOT")==0)
                    { bytePosPass1 = bytePosPass1 + 3;}
                    else if(strcmp((*tptr).text,"NOP")==0)
                    { bytePosPass1 = bytePosPass1 + 1;}
                    else
                    {
                         ERROR2("Pass1::processInstruction(): line %d,
                         invalid opcode (%s)\n",(*tptr).line,(*tptr).text);
                         return;
                    }
             }break;
             case 'O':
             {
                    if(strcmp((*tptr).text,"OR")==0)
                    { bytePosPass1 = bytePosPass1 + 4;}
                    else
                    {
                         ERROR2("Pass1::processInstruction(): line %d,
                         invalid opcode (%s)\n",(*tptr).line,(*tptr).text);
                         return;
                    }
             }break;
```

```
            case 'P':
            {
                  if(strcmp((*tptr).text,"PUSHB")==0)
                  { bytePosPass1 = bytePosPass1 + 2;}
                  else if(strcmp((*tptr).text,"PUSHW")==0)
                  { bytePosPass1 = bytePosPass1 + 2;}
                  else if(strcmp((*tptr).text,"PUSHD")==0)
                  { bytePosPass1 = bytePosPass1 + 2;}
                  else if(strcmp((*tptr).text,"PUSHQ")==0)
                  { bytePosPass1 = bytePosPass1 + 2;}
                  else if(strcmp((*tptr).text,"PUSHF1")==0)
                  { bytePosPass1 = bytePosPass1 + 2;}
                  else if(strcmp((*tptr).text,"PUSHF2")==0)
                  { bytePosPass1 = bytePosPass1 + 2;}
                  else if(strcmp((*tptr).text,"POPB")==0)
                  { bytePosPass1 = bytePosPass1 + 2;}
                  else if(strcmp((*tptr).text,"POPW")==0)
                  { bytePosPass1 = bytePosPass1 + 2;}
                  else if(strcmp((*tptr).text,"POPD")==0)
                  { bytePosPass1 = bytePosPass1 + 2;}
                  else if(strcmp((*tptr).text,"POPQ")==0)
                  { bytePosPass1 = bytePosPass1 + 2;}
                  else if(strcmp((*tptr).text,"POPF1")==0)
                  { bytePosPass1 = bytePosPass1 + 2;}
                  else if(strcmp((*tptr).text,"POPF2")==0)
                  { bytePosPass1 = bytePosPass1 + 2;}
                  else
                  {
                        ERROR2("Pass1::processInstruction(): line %d,
                        invalid opcode (%s)\n",(*tptr).line,(*tptr).text);
                        return;
                  }
            }break;
            case 'S':
            {
                  if(strcmp((*tptr).text,"SB")==0)
                  { bytePosPass1 = bytePosPass1 + 3;}
                  else if(strcmp((*tptr).text,"SW")==0)
                  { bytePosPass1 = bytePosPass1 + 3;}
                  else if(strcmp((*tptr).text,"SD")==0)
                  { bytePosPass1 = bytePosPass1 + 3;}
                  else if(strcmp((*tptr).text,"SQ")==0)
                  { bytePosPass1 = bytePosPass1 + 3;}
                  else if(strcmp((*tptr).text,"SF1")==0)
                  { bytePosPass1 = bytePosPass1 + 3;}
                  else if(strcmp((*tptr).text,"SF2")==0)
                  { bytePosPass1 = bytePosPass1 + 3;}
                  else if(strcmp((*tptr).text,"SRA")==0)
                  { bytePosPass1 = bytePosPass1 + 4;}
                  else if(strcmp((*tptr).text,"SRL")==0)
                  { bytePosPass1 = bytePosPass1 + 4;}
                  else if(strcmp((*tptr).text,"SL")==0)
                  { bytePosPass1 = bytePosPass1 + 4;}
                  else if(strcmp((*tptr).text,"SUB")==0)
```

```
                    { bytePosPass1 = bytePosPass1 + 4;}
                    else if(strcmp((*tptr).text,"SLT")==0)
                    { bytePosPass1 = bytePosPass1 + 4;}
                    else
                    {
                         ERROR2("Pass1::processInstruction(): line %d,
                         invalid opcode (%s)\n",(*tptr).line,(*tptr).text);
                         return;
                    }
              }break;
              case 'X':
              {
                    if(strcmp((*tptr).text,"XOR")==0)
                    { bytePosPass1 = bytePosPass1 + 4;}
                    else
                    {
                         ERROR2("Pass1::processInstruction(): line %d,
                         invalid opcode (%s)\n",(*tptr).line,(*tptr).text);
                         return;
                    }
              }break;
              default:
              {
                    ERROR1("Pass1::processInstruction(): %s not a
                    valid opcode\n",(*tptr).text);
                    return;
              }
         }/*end switch*/

         return;

    }/*end processInstruction*/
```

Every time identifier information is entered into the symbol repository, the same basic order of operations is performed. First, the identifier's text is stored in the string table. Next, the rest of the identifier's metadata is placed in the symbol table. Finally, an index for the identifier is created in the hash table. We will now look at the string table, symbol table, and hash table in that order.

StringTable

The string table is nothing more than a list of null-terminated strings. It is implemented using an extendable array. The string table is useful because it allows identifier names to all be stored in a single place. If an identifier's text is stored in more than one place, memory is wasted on redundant storage. Rather than store the text of the identifier directly, an index to the string table can be referenced. This kind of space savings adds up over the course of an application.

```
#define STR_TBL_INIT  2*1024          /*initial size of string table*/
#define STR_TBL_INC   1024            /*amount increment when expand*/
```

```
class StringTable
{
    U8 nStr;    /*current capacity*/

    public:
    U1 *text;
    U8 iStr;    /*next free space*/

    StringTable();
    ~StringTable();
    void addStrTbl(char *str);
    void printStrTbl();
};

StringTable::StringTable()
{
    text = (U1*)malloc(STR_TBL_INIT);
    if(text==NULL)
    {
        ERROR0("StringTable::StringTable(): out of memory\n");
        FATAL_ERROR();
    }
    iStr = 0;
    nStr = STR_TBL_INIT;
    return;

}/*end constructor*/

StringTable::~StringTable()
{
    free(text);
    return;

}/*end destructor*/

/*
add string to strTbl (re-size if necessary)
*/

void StringTable::addStrTbl(char *str)
{
    U8 len;
    U8 i;
    U8 final_index;
    U1 *ptr;

    len = strlen(str);          /*note: null not included*/
    len++;                      /*count null*/
    final_index = iStr + len - 1;

    /* capacity n will have indices 0,...,n-1 */
```

```
            if(final_index >= nStr)
            {
                  ptr = (U1*)malloc((size_t)(nStr+STR_TBL_INC));
                  if(ptr==NULL)
                  {
                        ERRORO("StringTable::addStrTbl(): no more memory\n");
                        FATAL_ERROR();
                  }
                  else
                  {
                        for(i=0;i<nStr;i++){ ptr[i] = text[i]; }
                        free(text);
                        text = ptr;
                        nStr = nStr+STR_TBL_INC;
                  }
            }

            for(i=0;i<=len;i++)
            {
                  text[iStr+i] = str[i];
            }
            iStr = final_index+1; /* next EMPTY space */
            return;

}/*end addStrTbl*/

void StringTable::printStrTbl()
{
      U8 i;
      U8 nstr;

      printf("\nSTRING TABLE----------------------\n");
      printf("capacity nStr ="); pU8(nStr); printf("\n");
      printf("next free index iStr ="); pU8(iStr); printf("\n\n");
      nstr = 1;

      for(i=0;i<iStr;i++)
      {
            if(i==0){printf("0)");}

            /*either print char or handle null char*/

            if(text[i]!='\0')
            {
                  putchar(text[i]);
            }
            else if(i<(iStr-1))
            {
                  printf("(null)\n%lu)",nstr); nstr++;
            }
            else if(i==(iStr-1))
            {
                  printf("(null)\n");
            }
```

```
        }
        return;

}/*printStrTbl*/
```

SymbolTable

The symbol table is an archive of symbol metadata. It stores information on all the global variables, procedures, and procedure-specific entities that exist in an assembly language program. The `SymbolTable` class, which embodies the symbol table of the assembler, has the following declaration:

```
class SymbolTable
{
    StringTable *strTbl;

    /*called via public constructors/destructors*/
    void initProc(struct Procedure *ptr);
    void freeProc(struct Procedure *ptr);

    /*called via public addProc___HL */
    void setProcRet(struct Procedure *ptr, struct StackFrame *add);
    void addProcArg(struct Procedure *ptr, struct StackFrame *add);
    void addProcLoc(struct Procedure *ptr, struct StackFrame *add);
    void addProcLbl(struct Procedure *ptr, struct Label *add);

    /*called via public printSymTbl*/
    void printGlobVar(struct GlobalVariable *ptr);
    void printProc(struct Procedure *ptr);

    public:
    struct GlobalVariable *globVar;
    U4 nGlobVar;
    U4 iGlobVar;

    struct Procedure *proc;
    U4 nProc;
    U4 iProc;

    SymbolTable(StringTable *st);
    ~SymbolTable();

    void addGlobVar(struct GlobalVariable *add);
    void addProc(struct Procedure *add);

    /*set elements of current procedure*/
    void setProcRetHL(struct StackFrame *add);
    void addProcArgHL(struct StackFrame *add);
    void addProcLocHL(struct StackFrame *add);
    void addProcLblHL(struct Label *add);

    void printSymTbl();
};
```

The core functionality of the `SymbolTable` class is to maintain a list of `Global-Variable` structures and a list of `Procedure` structures. These lists are implemented as extendable arrays.

```
#defineSZ_BYTE  1      /*used to indicate GlobVar type*/
#define SZ_WORD 2
#define SZ_DWORD    4
#define SZ_QWORD    8


char *globSz[]={"","SZ_BYTE","SZ_WORD","","SZ_DWORD",
                "","","","SZ_QWORD"};

struct GlobalVariable
{
    U8 text;    /* index into StrTbl of where identifier begins*/
    U1 dType;   /* SZ_BYTE, SZ_WORD, SZ_DWORD, SZ_QWORD */
    U8 len;     /* # elements if array */
    U8 size;    /* total byte size */
    U8 offset;  /* offset below $TOP, address(g) = $TOP - offset*/
    U4 line;    /* source code line containing declaration */
};

struct Procedure
{
    U8 text;            /* index into StrTbl of where identifier begins */
    U8 address;         /* address of procedure */
    U4 line;            /* source code line containing declaration */

    struct StackFrame ret;
    U1 nRet;            /* 0 = void return, 1 = returns a value*/
    struct StackFrame *arg;
    U1 nArg;
    U1 iArg;
    struct StackFrame *local;
    U1 nLocal;
    U1 iLocal;
    struct Label *label;
    U2 nLabel;
    U2 iLabel;
};
```

The `Procedure` structure uses `StackFrame` structures to represent the return value, arguments, and local variables of an assembly language procedure. Procedure labels are represented by `Label` structures. Thus, every `Procedure` structure has its own collection of `StackFrame` and `Label` structure lists. These lists are implemented as extendable arrays.

```
struct StackFrame
{
    U8 text;            /* index into StrTbl of where identifier begins */
    S4 fpOffset;        /* +n or -n from $FP */
    U4 line;            /* source code line containing declaration */
};
```

```
struct Label
{
    U8 text;        /* index into StrTbl of where identifier begins */
    U8 address;     /* address of label*/
    U4 line;        /* source code line containing declaration */
};
```

Figure 5-17 illustrates the basic hierarchy of structures that exist in the `SymbolTable` class.

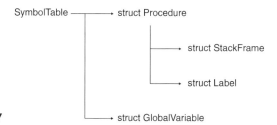

Figure 5-17

Given that all the list data structures in the symbol table are implemented as extendable arrays, the following macros in `SymTbl.cpp` control how large these arrays are and how much they are extended when they run out of room:

```
#define GLOB_INIT    10    /* _INIT = initial array size */
#define GLOB_INC     5     /* _INC = increment size when expand array */

#define PROC_INIT    10
#define PROC_INC     5

#define ARG_INIT     5
#define ARG_INC 5

#define LOC_INIT     5
#define LOC_INC 5

#define LBL_INIT     10
#define LBL_INC 10
```

The hierarchy of the 17 function calls in the `SymbolTable` class is a little more complicated. The best way to view the organization of functions is to start with the public functions and observe which private functions they call.

```
SymbolTable( )   ────────→ initProc( )
~SymbolTable( )  ────────→ freeProc( )

addGlobVar( )
addProc( )

setProcRetHL( )  ────────→ setProcRet( )
addProcArgHL( )  ────────→ addProcArg( )
addProcLocHL( )  ────────→ addProcLoc( )
addProcLblHL( )  ────────→ addProcLbl( )

printSymTbl( )   ──┬────→ printGlobVar( )
                   └────→ printProc( )
```

Figure 5-18

The constructor of the `SymbolTable` class allocates the initial lists of `Global-Variable` and `Procedure` structures. To initialize the list of `Procedure` structures, the constructor calls a helper function named `initProc()`.

```
SymbolTable::SymbolTable(StringTable *st)
{
    U4 i;

    strTbl = st;

    globVar = (struct GlobalVariable*)
            malloc(GLOB_INIT*sizeof(struct GlobalVariable));

    if(globVar==NULL)
    {
        ERROR0("SymbolTable::SymbolTable(): out of memory\n");
        FATAL_ERROR();
    }
    nGlobVar = GLOB_INIT;
    iGlobVar = 0;

    proc = (struct Procedure*) malloc(PROC_INIT*sizeof(struct Procedure));

    if(proc==NULL)
    {
        ERROR0("SymbolTable::SymbolTable(): out of memory\n");
        FATAL_ERROR();
    }
    nProc = PROC_INIT;
    iProc = 0;
    for(i=0;i<PROC_INIT;i++){ initProc(&proc[i]); }

    SYM_DEBUG1("SymbolTable::SymbolTable(): %lu globals\n",GLOB_INIT);
    SYM_DEBUG1("SymbolTable::SymbolTable(): %lu procs\n",PROC_INIT);

    return;

}/*end constructor*/

void SymbolTable::initProc(struct Procedure *ptr)
{
    (*ptr).text = 0;
    (*ptr).address = 0;
    (*ptr).line = 0;

    /*exactly one struct StackFrame ret*/
    (*ptr).nRet = 0;

    (*ptr).arg = (struct StackFrame*) malloc(ARG_INIT*sizeof(struct StackFrame));
    if((*ptr).arg==NULL)
    {
        ERROR0("SymbolTable::initProc(): out of memory\n");
        FATAL_ERROR();
    }
```

```
    (*ptr).nArg = ARG_INIT;
    (*ptr).iArg = 0;

    (*ptr).local = (struct StackFrame*) malloc(LOC_INIT*sizeof(struct StackFrame));
    if((*ptr).local==NULL)
    {
        FRRORO("SymbolTable::initProc(): out of memory\n");
        FATAL_ERROR();
    }
    (*ptr).nLocal = LOC_INIT;
    (*ptr).iLocal = 0;

    (*ptr).label = (struct Label*) malloc(LBL_INIT*sizeof(struct Label));
    if((*ptr).label==NULL)
    {
        ERRORO("SymbolTable::initProc(): out of memory\n");
        FATAL_ERROR();
    }
    (*ptr).nLabel = LBL_INIT;
    (*ptr).iLabel = 0;
    return;

}/*end initProc*/
```

I decided to be slightly anal retentive and design destructors that free all the allocated memory. Because a `Procedure` structure usually has its own set of dynamically allocated memory areas, the destructor calls a function named `freeProc()` to help reclaim `Procedure` structure storage.

All this reclamation work wasn't absolutely necessary. The symbol table is used for the duration of the assembler's life span and could be reclaimed by the operating system when the assembler exits instead of doing it manually.

```
SymbolTable::~SymbolTable()
{
    free(globVar);
    SYM_DEBUG1("SymbolTable::~SymbolTable(): free %lu globals\n",nGlobVar);
    freeProc(proc);
    return;

}/*end destructor*/

void SymbolTable::freeProc(struct Procedure *ptr)
{
    U4 i;
    SYM_DEBUG1("SymbolTable::freeProc(): freeing %lu procs\n",nProc);
    for(i=0;i<nProc;i++)
    {
        free(ptr[i].arg);
        free(ptr[i].local);
        free(ptr[i].label);
    }
    free(ptr);
    SYM_DEBUG0("SymbolTable::freeProc(): done freeing procs\n");
```

```
            return;

    }/*end freeProc*/
```

The `addGlobVar()` and `addProc()` functions add new global variables and procedures to the symbol table. If the symbol table's arrays run out of space, larger arrays will be
allocated.

```
void SymbolTable::addGlobVar(struct GlobalVariable *add)
{
    U4 i;
    struct GlobalVariable *new_gv;

    /* capacity n will have indices 0,...,n-1 */

    if(iGlobVar == nGlobVar)
    {
        U4 newsize = nGlobVar + GLOB_INC;
        new_gv = (struct GlobalVariable*)
                    malloc((newsize)*(sizeof(struct GlobalVariable)));
        if(new_gv==NULL)
        {
            ERROR0("SymbolTable::addGlobVar(): out of memory\n");
            FATAL_ERROR();
        }
        else
        {
            for(i=0;i<nGlobVar;i++){ new_gv[i] = globVar[i]; }
            free(globVar);
            globVar = new_gv;
            nGlobVar = nGlobVar+GLOB_INC;
        }
    }

    globVar[iGlobVar]=*add;
    iGlobVar++;
    return;

}/*end addGlobVar*/

void SymbolTable::addProc(struct Procedure *add)
{
    U4 i;
    Procedure *new_p;

    /* capacity n will have indices 0,...,n-1 */

    if(iProc == nProc)
    {
        U4 newsize = nProc + PROC_INC;
        new_p = (struct Procedure*)
                    malloc(newsize*sizeof(struct Procedure));
        if(new_p==NULL)
        {
```

```
                            ERRORO("SymbolTable::addProc(): out of memory\n");
                            FATAL_ERROR();
                    }
                    else
                    {
                            for(i=nProc;i<newsize;i++){ initProc(&new_p[i]); }
                            for(i=0;i<nProc;i++){ new_p[i] = proc[i]; }
                            delete(proc);
                            proc = new_p;
                            nProc = nProc+PROC_INC;
                    }
            }

            /*
            adding virgin proc, no internal elements yet
            (i.e. args, locals, labels)
            */

            proc[iProc].text=(*add).text;
            proc[iProc].address=(*add).address;
            proc[iProc].line=(*add).line;

            iProc++;
            return;

    }/*end addProc*/
```

The `setProcRetHL()`, `addProcArgHL()`, `addProcLocHL()`, and `addProc-LblHL()` functions are high-level (hence the HL suffix) routines that allow elements to be associated with the most recent procedure added to the symbol table. Typically, a procedure will be added to the symbol table with a call to `addProc()`. As the procedure's arguments, local variables, and labels are swallowed by the assembler, they will be added to the procedure's entry in the symbol table via calls to the HL routines.

```
void SymbolTable::setProcRetHL(struct StackFrame *add)
{
    /*
    add arg while processing current procedure
    current proc is at (iProc-1)
    */
    setProcRet(&proc[iProc-1],add);
    return;

}/*end setProcRetHL*/

void SymbolTable::setProcRet(struct Procedure *ptr, struct StackFrame *add)
{
    (*ptr).nRet=1;
    (*ptr).ret=*add;
    return;

}/*end setProcRet*/
```

```
void SymbolTable::addProcArgHL(struct StackFrame *add)
{
    /*
    add arg while processing current procedure
    current proc is at (iProc-1)
    */
    addProcArg(&proc[iProc-1],add);
    return;

}/*end addProcArgHL*/

void SymbolTable::addProcArg(struct Procedure *ptr, struct StackFrame *add)
{
    U4 i;
    struct StackFrame *new_sf;

    /* capacity n will have indices 0,...,n-1 */

    if((*ptr).iArg == (*ptr).nArg)
    {
        U4 newsize = (*ptr).nArg + ARG_INC;
        new_sf = (struct StackFrame*) malloc((newsize)*(sizeof(struct StackFrame)));
        if(new_sf==NULL)
        {
            ERRORO("SymbolTable::addProcArg(): out of  memory\n");
            FATAL_ERROR();
        }
        else
        {
            for(i=0;i<((*ptr).nArg);i++)
            { new_sf[i] = (*ptr).arg[i]; }
            free((*ptr).arg);
            (*ptr).arg = new_sf;
            (*ptr).nArg = (*ptr).nArg+ARG_INC;
        }
    }

    (*ptr).arg[(*ptr).iArg]=*add;
    (*ptr).iArg++;
    return;

}/*end addProcArg*/

void SymbolTable::addProcLocHL(struct StackFrame *add)
{
    /*
    add local while processing current procedure
    current proc is at (iProc-1)
    */
    addProcLoc(&proc[iProc-1],add);
    return;

}/*end addProcLocHL*/
```

```
void SymbolTable::addProcLoc(struct Procedure *ptr, struct StackFrame *add)
{
    U4 i;
    struct StackFrame *new_sf;

    /* capacity n will have indices 0,...,n-1 */

    if((*ptr).iLocal == (*ptr).nLocal)
    {
        U4 newsize = (*ptr).nLocal + LOC_INC;
        new_sf = (struct StackFrame*)
                    malloc((newsize)*(sizeof(struct StackFrame)));
        if(new_sf==NULL)
        {
            ERRORO("SymbolTable::addProcArg(): out of memory\n");
            FATAL_ERROR();
        }
        else
        {
            for(i=0;i<((*ptr).nLocal);i++)
            { new_sf[i] = (*ptr).local[i]; }
            free((*ptr).local);
            (*ptr).local = new_sf;
            (*ptr).nLocal = (*ptr).nLocal+LOC_INC;
        }
    }

    (*ptr).local[(*ptr).iLocal]=*add;
    (*ptr).iLocal++;
    return;

}/*end addProcLoc*/

void SymbolTable::addProcLblHL(struct Label *add)
{
    /*
    add label while processing current procedure
    current proc is at (iProc-1)
    */
    addProcLbl(&proc[iProc-1],add);
    return;

}/*end addProcLblHL*/

void SymbolTable::addProcLbl(struct Procedure *ptr,  struct Label *add)
{
    U4 i;
    struct Label *new_sf;

    /* capacity n will have indices 0,...,n-1 */

    if((*ptr).iLabel == (*ptr).nLabel)
    {
        U4 newsize = (*ptr).nLabel + LBL_INC;
```

```
            new_sf = (struct Label*) malloc((newsize)*(sizeof(struct Label)));
            if(new_sf==NULL)
            {
                    ERRORO("SymbolTable::addProcArg(): out of memory\n");
                    FATAL_ERROR();
            }
            else
            {
                    for(i=0;i<((*ptr).nLabel);i++)
                    { new_sf[i] = (*ptr).label[i]; }
                    free((*ptr).label);
                    (*ptr).label = new_sf;
                    (*ptr).nLabel = (*ptr).nLabel+LBL_INC;
            }
        }

        (*ptr).label[(*ptr).iLabel]=*add;
        (*ptr).iLabel++;
        return;

    }/*end addProcLbl*/
```

To help debug the symbol table, I created a function that prints out the contents of the symbol table to the console in a human-readable format. The `printSymTbl()` function invokes two helper functions, `printGlobVar()` and `printProc()`, to do its job.

```
    void SymbolTable::printSymTbl()
    {
        U4 i;
        printf("\nSYMBOL TABLE-----------\n");
        for(i=0;i<iGlobVar;i++)
        {
            printf("%d) ",i);
            printGlobVar(&globVar[i]);
            printf("\n");
        }
        for(i=0;i<iProc;i++)
        {
            printf("%d) ",i);
            printProc(&proc[i]);
            printf("\n");
        }
        return;

    }/*end printSymTbl*/

    void SymbolTable::printGlobVar(struct GlobalVariable *ptr)
    {
        printf("GLOBAL VAR-------------\n");
        printf("identifier=%s\n",&((*strTbl).text[(*ptr).text]));
        printf("data type=%s\n",globSz[(*ptr).dType]);
        printf("length="); pU8((*ptr).len); printf("\n");
        printf("size="); pU8((*ptr).size); printf("\n");
        printf("offset="); pS8(-((S8)(*ptr).offset)); printf("\n");
```

```
        printf("line=%lu\n",(*ptr).line);
        return;

}/*end printGlobVar*/


void SymbolTable::printProc(struct Procedure *ptr)
{
    U4 i;
    printf("PROC-------------------\n");
    printf("identifier=%s\n",&((*strTbl).text[(*ptr).text]));
    printf("address="); pU8((*ptr).address); printf("\n");
    printf("line=%lu\n\n",(*ptr).line);

    if((*ptr).nRet)
    {
        printf("RET\n");
        printf("\tid=%s\n",&((*strTbl).text[((*ptr).ret).text]));
        printf("\tfpOffset=%ld\n",((*ptr).ret).fpOffset);
        printf("\tline=%lu\n",((*ptr).ret).line);
    }

    printf("ARGS\n");
    for(i=0;i<(*ptr).iArg;i++)
    {
        printf("\t%d)",i);
        printf("id=%s\n",&((*strTbl).text[((*ptr).arg[i]).text]));
        printf("\tfpOffset=%ld\n",((*ptr).arg[i]).fpOffset);
        printf("\tline=%lu\n",((*ptr).arg[i]).line);
    }
    printf("LOCALS\n");
    for(i=0;i<(*ptr).iLocal;i++)
    {
        printf("\t%d)",i);
        printf("id=%s\n",&((*strTbl).text[((*ptr).local[i]).text]));
        printf("\tfpOffset=%ld\n",((*ptr).local[i]).fpOffset);
        printf("\tline=%lu\n",((*ptr).local[i]).line);
    }
    printf("LABELS\n");
    for(i=0;i<(*ptr).iLabel;i++)
    {
        printf("\t%d)",i);
        printf("id=%s\n",&((*strTbl).text[((*ptr).label[i]).text]));
        printf("\taddress=");
        pU8(((*ptr).label[i]).address);
        printf("\n");
        printf("\tline=%lu\n",((*ptr).label[i]).line);
    }
    return;

}/*end printProc*/
```

HashTable

The hash table is the phone book for symbol information. When you want to find information on a specific symbol, you compute the hash value of the symbol and then look up the slot in the table corresponding to that value. The hash table I implemented is an array of HashTbl structures, so a particular hash value will index a particular hash structure.

```
struct HashTbl
{
    U1 empty;          /*indicates if entry is used or not*/
    U8 text;           /*index to strTbl*/
    U1 type;           /*GLOBAL_VAR -> PROC_LBL*/
    U4 index;          /*index to globVar, proc arrays in symbTbl*/
    U4 subIndex;       /*subindex for PROC_RET, ... , PROC_LBL*/
    struct HashTbl *left;
    struct HashTbl *right;
};
```

The type field of the HashTbl structure indicates the type of symbol being indexed. This field is populated by one of the following macros defined in hashtbl.cpp:

```
#define GLOBAL_VAR    0
#define PROC          1
#define PROC_RET      2
#define PROC_ARG      3
#define PROC_LOC      4
#define PROC_LBL      5
```

To get a string representation of the symbol type, the following array is used:

```
char *SymTypeStr[]={"GLOBAL_VAR",
                    "PROC",
                    "PROC_RET","PROC_ARG","PROC_LOC","PROC_LBL"};
```

The index field of the HashTbl structure is an index into either the Global-Variable structure array or the Procedure structure array in the SymbolTable. The subIndex array is used to index arrays that are local to a Procedure structure. If you recall, each Procedure structure has several array lists of its own (for arguments, local variables, and labels). So, if you want to locate a particular local variable belonging to some function, you will need to specify its index in addition to the index of the procedure.

The hash table implemented in HASM also uses a BST-based, separate chaining mechanism to handle hash table collisions. This is identical to the one explained earlier during the discussion of the dictionary ADT. This accounts for the left and right pointer fields in the HashTbl structure.

NOTE The reason that a hash table is necessary is that the symbol table and string table are not ordered data structures. Elements are added to the string table and symbol table as they are encountered in the assembly source code. This would mean that we might have to search the entire string table or symbol table to find information on an identifier, if that identifier exists at all. Using a hash table to index identifiers is an effective way to speed things up. Each hash table entry has fields that index the symbol table and string table. Once a hash table entry has been located, the associated symbol table and string table data can be obtained immediately. Thus, the only labor-intensive part of indexing a symbol is computing the hash value of the symbol.

The assembler's hash table starts off as an array of `HashTbl` structures. This array is wrapped by the `HashTable` class. The `HashTable` class has the following declaration:

```
#define PRIME 547

class HashTable
{
    StringTable *strTbl;

    int hashpjw(unsigned char *s);

    /*collision resolution BST routines*/
    struct HashTbl* findNode(struct HashTbl* link, char *val);
    void insertNode(struct HashTbl** link, char *val, U8 text,
                    U1 type, U4 ind, U4 subInd, U4 line);
    void printTree(struct HashTbl* link, int level);
    void deleteAllNodes(struct HashTbl** link);

    public:
    struct HashTbl hashTbl[PRIME];

    HashTable(StringTable *st);
    ~HashTable();

    /*hash table routine calls corresponding BST routine*/
    struct HashTbl* queryHashTbl(char *str);
    void addHashTblEntry(char *val, U8 text, U1 type, U4 ind, U4 subInd, U4 line);
    void printHashTbl();
};
```

The constructor and destructor are relatively straightforward. The constructor basically intializes the array of `HashTbl` structures. The destructor applies a BST deletion operation to the right and left subtree of each `HashTbl` array entry to make sure that dynamically allocated memory is reclaimed.

```
HashTable::HashTable(StringTable *st)
{
    int i;
    for(i=0;i<PRIME;i++)
    {
        hashTbl[i].empty = TRUE;
        hashTbl[i].text = 0;
        hashTbl[i].left = NULL;
```

```
                    hashTbl[i].right = NULL;
        }
        strTbl = st;
        return;

}/*end constructor*/

HashTable::~HashTable()
{
        int i;
        for(i=0;i<PRIME;i++)
        {
                deleteAllNodes(&(hashTbl[i].left));
                deleteAllNodes(&(hashTbl[i].right));
        }
        return;

}/*end destructor*/

void HashTable::deleteAllNodes(struct HashTbl** link)
{
        if(*link==NULL){ return; }

        deleteAllNodes(&(*(*link)).left);
        deleteAllNodes(&(*(*link)).right);

        //printf("freeing node %s\n",&((*strTbl).text[(*(*link)).text]));
        free(*link);
        *link=NULL;

        return;

}/*end deleteAllNodes*/
```

In addition to the constructor and destructor, this class has three public member functions that it exposes to the world: addHashTblEntry(), queryHashTbl(), and printHashTbl(). In general, each public function ends up calling a related BST function. This is illustrated in Figure 5-19.

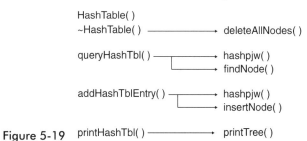

Figure 5-19

The queryHashTbl() function computes the hash value of a string. If the symbol exists in a hash table we get a pointer to the node; otherwise we get NULL.

```
struct HashTbl* HashTable::queryHashTbl(char *str)
{
    int hash;

    hash = hashpjw((unsigned char*)str);
    if(hashTbl[hash].empty==TRUE){ return(NULL); }
    return(findNode(&(hashTbl[hash]), str));

}/*end queryHashTbl*/

int HashTable::hashpjw(unsigned char *s)
{
    unsigned char * p;
    unsigned h = 0, g;

    for (p = s; *p != '\0'; p = p + 1)
    {
        h = (h < 4) + (*p);
        if (g = (h & 0xf0000000))
        {
            h = h ^ (g > 24);
            h = h ^ g;
        }
    }

    return h % PRIME;

}/*end hashpjw*/

struct HashTbl* HashTable::findNode(struct HashTbl* link, char *val)
{
    if(link==NULL)
    {
        return(NULL);
    }
    else if(strcmp(val,(char*)&((*strTbl).text[(*link).text]))==0)
    {
        return(link);
    }
    else if(strcmp(val,(char*)&((*strTbl).text[(*link).text]))>0)
    {
        return(findNode((*link).right,val));
    }
    else
    {
        return(findNode((*link).left,val));
    }

}/*end findNode*/
```

To add a new symbol definition to the hash table, the addHashTblEntry() function is invoked. This function uses the BST insertNode() routine to handle collisions by creating a binary tree.

```
void HashTable::addHashTblEntry(char *val,
                                U8 text,
                                U1 type,
                                U4 ind,
                                U4 subInd,
                                U4 line)
{
    struct HashTbl *ptr;
    int hash;

    hash = hashpjw((unsigned char*)val);

    if(hashTbl[hash].empty==TRUE)
    {
        hashTbl[hash].empty=FALSE;
        hashTbl[hash].text=text;
        hashTbl[hash].type=type;
        hashTbl[hash].index=ind;
        hashTbl[hash].subIndex=subInd;
        hashTbl[hash].left = NULL;
        hashTbl[hash].right = NULL;
        return;
    }

    ptr = &hashTbl[hash];
    insertNode(&ptr, val, text, type, ind, subInd, line);
    return;

}/*end addHashTblEntry*/

void HashTable::insertNode(struct HashTbl** link,
                           char *val,
                           U8 text,
                           U1 type,
                           U4 ind,
                           U4 subInd,
                           U4 line)
{
    if((*link) == NULL)
    {
        (*link) = (struct HashTbl*)malloc(sizeof(struct HashTbl));
        (*(*link)).empty     = FALSE;
        (*(*link)).text      = text;
        (*(*link)).type      = type;
        (*(*link)).index     = ind;
        (*(*link)).subIndex  = subInd;
        (*(*link)).left      = NULL;
        (*(*link)).right     = NULL;
    }
    else if(strcmp(val,(char*)&((*strTbl).text[(*(*link)).text])) == 0)
    {
     ERROR2("re-defined identifier %s on line %lu\n",val,line);
        return;
    }
```

```
    else if(strcmp(val,(char*)&((*strTbl).text[(*(*link)).text])) < 0)
    {
        insertNode(&((*(*link)).left) , val, text, type, ind, subInd, line);
    }
    else
    {
        insertNode(&((*(*link)).right) ,val, text, type, ind, subInd, line);
    }
    return;

}/*end insertNode*/
```

For the sake of debugging, I included a routine to print the hash table contents to the console in a human-readable format. The `printTree()` routine performs an inorder traversal of the binary tree and prints out node information during the traversal.

```
void HashTable::printHashTbl()
{
    int i;
    printf("\nHASH TABLE-------------\n");
    for(i=0;i<PRIME;i++)
    {
        if(hashTbl[i].empty == FALSE)
        {
            printf("Hash Slot %d)------\n",i);
            printTree(&(hashTbl[i]), 0);
            printf("\n");
        }
    }
    printf("\n");
    return;

}/*end printHashTbl*/

void HashTable::printTree(struct HashTbl* link, int level)
{
    int i;
    if(link==NULL)
    {
        return;
    }
    printTree((*link).right,level+1);
    for(i=0;i<level;i++){ printf("-"); }

    printf("id =%s\t",&((*strTbl).text[(*link).text]));
    printf("type=%s\t",SymTypeStr[(*link).type]);
    printf("(i,si)=(%d,%d)\n",(*link).index,(*link).subIndex);

    printTree((*link).left,level+1);
    return;

}/*end printTree*/
```

Pass 2 – Generate Bytecode and Listings

The basic operations involved in the second pass are very similar to those of the first pass. Just like the first pass, there is a `LineScanner` object, a `LineTokenizer` object, and a symbol repository. In fact, the source file listing of the second pass in `main.cpp` is almost identical to that of the first pass. The crucial difference that exists is that the `Pass1` object has been replaced by a `Pass2` object. Instead of populating the symbol repository with information, the `Pass2` object is generating bytecode and using the symbol repository to resolve memory address values. The bytecode emitted by the `Pass2` object is stored in an intermediate file. This intermediate file is used to generate the bytecode executable when the second pass is over.

```
/*3) PASS2 - create bytecode temp file and listing file */

MAIN_DEBUG0("initiating second pass\n");
{
  Pass2 pass2(&cmdLine,&strTbl,&symTbl,&hashTbl);
  LineScanner scanner(&cmdLine);
  line = scanner.getInputLine();
  while(line.end!=TRUE)
  {
    pass2.parseLine(&line);
    line = scanner.getInputLine();
  }
  pass2.parseLine(&line);
  if(cmdLine.listing==TRUE){ pass2.generateSymbolSummary(); }
}
MAIN_DEBUG1("%lu bytes written to tempfile\n",pass2.bytePosPass2);


/*if errors exist after 2nd pass, shutdown */

if(nErrors > 0)
{
  printf("main(): %d Error(s) during second pass\n",nErrors);
  printf("main(): build failed\n");
  FATAL_ERROR();
}
```

In addition to generating bytecode, the `Pass2` object also creates a listing file. The intermediate bytecode file has a .TMP file extension (as in "temporary"), and the listing file has a .lst file extension.

The `Pass2` object does a lot of work in terms of generating bytecode and a listing file. This is reflected in the somewhat monolithic nature of the `Pass2` class declaration:

```
class Pass2
{
    U4 bytePosPass2;            /*current index of bytecode being generated*/

    FILE *lfptr;               /*pointer to list file*/
    FILE *tfptr;               /*pointer to temporary bytecode file*/
```

```
char *lfile;                    /*pointer to list file name*/
char *tfile;                    /*pointer to temporary bytecode file name*/

char lfBuffer[BUFFER_SIZE];    /*output buffer for list file*/
char tfBuffer[BUFFER_SIZE];    /*output buffer for temp file*/

int iLFChar;                    /*index into lfBuffer*/
int iTFChar;                    /*index into tfBuffer*/

CommandLine *cmdLine;
StringTable *strTbl;
SymbolTable *symTbl;
HashTable *hashTbl;
LineTokenizer *toker;

char listing[LINE_SIZE];       /*line of text file to place in listing file*/

char lineNumber[32];           /*line number to place in listing file*/
U1 encoded[11];                /*holds bytes to write to temp file*/

void putByteTempBuff(U1 byte);
void flushTempBuff();

void putStrLstBuff(char *str);
void putByteLstBuff(U1 byte);
void flushLstBuff();

void  processDirective(struct Token *tptr, struct Line *line);
void  processGDirective(struct Token *tptr, struct Line *line);
void  processPDirective(struct Token *tptr, struct Line *line);

void  processInstruction(struct Token *tptr);

/*print symbol table, called by generateSymbolSummary()*/
void printGlobVarToLst(struct GlobalVariable *ptr);
void printProcToLst(struct Procedure *ptr);
void printTreeToLst(struct HashTbl* link, int level);

void I(U1 opcode, struct Token *tptr);

void IB(U1 opcode, struct Token *tptr);
void IRC(U1 opcode, U1 bytes, struct Token *tptr);
void IRA(struct Token *tptr);
void I2RA(struct Token *tptr);

void IR(U1 opcode, struct Token *tptr);
void I2R(U1 opcode,struct Token *tptr);
void I3R(U1 opcode, struct Token *tptr);
void I4R(U1 opcode, struct Token *tptr);

void IRF(U1 opcode, struct Token *tptr);
void IRD(U1 opcode, struct Token *tptr);

void IFC(U1 opcode, struct Token *tptr);
```

```
        void IF(U1 opcode, struct Token *tptr);
        void I2F(U1 opcode, struct Token *tptr);
        void I3F(U1 opcode, struct Token *tptr);
        void IFR(U1 opcode, struct Token *tptr);
        void IFD(U1 opcode, struct Token *tptr);

        void IDC(U1 opcode, struct Token *tptr);
        void ID(U1 opcode, struct Token *tptr);
        void I2D(U1 opcode, struct Token *tptr);
        void I3D(U1 opcode, struct Token *tptr);
        void IDR(U1 opcode, struct Token *tptr);
        void IDF(U1 opcode, struct Token *tptr);

        void commitToFiles(U1 len);

        public:
        Pass2(CommandLine *cptr, StringTable *st, SymbolTable *syt, HashTable *ht);
        ~Pass2();

        void parseLine(struct Line *line);
        void generateSymbolSummary();
};
```

Fortunately, the `Pass2` class has only four public functions. So at least we have some sort of starting point. In fact, to help understand the organization of the public and private member functions of the `Pass2` class, you might want to glance at Figure 5-20 and keep it in mind as you trace through the source code.

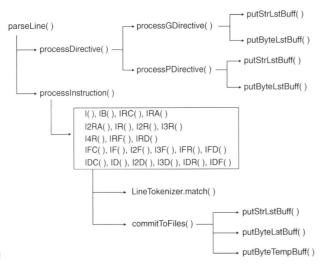

Figure 5-20

Because the `Pass2` class creates two files, a listing file and a temporary bytecode file, it uses two output buffers. The file pointers to the two output files and their associated output buffers are initialized by the constructor. The destructor makes sure that these resources are reclaimed properly.

```
Pass2::Pass2(CommandLine *cptr, StringTable *st, SymbolTable *syt, HashTable *ht)
{
    cmdLine = cptr;
    strTbl = st;
    symTbl = syt;
    hashTbl = ht;

    lfile = (*cptr).listFile;
    tfile = (*cptr).tempFile;

    if(lfile==NULL)
    {
        ERROR0("Pass2::Pass2(): listing file name not specified\n");
        FATAL_ERROR();
    }
    if(tfile==NULL)
    {
        ERROR0("Pass2::Pass2(): temporary file's name is NULL\n");
        FATAL_ERROR();
    }
    lfptr = fopen(lfile,"wb");
    tfptr = fopen(tfile,"wb");
    if(lfptr==NULL)
    {
        ERROR0("Pass2::Pass2(): could not open listing file\n");
        FATAL_ERROR();
    }
    if(tfptr==NULL)
    {
        ERROR0("Pass2::Pass2(): could not open temporary file\n");
        FATAL_ERROR();
    }
    bytePosPass2 = 0;
    iLFChar = 0;
    iTFChar = 0;
    return;

}/*end constructor*/

Pass2::~Pass2()
{
    flushTempBuff();
    flushLstBuff();
    if(fclose(lfptr))
    { ERROR1("Pass2::~Pass2(): problem closing listing file\n",lfile); }
    if(fclose(tfptr))
    { ERROR1("Pass2::~Pass2(): problem closing temp file\n",tfile); }
    return;

}/*end destructor*/
```

The two output buffers are managed by a series of functions. Strings and individual characters can be written to the listing file using the `putStrLstBuff()` and `putByteLstBuff()` functions. Bytes are written to the temporary bytecode file via the `putByteTempBuff()` function. When the `Pass2` object is about to leave its scope, it will need to flush whatever is left in the buffers. To do this, the `flushLstBuff()` and `flushTempBuff()` member functions are called by the `Pass2` destructor.

The arrangement of the `Pass2` buffers, with regard to the private data members and functions they use, is displayed in Figure 5-21.

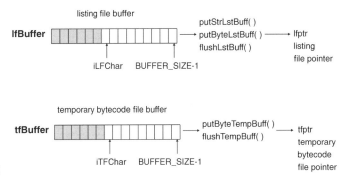

Figure 5-21

Given the preceding figure, it should be easier to understand the source code for the functions that manage the two output buffers:

```
void Pass2::putByteTempBuff(U1 byte)
{
    int nbytes;
    nbytes = 0;

    tfBuffer[iTFChar] = byte;
    iTFChar++;

    if(iTFChar==BUFFER_SIZE)
    {
        nbytes = fwrite(tfBuffer,sizeof(U1),BUFFER_SIZE,tfptr);
        if(nbytes!=BUFFER_SIZE)
        {
        ERROR1("Pass2::putByteTempBuff(): error fwrite to %s\n",tfile);
            FATAL_ERROR();
        }
        iTFChar = 0;
    }
    return;

}/*end putByteTempBuff*/

void Pass2::flushTempBuff()
{
    int nbytes;
    nbytes = 0;
```

```
        if(iTFChar>0)
        {
            nbytes = fwrite(tfBuffer,sizeof(U1),iTFChar,tfptr);
            if(nbytes!=iTFChar)
            {
            ERROR1("Pass2::flushTempBuff(): only flushed %lu bytes\n",nbytes);
            ERROR1("Pass2::flushTempBuff(): error on flush to %s\n",tfile);
                FATAL_ERROR();
            }
            iTFChar = 0;
        }
        return;

}/*end flushTempBuff*/


void Pass2::putStrLstBuff(char *str)
{
    U4 i;
    U4 j;
    U4 size;
    size = strlen(str);
    j=0;
    while((str[j]==' ')||(str[j]=='\t')){ j++; }
    for(i=j;i<size;i++){ putByteLstBuff(str[i]); }
    return;

}/*end putStrLstBuff*/


void Pass2::putByteLstBuff(U1 byte)
{
    int nbytes;

    nbytes = 0;

    lfBuffer[iLFChar] = byte;
    iLFChar++;

    if(iLFChar==BUFFER_SIZE)
    {
        nbytes = fwrite(lfBuffer,sizeof(U1),BUFFER_SIZE,lfptr);
        if(nbytes!=BUFFER_SIZE)
        {
        ERROR1("Pass2::putByteLstBuff(): flushed %lu bytes\n",nbytes);
        ERROR1("Pass2::putByteLstBuff(): error on fwrite to %s\n",lfile);
            FATAL_ERROR();
        }
        iLFChar = 0;
    }
    return;

}/*end putByteLstBuff*/


void Pass2::flushLstBuff()
```

```
{
    int nbytes;

    nbytes = 0;

    if(iLFChar>0)
    {
        nbytes = fwrite(lfBuffer,sizeof(U1),iLFChar,lfptr);
        if(nbytes!=iLFChar)
        {
        ERROR1("Pass2::flushLstBuff(): only flushed %lu bytes\n",nbytes);
        ERROR1("Pass2::flushLstBuff(): error on fwrite to %s\n",lfile);
            FATAL_ERROR();
        }
        iLFChar = 0;
    }
    return;

}/*end flushLstBuff*/
```

Like the `Pass1` class, the `Pass2` class has a `parseLine` public member function. It accepts a `Line` structure as an argument, which is passed to it by the `LineScanner` object in `main.cpp`. Using a `LineTokenizer` object, the `parseLine()` function will determine if the line of source code wrapped by the `Line` structure is a directive or an instruction. If the line of source code being scrutinized is a directive, and the listing switch has been set on the assembler's command line, the `processDirective()` function will be called. Otherwise, the `processInstruction()` function is invoked.

```
void Pass2::parseLine(struct Line *line)
{
    struct Token token;

    /*
    line can be
        i) a directive (starts with a period, i.e., .IP)
        ii) an instruction (opcode operand(s))
        iii) a comment (starts with #)
    */

    LineTokenizer t(line);
    toker = &t;

    token = (*toker).getNextLineToken();

    switch(token.text[0])
    {
        case '.':
        {
            if((*cmdLine).listing==TRUE)
            { processDirective(&token,line); }
        }break;
        case '#':
        {
```

```
                            /*ignore line*/
                    }break;
                default:{ processInstruction(&token); }
        }
        return;

}/*end parseLine*/
```

The processDirective() function, and the two functions that it invokes, serve the sole purpose of generating listing file entries. If you recall, directives are not translated into bytecode. However, they still need to show up in the listing file. The process-Directive(), processGDirective(), and processPDirective() functions all take directive information and emit it to the listing file. If the listing flag is not set on HASM's command line, none of these three functions are called.

```
void  Pass2::processDirective(struct Token *tptr, struct Line *line)
{
    if((*tptr).type==TOK_IDENTIFIER)
    {
        switch((*tptr).text[1])
        {
                case 'G':{ processGDirective(tptr,line); }break;
                case 'P':{ processPDirective(tptr,line); }break;
                default:
                {
                    ERROR1("Pass2::processDirective():
                    %s not a directive\n",(*tptr).text);
                }
        }
    }
    else
    {
        ERROR1("Pass2::processDirective(): %s
        not a directive\n",(*tptr).text);
    }
    return;

}/*end processDirective*/

void  Pass2::processGDirective(struct Token *tptr, struct Line *line)
{
    sprintf(lineNumber,"%lu",(*tptr).line);
    putStrLstBuff(lineNumber);
    putByteLstBuff(')');

    putStrLstBuff((*line).src);
    putByteLstBuff('\n');

    return;

}/*end processGDirective*/

void  Pass2::processPDirective(struct Token *tptr, struct Line *line)
{
```

```
if(strcmp((*tptr).text,".PB")==0)/*.PB  identifier [ EXPORT ]*/
{
    putStrLstBuff("#++++++++++++++++++++++++++++++++++++++++++++++\n");

    sprintf(lineNumber,"%lu",(*tptr).line);
    putStrLstBuff(lineNumber);
    putByteLstBuff(')');

    putStrLstBuff((*line).src);
    putByteLstBuff('\n');

}/*end .PB*/
else
{
    sprintf(lineNumber,"%lu",(*tptr).line);
    putStrLstBuff(lineNumber);
    putByteLstBuff(')');
    putByteLstBuff('\t');

    putStrLstBuff((*line).src);
    putByteLstBuff('\n');
}
return;

}/*end processPDirective*/
```

The `processInstruction()` function is like Grand Central Station in New York City. It is a central hub that branches off to over 20 different paths of execution. The `processInstruction()` function looks at the first token of the line of text, passed to the `Pass2` object by the `LineScanner`. If this first token is an instruction, the appropriate instruction handler function will be called to process the instruction text and produce the necessary bytecode and listing file entries.

The instruction handlers are constructed to process a specific instruction format. This allows a single instruction handler to be used to process multiple instructions and eliminates redundant code, to an extent. The instruction format a particular handler processes is indicated by the name of the function. The following naming scheme is applied:

- I = Instruction
- B = Byte constant
- C = Constant
- R = Integer register
- F = Float register
- D = Double register
- A = Identifier (i.e., resolved to an address)

The instruction handler `IB()` processes instructions that consist of an instruction followed by a byte constant (i.e., INT 4). If a certain type of register is used more than once, it will be prefixed with an integer indicating how many instances of the register type exist.

For example, the instruction handler I2RA() processes instructions that consist of an instruction, followed by two integer registers and an identifier (i.e., LAI $R2, $TOP, gvar1).

Regardless of the fact that there are over 20 instruction handlers, they all have the same basic goal. Specifically, the instruction handlers all populate the listing[], lineNumber[], and encoded[] private member arrays of the Pass2 class. The listing[] array holds a line of text to be written to the listing file. Similarly, because the listing file has line numbers, the lineNumber[] array stores the string version of the next line number. The encoded[] array is used to accumulate bytecode that will be written to the temporary bytecode file.

A call to the commitToFiles() function, which usually occurs at the end of an instruction handler, writes these arrays to the listing and intermediate bytecode files.

```
void  Pass2::processInstruction(struct Token *tptr)
{
    if((*tptr).type==TOK_IDENTIFIER)
    {
        switch((*tptr).text[0])
        {
            case 'A':
            {
                if(strcmp((*tptr).text,"ADD")==0)
                { I3R(ADD,tptr); }
                else if(strcmp((*tptr).text,"AND")==0)
                { I3R(AND,tptr); }
                else
                {
                ERROR2("processInstructionPass1(): line %d,
                invalid opcode (%s)\n",(*tptr).line,(*tptr).text);
                    return;
                }

            }break;
            case 'B':
            {
                if(strcmp((*tptr).text,"BS")==0)
                { I2R(BS,tptr); }
                else if(strcmp((*tptr).text,"BT")==0)
                { I3R(BT,tptr); }
                else
                {
                ERROR2("processInstructionPass1(): line %d,
                invalid opcode (%s)\n",(*tptr).line,(*tptr).text);
                    return;
                }

            }break;
            case 'C':
            {
                if(strcmp((*tptr).text,"CAST_IF")==0)
                { IRF(CAST_IF,tptr);}
                else if(strcmp((*tptr).text,"CAST_ID")==0)
```

```
                              { IRD(CAST_ID,tptr);}
                              else if(strcmp((*tptr).text,"CAST_FI")==0)
                              { IFR(CAST_FI,tptr);}
                              else if(strcmp((*tptr).text,"CAST_FD")==0)
                              { IFD(CAST_FD,tptr);}
                              else if(strcmp((*tptr).text,"CAST_DI")==0)
                              { IDR(CAST_DI,tptr);}
                              else if(strcmp((*tptr).text,"CAST_DF")==0)
                              { IDF(CAST_DF,tptr);}
                              else
                              {
                              ERROR2("processInstructionPass1(): line %d,
                              invalid opcode (%s)\n",(*tptr).line,(*tptr).text);
                                    return;
                              }

                    }break;
                    case 'D':
                    {
                         if(strcmp((*tptr).text,"DIV")==0)
                         { I4R(DIV,tptr);}
                         else if(strcmp((*tptr).text,"DI")==0)
                         { I(DI,tptr);}
                         else if(strcmp((*tptr).text,"DADD")==0)
                         { I3D(DADD,tptr);}
                         else if(strcmp((*tptr).text,"DSUB")==0)
                         { I3D(DSUB,tptr);}
                         else if(strcmp((*tptr).text,"DMULT")==0)
                         { I3D(DMULT,tptr);}
                         else if(strcmp((*tptr).text,"DDIV")==0)
                         { I3D(DDIV,tptr);}
                         else if(strcmp((*tptr).text,"DSLT")==0)
                         { I3D(DSLT,tptr);}
                         else
                         {
                         ERROR2("processInstructionPass1(): line %d,
                         invalid opcode (%s)\n",(*tptr).line,(*tptr).text);
                               return;
                         }

                    }break;
                    case 'E':
                    {
                         if(strcmp((*tptr).text,"EI")==0)
                         { I(EI,tptr);}
                         else
                         {
                         ERROR2("processInstructionPass1(): line %d,
                         invalid opcode (%s)\n",(*tptr).line,(*tptr).text);
                               return;
                         }

                    }break;
                    case 'F':
```

```
{
    if(strcmp((*tptr).text,"FADD")==0)
    { I3F(FADD,tptr);}
    else if(strcmp((*tptr).text,"FSUB")==0)
    { I3F(FSUB,tptr);}
    else if(strcmp((*tptr).text,"FMULT")==0)
    { I3F(FMULT,tptr);}
    else if(strcmp((*tptr).text,"FDIV")==0)
    { I3F(FDIV,tptr);}
    else if(strcmp((*tptr).text,"FSLT")==0)
    { I3F(FSLT,tptr);}
    else
    {
    ERROR2("processInstructionPass1(): line %d,
    invalid opcode (%s)\n",(*tptr).line,(*tptr).text);
        return;
    }

}break;
case 'H':
{
    if(strcmp((*tptr).text,"HALT")==0)
    { I(HALT,tptr);}
    else
    {
    ERROR2("processInstructionPass1(): line %d,
    invalid opcode (%s)\n",(*tptr).line,(*tptr).text);
        return;
    }

}break;
case 'I':
{
    if(strcmp((*tptr).text,"INT")==0)
    { IB(INT,tptr);}
    else
    {
    ERROR2("processInstructionPass1(): line %d,
    invalid opcode (%s)\n",(*tptr).line,(*tptr).text);
        return;
    }

}break;
case 'J':
{
    if(strcmp((*tptr).text,"JMP")==0)
    { IR(JMP,tptr);}
    else if(strcmp((*tptr).text,"JE")==0)
    { I3R(JE,tptr);}
    else if(strcmp((*tptr).text,"JNE")==0)
    { I3R(JNE,tptr);}
    else
    {
    ERROR2("processInstructionPass1(): line %d,
```

```
                            invalid opcode (%s)\n",(*tptr).line,(*tptr).text);
                                return;
                            }

                    }break;
                    case 'L':
                    {
                        if(strcmp((*tptr).text,"LBI")==0)
                        { IRC(LBI,1,tptr);}
                        else if(strcmp((*tptr).text,"LWI")==0)
                        { IRC(LWI,2,tptr);}
                        else if(strcmp((*tptr).text,"LDI")==0)
                        { IRC(LDI,4,tptr);}
                        else if(strcmp((*tptr).text,"LQI")==0)
                        { IRC(LQI,8,tptr);}
                        else if(strcmp((*tptr).text,"LF1I")==0)
                        { IFC(LF1I,tptr);}
                        else if(strcmp((*tptr).text,"LF2I")==0)
                        { IDC(LF2I,tptr);}
                        else if(strcmp((*tptr).text,"LB")==0)
                        { I2R(LB,tptr);}
                        else if(strcmp((*tptr).text,"LW")==0)
                        { I2R(LW,tptr);}
                        else if(strcmp((*tptr).text,"LD")==0)
                        { I2R(LD,tptr);}
                        else if(strcmp((*tptr).text,"LQ")==0)
                        { I2R(LQ,tptr);}
                        else it(strcmp((*tptr).text,"LF1")==0)
                        { IFR(LF1,tptr);}
                        else if(strcmp((*tptr).text,"LF2")==0)
                        { IDR(LF2,tptr);}
                        else if(strcmp((*tptr).text,"LAD")==0)
                        { IRA(tptr);}
                        else if(strcmp((*tptr).text,"LAI")==0)
                        { I2RA(tptr);}
                        else
                        {
                        ERROR2("processInstructionPass1(): line %d,
                        invalid opcode (%s)\n",(*tptr).line,(*tptr).text);
                                return;
                        }

                    }break;
                    case 'M':
                    {
                        if(strcmp((*tptr).text,"MOV")==0)
                        { I2R(MOV,tptr); }
                        else if(strcmp((*tptr).text,"MOVF")==0)
                        { I2F(MOVF,tptr); }
                        else if(strcmp((*tptr).text,"MOVD")==0)
                        { I2D(MOVD,tptr); }
                        else if(strcmp((*tptr).text,"MULT")==0)
                        { I3R(MULT,tptr);}
                        else
```

```
                {
                ERROR2("processInstructionPass1(): line %d,
                invalid opcode (%s)\n",(*tptr).line,(*tptr).text);
                    return;
                }

        }break;
        case 'N':
        {
            if(strcmp((*tptr).text,"NOT")==0)
            { I2R(NOT,tptr);}
            else if(strcmp((*tptr).text,"NOP")==0)
            { I(NOP,tptr);}
            else
            {
            ERROR2("processInstructionPass1(): line %d,
            invalid opcode (%s)\n",(*tptr).line,(*tptr).text);
                return;
            }

        }break;
        case 'O':
        {
            if(strcmp((*tptr).text,"OR")==0)
            { I3R(OR,tptr);}
            else
            {
            ERROR2("processInstructionPass1(): line %d,
            invalid opcode (%s)\n",(*tptr).line,(*tptr).text);
                return;
            }

        }break;
        case 'P':
        {
            if(strcmp((*tptr).text,"PUSHB")==0)
            { IR(PUSHB,tptr);}
            else if(strcmp((*tptr).text,"PUSHW")==0)
            { IR(PUSHW,tptr);}
            else if(strcmp((*tptr).text,"PUSHD")==0)
            { IR(PUSHD,tptr);}
            else if(strcmp((*tptr).text,"PUSHQ")==0)
            { IR(PUSHQ,tptr);}
            else if(strcmp((*tptr).text,"PUSHF1")==0)
            { IF(PUSHF1,tptr);}
            else if(strcmp((*tptr).text,"PUSHF2")==0)
            { ID(PUSHF2,tptr);}
            else if(strcmp((*tptr).text,"POPB")==0)
            { IR(POPB,tptr);}
            else if(strcmp((*tptr).text,"POPW")==0)
            { IR(POPW,tptr);}
            else if(strcmp((*tptr).text,"POPD")==0)
            { IR(POPD,tptr);}
            else if(strcmp((*tptr).text,"POPQ")==0)
```

```
                    { IR(POPQ,tptr);}
                    else if(strcmp((*tptr).text,"POPF1")==0)
                    { IF(POPF1,tptr);}
                    else if(strcmp((*tptr).text,"POPF2")==0)
                    { ID(POPF2,tptr);}
                    else
                    {
                    ERROR2("processInstructionPass1(): line %d,
                    invalid opcode (%s)\n",(*tptr).line,(*tptr).text);
                            return;
                    }

            }break;
            case 'S':
            {
                    if(strcmp((*tptr).text,"SB")==0)
                    { I2R(SB,tptr);}
                    else if(strcmp((*tptr).text,"SW")==0)
                    { I2R(SW,tptr);}
                    else if(strcmp((*tptr).text,"SD")==0)
                    { I2R(SD,tptr);}
                    else if(strcmp((*tptr).text,"SQ")==0)
                    { I2R(SQ,tptr);}
                    else if(strcmp((*tptr).text,"SF1")==0)
                    { IFR(SF1,tptr);}
                    else if(strcmp((*tptr).text,"SF2")==0)
                    { IDR(SF2,tptr);}
                    clsc if(strcmp((*tptr).tcxt,"SRA")--0)
                    { I3R(SRA,tptr);}
                    else if(strcmp((*tptr).text,"SRL")==0)
                    { I3R(SRL,tptr);}
                    else if(strcmp((*tptr).text,"SL")==0)
                    { I3R(SL,tptr);}
                    else if(strcmp((*tptr).text,"SUB")==0)
                    { I3R(SUB,tptr);}
                    else if(strcmp((*tptr).text,"SLT")==0)
                    { I3R(SLT,tptr);}
                    else
                    {
                    ERROR2("processInstructionPass1(): line %d,
                    invalid opcode (%s)\n",(*tptr).line,(*tptr).text);
                            return;
                    }

            }break;
            case 'X':
            {
                    if(strcmp((*tptr).text,"XOR")==0)
                    { I3R(XOR,tptr);}
                    else
                    {
                    ERROR2("processInstructionPass1(): line %d,
                    invalid opcode (%s)\n",(*tptr).line,(*tptr).text);
                            return;
```

```
                    }
                }break;
                default:
                {
                        ERROR1("%s not a valid opcode\n",(*tptr).text);
                        return;
                }
            }/*end switch*/
    }
    else
    {
            ERROR1("%s not a valid opcode\n",(*tptr).text);
    }
    return;

}/*end processInstruction*/

void Pass2::I(U1 opcode, struct Token *tptr)
{
    struct Token t;
    U1 bret;
    U1 nBYTES;
    nBYTES = 1;

    sprintf(lineNumber,"%lu",(*tptr).line);

    strcpy(listing,(*tptr).text);
    strcat(listing," ");
    encoded[0]=opcode;

    bret = (*toker).match(&t,TOK_NO_MORE);
    if(bret!=TRUE)
    {
            return;
    }

    commitToFiles(nBYTES);

    bytePosPass2 = bytePosPass2 + nBYTES;
    return;

}/*end I*/

void Pass2::IB(U1 opcode, struct Token *tptr)
{
    struct Token t;
    U1 bret;
    U1 nBYTES;
    nBYTES = 2;

    sprintf(lineNumber,"%lu",(*tptr).line);

    strcpy(listing,(*tptr).text);
    strcat(listing," ");
```

```
            encoded[0]=opcode;
            bret = (*toker).match(&t,TOK_INT_CONST);
            if(bret==TRUE)
            {
                  strcat(listing,t.text);
                  encoded[1]=(U1)t.val;
            }
            else
            {
                  return;
            }

            bret = (*toker).match(&t,TOK_NO_MORE);
            if(bret!=TRUE)
            {
                  return;
            }

            commitToFiles(nBYTES);

            bytePosPass2 = bytePosPass2 + nBYTES;
            return;

      }/*end IB*/

      void Pass2::IR(U1 opcode, struct Token *tptr)
      {
            struct Token t;
            U1 bret;
            U1 nBYTES;
            nBYTES = 2;

            sprintf(lineNumber,"%lu",(*tptr).line);

            strcpy(listing,(*tptr).text);
            strcat(listing," ");
            encoded[0]=opcode;

            bret = (*toker).match(&t,TOK_INT_REG);
            if(bret==TRUE)
            {
                  strcat(listing,t.text);
                  encoded[1]=(U1)t.val;
            }
            else
            {
                  return;
            }

            bret = (*toker).match(&t,TOK_NO_MORE);
            if(bret!=TRUE)
            {
                  return;
            }
```

```
        commitToFiles(nBYTES);

        bytePosPass2 = bytePosPass2 + nBYTES;
        return;

}/*end IR*/

void Pass2::IRC(U1 opcode, U1 bytes, struct Token *tptr)
{
        struct Token t;
        U1 bret;
        U1 nBYTES;
        nBYTES = 2+bytes; /*bytes = 1,2,4,8 (byte->qword)*/

        sprintf(lineNumber,"%lu",(*tptr).line);

        strcpy(listing,(*tptr).text);
        strcat(listing," ");
        encoded[0]=opcode;

        bret = (*toker).match(&t,TOK_INT_REG);
        if(bret==TRUE)
        {
                strcat(listing,t.text);
                encoded[1]=(U1)t.val;
        }
        else
        {
                return;
        }

        bret = (*toker).match(&t,TOK_COMMA);
        if(bret==TRUE){ strcat(listing,t.text); }
        else
        {
                return;
        }

        t = (*toker).getNextLineToken();
        if(t.type==TOK_INT_CONST)
        {
                strcat(listing,t.text);
                switch(bytes)
                {
                        case 1:
                        {
                                encoded[2] = (U1)t.val;
                        }break;
                        case 2:
                        {
                                wordToBytecode((U2)t.val, &encoded[2]);
                        }break;
                        case 4:
```

```
                            {
                                    dwordToBytecode((U4)t.val, &encoded[2]);
                            }break;
                        case 8:
                            {
                                    qwordToBytecode(t.val, &encoded[2]);
                            }break;
                    }
            }
            else if(t.type==TOK_CHAR_CONST)
            {
                    strcat(listing,t.text);
                    encoded[2]=0;encoded[3]=0;encoded[4]=0;encoded[5]=0;
                    encoded[6]=0;encoded[7]=0;encoded[8]=0;encoded[9]=0;

                    /*encode in big-endian format*/

                    switch(bytes)
                    {
                        case 1:{ encoded[2] = (U1)t.val; }break;
                        case 2:{ encoded[3] = (U1)t.val; }break;
                        case 4:{ encoded[5] = (U1)t.val; }break;
                        case 8:{ encoded[9] = (U1)t.val; }break;
                    }
            }
            else
            {
                    return;
            }

            bret = (*toker).match(&t,TOK_NO_MORE);
            if(bret!=TRUE)
            {
                    return;
            }

            commitToFiles(nBYTES);

            bytePosPass2 = bytePosPass2 + nBYTES;
            return;

}/*end IRC*/

void Pass2::IRA(struct Token *tptr)
{
        struct Token t;
        U1 bret;
        U1 nBYTES;
        struct HashTbl *hptr;

        nBYTES = 2+8; /*address = 8 bytes*/

        sprintf(lineNumber,"%lu",(*tptr).line);
```

```
strcpy(listing,(*tptr).text);
strcat(listing," ");
encoded[0]=LAD;

bret = (*toker).match(&t,TOK_INT_REG);
if(bret==TRUE)
{
     strcat(listing,t.text);
     encoded[1]=(U1)t.val;
}
else
{
     return;
}

bret = (*toker).match(&t,TOK_COMMA);
if(bret==TRUE)
{
     strcat(listing,t.text);
}
else
{
     return;
}

t = (*toker).getNextLineToken();
if(t.type==TOK_IDENTIFIER)
{
     strcat(listing,t.text);

     /*symbol must exist*/

     hptr =  (*hashTbl).queryHashTbl(t.text);
     if(hptr==NULL)
     {
          ERROR2("IRA(): line %lu, undefined
          identifier %s\n",t.line,t.text);
          return;
     }
     else
     {
          /*must be symbol type =  PROC, PROC_LBL */

          U8 val;
          if((*hptr).type==PROC)
          {
               /*resolve offset/address */
               val = ((*symTbl).proc[(*hptr).index]).address;
               qwordToBytecode(val, &encoded[2]);
          }
          else if((*hptr).type==PROC_LBL)
          {
               /*resolve offset/address */
               val = (((*symTbl).proc[(*hptr).index]).
```

```
                                    label[(*hptr).subIndex]).address;
                                    qwordToBytecode(val, &encoded[2]);
                    }
                    else
                    {
                            ERROR2("IRA(): line %lu, invalid operand for LAD
                                %s\n",t.line,t.text);
                            return;
                    }
            }
    }
    else
    {
            ERROR2("IRA(): line %lu, invalid constant %s\n",t.line,t.text);
            return;
    }

    bret = (*toker).match(&t,TOK_NO_MORE);
    if(bret!=TRUE){ return; }

    commitToFiles(nBYTES);

    bytePosPass2 = bytePosPass2 + nBYTES;
    return;

}/*end IRA*/

void Pass2::I2RA(struct Token *tptr)
{
    struct Token t;
    U1 bret;
    U1 nBYTES;
    struct HashTbl *hptr;
    nBYTES = 3+8; /*address = 8 bytes*/

    sprintf(lineNumber,"%lu",(*tptr).line);

    strcpy(listing,(*tptr).text);
    strcat(listing," ");
    encoded[0]=LAI;

    bret = (*toker).match(&t,TOK_INT_REG);
    if(bret==TRUE)
    {
            strcat(listing,t.text);
            encoded[1]=(U1)t.val;
    }
    else{ return; }

    bret = (*toker).match(&t,TOK_COMMA);
    if(bret==TRUE){ strcat(listing,t.text); }
    else{ return; }
    bret = (*toker).match(&t,TOK_INT_REG);
    if(bret==TRUE)
```

```
                    {
                          strcat(listing,t.text);
                          encoded[2]=(U1)t.val;
                    }
                    else{ return; }

                    brct - (*toker).match(&t,TOK_COMMA);
                    if(bret==TRUE){ strcat(listing,t.text); }
                    else{ return; }

                    t = (*toker).getNextLineToken();
                    if(t.type==TOK_IDENTIFIER)
                    {
                          strcat(listing,t.text);

                          /*symbol must exist*/

                          hptr =  (*hashTbl).queryHashTbl(t.text);
                          if(hptr==NULL)
                          {
                                ERROR2("I2RA(): line %lu, undefined identifier %s\n",t.line,t.text);
                                return;
                          }
                          else
                          {
/*must be symbol type = GLOBAL_VAR, PROC_RET, PROC_ARG, PROC_LOC */

                                S8 val;
                                if((*hptr).type==GLOBAL_VAR)
                                {
                                      /*resolve offset/address */
                                      val = -((S8)((*symTbl).globVar[(*hptr).index]).offset);
                                      qwordToBytecode(val, &encoded[3]);
                                }
                                else if((*hptr).type==PROC_RET)
                                {
                                      /*resolve offset/address */
                                      val = (((*symTbl).proc[(*hptr).index]).ret).fpOffset;
                                      qwordToBytecode(val, &encoded[3]);
                                }
                                else if((*hptr).type==PROC_ARG)
                                {
                                      /*resolve offset/address */
                                      val = (((*symTbl).proc[(*hptr).index]).
                                                  arg[(*hptr).subIndex]).fpOffset;
                                      qwordToBytecode(val, &encoded[3]);
                                }
                                else if((*hptr).type==PROC_LOC)
                                {
                                      /*resolve offset/address */
                                      val = (((*symTbl).proc[(*hptr).index]).
                                                  local[(*hptr).subIndex]).fpOffset;
                                      qwordToBytecode(val, &encoded[3]);
                                }
```

```
                    else
                    {
                            ERROR2("I2RA(): line %lu, invalid operand for LAD
                                    %s\n",t.line,t.text);
                            return;
                    }
            }
    }
    else
    {
            ERROR2("I2RA(): line %lu, invalid constant %s\n",t.line,t.text);
            return;
    }

    bret = (*toker).match(&t,TOK_NO_MORE);
    if(bret!=TRUE){ return; }

    commitToFiles(nBYTES);

    bytePosPass2 = bytePosPass2 + nBYTES;
    return;

}/*end I2RA*/

void Pass2::I2R(U1 opcode, struct Token *tptr)
{
    struct Token t;
    U1 bret;
    U1 nBYTES;
    nBYTES = 3;

    sprintf(lineNumber,"%lu",(*tptr).line);

    strcpy(listing,(*tptr).text);
    strcat(listing," ");
    encoded[0]=opcode;

    bret = (*toker).match(&t,TOK_INT_REG);
    if(bret==TRUE)
    {
            strcat(listing,t.text);
            encoded[1]=(U1)t.val;
    }
    else{ return; }

    bret = (*toker).match(&t,TOK_COMMA);
    if(bret==TRUE){ strcat(listing,t.text); }
    else{ return; }

    bret = (*toker).match(&t,TOK_INT_REG);
    if(bret==TRUE)
    {
            strcat(listing,t.text);
            encoded[2]=(U1)t.val;
```

```
        }
        else{ return; }

        bret = (*toker).match(&t,TOK_NO_MORE);
        if(bret!=TRUE){ return; }

        commitToFiles(nBYTES);

        bytePosPass2 = bytePosPass2 + nBYTES;
        return;

}/*end I2R*/

void Pass2::I3R(U1 opcode, struct Token *tptr)
{
        struct Token t;
        U1 bret;
        U1 nBYTES;
        nBYTES = 4;

        sprintf(lineNumber,"%lu",(*tptr).line);

        strcpy(listing,(*tptr).text);
        strcat(listing," ");
        encoded[0]=opcode;

        bret = (*toker).match(&t,TOK_INT_REG);
        if(bret==TRUE)
        {
                strcat(listing,t.text);
                encoded[1]=(U1)t.val;
        }
        else{ return; }

        bret = (*toker).match(&t,TOK_COMMA);
        if(bret==TRUE){ strcat(listing,t.text); }
        else{ return; }

        bret = (*toker).match(&t,TOK_INT_REG);
        if(bret==TRUE)
        {
                strcat(listing,t.text);
                encoded[2]=(U1)t.val;
        }
        else{ return; }

        bret = (*toker).match(&t,TOK_COMMA);
        if(bret==TRUE){ strcat(listing,t.text); }
        else{ return; }

        bret = (*toker).match(&t,TOK_INT_REG);
        if(bret==TRUE)
        {
                strcat(listing,t.text);
```

```
            encoded[3]=(U1)t.val;
    }
    else{ return; }

    bret = (*toker).match(&t,TOK_NO_MORE);
    if(bret!=TRUE){ return; }

    commitToFiles(nBYTES);

    bytePosPass2 = bytePosPass2 + nBYTES;
    return;

}/*end I3R*/

void Pass2::I4R(U1 opcode, struct Token *tptr)
{
    struct Token t;
    U1 bret;
    U1 nBYTES;
    nBYTES = 5;

    sprintf(lineNumber,"%lu",(*tptr).line);

    strcpy(listing,(*tptr).text);
    strcat(listing," ");
    encoded[0]=opcode;

    bret = (*toker).match(&t,TOK_INI_REG);
    if(bret==TRUE)
    {
        strcat(listing,t.text);
        encoded[1]=(U1)t.val;
    }
    else{ return; }

    bret = (*toker).match(&t,TOK_COMMA);
    if(bret==TRUE){ strcat(listing,t.text); }
    else{ return; }

    bret = (*toker).match(&t,TOK_INT_REG);
    if(bret==TRUE)
    {
        strcat(listing,t.text);
        encoded[2]=(U1)t.val;
    }
    else{ return; }

    bret = (*toker).match(&t,TOK_COMMA);
    if(bret==TRUE){ strcat(listing,t.text); }
    else{ return; }
    bret = (*toker).match(&t,TOK_INT_REG);
    if(bret==TRUE)
    {
        strcat(listing,t.text);
```

```
                    encoded[3]=(U1)t.val;
        }
        else{ return; }

        bret = (*toker).match(&t,TOK_COMMA);
        if(bret==TRUE){ strcat(listing,t.text); }
        else{ return; }

        bret = (*toker).match(&t,TOK_INT_REG);
        if(bret==TRUE)
        {
            strcat(listing,t.text);
            encoded[4]=(U1)t.val;
        }
        else{ return; }

        bret = (*toker).match(&t,TOK_NO_MORE);
        if(bret!=TRUE){ return; }

        commitToFiles(nBYTES);

        bytePosPass2 = bytePosPass2 + nBYTES;
        return;

}/*end I4R*/

void Pass2::IFC(U1 opcode, struct Token *tptr)
{
        struct Token t;
        U1 bret;
        U1 nBYTES;
        nBYTES = 6; /* float = 4 bytes */

        sprintf(lineNumber,"%lu",(*tptr).line);

        strcpy(listing,(*tptr).text);
        strcat(listing," ");
        encoded[0]=opcode;

        bret = (*toker).match(&t,TOK_FLT_REG);
        if(bret==TRUE)
        {
            strcat(listing,t.text);
            encoded[1]=(U1)t.val;
        }
        else{ return; }

        bret = (*toker).match(&t,TOK_COMMA);
        if(bret==TRUE){ strcat(listing,t.text); }
        else{ return; }
        t = (*toker).getNextLineToken();
        if(t.type==TOK_FLT_CONST)
        {
            strcat(listing,t.text);
```

```
                    floatToBytecode((F4)t.fval, &encoded[2]);
        }
        else
        {
                ERROR2("IFC(): line %lu, expecting float constant %s\n",t.line,t.text);
                return;
        }

        bret = (*toker).match(&t,TOK_NO_MORE);
        if(bret!=TRUE){ return; }

        commitToFiles(nBYTES);

        bytePosPass2 = bytePosPass2 + nBYTES;
        return;

}/*end IFC*/

void Pass2::IFR(U1 opcode, struct Token *tptr)
{
        struct Token t;
        U1 bret;
        U1 nBYTES;
        nBYTES = 3;

        sprintf(lineNumber,"%lu",(*tptr).line);

        strcpy(listing,(*tptr).text);
        strcat(listing," ");
        encoded[0]=opcode;

        bret = (*toker).match(&t,TOK_FLT_REG);
        if(bret==TRUE)
        {
                strcat(listing,t.text);
                encoded[1]=(U1)t.val;
        }
        else{ return; }

        bret = (*toker).match(&t,TOK_COMMA);
        if(bret==TRUE){ strcat(listing,t.text); }
        else{ return; }

        bret = (*toker).match(&t,TOK_INT_REG);
        if(bret==TRUE)
        {
                strcat(listing,t.text);
                encoded[2]=(U1)t.val;
        }
        else{ return; }

        bret = (*toker).match(&t,TOK_NO_MORE);
        if(bret!=TRUE){ return; }
```

```
        commitToFiles(nBYTES);

        bytePosPass2 = bytePosPass2 + nBYTES;
        return;

}/*end IFR*/

void Pass2::IF(U1 opcode, struct Token *tptr)
{
        struct Token t;
        U1 bret;
        U1 nBYTES;
        nBYTES = 2;

        sprintf(lineNumber,"%lu",(*tptr).line);

        strcpy(listing,(*tptr).text);
        strcat(listing," ");
        encoded[0]=opcode;

        bret = (*toker).match(&t,TOK_FLT_REG);
        if(bret==TRUE)
        {
                strcat(listing,t.text);
                encoded[1]=(U1)t.val;
        }
        else{ return; }

        bret = (*toker).match(&t,TOK_NO_MORE);
        if(bret!=TRUE){ return; }

        commitToFiles(nBYTES);

        bytePosPass2 = bytePosPass2 + nBYTES;
        return;

}/*end IF*/

void Pass2::I2F(U1 opcode, struct Token *tptr)
{
        struct Token t;
        U1 bret;
        U1 nBYTES;
        nBYTES = 3;

        sprintf(lineNumber,"%lu",(*tptr).line);

        strcpy(listing,(*tptr).text);
        strcat(listing," ");
        encoded[0]=opcode;

        bret = (*toker).match(&t,TOK_FLT_REG);
        if(bret==TRUE)
        {
```

```
                strcat(listing,t.text);
                encoded[1]=(U1)t.val;
        }
        else{ return; }

        bret = (*toker).match(&t,TOK_COMMA);
        if(bret==TRUE){ strcat(listing,t.text); }
        else{ return; }

        bret = (*toker).match(&t,TOK_FLT_REG);
        if(bret==TRUE)
        {
                strcat(listing,t.text);
                encoded[2]=(U1)t.val;
        }
        else{ return; }

        bret = (*toker).match(&t,TOK_NO_MORE);
        if(bret!=TRUE){ return; }

        commitToFiles(nBYTES);

        bytePosPass2 = bytePosPass2 + nBYTES;
        return;

}/*end I2F*/

void Pass2::I3F(U1 opcode, struct Token *tptr)
{
        struct Token t;
        U1 bret;
        U1 nBYTES;
        nBYTES = 4;

        sprintf(lineNumber,"%lu",(*tptr).line);

        strcpy(listing,(*tptr).text);
        strcat(listing," ");
        encoded[0]=opcode;

        bret = (*toker).match(&t,TOK_FLT_REG);
        if(bret==TRUE)
        {
                strcat(listing,t.text);
                encoded[1]=(U1)t.val;
        }
        else{ return; }

        bret = (*toker).match(&t,TOK_COMMA);
        if(bret==TRUE){ strcat(listing,t.text); }
        else{ return; }

        bret = (*toker).match(&t,TOK_FLT_REG);
        if(bret==TRUE)
```

```
    {
        strcat(listing,t.text);
        encoded[2]=(U1)t.val;
    }
    else{ return; }

    bret = (*toker).match(&t,TOK COMMA);
    if(bret==TRUE){ strcat(listing,t.text); }
    else{ return; }

    bret = (*toker).match(&t,TOK_FLT_REG);
    if(bret==TRUE)
    {
        strcat(listing,t.text);
        encoded[3]=(U1)t.val;
    }
    else{ return; }

    bret = (*toker).match(&t,TOK_NO_MORE);
    if(bret!=TRUE){ return; }

    commitToFiles(nBYTES);

    bytePosPass2 = bytePosPass2 + nBYTES;
    return;

}/*end I3F*/

void Pass2::IRF(U1 opcode, struct Token *tptr)
{
    struct Token t;
    U1 bret;
    U1 nBYTES;
    nBYTES = 3;

    sprintf(lineNumber,"%lu",(*tptr).line);

    strcpy(listing,(*tptr).text);
    strcat(listing," ");
    encoded[0]=opcode;

    bret = (*toker).match(&t,TOK_INT_REG);
    if(bret==TRUE)
    {
        strcat(listing,t.text);
        encoded[1]=(U1)t.val;
    }
    else{ return; }

    bret = (*toker).match(&t,TOK_COMMA);
    if(bret==TRUE){ strcat(listing,t.text); }
    else{ return; }
```

```
        bret = (*toker).match(&t,TOK_FLT_REG);
        if(bret==TRUE)
        {
             strcat(listing,t.text);
             encoded[2]=(U1)t.val;
        }
        else{ return; }

        bret = (*toker).match(&t,TOK_NO_MORE);
        if(bret!=TRUE){ return; }

        commitToFiles(nBYTES);

        bytePosPass2 = bytePosPass2 + nBYTES;
        return;

}/*end IRF*/

void Pass2::IDF(U1 opcode, struct Token *tptr)
{
    struct Token t;
    U1 bret;
    U1 nBYTES;
    nBYTES = 3;

    sprintf(lineNumber,"%lu",(*tptr).line);

    strcpy(listing,(*tptr).text);
    strcat(listing," ");
    encoded[0]=opcode;

    bret = (*toker).match(&t,TOK_DBL_REG);
    if(bret==TRUE)
    {
         strcat(listing,t.text);
         encoded[1]=(U1)t.val;
    }
    else{ return; }

    bret = (*toker).match(&t,TOK_COMMA);
    if(bret==TRUE){ strcat(listing,t.text); }
    else{ return; }

    bret = (*toker).match(&t,TOK_FLT_REG);
    if(bret==TRUE)
    {
         strcat(listing,t.text);
         encoded[2]=(U1)t.val;
    }
    else{ return; }
    bret = (*toker).match(&t,TOK_NO_MORE);
    if(bret!=TRUE){ return; }
```

```
                commitToFiles(nBYTES);

                bytePosPass2 = bytePosPass2 + nBYTES;
                return;

        }/*end IDF*/

        void Pass2::IDC(U1 opcode, struct Token *tptr)
        {
                struct Token t;
                U1 bret;
                U1 nBYTES;
                nBYTES = 10; /* double = 8 bytes */

                sprintf(lineNumber,"%lu",(*tptr).line);

                strcpy(listing,(*tptr).text);
                strcat(listing," ");
                encoded[0]=opcode;

                bret = (*toker).match(&t,TOK_DBL_REG);
                if(bret==TRUE)
                {
                        strcat(listing,t.text);
                        encoded[1]=(U1)t.val;
                }
                else{ return; }

                bret = (*toker).match(&t,TOK_COMMA);
                if(bret==TRUE){ strcat(listing,t.text); }
                else{ return; }

                t = (*toker).getNextLineToken();
                if(t.type==TOK_FLT_CONST)
                {
                        strcat(listing,t.text);
                        doubleToBytecode(t.fval, &encoded[2]);
                }
                else
                {
                        ERROR2("IDC(): line %lu, expecting double constant %s\n",t.line,t.text);
                        return;
                }

                bret = (*toker).match(&t,TOK_NO_MORE);
                if(bret!=TRUE){ return; }

                commitToFiles(nBYTES);

                bytePosPass2 = bytePosPass2 + nBYTES;
                return;

        }/*end IDC*/
```

```
void Pass2::IDR(U1 opcode, struct Token *tptr)
{
    struct Token t;
    U1 bret;
    U1 nBYTES;
    nBYTES = 3;

    sprintf(lineNumber,"%lu",(*tptr).line);

    strcpy(listing,(*tptr).text);
    strcat(listing," ");
    encoded[0]=opcode;

    bret = (*toker).match(&t,TOK_DBL_REG);
    if(bret==TRUE)
    {
        strcat(listing,t.text);
        encoded[1]=(U1)t.val;
    }
    else{ return; }

    bret = (*toker).match(&t,TOK_COMMA);
    if(bret==TRUE){ strcat(listing,t.text); }
    else{ return; }

    bret = (*toker).match(&t,TOK_INT_REG);
    if(bret==TRUE)
    {
        strcat(listing,t.text);
        encoded[2]=(U1)t.val;
    }
    else{ return; }

    bret = (*toker).match(&t,TOK_NO_MORE);
    if(bret!=TRUE){ return; }

    commitToFiles(nBYTES);

    bytePosPass2 = bytePosPass2 + nBYTES;
    return;

}/*end IDR*/

void Pass2::ID(U1 opcode, struct Token *tptr)
{
    struct Token t;
    U1 bret;
    U1 nBYTES;
    nBYTES = 2;

    sprintf(lineNumber,"%lu",(*tptr).line);

    strcpy(listing,(*tptr).text);
    strcat(listing," ");
```

```
                encoded[0]=opcode;

                bret = (*toker).match(&t,TOK_DBL_REG);
                if(bret==TRUE)
                {
                     strcat(listing,t.text);
                     encoded[1]=(U1)t.val;
                }
                else{ return; }

                bret = (*toker).match(&t,TOK_NO_MORE);
                if(bret!=TRUE){ return; }

                commitToFiles(nBYTES);

                bytePosPass2 = bytePosPass2 + nBYTES;
                return;

     }/*end ID*/

     void Pass2::I2D(U1 opcode, struct Token *tptr)
     {
                struct Token t;
                U1 bret;
                U1 nBYTES;
                nBYTES = 3;

                sprintf(lineNumber,"%lu",(*tptr).line);

                strcpy(listing,(*tptr).text);
                strcat(listing," ");
                encoded[0]=opcode;

                bret = (*toker).match(&t,TOK_DBL_REG);
                if(bret==TRUE)
                {
                     strcat(listing,t.text);
                     encoded[1]=(U1)t.val;
                }
                else{ return; }

                bret = (*toker).match(&t,TOK_COMMA);
                if(bret==TRUE){ strcat(listing,t.text); }
                else{ return; }

                bret = (*toker).match(&t,TOK_DBL_REG);
                if(bret==TRUE)
                {
                     strcat(listing,t.text);
                     encoded[2]=(U1)t.val;
                }
                else{ return; }
```

```
        bret = (*toker).match(&t,TOK_NO_MORE);
        if(bret!=TRUE){ return; }

        commitToFiles(nBYTES);

        bytePosPass2 = bytePosPass2 + nBYTES;
        return;

}/*end I2D*/

void Pass2::I3D(U1 opcode, struct Token *tptr)
{
        struct Token t;
        U1 bret;
        U1 nBYTES;
        nBYTES = 4;

        sprintf(lineNumber,"%lu",(*tptr).line);

        strcpy(listing,(*tptr).text);
        strcat(listing," ");
        encoded[0]=opcode;

        bret = (*toker).match(&t,TOK_DBL_REG);
        if(bret==TRUE)
        {
                strcat(listing,t.text);
                encoded[1]=(U1)t.val;
        }
        else{ return; }

        bret = (*toker).match(&t,TOK_COMMA);
        if(bret==TRUE){ strcat(listing,t.text); }
        else{ return; }

        bret = (*toker).match(&t,TOK_DBL_REG);
        if(bret==TRUE)
        {
                strcat(listing,t.text);
                encoded[2]=(U1)t.val;
        }
        else{ return; }

        bret = (*toker).match(&t,TOK_COMMA);
        if(bret==TRUE){ strcat(listing,t.text); }
        else{ return; }

        bret = (*toker).match(&t,TOK_DBL_REG);
        if(bret==TRUE)
        {
                strcat(listing,t.text);
                encoded[3]=(U1)t.val;
        }
        else{ return; }
```

```
        bret = (*toker).match(&t,TOK_NO_MORE);
        if(bret!=TRUE){ return; }

        commitToFiles(nBYTES);

        bytePosPass2 = bytePosPass2 + nBYTES;
        return;

}/*end I3D*/

void Pass2::IRD(U1 opcode, struct Token *tptr)
{
        struct Token t;
        U1 bret;
        U1 nBYTES;
        nBYTES = 3;

        sprintf(lineNumber,"%lu",(*tptr).line);

        strcpy(listing,(*tptr).text);
        strcat(listing," ");
        encoded[0]=opcode;

        bret = (*toker).match(&t,TOK_INT_REG);
        if(bret==TRUE)
        {
            strcat(listing,t.text);
            encoded[1]=(U1)t.val;
        }
        else{ return; }

        bret = (*toker).match(&t,TOK_COMMA);
        if(bret==TRUE){ strcat(listing,t.text); }
        else{ return; }

        bret = (*toker).match(&t,TOK_DBL_REG);
        if(bret==TRUE)
        {
            strcat(listing,t.text);
            encoded[2]=(U1)t.val;
        }
        else{ return; }

        bret = (*toker).match(&t,TOK_NO_MORE);
        if(bret!=TRUE){ return; }

        commitToFiles(nBYTES);

        bytePosPass2 = bytePosPass2 + nBYTES;
        return;
}/*end IRD*/

void Pass2::IFD(U1 opcode, struct Token *tptr)
{
```

```
        struct Token t;
        U1 bret;
        U1 nBYTES;
        nBYTES = 3;

        sprintf(lineNumber,"%lu",(*tptr).line);

        strcpy(listing,(*tptr).text);
        strcat(listing," ");
        encoded[0]=opcode;

        bret = (*toker).match(&t,TOK_FLT_REG);
        if(bret==TRUE)
        {
            strcat(listing,t.text);
            encoded[1]=(U1)t.val;
        }
        else{ return; }

        bret = (*toker).match(&t,TOK_COMMA);
        if(bret==TRUE){ strcat(listing,t.text); }
        else{ return; }

        bret = (*toker).match(&t,TOK_DBL_REG);
        if(bret==TRUE)
        {
            strcat(listing,t.text);
            encoded[2]=(U1)t.val;
        }
        else{ return; }

        bret = (*toker).match(&t,TOK_NO_MORE);
        if(bret!=TRUE){ return; }

        commitToFiles(nBYTES);

        bytePosPass2 = bytePosPass2 + nBYTES;
        return;

}/*end IFD*/

void Pass2::commitToFiles(U1 len)
{
    U4 i;

    /*populate list file*/

    if((*cmdLine).listing==TRUE)
    {
        /*line number*/
        putStrLstBuff(lineNumber);
        putByteLstBuff(')');
```

```
                        /*address*/
                        putByteLstBuff('[');
                        sprintf(lineNumber,"%lu",bytePosPass2);
                        putStrLstBuff(lineNumber);
                        putByteLstBuff(']');

                        /*instruction*/

                        putByteLstBuff('\t');
                        putByteLstBuff('\t');
                        putStrLstBuff(listing);
                        i = strlen(listing);
                        while(i<=30){ putByteLstBuff(' '); i++; }

                        /*binary version*/

                        putByteLstBuff('\t');
                        for(i=0;i<len;i++)
                        {
                                putByteLstBuff('[');
                                sprintf(lineNumber,"%lu",encoded[i]);
                                putStrLstBuff(lineNumber);
                                putByteLstBuff(']');
                        }
                        putByteLstBuff('\n');
                }

        /*populate temp file*/

        for(i=0;i<len;i++){ putByteTempBuff(encoded[i]); }

        return;

}/*end commitToFiles*/
```

The `generateSymbolSummary()` function is used to append a symbol table summary to the end of the listing file. The `generateSymbolSummary()` function iterates through the entire symbol repository. It offers information on global variables, procedures, the hash table, and the string table. To do all this, it invokes three other functions: `printGlobVarToLst()`, `printProcToLst()`, and `printTreeToLst()`.

```
void Pass2::generateSymbolSummary()
{
    U4 i;
    U8 nstr;

    /* 1) print out symbol table to listing file*/

    putByteLstBuff('\n');
    sprintf(listing,"%s","#++++SYMBOL TABLE++++++");
    putStrLstBuff(listing);
    putByteLstBuff('\n');
```

```c
for(i=0;i<(*symTbl).iGlobVar;i++)
{
     sprintf(listing,"->GLOBAL VARIABLE %d)",i);
     putStrLstBuff(listing);
     printGlobVarToLst(&((*symTbl).globVar[i]));
     putByteLstBuff('\n');
}
for(i=0;i<(*symTbl).iProc;i++)
{
     sprintf(listing,"->PROCEDURE %d)",i);
     putStrLstBuff(listing);
     printProcToLst(&((*symTbl).proc[i]));
     putByteLstBuff('\n');
}

/* 2) print out hash table to listing file*/

putByteLstBuff('\n');
sprintf(listing,"%s","#++++HASH TABLE++++++");
putStrLstBuff(listing);
putByteLstBuff('\n');

for(i=0;i<PRIME;i++)
{
     if((*hashTbl).hashTbl[i].empty == FALSE)
     {
          sprintf(listing,"Hash Slot %d)\n",i);
          putStrLstBuff(listing);

          printTreeToLst(&((*hashTbl).hashTbl[i]), 0);
          putByteLstBuff('\n');
     }
}

/* 3) print out string table to listing file*/

putByteLstBuff('\n');
sprintf(listing,"%s","#++++STRING TABLE++++++");
putStrLstBuff(listing);
putByteLstBuff('\n');

nstr = 1;

for(i=0;i<(*strTbl).iStr;i++)
{
     if(i==0)
     {
          putByteLstBuff('0');
          putByteLstBuff(')');
     }
     if((*strTbl).text[i]!='\0')
     {
          putByteLstBuff((*strTbl).text[i]);
     }
```

```
            else if(i<((*strTbl).iStr-1))
            {
                    putByteLstBuff('\n');
                    sprintf(lineNumber,"%d)",nstr);
                    putStrLstBuff(lineNumber);
                    nstr++;
            }
            else if(i==((*strTbl).iStr-1)){ putByteLstBuff('\n');}
    }

    return;

}/*end generateSymbolSummary*/

void Pass2::printGlobVarToLst(struct GlobalVariable *ptr)
{
    sprintf(listing,"identifier=%s\n",&((*strTbl).text[(*ptr).text]));
    putStrLstBuff(listing);

    sprintf(listing,"data type=%s\n",globSz[(*ptr).dType]);
    putStrLstBuff(listing);

    sprintf(listing,"array length=%lu\n",(*ptr).len);
    putStrLstBuff(listing);

    sprintf(listing,"total size=%lu\n",(*ptr).size);
    putStrLstBuff(listing);

    sprintf(listing,"line=%lu\n",(*ptr).line);
    putStrLstBuff(listing);

    sprintf(listing,"offset_$TOP=%lu\n",(*ptr).offset);
    putStrLstBuff(listing);

    return;

}/*end printGlobVarToLst*/

void Pass2::printProcToLst(struct Procedure *ptr)
{
    U2 i;

    sprintf(listing,"identifier=%s\n",&((*strTbl).text[(*ptr).text]));
    putStrLstBuff(listing);

    sprintf(listing,"address=%lu\n",(*ptr).address);
    putStrLstBuff(listing);

    sprintf(listing,"source file line=%lu\n",(*ptr).line);
    putStrLstBuff(listing);

    if((*ptr).nRet)
    {
```

```
                sprintf(listing,"RET\n");
                putStrLstBuff(listing);

                putByteLstBuff('\t');
                sprintf(listing,"identifier=%s\n", &((*strTbl).text[((*ptr).ret).text]));
                putStrLstBuff(listing);

                putByteLstBuff('\t');
                sprintf(listing,"fpOffset=%d\n",((*ptr).ret).fpOffset);
                putStrLstBuff(listing);

                putByteLstBuff('\t');
                sprintf(listing,"line=%lu\n",((*ptr).ret).line);
                putStrLstBuff(listing);

        }

        sprintf(listing,"ARGS\n");
        putStrLstBuff(listing);

        for(i=0;i<(*ptr).iArg;i++)
        {
                sprintf(listing,"%d)",i);
                putStrLstBuff(listing);

                sprintf(listing," identifier=%s\n",&((*strTbl).text[((*ptr).arg[i]).text]));
                putStrLstBuff(listing);

                putByteLstBuff('\t');
                sprintf(listing,"fpOffset=%d\n",((*ptr).arg[i]).fpOffset);
                putStrLstBuff(listing);

                putByteLstBuff('\t');
                sprintf(listing,"line=%lu\n",((*ptr).arg[i]).line);
                putStrLstBuff(listing);

        }
        sprintf(listing,"LOCALS\n");
        putStrLstBuff(listing);
        for(i=0;i<(*ptr).iLocal;i++)
        {
                sprintf(listing,"%d)",i);
                putStrLstBuff(listing);

                putByteLstBuff('\t');
                sprintf(listing,"
                        identifier=%s\n",&((*strTbl).text[((*ptr).local[i]).text]));
                putStrLstBuff(listing);

                putByteLstBuff('\t');
                sprintf(listing,"fpOffset=%d\n",((*ptr).local[i]).fpOffset);
                putStrLstBuff(listing);
```

```
                    putByteLstBuff('\t');
                    sprintf(listing,"line=%lu\n",((*ptr).local[i]).line);
                    putStrLstBuff(listing);

            }
        sprintf(listing,"LABELS\n");
        putStrLstBuff(listing);
        for(i=0;i<(*ptr).iLabel;i++)
        {
                sprintf(listing,"%d)",i);
                putStrLstBuff(listing);

                sprintf(listing,"
                        identifier=%s\n",&((*strTbl).text[((*ptr).label[i]).text]));
                putStrLstBuff(listing);

                putByteLstBuff('\t');
                sprintf(listing,"address=%lu\n",((*ptr).label[i]).address);
                putStrLstBuff(listing);

                putByteLstBuff('\t');
                sprintf(listing,"line=%lu\n",((*ptr).label[i]).line);
                putStrLstBuff(listing);

        }
        return;

}/*end printProcToLst*/

void Pass2::printTreeToLst(struct HashTbl* link, int level)
{
    int i;
    int size;

    if(link==NULL)
    {
            return;
    }

    printTreeToLst((*link).left,level+1);
    for(i=0;i<level;i++){ putByteLstBuff('-'); }

    sprintf(listing,"id =%s",&((*strTbl).text[(*link).text]));
    size = strlen(listing);
    for(i=0;i<size;i++){ putByteLstBuff(listing[i]);}
    while(i<20){ i++; putByteLstBuff(' '); }

    sprintf(listing," type=%s",SymTypeStr[(*link).type]);
    size = strlen(listing);
    for(i=0;i<size;i++){ putByteLstBuff(listing[i]);}
    while(i<20){ i++; putByteLstBuff(' '); }
    sprintf(listing,"(i,si)=(%d,%d)\n",(*link).index,(*link).subIndex);
    putStrLstBuff(listing);
```

```
            printTreeToLst((*link).right,level+1);
            return;

    }/*end printTreeToLst*/
```

Building the Compilation Unit

Once the first and second pass have completed, the assembler generates the bytecode executable and then safely shuts down. Again, the action begins in `main.cpp`.

```
    /*4) build compilation unit */

    MAIN_DEBUG0("building bytecode executable\n");
    {
        BuildFile bldfile(&cmdLine,&strTbl, &symTbl);
        bldfile.buildFileFormat();
    }

    /*5) safe-shutdown */

    printf("main(): exiting with (%d) errors\n",nErrors);
    shutDown(SHUTDOWN_OK);
    return;
```

From looking at the source code in `main.cpp`, you can see that most of the work is done by the `BuildFile` class. The `BuildFile` object spends its CPU cycles on creating the first three sections of the bytecode executable (the header section, the symbol table section, and the string table section). The instructions in the assembly language source file have already been translated into bytecode during the second pass. Once the first three sections of the final executable are built, the `BuildFile` object appends the contents of the intermediate bytecode file, generated by the `Pass2` object, to the end of what it has constructed. This is illustrated in Figure 5-22.

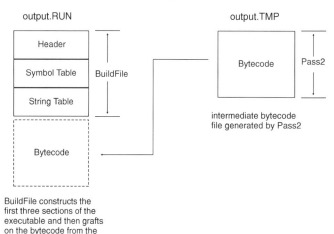

Figure 5-22   BuildFile constructs the first three sections of the executable and then grafts on the bytecode from the second pass

The declaration of the `BuildFile` class is as follows:

```
class BuildFile
{
    CommandLine *cmdLine;
    SymbolTable *symTbl;
    StringTable *strTbl;

    FILE *ofptr;                  /*pointer to output file*/
    FILE *afptr;                  /*pointer to temporary bytecode file*/

    char *ofile;                  /*pointer to output file name*/
    char *afile;                  /*pointer to temporary file name*/

    char ofBuffer[BUFFER_SIZE];   /*buffer for output file*/
    int iOFChar;                  /*index into ofBuffer*/

    U1 output[8];                 /*holds bytes to write to output file*/

    /*manage output buffer*/
    void putByteOutBuff(U1 byte);
    void flushOutBuff();

    /*these functions convert a number to big endian and write to output*/
    void commit2Bytes(U2 val);
    void commit4Bytes(U4 val);
    void commit8Bytes(U8 val);

    public:

    BuildFile(CommandLine *cptr, StringTable *st, SymbolTable *syt);
    ~BuildFile();
    void buildFileFormat();

};
```

To build the first three sections of the bytecode executable, the `BuildFile` object must maintain an output buffer. It initializes the buffer and the relevant file pointers in its constructor. The `BuildFile` object maintains an output `FILE` pointer to generate the bytecode executable and it also maintains a `FILE` pointer to read in the temporary bytecode file generated during the second pass. The `BuildFile` destructor makes sure that the output buffer is flushed and the files are all closed:

```
BuildFile::BuildFile(CommandLine *cptr, StringTable *st, SymbolTable *syt)
{
    cmdLine = cptr;
    strTbl = st;
    symTbl = syt;

    ofile = (*cptr).outputFile;
    afile = (*cptr).tempFile;

    ofptr = fopen(ofile,"wb");
    afptr = fopen(afile,"rb");
```

```
            if(ofptr==NULL)
            {
                ERROR1("BuildFile::BuildFile(): could not open %s\n",ofile);
                FATAL_ERROR();
            }
            if(afptr==NULL)
            {
                ERROR1("BuildFile::BuildFile(): could not open %s\n",afile);
                FATAL_ERROR();
            }
            iOFChar = 0;
            return;

}/*end constructor*/

BuildFile::~BuildFile()
{
        flushOutBuff();

        if(fclose(ofptr))
        { ERROR1("BuildFile::BuildFile(): problem closing %s\n",ofile); }
        if(fclose(afptr))
        { ERROR1("BuildFile::BuildFile(): problem closing %s\n",afile); }

        return;

}/*end finalizePass3*/
```

To actually manage the output buffer, the `BuildFile` class uses the `putByte-OutBuff()` and `flushOutBuff()` functions. The `putByteOutBuff()` function, in particular, is called by the other members of the class that need to write to the bytecode executable (i.e., the `commit2Bytes()`, `commit4Bytes()`, and `commit8-Bytes()` member functions).

```
void BuildFile::putByteOutBuff(U1 byte)
{
        int nbytes;

        nbytes = 0;

        ofBuffer[iOFChar] = byte;
        iOFChar++;

        if(iOFChar==BUFFER_SIZE)
        {
                nbytes = fwrite(ofBuffer,sizeof(U1),BUFFER_SIZE,ofptr);
                if(nbytes!=BUFFER_SIZE)
                {
                        ERROR1("BuildFile::putByteOutBuff(): fwrite error to %s\n",ofile);
                        FATAL_ERROR();
                }
                iOFChar = 0;
        }
        return;
```

```
}/*end putByteOutBuff*/

void BuildFile::flushOutBuff()
{
    int nbytes;

    nbytes = 0;

    if(iOFChar>0)
    {
        nbytes = fwrite(ofBuffer,sizeof(U1),iOFChar,ofptr);
        if(nbytes!=iOFChar)
        {
            ERROR1("BuildFile::flushOutBuff(): flushed %lu bytes\n",nbytes);
            ERROR1("BuildFile::flushOutBuff(): fwrite error to %s\n",ofile);
            FATAL_ERROR();
        }
        iOFChar = 0;
    }
    return;

}/*end flushOutBuff*/
```

The construction of the first three file sections and the subsequent appending of the .TMP bytecode file is handled by the buildFileFormat() member function. To determine the size of the symbol table, in an effort to build the header section, the buildFileFormat() function uses the following macros:

```
#define SIZE_GLOBREC      37
#define SIZE_PROCREC      25
#define SIZE_RETREC       16
#define SIZE_ARGREC       16
#define SIZE_LOCREC       16
#define SIZE_LBLREC       20
```

If you trace through the buildFileFormat() member function, you'll see that the path of execution of the buildFileFormat() function ends up resolving to a series of calls to the commit2Bytes(), commit4Bytes(), and commit8Bytes() functions. These functions commit word, double-word, and quad-word size values to the output buffer after converting them to big-endian format.

```
void BuildFile::buildFileFormat()
{
    U8 size_symtbl;
    U8 size_strtbl;
    U8 size_bc;
    U8 i;
    U8 j;
    int ch;

    size_symtbl = 0;
    size_strtbl = 0;
    size_bc     = 0;
```

```
/* 1) determine size of symbol table*/

size_symtbl = size_symtbl + 8; /*table of contents */
size_symtbl = size_symtbl + SIZE_GLOBREC*((*symTbl).iGlobVar);
size_symtbl = size_symtbl + SIZE_PROCREC*((*symTbl).iProc);

for(i=0;i<(*symTbl).iProc;i++)
{
     size_symtbl = size_symtbl + SIZE_RETREC*(((*symTbl).proc[i]).nRet);
     size_symtbl = size_symtbl + SIZE_ARGREC*(((*symTbl).proc[i]).iArg);
     size_symtbl = size_symtbl + SIZE_LOCREC*(((*symTbl).proc[i]).iLocal);
     size_symtbl = size_symtbl + SIZE_LBLREC*(((*symTbl).proc[i]).iLabel);
}

/* 2) determine size of string table*/

size_strtbl = (*strTbl).iStr;

/* 3) determine size of bytecode */

size_bc = getFileSize(afile);

/* 4) commit header to output file */

putByteOutBuff(0xDE); /*magic word to output file */
putByteOutBuff(0xED);

if((*cmdLinc).omitDebugData==TRUC)
{
     commit8Bytes((U8)0);
     commit8Bytes((U8)0);
     commit8Bytes(size_bc);

     ch = fgetc(afptr);
     while(ch!=EOF)
     {
          putByteOutBuff((U1)ch);
          ch = fgetc(afptr);
     }
     return;
}

commit8Bytes(size_symtbl);
commit8Bytes(size_strtbl);
commit8Bytes(size_bc);

/* 5) commit tables of contents (# globals and # procs) */

commit4Bytes((*symTbl).iGlobVar);
commit4Bytes((*symTbl).iProc);
/* 6) commit global vars to output file */

for(i=0;i<(*symTbl).iGlobVar;i++)
{
```

```
            commit8Bytes(((*symTbl).globVar[i]).text);
            putByteOutBuff(((*symTbl).globVar[i]).dType);
            commit8Bytes(((*symTbl).globVar[i]).len);
            commit8Bytes(((*symTbl).globVar[i]).size);
            commit8Bytes(-((S8)((*symTbl).globVar[i]).offset));
            commit4Bytes(((*symTbl).globVar[i]).line);
}

/* 7) commit procedures to output file */

for(i=0;i<(*symTbl).iProc;i++)
{
            commit8Bytes(((*symTbl).proc[i]).text);
            commit8Bytes(((*symTbl).proc[i]).address);
            commit4Bytes(((*symTbl).proc[i]).line);
            putByteOutBuff(((*symTbl).proc[i]).nRet);
            putByteOutBuff(((*symTbl).proc[i]).iArg);
            putByteOutBuff(((*symTbl).proc[i]).iLocal);
            commit2Bytes(((*symTbl).proc[i]).iLabel);

            for(j=0;j<((*symTbl).proc[i]).nRet;j++)
            {
                  commit8Bytes((((*symTbl).proc[i]).ret).text);
                  commit4Bytes((((*symTbl).proc[i]).ret).fpOffset);
                  commit4Bytes((((*symTbl).proc[i]).ret).line);
            }
            for(j=0;j<((*symTbl).proc[i]).iArg;j++)
            {
                  commit8Bytes((((*symTbl).proc[i]).arg[j]).text);
                  commit4Bytes((((*symTbl).proc[i]).arg[j]).fpOffset);
                  commit4Bytes((((*symTbl).proc[i]).arg[j]).line);
            }
            for(j=0;j<((*symTbl).proc[i]).iLocal;j++)
            {
                  commit8Bytes((((*symTbl).proc[i]).local[j]).text);
                  commit4Bytes((((*symTbl).proc[i]).local[j]).fpOffset);
                  commit4Bytes((((*symTbl).proc[i]).local[j]).line);
            }
            for(j=0;j<((*symTbl).proc[i]).iLabel;j++)
            {
                  commit8Bytes((((*symTbl).proc[i]).label[j]).text);
                  commit8Bytes((((*symTbl).proc[i]).label[j]).address);
                  commit4Bytes((((*symTbl).proc[i]).label[j]).line);
            }
}

/* 8) commit string table to output file */

for(i=0;i<(*strTbl).iStr;i++){ putByteOutBuff((*strTbl).text[i]); }

/* 9) append bytecode in temp to output file */

ch = fgetc(afptr);
while(ch!=EOF)
```

```
        {
            putByteOutBuff((U1)ch);
            ch = fgetc(afptr);
        }

        return;

}/*end buildFileFormat*/

void BuildFile::commit2Bytes(U2 val)
{
    wordToBytecode(val,output);
    putByteOutBuff(output[0]);
    putByteOutBuff(output[1]);
    return;

}/*end commit2Bytes*/

void BuildFile::commit4Bytes(U4 val)
{
    dwordToBytecode(val,output);
    putByteOutBuff(output[0]);
    putByteOutBuff(output[1]);
    putByteOutBuff(output[2]);
    putByteOutBuff(output[3]);
    return;

}/*end commit4Bytcs*/

void BuildFile::commit8Bytes(U8 val)
{
    qwordToBytecode(val,output);
    putByteOutBuff(output[0]);
    putByteOutBuff(output[1]);
    putByteOutBuff(output[2]);
    putByteOutBuff(output[3]);
    putByteOutBuff(output[4]);
    putByteOutBuff(output[5]);
    putByteOutBuff(output[6]);
    putByteOutBuff(output[7]);
    return;

}/*end commit8Bytes*/
```

Reading a Listing File

As stated earlier, the `Pass2` object will generate a listing file if the listing flag is set on the HASM command line. A listing file is really just a processed regurgitation of the assembly source file. The difference between a listing file and the original source file is that the listing file is annotated with line numbers, address offset information, and bytecode translations. The listing file also has a symbol table summary appended to the end that offers detailed information on symbols within the assembly program.

I will start by showing you a brief snippet of a program listing. Then I will dissect it into its various parts.

```
17)[0]    LBI $R1,-23      [0][8][233]
18)[3]    LWI $R2,280      [1][9][1][24]
19)[7]    LDI $R3,-70000   [2][10][255][254][238][144]
```

The first value (the leftmost entry) is a line number that indicates which line the text is located on in the original source file. In the preceding program listing snippet, there are three lines of source code taken from lines 17, 18, and 19 of the original source file. The next value, in brackets, is the address in memory the instruction will be assigned when the bytecode executable is loaded and run. For example, the instruction `LWI $R2, 280` will, according to the listing file, begin at the fourth byte in memory. Given that directives are not translated into bytecode, lines that have directives will not have an associated address value. The third entry you will see is the instruction text as it appears in the source file. This ASCII text version of the instruction will be followed by its bytecode translation. Note that all numeric values in the bytecode translation will appear in big-endian format. If you look at the bytecode translation of `LWI $R2, 280`, you will see that the value `280` is in the big-endian format.

The general layout of a listing file line is displayed in Figure 5-23.

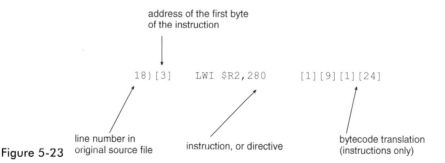

address of the first byte of the instruction

```
18)[3]    LWI $R2,280      [1][9][1][24]
```

line number in original source file

instruction, or directive

bytecode translation (instructions only)

Figure 5-23

Taking HASM for a Test Drive

Now that HASM is complete, we need to verify that it works correctly. One method that I discovered is to assemble a source code file and examine the listing file for discrepancies. Another, more involved technique is to dump the contents of the bytecode executable to the screen and validate the executable file one byte at a time. After sufficient experimentation, I developed a check list with six items that may be used to verify that the assembler is functioning properly:

- Listing file line numbers are correct.
- Listing file address values are valid.
- Listing file symbol table summary is correct.
- Listing file instruction encodings are correct.
- Bytecode executable has the correct size.
- Four sections of the bytecode executable are encoded correctly.

Some of these list items may seem like they involve an absurd amount of work. Indeed, this impression is correct. Manually verifying the contents of a bytecode executable can take hours. Fortunately, I have developed a set of small utility programs to automate some of the checks. Two of these tools are presented in the appendix.

NOTE   This six-point list will come in handy if you make changes to the assembler and want to be able to check your work.

Checking the line numbers is the easiest item on the list. Nevertheless, that does not mean that it is unimportant. Incorrect line numbering may indicate that an error has cropped up in the scanner or a component which uses the scanner. In the worst case, lines of code may be absent. Thus, it never hurts to perform a cursory check of the line numbers. It's easy and it pays dividends.

To check address values, the first thing you'll need to do is to manually compute the address of each byte of every bytecode instruction. Then you should compare the address of the last encoded byte against the size of the intermediate bytecode file (i.e., the .TMP file). If the two values are the same, that's a good sign. This is because the .TMP file consists entirely of bytecode, so the number of bytes in this file should equal the address of the last byte of the bytecode. Once you have demonstrated that the addresses of the individual bytes are kosher, you should check to make sure that every instruction that references an address (i.e., the LAD and LAI instructions) references a valid address.

To verify that the instruction encodings are correct, you will need to use the macros defined in `iset.c` and `exenv.c`. These two files will give the numeric equivalents for instructions and registers. To verify numeric values you should use the `numfmt` utility, which is explained in the appendix. The `numfmt` utility allows a numeric value to be decomposed into its constituent bytes. Keep in mind that numeric values are encoded in bytecode using the big-endian format.

Manually computing the size of the bytecode executable can be tedious, but it is the best way to make sure that the file has the correct size. This is probably the single most tedious step. To help you manually compute the size of the bytecode executable, you need to rely on the following facts:

- The header is always 26 bytes in size.

- Each global variable record in the symbol table is 37 bytes in size.

- Each procedure record in the symbol table is 25 bytes in size.

- Each procedure return value record in the symbol table is 16 bytes in size.

- Each procedure argument record in the symbol table is 16 bytes in size.

- Each procedure local variable record in the symbol table is 16 bytes in size.

- Each procedure label record in the symbol table is 20 bytes in size.

These facts will help you compute the size of the first two file sections. When you compute the size of the string table you should keep in mind that the null character at the end of each string is included in the string table. If you have performed the second check, there is no need to recompute the size of the bytecode section, because it is the same as the size of the .TMP file.

To check that the four sections of the bytecode executable have been built correctly, you should use the `filedmp` utility. In fact, I designed `filedmp` explicitly for this purpose. The `filedmp` utility is described at length in the appendix. Trying to do it all by hand could give you a nosebleed.

NOTE Unlike you, I initially did not have access to automation tools. I did everything by hand and it was an exhaustive byte-by-byte procedure. It took me the better part of a weekend to contrive ways to check my own work, manually translate an entire assembly language program into bytecode, and recreate the symbol table by hand.

While I was testing the assembler, I ran the following source code through HASM:

```
#------------------------------------------------------------
# globals
#
.GB gvar1
.GW gvar2
.GD gvar3   10
.GQ gvar4   15


#------------------------------------------------------------
.PB myproc1
    .PR   retval 6
    .PA   arg1   4
    .PA arg2  3
    .PA arg3  1
    .PV var1  -6
    .PV var2 -11
```

```
        .PV var3 -18
LBI $R1,-23
LWI $R2,280
LDI $R3,-70000
LQI $R4,1234567890123
LF1I $F1, -2.3e-4
LF2I $D1,100e2
LAD $R5,myproc2
LAI $R6,$TOP,gvar4
LWI $R7,600
SB $R1,$R7
LB $R8,$R7
SW $R2,$R7
LW $R9,$R7
SD $R3,$R7
LD $R10,$R7
SQ $R4,$R7
LQ $R11,$R7
SF1 $F1,$R7
LF1 $F2,$R7
SF2 $D1,$R7
LF2 $D2,$R7
PUSHB $R4
PUSHW $R4
PUSHD $R4
PUSHQ $R4
PUSHF1 $F1
PUSHF2 $D1
.PL proc1label1
POPB $R4
POPW $R4
POPD $R4
POPQ $R4
POPF1 $F3
POPF2 $D3
.PE


#-------------------------------------------------------------
.PB myproc2
    .PR  p2ret 10
    .PA  p2arg1  5
    .PA  p2arg2  2
    .PA  p2arg3  1
    .PV p2var1  -5
    .PV  p2var2 -12
    .PV  p2var3 -19
MOV $R4,$R12
MOVF $F3,$F4
MOVD $D3,$D4
LAD $R13,proc2label1
JMP $R13
NOP
NOP
NOP
```

```
          .PL proc2label1
          LAD $R13,proc2label2
          JE $R4,$R12,$R13
          NOP
          .PL proc2label2
          JNE $R4,$R12,$R13
          SLT $R1,$R4,$R13
          INT 12
          DI
          EI
          LBI $R2,10
          LBI $R3,112
          AND $R1,$R2,$R3
          OR  $R1,$R2,$R3
          XOR $R1,$R2,$R3
          NOT $R1,$R2
          LBI $R2,4
          BT  $R1,$R3,$R2
          BS  $R1,$R2
          SRA $R1,$R3,$R2
          SRL $R1,$R3,$R2
          SL  $R1,$R3,$R2
          LBI $R2,10
          LBI $R3,56
          ADD $R1,$R2,$R3
          SUB $R1,$R2,$R3
          MULT $R1,$R2,$R3
          DIV $R1,$R4,$R2,$R3
          CAST_IF $R1,$F3
          CAST_ID $R1,$D3
          CAST_FI $F1,$R3
          CAST_FD $F1,$D3
          CAST_DI $D3,$R1
          CAST_DF $D3,$F3
          LF1I $F2,340.5e-12
          LF1I $F3,12.456
          FADD $F1,$F2,$F3
          FSUB $F1,$F2,$F3
          FMULT $F1,$F2,$F3
          FDIV $F1,$F2,$F3
          FSLT $F1,$F2,$F3
          LF2I $D2,567.89
          LF2I $D3,75.23e5
          DADD $D1,$D2,$D3
          DSUB $D1,$D2,$D3
          DMULT $D1,$D2,$D3
          DDIV $D1,$D2,$D3
          DSLT $D1,$D2,$D3
          HALT

          .PE
```

The HASM assembler gave me the following listing file, which I successfully subjected to the six checks that I enumerated earlier:

```
 3).GB gvar1
 4).GW gvar2
 5).GD gvar3   10
 6).GQ gvar4   15
#++++++++++++++++++++++++++++++++++++++++++
 9).PB myproc1
10)  .PR retval 6
11)  .PA arg1   4
12)  .PA arg2   3
13)  .PA arg3   1
14)  .PV var1   -6
15)  .PV var2  -11
16)  .PV var3  -18
17)[0]     LBI  $R1,-23            [0][8][233]
18)[3]     LWI  $R2,280            [1][9][1][24]
19)[7]     LDI  $R3,-70000         [2][10][255][254][238][144]
20)[13]    LQI  $R4,1234567890123  [3][11][0][0][1][31][113][251][4][203]
21)[23]    LF1I $F1,-2.3e-4        [4][0][185][113][44][40]
22)[29]    LF2I $D1,100e2          [5][0][64][195][136][0][0][0][0][0]
23)[39]    LAD  $R5,myproc2        [6][12][0][0][0][0][0][0][0][124]
24)[49]    LAI  $R6,$TOP,gvar4     [7][13][7][255][255][255][255][255][255][255][93]
25)[60]    LWI  $R7,600            [1][14][2][88]
26)[64]    SB   $R1,$R7            [14][8][14]
27)[67]    LB   $R8,$R7            [8][15][14]
28)[70]    SW   $R2,$R7            [15][9][14]
29)[73]    LW   $R9,$R7            [9][16][14]
30)[76]    SD   $R3,$R7            [16][10][14]
31)[79]    LD   $R10,$R7           [10][17][14]
32)[82]    SQ   $R4,$R7            [17][11][14]
33)[85]    LQ   $R11,$R7           [11][18][14]
34)[88]    SF1  $F1,$R7            [18][0][14]
35)[91]    LF1  $F2,$R7            [12][1][14]
36)[94]    SF2  $D1,$R7            [19][0][14]
37)[97]    LF2  $D2,$R7            [13][1][14]
38)[100]   PUSHB  $R4             [20][11]
39)[102]   PUSHW  $R4             [21][11]
40)[104]   PUSHD  $R4             [22][11]
41)[106]   PUSHQ  $R4             [23][11]
42)[108]   PUSHF1 $F1             [24][0]
43)[110]   PUSHF2 $D1             [25][0]
44)  .PL   proc1label1
45)[112]   POPB  $R4              [26][11]
46)[114]   POPW  $R4              [27][11]
47)[116]   POPD  $R4              [28][11]
48)[118]   POPQ  $R4              [29][11]
49)[120]   POPF1 $F3              [30][2]
50)[122]   POPF2 $D3              [31][2]
51)  .PE
#++++++++++++++++++++++++++++++++++++++++++
54)  .PB   myproc2
55)  .PR   p2ret .10
56)  .PA   p2arg1  5
57)  .PA   p2arg2  2
58)  .PA   p2arg3  1
```

```
59) .PV    p2var1  -5
60) .PV    p2var2  -12
61) .PV    p2var3  -19
62)[124]   MOV  $R4,$R12                    [32][11][19]
63)[127]   MOVF $F3,$F4                     [33][2][3]
64)[130]   MOVD $D3,$D4                     [34][2][3]
65)[133]   LAD  $R13,proc2label1            [6][20][0][0][0][0][0][0][0][148]
66)[143]   JMP  $R13                        [35][20]
67)[145]   NOP                             [43]
68)[146]   NOP                             [43]
69)[147]   NOP                             [43]
70) .PL    proc2label1
71)[148]   LAD  $R13,proc2label2            [6][20][0][0][0][0][0][0][0][163]
72)[158]   JE   $R4,$R12,$R13               [36][11][19][20]
73)[162]   NOP                             [43]
74) .PL    proc2label2
75)[163]   JNE  $R4,$R12,$R13               [37][11][19][20]
76)[167]   SLT  $R1,$R4,$R13                [38][8][11][20]
77)[171]   INT  12                          [39][12]
78)[173]   DI                               [40]
79)[174]   EI                               [41]
80)[175]   LBI  $R2,10                      [0][9][10]
81)[178]   LBI  $R3,112                     [0][10][112]
82)[181]   AND  $R1,$R2,$R3                 [44][8][9][10]
83)[185]   OR   $R1,$R2,$R3                 [45][8][9][10]
84)[189]   XOR  $R1,$R2,$R3                 [46][8][9][10]
85)[193]   NOT  $R1,$R2                     [47][8][9]
86)[196]   LBI  $R2,4                       [0][9][4]
87)[199]   BT   $R1,$R3,$R2                 [48][8][10][9]
88)[203]   BS   $R1,$R2                     [49][8][9]
89)[206]   SRA  $R1,$R3,$R2                 [50][8][10][9]
90)[210]   SRL  $R1,$R3,$R2                 [51][8][10][9]
91)[214]   SL   $R1,$R3,$R2                 [52][8][10][9]
92)[218]   LBI  $R2,10                      [0][9][10]
93)[221]   LBI  $R3,56                      [0][10][56]
94)[224]   ADD  $R1,$R2,$R3                 [53][8][9][10]
95)[228]   SUB  $R1,$R2,$R3                 [54][8][9][10]
96)[232]   MULT $R1,$R2,$R3                 [55][8][9][10]
97)[236]   DIV  $R1,$R4,$R2,$R3             [56][8][11][9][10]
98)[241]   CAST_IF $R1,$F3                  [57][8][2]
99)[244]   CAST_ID $R1,$D3                  [58][8][2]
100)[247]  CAST_FI $F1,$R3                  [59][0][10]
101)[250]  CAST_FD $F1,$D3                  [60][0][2]
102)[253]  CAST_DI $D3,$R1                  [61][2][8]
103)[256]  CAST_DF $D3,$F3                  [62][2][2]
104)[259]  LF1I $F2,340.5e-12               [4][1][47][187][49][29]
105)[265]  LF1I $F3,12.456                  [4][2][65][71][75][199]
106)[271]  FADD $F1,$F2,$F3                 [63][0][1][2]
107)[275]  FSUB $F1,$F2,$F3                 [64][0][1][2]
108)[279]  FMULT $F1,$F2,$F3                [65][0][1][2]
109)[283]  FDIV $F1,$F2,$F3                 [66][0][1][2]
110)[287]  FSLT $F1,$F2,$F3                 [67][0][1][2]
111)[291]  LF2I $D2,567.89                  [5][1][64][129][191][30][184][81][235][133]
112)[301]  LF2I $D3,75.23e5                 [5][2][65][92][178][174][0][0][0][0]
```

```
113)[311] DADD $D1,$D2,$D3            [68][0][1][2]
114)[315] DSUB $D1,$D2,$D3            [69][0][1][2]
115)[319] DMULT $D1,$D2,$D3           [70][0][1][2]
116)[323] DDIV $D1,$D2,$D3            [71][0][1][2]
117)[327] DSLT $D1,$D2,$D3            [72][0][1][2]
118)[331] HALT                       [42]
120).PE


#++++SYMBOL TABLE++++++
->GLOBAL VARIABLE 0)identifier=gvar1
data type=SZ_BYTE
array length=1
total size=1
line=3
offset_$TOP=1

->GLOBAL VARIABLE 1)identifier=gvar2
data type=SZ_WORD
array length=1
total size=2
line=4
offset_$TOP=3

->GLOBAL VARIABLE 2)identifier=gvar3
data type=SZ_DWORD
array length=10
total size=40
line-5
offset_$TOP=43

->GLOBAL VARIABLE 3)identifier=gvar4
data type=SZ_QWORD
array length=15
total size=120
line=6
offset_$TOP=163

->PROCEDURE 0)identifier=myproc1
address=0
source file line=9
RET
    identifier=retval
    fpOffset=6
    line=10
ARGS
0)identifier=arg1
    fpOffset=4
    line=11
1)identifier=arg2
    fpOffset=3
    line=12
2)identifier=arg3
    fpOffset=1
    line=13
```

```
LOCALS
0)   identifier=var1
     fpOffset=-6
     line=14
1)   identifier=var2
     fpOffset=-11
     line=15
2)   identifier=var3
     fpOffset=-18
     line=16
LABELS
0)identifier=proc1label1
     address=112
     line=44


->PROCEDURE 1)identifier=myproc2
address=124
source file line=54
RET
     identifier=p2ret
     fpOffset=10
     line=55
ARGS
0)identifier=p2arg1
     fpOffset=5
     line=56
1)identifier=p2arg2
     fpOffset=2
     line=57
2)identifier=p2arg3
     fpOffset=1
     line=58
LOCALS
0)   identifier=p2var1
     fpOffset=-5
     line=59
1)   identifier=p2var2
     fpOffset=-12
     line=60
2)   identifier=p2var3
     fpOffset=-19
     line=61
LABELS
0)identifier=proc2label1
     address=148
     line=70
1)identifier=proc2label2
     address=163
     line=74

#++++HASH TABLE++++++
Hash Slot 22)
id =proc2label1      type=PROC_LBL      (i,si)=(1,0)
```

```
Hash Slot 23)
id =proc2label2     type=PROC_LBL     (i,si)=(1,1)

Hash Slot 38)
id =myproc1         type=PROC         (i,si)=(0,0)

Hash Slot 39)
id =myproc2         type=PROC         (i,si)=(1,0)

Hash Slot 111)
id =p2var1          type=PROC_LOC     (i,si)=(1,0)

Hash Slot 112)
id =p2var2          type=PROC_LOC     (i,si)=(1,1)

Hash Slot 113)
id =p2var3          type=PROC_LOC     (i,si)=(1,2)

Hash Slot 229)
id =var1            type=PROC_LOC     (i,si)=(0,0)

Hash Slot 230)
id =var2            type=PROC_LOC     (i,si)=(0,1)

Hash Slot 231)
id =var3            type=PROC_LOC     (i,si)=(0,2)

Hash Slot 321)
id =p2arg1          type=PROC_ARG     (i,si)=(1,0)

Hash Slot 322)
id =p2arg2          type=PROC_ARG     (i,si)=(1,1)

Hash Slot 323)
id =p2arg3          type=PROC_ARG     (i,si)=(1,2)

Hash Slot 345)
id =p2ret           type=PROC_RET     (i,si)=(1,0)

Hash Slot 390)
id =proc1label1     type=PROC_LBL     (i,si)=(0,0)

Hash Slot 439)
id =arg1            type=PROC_ARG     (i,si)=(0,0)

Hash Slot 440)
id =arg2            type=PROC_ARG     (i,si)=(0,1)

Hash Slot 441)
id =arg3            type=PROC_ARG     (i,si)=(0,2)

Hash Slot 457)
id =gvar1           type=GLOBAL_VAR   (i,si)=(0,0)
```

```
Hash Slot 458)
id =gvar2              type=GLOBAL_VAR    (i,si)=(1,0)


Hash Slot 459)
id =gvar3              type=GLOBAL_VAR    (i,si)=(2,0)


Hash Slot 460)
id =gvar4              type=GLOBAL_VAR    (i,si)=(3,0)


Hash Slot 484)
id =retval             type=PROC_RET      (i,si)=(0,0)


#+++++STRING TABLE++++++
0)gvar1
1)gvar2
2)gvar3
3)gvar4
4)myproc1
5)retval
6)arg1
7)arg2
8)arg3
9)var1
10)var2
11)var3
12)proc1label1
13)myproc2
14)p2ret
15)p2arg1
16)p2arg2
17)p2arg3
18)p2var1
19)p2var2
20)p2var3
21)proc2label1
22)proc2label2
```

The symbol table summary at the end of the listing file may require some explanation. It makes frequent references to values that only someone who is intimately familiar with the assembler's source code would recognize. Let's begin with the global variable entries.

```
->GLOBAL VARIABLE 1)identifier=gvar2
data type=SZ_WORD
array length=1
total size=2
line=4
offset_$TOP=3
```

These entries are actually pretty straightforward. The only potentially confusing field is the last, the `offset_$TOP` field. This field specifies the location of the first byte of a global variable in terms of the number of bytes below the address stored in the `$TOP` register. For example, if a global variable has an `offset_$TOP` value of 3, we know that the first byte of the global variable is located three bytes below the address stored in `$TOP`. In other words, the `offset_$TOP` field determines a global variable's offset from the address in `$TOP`.

Procedure entries in the symbol table summary also have a couple of idiosyncrasies.

```
->PROCEDURE 0)identifier=myproc1
address=0
source file line=9
RET
    identifier=retval
    fpOffset=6
    line=10
ARGS
0)identifier=arg1
    fpOffset=4
    line=11

LABELS
0)identifier=proc1label1
    address=112
    line=44
```

Each procedure entry is followed by the symbol table entries for the elements local to the procedure, like arguments, local variables, labels, and a return value. Return values, arguments, and local variable records will all have a field named `fpOffset`. This field specifies the offset of the element relative to the address stored in `$FP` and is used to locate data in a procedure's stack frame.

Hash table entries are probably the most cryptic. For example:

```
Hash Slot 23)
id =proc2label2     type=PROC_LBL     (i,si)=(1,1)
```

If you recall from the `hashtbl.cpp` assembler source file, hash table entries in the assembler are assigned a type, an index, and a subindex.

```
/*hash table type*/

#define GLOBAL_VAR    0
#define PROC          1
#define PROC_RET      2
#define PROC_ARG      3
#define PROC_LOC      4
#define PROC_LBL      5


char *SymTypeStr[]={"GLOBAL_VAR",
                    "PROC",
                    "PROC_RET","PROC_ARG","PROC_LOC","PROC_LBL"};

struct HashTbl
{
    U1 empty;          /*indicates if entry is used or not*/
    U8 text;           /*index to strTbl*/
    U1 type;           /*GLOBAL_VAR -> PROC_LBL*/
    U4 index;          /*index to globVar, proc arrays in symbTbl*/
    U4 subIndex;       /*subindex for PROC_RET, ... , PROC_LBL*/
```

```
    struct HashTbl *left;
    struct HashTbl *right;
};
```

The `type` field indicates what kind of symbol is being dealt with. This field is populated by one of the macro values GLOBAL_VAR, PROC, PROC_RET, etc. The `index` field is an offset into the symbol table's array of `GlobalVariable` structures or its array of `Procedure` structures. If the symbol is a procedure, or belongs inside of one, the `subIndex` field is an offset into one of the structure arrays in the corresponding `Procedure` structure.

The hash table entry in the listing file's symbol table summary specifies the type of the entry, the index, and the subindex. The index and subindex of a hash table entry are paired together in parentheses (i.e., `(i,si) = (1,1)`). Essentially, the listing file's hash table entries are a summary of what is used by the assembler. So, in a sense, this information is intended to help me debug the assembler rather than convey useful information to the reader.

References

Cormen, Thomas, Charles Leiserson, and Ronald Rivest. *Introduction to Algorithms.* McGraw-Hill, 2000. ISBN: 0070131430.

> By far, my favorite book on algorithms is Sedgewick's, which I mention in the references section of Chapter 2. Having said that, I've referenced this book because it covers topics that are hard to find elsewhere, such as B-trees. The downside is that the algorithms are all implemented in psuedocode, and very cryptic psuedocode at that.

Ford, William, and William Topp. *Assembly Language and Systems Programming for the M68000 Family.* D. C. Heath and Company, 1992. ISBN: 0669281999.

> This book focuses on Motorola hardware, but it is also one of those rare books that actually describes how a two-pass assembler functions. The operation of the HASM assembler closely matches the model described in this book.

Fowler, Martin. *Refactoring: Improving the Design of Existing Code.* Addison-Wesley, 2000. ISBN: 0201485672.

Goodrich, Michael, and Roberto Tamassia. *Data Structures and Algorithms in Java.* John Wiley and Sons, 2001. ISBN: 0471383678.

> A fairly rigorous and complete treatment of fundamental data structures. The strong point of this book is its formal and methodical organization. In a few places, however, I feel like the authors get caught up in the object-oriented aspects of Java, and this obscures the implementations somewhat.

Rideau, François-René. *Linux Assembler HOW-TO.* rideau@ens.fr, 1997.

> This is an excellent introduction to free Intel assembler tools. In particular, this article takes a look at GAS, GASP, NASM, and AS86. There may be a more recent version of this HOW-TO on the Internet. Check out the Linux sites on the Net. The

last time I checked, NASM was available at http://www.cryogen.com/Nasm, but this may have changed.

Shaffer, Clifford. *A Practical Introduction to Data Structures and Algorithm Analysis.* Prentice Hall, 1997. ISBN: 0131907522.

This book does a good job of examining the costs and benefits of different data structure implementations. Like a lot of texts on data structures, however, many of the implementations are incomplete and left as homework assignments. I hate it when they do that. I wish someone would write a book on data structures in C that was on the same level as *Numerical Recipes in C* by Press, Teukolsky, Vetterling, and Flannery.

Terry, P.D. *Compilers and Compiler Generators: An Introduction with C++.* Thomson Computer Press, 1997. ISBN: 1850322988.

This book gives the best exposition on assemblers that I have ever read. In fact, Terry devotes two whole chapters to the topic of assemblers! After hunting through almost 100 books on assembly language programming, Terry's book is the only one I've found that offers a lengthy and complete exposition of how an assembler does what it does.

Virtual Machine Interrupts

Overview and Organization

The HEC virtual machine relies upon the native operating system to provide basic services like input/output and IPC. Insulating itself from the details of communicating with hardware is what gives the HEC virtual machine its portability. Instead of directly fraternizing with the hardware, the virtual machine lets the operating system act as the middleman. To this end, the operating system is the agent that makes requests and handles low-level minutiae on behalf of the virtual machine.

All operating systems expose a set of primitive functions called *system calls*, which can be invoked to manage the computer's available resources and facilitate interaction with the hardware. For example, the MMURTL operating system provides a collection of almost 100 public system calls. The following 14 system calls are used by MMURTL to manage console input/output.

- SetVidOwner
- GetVidOwner
- GetNormVid
- SetNormVid
- ClrScr
- GetXY
- SetXY
- PutVidChars
- GetVidChars
- PutVidAttrs
- ScrollVid
- ReadKbd
- TTYOut
- EditLine

Every single variation of console input/output that MMURTL can perform must inevitably be spelled out in terms of the previous 14 functions. In this sense, system calls are like *atomic* elements that merge together, in various combinations, to form everything else in an operating system's universe. You can break every command shell feature and user program into a series of system calls.

You might notice that I didn't use C-like syntax to describe MMURTL's console I/O system calls. This is because system calls tend to be very low level; their operation can only be spelled out using machine-specific constructs. In other words, system calls often are written in assembly language. Contrary to the popular misconception, the motivation behind this is not speed. The marginal gain in execution speed does not justify the mind-numbing complexity that thousands of lines of assembly code entails. The truth is that the primary reason for coding system calls in assembler is that there are some things you can only do in assembler. Good examples of this are managing interrupts and sending data to hardware subsystems. In addition, the input and output parameters for a system call must be specified in terms of certain machine registers. Consider the following DOS system call:

Interrupt:	0x21 (i.e., INT 0x21)
Function:	0x09
Description:	Prints a string terminated by a $
Inputs:	AH = 9
	DS = segment address of string
	DX = offset address of string

A wise system engineer will attempt to ward off complexity by banishing the system-related assembly to the basement of the OS. There, in the darkness, only a trained plumber with a flashlight can muck around with the plumbing. Even then, an experienced developer will attempt to wrap the assembly code in C/C++ to make it more palatable.

 NOTE   I had the opportunity to speak with an engineer who helped manage the construction of the original OS/2 platform. He told me that around 20 percent of the kernel code was assembler. This is a lot of assembler, especially when you consider that Unix operating systems, like FreeBSD 4.4, have less than 2 percent of the kernel coded in assembly language. I am sure that the proliferation of assembly code in OS/2 had an impact on the development team's ability to port the code and institute design changes.

Representing a machine by a set of system calls is a judicious approach. However, it is not the final layer of abstraction. Higher level languages tend to wrap system calls in an effort to abstract functionality even further away from the machine. So there are always at least two levels of abstraction: system calls that isolate core assembly language routines and library calls that enclose the system calls.

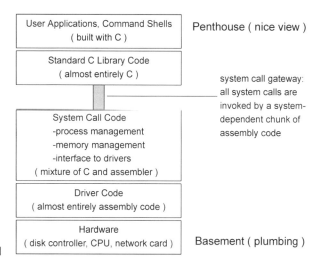

Figure 6-1

The C programming language's standard library is a classic example of this tactic. Let's look at a somewhat forced implementation of the putchar() function to see how library functions build upon system functions.

To begin with, most standard library implementations define putchar() in terms of its more general sibling, putc(), which writes a character to a given output stream. In the case of putchar(), the output stream is fixed as standard output (stdout).

```
#define putchar(c)       putc(c,stdout)
```

Thus, to understand putchar(), we must dissect putc():

```
int putc(int ch, FILE *stream)
{
    int ret;
    ret = write(stream,&ch,1);
    if(ret!=1){ return(EOF); }else{ return(c); }
}
```

The putc() function, in turn, wraps a system call named write(). A recurring theme you will notice is the tendency of functions with specific duties to invoke more general and primitive routines.

```
/*
stream = output stream to write to
buffer = buffer of bytes to write to stream
nbytes = number of bytes to write
returns: number of bytes written to stream
*/
int write(FILE *stream, void *buffer, int nbytes)
{
    struct call_struct;
    call_struct.type = FILE_SYSTEM;
    call_struct.subtype = BUFF_OUTPUT;
    call_struct.param1 = (long)stream;
    call_struct.param2 = (long)buffer;
    call_struct.param3 = nbytes;
```

```
    asm
    {
        MOV ECX,USER_LIBRARY
        LEA EAX,call_struct
        INT SYSTEM_CALL
    }
}
```

Notice how the `write()` function is actually a front man for a more general system call gateway named `system_call`. Typically, operating systems have a single, centralized dispatch mechanism to handle system call requests. This is necessary because system calls are typically implemented as software-generated interrupts, and there's only one way to generate a software interrupt (on the Intel platform, you use the INT instruction). Implementing a series of system calls becomes a matter of creating different variations of the same basic instruction.

In Figure 6-1, you can see how the system call gateway is a choke point between the user libraries and the implementation of the system calls. In an operating system that utilizes memory protection, the system call gateway is the only way for a user to initiate the execution of system call instructions. There's no other way to sneak to the location of the system call. This fact leads to the distinction of a computer running in *kernel mode* and *user mode*. A computer is in kernel mode when the CPU is executing system call instructions. Otherwise, a computer is in user mode, which means that it is executing instructions belonging to a library function or written by a user.

 NOTE In an operating system like DOS, which has no memory protection, it is possible to execute an interrupt service routine by using a long JMP instruction with some assorted assembly language acrobatics. There's nothing in place to prevent a program from jumping to the location of the system call's instructions and executing them. This is bad if you are trying to defend yourself against malicious programs. This is good if you are interested in playing around with your own memory management scheme.

To an extent, an operating system can be viewed in terms of its system calls. They give an operating system a kind of signature. However, a particular operating system is not completely defined by its system call interface. For example, a *clone operating system* mimics the operation of another operating system by offering an identical system call interface. However, the clone differs from the original because those system calls are implemented using different algorithms and data structures. It is a well-documented fact that Microsoft's 1982 release of its DOS operating system was a clone of IBM's PC DOS. Hence, an operating system is defined by the combination of its system call interface and the manner in which it implements those system calls.

NOTE The Portable Operating System Interface for Unix (POSIX) collection of standards was an attempt by the Institute of Electrical and Electronics Engineers (IEEE) to, among other things, establish a consistent system call interface for Unix. The motivation behind this initiative was the creeping divergence among Unix implementations, which blossomed in the 1980s.

Given that the HEC virtual machine is implemented in C, it is only natural that I would want the virtual machine to take advantage of the C standard library. The C standard library provides access to several fundamental operating system services, like file I/O and memory management. There are, however, some system services that require using a particular vendor's proprietary API. An example of this is network communication. You can't do everything in ANSI C. This is an unpleasant characteristic of the standard. Thus, I was forced to rely on a combination of standard C library functions and vendor-specific routines in order to give the HEC virtual machine access to the full range of operating system services.

The HEC virtual machine's connection to the C standard library and vendor-specific APIs is provided by the INT instruction. The execution of the INT instruction by the virtual machine leads to the invocation of the `handleInt()` function in `interupt.c`. This, in turn, leads to the execution of functions that wrap C standard library functions and platform-specific modules. The `handleInt()` function is analogous to an operating system's kernel mode gateway. It is the choke point through which all system services are accessed. The difference is that `handleInt()` does not invoke kernel routines. Instead, the `handleInt()` function invokes user-mode library procedures, which then invoke kernel routines on behalf of the virtual machine. With a virtual machine, you basically are adding a couple more layers of function wrapping into the execution path. This is illustrated in Figure 6-2.

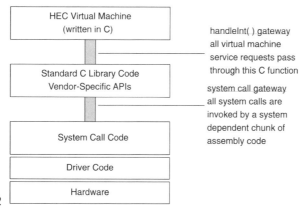

Figure 6-2

The byte-size literal operand following the INT instruction, also known as the *interrupt vector*, will determine which interrupt handler is invoked.

```
void handleInt(U1 byte)
{
    DBG_RUN1("handleInt(): received vector (%u)\n",byte);

    if(interruptOn==FALSE)
    {
        DBG_RUN0("handleInt(); interrupts are disabled\n");
        return;
    }

    switch(byte)
    {
        case 0:
        {
            DBG_RUN0("handleInt(): handling vector 0\n");
            handlefileIO();
        }break;
        case 1:
        {
            DBG_RUN0("handleInt(): handling vector 1\n");
            handleFileManagement();
        }break;
        case 2:
        {
            DBG_RUN0("handleInt(): handling vector 2\n");
            handleProcessManagement();

        }break;
        case 3:
        {
            DBG_RUN0("handleInt(): handling vector 3\n");
            debug = TRUE;
        }break;
        case 4:
        {
            DBG_RUN0("handleInt(): handling vector 4\n");
            handleTimeDateCall();

        }break;
        case 5:
        {
            DBG_RUN0("handleInt(): handling vector 5\n");
            handleCommandLine();

        }break;
        case 6:
        {
            DBG_RUN0("handleInt(): handling vector 6\n");
            handleMemoryStatus();
```

```
                              }break;
                              case 7:
                              {
                                    DBG_RUN0("handleInt(): handling vector 7\n");
                                    handleAllocCall();

                              }break;
                              case 8:
                              {
                                    DBG_RUN0("handleInt(): handling vector 8\n");
                                    handleMathCall();

                              }break;
                              case 9:
                              {
                                    DBG_RUN0("handleInt(): handling vector 9\n");
                                    handleNativeCall();

                              }break;
                              case 10:
                              {
                                    DBG_RUN0("handleInt(): handling vector 10\n");
                                    handleIPC();

                              }break;
                              default:
                              {
                                    DBG_RUN1("handleInt(): vector not handled (%u)\n",byte);
                              }
                    }

          return;

 }/*end handleInt*/
```

For example, if the INT 4 instruction is executed, the `handleTimeDateCall()` interrupt handler will be called. Each interrupt vector actually corresponds to a number of related functions. This means that each function invoked by `handleInt()` is capable of calling several different subfunctions. The handler routine for each vector value merely serves as a gateway to those subfunctions. The particular subfunction invoked will depend upon the value in the `$R1` register. This means that each interrupt handler will consist of a switch statement, which takes different execution paths depending on the value of `$R1`. For example:

```
 void handle---Call()
 {
     switch(R[$R1])
     {
          case 0:{}break;
          case 1:{}break;
          case 2:{}break;
          :
          :
```

```
        }
    return;
}
```

NOTE This is an important point, so I'm going to repeat myself in an effort to help you remember. Each interrupt vector value (INT 0, INT 10, etc.) corresponds to a specific interrupt handler (`handleFileIO()`, `handleIPC()`, etc.). Each handler, in turn, will call a different function depending on the value of the `$R1` register. Thus, each interrupt handler is associated with several possible routines.

NOTE During the implementation of the virtual machine's interrupt handlers, I was torn between using ANSI C standard libraries and using high-performance, low-level vendor functions. In particular, the platform-specific, low-level I/O routines presented me with the opportunity to bypass the operating system and user library buffering. I was tempted by the thought of how much redundant code I could sidestep. On the other hand, the low-level functions didn't offer all the bells and whistles that the C standard library did. I would probably have had to reproduce a lot of things myself. Not to mention that I would have had to rewrite everything when I ported the virtual machine. To reach a decision I went back to my three fundamental design criteria: portability, simplicity, and performance. In the end, portability won out. I only relied on platform-specific routines if the C standard libraries didn't have what I needed.

I was able to provide a whole series of different interrupt handlers. I tried to cover as many bases as I could, but at the same time I was also under pressure to focus on offering solid support for the basic services. A lake can be one mile wide or one mile deep, so to speak. I tried to compromise between providing an exhaustive set of handlers in a select set of core areas and giving the developer access to every nook and cranny of the native platform. The following is a summary of the types of interrupt handlers I implemented.

Table 6-1

Interrupt	Family of Functions
0	File input/output
1	File management
2	Process management
3	Breakpoints
4	Time and date calls
5	Handling command-line arguments
6	Memory diagnostics
7	Dynamic memory allocation
8	Mathematical functions
9	Interfacing with native code
10	Interprocess communication

The implementation of the virtual machine's various interrupt handlers is located in `intwin32.c`. I placed everything in one file in an effort to quarantine system-dependent code.

RANT You'll notice that I didn't include any GUI-related interrupts. This is because I have a sneaking suspicion that trying to support such an API on multiple platforms would prove to be a nightmare. Remember my three design goals for the virtual machine? Well, the requirement to support GUI controls cross-platform violates all three. Take a good look at the speed, responsiveness, and stability of Java GUI components. Then go see what you can whip up with Visual Basic in 15 minutes. There's no comparison.

I consider myself to be a Java proponent. I was using Java on Windows when the JDK had a DOS-based installer and ran on Windows 3.1. After working with Java professionally for over five years, it pains me to admit Java's GUI shortcomings. It's a sad fact, but Microsoft has won the battle for the desktop. I have worked with all of the current contenders. I have worked with Apple computers, which still do not know how to right-click. I have worked with KDE and GNOME, which lack the polish and slick integration of Windows. I use Visual Studio because it is the best GUI development suite in production. Bill Gates pours millions of dollars into Microsoft's development environment and it shows.

The best shot at cross-platform GUI support that developers have now is the Internet browser. You can use HTML and JavaScript to create widgets without selling out to somebody's brand of C++. You'll also have the distinct advantage of being able to run your presentation code on multiple platforms. A web page that does not rely on proprietary HTML tags will show up as easily on a Netscape browser running on a Solaris machine as it will on Internet Explorer. It also goes without saying that HTML and JavaScript are much easier to master than C++. From my own experience, I'd say that it takes a couple of years to really master MFC programming. It only takes a month or two for the same programmer to get the hang of HTML and JavaScript.

In the future, I think the next big thing will be an XML-based browser. HTML is somewhat limited in terms of the components it supports and the GET/POST transaction format it allows. This is particularly true when it comes to things like tree controls and multidocument views. XML will, no doubt, give birth to a much more powerful and general set of user interface tools.

Given that the browser has become the de facto UI, I decided to design the HEC virtual machine to be a server-side application engine. Nestled away on a sturdy server box, the HEC virtual machine can merrily chug away without needing to generate or manage GUI components.

INT 0 – File Input/Output

File input and output constitutes a core area of functionality. In some operating systems, like Unix, almost everything is viewed as a file. Performing file I/O typically involves three steps. First, before you can do anything else, you must open a file. Then you are free to perform any number of file-related actions. When you are done, you must clean up your toys and close the file.

Naturally, there is an exception to this rule. The C standard library provides three files that it opens and closes automatically. This means that you can read and write to these files without having to worry about performing the requisite bookkeeping. These three files are standard input, standard output, and standard error (`stdin`, `stdout`, and `stderr`). Standard input is a file that represents character input from the keyboard. You read from standard input in order to determine what the user has recently typed in. Standard output is a file that represents the screen. You write data to standard output in order to display data on the screen. Standard error is like standard output, with the exception that it cannot be redirected and is not buffered. What this means is that standard error messages will always be displayed on the screen.

 NOTE   What do I mean by "everything in Unix is viewed as a file"? This is an important question to ask. Unix was designed to be terse and simple, and present a hardware-independent interface to the user. Every device on a Unix machine is treated as a file in an effort to establish a consistent I/O mechanism. Files that represent devices belong to a class of files known as *special files* (as opposed to a *regular file*, which just stores data). From a programmer's perspective, writing data to a tape drive is no different than writing data to the console. The C library functions used are the same in both cases. In addition, by treating every device as a file, the number of system calls which Unix has to expose is kept to a minimum. Unix uses the same set of file I/O system calls to facilitate communication with all of its hardware components.

 NOTE   During my first year as a software engineer, I ran into a guy who had neglected to close his file handles in a mission-critical program. He was a college student who was interning over the summer. He had been charged with tweaking a job monitoring application. The monitor interacted with other related processes through an ancient VSAM (Virtual Storage Access Mechanism) database. VSAM was developed by IBM back when dinosaurs roamed the earth. The monitoring application, which the intern had modified, crashed. Fortunately, the scheduler was running on a mainframe, so it did not take the operating system down with it. After several frantic days of manually tracing program execution, debugging, and losing sleep, the problem was discovered. By the time we were done, the mainframe console was buried in a pile of fast-food containers. The team lead was none too happy that his pride and joy had keeled over and brought business to a screeching halt while the system admins scrambled to crank up the legacy applications. As an act of penance, the intern was forced to place a sign in his cube that said: "I will not forget to close my file handles."

Table 6-2 displays a summary of the file I/O functions implemented.

Table 6-2

Interrupt	Function ($R1)	Description
0	0	Opens a file
0	1	Closes a file
0	2	Flushes a file's buffer
0	3	Flushes the buffer to stdin
0	4	Flushes the buffer to stdout
0	5	Flushes the buffer to stderr
0	6	Moves the file position marker to the first byte in a file
0	7	Returns the current location of the file position marker
0	8	Sets the location of the file position marker
0	9	Tests for EOF

Interrupt	Function ($R1)	Description
0	10	Tests for an I/O error
0	11	Reads bytes from a file
0	12	Writes bytes to a file
0	13	Reads bytes from stdin
0	14	Writes bytes to stdout
0	15	Writes bytes to stderr
0	16	Prints a character to stdout
0	17	Prints a wide character to stdout
0	18	Prints a string to stdout
0	19	Prints a wide string to stdout
0	20	Prints an integer to stdout
0	21	Prints a floating-point value to stdout
0	22	Reads a string from stdin
0	23	Reads a wide string from stdin
0	24	Reads an integer from stdin
0	25	Reads a floating-point value from stdin

Now we'll take a look at the INT 0 functions individually.

INT 0 $R1=0   Opens a file

When you open a file, you will be given the address of a structure that represents the open file. This address is needed to perform operations on the file, but is merely a numeric value that can be stored in an integer register. Think of the structure address like a room key in a hotel: You can't do anything in the room without having the key.

Inputs $R2= Address of the null-terminated string storing the filename
$R3= Mode to open the file

$R3	Mode
0	Opens a file for reading
1	Creates a new file or truncates an existing one for output
2	Creates a new file for output or appends to an existing one
3	Creates a new file or truncates an existing one for input/output
4	Creates a new file or appends to an existing one for input/output

Outputs $R4= Pointer to a system file structure, or 0 if an error occurs

INT 0 $R1=1   Closes a file

Don't forget to close your files when you are done with them. It's like handing back your room key when you check out of a hotel. Forgetting to do so can get you in a load of trouble.

Inputs $R2= Pointer to a system file structure
Outputs $R3= 0 if the operation succeeded; nonzero otherwise

INT 0 $R1=2   Flushes a file's buffer

The C standard I/O libraries maintain their own buffers for performing input and output.
    If a file has been opened for output, flushing its buffer will write all remaining data still in the buffer to the file. If a file has been opened for input, flushing its buffer will merely clear the buffer and discard any data still remaining.
    Inputs $R2= Pointer to a system file structure
    Outputs $R3= 0 if the operation succeeded; nonzero otherwise

INT 0 $R1=3   Flushes the buffer to standard input (stdin)

The C standard I/O libraries maintain their own buffers for performing input and output.
    This call will clear the bytes remaining in standard input's buffer and discard them.
    Inputs   None
    Outputs $R3= 0 if the operation succeeded; nonzero otherwise

INT 0 $R1=4   Flushes the buffer to standard output (stdout)

The C standard I/O libraries maintain their own buffers for performing input and output.
    This call will take the bytes remaining in standard output's buffer and write them to a file.
    Inputs   None
    Outputs $R3= 0 if the operation succeeded; nonzero otherwise

INT 0 $R1=5   Flushes the buffer to standard error (stderr)

Most implementations of the C standard library do not buffer the standard error stream. So this function is more of a contingency than anything else.
    Inputs   None
    Outputs $R3= 0 if the operation succeeded; nonzero otherwise

INT 0 $R1=6   Moves the file position marker to the first byte in the file

When working with a file, you can specify where in the file you want an operation to be performed by modifying the file position marker. The location of the file position marker is given in bytes from the beginning of the file.
    Inputs $R2= Pointer to a system file structure
    Outputs   None

INT 0 $R1=7   Returns the current location of the file position marker

When working with a file, you can specify where in the file you want an operation to be performed by modifying the file position marker. The location of the file position marker is measured in bytes from the beginning of the file.
    Inputs $R2= Pointer to a system file structure
    Outputs $R3= Location of file position marker

INT 0 $R1=8   Sets the location of the file position marker

When working with a file, you can specify where in the file you want an operation to be performed by modifying the file position marker. The location of the file position marker is given in bytes from the beginning of the file.

The final location of the file position marker is determined by adding the offset in $R3 to the position specified by $R4.

Inputs $R2= Pointer to a system file structure

$R3= Offset in bytes from the position specified by $R4

$R4= Specifies the general position to place the file position marker

$R4	Location
0	Beginning of the file
1	End of the file
2	Current position

Outputs $R5= 0 if the operation succeeded; nonzero otherwise

INT 0 $R1=9   Tests for the end of file marker (EOF)

This function can be invoked after a file I/O operation to see if the end of the file has been reached.

Inputs $R2= Pointer to a system file structure

Outputs $R3= 0 if the file position marker is not at the end of the file

INT 0 $R1=10   Tests for a file I/O error

This function can be invoked after a file I/O operation to see if an error has occurred.

Inputs $R2= Pointer to a system file structure

Outputs $R3= 0 if no error has occurred; nonzero otherwise

INT 0 $R1=11   Reads bytes from a file

Inputs $R2= Pointer to a system file structure

$R3= Number of bytes to read

$R4= Address of buffer to receive data that is read in

Outputs $R5= Number of bytes actually read

$R6= 0 if no error has occurred; 1 otherwise

INT 0 $R1=12   Writes bytes to a file

Inputs $R2= Pointer to a system file structure

$R3= Number of bytes to write

$R4= Address of buffer of data to write to file

Outputs $R5= Number of bytes actually written

$R6= 0 if no error has occurred; 1 otherwise

INT 0 $R1=13   Reads bytes from standard input

Inputs $R3= Number of bytes to write

$R4= Address of buffer of data to write to file

Outputs $R5= Number of bytes actually written
$R6= 0 if no error has occurred; 1 otherwise

INT 0 $R1=14   Writes bytes to standard output
Inputs $R3= Number of bytes to write
$R4= Address of buffer of data to write to file
Outputs $R5= Number of bytes actually written
$R6= 0 if no error has occurred; 1 otherwise

INT 0 $R1=15   Writes bytes to standard error
Inputs $R3= Number of bytes to write
$R4= Address of buffer of data to write to file
Outputs $R5= Number of bytes actually written
$R6= 0 if no error has occurred; 1 otherwise

INT 0 $R1=16   Prints a character to standard output
Inputs $R2= Character to print
Outputs $R3= Number of characters printed
$R4= 0 if no error has occurred; 1 otherwise

INT 0 $R1=17   Prints a wide (16-bit) character to standard output
Inputs $R2= Wide character to print
Outputs $R3= Number of characters printed
$R4= 0 if no error has occurred; 1 otherwise

INT 0 $R1=18   Prints a null-terminated string to standard output
Inputs $R2= Address of null-terminated string
Outputs $R3= Number of characters printed
$R4= 0 if no error has occurred; 1 otherwise

INT 0 $R1=19   Prints a null-terminated wide string to standard output

A wide string is a string consisting of wide (16-bit) characters.
Inputs $R2= Address of null-terminated wide string
Outputs $R3= Number of characters printed
$R4= 0 if no error has occurred; 1 otherwise

INT 0 $R1=20   Prints an integer to standard output
Inputs $R2= Integer value to print
$R3= 1 if treating integer as unsigned; otherwise will print as signed
Outputs $R3= Number of characters printed
$R4= 0 if no error has occurred; 1 otherwise

INT 0 $R1=21   Prints a floating-point value to standard output
Inputs $D1= Floating-point value to print
Outputs $R3= Number of characters printed
$R4= 0 if no error has occurred; 1 otherwise

INT 0 $R1=22   Reads a null-terminated string from standard input
    Inputs $R2= Address of buffer where string can be placed
    Outputs $R3= 0 if an error has occurred; nonzero otherwise

INT 0 $R1=23   Reads a null-terminated wide string from standard input
    Inputs $R2= Address of buffer where wide string can be placed
    Outputs $R3= 0 if an error has occurred; nonzero otherwise

INT 0 $R1=24   Reads an integer in from standard input
    Inputs $R3= 1 if treating integer as unsigned; otherwise will read as signed
    Outputs $R2= Integer value read in
                $R3= 0 if an error has occurred; nonzero otherwise

INT 0 $R1=25   Reads a floating-point value in from standard input
    Outputs $D1= Floating-point value read in
                $R3= 0 if an error has occurred; nonzero otherwise

The following is an example of HEC assembly code that uses INT 0 functions. This code is in a file named `fileio.asm` on the companion CD-ROM.

```
#fileIO.asm---------------------------------------------
.PB main
.PV buffer -32
.PV fname -64

#allocate local storage on stack
PUSHQ $FP
MOV $FP,$SP
LQI $R7,64
SUB $SP,$SP,$R7

#read and print floating-point value
LQI $R1,25
INT 0
LQI $R1,21
INT 0

LQI $R2,10
LQI $R1,16
INT 0
LQI $R2,13
LQI $R1,16
INT 0

#read and print an integer
LQI $R3,0
LQI $R1,24
INT 0
LQI $R3,0
LQI $R1,20
INT 0
```

```
LQI $R2,10
LQI $R1,16
INT 0
LQI $R2,13
LQI $R1,16
INT 0

#read and print a string
LAI $R2,$FP,buffer
MOV $R7,$R2
LQI $R1,22
INT 0
LQI $R1,18
INT 0

LQI $R2,10
LQI $R1,16
INT 0
LQI $R2,13
LQI $R1,16
INT 0

#set file name
LAI $R2,$FP,fname
MOV $R9,$R2
LQI $R1,22
INT 0

#open a file, write a few bytes, then close
LQI $R3,1
LQI $R1,0
INT 0
MOV $R8,$R4

MOV $R2,$R8
LQI $R3,8
MOV $R4,$R7
LQI $R1,12
INT 0

MOV $R2,$R8
LQI $R1,1
INT 0

#open file, move around, read a byte, then close
MOV $R2,$R9
LQI $R3,0
LQI $R1,0
INT 0
MOV $R8,$R4
```

```
MOV $R2,$R8
LQI $R3,3
LQI $R4,0
LQI $R1,8
INT 0

MOV $R2,$R8
LQ1 $R1,7
INT 0
MOV $R2,$R3
LQI $R1,20
INT 0

LQI $R2,10
LQI $R1,16
INT 0
LQI $R2,13
LQI $R1,16
INT 0

MOV $R2,$R8
LQI $R3,3
MOV $R4,$R9
LQI $R1,11
INT 0

MOV $R2,$R9
LQI $R1,18
INT 0

MOV $R2,$R8
LQI $R1,1
INT 0

#reclaim local storage
MOV $SP,$FP
POPQ $FP

HALT
.PE
```

Running this program would produce the following type of session at the command line:

```
C:\DOCS\HEC\engine\Debug>engine fileio.RUN
allocating 131624 bytes
9.9994
9.999400e+000
-67
-67
allyoopsadazydo
allyoopsadazydo
file.bin
3
yooe.bin
```

The INT 0 functions are implemented within the `handleFileIO()` routine:

```
void handleFileIO()
{
    int retval;

    switch((U1)R[$R1])
    {
        case 0:
        {
            char *modes[]={"rb","wb","ab","wb+","ab+"};
            FILE *fptr;
            if(R[$R3]>4){ R[$R4]=0; return; }
            fptr = fopen(&RAM[R[$R2]],modes[R[$R3]]);
            if(fptr==NULL){ R[$R4]=0; }
            else{ R[$R4] = (U8)fptr; }

        }break;
        case 1:
        {
            R[$R3]=fclose((FILE *)R[$R2]);

        }break;
        case 2:
        {
            R[$R3]=fflush((FILE *)R[$R2]);

        }break;
        case 3:
        {
            R[$R3]=fflush(stdin);

        }break;
        case 4:
        {
            R[$R3]=fflush(stdout);

        }break;
        case 5:
        {
            R[$R3]=fflush(stderr);

        }break;
        case 6:
        {
            rewind((FILE *)R[$R2]);

        }break;
        case 7:
        {
            long pos;
            pos = ftell((FILE *)R[$R2]);
            if(pos==-1L){ R[$R3]=0; R[$R4]=1; }
            else{ R[$R3]=pos; R[$R4]=0; }
```

```
}break;
case 8:
{
     switch(R[$R4])
     {
          case 0:
          {
               R[$R5] =
               fseek((FILE *)R[$R2],(long)R[$R3],SEEK_SET);
          }break;
          case 1:
          {
               R[$R5] =
               fseek((FILE *)R[$R2],(long)R[$R3],SEEK_END);
          }break;
          case 2:
          {
               R[$R5] =
               fseek((FILE *)R[$R2],(long)R[$R3],SEEK_CUR);
          }break;
          default:
          {
               R[$R5] =
               fseek((FILE *)R[$R2],(long)R[$R3],SEEK_SET);
          }
     }

}break;
case 9:
{
     R[$R3]=feof((FILE *)R[$R2]);

}break;
case 10:
{
     R[$R3]=ferror((FILE *)R[$R2]);

}break;
case 11:
{
     size_t nbytes;
     nbytes = fread(&RAM[R[$R4]],1,(size_t)R[$R3],(FILE *)R[$R2]);
     if(nbytes<(size_t)R[$R3])
     {
          if(feof((FILE *)R[$R2])){ R[$R5]=nbytes; R[$R6]=0; }
          else if(ferror((FILE *)R[$R2]))
          { R[$R5]=nbytes; R[$R6]=1;}
          else{ R[$R5]=nbytes; R[$R6]=0; }
     }
     else{ R[$R5]=nbytes; R[$R6]=0; }

}break;
case 12:
{
```

```
        size_t nbytes;
        nbytes =
        fwrite(&RAM[R[$R4]],1,(size_t)R[$R3],(FILE *)R[$R2]);
        if(nbytes<(size_t)R[$R3])
        {
            if(feof((FILE *)R[$R2])){ R[$R5]=nbytes; R[$R6]=0; }
            else if(ferror((FILE *)R[$R2]))
            { R[$R5]=nbytes; R[$R6]=1;}
            else{ R[$R5]=nbytes; R[$R6]=0; }
        }
        else{ R[$R5]=nbytes; R[$R6]=0; }

}break;
case 13:
{
    size_t nbytes;
    nbytes = fread(&RAM[R[$R4]],1,(size_t)R[$R3],stdin);
    if(nbytes<(size_t)R[$R3])
    {
        if(feof(stdin)){ R[$R5]=nbytes; R[$R6]=0; }
        else if(ferror(stdin)){ R[$R5]=nbytes; R[$R6]=1;}
        else{ R[$R5]=nbytes; R[$R6]=0; }
    }
    else{ R[$R5]=nbytes; R[$R6]=0; }

}break;
case 14:
{
    size_t nbytes;
    nbytes = fwrite(&RAM[R[$R4]],1,(size_t)R[$R3],stdout);
    if(nbytes<(size_t)R[$R3])
    {
        if(feof(stdout)){ R[$R5]=nbytes; R[$R6]=0; }
        else if(ferror(stdout)){ R[$R5]=nbytes; R[$R6]=1;}
        else{ R[$R5]=nbytes; R[$R6]=0; }
    }
    else{ R[$R5]=nbytes; R[$R6]=0; }

}break;
case 15:
{
    size_t nbytes;
    nbytes = fwrite(&RAM[R[$R4]],1,(size_t)R[$R3],stderr);
    if(nbytes<(size_t)R[$R3])
    {
        if(feof(stderr)){ R[$R5]=nbytes; R[$R6]=0; }
        else if(ferror(stderr)){ R[$R5]=nbytes; R[$R6]=1;}
        else{ R[$R5]=nbytes; R[$R6]=0; }
    }
    else{ R[$R5]=nbytes; R[$R6]=0; }

}break;
case 16:
{
```

```
        retval = printf("%c",(char)R[$R2]);
        if(retval < 0){ R[$R3]=0; R[$R4]=1; }
        else{ R[$R3]=retval; R[$R4]=0; }

}break;
case 17:
{
        retval = wprintf(L"%lc",(wchar_t)R[$R2]);
        if(retval < 0){ R[$R3]=0; R[$R4]=1; }
        else{ R[$R3]=retval; R[$R4]=0; }
}break;
case 18:
{
        retval = printf("%s",(char *)&RAM[R[$R2]]);
        if(retval < 0){ R[$R3]=0; R[$R4]=1; }
        else{ R[$R3]=retval; R[$R4]=0; }

}break;
case 19:
{
        retval = wprintf(L"%ls",(wchar_t *)&RAM[R[$R2]]);
        if(retval < 0){ R[$R3]=0; R[$R4]=1; }
        else{ R[$R3]=retval; R[$R4]=0; }

}break;
case 20: /* note signed vs. unsigned */
{
        if(R[$R3]==1){ retval = printf("%I64u",R[$R2]); }
        else{ retval = printf("%I64d",R[$R2]); }
        if(retval < 0){ R[$R3]=0; R[$R4]=1; }
        else{ R[$R3]=retval; R[$R4]=0; }

}break;
case 21:
{
        retval = printf("%le",Rd[$D1]);
        if(retval < 0){ R[$R3]=0; R[$R4]=1; }
        else{ R[$R3]=retval; R[$R4]=0; }

}break;
case 22:
{
        retval = scanf("%s",(char *)&RAM[R[$R2]]);
        if((retval==EOF)||(retval==0))
        { R[$R3]=0; }else{ R[$R3]=retval; }

}break;
case 23:
{
        retval = wscanf(L"%ls",(wchar_t *)&RAM[R[$R2]]);
        if((retval==EOF)||(retval==0))
        { R[$R3]=0; }else{ R[$R3]=retval; }
```

```
        }break;
        case 24:
        {
                if(R[$R3]==1){ retval = scanf("%I64u",&R[$R2]); }
                else{ retval = scanf("%I64d",&R[$R2]); }
                if((retval==EOF)||(retval==0))
                { R[$R3]=0; }else{ R[$R3]=retval; }

        }break;
        case 25:
        {
                retval = scanf("%le",&Rd[$D1]);
                if((retval==EOF)||(retval==0))
                { R[$R3]=0; }else{ R[$R3]=retval; }

        }break;
        default:
        {
                ERROR1_LVL2("fileIO %lu function not handled",(U1)R[$R1]);
        }
    }
    return;

}/*end handlefileIO*/
```

INT 1 – File Management

There is life beyond just reading, writing, and updating files. Instances will arise where you will need to rename a file, move a file, delete a file, or examine the attributes of a file. In other words, you will need to invoke a file-related call that doesn't have anything to do with pure I/O. This is what the INT 1 file management functions are all about — interacting with a computer's file system.

A *file system* refers to both an arranged collection of files and the facilities in an operating system that determine how the files are organized, identified, and accessed. The exact meaning of the word is context sensitive. Thus, you'll hear a software engineer discuss the merits of the Linux ext2 file system (in which case he's talking about an operating system's file management facilities), and you'll also hear a system admin complain about how the file system on his servers is corrupted (in which case the files themselves are being referenced). In the following discussion, I will be using the term "file system" to designate an organized collection of files.

Most file systems use a mechanism known as a *directory* to organize their files. The physical implementation of a directory varies from one platform to the next. However, the basic purpose of a directory remains fairly consistent. In abstract terms, a directory is a component of a file system that stores files and other directories.

Most file system implementations organize their files into a hierarchical tree of directories. Such a tree is displayed in Figure 6-3.

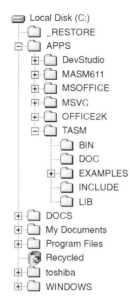

Figure 6-3

Like the tree abstract data type, a file system will have a directory that serves as a root node. All flavors of the Unix operating system refer to this root node as the *root directory*. In the Windows operating system, the root node of a file system is typically associated with a physical drive, like the Local Disk (C:) in Figure 6-3.

A file's *path* is a specification of its location in the computer's file system.

NOTE　To help confuse you, most operating system command shells also define an environmental variable named PATH, which is used to help the command shell find executable files at run time.

The *absolute path* of a file is a fully qualified specification of the file's location. The absolute path of a file begins with the root of the directory structure and includes every directory encountered in the traversal from the root to the file. For example, assume there is a file named make.exe in the BIN directory of the TASM folder in Figure 6-3. The fully qualified path of this executable is:

```
C:\APPS\TASM\BIN\make.exe
```

The *relative path* of a file is a path that does not begin with the root of the directory tree. Relative paths begin with the *current working directory*, which is where the command shell is currently situated. The current working directory is denoted, in a file's path, by a period (.). If the command shell has the TASM directory as its current working directory, the relative path of the make.exe file would be:

```
.\BIN\make.exe
```

Given that we have this background material under our belts, we are now ready to look at the virtual machine's file management interrupts. Table 6-3 displays a summary of the file management functions.

Table 6-3

Interrupt	Function ($R1)	Description
1	0	Indicates if file exists
1	1	Indicates if the file is a directory
1	2	Indicates if file can be read
1	3	Indicates if file can be written to
1	4	Returns the size of a file in bytes
1	5	Returns the time when the file was last modified
1	6	Deletes a file
1	7	Creates a directory
1	8	Deletes a directory
1	9	Returns the absolute path of a file
1	10	Returns the maximum length of a file path
1	11	Returns the contents of a directory
1	12	Renames a file or directory

Now we'll take a look at the INT 1 functions individually.

INT 1 $R1=0   Indicates if a file exists
  Inputs $R2= Address of the null-terminated string storing the filename
  Outputs $R3= 1 if the file exists, 0 otherwise

INT 1 $R1=1   Indicates if a file is a directory

In most operating systems, directories are just a certain kind of file. Like other files, directories store data and have entries in the file system. Think of directories as a particular species of the file genus. This call will check the attributes of a file to see if it is a directory.
  Inputs $R2= Address of the null-terminated string storing the filename
  Outputs $R3= 1 if the file is a directory, 0 if it is not, and 2 if an error occurs

INT 1 $R1=2   Indicates if a file can be read
  Inputs $R2= Address of the null-terminated string storing the filename
  Outputs $R3= 1 if the file can be read, 0 otherwise

INT 1 $R1=3   Indicates if a file can be written to
  Inputs $R2= Address of the null-terminated string storing the filename
  Outputs $R3= 1 if the file can be written to, 0 otherwise

INT 1 $R1=4   Returns the size of a file in bytes

I've always been curious about why the ANSI C standard library never had a function that returned the size of a file. The size of a file, measured in bytes, always seemed to me to be a universal metric. Every operating system that I've ever worked with offers a mechanism to determine the length of a file in terms of bytes.
  Inputs $R2= Address of the null-terminated string storing the filename
  Outputs $R3= Size of file in bytes
            $R4= 1 if an error has occurred (i.e., file does not exist), 0 otherwise

INT 1 $R1=5   Returns the time that a file was last modified

Time is measured in seconds elapsed since midnight (00:00:00), January 1, 1970, coordinated universal time (UTC).

    Inputs $R2= Address of the null-terminated string storing the filename
    Outputs $R3= Time when the file was last modified
                    $R4= 1 if an error has occurred (i.e., file does not exist), 0 otherwise

INT 1 $R1=6   Deletes a file

    Inputs $R2= Address of the null-terminated string storing the filename
    Outputs $R3= 1 if an error has occurred (i.e., file does not exist), 0 otherwise

INT 1 $R1=7   Creates a directory file

In most operating systems, directories are just a certain kind of file. Like other files, directories store data and have entries in the file system. Think of directories as a particular species of the file genus. This call will create a directory file.

    Inputs $R2= Address of the null-terminated string storing the directory path
    Outputs $R3= 1 if an error has occurred, 0 otherwise

INT 1 $R1=8   Deletes a directory file

In most operating systems, directories are just a certain kind of file. Like other files, directories store data and have entries in the file system. Think of directories as a particular species of the file genus. This call will delete a directory file.

    Inputs $R2= Address of the null-terminated string storing the directory path
    Outputs $R3= 1 if an error has occurred, 0 otherwise

INT 1 $R1=9   Returns the absolute path of a file

    Inputs $R2= Address of the null-terminated string storing the relative path
                    $R3= Address of the buffer where the full file path can be stored
    Outputs $R4= 1 if an error occurs, 0 otherwise
                    $R5= Length of the full path

INT 1 $R1=10   Returns the maximum length of a file path

Different host operating systems will have different length restrictions on the size of a fully qualified file path. This call is a way to query what this maximum value is.

    Inputs   None
    Outputs $R2= The maximum length of a file path

INT 1 $R1=11   Returns the contents of a directory

This function returns the contents of a directory as a large string which consists of a series of filenames separated by carriage returns and line feeds. If you want to determine the length of this string without actually returning a string, you should set $R3 to 1.

    Be warned; this is a relatively expensive operation.

    Inputs $R2= Address of a null-terminated string containing a directory path
                    $R3= 1 if should only populate $R5 and skip filling the buffer

$R4= Address of a buffer where a directory contents string can be placed

Outputs $R5= Size of the directory contents string stored in the buffer

$R6= 1 if an error has occurred, and 0 otherwise

INT 1 $R1=12 Renames a file or a directory

Inputs $R2= Address of the null-terminated string storing the old name

$R3= Address of the null-terminated string storing the new name

Outputs $R4= 1 if an error has occurred, and 0 otherwise

The following is an example of HEC assembly code that uses INT 1 functions. This code is in a file named `filemgmt.asm` on the companion CD-ROM.

```
.PB main
.PV filename1 -16
.PV filename2 -32
.PV dirname -40
.PV buffer -512

#allocate local storage
PUSHQ $FP
MOV $FP,$SP
LQI $R7,512
SUB $SP,$SP,$R7

#populate local dirName = C:\_a
LAI $R10,$FP,dirname
MOV $R14,$R10
LBI $R2,1

LBI $R1,'C'
SB $R1,$R10
ADD $R10,$R10,$R2

LBI $R1,':'
SB $R1,$R10
ADD $R10,$R10,$R2

LBI $R1,'\'
SB $R1,$R10
ADD $R10,$R10,$R2

LBI $R1,'_'
SB $R1,$R10
ADD $R10,$R10,$R2

LBI $R1,'a'
SB $R1,$R10
ADD $R10,$R10,$R2
```

```
LBI $R1,0
SB $R1,$R10

#populate local filename1 = C:\_a\t.txt
LAI $R10,$FP,filename1
MOV $R11,$R10
LBI $R2,1

LBI $R1,'C'
SB $R1,$R10
ADD $R10,$R10,$R2

LBI $R1,':'
SB $R1,$R10
ADD $R10,$R10,$R2

LBI $R1,'\'
SB $R1,$R10
ADD $R10,$R10,$R2

LBI $R1,'_'
SB $R1,$R10
ADD $R10,$R10,$R2

LBI $R1,'a'
SB $R1,$R10
ADD $R10,$R10,$R2

LBI $R1,'\'
SB $R1,$R10
ADD $R10,$R10,$R2

LBI $R1,'t'
SB $R1,$R10
ADD $R10,$R10,$R2

LBI $R1,'.'
SB $R1,$R10
ADD $R10,$R10,$R2

LBI $R1,'t'
SB $R1,$R10
ADD $R10,$R10,$R2

LBI $R1,'x'
SB $R1,$R10
ADD $R10,$R10,$R2

LBI $R1,'t'
SB $R1,$R10
ADD $R10,$R10,$R2
```

```
LBI $R1,0
SB $R1,$R10

#populate local filename2 = C:\_a\w.txt
LAI $R10,$FP,filename2
MOV $R12,$R10
LBI $R2,1

LBI $R1,'C'
SB $R1,$R10
ADD $R10,$R10,$R2

LBI $R1,':'
SB $R1,$R10
ADD $R10,$R10,$R2

LBI $R1,'\'
SB $R1,$R10
ADD $R10,$R10,$R2

LBI $R1,'_'
SB $R1,$R10
ADD $R10,$R10,$R2

LBI $R1,'a'
SB $R1,$R10
ADD $R10,$R10,$R2

LBI $R1,'\'
SB $R1,$R10
ADD $R10,$R10,$R2

LBI $R1,'w'
SB $R1,$R10
ADD $R10,$R10,$R2

LBI $R1,'.'
SB $R1,$R10
ADD $R10,$R10,$R2

LBI $R1,'t'
SB $R1,$R10
ADD $R10,$R10,$R2

LBI $R1,'x'
SB $R1,$R10
ADD $R10,$R10,$R2

LBI $R1,'t'
SB $R1,$R10
ADD $R10,$R10,$R2
```

```
LBI $R1,0
SB $R1,$R10

#check to see if filename1 exists and print return code
LBI $R1,0
MOV $R2,$R11
INT 1

MOV $R2,$R3
LBI $R1,20
INT 0

LQI $R2,10
LQI $R1,16
INT 0
LQI $R2,13
LQI $R1,16
INT 0

#check to see if filename1 is a directory
MOV $R2,$R11
LBI $R1,1
INT 1

MOV $R2,$R3
LBI $R1,20
INT 0

LQI $R2,10
LQI $R1,16
INT 0
LQI $R2,13
LQI $R1,16
INT 0

#check to see if can read filename1
LBI $R1,2
MOV $R2,$R11
INT 1

MOV $R2,$R3
LBI $R1,20
INT 0

LQI $R2,10
LQI $R1,16
INT 0
LQI $R2,13
LQI $R1,16
INT 0
```

```
#check to see if can write to filename1
LBI $R1,3
MOV $R2,$R11
INT 1

MOV $R2,$R3
LBI $R1,20
INT 0

LQI $R2,10
LQI $R1,16
INT 0
LQI $R2,13
LQI $R1,16
INT 0

#get size of filename1 in bytes
LBI $R1,4
MOV $R2,$R11
INT 1

MOV $R2,$R3
LBI $R1,20
INT 0

LQI $R2,10
LQI $R1,16
INT 0
LQI $R2,13
LQI $R1,16
INT 0

#get time of last modification of filename1
LBI $R1,5
MOV $R2,$R11
INT 1

MOV $R2,$R3
LBI $R1,20
INT 0

LQI $R2,10
LQI $R1,16
INT 0
LQI $R2,13
LQI $R1,16
INT 0

#delete filename1
LBI $R1,6
MOV $R2,$R11
INT 1
```

```
MOV $R2,$R3
LBI $R1,20
INT 0

LQI $R2,10
LQI $R1,16
INT 0

LQI $R2,13
LQI $R1,16
INT 0
#create a directory
LBI $R1,7
MOV $R2,$R12
INT 1

MOV $R2,$R3
LBI $R1,20
INT 0

LQI $R2,10
LQI $R1,16
INT 0
LQI $R2,13
LQI $R1,16
INT 0

#delete a directory
LBI $R1,8
MOV $R2,$R12
INT 1

MOV $R2,$R3
LBI $R1,20
INT 0

LQI $R2,10
LQI $R1,16
INT 0
LQI $R2,13
LQI $R1,16
INT 0

#obtain the full path of filename2
LBI $R1,9
LAI $R3,$FP,buffer
MOV $R13,$R3
MOV $R2,$R12
INT 1

MOV $R2,$R13
LBI $R1,18
INT 0
```

```
LQI $R2,10
LQI $R1,16
INT 0
LQI $R2,13
LQI $R1,16
INT 0

#get the maximum path length
LBI $R1,10
INT 1

LBI $R1,20
INT 0

LQI $R2,10
LQI $R1,16
INT 0
LQI $R2,13
LQI $R1,16
INT 0

#get the contents of C:\_a
LBI $R1,11
MOV $R2,$R14
LBI $R3,0
MOV $R4,$R13
INT 1

MOV $R2,$R13
LBI $R1,18
INT 0

LQI $R2,10
LQI $R1,16
INT 0
LQI $R2,13
LQI $R1,16
INT 0

#rename w.txt to t.txt
LBI $R1,12
MOV $R2,$R12
MOV $R3,$R11
INT 1

#reclaim local storage
MOV $SP,$FP
POPQ $FP

HALT
.PE
```

Running this program would produce the following type of session at the command line:

```
1
0
1
1
32
996101851
0
1
1
C:\_a\w.txt
260
w.txt
backup
```

NOTE The previous program assumes that a directory exists named C:_a that has two files (t.txt and w.txt) and a subdirectory named C:_a\backup. If you intend to duplicate the output above, you will need to create these file structures ahead of time.

The INT 1 functions are implemented within the handleFileManagement() routine, located in intwin32.c.

```c
#include<io.h>
#include<fcntl.h>
#include<sys\stat.h>
#include<direct.h>

void handleFileManagement()
{
    int retval;

    switch((U1)R[$R1])
    {
        case 0:
        {
            retval = _access(&RAM[R[$R2]],0); /*exist*/
            if(retval==0){ R[$R3]=1; }
            else{ R[$R3]=0; }

        }break;
        case 1:
        {
            DWORD result;
            result = GetFileAttributes(&RAM[R[$R2]]);
            if(result==0xFFFFFFFF)
            {
                R[$R3]=2;
            }
            else
            {
                if(result&FILE_ATTRIBUTE_DIRECTORY)
```

```
                {
                        R[$R3]=1;
                }
                else
                {
                        R[$R3]=0;
                }
        }

}break;
case 2:
{
    retval = _access(&RAM[R[$R2]],4); /*read*/
    if(retval==0){ R[$R3]=1; }
    else{ R[$R3]=0; }

}break;
case 3:
{
    retval = _access(&RAM[R[$R2]],2); /*write*/
    if(retval==0){ R[$R3]=1; }
    else{ R[$R3]=0; }

}break;
case 4:
{
    int handle;
    handle - _open(&RAM[R[$R2]],_O_RDONLY);
    if(handle==-1)
    {
        R[$R3] = 0;
        R[$R4] = 1;
    }
    else
    {
        long size;
        size = _filelength(handle);
        if(size==-1L)
        {
            R[$R3] = 0;
            R[$R4] = 1;
        }
        else
        {
            R[$R3] = size;
            R[$R4] = 0;
        }
        _close(handle);
    }

}break;
case 5:
{
    int handle;
```

```
handle = _open(&RAM[R[$R2]],_O_RDONLY);
if(handle==-1)
{
    R[$R3] = 0;
    R[$R4] = 1;
}
else
{
    struct _stat fields;
    retval = _fstat(handle,&fields);
    if(retval==-1L)
    {
        R[$R3] = 0;
        R[$R4] = 1;
    }
    else
    {
        /*
        typedef long time_t
        time_t st_mtime
        */

        R[$R3] = fields.st_mtime;
        R[$R4] = 0;
    }
    _close(handle);
}

}break;
case 6:
{
    if(remove(&RAM[R[$R2]])==-1){ R[$R3]=1; }
    else{ R[$R3]=0; }

}break;
case 7:
{
    if(_mkdir(&RAM[R[$R2]])==-1){ R[$R3]=1; }
    else{ R[$R3]=0; }

}break;
case 8:
{
    if(_rmdir(&RAM[R[$R2]])==-1){ R[$R3]=1; }
    else{ R[$R3]=0; }

}break;
case 9:
{
    char full[_MAX_PATH];
    if(_fullpath(full,&RAM[R[$R2]],_MAX_PATH)!=NULL)
    {
        int len;
        len = strlen(full);
```

```
                strcpy(&RAM[R[$R3]],full);
                R[$R4]=0;
                R[$R5]=len+1; /*include null*/
        }
        else
        {
                R[$R4]=1;
                R[$R5]=0;
        }
}break;
case 10:
{
        R[$R2]=_MAX_PATH;

}break;
case 11:
{
        /* execute dir /b */
        FILE *pipe;
        char buffer[16*1024];

        strcpy(buffer,"dir ");

        /*max windows filename is 215 chars in length*/

        if(strlen(&RAM[R[$R2]])>215)
        {
                R[$R5]=0;
                R[$R6]=1;
        }
        else
        {
                strcat(buffer,&RAM[R[$R2]]);
                strcat(buffer," /b");
                pipe = _popen(buffer,"rb");
                if(pipe==NULL)
                {
                        R[$R5]=0;
                        R[$R6]=1;
                }
                else
                {
                        R[$R5]=fread(buffer,1,16*1024,pipe);
                        if(R[$R3]!=1)
                        {
                                strcpy(&RAM[R[$R4]],buffer);
                        }
                        R[$R6]=0;
                        _pclose(pipe);
                }
        }

}break;
case 12:
```

```
          {
                    if(rename(&RAM[R[$R2]],&RAM[R[$R3]]))
                    {
                              R[$R4]=1;
                    }
                    else
                    {
                              R[$R4]=0;
                    }
          }break;
          default:
          {
                    ERROR1_LVL2("INT 1 %lu function not handled",(U1)R[$R1]);
          }
     }
     return;

}/*end handleFileManagement*/
```

INT 2 – Process Management

The ability of one process to launch and manage other processes is important because it facilitates a variation of *load balancing*. Certain problems, like a brute force assault against an encrypted message, are susceptible to being broken up into distinct subproblems. An executing process can spawn several *child processes* and assign each of them a part of the problem. In a multitasking environment, these child processes will be able to tackle the different parts of the problem in parallel.

When a process creates one or more child processes, it is known as the *parent process* of the children. In fact, children processes can spawn their own offspring and create a tree-like set of parent-child relationships. Such is the case with operating systems like Unix, where every process can inevitably be traced back to a single root process. Most variations of Unix, including Linux, christen this root process as the *init* process (as in the INITial process).

 NOTE A system is said to be *scalable* if it can handle arbitrarily large amounts of work. Load balancing is one of the principal techniques used to allow computer systems to scale. In abstract terms, load balancing is performed by taking a set of related instructions and distributing them among the available resources in a system.

Load balancing can be implemented in several ways and at several different levels. For example, load balancing can be implemented in a network of related computers using TCP routing. In TCP routing, a cluster of servers interfaces to a network using a router device that represents the cluster in terms of a single address. The TCP router receives all the traffic sent to the cluster and distributes it among the members of the cluster. This prevents particular members of the cluster from being weighed down with too much work and developing into bottlenecks.

Load balancing can also be implemented inside a single computer that has multiple processors, tightly coupled together, in the same memory space. In this case, there will be a system-level agent that partitions the machine's processors and memory among the set of existing tasks so that the resources assigned to a given process are proportional to the amount of computation required. The agent performing the partitioning will use some special internal algorithm involving platform-specific performance metrics to dynamically allocate resources.

Table 6-4 displays a summary of the process management functions implemented.

Table 6-4

Interrupt	Function ($R1)	Description
2	0	Spawns a new process
2	1	Waits for a child process to terminate
2	2	Executes a command
2	3	Executes a command with streamed output

Now we'll take a look at the INT 2 functions individually.

INT 2 $R1=0   Spawns a new process

This function spawns a new process where the parent process and the child process execute concurrently. This means that the parent process, once it has spawned the child process, will not wait for the child process to end before it continues with its own execution.

The spawned process will be launched from the current working directory. Also, the spawned process will inherit the environment of the parent process. This means that environmental variables like PATH will have parent values passed on to the child process.

     Inputs $R2= The address of a null-terminated string containing the filename

     Outputs $R4= A handle to the new process

                 $R5= 1 if an error occurs, and 0 otherwise

INT 2 $R1=1   Waits for a child process to terminate

This function causes the invoking process to suspend its own execution until the specified process has completed its work and exited.

     Inputs $R2= Handle to the process on which to wait

     Outputs $R3= Return code from process that is waited upon

                 $R4= 1 if there is an error, and 0 otherwise

INT 2 $R1=2   Executes a command shell interpreter command

This function causes a shell command to be loaded and run. This function does not force the invoking process to wait for the command to terminate before it resumes execution. Both processes execute concurrently.

     Inputs $R2= The address of a null-terminated string containing the

                 command

     Outputs $R3= 1 if there is an error, and 0 otherwise

INT 2 $R1=3   Executes a command with streamed output

This function is similar to the previous one. The difference is that this function will buffer and return everything the command printed to standard output while it ran. The previous version ($R1=2) is not very talkative; the only way to receive any information is through a returned integer value. This version supplies a more sophisticated form of command-process communication.

Inputs	$R2= The address of a null-terminated string containing the command
	$R3= The address of a buffer to store command output
	$R4= The size of the $R3 buffer
Outputs	$R5= The number of bytes streamed back as output by the command
	$R6= 1 if there is an error, and 0 otherwise

The following is an example of HEC assembly code that uses INT 2 functions. This code is in a file named procmgmt.asm on the companion CD-ROM.

```
.PB main
.PV filename1 -16
.PV filename2 -32
.PV buffer -512

#allocate local storage
PUSHQ $FP
MOV $FP,$SP
LQI $R7,512
SUB $SP,$SP,$R7

#populate filename1 = notepad
LAI $R10,$FP,filename1
MOV $R11,$R10
LBI $R2,1

LBI $R1,'n'
SB $R1,$R10
ADD $R10,$R10,$R2

LBI $R1,'o'
SB $R1,$R10
ADD $R10,$R10,$R2

LBI $R1,'t'
SB $R1,$R10
ADD $R10,$R10,$R2

LBI $R1,'e'
SB $R1,$R10
ADD $R10,$R10,$R2

LBI $R1,'p'
SB $R1,$R10
ADD $R10,$R10,$R2
```

```
LBI $R1,'a'
SB $R1,$R10
ADD $R10,$R10,$R2

LBI $R1,'d'
SB $R1,$R10
ADD $R10,$R10,$R2

LBI $R1,'.'
SB $R1,$R10
ADD $R10,$R10,$R2

LBI $R1,'e'
SB $R1,$R10
ADD $R10,$R10,$R2

LBI $R1,'x'
SB $R1,$R10
ADD $R10,$R10,$R2

LBI $R1,'e'
SB $R1,$R10
ADD $R10,$R10,$R2

LBI $R1,0
SB $R1,$R10

#populate local filename2 = mem /f
LAI $R10,$FP,filename2
MOV $R12,$R10
LBI $R2,1

LBI $R1,'m'
SB $R1,$R10
ADD $R10,$R10,$R2

LBI $R1,'e'
SB $R1,$R10
ADD $R10,$R10,$R2

LBI $R1,'m'
SB $R1,$R10
ADD $R10,$R10,$R2

LBI $R1,' '
SB $R1,$R10
ADD $R10,$R10,$R2

LBI $R1,'/'
SB $R1,$R10
ADD $R10,$R10,$R2
```

```
LBI $R1,'f'
SB $R1,$R10
ADD $R10,$R10,$R2

LBI $R1,0
SB $R1,$R10

#spawn notepad
LBI $R1,0
LBI $R3,0
MOV $R2,$R11
INT 2

#wait for notepad to die, then print return code
MOV $R2,$R4
LBI $R1,1
INT 2

MOV $R2,$R3
LBI $R1,20
INT 0

LQI $R2,10
LQI $R1,16
INT 0
LQI $R2,13
LQI $R1,16
INT 0

#spawn notepad again using different function
LBI $R1,2
MOV $R2,$R11
INT 2

MOV $R2,$R3
LBI $R1,20
INT 0

LQI $R2,10
LQI $R1,16
INT 0
LQI $R2,13
LQI $R1,16
INT 0

#call mem /f and print output
LBI $R1,3
MOV $R2,$R12
LAI $R3,$FP,buffer
LQI $R4,512
INT 2
```

```
LAI $R3,$FP,buffer
MOV $R2,$R3
LBI $R1,18
INT 0

LQI $R2,10
LQI $R1,16
INT 0
LQI $R2,13
LQI $R1,16
INT 0

#reclaim local storage
MOV $SP,$FP
POPQ $FP

HALT
.PE
```

Running this program will launch `notepad.exe` twice. The first time `notepad.exe` is launched, the parent process will wait for it to terminate. The second time, it will not. Finally, the output from the `mem` DOS shell command is piped to the console using the $R2=3 function. The session produced by this program looks like:

```
0
0

Free Conventional Memory:

    Segment        Total
    -------    -----------------
    00DD8          112     (0K)
    014C1          256     (0K)
    014D1       90,464    (88K)
    02AE7      475,536   (464K)

    Total Free: 566,368   (553K)

No upper memory available
```

The INT 2 functions are implemented within the `handleProcessManagement()` routine, located in `intwin32.c`.

```c
#include<process.h>

void handleProcessManagement()
{
    switch((U1)R[$R1])
    {
        case 0:
        {
            BOOL retval;
            STARTUPINFO sinfo;
            PROCESS_INFORMATION pinfo;
```

```
                  GetStartupInfo(&sinfo);

                  retval = CreateProcess(NULL,
                                          &RAM[R[$R2]],
                                          NULL,
                                          NULL,
                                          FALSE,
                                          0,
                                          NULL,
                                          NULL,
                                          &sinfo,
                                          &pinfo);
                  if(retval==FALSE)
                  {
                      R[$R4]=0;
                      R[$R5]=1;
                  }
                  else
                  {

                      R[$R4]=(int)pinfo.hProcess;
                      R[$R5]=0;
                  }

              }break;
              case 1:
              {
                  BOOL retval;
                  int code;
                  code=STILL_ACTIVE;
                  while(code==STILL_ACTIVE)
                  {
                      retval = GetExitCodeProcess((HANDLE)R[$R2],&code);
                  }
                  if(retval==FALSE)
                  {
                      R[$R3]=0;
                      R[$R4]=1;
                  }
                  else
                  {
                      R[$R3]=code;
                      R[$R4]=0;
                  }

              }break;
              case 2:
              {
                  int retval;
                  retval = system(&RAM[R[$R2]]);
                  if(retval==-1)
                  {
                      R[$R3]=0;
                      R[$R4]=1;
```

```
                    }
                    else
                    {
                        R[$R3]=retval;
                        R[$R4]=0;
                    }

                }break;
                case 3:
                {
                    FILE *pipe;

                    pipe = _popen(&RAM[R[$R2]],"rb");
                    if(pipe==NULL)
                    {
                        R[$R5]=0;
                        R[$R6]=1;
                    }
                    else
                    {
                        R[$R5]=fread(&RAM[R[$R3]],1,(size_t)R[$R4],pipe);
                        RAM[R[$R3]+R[$R5]]='\0';
                        R[$R6]=0;
                        _pclose(pipe);
                    }

                }break;
                default:
                {
                    ERROR1_LVL2("INT 2 %lu function not handled",(U1)R[$R1]);
                }
            }
        }
        return;

}/*end handleProcessManagement*/
```

INT 3 – Breakpoints

The breakpoint interrupt is very simple. It does not even have a handler function. When the INT 3 instruction is processed, it toggles the debug variable, which places the virtual machine into debug mode.

```
void handleInt(U1 byte)
{
    DBG_RUN1("handleInt(): received vector (%u)\n",byte);

    if(interruptOn==FALSE)
    {
        DBG_RUN0("handleInt(); interrupts are disabled\n");
        return;
    }
```

```
        switch(byte)
        {
            .
            .
            .
            case 3:
            {
                    DBG_RUN0("handleInt(): handling vector 3\n");
                    debug = TRUE;
            }break;
            .
            .
            .
            default:
            {
                    DBG_RUN1("handleInt(): vector not handled (%u)\n",byte);
            }
        }

        return;

}/*end handleInt*/
```

INT 4 – Time and Date Calls

The functions in this section are used to obtain the calendar date and time. Calendar time is useful for specifying the date when an event occurred, such as when a file was last modified. Successive measurements of the current time can be used to determine how quickly an application executed.

In API descriptions for time functions, you'll see a lot of terms thrown around, like Greenwich Mean Time and coordinated universal time. None of the dozens of specifications that I read went to the trouble of attempting to tell you what these terms mean. Rather than do you the disservice of skipping over this material, I'm going to dive into it and begin at ground zero.

Any phenomena that repeats itself on a regular basis can be used to create a time standard. Originally, the rotation of the earth was used to define the scientific unit of time (the second) because the rotation of the earth is periodic. In fact, up until the 1960s the second was expressed in terms of astronomical events. In 1967, an international group of scientists (the 13th General Conference on Weights and Measures) defined time using the following interpretation:

One second is the time occupied by 9,192,631,770 oscillations of the light emitted by a cesium-133 atom.

You see, when an atom changes from a high energy state to a low energy state, it emits radiation. Radiation is nothing more than waves made up of interconnected electrical and magnetic fields. Like other waves, these electromagnetic waves vibrate in space. They have periodic crests and troughs, just like the waves in the ocean. The length of time between successive crests is used to define a second of time.

Greenwich Mean Time (GMT) is a time standard that uses the Old Greenwich Observatory in England as a reference point (the official Royal Greenwich Observatory is currently located in Sussex). GMT became a standard because it was used by the British Royal Navy, which had a strong international presence in the nineteenth century. The old royal observatory in Greenwich lies on what is known as the *prime meridian* (zero degrees longitude). GMT refers to the time observed on the prime meridian. When someone says that it is 05:00:00 GMT, they are saying that it is currently 5:00 A.M. on the prime meridian. GMT has traditionally been calculated using astronomical observations. So when someone mentions GMT, it could potentially mean that astronomical algorithms are being used. This source of confusion, and the lack of precision of astronomical measurements, is what leads scientists to state time using a different standard.

The GMT standard and its descendents were replaced in the 1960s by the coordinated universal time standard, also called Universal Time Coordinate (UTC), which is based on an atomic clock. The UTC time standard is maintained by laboratories around the world. The National Bureau of Standards in Boulder, Colorado, sets the UTC time in the United States using cesium atomic frequency standard No. NBS-6. The time observed by the bureau is broadcast on shortwave and over the telephone (303-499-7111). Global Positioning System (GPS) satellites also broadcast UTC time. For all intents and purposes, GMT and UTC are the same. They differ by less than 0.9 seconds. The UTC time scale was created with the intention of allowing it to keep in approximate sync with GMT.

In computers, UTC time is typically expressed in terms of seconds since the *epoch*. The epoch is just a point in time which serves as a reference point. In the case of UTC, the epoch is defined as January 1, 1970 00:00:00. I remember the UTC epoch date by recalling a bit of computer history: 1970 was the year after Unix was born.

Local time is an observation of time that takes the standard time zone and daylight savings into account. Given a particular standard time zone, local time can be derived from UTC and vice versa. This allows the local time in any of the 24 standard time zones to be calculated from UTC.

Anyone who has ever read Patterson and Hennesay's *Computer Architecture: A Quantitative Approach* will know that there is only one truly consistent measure of performance: time. There have been any number of special metrics invented to measure performance, but most of them tend to obscure things. The best measure of the execution speed of a program is very simple: How long did it take for the program to run from the time it was loaded until the time it terminated? In light of this, the performance timer interrupt function is useful for measuring how quickly an application executes or for comparing the relative performance of two applications.

Table 6-5 displays a summary of the time and date functions implemented.

Table 6-5

Interrupt	Function ($R1)	Description
4	0	Returns the current UTC time
4	1	Decomposes UTC time into its date and time components
4	2	Converts UTC to local time

Interrupt	Function ($R1)	Description
4	3	Converts a date into seconds since the epoch
4	4	Creates a string representation of time
4	5	Computes the difference between two times
4	6	Performance timer

Now we'll take a look at the INT 4 functions individually.

INT 4 $R1=0   Returns the current UTC time

     Inputs   None

     Outputs $R2= The number of seconds elapsed since midnight (00:00:00), January 1, 1970, coordinated universal time (UTC) as measured by the computer's system clock.

INT 4 $R1=1   Decomposes UTC time into its date and time components

     Inputs $R2= Number of seconds since the epoch

     Outputs $R3= Seconds (0..59)

                     $R4= Minutes (0..59)

                     $R5= Hours (0..23)

                     $R6= Days (1..31)

                     $R7= Months (0..11)

                     $R8= Years (years passed since 1900)

INT 4 $R1=2   Converts UTC to local time

     Inputs $R2= Number of seconds since the epoch

     Outputs $R3= Seconds (0..59)

                     $R4= Minutes (0..59)

                     $R5= Hours (0..23)

                     $R6= Days (1..31)

                     $R7= Months (0..11)

                     $R8= Years (years passed since 1900)

INT 4 $R1=3   Converts a date into seconds since the epoch

     Inputs $R2= Seconds (0..59)

                     $R3= Minutes (0..59)

                     $R4= Hours (0..23)

                     $R5= Days (1..31)

                     $R6= Months (0..11)

                     $R7= Years (years passed since 1900)

     Outputs $R8= Seconds since the epoch

INT 4 $R1=4   Creates a 26-byte string representation of the time

This function takes a time, in seconds since the epoch, and converts it into a 26-byte ASCII string where the 25th byte and 26th byte are null characters.

     Inputs $R2= Number of seconds since the epoch

                     $R3= Address of a 26-byte buffer to hold the date string

Outputs   None

INT 4 $R1=5   Computes the difference between two times

Inputs $R2=$ Initial time, in seconds since the epoch

$R3=$ Final time, in seconds since the epoch

Outputs $R4=$ Difference, in seconds, between the two times

INT 4 $R1=6   Performance timer

The other functions in this section all yield time on the granularity of a second. This isn't useful for measuring application performance because a lot can happen in a second. In other words, a program that completes its work in 1 millisecond is much faster than a program that requires 100 milliseconds. If you used the second as a measuring rod, you would incorrectly conclude that both programs are equally fast. It's far easier to get a better look at relative performance using milliseconds as the unit of measure.

This function returns the number of milliseconds from some system-dependent reference point, like the epoch or when the machine was turned on. Some implementations return microseconds instead of milliseconds (i.e., the Linux port). The best way to use this function is to call it twice and then subtract the initial value from the final value to determine how many milliseconds elapsed between the two calls. This facilitates a way to determine how quickly a portion of code executed.

Depending on the reference point, this value may occasionally roll over to 0. Keep this in mind.

Inputs   None

Outputs $R2=$ The number of milliseconds from the reference point

The following is an example of HEC assembly code that uses INT 4 functions. This code is in a file named `timedate.asm` on the companion CD-ROM.

```
.PB main
.PV buffer -26

#allocate local storage
PUSHQ $FP
MOV $FP,$SP
LQI $R7,26
SUB $SP,$SP,$R7

#get the current UTC time
LQI $R1,0
INT 4
MOV $R20,$R2

LQI $R1,20
INT 0

LQI $R2,10
LQI $R1,16
INT 0
```

```
LQI $R2,13
LQI $R1,16
INT 0

#decompose into time/date components
MOV $R2,$R20
LQI $R1,1
INT 4

MOV $R9,$R3
MOV $R10,$R4
MOV $R11,$R5
MOV $R12,$R6
MOV $R13,$R7
MOV $R14,$R8

MOV $R2,$R9
LQI $R1,20
INT 0
LQI $R2,32
LQI $R1,16
INT 0
MOV $R2,$R10
LQI $R1,20
INT 0
LQI $R2,32
LQI $R1,16
INT 0
MOV $R2,$R11
LQI $R1,20
INT 0
LQI $R2,32
LQI $R1,16
INT 0
MOV $R2,$R12
LQI $R1,20
INT 0
LQI $R2,32
LQI $R1,16
INT 0
MOV $R2,$R13
LQI $R1,20
INT 0
LQI $R2,32
LQI $R1,16
INT 0
MOV $R2,$R14
LQI $R1,20
INT 0
LQI $R2,32
LQI $R1,16
INT 0
```

```
LQI $R2,10
LQI $R1,16
INT 0
LQI $R2,13
LQI $R1,16
INT 0

#get the equivalent local time
MOV $R2,$R20
LQI $R1,2
INT 4
MOV $R9,$R3
MOV $R10,$R4
MOV $R11,$R5
MOV $R12,$R6
MOV $R13,$R7
MOV $R14,$R8

MOV $R2,$R9
LQI $R1,20
INT 0
LQI $R2,32
LQI $R1,16
INT 0
MOV $R2,$R10
LQI $R1,20
INT 0
LQI $R2,32
LQI $R1,16
INT 0
MOV $R2,$R11
LQI $R1,20
INT 0
LQI $R2,32
LQI $R1,16
INT 0
MOV $R2,$R12
LQI $R1,20
INT 0
LQI $R2,32
LQI $R1,16
INT 0
MOV $R2,$R13
LQI $R1,20
INT 0
LQI $R2,32
LQI $R1,16
INT 0
MOV $R2,$R14
LQI $R1,20
INT 0
LQI $R2,32
LQI $R1,16
INT 0
```

```
LQI $R2,10
LQI $R1,16
INT 0
LQI $R2,13
LQI $R1,16
INT 0

#create a new time
LQI $R1,3
LQI $R2,0
LQI $R3,10
LQI $R4,23
LQI $R5,1
LQI $R6,8
LQI $R7,101
INT 4
MOV $R16,$R8

#get string rep of current time
MOV $R2,$R20
LAI $R3,$FP,buffer
LQI $R1,4
INT 4

LAI $R3,$FP,buffer
MOV $R2,$R3
LBI $R1,18
INT 0

LQI $R2,10
LQI $R1,16
INT 0
LQI $R2,13
LQI $R1,16
INT 0

#get string rep of new time
MOV $R2,$R16
LAI $R3,$FP,buffer
LQI $R1,4
INT 4

LAI $R3,$FP,buffer
MOV $R2,$R3
LBI $R1,18
INT 0

LQI $R2,10
LQI $R1,16
INT 0
LQI $R2,13
LQI $R1,16
INT 0
```

```
#compare previous date with today's
MOV $R2,$R20
MOV $R3,$R16
LQI $R1,5
INT 4

MOV $R2,$R4
LQI $R1,20
INT 0

LQI $R2,10
LQI $R1,16
INT 0
LQI $R2,13
LQI $R1,16
INT 0

#reclaim local storage
MOV $SP,$FP
POPQ $FP

HALT
.PE
```

Running this program would produce the following type of session at the command line:

```
996383467
7 11 5 29 6 101
7 11 22 28 6 101
Sat Jul 28 22:11:07 2001
Sat Sep 01 23:10:00 2001
3027533
```

The INT 4 functions are implemented within the `handleTimeDateCall()` routine, located in `intwin32.c`.

```c
void handleTimeDateCall()
{
    switch((U1)R[$R1])
    {
        case 0:
        {
            R[$R2]= time(NULL);

        }break;
        case 1:
        {
            struct tm *tptr;
            time_t t;
            t=(time_t)R[$R2];
            tptr = gmtime(&t);
            R[$R3]=(*tptr).tm_sec;
            R[$R4]=(*tptr).tm_min;
            R[$R5]=(*tptr).tm_hour;
            R[$R6]=(*tptr).tm_mday;
```

```
                        R[$R7]=(*tptr).tm_mon;
                        R[$R8]=(*tptr).tm_year;

                }break;
                case 2:
                {
                        struct tm *tptr;
                        time_t t;
                        t=(time_t)R[$R2];
                        tptr = localtime(&t);
                        R[$R3]=(*tptr).tm_sec;
                        R[$R4]=(*tptr).tm_min;
                        R[$R5]=(*tptr).tm_hour;
                        R[$R6]=(*tptr).tm_mday;
                        R[$R7]=(*tptr).tm_mon;
                        R[$R8]=(*tptr).tm_year;

                }break;
                case 3:
                {
                        struct tm ts;
                        time_t t;
                        (ts).tm_sec= (int)R[$R2];
                        (ts).tm_min= (int)R[$R3];
                        (ts).tm_hour= (int)R[$R4];
                        (ts).tm_mday= (int)R[$R5];
                        (ts).tm_mon= (int)R[$R6];
                        (ts).tm_year= (int)R[$R7];

                        t = mktime(&ts);
                        R[$R8]=t;

                }break;
                case 4:
                {
                        char datestr[26];
                        time_t t;
                        t = (time_t)R[$R2];
                        strcpy(datestr,ctime(&t));
                        strcpy(&RAM[R[$R3]],datestr);
                        RAM[R[$R3]+24]=0;

                }break;
                case 5:
                {
                        R[$R4] = (long)difftime((time_t)R[$R3],(time_t)R[$R2]);

                }break;
                case 6:
                {
                        R[$R2] = GetTickCount();

                }break;
                default:
```

```
                {
                        ERROR1_LVL2("INT 4 %lu function not handled",(U1)R[$R1]);
                }
        }
        return;

}/*end handleTimeDateCall*/
```

INT 5 – Handling Command-Line Arguments

The HEC virtual machine stores arguments to the bytecode executable using the ProgramArgs structure defined and used in cmdline.c. The ceiling of 32 program arguments might seem a little strict. However, if you need to pass more than 32 parameters to the executable, you should use a configuration file, in which case you will only require a single argument (the name of the configuration file).

```
#define MAX_PROGRAM_ARGS    32
struct ProgramArgs
{
    char *args[MAX_PROGRAM_ARGS];    /* program arguments */
    U1 nArgs;                        /* number of arguments */
};
struct ProgramArgs programArgs;
```

Table 6-6 displays a summary of the command-line functions implemented.

Table 6-6

Interrupt	Function ($R1)	Description
5	0	Returns the number of arguments
5	1	Returns a command-line argument

Now we'll take a look at the INT 5 functions individually.

INT 5 $R1=0   Returns the number of arguments
    Inputs   None
    Outputs $R2= The number of program arguments

INT 5 $R1=1   Returns a command-line argument

This function takes one of the program arguments and copies it into a buffer. Program arguments are allowed to be up to 255 characters long, so this function expects the buffer to be at least 256 bytes in length (which leaves space for a null character).
    Inputs $R2= Index into the array of arguments
                $R3= Address of a buffer where the argument can be stored
    Outputs $R4= 1 if a request is made for an argument that is not there
                $R5= Length of the argument string, including the null character

The following is an example of HEC assembly code that uses INT 5 functions. This code is in a file named cmdline.asm on the companion CD-ROM.

```
.PB main
.PV buffer -256

#allocate local storage
PUSHQ $FP
MOV $FP,$SP
LQI $R7,256
SUB $SP,$SP,$R7

#get the number of arguments
LQI $R1,0
INT 5
MOV $R20,$R2

LQI $R1,20
INT 0

LQI $R2,10
LQI $R1,16
INT 0
LQI $R2,13
LQI $R1,16
INT 0

#get the first two arguments
LAI $R3,$FP,buffer
LQI $R2,0
LQI $R1,1
INT 5

LAI $R3,$FP,buffer
MOV $R2,$R3
LBI $R1,18
INT 0

LQI $R2,10
LQI $R1,16
INT 0
LQI $R2,13
LQI $R1,16
INT 0

LAI $R3,$FP,buffer
LQI $R2,1
LQI $R1,1
INT 5

LAI $R3,$FP,buffer
MOV $R2,$R3
LBI $R1,18
INT 0
```

```
LQI $R2,10
LQI $R1,16
INT 0
LQI $R2,13
LQI $R1,16
INT 0

#reclaim local storage
MOV $SP,$FP
POPQ $FP

HALT
.PE
```

Running this program would produce the following type of session at the command line:

```
C:\DOCS\HEC\engine\Debug>engine cmdline.RUN arg1 arg2 arg3
allocating 131360 bytes
3
arg1
arg2
```

The INT 5 functions are implemented within the handleCommandLine() routine, located in intwin32.c.

```c
void handleCommandLine()
{
    switch((U1)R[$R1])
    {
        case 0:
        {
            R[$R2]= programArgs.nArgs;

        }break;
        case 1:
        {
            if(R[$R2]<programArgs.nArgs)
            {
                strncpy(&RAM[R[$R3]],programArgs.args[R[$R2]],256);
                RAM[R[$R3]+256]=0;
                R[$R4]=0;
                R[$R5]= strlen(&RAM[R[$R3]]);
                R[$R5]= R[$R5] + 1;
            }
            else
            {
                R[$R4]=1;
                R[$R5]=0;
            }

        }break;
        default:
        {
            ERROR1_LVL2("INT 5 %lu function not handled",(U1)R[$R1]);
        }
```

```
        }
        return;

    }/*end handleCommandLine*/
```

INT 6 – Memory Diagnostics

The HEC virtual machine has a relatively simple memory arrangement. There are three memory segments: a bytecode segment, a heap segment, and a stack segment. This interrupt provides a function that offers status information on the size of these segments. In addition, this interrupt also provides a routine that allows the memory status of the host operating system to be queried. This could be useful in the event that the HEC virtual machine needs to launch other virtual machines and wants to see if there is enough available memory to support new virtual machines.

Table 6-7 displays a summary of the memory status functions implemented.

Table 6-7

Interrupt	Function ($R1)	Description
6	0	Returns the status of virtual machine memory
6	1	Returns the status of host OS memory

Now we'll take a look at the INT 6 functions individually.

INT 6 $R1=0   Returns the status of virtual machine memory
    Inputs   None
    Outputs $R2= Size, in bytes, of the bytecode segment
                $R3= Size, in bytes, of the heap segment
                $R4= Size, in bytes, of the stack segment
                $R5= Total memory allocated by the virtual machine

INT 6 $R1=1   Returns the status of the host operating system's memory
    Inputs   None
    Outputs $R2= Total physical memory available
                $R3= Total physical memory in use
                $R4= Total paging memory available
                $R5= Total paging memory in use

The following is an example of HEC assembly code that uses INT 6 functions. This code is in a file named `memtest.asm` on the companion CD-ROM.

```
.PB main

#get VM memory stats
LQI $R1,0
INT 6
MOV $R20,$R2
MOV $R21,$R3
MOV $R22,$R4
MOV $R23,$R5
```

```
          MOV $R2,$R20
          LQI $R1,20
          INT 0

          LQI $R2,10
          LQI $R1,16
          INT 0
          LQI $R2,13
          LQI $R1,16
          INT 0

          MOV $R2,$R21
          LQI $R1,20
          INT 0

          LQI $R2,10
          LQI $R1,16
          INT 0
          LQI $R2,13
          LQI $R1,16
          INT 0

          MOV $R2,$R22
          LQI $R1,20
          INT 0

          LQI $R2,10
          LQI $R1,16
          INT 0
          LQI $R2,13
          LQI $R1,16
          INT 0

          MOV $R2,$R23
          LQI $R1,20
          INT 0

          LQI $R2,10
          LQI $R1,16
          INT 0
          LQI $R2,13
          LQI $R1,16
          INT 0

          #get host OS memory stats
          LQI $R1,1
          INT 6
          MOV $R20,$R2
          MOV $R21,$R3
          MOV $R22,$R4
          MOV $R23,$R5
```

```
MOV $R2,$R20
LQI $R1,20
INT 0

LQI $R2,10
LQI $R1,16
INT 0
LQI $R2,13
LQI $R1,16
INT 0

MOV $R2,$R21
LQI $R1,20
INT 0

LQI $R2,10
LQI $R1,16
INT 0
LQI $R2,13
LQI $R1,16
INT 0

MOV $R2,$R22
LQI $R1,20
INT 0

LQI $R2,10
LQI $R1,16
INT 0
LQI $R2,13
LQI $R1,16
INT 0

MOV $R2,$R23
LQI $R1,20
INT 0

LQI $R2,10
LQI $R1,16
INT 0
LQI $R2,13
LQI $R1,16
INT 0
HALT
.PE
```

Running this program would produce the following type of session at the command line:

```
521
65536
65536
131593
66527232
```

```
62783488
2080952320
49790976
```

The INT 6 functions are implemented within the `handleMemoryStatus()` routine, located in `intwin32.c`.

```c
void handleMemoryStatus()
{
    switch((U1)R[$R1])
    {
        case 0:
        {
            R[$R2]=R[$BE]+1;
            R[$R3]=R[$HE]-R[$HS]+1;
            R[$R4]=R[$TOP]-R[$SS]+1;
            R[$R5]=R[$TOP]+1;

        }break;
        case 1:
        {
            MEMORYSTATUS ms;
            GlobalMemoryStatus(&ms);
            R[$R2]=ms.dwTotalPhys;
            R[$R3]=ms.dwTotalPhys - ms.dwAvailPhys;
            R[$R4]=ms.dwTotalPageFile;
            R[$R5]=ms.dwTotalPageFile - ms.dwAvailPageFile;

        }break;
        default:
        {
            ERROR1_LVL2("INT 6 %lu function not handled",(U1)R[$R1]);
        }
    }
    return;

}/*end handleMemoryStatus*/
```

INT 7 – Dynamic Memory Allocation

The heap segment of the virtual machine's address space is a repository for memory that can be acquired by a program during execution. Thus, dynamic memory allocation is really more a matter of managing the heap effectively.

In Chapter 2, I presented a survey of dynamic memory allocation techniques. My basic design requirements (portability, simplicity, and performance) led me to adopt a manual memory management scheme for allocating and reclaiming real estate in the virtual machine's heap segment. I looked, with keen anticipation, at several garbage collection implementations. In the end, they usually violated at least two of my three design requirements. They were either complicated or they performed poorly.

As it stands now, if garbage collection is to be implemented, it will have to be done at the compiler level. In other words, the compiler will have to emit special code to provide the infrastructure for automatic memory reclamation.

For the sake of protecting the host operating system from the virtual machine, I decided to set the heap size at a fixed value when the virtual machine initializes. This prevents a single virtual machine from commandeering all of the host machine's resources. In this sense, a HEC virtual machine cannot produce the type of behavior associated with a memory leak.

Table 6-8 displays a summary of the dynamic memory allocation functions implemented.

Table 6-8

Interrupt	Function ($R1)	Description
7	0	Allocates memory in the heap
7	1	Frees memory in the heap
7	2	Prints out memory arrangement summary to stdout
7	3	Initializes the heap

Now we'll take a look at the INT 7 functions individually.

INT 7 $R1=0   Allocates memory in the heap

If an error occurs, or there is no free memory, then $R3 will be set to 0. The 0 address is always in the bytecode segment of the virtual machine's address space, so this is a natural way to indicate a problem.

Inputs $R2= The number of bytes to allocate

Outputs $R3= The address of the first byte of the allocated block of memory, or 0 if an error occurs

INT 7 $R1=1   Frees memory in the heap

Inputs $R2= The address of the memory block in the heap to free

Outputs $R3= 1 if an error has occurred, 0 otherwise

INT 7 $R1=2   Prints out memory arrangement summary to stdout

This function is useful for debugging the heap. The status of each allocated and free block of heap memory will be printed out in the order in which the blocks appear in memory, starting at the bottom of the heap. The information for each block will be printed in the following format:

```
[ previous, current, next, status ]
```

previous = The address of the previous block (or 0 if there is none)

current = The address of the current block of heap memory

next   = The address of the following block (or 0 if there is none)

status   = FREE or RESERVED

Inputs   None

Outputs   None

INT 7 $R1=3   Initializes the heap

This function has to be invoked before any of the other heap management functions are called. A compiler would automatically place a call to this function at the beginning of a program.

    Inputs   None
    Outputs   None

The following is an example of HEC assembly code that uses INT 7 functions. This code is in a file named `alloc.asm` on the companion CD-ROM.

```
.PB main

#init the heap
LQI $R1,3
INT 7

#allocate memory, place address in $R20
LQI $R2,20
LQI $R1,0
INT 7
MOV $R20,$R3

MOV $R2,$R20
LQI $R1,20
INT 0

LQI $R2,10
LQI $R1,16
INT 0
LQI $R2,13
LQI $R1,16
INT 0

#allocate memory, place address in $R21
LQI $R2,11
LQI $R1,0
INT 7
MOV $R21,$R3

MOV $R2,$R21
LQI $R1,20
INT 0

LQI $R2,10
LQI $R1,16
INT 0
LQI $R2,13
LQI $R1,16
INT 0

#allocate memory, place address in $R22
LQI $R2,1
LQI $R1,0
```

```
                  INT 7
                  MOV $R22,$R3

                  MOV $R2,$R22
                  LQI $R1,20
                  INT 0

                  LQI $R2,10
                  LQI $R1,16
                  INT 0
                  LQI $R2,13
                  LQI $R1,16
                  INT 0

                  #print out heap
                  LQI $R1,2
                  INT 7

                  #dealloc memory
                  MOV $R2,$R20
                  LQI $R1,1
                  INT 7

                  #print out heap
                  LQI $R1,2
                  INT 7

                  #dealloc memory
                  MOV $R2,$R21
                  LQI $R1,1
                  INT 7

                  #print out heap
                  LQI $R1,2
                  INT 7

                  #dealloc memory
                  MOV $R2,$R22
                  LQI $R1,1
                  INT 7

                  #print out heap
                  LQI $R1,2
                  INT 7

                  HALT
                  .PE
```

Running this program would produce the following type of session at the command line:

```
375
412
440
--HEAP--
[0,358,395,RESERVED]
```

```
[358,395,423,RESERVED]
[395,423,441,RESERVED]
[423,441,0,FREE]
--HEAP--
[0,358,395,FREE]
[358,395,423,RESERVED]
[395,423,441,RESERVED]
[423,441,0,FREE]
--HEAP--
[0,358,423,FREE]
[358,423,441,RESERVED]
[423,441,0,FREE]
--HEAP--
[0,358,0,FREE]
```

The INT 7 functions are implemented within the `handleAllocCall()` routine, which is located in `intwin32.c`.

Heap memory is organized as a series of free and reserved memory blocks. Each memory block in the heap, be it free or reserved, is linked to a previous block and a following block (with the exception of the first and last memory blocks). I decided to eschew the use of external data structures in favor of using heap memory itself to construct the linked list mechanism. Thus, each heap memory block is partitioned into four different sections. This is illustrated in Figure 6-4.

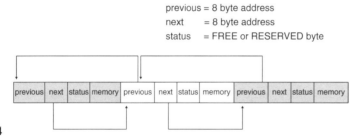

Figure 6-4

The first section takes up the first eight bytes of the memory block and is used to store the address of the first byte of the previous memory block. The second section also takes up eight bytes and is used to store the address of the first byte of the memory block following the current memory block. The third section of the memory block is a status byte that indicates if the block is FREE or RESERVED. The fourth section of the memory block is the memory that is allocated. The fourth section is the "payload," so to speak.

The first three sections of a memory block constitute a 17-byte header. It is pure overhead and will prefix every block of memory allocated. This header is what allows the memory management code to traverse the list of blocks in order to allocate and free memory. For the sake of making the following explanation easier to follow, I will represent heap memory blocks using a notation that is different from the actual layout of the memory block (see Figure 6-5).

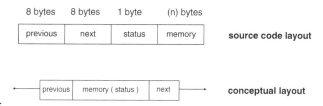

Figure 6-5

Heap memory initially starts out as a single, free memory block. The pointers to the previous and next memory blocks (the first two sections of the memory block header) have their values set to 0, to indicate that there is no previous or next block. This is displayed in Figure 6-6.

Figure 6-6

When the memory management code needs to allocate memory, it will search the list of heap blocks for the first free memory block that is large enough to satisfy the memory allocation request. This is known as a first fit allocation policy. What happens next depends upon the actual size of the free memory block. If enough memory exists, the memory manager will split the existing free block of memory into a reserved block and another free block. Otherwise, the memory manager will allocate the entire block of memory for the request and mark the block as reserved. This is illustrated in Figure 6-7.

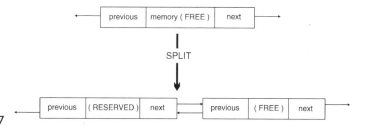

Figure 6-7

If the memory manager does not find a memory block big enough to answer the request, then it will return an address of 0. It just so happens that 0 is the address of the first byte in the bytecode segment of the virtual machine. This is nowhere near the heap segment, so it should be obvious that returning the 0 address indicates an error.

When a block of memory is set free, the status section of its header is set from RESERVED to FREE. Reclaiming an allocated memory block in the heap is typically a matter of merging the allocated block with the free blocks of memory. Given that all memory blocks, with the exception of the first and the last, have adjacent memory blocks preceding and following them, there are four distinct cases to handle (see Table 6-9):

Table 6-9

Scenario	Previous Block	Allocated Block	Next Block	Shorthand
1	free	reserved	free	FRF
2	free	reserved	reserved	FRR
3	reserved	reserved	free	RRF
4	reserved	reserved	reserved	RRR

In each case, the allocated block's status will go from RESERVED to FREE. The goal then becomes to merge free blocks together. In the first scenario (FRF), the allocated block will merge with both the free block preceding it and the free block following it to form one large free block. In the second scenario (FRR), the allocated block will merge with the free block preceding it. In the third scenario (RRF), the allocated block will merge with the free block following it. The fourth case, where all three blocks are reserved, is the only scenario in which there is no merging.

This merging procedure is illustrated in Figure 6-8.

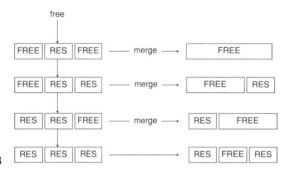

Figure 6-8

Now that you've waded through the theory, here is the source. I recommend starting with the `handleAllocCall()` function and tracing through the various interrupt functions.

```
#define FREE        0
#define RESERVED    1
char *statStr[] = {"FREE","RESERVED"};

/* Memory block header = 17 bytes = 8 previous + 8 next + status */

#define MEM_HEADER   17

#define prev(i)    *((U8 *)&memory[i])
#define next(i)    *((U8 *)&memory[i+8])
#define status(i)  memory[i+16]
#define size(i)    next(i)-i-MEM_HEADER

/* if going to split free block, need at least 8 bytes in new free part */

#define MIN_FREE_BYTES  8
```

```
U1 *memory;      /*alias for RAM */
U8 first;        /*stores address of first byte of heap*/
U8 last;         /*store address of last byte of heap + 1*/

/* prototypes-------------------------------------------------------*/

void heapInit();
U8 alloc(U8 nbytes);
int currentNodeAlloc(U8 i,U8 nbytes);
void deAlloc(U8 address);
void printMemory();

/* definitions------------------------------------------------------*/

void handleAllocCall()
{
    switch((U1)R[$R1])
    {
        case 0:
        {
            R[$R3] = alloc(R[$R2]);

        }break;
        case 1:
        {
            deAlloc(R[$R2]);

        }break;
        case 2:
        {
            printMemory();

        }break;
        case 3:
        {
            heapInit();

        }break;
        default:
        {
            ERROR1_LVL2("INT 7 %lu function not handled",(U1)R[$R1]);
        }
    }
    return;

}/*end handleAllocCall*/

void heapInit()
{
    /* set up scale parameters*/
    memory=RAM;
    first=R[$HS];
    last=R[$HE]+1;
```

```
            /*initialize the entire heap*/
            prev(first)=0;
            next(first)=0;
            status(first)=FREE;

            return;

        }/*end heapInit*/

        U8 alloc(U8 nbytes)
        {
            int ret;
            U8 i;

            i=first;

            if(status(i)==FREE)
            {
                ret = currentNodeAlloc(i,nbytes);
                if(ret==TRUE)
                {
                    return(i+MEM_HEADER);
                }
            }

            while(next(i)!=0)
            {
                i=next(i);
                if(status(i)==FREE)
                {
                    ret = currentNodeAlloc(i,nbytes);
                    if(ret==TRUE)
                    {
                        return(i+MEM_HEADER);
                    }
                }
            }

            return(0);

        }/*end alloc*/

        int currentNodeAlloc(U8 i,U8 nbytes)
        {
            U8 size;

            /*handle case of current block being the last*/

            if(next(i)==0){ size = last-i-MEM_HEADER; }
            else{ size = size(i); }

            /*either split current block, use entire current block, or fail*/
```

```
                  if(size >= nbytes + MEM_HEADER + MIN_FREE_BYTES)
                  {
                      U8 old_next;
                      U8 old_block;
                      U8 new_block;

                      old_next = next(i);
                      old_block = i;

                      /*fix up original block*/

                      next(i)=i+MEM_HEADER+nbytes;
                      new_block = next(i);
                      status(i)=RESERVED;

                      /*set up new free block*/

                      i = next(i);
                      next(i)=old_next;
                      prev(i)=old_block;
                      status(i)=FREE;

                      /*right neighbor must point to new free block*/

                      if(next(i)!=0)
                      {
                          i = next(i);
                          prev(i)=new_block;
                      }

                      return(TRUE);
                  }
              else if(size >= nbytes)
              {
                      status(i)=RESERVED;
                      return(TRUE);
              }

              return(FALSE);

}/*end currentNodeAlloc*/

void deAlloc(U8 address)
{
      U8 block;
      U8 lblock;
      U8 rblock;

      block = address-MEM_HEADER;
      lblock = prev(block);
      rblock = next(block);

      if((address>R[$HE])||(address<R[$HS]))
      {
```

```
            ERROR1_LVL2("deAlloc(): %I64u address out of bounds!\n",address);
            return;
      }

      /*
      4 cases: FFF->F, FFR->FR, RFF->RF, RFR
      always want to merge free blocks
      */

      if((lblock!=0)&&(rblock!=0)&&(status(lblock)==FREE)&&(status(rblock)==FREE))
      {
            next(lblock)=next(rblock);
            status(lblock)=FREE;
            if(next(rblock)!=0){ prev(next(rblock))=lblock; }
      }
      else if((lblock!=0)&&(status(lblock)==FREE))
      {
            next(lblock)=next(block);
            status(lblock)=FREE;
            if(next(block)!=0){ prev(next(block))=lblock; }
      }
      else if((rblock!=0)&&(status(rblock)==FREE))
      {
            next(block)=next(rblock);
            status(block)=FREE;
            if(next(rblock)!=0){ prev(next(rblock))=block; }
      }
      else{ status(block)=FREE; }

      return;

}/*end deAlloc*/

void printMemory()
{
      U8 i;
      i=first;
      printf("--HEAP--\n");
      printf("[%I64u,%I64u,%I64u,%s]\n",prev(i),i,next(i),statStr[status(i)]);
      while(next(i)!=0)
      {
            i=next(i);
            printf("[%I64u,%I64u,%I64u,%s]\n",prev(i),i,next(i),statStr[status(i)]);
      }
      return;

}/*end printMemory*/
```

INT 8 – Mathematical Functions

Table 6-10 displays a summary of the mathematical functions implemented.

Table 6-10

Interrupt	Function ($R1)	Description
8	0	Converts a string to an integer
8	1	Converts a string to a floating-point value
8	2	Converts an integer to a string
8	3	Converts a floating-point value to a string
8	4	Determines the status of a floating-point value
8	5	Computes the absolute value of an integer
8	6	Computes the absolute value of a floating-point value
8	7	Computes the ceiling of a floating-point value
8	8	Computes the floor of a floating-point value
8	9	Exponential function
8	10	Natural logarithm function
8	11	Base 10 logarithm function
8	12	Power function
8	13	Computes the square root of a floating-point value
8	14	Cosine function
8	15	Sine function
8	16	Tangent function
8	17	Arc cosine function
8	18	Arc sine function
8	19	Arc tangent function
8	20	Hyperbolic cosine function
8	21	Hyperbolic sine function
8	22	Hyperbolic tangent function

Now we'll take a look at the INT 8 functions individually.

INT 8 $R1=0   Converts a string to an integer

Inputs $R2= The address of the null-terminated string to convert to an integer

Outputs $R3= Integer equivalent of the string, or 0 if the conversion could not be made

INT 8 $R1=1   Converts a string to a floating-point value

Inputs $R2= The address of the null-terminated string to convert to a floating-point value. This string must have the following format:

`[sign][digits][.digits][ e | E [sign] digits]`

Outputs $D1= Floating-point equivalent of the string, or 0 if the conversion could not be made

INT 8 $R1=2 Converts an integer to a string
    Inputs $R2= The integer to convert to a string
    Outputs $R3= The address of a buffer to receive the string equivalent

INT 8 $R1=3 Converts a floating-point value to a string
    Inputs $D1= The floating-point value to convert to a string
    Outputs $R3= The address of a buffer to receive the string equivalent

INT 8 $R1=4 Determines the status of a floating-point value

The status of a floating-point value may be one of the following:

Table 6-11

Status Value	Description
0	Negative infinity
1	Negative normalized
2	Negative denormalized
3	Negative 0
4	Positive 0
5	Positive denormalized
6	Positive normalized
7	Positive infinity
8	NAN

Nonzero finite values can be either normalized or denormalized. Normalized numbers are basically your everyday, run-of-the-mill, floating-point values that can be encoded in normal format. If a number is in normalized form, you've got nothing to worry about.

Denormalized numbers are too small, too close to zero, to represent using the normal format. Denormalized numbers represent an underflow condition.

A floating-point value is said to be Not A Number (NAN) if it cannot be represented in the IEEE 754 standard format. In other words, the number is nonsensical as it is not a part of the real number line.
    Inputs $D1= A double value to evaluate
    Outputs $R2= The status of the floating-point value

INT 8 $R1=5 Computes the absolute value of a 32-bit integer
    Inputs $R2= The 32-bit integer value
    Outputs $R3= The absolute value of the integer

INT 8 $R1=6 Computes the absolute value of a floating-point value
    Inputs $D1= A floating-point value
    Outputs $D2= The absolute value of the floating-point value

INT 8 $R1=7 Computes the ceiling of a floating-point value

The ceiling of a value is the smallest integer not less than the value.
    Inputs $D1= A value to find the ceiling of
    Outputs $D2= The ceiling integer

INT 8 $R1=8   Computes the floor of a floating-point value

The floor of a value is the largest integer less than the value.

    Inputs $D1= A value to find the floor of
    Outputs $D2= The floor integer

INT 8 $R1=9   Exponential function

    Inputs $D1= Argument to the function
    Outputs $D2= The return value of the function

INT 8 $R1=10   Natural logarithm function

    Inputs $D1= Argument to the function
    Outputs $D2= The return value of the function

INT 8 $R1=11   Base 10 logarithm function

    Inputs $D1= Argument to the function
    Outputs $D2= The return value of the function

INT 8 $R1=12   Power function

    Inputs $D1= Value to be taken to a power
                 $D2= Exponent value
    Outputs $D3= Computes $D1 taken to the power in $D2

INT 8 $R1=13   Computes the square root of a floating-point value

    Inputs $D1= A nonnegative floating-point value
    Outputs $D2= The square root of the floating-point value

INT 8 $R1=14   Cosine function

    Inputs $D1= Argument to the function
    Outputs $D2= The return value of the function

INT 8 $R1=15   Sine function

    Inputs $D1= Argument to the function
    Outputs $D2= The return value of the function

INT 8 $R1=16   Tangent function

    Inputs $D1= Argument to the function
    Outputs $D2= The return value of the function

INT 8 $R1=17   Arc cosine function

    Inputs $D1= Argument to the function
    Outputs $D2= The return value of the function

INT 8 $R1=18   Arc sine function

    Inputs $D1= Argument to the function
    Outputs $D2= The return value of the function

INT 8 $R1=19   Arc tangent function

    Inputs $D1= Argument to the function
    Outputs $D2= The return value of the function

INT 8 $R1=20   Hyperbolic cosine function
Inputs $D1= Argument to the function
Outputs $D2= The return value of the function

INT 8 $R1=21   Hyperbolic sine function
Inputs $D1= Argument to the function
Outputs $D2= The return value of the function

INT 8 $R1=22   Hyperbolic tangent function
Inputs $D1= Argument to the function
Outputs $D2= The return value of the function

The INT 8 functions are implemented within the `handleMathCall()` routine, located in `intwin32.c`.

```c
#include<float.h>
#include<math.h>

void handleMathCall()
{
    switch((U1)R[$R1])
    {
        case 0:
        {
            R[$R3]=_atoi64(&RAM[R[$R2]]);

        }break;
        case 1:
        {
            Rd[$D1]=atof(&RAM[R[$R2]]);

        }break;
        case 2:
        {
            sprintf(&RAM[R[$R3]],"%I64d",R[$R2]);

        }break;
        case 3:
        {
            sprintf(&RAM[R[$R3]],"%e",Rd[$D1]);

        }break;
        case 4:
        {
            switch(_fpclass(Rd[$D1]))
            {
                case _FPCLASS_NINF:{ R[$R2]= 0; }break;
                case _FPCLASS_NN:{ R[$R2]= 1; }break;
                case _FPCLASS_ND:{ R[$R2]= 2; }break;
                case _FPCLASS_NZ:{ R[$R2]= 3; }break;
                case _FPCLASS_PZ:{ R[$R2]= 4; }break;
                case _FPCLASS_PD:{ R[$R2]= 5; }break;
                case _FPCLASS_PN:{ R[$R2]= 6; }break;
```

```
                          case _FPCLASS_PINF:{ R[$R2]= 7; }break;
                          case _FPCLASS_SNAN:{ R[$R2]= 8; }break;
                          case _FPCLASS_QNAN:{ R[$R2]= 8; }break;
                          default:{ R[$R2]= 8; }break;
                }

        }break;
        case 5:
        {
                R[$R3] = labs((long)R[$R2]);

        }break;
        case 6:
        {
                Rd[$D2] = fabs(Rd[$D1]);

        }break;
        case 7:
        {
                Rd[$D2] = ceil(Rd[$D1]);

        }break;
        case 8:
        {
                Rd[$D2] = floor(Rd[$D1]);

        }break;
        case 9:
        {
                Rd[$D2] = exp(Rd[$D1]);

        }break;
        case 10:
        {
                Rd[$D2] = log(Rd[$D1]);

        }break;
        case 11:
        {
                Rd[$D2] = log10(Rd[$D1]);

        }break;
        case 12:
        {
                Rd[$D3] = pow(Rd[$D1],Rd[$D2]);

        }break;
        case 13:
        {
                Rd[$D2] = sqrt(Rd[$D1]);

        }break;
        case 14:
        {
```

```
                              Rd[$D2] = cos(Rd[$D1]);

             }break;
             case 15:
             {
                   Rd[$D2] = sin(Rd[$D1]);

             }break;
             case 16:
             {
                   Rd[$D2] = tan(Rd[$D1]);

             }break;
             case 17:
             {
                   Rd[$D2] = acos(Rd[$D1]);

             }break;
             case 18:
             {
                   Rd[$D2] = asin(Rd[$D1]);

             }break;
             case 19:
             {
                   Rd[$D2] = atan(Rd[$D1]);

             }break;
             case 20:
             {
                   Rd[$D2] = cosh(Rd[$D1]);

             }break;
             case 21:
             {
                   Rd[$D2] = sinh(Rd[$D1]);

             }break;
             case 22:
             {
                   Rd[$D2] = tanh(Rd[$D1]);

             }break;
             default:
             {
                   ERROR1_LVL2("INT 8 %lu function not handled",(U1)R[$R1]);
             }
      }
      return;

}/*end handleMathCall*/
```

INT 9 – Interfacing with Native Code

Legacy code is a fact of life. This is particularly true when it comes to an ancient behemoth like COBOL. In 1997, the Gartner Group estimated that there were over 180 billion lines of COBOL code in use and five million new lines of COBOL code being written each year. Authors like Carol Baroudi have even estimated the number of lines of legacy COBOL code at 500 billion lines. Needless to say, this mountain of code has taken on a life of its own and probably developed enough inertia to last at least another hundred years.

The preponderance of COBOL is partially due to historical forces. COBOL was adopted by the United States Department of Defense (DoD) in 1960 and became a de facto standard. The reason for this is that the DoD, the largest purchaser of computer hardware both then and now, would not buy hardware for data processing unless the vendor provided a COBOL compiler. Another reason COBOL is so widespread is due to the fact that COBOL is very good at what it is designed for—executing business calculations. When it comes to performing financial computations to fractions of a cent without introducing rounding errors, COBOL is still the king of the hill. The language features that support financial mathematics in COBOL are a very natural part of the language and extremely easy to use.

NOTE Some people have a love/hate relationship with COBOL. I am one of those people. In 1999 I was given the opportunity to get my hands dirty, like thousands of other developers, tackling the Y2K problem. I have worked primarily with MicroFocus COBOL on several high-end Unix machines and I have learned to appreciate its speed and straightforward syntax. From the viewpoint of a systems engineer, the lack of an activation record and the absence of dynamic memory allocation makes a COBOL application a lot easier to translate into assembler. Everything is global, and the code and data segments are a fixed-size chunk of memory. This can be a godsend in a production environment where it helps to know ahead of time what kind of load a set of applications is going to place on machine resources.

What I found agonizing about COBOL was how the programmers, in the days of yore, abused it. I found variables that were named after someone's pet. I found dozens of procedures that varied by only one or two lines of code. There was so much dead code littering the source repository that I usually had to crank up a debugger to successfully ferret out live sections of code.

Writing lucid COBOL relies upon the developer to be sensible enough to abide by a certain number of naming and organizational conventions. The problem with this is that the language does nothing to encourage a developer to abide by these conventions. A programmer is free to ignore all of them and just do whatever he wants. The result of this is what is known in software engineering as a "big ball of mud." More messy code gets slapped onto already messy code until a huge, amorphous ball of mud is produced that no one knows how to move.

Software architects at large banks and insurance companies do not have the luxury of being able to pick the latest tools and methodologies and rewrite everything from scratch. In fact, most seasoned architects are hesitant to replace legacy systems, and with good reason.

Legacy code may be old, but it supports core business functionality and has been painstakingly debugged. In this kind of situation, legacy code is seen as a corporate asset that represents the investment of hundreds of thousands of man-hours. An architect who actually does want to overhaul a system will, no doubt, face resistance from a CIO whose orientation tends towards dollars and cents. If a system does what it's supposed to and helps to generate income, why fix it? Throwing everything away for the sake of technology alone is a ridiculously poor excuse.

Another factor that inhibits the replacement of legacy code is the sheer size of an existing code base. In order to replace old code with new code, you have to completely understand the functionality the old code provides. In a million-line labyrinth of 80-column code, business logic is hard to extract and duplicate. Often times, the people who wrote the code have left the company or have been promoted to different divisions. Instituting even relatively simple changes can prove to be expensive and involve months of reverse engineering and testing. I've known Y2K programmers who were too scared to modify legacy code. The old code was so convoluted that they didn't know what kind of repercussions their changes would have.

Will COBOL ever die? Will it be replaced? I would like to think so. However, I suspect that COBOL houses will probably, fundamentally, stay COBOL houses. They may occasionally renovate with Object COBOL, or slap on a new layer of paint with Java, but replacing the plumbing of an aging mansion is a very expensive proposition. In fact, it's often cheaper just to tear the house down and build a new one. Try explaining this to the CEO of a Fortune 100 company.

Given that legacy code is not easily supplanted, the idea, then, is that new technology will serve to augment the existing legacy code instead of replacing it. To do this, a mechanism has to exist for the old and new code to interact.

As it turns out, almost every commercial vendor that markets a development tool will provide hooks to invoke C code. For example, MicroFocus supplies special features in its COBOL programming suite that allow C code to be called from within a COBOL application. Sun Microsystem's Java run-time has a native interface which allows the Java run-time to load and run C functions. Even Microsoft's Visual Basic provides a set of API calls that permit routines written in C to be invoked. The C language has turned out to be a kind of universal glue through which disparate development environments can fraternize.

 NOTE   I once worked for an ERP company whose middleware consisted of several distinct layers, each of which was implemented in a different programming language. Their presentation manager, written in Java, sent user requests to the transaction manager. The transaction manager, written in C, typically administered hundreds of business applications which were written in COBOL. The business applications, in turn, invoked routines written in C to commit information to the data store.

I can think of three ways that would allow the HEC run-time to interact with native code:

- Compiling to a common object file format

- Porting a native compiler to generate bytecode

- Loading and calling shared libraries

The first approach involves taking the HEC run-time and the corresponding bytecode executable, and merging them together into a single native object file. This object file can then be linked with the host platform's linker to produce a native executable. Naturally, this would require constructing another tool to perform the object file creation, but this isn't what scared me away. What scared me away was the fact that there are so many different object file formats and each one is sufficiently complicated. There is the OMF object file format, the COFF object file format, the ELF object file format, the A.OUT object file format, and the list goes on. Each object file format has its own peculiarities with regard to how the header, relocation records, and symbol table are stored and arranged. The specification of Intel's OMF format takes up page after page, so I immediately started looking for alternatives to this approach.

The second approach entails porting a native compiler (i.e., a FORTRAN compiler or a COBOL compiler) so that the back end of the compiler generates HEC bytecode instructions instead of native machine instructions. The intent is that all high-level source code, regardless of the language used, will be translated into bytecode. Again, I am but a single person. I could probably target the HEC virtual machine with a high-level language or two, but I don't have the time or energy to port every language. Because of this, I moved on to the third approach.

The third approach appealed to me the most. Loading a shared library (or a dynamic-link library (DLL), if you're on Windows) within the context of the HEC virtual machine is relatively easy. Most of the work has already been performed via vendor-specific library functions.

But what about mapping HEC data types to native C data types? Doesn't each platform have its own interpretation of the atomic C data types? Wouldn't this require special header files?

The Java run-time follows this route. Each port of the Java run-time has its own special header file that maps Java data types to native C data types. I decided to follow a different route. Rather than exchange data directly through a particular type mapping, I decided that the HEC run-time and the native code would exchange data using XML. This is a much more flexible and general data interchange technique. Naturally, there is a certain amount of overhead associated with parsing XML. However, I thought that the portability achieved would be worth the effort spent on parsing.

The HEC native interface is actually very simple. The interrupt function loads a shared library and feeds the shared library a string of XML text. The exposed DLL routine that receives this XML is what I will refer to as a *gateway*. The gateway routine is responsible for reading the XML and using the data within the XML to determine which secondary native function to invoke. The gateway routine is called such because it is the checkpoint that every native call, for a given shared library, must pass through. Think of the gateway as a native code middleman that delegates calls to other shared library functions. Note that each shared library will need to define its own gateway routine. When the native function which the gateway routine invoked on behalf of the HEC run-time is done, it will return a snippet of XML back to the gateway. The gateway will then return this XML back to the virtual machine. Thus, the input and output mechanism is nothing more than XML-formatted text.

This entire process is illustrated in Figure 6-9.

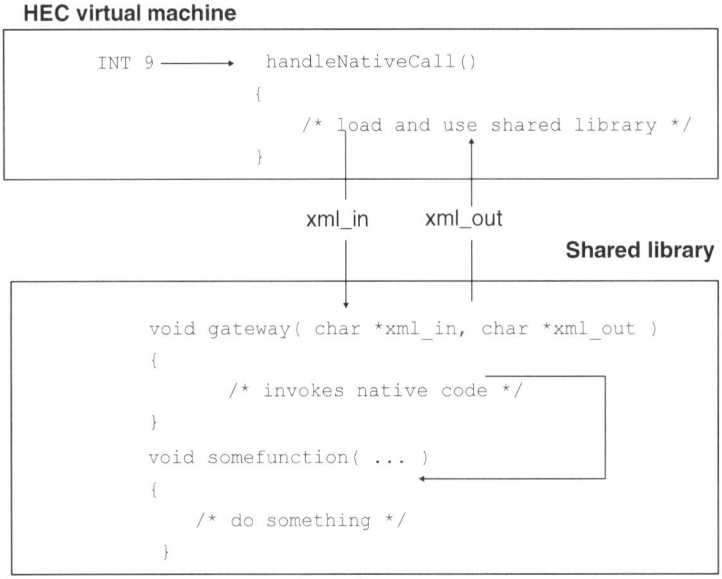

Figure 6-9

The format of the XML, which passes back and forth between the HEC run-time and the native code, is completely up to you. It is your responsibility to have the native client parse and process the XML. You can use any XML API that you like and construct your own DTD to use with it. For example, your XML documents could be constructed using the following DTD:

```
<?xml version="1.0" encoding="UTF-8" standalone="yes" ?>
<!DOCTYPE NativeCall [
    <!ELEMENT NativeCall (inputParameter*,returnParameter*)>
    <!ATTLIST  NativeCall
            function CDATA          #REQUIRED>
    <!ELEMENT inputParameter EMPTY>
    <!ATTLIST inputParameter
            name  CDATA            #REQUIRED
            type  (ATOMIC|COMPOUND) #REQUIRED
            value CDATA            #REQUIRED>
    <!ELEMENT returnParameter EMPTY>
    <!ATTLIST returnParameter
            name  CDATA            #REQUIRED
            type  (ATOMIC|COMPOUND) #REQUIRED
            value CDATA            #REQUIRED>
]>
```

As you can see, this DTD specifies the native function the gateway routine should invoke, and the parameters which should be passed back and forth to this native function. The actual XML passed to the gateway would look like:

```
<NativeCall function="updateStatus">
    <inputParameter name="average" type="ATOMIC"  value="56.5"/>
    <inputParameter name="status" type="COMPOUND" value="high;tight;77"/>
```

```
        <inputParameter name="alert" type="ATOMIC" value="true"/>
    </NativeCall>
```

The XML the native code passes back might look something like:

```
<NativeCall function="updateStatus">
    <returnParameter name="result" type="ATOMIC" value="3.143"/>
    <returnParameter name="levels" type="COMPOUND" value="23;47;86"/>
</NativeCall>
```

Notice how I have allowed for the passing of compound data types. In the previous XML snippet, the variable named `status` stores three values: two strings and an integer. These values are delimited by semicolons. I've also constructed the DTD so that the native code can return more than one output parameter to the virtual machine.

Table 6-12 displays a summary of the native code interface functions.

Table 6-12

Interrupt	Function ($R1)	Description
9	0	Acquires a handle to a shared library
9	1	Invokes a native method from a shared library
9	2	Frees the shared library

Now we'll take a look at the INT 9 functions individually.

INT 9 $R1=0   Acquires a handle to a shared library

This function loads a shared library into memory. Naturally, calling a shared library requires that it be available in memory, so calling this routine is a prerequisite.

Inputs $R2= Address of a null-terminated string storing the library's name
Outputs $R3= A handle to the shared library
            $R4= 1 if an error has occurred, and 0 otherwise

INT 9 $R1=1   Invokes a native method from a shared library

This method invokes the gateway routine and feeds it an XML document. The XML document returned from the native code is stored in a return buffer.

Inputs $R2= The handle to the shared library
            $R3= Address of a null-terminated string storing XML
            $R4= Address of a buffer to hold the XML returned
Outputs $R5= 1 if an error has occurred, and 0 otherwise

INT 9 $R1=2   Frees a shared library

When you're done with a shared library, you should set it free. Otherwise, you run the risk of wasting system resources and slowing down your machine.

Inputs $R2= The handle to the shared library
Outputs $R3= 1 if an error has occurred, and 0 otherwise

The following is an example of HEC assembly code that uses the INT 9 function. This code is in a file named `native.asm` on the companion CD-ROM.

```
.PB main
.PV filename -16
.PV input   -128
.PV output  -512

#allocate local storage
PUSHQ $FP
MOV $FP,$SP
LQI $R7,512
SUB $SP,$SP,$R7

#populate name of shared lib = sharedLib.dll
LAI $R10,$FP,filename
MOV $R14,$R10
LBI $R2,1

LBI $R1,'s'
SB $R1,$R10
ADD $R10,$R10,$R2

LBI $R1,'h'
SB $R1,$R10
ADD $R10,$R10,$R2

LBI $R1,'a'
SB $R1,$R10
ADD $R10,$R10,$R2

LBI $R1,'r'
SB $R1,$R10
ADD $R10,$R10,$R2

LBI $R1,'e'
SB $R1,$R10
ADD $R10,$R10,$R2

LBI $R1,'d'
SB $R1,$R10
ADD $R10,$R10,$R2

LBI $R1,'L'
SB $R1,$R10
ADD $R10,$R10,$R2

LBI $R1,'i'
SB $R1,$R10
ADD $R10,$R10,$R2

LBI $R1,'b'
SB $R1,$R10
ADD $R10,$R10,$R2

LBI $R1,'.'
SB $R1,$R10
```

```
        ADD $R10,$R10,$R2

        LBI $R1,'d'
        SB $R1,$R10
        ADD $R10,$R10,$R2

        LBI $R1,'l'
        SB $R1,$R10
        ADD $R10,$R10,$R2

        LBI $R1,'l'
        SB $R1,$R10
        ADD $R10,$R10,$R2

        LBI $R1,0
        SB $R1,$R10

        #populate XML input <IN>proc1</IN>
        LAI $R10,$FP,input
        MOV $R11,$R10
        LBI $R2,1

        LBI $R1,'<'
        SB $R1,$R10
        ADD $R10,$R10,$R2

        LBI $R1,'I'
        SB $R1,$R10
        ADD $R10,$R10,$R2

        LBI $R1,'N'
        SB $R1,$R10
        ADD $R10,$R10,$R2

        LBI $R1,'>'
        SB $R1,$R10
        ADD $R10,$R10,$R2

        LBI $R1,'p'
        SB $R1,$R10
        ADD $R10,$R10,$R2

        LBI $R1,'r'
        SB $R1,$R10
        ADD $R10,$R10,$R2

        LBI $R1,'o'
        SB $R1,$R10
        ADD $R10,$R10,$R2

        LBI $R1,'c'
        SB $R1,$R10
        ADD $R10,$R10,$R2
```

```
        LBI  $R1,'1'
        SB   $R1,$R10
        ADD  $R10,$R10,$R2

        LBI  $R1,'<'
        SB   $R1,$R10
        ADD  $R10,$R10,$R2

        LBI  $R1,'/'
        SB   $R1,$R10
        ADD  $R10,$R10,$R2

        LBI  $R1,'I'
        SB   $R1,$R10
        ADD  $R10,$R10,$R2

        LBI  $R1,'N'
        SB   $R1,$R10
        ADD  $R10,$R10,$R2

        LBI  $R1,'>'
        SB   $R1,$R10
        ADD  $R10,$R10,$R2

        LBI  $R1,0
        SB   $R1,$R10

        #load the library (put handle in $R20)
        LQI  $R1,0
        MOV  $R2,$R14
        INT  9
        MOV  $R20,$R3

        MOV  $R2,$R4
        LQI  $R1,20
        INT  0

        LQI  $R2,10
        LQI  $R1,16
        INT  0
        LQI  $R2,13
        LQI  $R1,16
        INT  0

        #execute native call
        LAI  $R4,$FP,output
        MOV  $R3,$R11
        MOV  $R2,$R20
        LQI  $R1,1
        INT  9

        LAI  $R2,$FP,output
        LQI  $R1,18
        INT  0
```

```
LQI $R2,10
LQI $R1,16
INT 0
LQI $R2,13
LQI $R1,16
INT 0

#free library
MOV $R2,$R20
LQI $R1,2
INT 9

MOV $R2,$R3
LQI $R1,20
INT 0

LQI $R2,10
LQI $R1,16
INT 0
LQI $R2,13
LQI $R1,16
INT 0

#reclaim local storage
MOV $SP,$FP
POPQ $FP

HALT
.PE
```

This assembly code calls a library named `sharedLib.dll`. I'm now going to provide an example implementation of `sharedLib.dll` on Windows. To give you an idea of where I started, I'm going to give you the source code skeleton that I began with. All Windows DLLs that want to interact with the HEC run-time will need to implement the following skeleton:

```
#include<windows.h>

__declspec(dllexport) void gateway(char *xml_in, char *xml_out)
{
    /*
    the gateway code should
    a) parse the XML
    b) invoke the native code requested by the XML
    */
    return;
}
```

The one function that the DLL absolutely must export is a function named `gateway`. This routine must have the exact type signature specified in the skeleton. There are two string parameters, one for XML input and one for XML output. When HEC invokes a native function, it calls `gateway()` and passes the routine an XML document. The XML is used to indicate to `gateway()` which native function should be invoked and what parameters should be passed.

NOTE Every platform will have its own special syntax for exporting a library method and command line for compiling the C code into a native binary. Windows, Solaris, AIX, and HP-UX all have their peculiarities. Nevertheless, the basic mechanism is the same. The exported (i.e., visible) function has to have the name `gateway()` and it expects two string parameters that facilitate data interchange via XML.

In this particular example, I fleshed out the previous skeleton as follows:

```c
#include<windows.h>
#include<stdio.h>
#include<string.h>

void proc1(char *in,char *out);
void proc2(char *in,char *out);

__declspec(dllexport) void gateway(char *xml_in, char *xml_out)
{
    int i;
    char *cptr;
    char proc[8];

    printf("Inside DLL\n");
    cptr = strchr(xml_in,(int)'p');

    for(i=0;i<5;i++){ proc[i]=cptr[i]; }
    proc[5]='\0';

    switch(proc[4])
    {
        case '1':
        {
            proc1(xml_in,xml_out);
        }break;
        case '2':
        {
            proc2(xml_in,xml_out);
        }break;
        default:
        {
            strcpy(xml_out,"sharedLib: function not found\n");
        }
    }

    return;

}/*end gateway*/

void proc1(char *in,char *out)
{
```

```
        printf("proc1() invoked via->%s\n",in);
        strcpy(out,"<proc1>0</proc1>");
        return;

}/*end proc1*/

void proc2(char *in,char *out)
{
        printf("proc2() invoked via->%s\n",in);
        strcpy(out,"<proc2>0</proc2>");
        return;

}/*end proc2*/
```

For the sake of keeping the example brief and easy to follow, I do not make use of an XML API to parse the input or generate the output. In general, I heartily admit that using raw `string.h` functions to parse XML is not a very powerful approach, but I was more interested in demonstrating the basic operation. I think you get the general idea. The gateway is really just a traffic cop that redirects traffic to the appropriate function based on the contents of the XML input.

 NOTE One thing to keep in mind if you attempt to run this program is that Windows DLLs must be located in a directory that is included in the PATH environmental variable. Otherwise, Windows will not be able to find the required DLL and the call to load it will fail.

Running this program would produce the following type of session at the command line:

```
allocating 131660 bytes
0
Inside DLL
proc1() invoked via-><IN>proc1</IN>
<proc1>0</proc1>
0
```

The INT 9 functions are implemented within the `handleNativeCall()` routine, located in `intwin32.c`.

```
void handleNativeCall()
{
    typedef void (*FunctionPtr)(char*, char*);
    FunctionPtr address;

    switch((U1)R[$R1])
    {
        case 0:
        {
            HINSTANCE file_handle;
            file_handle = LoadLibrary(&RAM[R[$R2]]);
            R[$R3]= (U8)file_handle;
            if(file_handle==NULL){ R[$R4]=1; }
            else{ R[$R4]=0; }
```

```
        }break;
        case 1:
        {
            address =
            (FunctionPtr)GetProcAddress((HINSTANCE)R[$R2],"gateway");
            if(address==NULL)
            {
                R[$R5]=1;
            }
            else
            {
                R[$R5]=0;
                (address)(&RAM[R[$R3]],&RAM[R[$R4]]);
            }

        }break;
        case 2:
        {
            int unload;
            unload = (int)FreeLibrary((HINSTANCE)R[$R2]);
            if(unload==0)
            {
                R[$R3]=1;
            }
            else
            {
                R[$R3]=0;
            }

        }break;
        default:
        {
            ERROR1_LVL2("INT 9 %lu function not handled",(U1)R[$R1]);
        }
    }
    return;

}/*end handleNativeCall*/
```

INT 10 – Interprocess Communication (IPC)

The INT 2 instruction provides the capability to proliferate processes in memory, but in order to truly reap the benefits of load balancing, there has to be a way for the different processes to communicate. There have to be facilities that permit *interprocess communication* (IPC). This section details the IPC functions available to the HEC virtual machine.

IPC Overview

As with all of the virtual machine's interrupts, HEC's IPC resources are based on existing services offered by the host platform. I did some research to explore the different IPC mechanisms I could build upon. I ended up with the following list of IPC primitives:

- Signals
- File locking and record locking
- Semaphores
- Shared memory segments
- Anonymous pipes
- Named pipes
- Remote procedure call
- Sockets

Signals

Signals are low-level alerts that are sent to a running process. There are any number of conditions that generate signals, but most of them have to do with circumstances that would normally require a process to terminate, such as when the user types Ctrl+C, or when the hardware catches a divide-by-zero error. Signals are implemented using interrupts, and typically the hardware details are wrapped by a set of functions that offer a more abstract interface. Signal APIs usually provide facilities to send, register for, and handle signals. If a process does not explicitly register to handle a signal, it can rely on a default signal handler that is provided by the native operating system. Most of the time, the default action is to terminate the process receiving the signal. Little or no information accompanies a signal, so they are really a very primitive notification mechanism.

File Locking

File locking is another basic communication technique. By locking a file, a process can guarantee that it is the only system entity that has ownership of the file. This ownership may be *mandatory* or *advisory*. A mandatory lock means the process owning the file is the only process that can read or write to the file. An advisory lock allows other processes to read and write to a locked file.

A file can be locked to indicate that a certain condition holds. For example, if you build a program and you only want one copy of it to be able to run at a time, you can have the program lock a specific file. If another user tries to launch another copy of your program, the newly created process will realize that the designated file is locked and shut down.

File locking can allow processes to communicate. For example, some database designs allow user processes to modify a database table only after the process has obtained locks on the table's index file and data file. At any given point in time, only a single process can perform an update. This would allow one process to deposit information that another process could retrieve later on. A database used in this way creates a type of asynchronous messaging system.

Record locking is just a special case of file locking where the host operating system allows specific ranges of bytes within a file to be locked. In other words, different processes can place locks on different parts of a file simultaneously.

Semaphores

A semaphore is a more general mechanism than a file lock. Semaphores are used to provide mutually exclusive access to some system resource, which may or may not be a file. The best way to think of a semaphore is to view it as a data structure that can be shared among different processes and acts as a counter. The simplest type of semaphore is what is known as a *binary semaphore*, or *mutex*. It has two possible values: 0 and 1. A binary semaphore provides exclusive access to a single resource. There are two operations, DOWN and UP, used to acquire and free a resource that is guarded by a binary semaphores.

The DOWN operation consists of three steps and can be performed by any process:

1. Examine the counter value of the semaphore.

2. If the value is 1, the process can decrement the counter to 0, assume control of the resource, and complete its DOWN operation.

3. If the value is 0, the process must sleep until the value has been set back to 1 and not be able to fully complete its DOWN operation.

The UP operation can only be performed by the process that set the semaphore to 0 and controls the shared resource. When the process controlling the resource is done, it can increment the semaphore's value back to 1 (an UP operation) and release the shared resource.

After an UP operation has been performed, processes sleeping on the semaphore will have the opportunity to access the shared resource. If there is more than one sleeping process, the operating system will pick a process to wake and allow that revived process to complete its DOWN operation and take control of the shared resource.

NOTE What allows binary semaphores to work so well is that the DOWN and UP operations are *atomic*. This is what separates semaphores from earlier, less successful attempts at implementing mutual exclusion. Once a process has started performing a DOWN or an UP operation, nothing short of pulling the power cord on the computer can stop the operation or access the semaphore until the operation is completed. On the Intel platform, atomic operations can be constructed using the CLI and STI instructions. By executing CLI and clearing the interrupts flag, we basically allow the CPU to ignore the rest of the world until the STI operation is executed. Because CLI and STI are such powerful commands, the management of semaphores is usually buried deep in the bowels of the operating system.

By themselves, semaphores do not really serve as an IPC mechanism. Unlike files, they do not store a payload of data that can be updated by separate processes. Instead, semaphores were meant to be used to provide mutually exclusive access to a shared resource. The shared resource itself is usually what provides the IPC mechanism. The semaphore is the sentinel that stands guard, making sure that only one process has control of the shared resource at any point in time. In this sense, the semaphore is said to *synchronize* access to the shared resource.

 NOTE If the platform you're working on doesn't provide semaphores, a file lock can potentially serve as a viable substitute in some cases. There will, however, be a performance discrepancy due to the overhead of performing file-related operations.

Shared Memory Segments

Shared memory segments are regions of memory that can be manipulated by more than one process. This form of IPC is extremely fast, but it does require the use of semaphores to synchronize access. Think of a shared memory segment like a whiteboard during a staff meeting. Several different people can get up and write to the same area of the board, but only one person at a time is allowed to modify the board. In this scenario, the whiteboard felt-tip pen is like a semaphore. Only the person who has the pen can get up and write on the whiteboard. When that person is done, he or she passes the pen on to someone else. The team supervisor, assuming the role of the operating system, usually decides who the pen gets passed to.

Anonymous Pipes

Anonymous pipes are communications channels that allow related processes to exchange data. When I use the term "related processes," I mean that one process must be a descendent of the other, or that the processes must have a common parent. Anonymous pipes provide the functionality behind the "|" redirector, which is a built-in feature for most command shells. The original impetus behind anonymous pipes originated during the early days of Unix. The founding fathers wanted a mechanism that would allow them to chain different programs together by using the output of one program as the input to another. In this context, the term "pipe" makes a lot of sense. Anonymous pipes serve to join applications by providing the plumbing necessary for them to communicate. One major restriction, which truly limits the utility of anonymous pipes, is that they are *half-duplex*. This is a fancy way of saying that the data can only flow in one direction between processes.

Most of the techniques I've discussed so far are fairly efficient ways for processes to communicate. This is particularly true for semaphores and shared memory segments. However, there is a catch: The real problem, in my opinion, with signals, file locking, shared memory, and anonymous pipes is that they can only be used by processes executing in the same physical address space. In other words, they can only be used by programs running on the same machine. I wanted the HEC virtual machine to be able to collaborate with other processes running on a network. In this day and age, not having network capabilities is like being stuck on an island.

NOTE   The requirement that the virtual machine be network enabled forced me to expand the list of IPC candidates to include named pipes, remote procedure call, and sockets.

Named Pipes

Named pipes are a more general extension of anonymous pipes. First and foremost, a named pipe is assigned a file path. This allows unrelated processes to access a named pipe because the named pipe has an entry in the file system. In fact, named pipes are typically implemented as a special type of file. Originally, named pipes were only half-duplex. The first byte written to a named pipe by the data producing process was also the first byte read from it by the data consuming process. This might account for why named pipes are sometimes referred to as FIFO files (first in, first out). Contemporary named pipes provide *full-duplex* communication so that data can flow both ways, and also provide the ability for different processes across a network to communicate.

I found that named pipes, on more than a couple of platforms, exhibited some rather odd system-dependent behavior. For example, on some versions of Windows the server end of a named pipe can only be instantiated on a machine that is a full-blown server. This eliminated named pipes from my list of hopefuls.

RPC

Remote procedure call (RPC) is a technique that was born in the 1980s. It was originally a part of Sun Microsystem's Open Network Computing (ONC) implementation. RPC is an attempt to simplify network programming by abstracting the process of network communication to the application level. In other words, a programmer can call procedures located on other machines with the same ease as invoking procedures on the local machine. The programmer does not have to be concerned with the details of establishing and managing a network connection; these are all taken care of by the RPC mechanism.

The problem with RPC is that the actions necessary to translate a function call into a set of equivalent network messages can entail a certain amount of overhead. There are a multitude of different steps that have to be performed in order to encode a function call into a network message on the local machine. These steps have to be repeated on the remote machine in order to decode the network message and invoke the remote function. This whole process has to be repeated again in order for the remote function to return a value to the invoking procedure on the local machine. Because of the performance hit and complexity associated with RPC, I decided against using it as an IPC mechanism.

In the end, I decided on allowing the HEC virtual machine to implement two forms of IPC. For synchronization and communication on the local host, I decided to implement mutexes. For network-based communication, I decided to implement sockets. Given the popularity of the Internet, I settled on TCP as the basic socket protocol. For me, the fault tolerance built into TCP is worth the extra overhead that it entails.

Sockets

The sockets paradigm was introduced in 1982 by engineers working on the Berkeley flavor of Unix. It ended up being very successful as an IPC mechanism. Facilities for sockets are implemented by almost every contemporary operating system. A socket is a full-duplex communication device which can be used to allow processes on the same machine, or on different machines, to communicate. Sockets is a programming interface that provides a set of function calls that programs can use to communicate over a network. As such, the sockets interface is able to somewhat divorce itself from network implementation details. The sockets interface is capable of supporting several different underlying network protocols.

A *network protocol* is a collection of rules defining how data is exchanged between computers on a network. A network protocol dictates the format and meaning of the data exchanged. A network protocol also specifies how machines on a network implement the operations of sending and receiving data.

A *connection-oriented* protocol is a protocol that takes steps to ensure that transmitted data has reached its destination intact. Connection-oriented protocols are useful in large networks, where data can be lost due to line noise and network congestion. A *connectionless* protocol does not check to see if transmitted data has reached its destination. Connectionless protocols are appropriate for situations where performance is crucial or where network bandwidth is limited.

There are dozens of different networking protocols. Some of them have survived purely because they support legacy systems, and others have been embraced as de facto standards. Related networking protocols that work together to provide communication are known as *protocol stacks*. A protocol stack is called such because the protocols in a stack are layered on top of each other. Each layer in the stack handles a different part of the communication process. The following is a partial list of well-known networking protocol stacks:

- AppleTalk
- SNA
- NetWare
- TCP/IP

AppleTalk is a suite of networking protocols developed by Apple. It's targeted at providing peer-to-peer file and printer sharing for Apple machines. It's my guess that AppleTalk will go the way of DECnet and become a historical footnote.

Systems Network Architecture (SNA) is a proprietary protocol stack originally developed by IBM in 1974. Given IBM's dominance in the production of large and expensive machines, the SNA suite is focused on shuttling transaction information to and from high-end computers (i.e., mainframes, enterprise servers, big iron, whatever you want to call them). This pretty much limits the target audience to large corporations.

The NetWare protocol stack was introduced by Novell in the early 1980s. The NetWare product originally started out as a file server operating system, but Novell broadened the product to include several other services. NetWare makes use of two proprietary protocols named IPX and SPX to handle lower-level networking details. However, NetWare can use other protocol stacks also, like TCP/IP. The success of Netware and its proprietary networking protocols will probably be tied to the success of Novell in the coming years.

In terms of widespread use, the undisputed king of protocol suites is TCP/IP. The Internet is one, very large TCP/IP network. TCP/IP is also the most popular protocol for private local and wide area networks. In fact, a systems admin establishing a new intranet for his company would be hard pressed to find a reason to implement a protocol other than TCP/IP.

Although TCP is a specific protocol (Transmission Control Protocol) and IP is a specific protocol (Internet Protocol), the term TCP/IP tends to refer to a whole stack of protocols developed by a project that was started by the DoD in 1969. Three central protocols to the TCP/IP suite are IP, TCP, and UDP (User Datagram Protocol). IP is a connectionless protocol that manages the actual transmission of data around the network. IP is at the lowest level of the protocol stack. TCP and UDP are both built on top of IP. TCP and UDP are higher-level protocols that serve as a liaison between user applications and the IP layer. The primary distinction between TCP and UDP is that TCP is a connection-oriented protocol and UDP is a connectionless protocol.

 NOTE   In general, TCP/IP networks are very resilient. This is because TCP/IP networks are *packet-switched*. Data transmitted from one network host to another is broken up into a series of packets. Because each packet of information stores the address of its intended destination, the packets that constitute a message can take different routes along the network to get to the destination. This means that if several nodes on a TCP/IP network fail, new routes through the network will be established. This kind of fault tolerance was important to the DoD because it was originally interested in designing a command and control network that could survive a nuclear war.

TCP/IP Sockets

Regardless of what you use them for, implementing TCP/IP sockets requires that the programmer follow a certain song and dance number. These dance steps will differ depending on the type of socket you're working with. Sockets come in two basic flavors: client sockets and server sockets.

Server sockets hang out and wait for clients to connect to them. Server sockets are like the telephone operators of days gone by, when switchboards were manually operated. They sit at the switchboard and wait for an incoming client call. Once a server socket has noticed that a client socket is attempting to connect, it will spawn a new socket on the server side which will be dedicated to communicating with the client socket. This new server-side connection socket will interact with the client socket until either the server connection socket decides by itself to shut down, or the client socket sends a message that tells the server connection socket to shut down.

Implementing a client socket involves the following steps:
1. Construct a client socket.
2. Send data to a server socket.
3. Receive data from server socket.
4. Goto step 2 or step 5.
5. Close the client socket.

Implementing a server socket involves the following steps:
1. Construct a server socket.
2. Allow the server socket to accept connections.
3. Receive data from a client using the connection socket.
4. Send data to a client using the connection socket.
5. Goto step 3 or step 6.
6. Close the connection socket.
7. Goto step 2 or step 8.
8. Close the server socket.

These steps are illustrated in Figure 6-10.

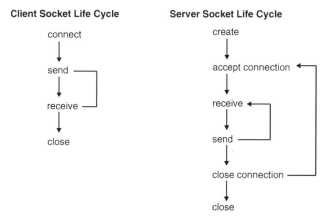

Figure 6-10

TCP/IP Addressing

Every computer on a TCP/IP network is assigned at least one *IP address*. Machines that have more than one network adapter can have multiple IP addresses. The assignment of IP addresses is analogous to the way in which houses on a street each have their own address. An IP address serves as a unique identifier so that machines on a network can be specified unambiguously.

An IP address is nothing more than a 32-bit number. Traditionally, this 32-bit number has been expressed in what is known as *dotted-decimal* form. In dotted-decimal form, the 32-bit number is divided into four bytes. Each byte is represented as an unsigned integer in the range from 0 to 255, and the four bytes are delimited by periods. For example, the IP address 167,775,892 in binary would look like:

```
00001010000000000000111010010100
(or 00001010.00000000.00001110.10010100)
```

and would be represented in dotted-decimal form as:

```
10.0.14.148
```

Specifying the IP address of a network machine, however, is still not enough to communicate with a process on that machine using TCP/IP. A computer may have several different applications running simultaneously that are all using TCP/IP. There has to be a way to distinguish which application on a given machine you want to talk to. This is where *port numbers* enter into the picture.

A port number is a 16-bit value that serves to identify an application on a given machine. Port numbers are represented as unsigned integers in the range from 0 to 65,535. Hence, there are actually two identifiers needed to communicate with an application on a network. You need to know the IP address of the machine executing the process, and you need to know the port address of that application on the machine.

The mapping of port numbers to applications has been taken up by the Internet Assigned Numbers Authority (IANA) and is described in RFC 1700. In a nutshell, port numbers 0 through 1,023 are reserved for well-known TCP/IP services (like Telnet, FTP, SMTP, etc.). Port numbers 1,024 through 65,535 can be used by user applications. There is really no enforcement mechanism to the IANA's mapping; it is purely a suggested convention.

In general, IP addresses can be difficult to remember. Even worse, computers on intranets usually have their IP address assigned dynamically so that the IP address of a given machine will change after a set period of time (automatic IP assignment is facilitated by a protocol named DHCP, which I don't have space to explain). This is why most people prefer to identify a computer on a network using the computer's *host name*.

A computer's host name is a symbolic name that is easy to remember, like Zeus or Spock. Host names are typically associated with IP addresses using the Domain Name System (DNS). DNS is a distributed database of name servers that map IP addresses to host names. The Internet has the largest DNS implementation. Most large organizations have at least one DNS name server that they expose to the Internet.

DNS allows host names to be qualified by *domain* and *subdomain* names. Domain and subdomain names give extra information about the organization that the host belongs to. Here are a few standard domain names:

- com — commerce
- edu — education
- gov — U.S. government
- mil — U.S. military
- net — networking organization
- org — private or nonprofit organization
- int — international

Unlike domain names, subdomain names are assigned arbitrarily by the sysop in charge of your network. For example, if you are working on a computer named sparky for a corporation named IPM, the fully qualified host name would look something like:

```
sparky.ipm.com
```

As you can see, the general format is: hostname.subdomain.domain.

Sometimes, a host will have more than one subdomain name. For instance:

```
borg.ipm.us.com
```

Implementation

Table 6-13 displays a summary of the IPC functions implemented.

Table 6-13

Interrupt	Function ($R1)	Description
10	0	Performs a DOWN operation on a mutex
10	1	Performs an UP operation on a mutex
10	2	Creates a client socket
10	3	Closes a client socket
10	4	Transmits data over a socket
10	5	Receives data from a socket
10	6	Gets the name of the local host
10	7	Resolves a host name to an IP address
10	8	Resolves an IP address to a host name
10	9	Creates a server socket
10	10	Allows a server socket to accept a client connection
10	11	Closes the connection socket on the server side
10	12	Closes the server socket

Now we'll take a look at the INT 10 functions individually.

INT 10 $R1=0   Performs a DOWN operation on a mutex

This function will either obtain a handle to a mutex and return immediately or cause the current process to block until it can obtain ownership of the mutex.

Inputs $R2= Address of a null-terminated string storing the name of the mutex

Outputs $R3= A handle to the mutex

$R4= 1 if an error has occurred, and 0 otherwise

INT 10 $R1=1   Performs an UP operation on a mutex

This function releases a mutex so that other waiting processes can obtain ownership.

Inputs $R2= A handle to a mutex

Outputs $R3= 1 if an error has occurred, and 0 otherwise

INT 10 $R1=2   Creates a client socket

This function constructs a client socket that will connect to a server socket. The IP address and port that specify the location of the server socket are supplied as arguments to this function.

    Inputs $R2= Address of a null-terminated string storing an IP address
                    $R3= Port to connect with
    Outputs $R4= Handle to the connected socket
                    $R5= 1 if an error has occurred, and 0 otherwise

INT 10 $R1=3   Closes a client socket

This call terminates a client socket and allows the native operating system to reclaim resources that were used by the client socket.

    Inputs $R2= Handle to the connected socket
    Outputs $R3= 1 if an error has occurred, and 0 otherwise

INT 10 $R1=4   Transmits data over a socket

This function is used by a socket to transmit data. This function can be invoked by both client and server sockets.

    Inputs $R2= Handle to the connected socket
                    $R3= Address of a buffer containing the message
                    $R4= The length of the message to transmit
    Outputs $R5= 1 if an error has occurred, and 0 otherwise

INT 10 $R1=5   Receives data from a socket

This function is used by a socket to receive data. This function can be invoked by both client and server sockets.

    Inputs $R2= Handle to the connected socket
                    $R3= Address of a buffer where message will be received
                    $R4= The length of the message to receive
    Outputs $R5= 1 if an error has occurred, and 0 otherwise

INT 10 $R1=6   Gets the name of the local host

    Inputs $R2= Address of a buffer where the host name can be stored
                    $R3= The size of the buffer pointed to by $R2
    Outputs $R4= 1 if an error has occurred, and 0 otherwise

INT 10 $R1=7   Resolves a host name to an IP address

This function takes a string containing a host name and returns a string containing one or more IP addresses. If a given host name resolves to multiple IP addresses because it has several network interfaces, the different addresses will be delimited by colons in the output buffer (i.e., "10.0.14.145:10.0.14.126:10.0.14.146").

    Inputs $R2= Address of null-terminated string containing the host name
                    $R3= Address of a buffer where the IP address can be stored
    Outputs $R4= 1 if an error has occurred, and 0 otherwise

INT 10 $R1 = 8   Resolves an IP address to a host name

This function takes a string containing an IP address and returns a string containing the host name.

      Inputs $R2= Address of null-terminated string containing the IP address

                  $R3= Address of a buffer where the host name can be stored

      Outputs $R4= 1 if an error has occurred, and 0 otherwise

INT 10 $R1 = 9   Creates a server socket

Sockets come in two flavors: client sockets and server sockets. Server sockets sit on a computer and wait for a client to connect with them. The IP address and port the server socket will bind to are specified as arguments to this function. The IP address must be specified because a computer may have several network interfaces.

      Inputs $R2= Address of null-terminated string containing the IP address

                  $R3= Port at which server socket will listen to

      Outputs $R4= Handle to the server socket

                  $R5= 1 if an error has occurred, and 0 otherwise

INT 10 $R1 = 10   Allows a server socket to accept a client connection

Server sockets spawn a new socket when a client connects with them. This connection socket is what actually interacts with the client socket. The original server socket really doesn't do that much, other than accepting connections and spawning connection sockets.

      Inputs $R2= A handle to the original server socket

                  $R3= The address of a buffer for storing the address of the client

                        socket

      Outputs $R4= A handle to the connection socket

                  $R5= 1 if an error has occurred, and 0 otherwise

INT 10 $R1 = 11   Closes the connection socket on the server side

This call terminates a connection socket and allows the native operating system to reclaim resources that were used by the connection socket. This call must be invoked before the server socket that spawned it is closed.

      Inputs $R2= A handle to the connection socket

      Outputs $R3= 1 if an error has occurred, and 0 otherwise

INT 10 $R1 = 12   Closes the server socket

This call terminates a server socket and allows the native operating system to reclaim resources that were used by the server socket. This can only be called after the connection socket has been closed.

      Inputs $R2= A handle to the server socket

      Outputs $R3= 1 if an error has occurred, and 0 otherwise

The following is an example of HEC assembly code that uses mutex functions. The code is in a file named `ipc1.asm` on the companion CD-ROM. The code in `ipc1.asm` grabs a mutex, prints out a string (to show that the mutex has been obtained), and then reads in a string from the user. When the user is done entering the string, the string entered is printed out and the process releases the mutex via an UP operation.

```
.PB main
.PV buffer -40
.PV mutex -64

#allocate local storage on stack
PUSHQ $FP
MOV $FP,$SP
LQI $R7,64
SUB $SP,$SP,$R7

#set name of mutex and store address in $R14
LAI $R10,$FP,mutex
MOV $R14,$R10
LBI $R2,1

LBI $R1,'m'
SB $R1,$R10
ADD $R10,$R10,$R2

LBI $R1,'i'
SB $R1,$R10
ADD $R10,$R10,$R2

LBI $R1,'n'
SB $R1,$R10
ADD $R10,$R10,$R2

LBI $R1,'e'
SB $R1,$R10
ADD $R10,$R10,$R2
LBI $R1,0
SB $R1,$R10

#obtain a mutex
MOV $R2,$R14
LQI $R1,0
INT 10
MOV $R15,$R3

#print string to signal that mutex obtained
MOV $R2,$R14
LQI $R1,18
INT 0

LQI $R2,10
LQI $R1,16
INT 0
LQI $R2,13
LQI $R1,16
INT 0
```

```
#read and print string
LAI $R2,$FP,buffer
LQI $R1,22
INT 0

LQI $R1,18
INT 0

LQI $R2,10
LQI $R1,16
INT 0
LQI $R2,13
LQI $R1,16
INT 0

#release mutex
MOV $R2,$R15
LQI $R1,1
INT 10


#reclaim local storage
MOV $SP,$FP
POPQ $FP

HALT
.PE
```

The best way to test this code is to crank up three or four command prompts and launch several copies of the virtual machine, all of them running ipc1.RUN. This will allow you to see how the DOWN and UP functions serve to pass around the semaphore from process to process.

The following is an example of HEC assembly code that uses name and address resolution functions. This code is in a file named ipc2.asm on the companion CD-ROM.

```
.PB main
.PV hostname -32
.PV ipaddr  -64

#allocate local storage on stack
PUSHQ $FP
MOV $FP,$SP
LQI $R7,64
SUB $SP,$SP,$R7

#get the local host name and print it
LAI $R2,$FP,hostname
LQI $R3,32
LBI $R1,6
INT 10

LQI $R1,18
INT 0
```

```
LQI $R2,10
LQI $R1,16
INT 0
LQI $R2,13
LQI $R1,16
INT 0

#get the ip address of local host
LAI $R2,$FP,hostname
LAI $R3,$FP,ipaddr
LQI $R1,7
INT 10

MOV $R2,$R3
LQI $R1,18
INT 0

LQI $R2,10
LQI $R1,16
INT 0
LQI $R2,13
LQI $R1,16
INT 0

#get the host name associated with this IP
LAI $R3,$FP,hostname
LAI $R2,$FP,ipaddr
LQI $R1,8
INT 10

MOV $R2,$R3
LQI $R1,18
INT 0

LQI $R2,10
LQI $R1,16
INT 0
LQI $R2,13
LQI $R1,16
INT 0

#reclaim local storage
MOV $SP,$FP
POPQ $FP

HALT
.PE
```

This program gets the local host name, resolves the IP address of the local host, and then reverse resolves the IP address to obtain the local host name. If the code from `ipc2.asm` is executed by the HEC virtual machine, the following kind of output will be printed to standard output:

```
DarkMatter
127.0.0.1
DarkMatter
```

When I ran this program, my machine was not connected to a network. So, as you can see, my machine (DarkMatter) resolves to the loopback address.

The following is an example of HEC assembly code that uses the client socket functions. This code is in a file named `ipc3.asm` on the companion CD-ROM.

```
.PB main
.PV message  -32
.PV ipaddr   -64

#allocate local storage on stack
PUSHQ $FP
MOV $FP,$SP
LQI $R7,64
SUB $SP,$SP,$R7

#set the ipaddress
LAI $R10,$FP,ipaddr
MOV $R14,$R10
LBI $R2,1

LBI $R1,'1'
SB $R1,$R10
ADD $R10,$R10,$R2

LBI $R1,'2'
SB $R1,$R10
ADD $R10,$R10,$R2
LBI $R1,'7'
SB $R1,$R10
ADD $R10,$R10,$R2

LBI $R1,'.'
SB $R1,$R10
ADD $R10,$R10,$R2

LBI $R1,'0'
SB $R1,$R10
ADD $R10,$R10,$R2

LBI $R1,'.'
SB $R1,$R10
ADD $R10,$R10,$R2

LBI $R1,'0'
SB $R1,$R10
ADD $R10,$R10,$R2

LBI $R1,'.'
SB $R1,$R10
ADD $R10,$R10,$R2
```

```
       LBI $R1,'1'
       SB $R1,$R10
       ADD $R10,$R10,$R2

       LBI $R1,0
       SB $R1,$R10

       #set the message contents (all 7 bytes of it, woo hoo!)
       LAI $R10,$FP,message
       MOV $R15,$R10
       LBI $R2,1

       LBI $R1,'h'
       SB $R1,$R10
       ADD $R10,$R10,$R2

       LBI $R1,'e'
       SB $R1,$R10
       ADD $R10,$R10,$R2

       LBI $R1,'l'
       SB $R1,$R10
       ADD $R10,$R10,$R2

       LBI $R1,'l'
       SB $R1,$R10
       ADD $R10,$R10,$R2

       LBI $R1,'o'
       SB $R1,$R10
       ADD $R10,$R10,$R2

       LBI $R1,'!'
       SB $R1,$R10
       ADD $R10,$R10,$R2

       LBI $R1,0
       SB $R1,$R10

       #create the client socket
       MOV $R2,$R14
       LQI $R3,30000
       LQI $R1,2
       INT 10
       MOV $R16,$R4

       #send some data
       MOV $R2,$R16
       MOV $R3,$R15
       LQI $R4,7
       LQI $R1,4
       INT 10
```

```
#shut the client socket down
MOV $R2,$R16
LQI $R1,3
INT 10

#reclaim local storage
MOV $SP,$FP
POPQ $FP

HALT
.PE
```

The following is an example of HEC assembly code that uses the server-side socket functions. This code is in a file named `ipc4.asm` on the companion CD-ROM.

```
.PB main
.PV buffer  -32
.PV ipaddr  -64

#allocate local storage on stack
PUSHQ $FP
MOV $FP,$SP
LQI $R7,64
SUB $SP,$SP,$R7

#set the ipaddress
LAI $R10,$FP,ipaddr
MOV $R14,$R10
LBI $R2,1

LBI $R1,'1'
SB $R1,$R10
ADD $R10,$R10,$R2

LBI $R1,'2'
SB $R1,$R10
ADD $R10,$R10,$R2

LBI $R1,'7'
SB $R1,$R10
ADD $R10,$R10,$R2

LBI $R1,'.'
SB $R1,$R10
ADD $R10,$R10,$R2

LBI $R1,'0'
SB $R1,$R10
ADD $R10,$R10,$R2

LBI $R1,'.'
SB $R1,$R10
ADD $R10,$R10,$R2
```

```
LBI $R1,'0'
SB $R1,$R10
ADD $R10,$R10,$R2

LBI $R1,'.'
SB $R1,$R10
ADD $R10,$R10,$R2

LBI $R1,'1'
SB $R1,$R10
ADD $R10,$R10,$R2

LBI $R1,0
SB $R1,$R10

#open a server socket
MOV $R2,$R14
LQI $R3,30000
LQI $R1,9
INT 10
MOV $R15,$R4

#accept a connection
MOV $R2,$R15
LAI $R3,$FP,buffer
LQI $R1,10
INT 10
MOV $R16,$R4

#print client address
LAI $R3,$FP,buffer
MOV $R2,$R3
LQI $R1,18
INT 0

LQI $R2,10
LQI $R1,16
INT 0
LQI $R2,13
LQI $R1,16
INT 0

#receive data from client ($R1=5)
MOV $R2,$R16
LAI $R3,$FP,buffer
LQI $R4,7
LQI $R1,5
INT 10

#print data
LAI $R3,$FP,buffer
MOV $R2,$R3
LQI $R1,18
INT 0
```

```
LQI $R2,10
LQI $R1,16
INT 0
LQI $R2,13
LQI $R1,16
INT 0

#close connection socket
MOV $R2,$R16
LQI $R1,11
INT 10

#close server socket
MOV $R2,$R15
LQI $R1,12
INT 10

#reclaim local storage
MOV $SP,$FP
POPQ $FP

HALT
.PE
```

To test `ipc3.asm` and `ipc4.asm`, you should run them together. Specifically, you should start the server first and then run the client. The server side of this tag team will print out the address of the client and then print out the message sent by the client.

```
127.0.0.1
hello!
```

The INT 10 functions are implemented using the `initSockets()` and `handleIPC()` routines, located in `intwin32.c`. As a final note, I think I should comment that networking on Windows is anything but straightforward, especially when you compare it to the networking API for Linux or any of the Unix flavors. In the tradition of DCOM, Microsoft decided to make the underlying mechanism very simple. As a result, a lot of complexity was shifted to the shoulders of the developer.

On the other hand, the API that Microsoft supplies to manage a mutex is notably easier to deal with when you compare it with the semaphore API on Linux.

```
int initSockets()
{
    WORD wVersionRequested;
    WSADATA wsaData;

    wVersionRequested = MAKEWORD(2, 2);

    if(WSAStartup(wVersionRequested, &wsaData))
    {
        return(1);
    }

    if(LOBYTE(wsaData.wVersion)!=2 ||
       HIBYTE(wsaData.wVersion)!=2)
```

```
            {
                    return(1);
            }

            return(0);

    }/*end initSockets*/

    void handleIPC()
    {
        switch((U1)R[$R1])
        {
            case 0:
            {
                HANDLE hmutex; // void*

                hmutex = CreateMutex(NULL,TRUE,&RAM[R[$R2]]);
                if(hmutex==NULL)
                {
                    if(GetLastError()==ERROR_ALREADY_EXISTS)
                    {
                        hmutex =
                        OpenMutex(MUTEX_ALL_ACCESS,FALSE,&RAM[R[$R2]]);
                        if(hmutex==FALSE)
                        {
                            R[$R4]=1;
                        }
                        else
                        {
                            WaitForSingleObject(hmutex,INFINITE);
                            R[$R3]=(U8)hmutex;
                            R[$R4]=0;
                        }
                    }
                    else
                    {
                        R[$R4]=1;
                    }
                }
                else
                {
                    WaitForSingleObject(hmutex,INFINITE);
                    R[$R3]=(U8)hmutex;
                    R[$R4]=0;
                }

            }break;
            case 1:
            {
                BOOL retval;
                retval = ReleaseMutex((HANDLE)R[$R2]);
                if(retval==FALSE)
                {
                    R[$R3]=1;
```

```
            }
            else
            {
                    retval = CloseHandle((HANDLE)R[$R2]);
                    if(retval==FALSE)
                    {
                        R[$R3]=1;
                    }
                    else
                    {
                        R[$R3]=0;
                    }
            }

    }break;
    case 2:
    {
        if(initSockets())
        {
            R[$R5]=1;
        }
        else
        {
            struct sockaddr_in address;
            SOCKET client;
            int err;

            address.sin_family=AF_INET;
            address.sin_port = htons((unsigned short)R[$R3]);
            address.sin_addr.s_addr = inet_addr(&RAM[R[$R2]]);

            client = socket(AF_INET,SOCK_STREAM,0);
            if(client==INVALID_SOCKET)
            {
                R[$R5]=1;
            }
            else
            {
                err = connect(client,
                            (SOCKADDR*)&address,
                             sizeof(address));
                if(err==SOCKET_ERROR)
                {
                    R[$R5]=1;
                }
                else
                {
                    R[$R5]=0;
                    R[$R4]=(U8)client;
                }
            }
        }
    }

    }break;
```

```
case 3:
{
    if(shutdown((SOCKET)R[$R2],0x02)==SOCKET_ERROR)
    {
        R[$R3]=1;
    }
    else
    {
        if(closesocket((SOCKET)R[$R2])==SOCKET_ERROR)
        {
            R[$R3]=1;
        }
        else
        {
            R[$R3]=0;
            WSACleanup();
        }
    }

}break;
case 4:
{

    int nLeft;
    int index;
    char *buffer;

    nLeft=(int)R[$R4];
    index=0;
    R[$R5]=0;
    buffer = &RAM[R[$R3]];
    while(nLeft>0)
    {
        int ret;
        ret = send((SOCKET)R[$R2],
                    &(buffer[index]),
                    nLeft,
                    0);
        if(ret==SOCKET_ERROR)
        {
            R[$R5]=1;
            break;
        }
        nLeft = nLeft - ret;
        index = index + ret;
    }

}break;
case 5:
{
    int nLeft;
    int index;
    char *buffer;
```

```
                nLeft=(int)R[$R4];
                index=0;
                R[$R5]=0;
                buffer = &RAM[R[$R3]];
                while(nLeft>0)
                {
                      int ret;
                      ret = recv((SOCKET)R[$R2],
                                  &(buffer[index]),
                                  nLeft,
                                  0);
                      if(ret==SOCKET_ERROR)
                      {
                            R[$R5]=1;
                            break;
                      }
                      nLeft = nLeft - ret;
                      index = index + ret;
                }

        }break;
        case 6:
        {
              if(initSockets())
              {
                    R[$R4]=1;
              }
              else
              {
                    if(gethostname(&RAM[R[$R2]],(int)R[$R3]))
                    {
                          R[$R4]=1;
                          WSACleanup();
                    }
                    else
                    {
                          R[$R4]=0;
                          WSACleanup();
                    }
              }

        }break;
        case 7:
        {
              HOSTENT *hp;
              int i;

              if(initSockets())
              {
                    R[$R4]=1;
              }
              else
              {
                    hp = gethostbyname(&RAM[R[$R2]]);
```

```
                        if(hp==NULL)
                        {
                              R[$R4]=1;
                              WSACleanup();
                        }
                        else
                        {
                              if((*hp).h_addr_list[0]!=0)
                              {
                                    struct in_addr addr;
                                    memcpy(&addr,
                                          (*hp).h_addr_list[0],
                                            sizeof(struct in_addr));
                                    strcpy(&RAM[R[$R3]],inet_ntoa(addr));
                              }
                              for (i =1;(*hp).h_addr_list[i]!=0;++i)
                              {
                                    struct in_addr addr;
                                    memcpy(&addr,
                                          (*hp).h_addr_list[i],
                                            sizeof(struct in_addr));
                                    strcat(&RAM[R[$R3]],":");

                                    strcat(&RAM[R[$R3]],inet_ntoa(addr));
                              }

                              R[$R4]=0;
                        }
                        WSACleanup();
                  }

            }break;
            case 8:
            {
                  HOSTENT *hp;
                  struct in_addr hostaddr;

                  if(initSockets())
                  {
                        R[$R4]=1;
                  }
                  else
                  {
                        hostaddr.s_addr = inet_addr(&RAM[R[$R2]]);

                        hp = gethostbyaddr((char *)&hostaddr,
                                          sizeof(struct in_addr),
                                          AF_INET);

                        if(hp==NULL)
                        {
                              R[$R4]=1;
                        }
                        else
```

```
                    {
                        strcpy(&RAM[R[$R3]],(*hp).h_name);
                        R[$R4]=0;
                    }

                    WSACleanup();
            }

    }break;
    case 9:
    {
        if(initSockets())
        {
            R[$R4]=1;
        }
        else
        {
            struct sockaddr_in address;
            SOCKET server;
            int err;
            address.sin_family=AF_INET;
            address.sin_port = htons((unsigned short)R[$R3]);
            address.sin_addr.s_addr = inet_addr(&RAM[R[$R2]]);

            server = socket(AF_INET,SOCK_STREAM,0);
            if(server==INVALID_SOCKET)
            {
                R[$R5]=1;
            }
            else
            {
                err = bind(server,
                        (SOCKADDR*)&address,
                         sizeof(address));
                if(err==SOCKET_ERROR)
                {
                    R[$R5]=1;
                }
                else
                {
                    err = listen(server,SOMAXCONN);
                    if(err==SOCKET_ERROR)
                    {
                        R[$R5]=1;
                    }
                    else
                    {
                        R[$R5]=0;
                        R[$R4]=(U8)server;
                    }
                }
            }
        }
    }
```

```
    }break;
    case 10:
    {
         SOCKET connection;
         struct sockaddr_in client;
         int length;
         connection = accept((SOCKET)R[$R2],
                             (SOCKADDR*)&client,
                             &length);
         if(connection==INVALID_SOCKET)
         {
              R[$R5]=1;
         }
         else
         {
              R[$R5]=0;
              strcpy(&RAM[R[$R3]],inet_ntoa(client.sin_addr));
              R[$R4]=(U8)connection;
         }

    }break;
    case 11:
    {
         if(shutdown((SOCKET)R[$R2],0x02)==SOCKET_ERROR)
         {
              R[$R3]=1;
         }
         else
         {
              if(closesocket((SOCKET)R[$R2])==SOCKET_ERROR)
              {
                   R[$R3]=1;
              }
              else
              {
                   R[$R3]=0;
              }
         }

    }break;
    case 12:
    {
         if(closesocket((SOCKET)R[$R2])==SOCKET_ERROR)
         {
              R[$R3]=1;
         }
         else
         {
              R[$R3]=0;
              WSACleanup();
         }

    }break;
    default:
```

```
            {
                    ERROR1_LVL2("INT 10 %lu function not handled",(U1)R[$R1]);
            }
        }
        return;

    }/*end handleIPC*/
```

References

Jones, Anthony, and Jim Ohlund. *Network Programming for Microsoft Windows.* Microsoft Press, 1999. ISBN: 0735605602.

Trying to write Windows networking code by reading the MSDN online documentation is a losing proposition. You have no choice but to fork over your cash and buy a few books. This fairly recent work gives a complete overview of the networking facilities provided by the Windows API.

Quinn, Bob, and Dave Shute. *Windows Sockets Network Programming.* Addison-Wesley, 1996. ISBN: 0201633728.

This book is a bit older than Jones and Ohlund, but is easier to read and focuses explicitly on sockets.

Rector, Brent, and Joseph Newcomer. *Win32 Programming.* Addison Wesley Longman, 1997. ISBN:0201634929.

Simon, Richard. *Windows NT Win32 API SuperBible.* Waite Group Press, 1997. ISBN: 1571690891.

This is an extremely useful book that surveys the Win32 API categorically. Simon is very successful at making his book easy to understand and use.

Sterling, Bruce. *The Hacker Crackdown: Law and Disorder on the Electronic Frontier.* Bantam Books, 1992. ISBN: 055356370X.

Bruce Sterling is both technically competent and an excellent writer. This is a rare commodity among authors who write documentaries on the technology subculture. Sterling gives a detailed and engrossing look at the evolution of the digital underground.

Stevens, Richard. *Advanced Programming in the UNIX Environment.* Addison-Wesley, 1993. ISBN: 0201563177.

Richard Stevens is on a level all his own when it comes to explaining the finer points of programming with UNIX. Every deep geek I know has Stevens' books on his shelf.

_____. *TCP/IP Illustrated, Volume 1.* Addison-Wesley, 1994. ISBN: 0201633469.

_____. *UNIX Network Programming.* Prentice Hall, 1990. ISBN: 0139498761.

HEC Assembly Language

We've examined the design and implementation of the HEC virtual machine and assembler. Now we're ready to take a better look at how assembly language programs are constructed. As with any complicated topic, the subject of HEC assembly language is more easily explained using an *evolutionary approach*. I will begin by introducing basic language features which are, by themselves, fairly simple and primitive. Then, I will take these features and either build upon them or use them to produce more elaborate constructs. This is analogous to how nature takes basic, microscopic forms of life and produces more complicated organisms. This chapter starts with very simple assembly language statements. By the end of this chapter, I will be discussing more sophisticated language features that facilitate recursion and enforce scope rules.

Constituents of an Assembly Language Program

All HEC assembly programs can be decomposed into a series of statements. Each statement takes up a single line in the assembly language source file. The HEC assembler allows a source file line to be up to 512 characters in length. Statements can be classified into three different subspecies:

- Instructions
- Directives
- Comments

Instructions

Instructions are statements that are translated into bytecode by the HEC assembler. An instruction consists of a single *opcode* and zero or more *operands*.

```
instruction ≡ opcode [ operand [ operand ... ] ]
```

An opcode is a symbol that defines both the action and the form the instruction takes. I defined all of the HEC opcodes so that they would completely determine both the number of operands following the opcode and the type of those operands.

Consider the following instruction:

```
ADD  $R14, $R3, $R2
```

The ADD opcode requires that it is followed by three integer registers (the assembler will enforce this rule). The ADD opcode also dictates that the sum of the values in $R2 and $R3 will be placed in $R14. Hence, you can see how the ADD opcode specifies the action that the instruction takes, and the overall format of the instruction.

An operand specifies the data that the instruction will act upon. The HEC assembly language recognizes five distinct types of instruction operands. These operand types are listed in Table 7-1.

Table 7-1

Operand Type	Examples
Register	$D5, $R14, $FP
Identifier	myfunction, @arg
Character literal	'c'
Integer literal	–56,353, +73, 54
Floating-point literal	45.03e–7

Register operands are simply any of the registers that exist in the HEC virtual machine's execution environment. You can directly access and manipulate all the virtual machine's registers. However, there are some registers, such as $BE, $HS, $HE, and $SS, that you will not want to modify. These registers are strictly used to delimit regions of memory and are intended to be used by the virtual machine only. If you do modify these registers (and you do so at your own risk), you'll want to make sure to save the old values somewhere so that you can restore these registers when you are done.

Identifiers are symbols that consist of a set of characters. Identifiers are used to name variables, procedures, and labels. The first character of an identifier must be a letter (i.e., a-z and A-Z), an @, an underscore, a question mark, or a period. Characters following the first may belong to the previously described class of characters in addition to numeric digits.

First character: a-z, A-Z, @, _, ?, .
Following characters: a-z, A-Z, @, _, ?, . , 0-9

The following are valid identifiers:

```
abacab_?7
?_variable20
__is_Number
.my_5_function
```

The following symbols are not valid identifiers:

```
12_proc
$my_value
my_#_function
```

A *literal* is a token whose value is a specified constant. I use the term "literal" to help distinguish these constant values from other language elements whose values do not change. The HEC assembly language permits the use of character, integer, and floating-point literals.

An *immediate operand* is an operand that is a literal value.

Character literals begin with a single quote, followed by a printable ASCII character, and then a closing single quote. Printable ASCII characters are those characters whose equivalent numeric values are in the range from 32 to 126 (space to ~).

For example:

```
'a'
'2'
'*'
```

Integer literals consist of a nonzero digit, followed by zero or more decimal digits. Integer literals may be preceded by a sign symbol.

```
[ sign ] nonzero-digit [ digits ]
```

For example:

```
6503
-2
+114
```

Floating-point literals are numbers that assume the standard scientific notation format. They are basically an extension of integer literals in that they can include a decimal point and an exponent. The HEC assembler will accept floating-point values that adhere to one of the following basic schemes:

```
[sign] 0 . digits [ (e|E) [ sign ] digits ]
[sign] digit [digits] . digits [ (e|E) [ sign ] digits ]
```

For example:

```
+0.12
7.73e5
-945.1e-2
```

Directives

Directives are statements that do not get directly translated into bytecode. Instead, they are used primarily to define symbols (i.e., the names of procedures, variables, and labels). When the assembler processes the assembly language source file during its first pass, directives are used to populate the assembler's symbol table. When it translates the source code into bytecode during the second pass, the symbol information gleaned from the directives will help the assembler replace each symbol in the source file with its equivalent memory address.

Thus, directives are intended to help the assembler resolve identifiers to addresses when the source file is assembled. For example, consider the following block of code which uses a label directive:

```
.PL  mylabel
LQI  $R1,-62
MOV  $R2,$R1
LAI  $R3, mylabel
```

The .PL directive defines a label. The assembler records the memory address of this label as the address of the first byte of the instruction following the label directive. In this case, the label `mylabel` will represent the address of the LQI opcode in the instruction directly beneath it. When this label's identifier is encountered elsewhere in the source file, the assembler will replace the identifier with the address associated with the label.

One thing you will notice as we discuss directives in this chapter is that all directive statements begin with a period (i.e., .PL, .PB, .GB, etc.).

Comments

Comments are pretty simple. The important characteristic of comments is that the assembler completely ignores them. Comments are intended to help make assembly source code more readable by providing in-code documentation. This is particularly important with assembly code, because it is a low-level language. It is very easy to become lost in details if the appropriate comments are not included. There have been times when a well-placed comment or two has saved me from having to reverse engineer my own code.

Comments begin with a hash character (i.e., #). Comments, like the other types of statements, take up an entire source file line. This hash character must be the first character of the source file line. The assembler will basically ignore every line that begins with a hash character. For example:

```
# print out the integer value 732
LQI $R2, 732
LQI $R1, 20
INT 0
```

NOTE The comment syntax I use is similar to the single-line comment syntax used by most Unix command shells, like the Korn shell and the Bash shell. I decided to adopt this syntax intentionally so that Unix people would feel right at home.

A graphical decomposition of the various parts of an assembly language source file in provided in Figure 7-1.

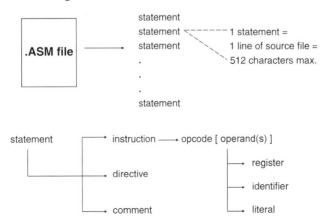

Figure 7-1

Defining Procedures and Labels

An assembly language program, from an organizational standpoint, is nothing more than a collection of procedures. A *procedure*, in terms of the HEC assembly language, is a set of contiguous instructions delimited by the .PB and .PE directives.

In general, the .PB and .PE directives are used together in the following way:

```
.PB identifier
     #
     # procedure's assembly code goes here
     #
.PE
```

Here is an example of a very simple procedure that reads and then prints an integer to the screen:

```
.PB myfunction
     LQI $R1,24
     INT 0
     LQI $R1,20
     INT 0
.PE
```

The .PB directive is used to specify the beginning of a procedure (i.e., .PB as in "Procedure Begin"). The .PB directive is always followed by an identifier that denotes the name of the procedure. A procedure's identifier represents the address of the first byte of the first instruction in the procedure. This means that, in the example above, when the identifier myfunction is used as an operand in an instruction, it will be replaced by the address of the first byte of the LQI $R1,24 instruction.

The .PE directive is used to terminate a procedure (i.e., .PE as in "Procedure End"). The .PE directive does not need to be followed by an identifier. It is assumed that it is coupled with the most recent .PB directive preceding it.

NOTE The HEC assembly language does not allow procedure definitions to be nested. You cannot have one procedure inside of another. This means that a .PB directive must always be delimited by a .PE before another .PB directive can be applied. Also, no procedure in a HEC assembly language program can have the same name as another. All procedures must have unique names.

NOTE The HEC assembler does not allow instructions to exist outside of a procedure. Every instruction must lie between a particular set of .PB and .PE directives.

Labels are used to mark a particular instruction inside of a procedure. Labels are created using the .PL directive. Like the .PB directive, the .PL directive is followed by an identifier. The .PL directive has the form:

```
.PL identifier
```

Labels represent the address of the first byte of the instruction immediately after them. For example, take the following procedure:

```
.PB myfunction
      LQI $R1,24
      INT 0
      .PL myfunction_L001
      LQI $R1,20
      INT 0
.PE
```

The label `myfunction_L001` represents the address of the first byte of the `LQI $R1,20` instruction. When this label is encountered as an operand in an instruction, the assembler will replace the `myfunction_L001` identifier with its equivalent address.

NOTE Label names must be unique in a HEC assembly language program. They cannot match any other name (i.e., procedure name or variable name). I've found that prefixing a label with the name of the function and suffixing it with a sequential numeric value is an effective way to guarantee that the label names in a program remain unique. Take another look at the previous example to see what I mean.

I initially designed HEC with the intention that all memory storage would be provided by either the stack or the heap segments. In accordance with this design restriction, I didn't include any instructions or directives that were explicitly meant to allocate memory storage within the bytecode segment of HEC's address space. Part of the reason for relying exclusively on the heap and the stack was bytecode verification. The verifier expects nothing but instructions in the bytecode section of the binary executable. This makes it easy for the verifier to scan quickly through the bytecode segment during virtual machine initialization and check for invalid instructions.

However, there actually is a way to allocate storage in the bytecode section. Yes, I'm afraid that there is a loophole that sneaky programmers can use to subvert my memory allocation strategy. This trick centers around the use of labels and the NOP instruction. The NOP instruction does nothing, hence the name "No Operation." The NOP instruction is a single byte in length. By preceding a set of NOP instructions with a label, you can effectively create a storage space. For example:

```
# jump over the following code
.PL  my_variable
NOP
NOP
NOP
NOP
.PL  my_variable_end
```

The previous code constructs a double word of bytecode storage. This storage can be accessed using the address that is represented by the `my_variable` label. The bytecode verifier is happy because there are instructions present during initialization. The only thing you need to be careful about is making sure that the path of execution jumps around the NOP instructions. If you use these four NOP instructions for storage, the values of these four bytes have the potential to change in value during execution such that they no longer represent NOP instructions. If program control runs into this series of bytes, it will interpret the storage bytes as instructions and potentially crash the virtual machine.

If you really wanted to go over the edge, you could create a procedure that is nothing but storage. This would give you one big statically allocated chunk of memory. In fact, you could get even more sophisticated by placing labels within this procedure to delimit specific areas of storage.

```
.PB  data_segment
     NOP
     NOP
     .PL data_segment_var2
     NOP
     NOP
     .PL data_segment_var3
     NOP
     .
     .
     .
     NOP
.PE
```

Those of you familiar with Intel assembly language will recognize that the previous static data item is similar to what is known as a *data segment*. Unlike me, the guy who designed the Intel 8086 execution environment decided that he would allow the programmer to define segments of memory to be statically allocated for storage.

This NOP-based, static memory allocation scheme is really more of an unintended consequence than anything else. Naturally, I would encourage you to stick to the data allocation techniques I outline later in this chapter. Nevertheless, I thought I should show you an unorthodox alternative just in case.

 NOTE Programming languages like COBOL do not have a stack or heap. All of the storage in COBOL is statically allocated at compile time. This is not just a matter of syntax. It's more an issue of underlying architecture and intent. Programs written in COBOL tend to be oriented towards shuttling fixed-size transaction information to and from a data store. You don't need sophisticated memory management to do this kind of repetitive, transaction-centric work. The benefit to using a language like COBOL is that you'll know at compile time how much storage space is needed by a program. This will allow the architect and sysop to get together and do some resource planning in advance. If you know that a program takes 512 KB of RAM, and that there will be a couple hundred instances of that program running at any point in time, you can get a decent idea of what kind of hardware commitment you will have to make.

Loading and Moving Immediate Data

There is a whole set of instructions in the HEC assembly language devoted to loading immediate data into registers. Recall that an immediate operand is just a literal operand. Thus, the following operations summarized in Table 7-2 are used to load literals into registers.

Table 7-2

Instruction	Meaning
LBI $R, byte	Loads the byte literal into the integer register $R
LWI $R, word	Loads the word literal into the integer register $R
LDI $R, dword	Loads the double word literal into the integer register $R
LQI $R, qword	Loads the quad word literal into the integer register $R
LF1I $F, float	Loads the single-precision floating-point literal into the register $F
LF2I $D, double	Loads the double-precision floating-point literal into the register $D

Obviously, LBI stands for Load Byte Immediate, LWI stands for Load Word Immediate, and so on. All of the instructions that handle integer literals (i.e., LBI, LWI, LDI, and LQI) assume that they are working with signed integers. The LF1I and LF2I instructions load floating-point values into single- and double-precision floating-point registers.

The only real distinction between the LBI, LWI, LDI, and LQI instructions is the size of the literal integer operand they handle. To refresh your memory, the signed and unsigned ranges of the different data types are enumerated in Table 7-3.

Table 7-3

Type	Byte Size	Signed Range	Unsigned Range
Byte	1	–128 to 127	0 to 255
Word	2	–32,768 to 32,767	0 to 65,535
Double word	4	-2^{31} to $2^{31}-1$	0 to 4,294,967,295
Quad word	8	-2^{63} to $2^{63}-1$	0 to $2^{64}-1$
Float	4	3.4×10^{-38} to 3.4×10^{38}	NA
Double	8	1.7×10^{-308} to 1.7×10^{308}	NA

The ranges for single- and double-precision floating-point values are approximate and tend to vary from one platform to the next.

Using these instructions is a piece of cake. You just pick a register and enter the literal you want loaded. For example:

```
LF1I   $F3, -3.404
LBI    $R11, 'c'
LWI    $R3, 7021
```

NOTE   The terms "load" and "store" have special meanings in the context of the HEC assembly language. The operation of loading means that an immediate value, or a value somewhere in memory, is being placed into a register. In a load operation, a register is the final destination, with a value in a register being placed somewhere in memory. In a store operation, a register is being used as the source and a location in memory as final destination.

There are nine instructions total in the entire instruction set that use immediate operands. Unless you write code that has a proliferation of hard-coded values, you will probably not use the previously discussed instructions frequently. Nevertheless, the instructions are easy to understand and will serve as a springboard to look at other instructions. This is why I introduced them first.

Once you have an immediate operand loaded into a register, you may want to copy the value to another register. This is what the three move instructions in Table 7-4 are for.

Table 7-4

Instruction	Meaning
MOV $r1, $r2	Copies the contents of integer register $r2 into $r1
MOVF $f1, $f2	Copies the contents of single-precision floating-point register $f2 into $f1
MOVD $d1, $d2	Copies the contents of double-precision floating-point register $d2 into $d1

In the instructions above, I used symbols like $r1 and $r2 to reinforce the fact that $r1 and $r2 could be any integer register. In other words, $r1 does not have to be $R1; it could be $R8 or $R14.

```
# load 32 into $R7 and then copy to $R4
LQI  $R7, 32
MOV $R4, $R7
```

Direct Memory Addressing Mode

There are a lot of HEC assembly language instructions that operate on data that is located strictly in registers. For example:

```
ADD $R1, $R2, $R3
```

The ADD instruction takes the values in $R2 and $R3 and places the sum in $R1. Everything that happens is localized to a set of registers. There are, however, a number of HEC assembly language instructions that operate on data located in memory. In order to work with data located in memory, we need to be able to specify the exact position of the data item in memory. This leads us to the topic of memory addressing modes.

 NOTE   When I use the term "memory" in the following discussion, I am referring to the HEC virtual machine's address space (i.e., the bytecode, heap, and stack segments). In addition, I will often use the term *data item* to refer to an area of memory being used to stockpile one or more pieces of information. In other words, a data item is an arbitrary storage space somewhere in memory.

A *memory addressing mode* is a particular technique for specifying the location of an instruction operand that is in memory.

There are two basic memory addressing modes: direct memory addressing mode and indirect memory addressing mode.

In the *direct memory addressing mode*, the address of an operand in memory is explicitly known after the assembler processes the source file. This means that the address of the data item will be embedded in the instruction's bytecode.

In the *indirect memory addressing mode*, the address of an operand in memory is not known until the instruction referencing the operand executes at run time. The indirect addressing mode uses values computed at run time to specify an address.

These explanations may seem a little vague. Especially because I haven't accompanied them with any concrete examples. However, as you progress through the chapter and see how these concepts are actually implemented, things will become clearer. For the remainder of this section, I'm going to examine the direct addressing mode. The indirect addressing mode will be introduced later on in this chapter.

The HEC assembly language has two instructions that use the direct addressing mode. These instructions are LQI and LAD. Both of these can be used to load an address into an integer register. You were introduced to the LQI instruction in the previous chapter.

The most direct, and primitive, way to load an address into a register is to specify the address as an integer literal using the LQI instruction:

```
LQI  $R15, 2147
```

The statement above loads the address `2147` into register `$R15`. Well, actually you're loading an integer literal into `$R15`, but you can interpret the integer as an address if you want to. It all depends on how you end up using the literal. This is possible because an address, in the context of the HEC virtual machine, is just a 64-bit unsigned integer.

One caveat of using LQI is that it treats its operands as signed 64-bit integer values. Hence, the range of valid address values that it can accept are limited to roughly half of the possible address values (because addresses are unsigned 64-bit integer values).

Another problem with using the LQI instruction is that it forces you to keep track of specific address values. Even worse, alterations made to a program can cause the addresses of certain data items to change, and you'll have to take this into account also. Unless you have a photographic memory and can constantly juggle a couple hundred numbers in your head, I would recommend against using LQI to handle address values. In general, manually specifying an address and loading it into a register using LQI is an undesirable solution and should only be used as a last resort.

It would be far easier to represent addresses in memory using identifiers and then let the assembler take responsibility for resolving an identifier to an address when it processes the source file. This is the motivation behind the LAD (Load Address Direct) instruction. The LAD instruction has the following format:

```
LAD  $R, identifier
```

The LAD instruction takes the address represented by the identifier and loads it into an integer register (`$R`). The identifier must be the name of a label or procedure. This restricts the LAD instruction to calculating the address of a procedure or the address of a label. When the assembler processes the LAD instruction, it will literally replace the identifier with a 64-bit address, such that the bytecode translation of the LAD instruction takes up 10 bytes (one byte for the opcode, one byte for the register, and eight for the address).

NOTE Don't forget, the LAD instruction can only be used in conjunction with label or procedure identifiers. This is because the assembler, during its first pass, computes the address of procedures and labels, and stores their addresses in the symbol table. When the assembler makes its second pass, it can replace the identifier in the instruction with its eight-byte address.

Looking at an example may help to clarify things. The following program uses the LAD instruction to calculate the address of a label and the address of a procedure. Then it prints these values. For the sake of readability, I follow these values with carriage return and line feed variables.

```
.PB proc1
    # print the address of a procedure
    LAD $R4,proc2
    MOV $R2,$R4
    LBI $R1,20
    INT 0
    .PL proc1_L001
    LQI $R2,10
    LQI $R1,16
    INT 0
    LQI $R2,13
    LQI $R1,16
    INT 0

    # print the address of a label
    LAD $R4,proc1_L001
    MOV $R2,$R4
    LBI $R1,20
    INT 0
    LQI $R2,10
    LQI $R1,16
    INT 0
    LQI $R2,13
    LQI $R1,16
    INT 0
    HALT
.PE
.PB proc2
    LQI $R1,23
    MOV $R3,$R1
.PE
```

This program will stream the following output to standard output:

```
125
18
```

By looking at the listing of this file, you can see how the assembler replaces the label and procedure identifiers with their addresses in the bytecode translation.

```
#++++++++++++++++++++++++++++++++++++++++++++
1).PB proc1
3)[0]          LAD $R4,proc2        [6][11][0][0][0][0][0][0][0][125]
4)[10]         MOV $R2,$R4          [32][9][11]
5)[13]         LBI $R1,20           [0][8][20]
6)[16]         INT 0                [39][0]
7)             .PL proc1_L001
8)[18]         LQI $R2,10           [3][9][0][0][0][0][0][0][0][10]
9)[28]         LQI $R1,16           [3][8][0][0][0][0][0][0][0][16]
10)[38]        INT 0                [39][0]
11)[40]        LQI $R2,13           [3][9][0][0][0][0][0][0][0][13]
12)[50]        LQI $R1,16           [3][8][0][0][0][0][0][0][0][16]
13)[60]        INT 0                [39][0]
16)[62]        LAD $R4,proc1_L001   [6][11][0][0][0][0][0][0][0][18]
17)[72]        MOV $R2,$R4          [32][9][11]
18)[75]        LBI $R1,20           [0][8][20]
19)[78]        INT 0                [39][0]
21)[80]        LQI $R2,10           [3][9][0][0][0][0][0][0][0][10]
22)[90]        LQI $R1,16           [3][8][0][0][0][0][0][0][0][16]
23)[100]       INT 0                [39][0]
24)[102]       LQI $R2,13           [3][9][0][0][0][0][0][0][0][13]
25)[112]       LQI $R1,16           [3][8][0][0][0][0][0][0][0][16]
26)[122]       INT 0                [39][0]
27)[124]       HALT                 [42]
28) .PE
#++++++++++++++++++++++++++++++++++++++++++++
29).PB proc2
30)[125]       LQI $R1,23           [3][8][0][0][0][0][0][0][0][23]
31)[135]       MOV $R3,$R1          [32][10][8]
32) .PE
```

When the assembler hits the two LAD instructions (lines 3 and 16), it will take the address of the procedure and label in the symbol table and use these values to replace the procedure identifier and label identifier.

Instruction	Opcode	Register	Address
LAD $R4, proc2	6	11	125
LAD $R4, proc1_L001	6	11	18

You can verify all this by checking the address values, which are located in the listing text directly after the line numbers on the left side. Sure enough, proc2 starts at byte 125, and proc1_L001 is at byte 18.

Loading and Storing Data

In the last section, I mentioned that there were a number of HEC assembly instructions that operate on data located in memory. We're going to look at a few of these instructions in this section. Tables 7-5 and 7-6 provide a summary of these instructions.

Table 7-5

Instruction	Meaning
LB $r1, $r2	Loads the byte located at the address in $r2 into $r1
LW $r1, $r2	Loads the word located at the address in $r2 into $r1
LD $r1, $r2	Loads the double word located at the address in $r2 into $r1
LQ $r1, $r2	Loads the quad word located at the address in $r2 into $r1
LF1 $f1, $f2	Loads the single-precision float located at the address in $f2 into $f1
LF2 $d1, $d2	Loads the double-precision float located at the address in $d2 into $d1

Table 7-6

Instruction	Meaning
SB $r1, $r2	Places the byte in $r1 at the address specified by $r2
SW $r1, $r2	Places the word in $r1 at the address specified by $r2
SD $r1, $r2	Places the double word in $r1 at the address specified by $r2
SQ $r1, $r2	Places the quad word in $r1 at the address specified by $r2
SF1 $f1, $f2	Places the single-precision float in $f1 at the address specified by $f2
SF2 $d1, $d2	Places the double-precision float in $d1 at the address specified by $d2

Unlike the load instructions you saw earlier, which act on immediate operands, these instructions operate on data that is either in memory or in a register. Now you know why I introduced direct memory addressing in the previous section. In order to use these instructions, you must have an address in one of the registers.

The following program is a simple illustration of loading and storing. The program stores a word in memory and then loads it back into a register. To prove that everything turns out OK, the program prints the loaded value to the screen.

```
.PB proc1
      # store -43 in memory and then load
      LAD $R10,proc2
      LQI $R2,-43
      SW  $R2,$R10
      LW  $R3,$R10

      # print what we loaded
      MOV $R2,$R3
      LBI $R1,20
      INT 0

      LQI $R2,10
      LQI $R1,16
      INT 0
      LQI $R2,13
      LQI $R1,16
      INT 0
      HALT
```

```
.PE
.PB proc2
    NOP
    NOP
.PE
```

When run, this program should simply print out the value −43 and then exit.

If you create a listing of the previous program, you will see that the proc2 procedure is located at address 79. The store operation takes a word containing the value −43 and places it at address 79. The load operation merely fetches this value.

As you can see, I violated my own principles and created a static block of storage in the bytecode segment under the guise of a procedure consisting of NOP instructions. This is a necessity, however, because I haven't introduced indirect addressing yet and indirect addressing is how data items are normally referenced.

Now, let's get a little more complicated. This time, I'm going to store a double word in memory, but then only load a part of that double word.

```
.PB proc1
    # store -43 in memory and then load
    LAD $R10,proc2
    LQI $R2,11329042
    SD  $R2,$R10
    LW  $R3,$R10

    # print what we loaded
    MOV $R2,$R3
    LBI $R1,20
    INT 0

    LQI $R2,10
    LQI $R1,16
    INT 0
    LQI $R2,13
    LQI $R1,16
    INT 0
    HALT
.PE
.PB proc2
    NOP
    NOP
    NOP
    NOP
.PE
```

When this program is run, the value −8686 is printed to standard output. Why?

Well, let's take a closer look at what happens and work through the program in slow motion. As before, the proc2 procedure starts at address 79, so this is where our make-shift storage area begins. The store instruction has the value 11,329,042 in its first register operand. In hexadecimal, this value looks like 0x00ACDE12. The store instruction takes this value and places it at address 79 (see Figure 7-2).

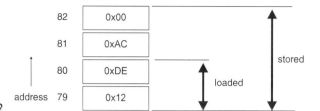

Figure 7-2

The Intel architecture I ran this on is little-endian, so the byte at address 79 will be set to the value 0x12. When the load instruction is executed, only the first two bytes are captured because the load instruction LW loads word-size values from memory. This means that the value 0xDE12 is placed in the $R3 register. Now, if we look at 0xDE12 in binary, we see:

1101111000010010

Given that the load and store instructions treat their operand values as signed, the leftmost bit will cause the value (via two's complement) to be interpreted as negative such that we end up with -8686.

Don't forget the distinction between loading and storing data. It's very easy to confuse these two because load and store have similar meanings in everyday English. Loading data transfers values from memory to a register. Storing data transfers values from a register to memory.

	Source		Destination
Load:	memory	→	register
Store:	register	→	memory

Another thing to keep in mind is that data is loaded and stored with a sign extension. This ensures that if you store –1 in memory, when you load it back you will still have –1. You might want to take a look at the virtual machine instruction implementations in `load.c` to get a better idea of what I mean.

Arithmetic

The HEC assembly language has the standard set of instructions to handle basic integer arithmetic. Table 7-7 provides a summary of these instructions.

Table 7-7

Instruction	Meaning
ADD $r1, $r2, $r3	Places the sum of $r2 and $r3 in $r1
SUB $r1, $r2, $r3	Subtracts $r3 from $r2 and place the result in $r1
MULT $r1, $r2, $r3	Places the product of $r2 and $r3 in $r1
DIV $r1, $r2, $r3, $r4	Divides $r3 by $r4, and puts the quotient in $r1and the remainder in $r2

Integer division always truncates the fractional portion of the quotient. This leaves us with an integer-valued quotient. The remainder is placed in another register (this only makes sense because an integer register is not capable of storing non-integer values). For example, consider the following scenario:

```
$R3 = 21    $R4 = 4
```

The instruction:

```
DIV $R1, $R2, $R3, $R4
```

would produce the following result:

```
$R1 = 5    $R2 = 1
```

There are a couple of other things to keep in mind with regard to integer arithmetic. First, the integer arithmetic instructions treat all the operands as signed values. Take a look at the virtual machine's intmath.c source file to get a better idea of how this is implemented.

Second, if a numeric overflow occurs, there are no exceptions thrown. Instead, a value will just quietly switch signs. Hence, it is the responsibility of the developer to stay on guard for overflows.

Here is an example that illustrates both of these points. In this program we take the largest integer value possible and then observe what happens when we increment it.

```
.PB mathproc

    # 8-byte integers roll over after 9,223,372,036,854,775,807
    LQI $R1,9223372036854775807
    LQI $R2,1
    ADD $R3,$R2,$R1

    # print what we have computed
    MOV $R2,$R3
    LBI $R1,20
    INT 0
    LQI $R2,10
    LQI $R1,16
    INT 0
    LQI $R2,13
    LQI $R1,16
    INT 0
    HALT
.PE
```

When run, this program prints the following value to standard output:

```
-9223372036854775808
```

As you can see, adding 1 to the largest possible positive signed value caused it to roll over and change sign.

The HEC virtual machine also has equivalent mathematical instructions for single-precision and double-precision floating-point values. These instructions are summarized in Tables 7-8 and 7-9.

Table 7-8

Instruction	Meaning
FADD $f1, $f2, $f3	Places the sum of $f2 and $f3 in $f1
FSUB $f1, $f2, $f3	Subtracts $f3 from $f2 and places the result in $f1
FMULT $f1, $f2, $f3	Places the product of $f2 and $f3 in $f1
FDIV $f1, $f2, $f3	Divides $f2 by $f3 and places the quotient in $f1

Table 7-9

Instruction	Meaning
DADD $d1, $d2, $d3	Places the sum of $d2 and $d3 in $d1
DSUB $d1, $d2, $d3	Subtracts $d3 from $d2 and places the result in $d1
DMULT $d1, $d2, $d3	Places the product of $d2 and $d3 in $d1
DDIV $d1, $d2, $d3	Divides $d2 by $d3 and places the quotient in $d1

As with the integer arithmetic functions, these functions do not openly complain when a floating-point number blows up to infinity or becomes nonsensical. It is the responsibility of the developer to check for bad values. Fortunately, in the case of floating-point values, the $R1= 4 function of the INT 8 instruction can be used to query the status of a floating-point value. See Chapter 6 for details on this invaluable interrupt function.

Bitwise Operations

I have mixed feelings about bitwise operations. Typically, they are used in situations where memory is scarce or where high-speed arithmetic must be performed. For example, one very space-efficient way to flag certain conditions in a program is to use the bits within an unsigned integer. Another situation in which you might need to use bitwise instructions is when you are interfacing with hardware. There are a number of peripheral components, like network cards, that communicate by packing several pieces of information into a single byte.

An unsigned byte is capable of indicating eight distinct states. In the following snippet of code, I define an unsigned character and a set of macros (one macro for each bit-sized flag in the character):

```
#define BIT_MASK_1    1     /* 00000001 */
#define BIT_MASK_2    2     /* 00000010 */
#define BIT_MASK_3    4     /* 00000100 */
#define BIT_MASK_4    8     /* 00001000 */
#define BIT_MASK_5    16    /* 00010000 */
#define BIT_MASK_6    32    /* 00100000 */
#define BIT_MASK_7    64    /* 01000000 */
#define BIT_MASK_8    128   /* 10000000 */

unsigned char flags;
```

Let's say you wanted to see if the current state of the program was such that the conditions associated with the second or fourth bitmask existed. In other words, you wanted to check to see if the second or fourth bits of the flag were set. You could check for this using the following code:

```
if(flags&(BIT_MASK_2|BIT_MASK_4))
{
    printf("condition %u holds\n",(BIT_MASK_2|BIT_MASK_4));
}
```

Another use for bitwise operations is to multiply and divide quickly. For example, in order to divide an unsigned number by 2, you would shift the number one bit to the right. To multiply an unsigned number by 2, you would shift the number one bit to the left.

$$10 / 2 = 5 \qquad 10 = 00001010 \qquad 5 = 00000101$$
$$15 \times 2 = 30 \qquad 15 = 00001111 \qquad 30 = 00011110$$

This same type of operation holds when you want to multiply and divide by a value that is a power of two. Shifting operations are much faster than normal multiplication and division operations. On some platforms, shifting operations are almost ten times faster than arithmetic operations.

 NOTE One of the absolutely most frustrating bugs to hunt down is one that occurs in code that twiddles bits around. If your symbolic debugger cannot display values in binary format, you are hosed. Sane languages, like Java, have instituted the Boolean data type in an attempt to encourage programmers to give each flag its own Boolean variable.

With all that said, and with a mild sense of trepidation, I will introduce HEC's bitwise instructions. Table 7-10 summarizes these.

Table 7-10

Instruction	Meaning
AND $r1, $r2, $r3	Places the bitwise AND of $r1 and $r2 in $r3
OR $r1, $r2, $r3	Places the bitwise OR of $r1 and $r2 in $r3
XOR $r1, $r2, $r3	Places the bitwise XOR of $r1 and $r2 in $r3
NOT $r1, $r2	Places the bitwise NOT of $r1 in $r2
BT $r1, $r2, $r3	If the bit specified by the value in $r3 is on, sets $r1 to 1; otherwise set $r1 to 0
BS $r1, $r2	Sets the bit specified by the value in $r2 in $r1
SRA $r1, $r2, $r3	Copies to $r1 the value of $r2 shifted exactly $r3 bits to the right
SRL $r1, $r2, $r3	Copies to $r1 the value of $r2 shifted exactly $r3 bits to the right
SL $r1, $r2, $r3	Copies to $r1 the value of $r2 shifted exactly $r3 bits to the left

If you haven't been exposed to bitwise operations in the past, you probably have a few questions you need answered. For example, what is a bitwise AND?

The bitwise AND, OR, XOR, and NOT instructions perform operations which are governed by the following truth table (Table 7-11).

Table 7-11

A	B	A AND B	A OR B	A XOR B	NOT A
1	0	0	1	1	0
0	1	0	1	1	1
1	1	1	1	0	0
0	0	0	0	0	1

When these bitwise operations are applied to two integer values, the operations displayed in Table 7-11 are performed for all the corresponding bits in each value. For example, assume the following two values:

```
$R1 = 179 (10110011 in binary)
$R2 = 121 (01111001 in binary)
```

If we were to bitwise AND these values together, we would get:

```
        10110011
AND     01111001
        00110001
```

 NOTE A bit (a single binary digit) is said to be set when its value has been changed to 1. When a bit's value is switched to 0, the bit is said to be *cleared*.

Bitwise ANDing is a useful technique for turning bits off. This is because if a particular bit in either of two values being ANDed is 0, the resulting bit will be 0. An effective way to check to see if a bit is set in a value is to AND the value with a mask that only has a single bit set (i.e., you can bitwise AND a value with the mask 00000010 to see if the second bit is set in that value).

```
        00000010
AND     01111001
        00000000
```

As you can see, the second bit is not set in $R2.

If we were to bitwise OR the values in $R1 and $R2 together, we would get:

```
        10110011
OR      01111001
        11111011
```

Bitwise ORing is a useful technique for turning bits on. This is because if a particular bit in either of two values being ORed is 1, the resulting bit will be 1.

If we were to bitwise XOR these values together, we would get:

```
        10110011
XOR     01111001
        11001010
```

If we were to bitwise NOT the value in $R1, we would get:

```
NOT     10110011
        01001100
```

The unary NOT instruction basically reverses the state of all the bits in an operand.

The SRA instruction stands for Shift Right Arithmetic. The SRA instruction is used to shift the bits in a byte to the right. In the case of the SRA, the two's complement sign bit (i.e., the leftmost bit) will enter in on the left side.

```
SRA  00010011 = 00001001
SRA  10011001 = 11001100
```

The SRL instruction stands for Shift Right Logical. It works like the SRA instruction with the exception that the zero bit enters in on the left side.

```
SRL  10011001 = 01001100
```

The SL instruction is used to shift the bits in a value to the left. When the bits shift left, zero bits will enter on the right.

```
SL  10011001 = 00110010
```

As I mentioned earlier, bitwise shifting is a clean way to do fast multiplication and division on unsigned integer values. A shift left is equivalent to multiplying a value by two, and a shift right (via SRL) is equivalent to dividing a value by two. The only problem I have with this is that, in a hardware driver program that is already rife with bitwise operations, using this technique may actually confuse the reader. They may not be sure if you are dividing by two or adjusting for status flags.

NOTE The bitwise instructions can only be applied to integer operands. Don't ever try to perform bitwise operations on floating-point values or you will end up with garbage. This is reflected by the fact that only integer registers show up in Table 7-10, in case you didn't notice. All the bitwise operations treat their operands as unsigned integer values. The only exception to this rule is the SRA instruction.

Here is an example program that works with a few of the recently introduced instructions:

```
.PB bitproc

        #do some ANDing and ORing
        LQI $R1,32
        LQI $R2,100
        AND $R3,$R2,$R1
        LQI $R1,25
        OR $R2,$R3,$R1
        MOV $R5,$R2

        # print value in $R2
        LBI $R1,20
        INT 0
        LQI $R2,10
        LQI $R1,16
        INT 0
        LQI $R2,13
        LQI $R1,16
        INT 0

        #now do a shift, just for fun
        LQI $R1,1
```

```
    SRA $R2,$R5,$R1

    # print value in $R2
    LBI $R1,20
    INT 0
    LQI $R2,10
    LQI $R1,16
    INT 0
    LQI $R2,13
    LQI $R1,16
    INT 0

    HALT
.PE
```

When this program is run, the following output is streamed to standard output:

```
57
28
```

The BT and BS instructions are used to test for bits and set bits, respectively. The BT (i.e., Bit Test) instruction takes the value in its second register operand and checks to see if the bit specified by the third register operand is set. If this bit is set, the first register operand will be set to 1. Otherwise, the first register operand will be set to 0.

```
Given $R2 = 70  (01000110 in binary) and  $R3 = 6
BT $R1, $R2, $R3 will set  $R1=1
```

The bit specifier in the third register can range from 0 to 63. In the previous example, the value 6 causes the seventh bit in $R2 to be tested.

The BS (i.e., Bit Set) instruction is used to set bits. The bit specified by the second register operand will be set in the value specified by the first register operand. For example:

```
Given  $R1 = 0  and  $R2 = 5
BS $R1, $R2 will set  $R1=32
```

As with BT, the bit index specified by the second register operand can range from 0 to 63 (such that all 64 bits can be accessed). In the previous example, the sixth bit was set in $R1, changing it from 0 to 32.

One type of bitwise operation that I have not covered is bitwise rotation. I have tried to avoid the topic partially because I don't want to encourage you to bit bash. However, like every parent who has had to deal with a teenager, I felt that if I openly discouraged you, you would make a point of focusing on bit manipulation.

One of the issues with bit shifting is that information is lost when bits are shifted out of range. Bitwise rotation is a way to deal with this problem. Left bitwise rotation takes bits shifted out on the left and places them on the right side. For example, assume we are dealing with a byte storing the unsigned value 218:

```
11011010
```

A single left bitwise rotation would shift every bit one position left. The leftmost bit shifted out, in this case a 1, would then be placed on the right side to produce the following value:

```
10110101
```

The right bitwise rotation is merely the inverse of left rotation. Bits are shifted right, and the rightmost bit shifted out is placed on the left side. If we took the byte in the previous example and performed a right bitwise rotation, we would end up with:

    01101101

Figure 7-3 illustrates the basic mechanism behind right and left bitwise rotation.

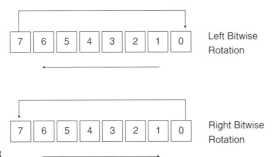

Figure 7-3

 NOTE I did not implement instructions that perform rotation. This does not mean I left you completely out at sea. You can simulate rotation using the BT instruction and bitwise shifts.

Data Conversion

There will be times when you will need to convert an integer into a floating-point value and vice versa. When this happens, the instructions in this section will come in handy. Table 7-12 summarizes the conversion functions supplied in the HEC instruction set.

Table 7-12

Instruction	Meaning
CAST_IF $R, $F	Casts the single-precision float in $F to an integer and places it in $R
CAST_ID $R, $D	Casts the double-precision float in $D to an integer and places it in $R
CAST_FI $F, $R	Casts the integer in $R to a single-precision float and places it in $F
CAST_FD $F, $D	Casts a double-precision float in $D to a single-precision float in $F
CAST_DI $D, $R	Casts the integer in $R to a double-precision float and places it in $D
CAST_DF $D, $F	Casts a single-precision float in $F to a double-precision float in $D

Each cast instruction has a two-character suffix. This suffix is intended to help indicate the conversion being performed. Naturally, when a floating-point value is cast to an integer, the fractional portion of the number is truncated.

Here is a sample program that demonstrates a few of these instructions.

```
.PB convertproc

        # convert a float to an integer
        LF1I $F1,-56.02e7
        CAST_IF $R2,$F1

        # print value in $R2
        LBI $R1,20
        INT 0
        LQI $R2,10
        LQI $R1,16
        INT 0
        LQI $R2,13
        LQI $R1,16
        INT 0

        # try it again with a different value
        LF1I $F1,127.0754
        CAST_IF $R2,$F1

        # print value in $R2
        LBI $R1,20
        INT 0
        LQI $R2,10
        LQI $R1,16
        INT 0
        LQI $R2,13
        LQI $R1,16
        INT 0

        #convert an integer to a float
        LQI $R1,89345768
        CAST_DI $D1,$R1

        # print value in $R2
        LBI $R1,21
        INT 0
        LQI $R2,10
        LQI $R1,16
        INT 0
        LQI $R2,13
        LQI $R1,16
        INT 0

        HALT
.PE
```

When run, this program sends the following values to standard output:

```
-560200000
127
8.934577e+007
```

Program Flow Control

Program flow control instructions have the ability to alter a program's flow of execution (i.e., its path of execution). There are three different categories of program flow control instructions:

- Jump instructions
- Selection instructions
- Iterative instructions

Jump instructions cause the execution path of a program to jump to another region of memory. Most of the jump instructions in HEC's instruction set are implemented by altering the contents of the $IP register.

Selection instructions provide several different potential paths of execution for an executing process. The path of execution actually taken, out of all the potential paths, usually depends upon the current machine state of the process. In other words, a selection instruction presents an oncoming process with several alternatives. The process chooses an alternative based on its current machine state.

Iterative instructions facilitate the repeated execution of a set of instructions. The number of times that the set of instructions is repeated (i.e., iterated) typically depends on the state of one or more conditional values. For example, a block of code will execute as long as the contents of $R1 are less than 25.

The best way to understand how to use these program control instructions is to look at how program control is implemented in a higher-level language, such as C, and offer equivalent implementations in assembly language. The C programming language has the following program flow control statements:

- Jump statements — goto, procedure calls
- Selection statements — if-else, switch
- Iterative statements — for, while

Jumping

The HEC assembly language provides the following instruction to implement program flow jumping (see Table 7-13).

Table 7-13

Instruction	Meaning
JMP $R	Jumps to the address specified by the $R integer register

The JMP instruction expects a single register operand. This register must be one of the general integer registers (i.e., $R7, $R13, etc.). The integer register specified must contain the address of the memory location to which program control is supposed to jump.

A program written in C can cause program execution to jump using the goto statement, or by making a procedure call. For example:

```
#include<stdio.h>

void myfunction()
{
    printf("%d\n",42);
}

void main()
{
    goto mylabel;
    printf("%d\n",7);
    mylabel:
    myfunction();
    printf("%d\n",6);
    return;
}
```

This program uses a goto statement to jump over the first print statement. This program also makes a function call, which again causes the path of execution to jump to the body of the invoked function.

We can recreate both of these using the JMP instruction and the direct addressing mode. Recall that direct addressing mode allows the address of the label or procedure to be loaded into an integer register. The JMP instruction can then use the loaded value to perform a jump.

```
.PB startproc

    # jump over the following print statement
    LAD $R1,startproc_L001
    JMP $R1

    # print value 7
    LQI $R2,7
    LBI $R1,20
    INT 0
    LQI $R2,10
    LQI $R1,16
    INT 0
    LQI $R2,13
    LQI $R1,16
    INT 0

    .PL startproc_L001

    # jump to function
    LAD $R1,myfunction
    JMP $R1

    .PL startproc_L002

    # print value 6
    LQI $R2,6
    LBI $R1,20
```

```
        INT 0
        LQI $R2,10
        LQI $R1,16
        INT 0
        LQI $R2,13
        LQI $R1,16
        INT 0

        HALT
    .PE

    .PB myfunction
        # print value 42
        LQI $R2,42
        LBI $R1,20
        INT 0
        LQI $R2,10
        LQI $R1,16
        INT 0
        LQI $R2,13
        LQI $R1,16
        INT 0
        LAD $R1,startproc_L002
        JMP $R1
    .PE
```

As you can see, this is pretty simple. You just apply the LAD instruction, and then perform a JMP operation.

NOTE The function call we made is, in a way, very constrained. We didn't pass arguments, use local variables with the function, or return a value. We will learn how to implement these features later on when I introduce the concept of an activation record.

Selection

The HEC assembly language provides five instructions to support selective program execution.

Table 7-14

Instruction	Meaning
JE $r1, $r2, $r3	If the contents of $r1 and $r2 are equal, jumps to the address in $r3
JNE $r1, $r2, $r3	If the contents of $r1 and $r2 are not equal, jumps to the address in $r3
SLT $r1, $r2, $r3	Sets $r1 to 1 if $r2 is less than $r3, otherwise sets $r1 to 0
FSLT $f1, $f2, $f3	Sets $f1 to 1 if $f2 is less than $f3, otherwise sets $f1 to 0
DSLT $d1, $d2, $d3	Sets $d1 to 1 if $d2 is less than $d3, otherwise sets $d1 to 0

The JE, JNE, and SLT instructions all require integer register operands. The FSLT instruction expects $F register operands containing single-precision floating-point values. The DSLT instruction expects $D register operands containing double-precision floating-point values.

You might notice that I did not include JE and JNE type instructions for floating-point values. This is because checking to see if two different floating-point values are equal is a waste of time. Ninety-nine point nine percent of the time, two different floating-point values will never be equal. Even two floating-point values that store the same basic quantity will vary by a small amount. Hence, as far as floating-point values go, it only makes sense to see if one value is greater than or less than another. This is what the FSLT and DSLT instructions are all about.

The C programming language has two basic statements that implement selective execution: if-else and switch. Here is an example illustrating the use of both of these constructs:

```c
#include<stdio.h>

void main()
{
    int i;
    i=127;

    if(i>300){ printf("%d\n",300); }
    else{ printf("%d\n",i); }

    switch(i)
    {
        case 0:{ printf("%d\n",0); }break;
        case 127:{ printf("%d\n",127); }break;
        default:{ printf("%d\n",-1); }
    }

    return;
}
```

We can recreate this code fairly easily in terms of HEC assembly language:

```
.PB selectproc

    #storage
    .PL selectproc_i
    NOP
    NOP
    NOP
    NOP
    NOP
    NOP
    NOP
    NOP

    # set i to 127
    LAD $R4,selectproc_i
```

```
LQI $R3,127
SQ  $R3,$R4

# check to see if i>300
LQ   $R3,$R4
LQI $R2,300
SLT $R1,$R2,$R3
LQI $R2,1
LAD $R3,selectproc_L1
LAD $R4,selectproc_L2
JE   $R1,$R2,$R3
JNE $R1,$R2,$R4

# go here if 300<i and print 300
.PL selectproc_L1
LQI  $R2,300
LAD $R10,selectproc_L3
LAD $R1,printNumber
JMP $R1

# go here if i<=300 and print i
.PL selectproc_L2
LAD $R4,selectproc_i
LQ   $R2,$R4
LAD $R10,selectproc_L3
LAD $R1,printNumber
JMP $R1

# end of the if-statement
.PL selectproc_L3

# start of the switch statement
LAD $R4,selectproc_i
LQ   $R1,$R4

LQI $R5,0
LQI $R6,127
LAD $R2,selectproc_L4
JE $R1,$R5,$R2
LAD $R2,selectproc_L5
JE $R1,$R6,$R2

#default here
LQI $R2,-1
LAD $R10,selectproc_end
LAD $R1,printNumber
JMP $R1

.PL selectproc_L4
LQI $R2,0
LAD $R10,selectproc_end
LAD $R1,printNumber
JMP $R1
```

```
        .PL selectproc_L5
        LQI $R2,127
        LAD $R10,selectproc_end
        LAD $R1,printNumber
        JMP $R1

        .PL selectproc_end
        HALT
.PE

# print value in $R2
# return to address in $R10
.PB printNumber
        LBI $R1,20
        INT 0
        LQI $R2,10
        LQI $R1,16
        INT 0
        LQI $R2,13
        LQI $R1,16
        INT 0
        JMP $R10
.PE
```

By looking at the previous code, you should be able to generalize the tactics being applied. For example, to perform a greater-than/less-than selection, you apply the SLT instruction (or DSLT or FSLT) and then pass the resulting 1 or 0 value in the first register operand of the SLT instruction to JE and JNE.

To be honest, the hardest part of building if-else selection statements is constructing the assembly code needed to evaluate the conditional expression specified by the if statement. For example, take the following snippet of C code:

```
#include<stdio.h>

void main()
{
    int k;
    int i=20;
    int j=56;
    if((i+j<80)&&(i!=j)&&(i/2==10))
    {
        k=34;
        printf("%d\n",k);
    }

    return;
}
```

The previous if statement's expression is going to resolve into a morass of assembly instructions. You would need to evaluate each of the three subexpressions in order and execute the enclosed code block only if all three subexpressions are true. It looks easy in C (which is the whole point of using C), but in assembly code evaluating the conditional expression is a little more harrowing. What you'll end up with is something that looks like:

```
.PB selectproc

    #storage
    .PL selectproc_k
    NOP
    .PL selectproc_i
    NOP
    .PL selectproc_j
    NOP

    # set i to 20
    LAD $R4,selectproc_i
    LBI $R3,20
    SB  $R3,$R4

    # set j to 56
    LAD $R4,selectproc_j
    LBI $R3,56
    SB  $R3,$R4

    # check for (i+j)<80
    LAD $R4,selectproc_i
    LB  $R2,$R4
    LAD $R4,selectproc_j
    LB  $R3,$R4
    ADD $R1,$R2,$R3
    LBI $R4,80
    SLT $R2,$R1,$R4
    LBI $R5,0
    LAD $R6,selectproc_end
    JE  $R2,$R5,$R6

    # check for i!=j
    LAD $R4,selectproc_i
    LB  $R2,$R4
    LAD $R4,selectproc_j
    LB  $R3,$R4
    LAD $R6,selectproc_end
    JE  $R2,$R3,$R6

    # check for i/10==2
    LAD $R4,selectproc_i
    LB  $R3,$R4
    LBI $R4,10
    DIV $R1,$R2,$R3,$R4
    LBI $R2,2
    LAD $R6,selectproc_end
    JNE $R1,$R2,$R6

    # if you made it this far set k=34 and print k
    LAD $R4,selectproc_k
    LBI $R3,34
    SB  $R3,$R4
    LB  $R2,$R4
```

```
        LAD $R10,selectproc_end
        LAD $R1,printNumber
        JMP $R1

        .PL selectproc_end
        HALT
.PE

# print value in $R2
# return to position in $R10
.PB printNumber
    LBI $R1,20
    INT 0
    LQI $R2,10
    LQI $R1,16
    INT 0
    LQI $R2,13
    LQI $R1,16
    INT 0
    JMP $R10
.PE
```

Performing a switch statement is far simpler. This is due to the switch statement's reliance on the JE instruction. You basically take an integer value and run it through a series of comparisons. The value that matches is the one that will have its code executed. The underlying nature of the JE instruction is the reason switch statements only work with integer arguments.

Iteration

There are no particular instructions that are specifically intended for iteration. Instead, iteration is implemented by using certain combinations of selective and jumping instructions.

The C programming language has a couple of widely used statements that are used to produce iteration. These are the for loop and the while loop. The for loop is useful when you know in advance how many times you want to execute a block of code.

```
#include<stdio.h>

void main()
{
    int i;
    for(i=0;i<10;i++){ printf("%d\n",i); }
    return;
}
```

The equivalent of this short program in HEC assembly code looks like:

```
.PB loopproc

    #storage
    .PL loopproc_i
    NOP
```

```
        # set i to 0
        LAD $R4,loopproc_i
        LBI $R3,0
        SB  $R3,$R4

        # check to see if i<10
        .PL loopproc_L1
        LQI $R3,10
        LB  $R2,$R4
        SLT $R1,$R2,$R3
        LQI $R4,0
        LAD $R5,loopproc_end
        JE  $R1,$R4,$R5

        # print out i
        LAD $R4,loopproc_i
        LB $R2,$R4
        LAD $R10,loopproc_L2
        LAD $R1,printNumber
        JMP $R1

        # increment i
        .PL loopproc_L2
        LBI $R3,1
        LAD $R4,loopproc_i
        LB  $R2,$R4
        ADD $R1,$R2,$R3
        SB  $R1,$R4
        LAD $R1,loopproc_L1
        JMP $R1

        .PL loopproc_end
        HALT
.PE

# print value in $R2
# return to position in $R10
.PB printNumber
    LBI $R1,20
    INT 0
    LQI $R2,10
    LQI $R1,16
    INT 0
    LQI $R2,13
    LQI $R1,16
    INT 0
    JMP $R10
.PE
```

The while loop is useful for iterating through a block of code when you don't know how many times you want to execute the block of code. In many ways, however, a while loop is just a for loop that has its initializer located outside the loop and its increment rule located inside the loop. In this sense, a while loop is just a lazy, spread-out for loop.

```
#include<stdio.h>

void main()
{
    int i;
    i=10;
    while(i>0){ printf("%d\n",i); i--; }
    return;
}
```

The equivalent of this short while loop program in HEC assembly code looks just like the previous assembly language equivalent of the for loop program. This just goes to show how similar the while loop and for loop are at the machine level.

As with selection statements, the most difficult part of implementing something like a for loop or a while loop will be constructing the code that evaluates the loop's conditional expression. Both the for loop and the while loop use conditional expressions to determine if they should stop or continue looping through their target block of code.

Manipulating the Stack

The stack is one of the primary organs of the HEC run-time's anatomy. In order to make use of indirect addressing and dynamic memory allocation, you must first master the art of stack manipulation because both of these highly coveted features rely on the stack.

The stack is prepared by the virtual machine during initialization. The stack is delimited by the contents of the $SS register (Stack Start) and the $TOP register (the top of memory). The $SS register points to the first byte of the stack segment, which is to say that it holds the address of the lowest byte in the stack segment. The $TOP register is set up to contain the address of the last byte of the address space, which also happens to be the end of the stack (see Figure 7-4).

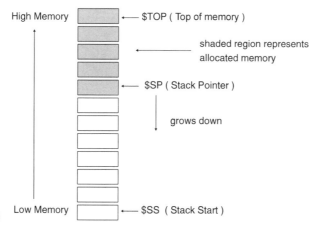

Figure 7-4

The $SP register (Stack Pointer) is initialized so that it points to the same byte as the $TOP register. This is done because the stack grows downward, towards $SS, as items are pushed on. By positioning the stack pointer at the top, we are giving it as much room as possible to grow. Running out of stack space can lead to tragedy, and this is one reason I allow the size of the stack to be specified on the virtual machine's command line.

There are two ways to manipulate the stack:

■ Direct modification of $SP

■ Using push and pop instructions

You can use the integer arithmetic functions discussed earlier to reposition the stack pointer. This is done by manually adding or subtracting a value from the contents of the $SP register. The other alternative is to use the push and pop instructions, which automatically increment and decrement the value of $SP behind the scenes.

The difference between the two techniques is that the push and pop instructions actually place values on the stack. Direct modification of the $SP register will allocate space, it just won't populate it. It will be up to you, the programmer, to populate memory storage that is allocated using direct manipulation of $SP.

Table 7-15 provides a summary of the push and pop instructions.

Table 7-15

Instruction	Meaning
PUSHB $R	Pushes the byte in $R on to the stack
PUSHW $R	Pushes the word in $R on to the stack
PUSHD $R	Pushes the double word in $R on to the stack
PUSHQ $R	Pushes the quad word in $R on to the stack
PUSHF1 $F	Pushes the single-precision floating-point value in $F onto the stack
PUSHF2 $D	Pushes the double-precision floating-point value in $D onto the stack
POPB $R	Pops the top byte off the stack and into $R
POPW $R	Pops the top word off the stack and into $R
POPD $R	Pops the top double word off the stack and into $R
POPQ $R	Pops the top quad word off the stack and into $R
POPF1 $F	Pops the top single-precision floating-point value off the stack and into $F
POPF2 $D	Pops the top double-precision floating-point value off the stack and into $D

The push instruction causes the stack pointer to be decremented. The space created by this operation will be populated by the push instruction's operand. The stack pointer will always point to the first byte of the data item on the top of the stack.

The pop instruction causes the stack pointer to be incremented. The storage reclaimed has its data stored in the pop instruction's operand. The push and pop operations are displayed in Figure 7-5 to give you a better idea how they function.

In Figure 7-5, I am assuming that I'm dealing with a native host that is little-endian, i.e., the low-order bytes of a value are in lower memory.

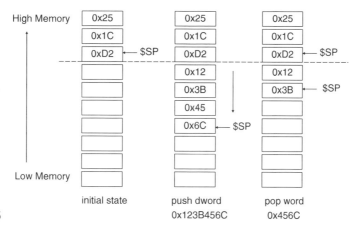

Figure 7-5

With manual stack pointer manipulation, storing and retrieving data is not as automated. Adding or subtracting values from the stack pointer does effectively change where it points. However, transferring data to and from the stack must be done manually. This is illustrated in Figure 7-6.

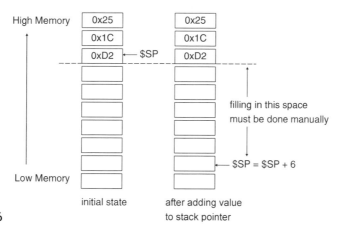

Figure 7-6

The stack is basically a data storage area. It is a kind of temporary scratch pad that applications can use to keep track of short-lived values. Recall, the stack is useful for operations that must be done and then undone. Thus, it is a good way to store, and then reclaim, temporary data. I designed the HEC virtual machine with the intent that the stack would provide storage space for variables and function parameters (this will be discussed in more depth later on). What distinguishes the stack from a free-for-all storage region, like the heap, is that there are rules that enforce a certain degree of regularity. In other words, the stack is predictable and the heap is chaotic. With the stack, you pretty much always know where the next chunk of memory will be allocated, regardless of how big or how small the data item to be allocated is.

The following short example illustrates stack management using both of the basic stack manipulation techniques:

```
    .PB stackproc

        #manually place word on stack
        LWI $R2,6570
        LQI $R3,2
        SUB $SP,$SP,$R3
        SW  $R2,$SP

        #pop word into $R2 then print
        POPW $R2
        LAD $R10,stackproc_L1
        LAD $R1,printNumber
        JMP $R1

        .PL stackproc_L1

        # push a quad word on to stack
        LQI $R2,-1234567890
        PUSHQ $R2

        # manually retrieve quad word and print
        LQ $R2,$SP
        LQI $R3,8
        SUB $SP,$SP,$R3
        LAD $R10,stackproc_end
        LAD $R4,printNumber
        JMP $R4

        .PL stackproc_end
        HALT
    .PE

# print value in $R2
# return to position in $R10
.PB printNumber
    LBI $R1,20
    INT 0
    LQI $R2,10
    LQI $R1,16
    INT 0
    LQI $R2,13
    LQI $R1,16
    INT 0
    JMP $R10
.PE
```

Indirect Memory Addressing Mode

Recall that earlier in this chapter I defined a memory addressing mode as a particular technique for specifying the location of an instruction operand that is located in memory. I also mentioned that the indirect memory addressing mode calculates the address of an operand in memory at run time, such that its address is not actually known until the program executes. This is because the indirect addressing mode uses values computed at run time to specify an address.

The indirect memory addressing mode is supported by the LAI instruction. It has the basic form:

```
LAI  $r1, $r2, identifer
```

The LAI instruction (Load Indirect Address) takes the integer offset associated with the third operand (the identifier) and adds it to the contents of the second register operand. The sum of the integer offset and register is placed in the first register operand. In other words:

```
$r1 = $r2  + idenfier_offset
```

The first two operands ($r1 and $r2) must both be integer-valued registers. The third operand is an identifier that is resolved to an integer offset by the HEC assembler. This is an important point: The identifier is resolved to an integer offset (exactly how this is done will be explained in later sections).

The second register operand ($r2) is assumed to hold the address of a byte somewhere in memory. The identifier represents a positive or negative integer offset from the base address in $r2. The final address of the data item to be referenced is determined by adding this offset to the base address (see Figure 7-7).

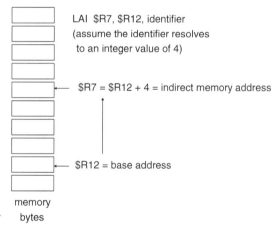

memory
bytes

Figure 7-7

 NOTE Now you know why indirect memory addresses cannot be resolved until run time. The value in $r2 will not be known until the program actually executes.

The key ingredient in the indirect memory addressing operation is the identifier, which I've been intentionally ambiguous about. The identifier can be the name of a function parameter, a local variable, or a global variable. The actual mechanism used to replace the identifier with its integer offset depends upon the type of identifier being used. I will discuss global variables and function-related storage items in the next couple of sections and spell out the particulars of each case.

NOTE The LAI instruction should not use the names of labels or procedures as operands. These identifiers are not resolved to integer offsets by the assembler; they are resolved to actual, full-fledged address values. The only identifiers that the LAI instruction can use are the names of global variables, function parameters, and local variables.

Defining Global Variable Storage

Up to this point, I have been using all sorts of unorthodox, and somewhat makeshift, techniques to allocate memory storage. I've used sections of a procedure, or entire procedures, along with dummy NOP instructions to meet my data storage needs.

However, we now have the tools necessary to allocate and access storage using the stack. Through stack manipulation we can create memory storage space. Using indirect memory addressing, we can reference that storage. In this section, I'm going to merge the material in the previous two sections to show you how to manage global data.

NOTE Originally, I assumed that all data would be allocated off the stack. This is due to the fact that the bytecode verifier assumes that it will encounter nothing but bytecode instructions during its traversal of the bytecode segment. The techniques I present in this chapter are the ones that I formally designed.

Global variables are declared programmatically using the set of directives in the following table.

Table 7-16

Directive	Meaning
.GB identifier [n]	Declares a global variable consisting of n bytes
.GW identifier [n]	Declares a global variable consisting of n words
.GD identifier [n]	Declares a global variable consisting of n double words
.GQ identifier [n]	Declares a global variable consisting of n quad words

For example, the following statement declares a global variable consisting of two words:

```
.GW  myglobal    2
```

The integer suffix is optional. If the integer suffix is not present, it means that only a single element of the given size is being declared. Thus, that the following two declarations are equivalent:

```
.GD  global_a    1
.GD  global_b
```

NOTE The previous directives declare global variables. By using the term "declare," I mean that the symbol table in the assembler is made aware of these variables. However, no storage is allocated. When storage is allocated for a variable, the variable is then defined. Declaration and definition are not the same thing.

For example, in the Java programming language, the following statement declares an object variable of type `String`:

```
String str_obj;
```

However, the memory storage for a `String` object is not allocated. All we have created up to this point is an implicit pointer (i.e., a 32-bit value) that will be used to store the address of the object when its storage is actually allocated.

The `String` object is defined when the following statement is applied:

```
str_obj = new String("this is my string");
```

This statement allocates memory from the Java virtual machine's heap and places the address of this object into the `str_obj` variable.

I will show you how to define global variables next.

At the beginning of an application, you will need to allocate storage for all the global variables. The easiest way to do this is to subtract the total size of all the global variables, measured in bytes, from the stack pointer. This effectively defines all of the global variables by allocating real estate for them on the stack.

The following code allocates 50 bytes for global storage:

```
LQI  $R1, 50
SUB  $SP, $SP, $R1
```

Because global variables should be accessible for the life span of a program, they will never need to be reclaimed. This means that you can execute the previous two instructions at the beginning of your application, and never have to worry about readjusting $SP. The initial decrementing is permanent and results in an informal redefinition of the top of the stack.

In an application, you can calculate the address of the first byte of a global variable using the following instruction:

```
LAI  $R, $TOP, global_name
```

The assembler resolves the name of the global variable to a negative integer offset from $TOP. The result of this is that the LAI instruction calculates the address of the first byte of the global variable and places it in $R. The assembler, during its first pass, keeps track of all the global variables it encounters and their individual sizes. The assembler also keeps a running tally of the total memory required for the global variables it has encountered. The address of the most recently declared global variable is merely the negative value of the running tally added to $TOP.

Here is an example to help clarify this. Assume a program declares the following global variables:

```
.GQ  gavr1
.GB  gvar2   3
.GD  gvar3
```

These variables require 15 bytes of storage. This means that at the beginning of the application, the following instructions will be needed to actually allocate the 15 bytes:

```
LQI $R1, 15
SUB $SP, $SP, $R1
```

The assembler keeps track of each global variable's offset from $TOP, such that when the memory from the stack is allocated for these variables, the following type of memory arrangement in the stack is produced:

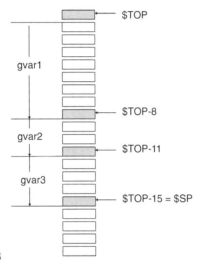

Figure 7-8

The program can reference these three global variables using the LAI instruction:

```
LAI  $R1, $TOP, gvar1
LAI  $R1, $TOP, gvar2
LAI  $R1, $TOP, gvar3
```

Behind the scenes, the assembler calculates an address to put in $R1 using the following sort of logic:

```
LAI $R1,$TOP,gvar1  →  LAI  $R1,$TOP,-8   →  $R1 = $TOP - 8  = address gvar1
LAI $R1,$TOP,gvar2  →  LAI  $R1,$TOP,-11  →  $R1 = $TOP - 11 = address gvar2
LAI $R1,$TOP,gvar3  →  LAI  $R1,$TOP,-15  →  $R1 = $TOP - 15 = address gvar3
```

The following program demonstrates how to declare, define, and access global variables:

```
.GQ gvar1
.GB gvar2 4

.PB globalproc

    # manually allocate global variable space
    LQI $R3,12
    SUB $SP,$SP,$R3

    # load values into variables
    LAI $R1,$TOP,gvar1
```

```
        LQI $R2,-320
        SQ  $R2,$R1

        LAI $R1,$TOP,gvar2
        LQI $R2,25
        SD  $R2,$R1

        # get values and print them
        LAI $R1,$TOP,gvar1
        LQ  $R2,$R1
        LAD $R10,globalproc_L1
        LAD $R4,printNumber
        JMP $R4

        .PL globalproc_L1

        # manually retrieve quad word and print
        LAI $R1,$TOP,gvar2
        LD  $R2,$R1
        LAD $R10,globalproc_end
        LAD $R4,printNumber
        JMP $R4

        .PL globalproc_end
        HALT
    .PE

# print value in $R2
# return to position in $R10
.PB printNumber
    LBI $R1,20
    INT 0
    LQI $R2,10
    LQI $R1,16
    INT 0
    LQI $R2,13
    LQI $R1,16
    INT 0
    JMP $R10
.PE
```

Constructing Activation Records

If you look at the previous examples in this chapter, you should see that my approach to handling functions has been, to say the least, improvised and informal. In this chapter, I'm going to introduce a formal approach to managing the invocation and execution of function calls.

As with global variables, we can use stack manipulation and indirect addressing to manage the parameters and local storage of a procedure.

NOTE When I talk about the *parameters* of a function, I am referring to the arguments fed to the function, the function's return value, and its return address.

 NOTE You could potentially use registers to pass parameter information to a function. However, using registers to pass parameters does not support recursion. Using the stack is a more flexible and powerful technique.

Managing the stack to facilitate a function call is the responsibility of both the procedure that is invoking the function and the function being invoked. Both entities must work together in order to pass information back and forth on the stack. I will start with the responsibilities that belong to the invoking function.

The following steps can be used to invoke a procedure and pass it arguments (see Figure 7-9):

1. Push the current function's state onto the stack.

2. Push the return value onto the stack.

3. Push function arguments onto the stack.

4. Push the return address onto the stack.

5. Jump to the location of the procedure.

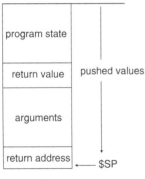

Figure 7-9   stack

When you invoke a function, it may use the same registers as the function that invoked it. To prevent the invoked function from affecting the function that invoked it, you might want to save a particular set of registers on the stack. This effectively saves the state of the current procedure so that the function call does not lead to unintentional side effects.

The second step (pushing the return value onto the stack) is really performed in order to allocate storage space for the return value. The function being invoked is the agent that is actually responsible for placing a meaningful value in this space. The invoking function is free to place garbage in this space if it wants to. An alternative to pushing a return value on the stack is to simply decrement the stack pointer. This operation serves the same basic purpose of allocating storage on the stack for a return value.

The return address passed to a function is typically the address of a label following the jump to the function. This way, execution after the function call picks up right where it left off.

Once the invoked function has done its business, the invoking function will need to take the following steps to get its hands on the return value and clean up the stack:

1. Pop the return address off the stack.

2. Pop the function arguments off the stack.

3. Pop the return value off the stack.

4. Pop the saved program state off the stack.

Another way to handle the return address and arguments is to simply increment the stack pointer. We really have no use for the function arguments and the return address once the invoked function has returned, so this is a cleaner and more efficient way to reclaim the corresponding stack space.

The function being invoked must also take a few steps to ensure that it can access the parameters passed to it and to create local storage:

1. Push $FP onto the stack (to save its value).

2. Copy the current $SP value into $FP.

3. Decrement $SP to allocate local storage.

4. Execute the function's instructions.

The result of all this stack manipulation is that we end up with a stack arrangement similar to that displayed in Figure 7-10.

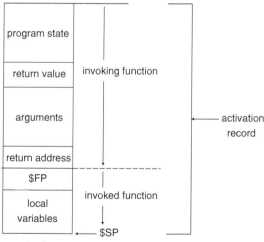

Figure 7-10   stack

The region of the stack used to store a function's parameters and local storage is referred to as the *activation record* because every time a procedure in activated (i.e., invoked) this information must be specified. An activation record is also known as a *stack frame*. The stack region displayed in Figure 7-10 is an example of an activation record.

After pushing the $FP register onto the stack, to save its value we copy the current value of $SP into $FP. Because $FP was just pushed on the stack, the $SP register will store the address of the first byte of the $FP value that we pushed on the stack. This allows us to use the new $FP value as a reference point with regard to the stack frame. Regardless of how the stack is manipulated inside the function, the $FP register will always point to the same byte. This is illustrated in Figure 7-11.

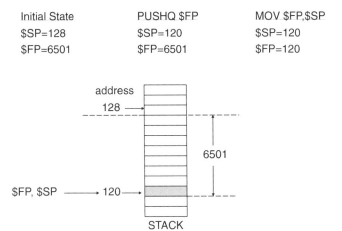

Initial State	PUSHQ $FP	MOV $FP,$SP
$SP=128	$SP=120	$SP=120
$FP=6501	$FP=6501	$FP=120

Figure 7-11

Inside the body of the invoked function, the various parameters and local storage can be accessed by adding an offset to the value in the $FP register. Now you know why the $FP register is called the *frame pointer*: It points to the stack frame and its constituents. I will explain the particulars of this technique later on.

When the function has done its thing and is ready to return, it must perform the following stack maintenance steps:

1. Construct the return address.

2. Reclaim local storage.

3. Pop $FP off the stack.

4. Jump to the return address.

This may all seem a little confusing. Let's look at a concrete example to expedite your understanding.

Let's assume that we're invoking a function, named myfunction, which takes a single word-size argument and generates a word-size return value. Furthermore, let's assume the function uses two local variables that are each a word in size. In C, this function would look like:

```
short int myfunction(short int arg)
{
        short int local1;
        short int local2;
        /* code goes here */
        return(retval);
}
```

If you invoked `myfunction` and followed all the previously described stack-based dance steps to push a return value, arguments, a return address, and local storage onto the stack, you would end up with a 24-byte activation record that looks like the one in Figure 7-12.

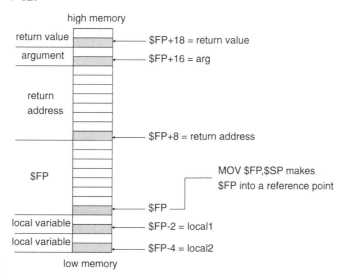

Figure 7-12

Inside of the function, once $FP is pushed on the stack and then assigned the value of $SP, the procedure's elements can be referenced using $FP as a base address:

Table 7-17

Element	Address
Return value	$FP+18
Argument	$FP+16
Return address	$FP+8
Local variable1	$FP–2
Local variable2	$FP–4

Using HEC assembly language, you could reference these variables with a couple of fairly straightforward instructions. For example, the following code computes the address of the function's single argument and places it in $R2:

```
LQI   $R1, 16
ADD   $R2, $FP, $R1
```

However, it can be a real pain to have to remember all the different offsets from $FP. Can you imagine how tedious this would become in a function that had five distinct arguments and 20 local variables? Wouldn't it be easier to be able to substitute an offset with a symbolic identifier? As it turns out, HEC assembly language does provide this kind of amenity.

There are three directives that procedures can use to declare procedure parameters and local storage (see Table 7-18).

Table 7-18

Directive	Meaning
.PR identifier +integer	Specifies the location of a procedure's return value
.PA identifier +integer	Specifies the location of a procedure's argument
.PV identifier –integer	Specifies the location of a procedure's local variable

More than anything else, these directives provide a symbolic way to refer to offsets in the activation record. These directives operate through a mechanism consisting of basic macro substitution. When the assembler encounters an identifier appearing in one of the previous three directives, it will replace the identifier with the integer value that follows it in the directive.

For example, to declare the various parameters and local variables in the `myfunction` routine, we would use the following set of directives:

```
.PR  retval  18
.PA  arg     16
.PV  local1  -2
.PV  local2  -4
```

To obtain the address of `myfunction`'s lone argument, instead of using:

```
LQI  $R1, 16
ADD  $R2, $FP, $R1
```

you can use the argument's identifier in conjunction with indirect addressing:

```
LAI  $R2, $FP, arg
```

This is because using the LAI instruction, in combination with an identifier from one of these three directives (.PR, .PA, .PV), is roughly equivalent to

```
LAI  $R2, $FP, arg  →  LAI  $R2, $FP, 16  →  $R2 = $FP  +16
```

As you can see, using the LAI instruction and an identifier is much simpler than using purely numeric offsets.

NOTE You, the programmer, are responsible for determining the value of the integer offset that follows the identifier in the .PR, .PA, and .PV directives. The assembler merely replaces the identifier with the integer value that you specified. If a compiler is generating the assembly code, then it is the compiler's job to keep track of and generate the numeric offset values.

NOTE The return address of a function will really only be referenced when the function is ready to return. Given this fact, I didn't think it was necessary to create a special directive to symbolically reference the return address. If you want to get around this restriction, you can always treat the return address as a function argument and use the .PA directive ot create storage space for the return address.

I will now demonstrate some of this section's concepts with a brief example.

```
.PB invokeproc

    #invoke the function computeAverage
    LQI $R1,4
    SUD $SP,$SP,$R1
    LDI $R1,100
    PUSHD $R1
    LDI $R1,50
    PUSHD $R1
    LDI $R1,30
    PUSHD $R1
    LAD $R1,invokeproc_L1
    PUSHQ $R1
    LAD $R1,computeAverage
    JMP $R1

    .PL invokeproc_L1
    LQI $R1,20
    ADD $SP,$SP,$R1
    POPD $R2

    #print the return value
    LBI $R1,20
    INT 0
    LQI $R2,10
    LQI $R1,16
    INT 0
    LQI $R2,13
    LQI $R1,16
    INT 0

    .PL invokeproc_end
    HALT
.PE

# function:     int computeAverage(int a,int b, int c)
# return value: average of the three arguments
.PB computeAverage
.PR avg        28
.PA arg_a 24
.PA arg_b 20
.PA arg_c 16
.PV total    -4

    #set up stack and local storage
    PUSHQ $FP
    MOV  $FP,$SP
    LQI  $R1,4
    SUB  $SP,$SP,$R1

    #take care of business
    LAI $R3,$FP,arg_a
```

```
        LD   $R2,$R3
        LAI  $R1,$FP,total
        SD   $R2,$R1

        LAI  $R3,$FP,arg_b
        LD   $R2,$R3
        LAI  $R3,$FP,total
        LD   $R4,$R3
        ADD  $R2,$R2,$R4
        SD   $R2,$R1

        LAI  $R3,$FP,arg_c
        LD   $R2,$R3
        LAI  $R3,$FP,total
        LD   $R4,$R3
        ADD  $R2,$R2,$R4
        SD   $R2,$R1

        LQI  $R4,3
        LD   $R2,$R1
        DIV  $R5,$R6,$R2,$R4
        LAI  $R1,$FP,avg
        SD   $R5,$R1

        #set up return address, reclaim local storage
        LQI  $R2,8
        ADD  $R3,$FP,$R2
        LQ   $R1,$R3
        MOV  $SP,$FP
        POPQ $FP
        JMP  $R1
    .PE
```

This program prints out the value 60, which is the average of 100, 50, and 30.

The invoking function in the previous example implements all but the first of the following eight steps:

1. Push the current function's state onto the stack.

2. Allocate storage on the stack for the return value.

3. Push function arguments onto the stack.

4. Push the return address onto the stack.

5. Jump to the location of the procedure.

6. Reclaim storage used for the return address and arguments.

7. Pop the return value off the stack.

8. Pop the saved program state off the stack.

From this example, it is also possible to build a generic skeleton for the body of a function. This skeleton implements the eight steps we mentioned earlier:

1. Push $FP onto the stack (to save its value).

2. Copy the current $SP value into $FP.

3. Decrement $SP to allocate local storage.

4. Execute the function's instructions.

5. Construct the return address.

6. Reclaim local storage.

7. Pop $FP off the stack.

8. Jump to the return address.

```
#---------------------------------------------------------------------------
.PB    function_name

# .PR, .PA, and .PV directives placed here

# (steps 1-3) set up $FP and allocate local storage
PUSHQ $FP
MOV    $FP,$SP
LQI    $R1,local_storage_size
SUB    $SP,$SP,$R1

# (step 4) function's code goes here

# (steps 5-8) set up the return address and reclaim local storage
LQI    $R2,8
ADD    $R3,$FP,$R2
LQ     $R1,$R3
MOV    $SP,$FP
POPQ   $FP
JMP    $R1

.PE
#---------------------------------------------------------------------------
```

 NOTE   The arrangement of elements in the activation record does not necessarily have to follow the conventions that I adhere to in this section. You are free to organize your activation records however you see fit. You can place the function arguments before the return value, or you can place your return address before the arguments. The key point to remember is that you must create, reclaim, and manage your activation records in a consistent manner. Doing things uniformly is the secret. Establish your conventions and then stick to them.

Data Type Mappings

The HEC assembly language deals with data that exists in multiples of four basic sizes: bytes, words, double words, and quad words. If you are building a development tool, however, it helps to know how to map high-level language data types to assembly-level constructs.

Take the following variable declarations in C:

```
struct mystruct
{
    char *name;
    short int age;
};
char            ch;
short int       si_var;
long  int       li_var;
float       flt;
double      dbl;
short       s_arr[5];
long int    *iptr;
struct mystruct  fields;
```

Using the global variable directives, I could declare the equivalent of these C variables in HEC assembly language:

```
.GB       ch
.GW       si_var
.GD       li_var
.GD       flt
.GQ       dbl
.GB       s_arr          20
.GQ       iptr
.GB       fields         10
```

It might be easier if we place the C and assembly declarations side by side.

Table 7-19

C Code		Assembly		
char	ch;	.GB	ch	
short int	si_var;	.GW	si_var	
long int	li_var;	.GD	li_var	
float	flt;	.GD	flt	
double	dbl;	.GQ	dbl	
short	s_arr[5];	.GB	s_arr	20
long int	*iptr;	.GQ	iptr	
struct mystruct	fields;	.GB	fields	10

The first five variables (ch through dbl) are relatively direct because they are declared as atomic data types. Character variables in C take up a single byte. Short integers in C require a word and long integers require a double word. The IEEE 754 floating-point standard defines single-precision floats as occupying 32 bits of storage and double-precision floating-point values as occupying 64 bits of storage. All of these storage requirements can be met by the .GB, .GW, .GD, and .GQ directives.

Pointers, in the C programming language, are used to store the address of another variable. This means that a pointer variable, like `iptr`, will need enough storage space of its own to hold an address. The HEC virtual machine has a 64-bit address space, which is another way of saying that the address of each byte of memory is specified by a 64-bit value. This means that `iptr` will require eight bytes of storage space. We can use the .GQ directive to satisfy this requirement.

The array variable, `s_arr`, and the structure variable, `fields`, are a whole different can of worms. In general, assembly languages tend to translate compound data types into large blobs of bytes. For example, the `s_arr` array is an array of five short integers. This is equivalent to an assembly language blob of 20 bytes. The `fields` structure variable requires at least ten bytes because it consists of a short integer (two bytes) and a character pointer (8 bytes). In assembly, we would create this structure variable using a blob of ten bytes. To create these blobs of arbitrary size, I use the .GB directive and specify an integer suffix equal to the size of the data item for which I want to allocate memory.

NOTE When I use the term "blob," I am referring to a contiguous sequence of bytes in memory that is being used for storing a compound data type.

As an example, let's look at how a commercial compiler like Visual Studio handles compound data types. Let's run the following code through the Visual C++ compiler and set the listing option.

```
struct mystruct
{
    char field0;
    char *field1;
    char *field2;
    short int field3;
};
struct mystruct  fields;
void main(){}
```

The assembly listing file that is generated looks something like:

```
_DATA     SEGMENT
COMM      _fields:BYTE:010H
_DATA     ENDS
PUBLIC    _main
_TEXT     SEGMENT
_main     PROC NEAR

; 9    : void main(){}

    push  ebp
    mov   ebp, esp
    pop   ebp
    ret   0
_main     ENDP
```

```
_TEXT    ENDS
END
```

As you can see, the Microsoft assembly code uses the COMM directive to create a communal variable. Communal variables do not have their storage allocated until load time, so I assume the compiler is trying to save space. Anyway, the COMM directive obeys the following scheme:

```
COMM   label:type:count
```

Thus, the statement:

```
COMM   _fields:BYTE:010H
```

declares a communal variable that is 16 bytes in size (note, 010H is the same as 0x10, which is hexadecimal for 16). Yes sir, there is your 16-byte blob. On the Win32 platform, pointers require 32 bits, so I suppose that Windows is padding this structure to meet a four-byte memory alignment restriction.

Arrays and structure variables are similar in that they are both allocated as contiguous blobs of bytes. However, arrays and structure variables differ in terms of how their elements are accessed. Specifically, an array consists of a series of elements that all have the same size in bytes. This means that the address of an array element can be calculated using the following type of logic:

```
address(i) = address of array element (i)
address(i) = address(0) +  (i x (sizeof(element)))
```

This is illustrated in Figure 7-13.

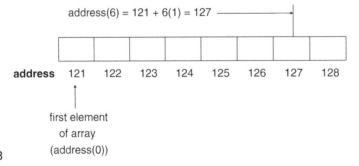

Figure 7-13

Thus, accessing an array element requires you to obtain the address of the first byte of the array and then perform some elementary arithmetic.

Structure variables consist of elements that differ in size. This means that in order to access the members of a structure, you will have to remember all of their byte offsets from the beginning of the variable. You cannot rely on a simple formula because the makeup of a structure is not necessarily uniform. Normally, high-level language compilers take care of recording the byte offsets of each structure member automatically. However, if you're writing an assembly program by hand, you'll have to keep track of things yourself.

For example, consider the following C structure:

```
struct fieldstruct
{
    char fld0;  /* 1 byte */
    short fld1; /* 2 bytes */
    char fld?;  /* 1 byte */
    long fld3;  /* 4 bytes */
};
```

We are going to have to bite the bullet and keep in mind that the `fld3` member variable is four bytes after the first byte of the structure (see Figure 7-14). Naturally, this becomes even more difficult for heavily nested structure declarations, and this is when a compiler comes in very handy.

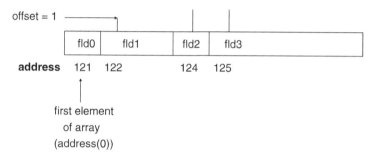

Figure 7-14

If you want to take the C variables that we discussed earlier and declare them as local variables in a function (instead of declaring them as global variables), you could construct the assembly language version of these variables using the `.PV` directive.

Table 7-20

C Code		Assembly		
char	ch;	.PV	ch	−1
short int	si_var;	.PV	si_var	−3
long int	li_var;	.PV	li_var	−7
float	flt;	.PV	flt	−11
double	dbl;	.PV	dbl	−19
short	s_arr[5];	.PV	s_arr	−39
long int	*iptr;	.PV	iptr	−47
struct mystruct	fields;	.PV	fields	−57

A function declaring the above local variables would have an activation record resembling that displayed in Figure 7-15.

In Figure 7-15, I'm only showing the bottom half of the stack frame. This is the part that is generated by the function being invoked.

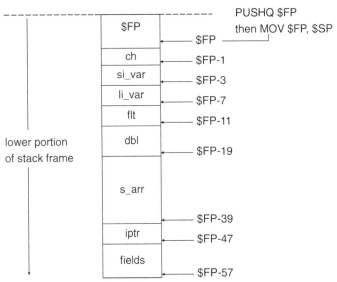

Figure 7-15

Scope

The *scope* of a program element (a variable declaration, a function, etc.) determines both the visibility and, potentially, the life span of the element. When a program element is *visible*, it can be accessed and manipulated. The *life span* of a program element determines when the element is created and destroyed.

NOTE The one caveat to this rule is for program elements which have their storage space allocated off the heap, dynamically, during execution. In this case, scope only defines the visibility of the program element. The element will exist until it is reclaimed, which may or may not be related to the scope of the element.

To explore the meaning of scope, let us examine how scope rules apply to variables in the C programming language.

Scope rules in C are implemented through the use of code blocks. A *block* of code is a region of source code that lies between a pair of brackets ({ }). A function definition is an example of a block of code.

```
void  myfunction()
{
    # block of code
}
```

In fact, functions are actually at the top of the block hierarchy in C. Functions may contain other blocks of code, as long as the blocks of code are not function definitions (function definitions cannot be nested in C). For example, the following function definition contains a few sub-blocks.

```
void myfunction()
{
     int i;
     for(i=0;i<10;i++)
     {
          if((i%2)==0)
          {
               printf("%d is even\n",i);
          }
     }

     {
          int j=10;
          printf("j=%d\n",j);
     }

     return;
}
```

From the previous function definition, we can see that blocks of code may be nested. In addition, although blocks of code are usually associated with program control statements, it is possible for blocks of code to exist completely by themselves. For example, the code that prints out the value of j is a stand-alone block.

Even though functions may contain other blocks of code, blocks of code (that are not function definitions) cannot independently exist outside of a function definition. For example, you would never see:

```
void myfunction1()
{
    # block of code
}

int i;
for(i=0;i<10;i++){ printf("%d\n",i); }

void myfunction2()
{
    # block of code
}
```

An ANSI C compiler processing the previous code would protest that the for loop does not belong to a function and would refuse to compile the code.

The scope of variables in C is block based. A variable declared inside of a block of code is known as a *local variable*. A local variable is visible in the block in which it is declared and all the sub-blocks within that block. A variable cannot be accessed outside of the block in which it was declared. For example, the following snippet of C code is completely legal:

```
void main()
{
     int i;
     for(i=0;i<10;i++)
     {
```

```
        int j=i*i;
        printf("i=%d, i^2=%d\n",i,j);
    }
}
```

The following snippet of C code is illegal:

```
void main()
{
    int i;
    for(i=0;i<10;i++)
    {
        int j=i*i;
        printf("i=%d, i^2=%d\n",i,j);
    }
    printf("i=%d, i^2=%d\n",i,j);
}
```

In the first case, we are perfectly within the syntactical rules of C when the variable i is accessed in a sub-block. In the second case, however, we try to access the variable j outside of its declaring block, and the compiler will emit an error.

Naturally, there are two special cases to this rule: global variables and the formal parameters of a function.

A global variable is a variable defined outside of any block of code. As such, a global variable is visible throughout a program by every section of code. Global variables also exist for the duration of a program's execution path.

Formal parameters are the variables specified in the prototype of a function. They are the variables that receive the arguments passed to a function when it is invoked. Formal parameters have visibility and a life span that is limited to the body of the function they belong to.

Figure 7-16 displays an example of these three types of variables (local, global, and formal parameters) in the context of different levels of scope.

Now that we've seen how the concept of scope operates in a high-level language, we have the necessary preparation to see how scope can be implemented using the HEC assembly language.

 NOTE There will, no doubt, be people who contest my labeling of C as a high-level language. From the perspective of assembly language, C is a high(er)-level language. However, when compared to object-oriented languages like Java, which have a lot of bells and whistles to make the programmer's life easy, C is a low(er)-level language. Thus, the best compromise would be to call C a mid-level language.

Two basic techniques come to mind with regard to managing scope within the body of a procedure:

- All-at-once (user/compiler enforced)
- Enforce scope using stack frames

One way to manage scope is to declare and allocate storage for all of a function's variables at the start of the function. In other words, we use the function's activation record to

```
#include<stdio.h>

int global var;

void function(int arg1, int arg2)
{
            int i=0;
            int n_even=0;

            for(i=arg1;i<arg2;i++)
            {
                        printf("i=%d\n",i);

                        if(i%2==0)
                        {
                                    char message []="(i) is even\n";
                                    printf("%s", message);
                                    n_even++;
                                    printf("number of even loops=%d\n\n", n_even);
                        }
                        else
                        {
                                    char warning[] = "(i) did not meet print condition\n\n";
                                    printf("%s", warning);
                        }
            }

            {
                        int local;
                        local = 100;
                        printf("local+globvar=%d\n",(local+globalvar));
            }

            return;

}/*end function*/
```

Figure 7-16

provide storage for every non-global variable accessed inside of the function, regardless of where it is used. This relies on the programmer to be vigilant about where and how he accesses a variable. If a compiler is generating the assembly code, instead of a programmer, then the compiler will use its symbol table to make sure that a local variable is not accessed outside of its declaring block.

In the section on activation records, we saw how procedure-based scope was implemented. By using the stack, we were able to create storage that had a scope and life span limited to the function. By using this same type of technique on a smaller scale, we can implement visibility and life span on a block-by-block basis. This is an alternative to relying on the programmer or compiler.

 NOTE In a way, stacks are really about storage life span. Visibility restrictions follow naturally as a result of life span constraints. Recall that stacks are good for situations in which you need to do, and then undo, an operation. This makes them perfect for creating temporary storage. The limited visibility is more of a side effect of the limited life span. Once a variable has been popped off the stack, it is gone and any reference to it will probably yield garbage.

The easiest way to think of a block of code is like a stripped-down type of function that has no return value and no return address. It only has local variables. Table 7-21 presents a basic comparison of functions and code blocks.

Table 7-21

	Saved State	Return Value	Arguments	Return Address	Locals
Function	yes	yes	yes	yes	yes
Code block	yes	no	yes	no	yes

As you can see from the table, a code block has saved program state information and local variables in its stack frame. Local variables declared outside the block but accessed inside the block can be treated as arguments. Figure 7-17 displays a comparison of the stack frames used by a function and a code block.

Naturally, there are tradeoffs between the all-at-once approach and the stack frame approach to scope management. These tradeoffs are listed in Table 7-21.

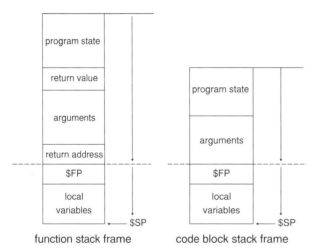

Figure 7-17 function stack frame   code block stack frame

Table 7-21

	All-At-Once Scope	Stack Frame Scope
Speed	Faster	Slower
Stack memory usage	More	Less
Executable size	Smaller	Larger

The stack frame scope technique requires stack manipulation be performed every time that a block is entered or exited. If a section of code has a heavily nested set of blocks, this translates into a lot of extra push and pop operations. This means that stack frame scope implementation will create an executable that is larger and slower because there are a lot more instructions to execute.

The downside of using the all-at-once tactic is that it requires a lot of storage overhead. Space in the activation record will be reserved even if a variable is not used. If a function has several different possible execution paths, a lot of storage is wasted.

If a compiler is generating the assembly code, then I'd feel secure in the all-at-once approach. However, if the assembly code is being manually written, I might be tempted to rely on the stack frame approach.

I'm now going to use a simple example to demonstrate the differences between the two approaches. Here is a simple example of a nested code block in C:

```
int i;
i=5;
{
    int j;
    j=14;
    {
        int k;
        k = i + j;
        printf("%d\n",k);
    }
}
```

Following is the HEC assembly language equivalent that uses the all-at-once approach:

```
.PB blocproc

    .PV blocproc_i -4
    .PV blocproc_j -8
    .PV blocproc_k -12

    # set up function locals
    PUSHQ $FP
    MOV $FP,$SP
    LQI $R1,12
    SUB $SP,$SP,$R1

    LAI $R1,$FP,blocproc_i
    LQI $R2,5
    SD  $R2,$R1

    LAI $R1,$FP,blocproc_j
    LQI $R2,14
    SD  $R2,$R1

    LAI $R1,$FP,blocproc_i
    LD  $R13,$R1

    LAI $R1,$FP,blocproc_j
    LD  $R12,$R1

    LAI $R1,$FP,blocproc_k
    ADD $R4,$R13,$R12
    SD  $R4,$R1

    LAI $R1,$FP,blocproc_k
    LD  $R2,$R1

    #print the return value
    LBI $R1,20
    INT 0
    LQI $R2,10
    LQI $R1,16
```

```
        INT 0
        LQI $R2,13
        LQI $R1,16
        INT 0

        # reclaim function local storage
        MOV $SP,$FP
        POPQ $FP
        HALT
    .PE
```

Here is the HEC assembly language version that uses the stack frame approach:

```
    .PB blocproc

        .PV blocproc_i -4

        # set up function locals
        PUSHQ $FP
        MOV $FP,$SP
        LQI $R1,4
        SUB $SP,$SP,$R1

        LAI $R1,$FP,blocproc_i
        LQI $R2,5
        SD  $R2,$R1

        LAI $R1,$FP,blocproc_i
        LD  $R13,$R1

        #enter first block
        .PV blocproc_j  -4
        PUSHQ $FP
        MOV $FP,$SP
        LQI $R1,4
        SUB $SP,$SP,$R1

        LAI $R1,$FP,blocproc_j
        LQI $R2,14
        SD  $R2,$R1

        LAI $R1,$FP,blocproc_j
        LD  $R12,$R1

        #enter second sub-block
        .PV blocproc_k  -4
        PUSHQ $FP
        MOV $FP,$SP
        LQI $R1,4
        SUB $SP,$SP,$R1

        LAI $R1,$FP,blocproc_k
        ADD $R4,$R13,$R12
        SD  $R4,$R1
```

```
        LAI $R1,$FP,blocproc_k
        LD $R2,$R1

        #print the return value
        LBI $R1,20
        INT 0
        LQI $R2,10
        LQI $R1,16
        INT 0
        LQI $R2,13
        LQI $R1,16
        INT 0

        #exit second sub-block
        MOV $SP,$FP
        POPQ $FP

        #exit first block
        MOV $SP,$FP
        POPQ $FP

        # reclaim function local storage
        MOV $SP,$FP
        POPQ $FP
        HALT
    .PE
```

In the previous example, I was able to avoid pushing outer-scope local variables onto the stack by saving them in registers. I got away with this because this example only has a couple of variables. In a scenario that involved 20 to 30 local variables, I would have no choice but to use the stack.

In general, from the previous assembly code you should be able to see that code blocks all use the following type of skeleton:

```
    # set up stack frame
    PUSHQ $FP
    MOV $FP,$SP
    LQI $R1, local-storage-size
    SUB $SP,$SP,$R1

    #
    # code block instructions here
    #

    # clean up the stack
    MOV $SP,$FP
    POPQ $FP
```

The stack frame scope implementation has over 40 instructions and produces an executable that is 379 bytes in size. The all-at-once example has 30 instructions and produces an executable that is 331 bytes in size. QED.

Instruction and Directive Summary

Assembly language, from a syntactic standpoint, is a walk in the park. An assembly language program consists of one or more statements. A statement can be an instruction, a directive, or a comment. An instruction consists of an opcode and zero or more operands. There are only ten directives to deal with and the comment symbol is like something right out of a Bourne shell script. The hierarchy of language components is displayed in Figure 7-18.

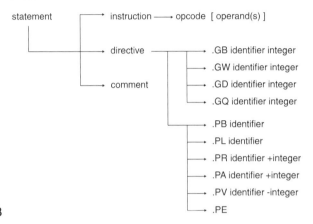

Figure 7-18

I really despise books that make you flip through chapters looking for related pieces of information. In light of this, I've decided to gather all of the instruction tables in one place in an effort to save you time and effort.

Type	Byte Size	Signed Range	Unsigned Range
Byte	1	–128 to 127	0 to 255
Word	2	–32,768 to 32,767	0 to 65,535
Double word	4	-2^{31} to $2^{31} - 1$	0 to 4,294,967,295
Quad word	8	-2^{63} to $2^{63} - 1$	0 to $2^{64} - 1$
Float	4	3.4×10^{-38} to 3.4×10^{38}	NA
Double	8	1.7×10^{-308} to 1.7×10^{308}	NA

Instruction	Meaning
LBI $R, byte	Loads the byte literal into the integer register $R
LWI $R, word	Loads the word literal into the integer register $R
LDI $R, dword	Loads the double word literal into the integer register $R
LQI $R, qword	Loads the quad word literal into the integer register $R
LF1I $F, float	Loads the single-precision floating-point literal into the register $F
LF2I $D, double	Loads the double-precision floating-point literal into the register $D
MOV $r1, $r2	Copies the contents of integer register $r2 into $r1
MOVF $f1, $f2	Copies the contents of single-precision floating-point register $f2 into $f1

Instruction	Meaning
MOVD $d1, $d2	Copies the contents of double-precision floating-point register $d2 into $d1
LB $r1, $r2	Loads the byte located at the address in $r2 into $r1
LW $r1, $r2	Loads the word located at the address in $r2 into $r1
LD $r1, $r2	Loads the double word located at the address in $r2 into $r1
LQ $r1, $r2	Loads the quad word located at the address in $r2 into $r1
LF1 $f1, $f2	Loads the single-precision float located at the address in $f2 into $f1
LF2 $d1, $d2	Loads the double-precision float located at the address in $d2 into $d1
LAD $r, identifier	Loads the address of a procedure or label into $r
LAI $r1, $r2, identifier	Constructs an indirect address and place it into $r1
SB $r1, $r2	Places the byte in $r1 at the address specified by $r2
SW $r1, $r2	Places the word in $r1 at the address specified by $r2
SD $r1, $r2	Places the double word in $r1 at the address specified by $r2
SQ $r1, $r2	Places the quad word in $r1 at the address specified by $r2
SF1 $f1, $f2	Places the single-precision float in $f1 at the address specified by $f2
SF2 $d1, $d2	Places the double-precision float in $d1 at the address specified by $d2
ADD $r1, $r2, $r3	Places the sum of $r2 and $r3 in $r1
SUB $r1, $r2, $r3	Subtracts $r3 from $r2 and places the result in $r1
MULT $r1, $r2, $r3	Places the product of $r2 and $r3 in $r1
DIV $r1, $r2, $r3, $r4	Divides $r3 by $r4, puts the quotient in $r1 and the remainder in $r2
FADD $f1, $f2, $f3	Places the sum of $f2 and $f3 in $f1
FSUB $f1, $f2, $f3	Subtracts $f3 from $f2 and places the result in $f1
FMULT $f1, $f2, $f3	Places the product of $f2 and $f3 in $f1
FDIV $f1, $f2, $f3	Divides $f2 by $f3 and places the quotient in $f1
DADD $d1, $d2, $d3	Places the sum of $d2 and $d3 in $d1
DSUB $d1, $d2, $d3	Subtracts $d3 from $d2 and places the result in $d1
DMULT $d1, $d2, $d3	Places the product of $d2 and $d3 in $d1
DDIV $d1, $d2, $d3	Divides $d2 by $d3 and places the quotient in $d1
AND $r1, $r2, $r3	Places the bitwise AND of $r1 and $r2 in $r3
OR $r1, $r2, $r3	Places the bitwise OR of $r1 and $r2 in $r3
XOR $r1, $r2, $r3	Places the bitwise XOR of $r1 and $r2 in $r3
NOT $r1, $r2	Places the bitwise NOT of $r1 in $r2
BT $r1, $r2, $r3	If the bit specified by the value in $r3 is on, sets $r1 to 1; otherwise sets $r1 to 0
BS $r1, $r2	Sets the bit specified by $r2 in $r1
SRA $r1, $r2, $r3	Copies to $r1 the value of $r2 shifted exactly $r3 bits to the right
SRL $r1, $r2, $r3	Copies to $r1 the value of $r2 shifted exactly $r3 bits to the right
SL $r1, $r2, $r3	Copies to $r1 the value of $r2 shifted exactly $r3 bits to the left
CAST_IF $R, $F	Casts the single-precision float in $F to an integer and places it in $R

Instruction	Meaning
CAST_ID $R, $D	Casts the double-precision float in $D to an integer and places it in $R
CAST_FI $F, $R	Casts the integer in $R to a single-precision float and places it in $F
CAST_FD $F, $D	Casts a double-precision float in $D to a single-precision float in $F
CAST_DI $D, $R	Casts the integer in $R to a double-precision float and places it in $D
CAST_DF $D, $F	Casts a single-precision float in $F to a double-precision float in $D
JMP $R	Jumps to the address specified by the $R integer register
INT byte	Executes the interrupt specified by the byte literal operand
NOP	Does nothing
HALT	Shuts down the virtual machine
JE $r1, $r2, $r3	If the contents of $r1 and $r2 are equal, jumps to the address in $r3
JNE $r1, $r2, $r3	If the contents of $r1 and $r2 are not equal, jumps to the address in $r3
SLT $r1, $r2, $r3	Sets $r1 to 1 if $r2 is less then $r3, otherwise sets $r1 to 0
FSLT $f1,$f2, $f3	Sets $f1 to 1 if $f2 is less then $f3, otherwise sets $f1 to 0
DSLT $d1,$d2,$d3	Sets $d1 to 1 if $d2 is less then $d3, otherwise sets $d1 to 0
PUSHB $R	Pushes the byte in $R onto the stack
PUSHW $R	Pushes the word in $R onto the stack
PUSHD $R	Pushes the double word in $R onto the stack
PUSHQ $R	Pushes the quad word in $R onto the stack
PUSHF1 $F	Pushes the single-precision floating-point value in $F onto the stack
PUSHF2 $D	Pushes the double-precision floating-point value in $D onto the stack
POPB $R	Pops the top byte off the stack and into $R
POPW $R	Pops the top word off the stack and into $R
POPD $R	Pops the top double word off the stack and into $R
POPQ $R	Pops the top quad word off the stack and into $R
POPF1 $F	Pops the top single-precision floating-point value off the stack and into $F
POPF2 $D	Pops the top double-precision floating-point value off the stack and into $D

References

The material in this chapter is fairly dry. Rather than just direct you to even more exhausting, detail-possessed ramblings, I thought I would break up the tedium by introducing a couple of books that might get your mind to work in different directions. Some of the following books are serious works of nonfiction, and others are just mind candy.

Bamford, James. *Body of Secrets: Anatomy of the Ultra-Secret National Security Agency from the Cold War through the Dawn of a New Century.* Doubleday, 2001. ISBN: 0385499078.

James Bamford has ventured deep into the NSA and lived to tell about it. This is the kind of book that everyone at the Pentagon will want to buy to see what their coworkers are up to. This gem has a couple of pieces of information that, in the intelligence community, are known as "burn your eyes" government secrets.

Blatner, David. *The Joy of Pi.* Walker Publishing, 1997. ISBN: 0802713327.

By far, the most engrossing part of this book is the discussion of David and Gregory Chudnovsky. These two brilliant Russian mathematicians built a supercomputer in their apartment to enumerate billions of digits of Pi. One might speculate that David and Gregory invented the sport of "extreme mathematics."

Bloom, Howard. *Global Brain: The Evolution of Mass Mind from the Big Bang to the 21st Century.* John Wiley and Sons, 2000. ISBN: 0471295841.

Howard Bloom is a scientist who has used the music industry as a vast experimental laboratory. Being a physicist myself, I can appreciate his approach and perspective. Howard presents some interesting ideas by looking at current trends, extrapolating them, and testing his predictions by contrasting them to similar historical developments. This is an excellent book to have on your nightstand.

Gleick, James. *Chaos: Making a New Science.* Penguin Books, 1987. ISBN: 0140092501.

"Chaos theory" is a very broad term used to collectively refer to a set of unconventional mathematical ideas that approach old problems in an effort to shed new light on them. In the past, scientists have approached difficult problems used analytic techniques that were deemed "good enough." With the advent of cheap, high-power computing, researchers have been able to transcend solutions that are merely "good enough" in a quest to foster greater insight into chaotic phenomena.

Kahn, David. *The Code-Breakers.* Scribner, 1996. ISBN: 0684831309.

This is a documentary of the history on cryptanalysis, the art of code breaking. It is probably the most pedantic and complete historical treatment to date. The moral that this book seems to offer is that there's nothing more dangerous than people who put blind faith in a cryptosystem that is assumed to be secure... amen.

Kelly-Bootle, Stan. *The Computer Contradictionary.* MIT Press, 1995. ISBN: 0262611120.

Stan Kelly-Bootle is the lord high commentator and elder statesman of the Unix order. If it were not for Stan, I would have nothing to read before going to bed. This book serves as a humorous respite from plodding technological works (like mine), and also offers a certain amount of cultural enrichment. Thank goodness for Stan and his love of ISAM.

Advanced Topics

Some run-time systems, like the Java virtual machine, are implemented with a particular language in mind. In opposition to this trend, I attempted to design the HEC virtual machine so that it would not be biased towards any particular programming language. If you are targeting the HEC run-time with a structured programming language, everything you need to know is in Chapter 7. However, if you wish to target the HEC run-time with an object-oriented language, you will also need to absorb the material in this chapter. The first half of this chapter is intended to give you an idea of how object-oriented features can be implemented with respect to the HEC virtual machine.

The second half of this chapter is concerned with porting and building the HEC virtual machine. Having placed a heavy emphasis on portability, I would not be able to look myself in the mirror every morning if I didn't at least make a Linux port available. To make it easy for you to tinker with the source code, I explain the steps that are necessary to build the HEC run-time on both Linux and Windows.

Finally, if the HEC virtual machine does not meet your expectations, I describe how to build your own virtual machine at the end of this chapter. Because building a virtual machine involves several of the steps necessary to construct an operating system, I thought it would be interesting to explain how you can go about implementing your own operating system. The idea of building an OS from scratch has always intrigued me. I had no idea where to begin until I met a couple of veteran systems engineers who had plied their trade at Control Data. I am going to share the basic methodology they explained to me.

Targeting HEC: Compiler Design

Managing Complexity

If you have worked through all the assembly source code examples in this book, you have probably come to a startling discovery: Writing assembly code is tedious work that bogs you down with mind-numbing details, and programming in assembly language is a tragic waste of your time and effort. Using assembly language can negatively impact maintainability, portability, and your sanity.

What? Then why spend almost all of this book on such an odious topic? Am I playing an elaborate prank on you?

No, I am not playing a prank on you. The truth is that learning assembly language and machine architecture is a necessary evil. In order to ascend to the next plane and construct useful, high-level development tools, you have to possess an intimate knowledge of the output these tools produce. You cannot construct a large, stable, and functional house without initially spending the requisite time building a foundation and installing the plumbing.

The punch line is not that you should program in assembly language. Rather, the idea is that you should master assembly language programming so that you have the necessary insight to build serviceable higher-level tools.

The fundamental, core issue encountered in software engineering is complexity. The evolution of programming languages has been driven by the need to manage and constrain complexity.

Initially, programs were hard-coded in raw binary. This was back in the days of Howard Aiken's MARK I, which was unveiled in 1944. As the years wore on, programs got to the size where coding in raw binary was simply too tedious. In 1949, the first assembly language was developed for the UNIVAC I. Assembly language made programming less complicated by replacing raw binary instructions with terse symbolic mnemonics. Originally a programmer would have had to manually write something like:

```
10010110   10101110   01101011
```

Using assembly language, the previous binary instruction could be replaced with:

```
INC  AR  0x6B
```

This primitive symbolic notation helped to make programming easier. Again, however, programs became larger and more complicated to the extent that something new was needed. This something new reared its head in the next decade. In the 1950s, with the emergence of transistor-based circuits, higher-level languages emerged. Two such languages were COBOL and FORTRAN. All of these early high-level languages were block-based and used the GOTO statement, or something resembling it, to move from block to block.

The emergence of block-based languages led to the development of structured programming in the late 1960s. One of the original essays that led to the birth of structured programming was written by Dijkstra in 1968. It was a letter in the *Communications of the ACM* entitled "GOTO Statement Considered Harmful." This revolutionary paper caused quite a stir. The state-of-the-art languages at the time, like COBOL II and FORTRAN IV, used GOTOs liberally.

Structured programming is the approach to writing procedure-based code where the use of the GOTO statement is either minimized or excluded entirely.

History sides with Dijkstra (big surprise). Structured programming was the paradigm that characterized software development in the 1970s and 1980s. When a software team in the 1970s wanted to design a business application, the first thing they would do is model the data that the application would manage. This usually meant designing database tables and memory resident data structures. This initial collection of schemas and data types would be the starting point around which everything else would revolve. Next, the team would decide on the algorithms and corresponding functions that would operate on the data. Structured programming is notably either data oriented or procedure oriented, but never both.

Even though structured programming was supposed to be a cure-all, it fell short of its expectations. Specifically, the structured approach proved to be inadequate with regard to maintaining large projects. This is a crucial flaw because most of the money invested in a software project is spent on maintenance. During the 1980s, structured programming was gradually replaced by the object-oriented approach that was promoted by languages like C++ and Smalltalk.

Can you see the trend I'm trying to illuminate?

I am of the opinion that every programming language has a complexity threshold. After a program reaches a certain number of lines of code, it becomes difficult to understand and modify. Naturally, lower-level languages will have a lower complexity threshold than the higher ones. To get an idea of what the complexity threshold is for different types of programming languages, we can take a look at a collection of well-known operating systems (see Table 8-1).

Table 8-1

OS	Lines of Code	Language	Source
MS DOS 2.0	20,000	Assembly	*Modern Operating Systems*, Andrew Tanenbaum
Minix	74,000	C	*Operating Systems: Design and Implementation*, Andrew Tanenbaum
FreeBSD	200,000 (kernel only)	C	*The Design and Implementation of the 4.4BSD Operating System*, Kirk McKusick
Windows 98	18 million (everything)	C/C++	February 2, 1999 (A.M. Session) United States vs. Microsoft et. al.

From Table 8-1, it seems that the number of lines of code that can be efficiently managed by a language increase by a factor of 10 as you switch to more sophisticated paradigms (see Table 8-2).

Table 8-2

Language	Paradigm	Complexity Threshold
Raw binary	Every man for himself (no rules)	10,000
Assembler	Block-based using GOTO	100,000
C	Structured programming	1,000,000
C++	Object-oriented	10,000,000

Inevitably, the languages that survive, and perhaps pass on their features to new languages, will be the ones that are the most effective at managing complexity. In the early days of Unix, almost every bit of system code was written in C. As operating systems have grown, the use of C, as a matter of necessity, has given way to implementation in C++. According to a July 29, 1996, *Wall Street Journal* article, the Windows NT operating system consisted of 16.5 million lines of code. It is no big surprise, then, that Microsoft had begun building some of its primary OS components entirely in C++. For example, a fundamental component of the Windows NT kernel, the Graphics Device Interface (GDI32.DLL), was written completely in C++. According to Microsoft engineers, this was done for the sake of keeping the component maintainable.

You might balk at this theory by pointing out that COBOL is still the most prolific development language. I would agree with you on this. However, I think that COBOL is also a legacy programming language. Remember, I'm talking about the evolution and development of new languages. COBOL has been around since the 1950s, when a team led by Rear Admiral Grace Murray Hopper developed it for the Department of Defense. COBOL is a language that survives only because of its existing inertia, not because it lends itself to easy maintenance. I am sure that tens of thousands of in-house COBOL programmers would agree with me.

If I had to offer an example of a recent programming language that facilitated the development of large-scale projects, and did an adequate job of limiting complexity, I would pick Java. When I came across Java in 1995, I was thrilled. Having worked at an ERP company that maintained a code base consisting of 16 million lines of K&R C, I had come to dread the prospect of hunting down header files and obscure libraries, which were invariably spread across a massive, cryptic, and completely undocumented source tree. Sometimes I would spend several hours just trying to find one source file or function definition. There were afternoons where I would start `grep` at the root of a machine's file system and go have a coffee break. In fact, I distinctly remember spending an entire afternoon trying to locate the following macro:

```
#define PrcBInNdNbr 14
```

(Just in case you're wondering, this ridiculous macro stands for Process Binary Instruction Node Number.) Java eliminated this problem in one fell swoop by enforcing a one-to-one mapping between package names and directory names. When I initially discovered that Java enforced this convention, I felt like jumping and shouting, "Amen!"

Some engineers may decry the package-directory naming scheme, claiming that it is a characteristic of a bondage-discipline language. These engineers have obviously never worked on a large project. On a large project, you need to maintain organization, even if it is instituted at the cost of flexibility. Sometimes the only thing between a million lines of code and absolute chaos is a set of well-enforced conventions.

In the past, it has been up to the software engineers involved on a project to be good citizens and obey the informal organizational schemes. However, there was usually nothing stopping a programmer from breaking the rules and introducing complexity into the system. Sure enough, there's always at least one guy who has to do things "his way." As part of the language's masterful design, the founding fathers at JavaSoft decided that the Java run-time would take an active role in maintaining an organized source tree by enforcing the package-directory naming scheme.

NOTE   According to *The Hacker's Dictionary*, a *bondage-discipline language* is a language, like PASCAL, that forces the programmer to abide by a certain set of strict syntactic and structural rules. The term is used derisively by programmers who feel that the rules have their origins in the language designer's arbitrary world view rather than pragmatic inspiration.

In his 1986 essay, "No Silver Bullet: Essence and Accidents of Software Engineering," Robert Brooks predicted that nothing would appear in the following decade that would improve software productivity by an order of magnitude. It would seem as though he was correct. The productivity tools that did present themselves in the 1990s seemed more like flavor-of-the-month phenomenon, or thinly veiled attempts by a single company to corner the market on design methodologies. In the 1990s, software design tools didn't do much more than draw pretty pictures. In fact, one of the architects that I worked with found that PowerPoint was easier to work with than the company's official design tool.

The next hundred years will be very telling. The laws of quantum mechanics place a barrier on how small we can make a computer. This means that speed improvements will eventually have to be based on better software mechanisms. This, in turn, implies that software will inexorably become more complicated (i.e., compare quicksort to bubble sort). The need to manage this complexity will give birth to at least a couple of tenable solutions, and probably several bad solutions. Necessity is the mother of invention. Software engineering will either find ways to manage complexity or be swallowed up by it.

Approach

All programs can be distilled into a collection of assembly language instructions and data. This is a crucial fact that compiler writers depend upon to design languages. Regardless of how sophisticated a feature is, it can always be spelled out using the primitive elements of assembly language. For example, in the early days of the C programming language, C code was translated into assembly language as an intermediate step. Some compilers still support this feature.

The assembly code generated by such a compiler is processed, by an assembler, to create a *compilation unit*. A compilation unit is basically a binary file that may contain unresolved references to symbols located elsewhere. To build an executable file, a linker is used to merge the compilation unit with other compilation units and user libraries in an effort to resolve external references.

These steps are illustrated in Figure 8-1.

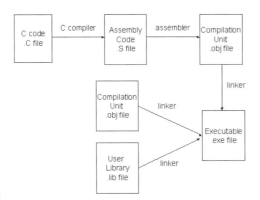

Figure 8-1

 NOTE The HEC assembler generates a complete executable, so the linking step is not included in the process of building the finished bytecode file.

If everything ends up as assembly code, how are object-oriented constructs represented in terms of HEC assembly language? That is the primary question this chapter attempts to answer. To understand how I address this question, I will begin by taking a look back at history.

When Bjarne Stroustrup designed and implemented the first C++ compiler at Bell Labs in 1983, it was initially a C++ to C translator. The tool that he wrote was named Cfront (as in a front end to a C compiler). Cfront took a C++ program and emitted an equivalent program in C. A C compiler would then be invoked to process the C code and generate assembly code.

Thus, it is possible to recreate C++ using nothing but C and some special notational conventions. In Chapter 7, I gave you the necessary tools to take a structured language, like C, and generate the corresponding assembly code. This means that if I give you the tools to create object-oriented constructs in terms of a procedure-based language, like C, you can use the material in Chapter 7 to translate the code the rest of the way to assembly language (see Figure 8-2).

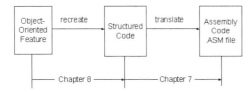

Figure 8-2

This is the way I will approach object implementation in terms of HEC assembly language. I will use Java to illustrate basic object-oriented concepts. Then I will show how similar object-oriented mechanisms can be implemented in C. If you wish to see how the C code translates into assembly code, you can revisit Chapter 7. One of the reasons I am taking this route is to save space. Another reason I'm adopting this tactic is to make my ideas as clear as possible. By breaking the process up into two distinct steps, I am hoping to ease the transition from object-oriented code to assembly code.

NOTE   I will not be translating Java directly into C. In other words, my C code will not be capable of recreating all the functionality of the Java language and run-time. Rather, I will use Java to highlight certain object-oriented mechanisms. Then I will try to demonstrate how each general object-oriented mechanism can be implemented in C.

ASIDE   Do not underestimate the power of notational conventions. The fact that an object-oriented language can be decomposed into a structured language, accompanied by a set of notational conventions, is not as pedestrian as you might think it is.

The implementation of simple notational changes can often produce profound results.

For example, take the mathematical subject of linear algebra. Linear algebra centers around manipulating a system of linear equations, which is a set of equations with the following form:

$$a_{11}x_1 + a_{12}x_2 + a_{13}x_3 + \ldots + a_{1n} x_n = b_1$$
$$a_{21}x_1 + a_{22}x_2 + a_{23}x_3 + \ldots + a_{2n} x_n = b_2$$
$$\vdots \qquad\qquad\qquad\qquad \vdots$$
$$a_{n1}x_1 + a_{n2}x_2 + a_{n3}x_3 + \ldots + a_{nn} x_n = b_n$$

Typically, the goal of manipulating these equations is to find a solution for $(x_1, x_2, \ldots x_n)$ that satisfies all of the equations. This is the fundamental starting point for the entire field of linear algebra. There are thousands of theorems and corollaries devoted to addressing this problem.

Originally, having to work with such equations was problematic because describing everything was very awkward and tedious. However, the introduction of matrix notation allowed the previous set of equations to be rewritten as:

$$Ax = b$$

where the symbol A represents a matrix of the form:

$$A = \begin{matrix} a_{11} & a_{12} & a_{13} & a_{1n} \\ a_{21} & a_{22} & a_{23} & a_{2n} \\ \cdot & & & \cdot \\ \cdot & & & \cdot \\ a_{n1} & a_{n2} & a_{n3} & a_{nn} \end{matrix}$$

And x and b are both n-dimensional vectors.

$$x = [x_1, x_2, \ldots x_n]^T \quad b = [b_1, b_2, \ldots b_n]^T$$

If you're interested in a better look at how the mechanics of this notation operate, you can reference Leon's book *Linear Algebra with Applications* that I mention at the end of the chapter.

Notational conventions allow details to be abstracted so that higher-level issues can be examined in a more efficient manner. They effectively remove mental clutter. By easing the manipulation of systems of linear equations, matrix notation has had a major role with regard to ushering in advances in mathematics and science. Experts estimate that roughly 75 percent of the problems encountered in scientific and industrial settings involve solving a system of linear equations at some point.

Now, look back on the history of programming languages; you should be able to recognize the same theme. Simple notational changes, enforced by development tools, have allowed more complicated models to be designed and managed.

Supporting Object-Oriented Features

The Basic Tenets

Structured programming tends to view a problem either in terms of the data being manipulated or the actions being performed. For example, let's say that you had an array of integers you wanted to sort in place.

If you asked an engineer who does structured programming what this sorting problem was all about, he would tell you one of two things. First, he might say that the problem was about an array of integers:

```
#define  ARR_SIZE 50
int values[ARR_SIZE];
```

Another possibility is that he would tell you that the problem was about a function named `sortIntegers()` that accepts an array of integers as an argument and does an in-place sort of those values:

```
sortIntegers(int * array);
```

Object-oriented programming merges data, and the instructions acting on that data, into software entities called *objects*. Using the object-oriented approach, we would merge the array of integers and the function used to sort the list into a single component. In the Java programming language, the corresponding class declaration would look something like:

```java
public class ArrayList
{
    private int[] array=null;

    public ArrayList(int[] arr){ array=arr; }

    public int[] getArray(){ return(array); }

    public void sortArray()
    {
        int size = array.length;
        for(int i=0;i<size;i++)
        {
            for(int j=i;(j>0)&&(array[j]<array[j-1]);j--)
            {
                int temp = array[j];
                array[j] = array[j-1];
                array[j-1]=temp;
            }
        }
    }

    public void printArray()
    {
        int size = array.length;
        for(int i=0;i<size;i++){ System.out.println("["+i+"]="+array[i]); }
    }
```

```
public static void main(String[] args)
{
    int[] arr = new int[5];
    arr[0]=12; arr[1]=7; arr[2]=1; arr[3]=20; arr[4]=14;
    ArrayList al = new ArrayList(arr);
    al.printArray();
    al.sortArray();
    al.printArray();
}

}/*end class*/
```

 NOTE In the discussions that follow, I will be using the terms "class" and "object." These two terms represent different things, so it's important to understand the distinction. A *class* is a declaration that describes the composition of an object. An *object* is an instance of a class type. When an object is defined/instantiated, memory is allocated for the object so that the object will have its own copy of the data members specified by the class description.

For example, the following code declares a class named `MyClass`:

```
public class MyClass
{
    private String str=null;
    public void setString(String s){ str = s; }
    public String getString(){ return(str); }
}
```

The next line of code defines an object of type `MyClass`:

```
MyClass obj = new MyClass();
```

In the case of Java, this means that memory is allocated from the Java virtual machine's heap to represent the object in memory.

When faced with a large project, the object-oriented school of thought dictates that the solution should consist of a set of independent, self-contained objects. Each object is a stand-alone "black box" that exposes a specific set of connection points to the outside world and hides the rest of its operation inside. This allows components to be pulled out and maintained separately without threatening the overall integrity of the solution.

Using the structured programming approach, large-scale software solutions are typically monolithic. What you usually end up with is a set of highly coupled functions passing around, and updating, the same data. The fundamental problem with this is that maintenance is a nightmare. You often can't change a single function without generating some sort of ripple effect that spreads out and impacts code somewhere else. Object-oriented programming solves this problem by making the software components of a solution pluggable.

Besides just decomposing a program into a set of objects, object-oriented programming implements three basic mechanisms that make it effective at limiting complexity.

■ Encapsulation

■ Inheritance

- Polymorphism

I will spend the remainder of this chapter examining each of these features in turn. I will explain what each feature does, how it is implemented in Java, and how the feature can be constructed using C. Translating the C code to HEC assembly language can then be performed using the techniques presented in Chapter 7.

NOTE I do not have the space to provide a comprehensive treatment of Java. In fact, it would help dramatically if you've already been exposed to Java. If you need to get up to speed quickly, I mention a couple of books in the reference section that should allow you to hit the ground running.

Encapsulation

Encapsulation is the object-oriented mechanism that allows data, and the procedures that act on that data, to be united into a single programming construct. Encapsulation is also what allows a class to hide its internal implementation. By declaring certain member variables and functions as private, a class can ensure that the outside world cannot access these class members. Likewise, a class can expose a member variable or member function to the outside world by declaring it public. The black box effect used to produce a pluggable software solution is facilitated primarily by encapsulation.

To recreate encapsulation, we will need to find a way to implement the following two features:

- Data and instruction binding

- Hiding/exposing implementation

For example, examine the following Java class which models a simple queue:

```
public class Queue
{
    private int[] queue=null;
    private int add_pos;
    private int get_pos;

    private void error(int type)
    {
        System.out.print("Queue.error(): ");
        switch(type)
        {
            case 1:{ System.out.println("end of line");}break;
            case 2:{ System.out.println("empty queue");}break;
            default:{System.out.println("not handled");}break;
        }
        return;

    }/*end error------------------------------------------------*/

    public Queue(int size)
    {
        queue = new int[size];
```

```
                add_pos =-1;
                get_pos =-1;
                return;

        }/*end constructor-----------------------------------------------*/

        public void enterQueue(int number)
        {
                if(add_pos==queue.length){ error(1); }
                add_pos = add_pos+1;
                queue[add_pos]=number;
                return;

        }/*end enter-----------------------------------------------------*/

        public int service()
        {
                if(get_pos==add_pos){ error(2); }
                get_pos=get_pos+1;
                return(queue[get_pos]);

        }/*end service---------------------------------------------------*/

        public static void main(String[] args)
        {
                Queue q = new Queue(10);
                q.enterQueue(22);
                q.enterQueue(3);
                q.enterQueue(17);
                System.out.println("servicing "+q.service());
                System.out.println("servicing "+q.service());
                System.out.println("servicing "+q.service());
                return;

        }/*end main------------------------------------------------------*/

}/*end class*/
```

Encapsulation is what allows the queue array and its associated functions to be bound together. Encapsulation also allows the Queue class to conceal its internal operation. The programmer can only invoke the three public methods. Nothing is known about the queue array, or the add_pos or get_pos private variables. They are hidden behind the cover of the black box.

How is encapsulation implemented? The following C code illustrates how encapsulation can be implemented in terms of a structured language.

```c
#include <stdio.h>
#include <stdlib.h>

struct Queue
{
    int *queue;
    int queue_length;
```

```
    int add_pos;
    int get_pos;
};

/*member function declarations------------------------------------*/

void error(int type);
struct Queue *new_Queue(int size);
void reclaim_Queue(struct Queue *qptr);
void Queue_enterQueue(struct Queue *qptr, int number);
int Queue_service(struct Queue *qptr);
void main();

/*member function definitions------------------------------------*/

void error(int type)
{
    printf("Queue.error(): ");
    switch(type)
    {
        case 1:{ printf("end of line\n");}break;
        case 2:{ printf("empty queue\n");}break;
        default:{ printf("not handled\n");}break;
    }
    return;

}/*end error*/

struct Queue *new_Queue(int size)
{
    struct Queue *qptr;
    qptr = malloc(sizeof(struct Queue));
    (*qptr).queue = malloc(size*(sizeof(int)));
    (*qptr).queue_length = size;
    (*qptr).add_pos = 0;
    (*qptr).get_pos = 0;
    return(qptr);

}/*end new_Queue*/

void reclaim_Queue(struct Queue *qptr)
{
    free((*qptr).queue);
    free(qptr);

}/*end reclaim_Queue*/

void Queue_enterQueue(struct Queue *qptr, int number)
{
    if(((*qptr).add_pos)==((*qptr).queue_length)){ error(1); }
    (*qptr).add_pos = ((*qptr).add_pos)+1;
    (*qptr).queue[(*qptr).add_pos]=number;
    return;
```

```
    }/*end enterQueue*/

    int Queue_service(struct Queue *qptr)
    {
        if(((*qptr).get_pos)==((*qptr).add_pos)){ error(2); }
        (*qptr).get_pos=((*qptr).get_pos)+1;
        return((*qptr).queue[(*qptr).get_pos]);

    }/*end service*/

    void main()
    {
        struct Queue *q = new_Queue(10);

        Queue_enterQueue(q,22);
        Queue_enterQueue(q,3);
        Queue_enterQueue(q,17);

        printf("servicing %d\n",Queue_service(q));
        printf("servicing %d\n",Queue_service(q));
        printf("servicing %d\n",Queue_service(q));

        reclaim_Queue(q);
        return;

    }/*end main---------------------------------------------------------*/
```

As you can see, the data members of the class are placed in a structure. To bind this data with the class's member functions, we add an implicit argument to the member functions that accepts a pointer to the structure, such that:

```
    q.enterQueue(22);
```

becomes:

```
    struct Queue *q = new_Queue(10);
    Queue_enterQueue(q,22);
```

This *implicit argument* technique is what allows a member function to access the data members of the object without having to give each object its own special copy of functions.

The C-based member functions of the Queue class are also prefixed with the class name (i.e., Queue_enterQueue) to distinguish them as belonging to the Queue class. This is another technique used to bind the class elements together.

Hiding implementation is not as easy. Ensuring that a private member stays private is typically a job handled by the compiler and its symbol table. Most object-oriented language compilers will check to make sure that an object's private members are not accessed illegally, and if they are, the compiler will generate an error. If you are writing object-oriented assembly code manually, there is nothing to prevent you from accessing an object's private members. You will just have to be disciplined and remember, perhaps through a naming convention, that some members should not be accessed from the outside.

```
struct Queue
{
    /* could apply private_ prefix to remind yourself */
    int *private_queue;
    int private_queue_length;
    int private_add_pos;
    int private_get_pos;
};
```

Remember from Chapter 7 that from the perspective of an assembly language programmer, a structure is just a blob of bytes. To create a member function with an implicit object argument, you merely have to expand the activation record to accommodate an extra blob of storage in the argument section of the stack frame.

Inheritance

Inheritance is a mechanism that allows one class to pass on its traits (its member variables and functions) to another class. Inheritance is useful because it facilitates the construction of class hierarchies that are characterized by incremental specialization, and this encourages code reuse.

In the context of inheritance, the class that is passing on its attributes is known as the *base class*, or the *superclass*. A base class can pass on both its member variables and its member functions. The class that inherits these elements is known as the *derived class*, or *subclass*.

For example, let's assume you need to write a set of classes that will be used to perform authentication when a user logs into your application. And let's say that you want to be able to provide several different types of authentication via a one-way hash function. To avoid having to rewrite the same code over and over, you can centralize all of the common functionality into a single base class. Then, when you need to add special features, you can extend the base class's functionality by creating a subclass. This type of arrangement is illustrated in Figure 8-3.

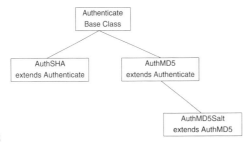

Figure 8-3

In Figure 8-3, the Authenticate class would provide basic functionality that all of its descendents would need (like reading in the user's pass phrase and comparing the hashed pass phrase against whatever the application has stored, etc.). The AuthMD5 and AuthSHA classes are subclasses of the Authenticate base class. They both implement different one-way hash functions (MD5 and the Secure Hash Algorithm (SHA)). The AuthMD5Salt class specializes the AuthMD5 class even further by adding salt to the hash of the user's pass phrase. Because of this, the `AuthMD5Salt` class is declared as a subclass of `AuthMD5`. This allows the `AuthMD5Salt` class to borrow functionality that was already built into `Authenticate` and `AuthMD5`, and this prevents a lot of redundant code from being written.

NOTE If you are not familiar with cryptographic topics like authentication, I have provided a couple of useful titles in the reference section.

Some languages allows a subclass to inherit the properties of two separate base classes. This can lead to a precarious relationship known as the *deadly diamond*. For example, assume a base class A has an integer member variable named i. According to the hierarchy in Figure 8-4, subclasses B and C will inherit i from A. However, D is a subclass of both B and C. Which copy of i will D inherit — B's or C's ?

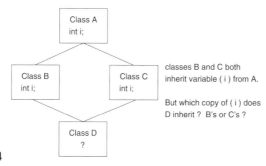

Figure 8-4

The C++ programming language has all sorts of awkward mechanisms in place to deal with the deadly diamond and facilitate multiple inheritance (like virtual base classes, scope resolution operators, and other such tripe). To be honest, I think that the multiple inheritance features in C++ end up creating more problems than they solve. In general, multiple inheritance is a menace which tends to breed complexity and side effects when it is applied.

Fortunately, more recent and enlightened languages, such as Java, do not allow a class to be a subclass of more than one base class. Here is a simple example that demonstrates inheritance using Java:

```java
public class Insurance
{
    private int limit=1000000;
    private int rate;

    public Insurance(){ rate=117;}
    public void setRate(int init_rate){ rate=init_rate;}
    public int getRate(){ return(rate);}
    public int getLimit(){ return(limit);}

    public static void main(String[] args)
    {
        CarInsurance ci = new CarInsurance();
        ci.setRate(125);
```

```
                    ci.setYear(1998);
                    System.out.print("year= "+ci.getYear()+" rate="+ci.getRate());
                    System.out.println(" limit= "+ci.getLimit());

                    HealthInsurance hi = new HealthInsurance();
                    hi.setRate(45);
                    hi.setAge(26);
                    System.out.print("age= "+hi.getAge()+" rate="+hi.getRate());
                    System.out.println(" limit= "+ci.getLimit());
                    return;
        }

}/*end class*/

class HealthInsurance extends Insurance
{
    private int age;
    public void setAge(int yrs){ age = yrs;}
    public int getAge(){ return(age);}

}/*end class*/

class CarInsurance extends Insurance
{
    private int car_year;
    public void setYear(int yrs){ car_year = yrs;}
    public int getYear(){ return(car_year);}

}/*end class*/
```

In the previous example there is a base class named Insurance, which is intended to represent an insurance policy. It is extended by two subclasses that specialize in different types of insurance. These two subclasses will inherit the members of their common base class.

This kind of hierarchical relationship can also be constructed in terms of C:

```
#include <stdio.h>
#include <stdlib.h>

/* INSURANCE +++++++++++++++++++++++++++++++++++++++++++++++++++++++++++*/

struct Insurance
{
    int limit;
    int rate;
};

/*member function declarations-------------------------------------*/

struct Insurance *new_Insurance();
void new_Insurance_init(struct Insurance *iptr);
void reclaim_Insurance(struct Insurance *iptr);

void Insurance_setRate(struct Insurance *iptr, int init_rate);
int Insurance_getRate(struct Insurance *iptr);
```

```
int Insurance_getLimit(struct Insurance *iptr);

/*member function definitions-------------------------------------*/

struct Insurance *new_Insurance()
{
    struct Insurance *iptr;
    iptr = malloc(sizeof(struct Insurance));
    new_Insurance_init(iptr);
    return(iptr);

}/*end constructor*/

void new_Insurance_init(struct Insurance *iptr)
{
    (*iptr).rate = 117;
    (*iptr).limit= 1000000;

}/*end new_Insurance_init*/

void reclaim_Insurance(struct Insurance *iptr)
{
    free(iptr);

}/*end reclaim_Insurance*/

void Insurance_setRate(struct Insurance *iptr, int init_rate)
{
    (*iptr).rate=init_rate;

}/*end Insurance_setRate*/

int Insurance_getRate(struct Insurance *iptr){ return((*iptr).rate);}
int Insurance_getLimit(struct Insurance *iptr){ return((*iptr).limit);}

/* HEALTH_INSURANCE ++++++++++++++++++++++++++++++++++++++++++++++++*/

struct HealthInsurance
{
    /*inherited members first*/
    int limit;
    int rate;
    /*HealthInsurance members*/
    int age;
};

/*member function declarations---------------------------------------*/

struct HealthInsurance *new_HealthInsurance();
void reclaim_HealthInsurance(struct HealthInsurance *iptr);

void HealthInsurance_setAge(struct HealthInsurance *iptr, int yrs);
int HealthInsurance_getAge(struct HealthInsurance *iptr);
```

```
/*member function definitions-------------------------------------*/

struct HealthInsurance *new_HealthInsurance()
{
    struct HealthInsurance *iptr = malloc(sizeof(struct HealthInsurance));
    new_Insurance_init((struct Insurance*)iptr);
    return(iptr);

}/*end constructor*/

void reclaim_HealthInsurance(struct HealthInsurance *iptr)
{
    free(iptr);

}/*end reclaim_HealthInsurance*/

void HealthInsurance_setAge(struct HealthInsurance *iptr, int yrs)
{
    (*iptr).age = yrs;

}/*end HealthInsurance_setAge*/

int HealthInsurance_getAge(struct HealthInsurance *iptr)
{
    return((*iptr).age);

}/*end HealthInsurance_getAge*/

/* CAR_INSURANCE ++++++++++++++++++++++++++++++++++++++++++++++++++*/

struct CarInsurance
{
    /*inherited members first*/
    int limit;
    int rate;
    /* CarInsurance members*/
    int car_year;
};

/*member function declarations------------------------------------*/

struct CarInsurance *new_CarInsurance();
void reclaim_CarInsurance(struct CarInsurance *iptr);

void CarInsurance_setYear(struct CarInsurance *iptr, int yrs);
int CarInsurance_getYear(struct CarInsurance *iptr);

/*member function definitions-------------------------------------*/

struct CarInsurance *new_CarInsurance()
{
    struct CarInsurance *iptr = malloc(sizeof(struct CarInsurance));
    new_Insurance_init((struct Insurance*)iptr);
```

```
            return(iptr);

    }/*end constructor*/

    void reclaim_CarInsurance(struct CarInsurance *iptr)
    {
            free(iptr);

    }/*end reclaim_CarInsurance*/

    void CarInsurance_setYear(struct CarInsurance *iptr, int yrs)
    {
            (*iptr).car_year = yrs;

    }/*end CarInsurance_setyear*/

    int CarInsurance_getYear(struct CarInsurance *iptr)
    {
            return((*iptr).car_year);

    }/*end CarInsurance_getYear*/

    /* MAIN_BOOTSTRAP+++++++++++++++++++++++++++++++++++++++++++++++++++++++*/

    void main()
    {
            struct CarInsurance *ci;
            struct HealthInsurance *hi;

            ci = new_CarInsurance();
            Insurance_setRate((struct Insurance*)ci,125);
            CarInsurance_setYear(ci,1998);
            printf("year=%d ",CarInsurance_getYear(ci));
            printf("rate=%d ",Insurance_getRate((struct Insurance*)ci));
            printf("limit=%d\n",Insurance_getLimit((struct Insurance*)ci));
            reclaim_CarInsurance(ci);

            hi = new_HealthInsurance();
            Insurance_setRate((struct Insurance*)hi,45);
            HealthInsurance_setAge(hi,26);
            printf("Age=%d ",HealthInsurance_getAge(hi));
            printf("rate=%d ",Insurance_getRate((struct Insurance*)hi));
            printf("limit=%d\n",Insurance_getLimit((struct Insurance*)hi));
            reclaim_HealthInsurance(hi);

            return;

    }/*end main-------------------------------------------------------*/
```

In the previous C code, inheritance is implemented by allowing the C structures, which represent the subclasses, to include the member variables of the superclass.

```
struct HealthInsurance
{
```

```
        /*inherited members first*/
        int limit;
        int rate;
        /*HealthInsurance members*/
        int age;
    };
```

Notice how the data members of the superclass are declared first. This is a subtle but important point. Declaring the base class variables first is done intentionally so that the subclass structures can be cast to the type of their superclass and passed to the superclass member functions. This is a tactic that allows base class functions to be inherited/used by subclasses.

```
    hi = new_HealthInsurance();
    Insurance_setRate((struct Insurance*)hi,45);
```

The previous code works because the cast operation merely truncates data members that do not belong to the `Insurance` class. This technique is also used to allow the constructor of a subclass to invoke the constructor of its superclass.

```
struct CarInsurance *new_CarInsurance()
{
    struct CarInsurance *iptr = malloc(sizeof(struct CarInsurance));
    new_Insurance_init((struct Insurance*)iptr);
    return(iptr);

}/*end constructor*/
```

From the perspective of an assembly language programmer, a subclass is just a blob of bytes that has a little extra storage space in it for data values declared by the superclass. In other words, subclass byte blobs are always greater than, or equal to, the size of base class byte blobs.

In terms of controlling which members are inherited and which ones are not, again this has typically been the responsibility of the compiler and its symbol table. If you're going to write object-oriented assembly code, you will have to rely on your own short-term memory and naming conventions. One caveat that you should watch out for: If you decide not to pass on a certain variable from a base class, you have to be careful not to pass on functions that use that variable.

Polymorphism

Polymorphism is a mechanism that allows an operation to be generalized so that it can be used to process several possible combinations of arguments or exhibit different types of behavior. Polymorphism has often been typified by the expression "one interface, multiple methods." In practice, polymorphism has been implemented by permitting several different functions to share the same name. Most object-oriented languages support two kinds of polymorphism: function overloading and function overriding.

Function overloading is an object-oriented feature that allows two methods belonging to the same class to share the same name. For example, the following class has an overloaded function named `myfunction`:

```
public class MyClass
{
      int myfunction(int arg1, int arg2){ return(arg1+arg2); }
      void myfunction(String str){ return(str+" returned"); }
}
```

When an overloaded function is invoked, the version of the function called is the one whose formal parameters match the number and type of arguments in the function invocation. This requires that overloaded functions differ in terms of the number and type of parameters that they accept. Under no circumstances can two overloaded functions have the same parameter declarations.

```
/*calls the second version of myfunction*/

MyClass obj = new MyClass();
obj.myfunction("this is a string argument");
```

Function overriding is an object-oriented feature that allows a subclass to redefine a function it has inherited from a superclass. For example, the following snippet of code shows how a subclass of MyClass can override myfunction:

```
public class MyClassChild extends MyClass
{
      /*re-implementation overrides the parent*/
      int myfunction(int arg1, int arg2){ return(arg1*arg2) }
}
```

When MyClassChild has its myfunction procedure invoked, the version defined within the MyClassChild class will be the one that is used. This effectively allows a subclass to override the behavior of a parent's function, hence the name "function overriding."

```
/* the following code prints out the value 14, instead of 9 */

MyClassChild child_obj = new MyClassChild();
System.out.println("return value = "+child_obj.myfunction(2,7));
```

But wait, there's more! Function overriding can be used to implement a technique known as *run-time polymorphism*. A superclass reference variable can store the address of an object whose type is one of its derived classes. If this is the case, and the superclass variable invokes an overridden function, the version of the function called will depend on the type of object being referenced when the call is made. The resolution of which function to call is made while the program is executing, hence the name "run-time polymorphism."

```
/* again, we print out the value 14 */

MyClass myclass = null;
myclass = new MyClassChild();
System.out.println("return value = "+myclass.myfunction(2,7));
```

NOTE With function overriding, the parameter declaration of the function in the subclass must exactly match the parameter declaration of the function in the base class that it is overriding. If the parameter declarations do not match, what is being performed is merely function overloading.

Try not to confuse function overloading and function overriding. Function overloading has to do with function definitions, defined within the same class, that share the same name but differ in terms of their parameter declarations. Function overriding is based on inheritance and permits a subclass to redefine a function inherited from the superclass.

The following example in Java demonstrates both function overloading and function overriding.

```java
/* CLASS SOLID+++++++++++++++++++++++++++++++++++++++++++++++++++++++++*/

public class Solid
{
    protected int length;

    public Solid(){ length=-1; }
    public double getVolume(){ return((double)length); }

    public static void main(String[] args)
    {
        Cube cube = new Cube(2,3,4);
        System.out.println("volume="+cube.getVolume());
        System.out.println("volume="+cube.getVolume(5,5,7));

        Solid solid;
        solid = new Cube(10,2,7);
        System.out.println("volume="+solid.getVolume());

        solid = new Cone(8,3);
        System.out.println("volume="+solid.getVolume());
        return;

    }/*end main*/

}/*end class*/

/* CLASS CUBE+++++++++++++++++++++++++++++++++++++++++++++++++++++++++*/

class Cube extends Solid
{
    private int width;
    private int height;

    public Cube(int len,int wdth, int ht)
    {
        length=len;
        width =wdth;
```

```
                    height=ht;

            }/*end constructor*/

            public double getVolume(){ return((double)(length*width*height)); }

            public double getVolume(int len,int wdth,int ht)
            {
                    length=len;
                    width =wdth;
                    height=ht;
                    return((double)(len*wdth*ht));

            }/*end getVolume*/

    }/*end class*/

    /* CLASS CONE++++++++++++++++++++++++++++++++++++++++++++++++++++++++++++++*/

    class Cone extends Solid
    {
        private int radius;

        public Cone(int ht,int rad)
        {
                length = ht;
                radius = rad;

        }/*end constructor*/

        public double getVolume(){ return(Math.PI*(radius*radius)*length); }

    }/*end class*/
```

When the `main()` method, defined within the `Solid` class, is executed by the virtual machine, the following output is sent to the console:

```
volume=24
volume=175
volume=140
volume=226.195
```

The `main()` function begins with an example of function overloading. In this case, the `Cube` class has two functions that calculate the volume of a three-dimensional cube. However, they differ in their parameter declarations, and this is what facilitates the overloading.

```
Cube cube = new Cube(2,3,4);
System.out.println("volume="+cube.getVolume());
System.out.println("volume="+cube.getVolume(5,5,7));
```

The next snippet of code in `main()` is a classic example of function overriding. We basically have a `Solid` object pointer (an *implicit* pointer) that is set to reference subclass objects. We then call the `getVolume()` function, which is overridden by both of the subclasses.

```
Solid solid;
solid = new Cube(10,2,7);
System.out.println("volume="+solid.getVolume());

solid = new Cone(8,3);
System.out.println("volume="+solid.getVolume());
return;
```

As in the previous examples, we can recreate polymorphism using nothing more than C code and notational conventions. But before we begin, I need to cover a topic that some of you may not be familiar with: *function pointers*.

To implement run-time polymorphism in C, I've been forced to rely on function pointers. Function pointers are pointers that store the address of a function. Like other pointers, function pointers can be indirectly referenced, such that a particular function can be invoked indirectly by the function pointer.

For example, given the function:

```
void compute(int a, int b){ /*code here*/ }
```

we can declare a function pointer using a statement like:

```
void (*fptr) (int, int);
```

which can be set to the address of `compute()` using:

```
fptr = compute;
```

The `compute()` function can now be invoked indirectly via:

```
(*fptr)(4, 11);
```

Here is a short example that illustrates some basic function pointer manipulation techniques:

```
#include<stdio.h>

int area(int length,int width){ return(length*width); }
int volume(int length,int width,int height){ return(length*width*height); }

struct functionList
{
    int (*fptr1)(int len, int wid);
    int (*fptr2)(int len, int wid, int ht);
};

void main()
{
    int (*fptr)(int,int);
    struct functionList flist = { area, volume };

    fptr=area;
    printf("area(5,7)=%d\n",(*fptr)(5,7));
    printf("volume(5,5,3)=%d\n",(*volume)(5,5,3));
```

```
      printf("area(4,7)=%d\n",(*(flist.fptr1))(4,7));
      printf("volume(4,5,3)=%d\n",(*(flist.fptr2))(4,5,3));
      return;
}
```

Now that you have the concept of function pointers under your belt, you are now ready to dive into the C equivalent of the previous Java program.

```c
#include<stdio.h>
#include<stdlib.h>

/*SOLID CLASS+++++++++++++++++++++++++++++++++++++++++++++++++++++++++++++++*/

struct Solid_universalInfo
{
    double (*getVolume)(struct Solid *sptr);
};

struct Solid
{
    struct Solid_universalInfo *iptr;
    int length;
};

double Solid_getVolume(struct Solid *sptr){ return((double)(*sptr).length); }

void new_Solid_init(struct Solid *sptr)
{
    (*sptr).length=-1;
    return;

}/*end new_Solid_init*/

struct Solid * new_Solid()
{
    struct Solid *sptr = malloc(sizeof(struct Solid));

    new_Solid_init(sptr);

    (*sptr).iptr=malloc(sizeof(struct Solid_universalInfo));
    (*(*sptr).iptr).getVolume = Solid_getVolume;

    return(sptr);

}/*end new_Solid*/

void Solid_reclaim(struct Solid *sptr)
{
    free((*sptr).iptr);
    free(sptr);
    return;

}/*end Solid reclaim*/
```

```
/*CUBE CLASS+++++++++++++++++++++++++++++++++++++++++++++++++++++++++++*/

struct Cube_universalInfo
{
    double (*getVolume)(struct Cube *cptr);
};

struct Cube
{
    /*universal info*/
    struct Cube_universalInfo *iptr;
    /*parent members*/
    int length;
    /*Cube members*/
    int width;
    int height;
};

double Cube_getVolume(struct Cube *cptr)
{
    double volume;
    volume = (*cptr).length * (*cptr).width * (*cptr).height;
    return(volume);

}/*end Cube_getVolume*/

double Cube_getVolume_Int_Int_Int(struct Cube *cptr,int len, int wdth, int ht)
{
    (*cptr).length = len;
    (*cptr).width = wdth;
    (*cptr).height = ht;
    return((double)(len*wdth*ht));

}/*end Cube_getVolume_Int_Int_Int*/

void new_Cube_init(struct Cube *cptr,int len, int wdth, int ht)
{
    new_Solid_init((struct Solid*)cptr);
    (*cptr).length = len;
    (*cptr).width = wdth;
    (*cptr).height = ht;
    return;

}/*end new_Cube_init*/

struct Cube * new_Cube(int len, int wdth, int ht)
{
    struct Cube *cptr = malloc(sizeof(struct Cube));

    new_Cube_init(cptr,len,wdth,ht);

    (*cptr).iptr = malloc(sizeof(struct Cube_universalInfo));
    (*(*cptr).iptr).getVolume = Cube_getVolume;
```

```
        return(cptr);

}/*end new_Cube*/

void Cube_reclaim(struct Cube *cptr)
{
    free((*cptr).iptr);
    free(cptr);
    return;

}/*end Cube_reclaim*/

/*CONE CLASS+++++++++++++++++++++++++++++++++++++++++++++++++++++++++*/

struct Cone_universalInfo
{
    double (*getVolume)(struct Cone *cptr);
};

struct Cone
{
    /*universal info*/
    struct Cone_universalInfo *iptr;
    /*parent members*/
    int length;
    /*Cone members*/
    int radius;
};

double Cone_getVolume(struct Cone *cptr)
{
    double volume;
    volume = 3.14159265358979323846426433832795;
    volume = volume*(*cptr).length *(*cptr).radius * (*cptr).radius;
    return(volume);

}/*end Cone_getVolume*/

void new_Cone_init(struct Cone *cptr,int ht, int rad)
{
    new_Solid_init((struct Solid*)cptr);
    (*cptr).length = ht;
    (*cptr).radius = rad;
    return;

}/*end new_Cone_init*/

struct Cone * new_Cone(int ht, int rad)
{
    struct Cone *cptr = malloc(sizeof(struct Cone));

    new_Cone_init(cptr,ht,rad);

    (*cptr).iptr = malloc(sizeof(struct Cone_universalInfo));
```

```
        (*(*cptr).iptr).getVolume = Cone_getVolume;

        return(cptr);

}/*end new_Cone*/

void Cone_reclaim(struct Cone *cptr)
{
        free((*cptr).iptr);
        free(cptr);
        return;

}/*end Cone_reclaim*/

/* MAIN++++++++++++++++++++++++++++++++++++++++++++++++++++++++++++++++++*/

void main()
{
        struct Solid *solid;
        struct Cube *cube;

        /*demonstrate function overloading*/

        cube = new_Cube(2,3,4);
        printf("volume=%g\n",Cube_getVolume(cube));
        printf("volume=%g\n",Cube_getVolume_Int_Int_Int(cube,5,5,7));
        Cube_reclaim(cube);

        /*demonstrate function overriding*/

        solid = (struct Solid*)new_Cube(10,2,7);
        printf("volume=%g\n",(*(*(*cube).iptr).getVolume)(cube));
        Cube_reclaim((struct Cube*)solid);

        solid = (struct Solid*)new_Cone(8,3);
        printf("volume=%g\n",(*(*(*cube).iptr).getVolume)(cube));
        Cone_reclaim((struct Cone*)solid);
        return;

}/*end main*/
```

NOTE Whoa! You can see now why I decided to go from Java to C instead of Java to HEC assembly. The original 71 lines of Java code, which was a relatively simple example, expanded to almost 200 lines of C. If I were to have used assembly language directly, we probably would have ended up with a couple thousand lines of assembly language, and I am sure you'd rather not wade through that much assembly code. After reading Chapter 7, you should have a pretty good idea of how to take the C code and create the corresponding assembly language equivalent. Think of the C code as an abstract, shorthand version of assembly language (I'm sure that's how Ken and Dennis saw it).

The previous C code uses a couple of new tactics. So I'm going to proceed carefully and try to cover most of the important points.

In the previous C code, the technique that facilitates function overloading is known as *name mangling*. Because every function in a C program must have a unique name, one way to ensure that overloaded functions end up with distinct names in C is to slightly alter their names (i.e., mangle them) by adding a suffix. In the case of the previous C code, I suffix parameter type information to the end of each overloaded function.

```
cube = new_Cube(2,3,4);
printf("volume=%g\n",Cube_getVolume(cube));
printf("volume=%g\n",Cube_getVolume_Int_Int_Int(cube,5,5,7));
Cube_reclaim(cube);
```

I ended up having to do a couple of things to support run-time polymorphism. The first thing I had to do was to alter the structure declarations that I've been using so that the first element of each declaration was a special pointer.

```
struct Cube
{
    /*universal info*/
    struct Cube_universalInfo *iptr;

    /*parent members*/
    int length;

    /*Cube members*/
    int width;
    int height;
};
```

This special pointer references a structure that holds standard information on each class (i.e., universally supplied information; every class supplies this type of data).

```
struct Cube_universalInfo
{
    double (*getVolume)(struct Cube *cptr);
};
```

In the case of the Cube class, I'm storing information about the superclass function which the Cube class overrides (i.e., the getVolume() function). This will allow run-time polymorphism to be performed using function pointers. Observe how I initialize the class. I make sure to call the constructor of the superclass first.

```
void new_Cube_init(struct Cube *cptr,int len, int wdth, int ht)
{
    new_Solid_init((struct Solid*)cptr);
    (*cptr).length = len;
    (*cptr).width = wdth;
    (*cptr).height = ht;
    return;

}/*end new_Cube_init*/

struct Cube * new_Cube(int len, int wdth, int ht)
{
```

```
        struct Cube *cptr = malloc(sizeof(struct Cube));
        new_Cube_init(cptr,len,wdth,ht);
        (*cptr).iptr = malloc(sizeof(struct Cube_universalInfo));
        (*(*cptr).iptr).getVolume = Cube_getVolume;
        return(cptr);

    }/*end new_Cube*/
```

Setting up the function pointers is a little extra work. But the final results are impressive.

```
    /*demonstrate function overriding*/

    solid = (struct Solid*)new_Cube(10,2,7);
    printf("volume=%g\n",(*(*(*cube).iptr).getVolume)(cube));
    Cube_reclaim((struct Cube*)solid);

    solid = (struct Solid*)new_Cone(8,3);
    printf("volume=%g\n",(*(*(*cube).iptr).getVolume)(cube));
    Cone_reclaim((struct Cone*)solid);
```

One last thing to keep in mind: In order to make run-time polymorphism seamless, I have to make sure that the names of the function pointers are all the same, that there is no mangling applied to them. In each case, I declare the function pointer with the name getVolume.

```
    struct Solid_universalInfo
    {
        double (*getVolume)(struct Solid *sptr);
    };

    struct Cube_universalInfo
    {
        double (*getVolume)(struct Cube *cptr);
    };

    struct Cone_universalInfo
    {
        double (*getVolume)(struct Cone *cptr);
    };
```

 NOTE Because a pointer, regardless of its type, takes up a fixed number of bytes, we can still cast a class structure from one type to another without worrying. Even though each class structure has a different universal data structure (i.e., Solid_universalInfo, Cube_universalInfo, Cone_universalInfo), we can still cast Cone to Solid, and Solid to Cone, because these pointers all take up the same amount of room.

Consider the Solid and Cone structures (assume we're running on 32-bit Intel):

```
    struct Solid
    {
        struct Solid_universalInfo *iptr;   //4 bytes
        int length;                         //4 bytes
    };

    struct Cone
```

```
    {
        struct Cone_universalInfo *iptr;    //4 bytes
        int length;                          //4 bytes
        int radius;                          //4 bytes
    };
```

These two structures only differ by the last four bytes at the end of the Cone structure. The first eight bytes of each declaration serve identical purposes. Thus, we could take a variable of type Cone, and treat it like a variable of type Solid. The cast operation would merely cause the compiler to ignore Cone's last four bytes.

```
    struct Cone *cone;
    struct Solid *solid;
    cone = new_Cone(1,5);
    solid = (struct Solid*)cone;
    printf("length=%g\n",(*solid).length);
```

Exceptions

Before the advent of exception handling, when something strange happened in your application, you had to rely on global variables and function return values to see what had happened.

```
    int retval;
    char str[32];
    retval= scanf("%s",str);
    if((retval==0)||(retval==EOF))
    {
        printf("error reading field\n");
        /*
        handle error
        */
    }
    printf("%s\n",str);
```

There are three significant problems with this approach:

- Code clutter

- Loss of state information

- Crashes caused by ignoring return values

If you are truly meticulous in terms of handling every single return value, you run the risk of losing your basic logic in a tar pit of minutiae. Following is a fun example — even the error handling code has error handling code.

```
    int retval;
    char str[32];
    retval= scanf("%s",str);
    if((retval==0)||(retval==EOF))
    {
        retval = printf("error reading field\n");
        if(retval<0)
        {
            retval = fprintf(stderr,"you are hosed\n");
```

```
                    if(retval<0)
                    {
                            /*you are truly hosed*/
                            exit(1);
                    }
            }
    }
    retval = printf("%s\n",str);
    if(retval<0)
    {
            retval = fprintf(stderr,"you are hosed\n");
            if(retval<0)
            {
                    /*you are truly hosed*/
                    exit(1);
            }
    }
```

In addition, you cannot expect a single error value to always offer enough information. Any programmer would be hard pressed to determine why and how a function fails when all they get from a call is an integer value like −1. The end result is that information about the state of the program is lost.

Finally, programmers are humans, and as such they are given to fits of lethargy. Even worse, they suffer from deadlines. Subjected to lethargy and deadlines, they may be in such a rush to complete a piece of code at the last minute that, in their haste, they forget to handle the return value of a function and bring everything crashing down.

```
FILE *fptr;
int ch;
fptr=fopen("myfile.txt","rb");

/*
forget to check for fptr==NULL
sends everything to the big room if the file is missing
*/

ch = fgetc(fptr);
while(ch!=EOF)
{
        printf("%c",(char)ch);
        ch = fgetc(fptr);
}
fclose(fptr);
```

Exception handling is a sane way to bring an end to this return value madness.

An *exception* is a construct that is generated when a program attempts to perform an abnormal operation. This does not mean that every exception represents an error due to some basic service failing. Rather, an exception is intended to represent a condition the programmer views as aberrant.

When an exception is generated, a potentially non-local jump will be performed from the code producing the exception to the code that has been designated to handle the exception. An exception is said to be *thrown* by the code that generates it and *caught* by the code that processes it. This is illustrated in Figure 8-5.

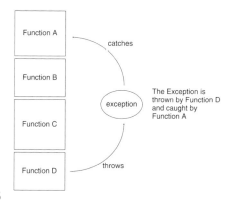

Figure 8-5

 NOTE Exception handling is a very powerful feature and, if applied judiciously, it can significantly ease the management of large, complicated software applications. This is why I am going to spend several sections on this topic.

Exceptions in Java

In Java, exceptions are implemented as objects. There are two ways to throw an exception in Java:

■ Internally by Java's virtual machine

■ Use the throw statement

Likewise, there are two ways to catch an exception:

■ Use the default virtual machine handler

■ Use a try-catch statement

The idea is to place statements that you want to monitor for exceptions within a try block. If the code you are watching actually generates an exception, then the catch block is intended to process the thrown exception.

```java
int i;
int j;
try
{
     i = 5;
     j=0;
     i = i/j;
}
catch(ArithmeticException ae)
{
     System.out.println("Divide by zero!");
     i = 0;
}
```

In the previous example, the Java virtual machine generated and threw the divide-by-zero exception. If you wanted to, you could throw the exception manually by using the throw statement.

```
int i;
int j;
try
{
    i = 5;
    j=0;
    if(j==0){ throw(new ArithmeticException()); }
    else{ i = i/j; }
}
catch(ArithmeticException ae)
{
    System.out.println("Divide by zero!");
    i = 0;
}
```

 NOTE If your code does not catch an exception with a try-catch statement, the default Java run-time exception handler will be used to catch it. The default handler basically dumps a stack trace to the console and kills the thread that threw the exception. If your program is not multithreaded, the Java run-time will cause your program to exit.

In general, the object declaration specified by the catch block should match the type of exception that you are trying to catch. If you're interested in catching more than one type of exception, you can follow a try block with multiple catch blocks.

```
try
{
    doSomeWork();
    doSomeMoreWork();
}
catch(IndexOutOfBoundesException e1)
{
    System.out.println("exception:"+e1.getMessage());
}
catch(NegativeArraySizeException e2)
{
    System.out.println(("exception:"+e2.getMessage());
}
```

The thrown exception will examine each catch statement, in the order in which they occur, until a match is found. If a match is not found, the exception is passed the Java run-time's default handler.

Another thing to keep in mind is that a given exception class can handle exceptions that are derived from it.

```
try
{
    doSomeWork();
    doSomeMoreWork();
```

```
    }
    catch(Exception e1)
    {
        System.out.println("exception:"+e1.getMessage());
    }
    catch(NegativeArraySizeException e2)
    {
        System.out.println(("exception:"+e2.getMessage());
    }
```

The second catch block in the above example will never be executed because the first catch statement captures every exception. This is due to the fact that all Java exceptions are derived from the `java.lang.Exception` class.

If a function generates an exception that it does not catch, then the function will need to be declared with the throws clause. The javac compiler enforces this rule to ensure that exceptions are handled properly. If a function throws multiple types of exceptions, then its throws clause will include a comma-separated list of exception types.

```
public void myfunction1(int arg1) throws SecurityException
{
    try
    {
        myfunction2(arg1);
    }
    catch(NullPointerException e)
    {
        System.out.println("exception:"+e.getMessage());
    }
}

public void myfunction2(int arg2) throws NullPointerException, SecurityException
{
    if(arg2==1){ throw(new NullPointerException()); }
    else{ throw(new SecurityException()); }
}
```

In the previous example, the first function (`myfunction1`) invokes another function (`myfunction2`) which throws two possible types of exceptions. Note the comma-separated list of exceptions in the `myfunction2` declaration. Because `myfunction1` only handles one of those types of exceptions, it must also have a throws clause in its declaration.

 NOTE Be careful to distinguish between throw and throws. The throw statement is used to manually throw an exception. The throws clause is used to indicate that a function generates an exception that it does not catch.

If you want to make sure that a certain set of instructions is executed after a particular try-catch statement, then you can suffix the try-catch statement with a finally block. The finally block will be executed regardless of whether the associated exceptions are caught.

```
try
{
      throw(new ArithmeticException());
}
catch(ArithmeticException ae)
{
      System.out.println("handle exception");
}
finally
{
      System.out.println("execute this always");
}
```

Naturally, there are all sorts of different exception handling variations that you can construct. You can nest try-catch statements or you can place a try-catch statement within another catch block. For example, here is a snippet of code that encompasses both of these ideas:

```
try
{
      try
      {
            throw(new ArithmeticException());
      }
      catch(ArithmeticException ae)
      {
            try
            {
                  System.out.println("inner-most try");
            }
            catch(Exception e)
            {
                  System.out.println("handle exception");
            }
            System.out.println("handle exception");
      }
      finally
      {
            System.out.println("execute this always");
      }
}
catch(Exception e)
{
      System.out.println("last line of defense!");
}
```

There are all sorts of different combinations. The fundamental thing to remember is that everything is built upon the proper utilization of five keywords:

■ try

■ catch

■ finally

- throw
- throws

Implementing Exceptions

From the research I have done, I have seen two different approaches used to implement exception handling:

- Dynamic registration approach
- Static table approach

Here, I am using Christensen's terminology. Different researchers have used other terms for these two approaches, like "portable" and "non-portable," but I like Christensen's the best, so I'll stick to them.

Dynamic registration relies upon a special stack-based data structure that stores information about the location and type of active exception handlers. I will refer to this data structure as the *exception handler stack*. When a try-catch statement is entered, the program pushes this block's metadata onto the exception handler stack. When program control leaves the try-catch block, the program must pop this block's information off the exception handler stack. This ensures that the exception handler stack will only include information on handlers which currently enclose the program counter. When an exception is thrown, the run-time system will query the exception handler stack for an exception handler that processes the type of exception being thrown. If such a handler is found, a potentially non-local jump will be made from the code generating the exception to the code that constitutes the handler. This is illustrated in Figure 8-6.

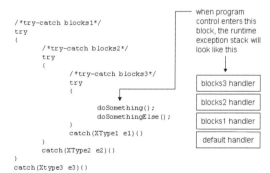

Figure 8-6

One of the performance issues with the dynamic registration approach is that the compiler has to emit special code to manage the run-time stack. This translates into extra instructions that must be executed by the application. If an exception happens only rarely (like they are supposed to), a lot of this is a waste of effort. On the other hand, the dynamic registration technique is fairly quick when it comes to actually handling the exception itself. This is because exception handling information is localized to a fairly lightweight stack structure that the program can zip through when it needs to find a handler.

Oddly enough, some dynamic registration implementations use the operating system to keep track of exception handling information. This is not exactly a wise idea because it adds the overhead of making a system call to the already expensive task of managing the exception data structure. The Borland article mentioned in the reference section talks about this approach with regard to OS/2. Why? I don't know. It seemed like a novelty to me more than anything else.

Most of the time, however, the dynamic registration approach does not rely at all on the native operating system, and this allows the dynamic registration approach to be fairly portable.

The static table approach relies on the compiler to create a static table that stores the start and end address of regions of code that are monitored by certain exception handlers. Naturally the static table stores other types of metadata, but the start-end address pairs are the crucial pieces of information. When an exception is thrown, the value of the instruction pointer (i.e., the IP register on the Intel platform) is examined. The instruction pointer holds the address of the current instruction being executed. If there is an exception handler that is capable of processing the exception being thrown and whose start-end address range encloses the current value of the instruction pointer, a (potentially) non-local goto will be performed that transfers program control to the exception handler. This operation is displayed in Figure 8-7.

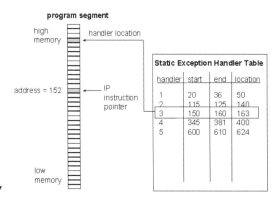

Figure 8-7

In Figure 8-7, the instruction pointer is pointing to address 152. There happens to be an exception handler monitoring the region from address 150 to 160. So, in this case, program control will jump to address 163, the location of the exception handler.

If an exception handler cannot be found for the current instruction pointer value, the return address of the current procedure will be extracted from its activation record. This return address will then be processed in a manner similar to the instruction pointer. In other words, the return address is treated like a new instruction pointer value. This process will continue until the call stack unwinds to the program's point of entry. If this is the case, a default exception will usually be invoked.

Because the static table is created at compile time, there is little or no overhead associated with its maintenance (because it has already been completely generated). The overhead that does occur can be attributed to the actual handling of the execution.

Given that applications are only rarely supposed to fail, some people would argue that the overhead associated with handling an exception is a non-issue. To an extent, I would have to agree with these people. However, if a program frequently uses exceptions as an opportunity to correct itself instead of heading to the nearest exit, the performance of exception handling is relevant.

One of the traditional problems with the static table method is that it is very low level. This adversely effects the portability of static table exception handling systems that are built on top of native hardware. However, with a virtual machine, this problem has been eliminated. The registers of a virtual machine, and the other components of the virtual execution environment, are basically the same everywhere. This makes the static table approach very attractive with regard to HEC.

Table 8-3 provides a comparison of the dynamic registration and static table approach.

Table 8-3

	Dynamic Registration	Static Table
Maintenance cost	Expensive	Cheap
Exception throw cost	Cheap	Expensive
Portability	Yes	No (Yes on a virtual machine)
Platform support	Yes ... but why?	No

As I've mentioned many times already, there are no perfect answers. There are only trade-offs and personal values; choosing a particular technique has a lot to do with your world view.

Example Implementation

This section includes an implementation that shows an example of how the dynamic registration approach to exception handling works. To give you a better idea of what the C code is attempting to do, I will begin with a version that is written in Java.

```java
public class TestExcept
{
    public static void main(String[] args)
    {
        TestExcept te = new TestExcept();
        te.testfunction();
    }/*end main*/

    public void createProblem(int arg)
    throws ExceptionTypeOne, ExceptionTypeTwo, ExceptionTypeThree
    {
        switch(arg)
        {
        case 0:{ throw(new ExceptionTypeOne("this is the first test")); }
        case 1:{ throw(new ExceptionTypeTwo("this is the first test")); }
        case 2:{ throw(new ExceptionTypeThree("this is the first test")); }
        }
    }/*end createProblem*/
    public void testfunction3()  throws ExceptionTypeOne, ExceptionTypeTwo
```

```java
    {
        try
        {
            createProblem(1);
        }
        catch(ExceptionTypeThree et3)
        {
            System.out.println("ExceptionTypeThree catch block(3)");
            System.out.println("message="+et3.getMessage());
        }
    }/*end testfunction3*/

    public void testfunction2() throws ExceptionTypeOne
    {
        try
        {
            testfunction3();
        }
        catch(ExceptionTypeTwo et2)
        {
            System.out.println("inside ExceptionTypeTwo catch block(2)");
            System.out.println("message="+et2.getMessage());
        }
    }/*end testfunction2*/

    public void testfunction()
    {
        try
        {
            testfunction2();
        }
        catch(ExceptionTypeOne et1)
        {
            System.out.println("inside ExceptionTypeOne catch block(1)");
            System.out.println("message="+et1.getMessage());
        }
    }/*end test function*/

}/*end class*/

class ExceptionTypeOne extends Exception
{
    public ExceptionTypeOne(String str){ super(str); }
}
class ExceptionTypeTwo extends Exception
{
    public ExceptionTypeTwo(String str){ super(str); }
}
class ExceptionTypeThree extends Exception
{
    public ExceptionTypeThree(String str){ super(str); }
}
```

The previous Java code invokes three functions serially. A function named test-function() calls a function named testfunction2(), which in turn calls a function named testfunction3(). Each function handles a different kind of exception. The testfunction3() function invokes createProblem() which, naturally, creates a problem by throwing an exception. By toggling the argument to createProblem(), you can vary which type of exception gets thrown.

The C equivalent of the previous Java program is rather involved. I have attempted to make it easier to understand by delimiting the various portions of code according to functionality. Hang on to your hat...

```c
#include<stdio.h>
#include<stdlib.h>
#include<setjmp.h>
#include<string.h>

/* EXCEPTION CLASS+++++++++++++++++++++++++++++++++++++++++++++++++++++++++*/

struct Exception
{
    char *name;
    int hashcode;
    char *message;
};

int getHash(unsigned char *cptr)
{
    unsigned char * p;
    unsigned h, g;
    unsigned short PRIME;

    h=0;
    PRIME=503;

    for (p = cptr; *p != '\0'; p = p + 1)
    {
        h = (h << 4) + (*p);
        if (g = (h & 0xf0000000))
        {
            h = h ^ (g >> 24);
            h = h ^ g;
        }
    }

    return(h % PRIME);

}/*end getHash*/

struct Exception* new_Exception(char *name)
{
    struct Exception *eptr;
    eptr=malloc(sizeof(struct Exception));
    (*eptr).name=malloc(strlen(name)+1);
    strcpy((*eptr).name,name);
```

```c
        (*eptr).hashcode = getHash(name);
        return(eptr);
}/*end new_Exception*/

void Exception_setMessage(struct Exception *eptr,char *msg)
{
        (*eptr).message=malloc(strlen(msg)+1);
        strcpy((*eptr).message,msg);

}/*end Exception_setMessage*/

char *Exception_getMessage(struct Exception *eptr)
{
        return((*eptr).message);

}/*end Exception_getMessage*/

void reclaim_Exception(struct Exception *eptr)
{
        free((*eptr).name);
        free((*eptr).message);
        free(eptr);
}/*end reclaim_Exception*/

/* EXCEPTION HANDLER+++++++++++++++++++++++++++++++++++++++++++++++++++++*/

int capacity;
int size;
struct ExceptionHandler
{
        char *type;
        int hashcode;
        jmp_buf location;
};
struct ExceptionHandler *HandlerList;

void initExceptionHandlerList()
{
        capacity = 20;
        size=0;
        HandlerList = malloc((capacity)*(sizeof(struct ExceptionHandler)));
        if(HandlerList==NULL)
        {
                printf("could not allocate handler list\n");
                exit(1);
        }
        return;
}/*end initExceptionHandlerList*/

void reclaimExceptionHandlerList()
{
        free(HandlerList);
}/*end reclaimExceptionHandlerList*/
```

```
struct ExceptionHandler* pushExceptionHandler(char *e_type)
{
    int index;
    size++;
    index=size-1;

    if(index < capacity)
    {
        HandlerList[index].type = e_type;
        HandlerList[index].hashcode = getHash(e_type);
    }
    else
    {
        int i;
        struct ExceptionHandler* temp;

        capacity = capacity+20;
        temp = malloc((capacity)*(sizeof(struct ExceptionHandler)));
        if(temp==NULL)
        {
            printf("could not allocate handler list\n");
            exit(1);
        }
        for(i=0;i<index;i++){ temp[0]=HandlerList[0]; }
        free(HandlerList);
        HandlerList = temp;
        HandlerList[index].type = e_type;
        HandlerList[index].hashcode = getHash(e_type);
    }
    return(&HandlerList[index]);
}/*end pushExceptionHandler*/

void popExceptionHandler(){ size--; }/*end popExceptionHandler*/

void throwException(struct Exception *eptr)
{
    int i;
    int position;
    position = size-1;

    for(i=position;i>=0;i--)
    {
        if((*eptr).hashcode==HandlerList[i].hashcode)
        {
            if(strcmp((*eptr).name,HandlerList[i].type)==0)
            {
                printf("found handler at index=%d\n",i);
                longjmp(HandlerList[i].location,(int)eptr);
            }
        }
    }
    printf("exception not caught!\n");
    printf("name= %s ",(*eptr).name);
    printf("message= %s\n",(*eptr).message);
```

```
        exit(1);
}/*end throwException*/

void printExceptionHandlerList()
{
    int i;
    int position;
    position = size-1;

    for(i=position;i>=0;i-)
    {
        printf("Handler[%d] (type,hash)=",i);
        printf("(%s,%d)\n",HandlerList[i].type,HandlerList[i].hashcode);
    }
    return;
}/*end printExceptionHandlerList*/

/* DRIVER+++++++++++++++++++++++++++++++++++++++++++++++++++++++++++++*/

void createProblem()
{
    struct Exception *eptr;
    eptr = new_Exception("ExceptionTypeTwo");
    Exception_setMessage(eptr,"this is the first test");
    throwException(eptr);

}/*end createProblem*/

void testfunction3()
{
    struct ExceptionHandler* hptr;
    int retval;
    char e_name[] ="ExceptionTypeThree";

    hptr = pushExceptionHandler(e_name);
    retval = setjmp((*hptr).location);

    switch(retval)
    {
        case 0:
        {

            printf("code inside third try block\n");
            printf("current list of handled exceptions\n");
            printExceptionHandlerList();
            createProblem();

        }break;
        default:
        {
            struct Exception *eptr;
            eptr = (struct Exception*)retval;
            printf("inside %s catch block(3)\n",e_name);
            printf("message=%s\n\n",Exception_getMessage(eptr));
```

```
                            reclaim_Exception(eptr);
                }
        }

        popExceptionHandler();

        return;
}/*end testfunction3*/

void testfunction2()
{
        struct ExceptionHandler* hptr;
        int retval;
        char e_name[] ="ExceptionTypeTwo";

        hptr = pushExceptionHandler(e_name);
        retval = setjmp((*hptr).location);

        switch(retval)
        {
            case 0:
            {

                    printf("code inside second try block\n");
                    testfunction3();

            }break;
            default:
            {
                    struct Exception *eptr;
                    eptr = (struct Exception*)retval;
                    printf("inside %s catch block(2)\n",e_name);
                    printf("message=%s\n\n",Exception_getMessage(eptr));
                    reclaim_Exception(eptr);
            }
        }

        popExceptionHandler();

        return;
}/*end testfunction2*/

void testfunction()
{
        struct ExceptionHandler* hptr;
        int retval;
        char e_name[] ="ExceptionTypeOne";

        hptr = pushExceptionHandler(e_name);
        retval = setjmp((*hptr).location);

        switch(retval)
        {
                case 0:
```

```
                {
                    printf("code inside first try block\n");
                    testfunction2();

                }break;
                default:
                {
                    struct Exception *eptr;
                    eptr = (struct Exception*)retval;
                    printf("inside %s catch block(1)\n",e_name);
                    printf("message=%s\n\n",Exception_getMessage(eptr));
                    reclaim_Exception(eptr);
                }
            }

        popExceptionHandler();

        return;
}/*end testfunction*/

void main()
{
    initExceptionHandlerList();
    testfunction();
    reclaimExceptionHandlerList();
    return;
}/*end main*/
```

If you are a little confused, take a look at Figure 8-8. It should give a rough idea of the basic motivation behind this source code.

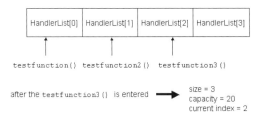

Figure 8-8

The primary data structure is the `HandlerList` stack. It is a dynamically resizable array that `ExceptionHandler` structures are pushed on and popped off of.

Each time a try block is entered, we need to register its exception handler with the stack. This will result in an `ExceptionHandler` structure being pushed on the exception handler stack.

```
struct ExceptionHandler* hptr;
int retval;
char e_name[] ="ExceptionTypeThree";

hptr = pushExceptionHandler(e_name);
retval = setjmp((*hptr).location);
```

The try-catch blocks are realized as a switch statement. The zero case is the try block and the default case is the catch block.

```
switch(retval)
{
    case 0:
    {

        printf("code inside third try block\n");
        printf("current list of handled exceptions\n");
        printExceptionHandlerList();
        createProblem();

    }break;
    default:
    {
        struct Exception *eptr;
        eptr = (struct Exception*)retval;
        printf("inside %s catch block(3)\n",e_name);
        printf("message=%s\n\n",Exception_getMessage(eptr));
        reclaim_Exception(eptr);
    }
}
```

If program control executes the zero case without throwing an exception, the handler must remove itself from the list of registered handlers by pushing itself off the stack.

```
popExceptionHandler();
```

The subtle key to the C implementation is the utilization of the ANSI setjmp() and longjmp() functions. Normally, a C goto statement will only let you hop around within a single function. You cannot use goto to jump from one function to another. The problem is that handling exceptions requires non-local transfers of program control. Fortunately, the C standard library comes to the rescue with a couple of functions that do some stack-based acrobatics on our behalf.

The trick is to implement setjmp() and longjmp() in terms of HEC assembly. To get an idea of how to do that, we need to take a closer look at these functions.

The setjmp() function takes the entire stack frame of the invoking function, stores it in a jmp_buf structure, and returns the value 0. The longjmp() routine accepts this jmp_buf structure as an argument and transfers program control (or at least appears to) to the point just before the corresponding setjmp(), such that the function is effectively reinvoked. The difference is that this time, the setjmp() call will return a nonzero value to signal that it is being called by longjmp(). Implementation of these functions varies greatly from one platform to the next, so it's hard to pin down exactly what is going on.

What this means is that, rather than recreate these functions down to the smallest detail, we need to recreate their general intent: a non-local jump. Given that the JMP instruction facilitates non-local transfers of program control in the HEC assembly language, you'd probably want to use some variation of the JMP instruction to facilitate exception handling.

Abusing Exceptions

Programmers who abuse exceptions are like ambulance drivers who turn on their siren when going on a doughnut run. Don't get me wrong: I like an occasional doughnut myself, but doughnuts are no reason to power up the lights and stop traffic.

Like almost every other language feature, exception handling can be abused. Some underhanded programmers have been known to use exception handling as the equivalent of a non-local goto statement. In other words, instead of returning through the normal chain of command, a function can jump several functions back with return value information stored in the exception.

The difference between this use and the intended use of exception handling is that exception handling is intended to imply that an exceptional, out-of-the-ordinary event has occurred that demands attention. If you use exception handling casually, you might cause someone reading your code to wonder what's going on. Where is the fire?

Porting

Observations on Linux

There has been a lot of hype surrounding Linux over the past couple of years. I decided to put the penguin to the test and port the HEC suite of programs to Linux. I went out and bought a copy of Caldera's distribution to see how commercial-grade Linux measured up.

I have to admit, I was looking forward to using Linux for a nontrivial chunk of programming. Like everyone else, I have seen IBM's peace, love, and Linux advertisements. My expectations were pretty high. I plunked down some cash and went home to do a full installation. The install took up over a gigabyte of drive space.

My reactions are mixed. Before I begin, I think I would like to say that it's very seductive to get swept away by fashionable technology without trying to weigh things objectively. Now that I have developed software on both Linux and Microsoft, I'm going to try and step back and make a judgment. I paid good money for both the Linux and Microsoft development suites that I tested. What follows is nothing more than my honest take on the state of programming tools on both platforms.

While Linux does have the typical set of command-line tools, they do not come close to what Microsoft offers. The Linux environment that I worked with was complicated, incomplete, and poorly documented. But before you Linux fanatics flame me, please hear me out.

These are some of the outstanding issues that I encountered:

- Library support (or lack thereof)
- IDE usability
- IDE extensibility
- Documentation

First, and most importantly, Microsoft's Visual C++ compiler sports a complete ISO/ANSI C standard library. I did not have to download a third-party API and then figure out how to integrate it into my source tree. In addition, the Visual Studio documentation is consistent, all in one place, and integrated into the environment. The MSDN documentation may take up a lot of disk space, but it's well organized and everything, and I mean everything, is all in one place.

For example, when I needed to determine the amount of free physical memory available, there was a well-documented system call that I could take advantage of (if you recall from win32.c, `GlobalMemoryStatus()`). I didn't have to go digging through HOWTOs, or wade through obsolete man pages, or try to hunt down clues hidden in textinfo files. I browsed through the Win32 API and there it was.

Furthermore, the necessary extension functions that I needed in order to deal with 64-bit integers were all there in Windows. They were grouped in with the other ANSI calls so that I wouldn't have to go far to find them. For example, if you need to convert a string to a 64-bit integer, all you have to do is call `_atoi64()`. Using 64-bit values on Windows is a cakewalk.

This is more than I can say for Caldera's development tool set. The C standard library was blatantly lacking in several areas, like wide-character support (i.e., `wprintf()`). Caldera's installation program claimed that I would be getting a fully functional development machine. How can they call it that when the `wchar.h` header file is missing its most useful components? The least they could do would be to give me a complete standard library! I was hoping for a little more from a company that had prided itself on beating Microsoft at its own game.

Now, I'm sure that there will be those Linux gurus in the audience who say: "Oh, see, it's really not that hard to use wide characters, all you have to do is download the so-and-so tar file and…"

The ugly truth is that the wide-character ANSI/ISO functions should be there to begin with. I shouldn't have to download anything to access such rudimentary API calls. The `wprintf()` function should be right where the ISO standard says it should. In the case of Caldera's OpenLinux, they were not. I find this reprehensible, to say the least. If Microsoft can get it right, it shouldn't be so hard for Caldera to put a little extra work in and offer a fully functional standard library. They should make life easy for me, not point me in the direction of some web link and wish me good luck.

 NOTE I knew I was hosed when I typed in:

        man wprintf

and I got back:

        No manual entry for wprintf

If there are Linux distributions that actually do have a complete ANSI/ISO library, this does not bode well for Linux because it gives the impression of fragmentation. There is only one true version of Windows XP, and it is built by Microsoft. When someone talks about Linux, you can't be sure which frame of reference they are using. Are they talking about Caldera? Red Hat? SuSE? Slackware?

Regardless of what Linux zealots say, there are marked differences between the distributions. For example, I've found that PAM-related services, which are used to provide configurable authentication, operate differently among the various distributions. Another problem is the proliferation of incompatible user interfaces. Some development tools only work on KDE, and others only work on GNOME. This makes it hard to develop a consistent and predictable GUI tool set.

Usability is another big issue. One tool that I have found extremely easy to use is Microsoft's Visual Source Safe. It's completely visual, self-evident, and allows me to do a lot of complicated manipulation without having to remember 25 different command-line options. Most importantly, you can see everything that's going on. I've worked extensively with CVS on Solaris, and compared to Visual Source Safe, using CVS is like working in the dark.

There are GUI front ends to CVS, and I have worked with more than a couple of them, but they are all fairly primitive when you compare them to Visual Source Safe. In fact, if I had to pick the one Microsoft product that I liked the most, it would probably be a toss-up between PowerPoint and Visual Source Safe.

 NOTE   Here is a canonical usability test. Take someone who has had minimal exposure to computers (i.e., your mother). Allow them to play with Microsoft WordPad and then give them a chance to fiddle with vi. WordPad will win every time. Normal people realize that having to memorize dozens of obscure commands is a waste of time, and they would rather interact with a tool that is intuitive and easy to work with. Naturally, there will be those members of the audience who think otherwise. They would say: "But, but, but ... vi has far more powerful features than WordPad." These are the same people who yearn for the good old days of the 25x80 dummy terminals. The vi editor is nothing more than a relic from the pre-GUI era.

 NOTE   I have not been compensated in any way by Microsoft. What I am offering is my unadulterated opinion. I work with software tools every day and I feel like I know what distinguishes an effective and usable tool from one that isn't. In general, if you have read this book in its entirety, you will notice that I have positive and negative things to say about both Linux and Windows.

Microsoft's IDE also does a decent job of generating and automatically maintaining make files. For a beginner who does not understand the nuances of suffix rules, this is a godsend. While working in the Linux domain, I found myself constantly switching windows to manually invoke the GNU make utility. Yes, I know that invoking a make can be done from emacs; it is just that I don't consider emacs to exactly be a self-evident application and I'd rather not waste my time learning it.

In terms of extensibility, again, Microsoft is the undisputed champion. The Visual Studio IDE is renowned for its ability to be reconfigured. You can drag and drop menu bars or create your own customized controls. You can anchor IDE widgets, or you can let them float freely around the IDE. The list goes on and on.

Documentation is a pet peeve of mine. Microsoft does a notably good job of organizing its documentation and making it easy to use. In fact, Microsoft's ANSI C run-time libraries are organized both by category and alphabetically, which almost guarantees that I'll be able to find what I need. Furthermore, Microsoft centralizes everything in one place and gives it all a consistent user interface.

Caldera, on the other hand, has a confusing collection of man pages, textinfo files, and HTML. Unlike Microsoft's documentation, the Linux man pages do not indicate which library binary a function belongs to. If you're lucky, you'll get a reference to a header file.

This is a really big problem. I had to spend a couple of hours during my Linux port just trying to find which shared library the `math.h` functions belonged to. As it turns out, they belong to `/lib/libm-2.1.1.so`. The problem is that I only discovered this after executing the `nm` command on every shared object in my file system — not a pleasant way to spend a Saturday afternoon.

What this leads me to conclude is that Linux is not an operating system for beginners. It is an operating system for hobbyists who like to spend their spare time wading around in the kernel and investing the time necessary to learn how to use it. If this is the case, then Linux is doomed to the server-side backwaters of the computing industry. History has shown that the public will adopt and use technology that is both accessible and easy to use. I'm not exactly a neophyte when it comes to building software, and even I was a little put off by all the missing pieces that I encountered. I doubt very highly that I will buy another Linux distribution in the future.

 NOTE At the end of the day, Bill Gates has pumped hundreds of millions of dollars into the Windows operating system and it shows. Comparing Windows to Linux is like comparing a Porsche to a used Honda Civic. With a used Civic, you can usually get from point A to point B. But with a Porsche, you get everything else. The Honda is cheap and has a notable life span. The Porsche costs more but is really fun to drive.

 NOTE Linux and other open source operating systems still have a trump card left to play: The source code is publicly available. This is a very important feature for engineers who are concerned about security. On March 17, 2001, a report in *Der Spiegel* stated that Germany's military would not use Microsoft software in sensitive areas. The report claimed that officials in the German military were concerned that Microsoft had installed secret back doors that would allow American intelligence agencies to access German secrets.

The report has since been revoked by German military spokesmen, but the point is still valid. There are millions of lines of code in Windows XP. Who knows what is really going on beneath the hood? You could crank up a disassembler, but I don't know anyone who has the patience, or time, to reverse engineer that amount of code. If your life depended upon the ability of your computer to maintain confidentiality, would you use Windows? Personally, I think I would give up the convenience of the Windows GUI in favor of peace of mind.

With open source operating systems, this problem is not as pressing. The inner workings are completely exposed for all to see. Flaws that do exist can be identified and eliminated. This is particularly true when it comes to a BSD variant named OpenBSD. OpenBSD is an open source operating system whose claim to fame is security and stability. The OpenBSD development team performs ongoing, and rigorous, source code auditing. These audits are a core component of the development cycle. OpenBSD is the only platform I know of where the development team stresses the need to simplify and add security, as opposed to haphazardly piling on new features.

This does not mean that OpenBSD is antiquated. In fact, OpenBSD was the first operating system to have an IPsec stack. OpenBSD's IPsec stack was introduced in 1997, while Windows NT admins were treading water just trying to keep up with their service packs.

In short, if I had to expose a machine to the wild West that is the Internet, I would want that gateway to be an OpenBSD box. For information, visit http://www.openbsd.org.

Now that I've discussed my take on the state of Linux, I can discuss how I handled the Linux port.

If you remember my design goals (portability, simplicity, and performance) my number one priority was making sure that I could port the virtual machine. Given that portability was my primary concern, I tried to isolate platform-dependent code to two source files: `win32.c` and `intwin32.c`.

I rewrote these files as `linux.c` and `intlinux.c`.

linux.c

Porting the code to Linux and constructing the necessary make files took about 60 hours of work (60 very frustrating hours). Porting `win32.c` was fairly simple; Linux on Intel works with integer values in little-endian format, so I didn't have to modify any of the code related to endianness.

In fact, most of the porting involved changing "`%I64u`" to "`%llu`" in order to print out 64-bit numbers.

```
/*+++++++++++++++++++++++++++++++++++++++++++++++++++++++++++++++++++++++++
+  macros                                                                 +
+++++++++++++++++++++++++++++++++++++++++++++++++++++++++++++++++++++++++*/

#define S1      signed char
#define S2      signed short
#define S4      signed long
#define S8      signed long long

#define U1      unsigned char
#define U2      unsigned short
#define U4      unsigned long
#define U8      unsigned long long

/*
    Use ANSI-754 standard for single and double precision floats
    single precision = 4 bytes
    double precision = 8 bytes
*/

#define F4      float
```

```
#define F8        double

/* platform-specific I/O -----------------------------------------*/

#define PRINT_UREG(rstr,reg)     printf("%-6s=%-21llu",rstr,reg)
#define PRINT_SREG(rstr,reg)     printf("%-6s=%-21lld",rstr,reg)
#define PRINT_FREG(rstr,reg)     printf("%-6s-%g",rstr,(F4)reg)
#define PRINT_DREG(rstr,reg)     printf("%-6s=%g",rstr,(F8)reg)


#define pU1(arg)      printf("%u",arg)
#define pU2(arg)      printf("%hu",arg)
#define pU4(arg)      printf("%lu",arg)
#define pU8(arg)      printf("%llu",arg)


#define pS1(arg)      printf("%d",arg)
#define pS2(arg)      printf("%hd",arg)
#define pS4(arg)      printf("%ld",arg)
#define pS8(arg)      printf("%lld",arg)


#define PRINT_MEM(index)    printf("RAM[%llu]=%u",index,RAM[index])


#define rU8(arg)      scanf("%llu",arg)


#define fpU8(ptr,arg) fprintf(ptr,"%llu",arg)
#define fpS8(ptr,arg) fprintf(ptr,"%lld",arg)


/* macros below used during reformatting --------------------------*/

/*
    reverse the order of bytes within an array
*/

U1 fb[8];

#define FORMAT_WORD(arr,start) { fb[0]=arr[start+1];\
                                 fb[1]=arr[start];\
                                 arr[start]=fb[0];\
                                 arr[start+1]=fb[1]; }

#define FORMAT_DWORD(arr,start) {fb[0]=arr[start+3];\
                                 fb[1]=arr[start+2];\
                                 fb[2]=arr[start+1];\
                                 fb[3]=arr[start];\
                                 arr[start]=fb[0];\
                                 arr[start+1]=fb[1];\
                                 arr[start+2]=fb[2];\
                                 arr[start+3]=fb[3]; }

#define FORMAT_QWORD(arr,start){ fb[0]=arr[start+7];\
                                 fb[1]=arr[start+6];\
                                 fb[2]=arr[start+5];\
                                 fb[3]=arr[start+4];\
                                 fb[4]=arr[start+3];\
                                 fb[5]=arr[start+2];\
```

```
                                    fb[6]=arr[start+1];\
                                    fb[7]=arr[start];\
                                    arr[start]=fb[0];\
                                    arr[start+1]=fb[1];\
                                    arr[start+2]=fb[2];\
                                    arr[start+3]=fb[3];\
                                    arr[start+4]=fb[4];\
                                    arr[start+5]=fb[5];\
                                    arr[start+6]=fb[6];\
                                    arr[start+7]=fb[7]; }


/*+++++++++++++++++++++++++++++++++++++++++++++++++++++++++++++++++++++
+  public prototypes                                                 +
+++++++++++++++++++++++++++++++++++++++++++++++++++++++++++++++++++++*/

void checkEndian();
void printBytes(U1 bytes[], int nbytes);
void testConversion();

U2 bytecodeToWord(U1 bytes[]);
U4 bytecodeToDWord(U1 bytes[]);
U8 bytecodeToQWord(U1 bytes[]);
F4 bytecodeToFloat(U1 bytes[]);
F8 bytecodeToDouble(U1 bytes[]);

void wordToBytecode(U2 word, U1 arr[]);
void dwordToBytecode(U4 dword, U1 arr[]);
void qwordToBytecode(U8 qword, U1 arr[]);
void floatToBytecode(F4 flt, U1 arr[]);
void doubleToBytecode(F8 dbl, U1 arr[]);

U4 getAvailableMemory();
U4 getFileSize(char *name);
void testNativeFunctions();

/* added for assembler */

U8 stringToU8(char *str);

/*+++++++++++++++++++++++++++++++++++++++++++++++++++++++++++++++++++++
+ definitions                                                        +
+++++++++++++++++++++++++++++++++++++++++++++++++++++++++++++++++++++*/

/*
    Note: bytecode format for numbers must be platform neutral
          ... So we must agree on a convention ahead of time.

    Integers - Stored in big-endian (high byte first) order,
               AKA network order

                OxDEED1234  = OxDE  OxED  Ox12  Ox34
                                   [0]   [1]   [2]   [3]
```

```
        Floats - Stored using IEEE 754 format using big-endian order

            Intel floating-point values are little endian

            [0 --decimal part -- 22][23 --exponent-- 30] [31=sign]
            byte[0]                                       byte[4]

            [0 --decimal part -- 51][52 --exponent-- 62][63=sign]
            byte[0]                                       byte[7]

            For both, you'll need to convert to and from big-endian

        NOTA BENE: should convert values once upon loading application,
                   to avoid redundant computation at runtime
*/


/*-------------------------------------------------------------------*/
/*

    This method checks the current platform's endianess
    big-endian        higher-order bytes first (are at lower mem)
    little endian     lower-order bytes first (are at lower mem)

    On Intel Hardware using NT 4.0 we get:
    value = 0xDEED1234
    machine is LITTLE endian - LOWER order bytes come first
    here are the bytes
    [0]=0x34 [1]=0x12 [2]=0xED [3]=0xDE
*/

void checkEndian()
{
    int i=0xDEED1234;
    int j;
    unsigned char *buff;

    printf("value = %lx\n",i);
    buff = (unsigned char*)&i;
    if(buff[0]==0x34)
    {
        printf("machine is LITTLE endian - LOWER order bytes come first");
    }
    else
    {
        printf("machine is BIG endian - HIGHER order bytes come first");
    }

    printf("\nhere are the 4 bytes\n");
    for(j=0;j<4;j++){ printf(" byte [%d]=%x ",j,buff[j]); }
    printf("\n");
    return;

}/*end checkEndian*/
```

```
/*----------------------------------------------------------------*/

/*
    Routines below convert bytecode values to native Intel format
*/

U2 bytecodeToWord(U1 bytes[])
{
    U2 word;
    U1 *buffer;

    buffer = (U1*)&word;
    buffer[0] = bytes[1];
    buffer[1] = bytes[0];

    return(word);

}/*end bytecodeToWord*/

U4 bytecodeToDWord(U1 bytes[])
{
    U4 dword;
    U1 *buffer;

    buffer = (U1*)&dword;
    buffer[0] = bytes[3];
    buffer[1] = bytes[2];
    buffer[2] = bytes[1];
    buffer[3] = bytes[0];

    return(dword);

}/*end bytecodeToDWord*/

U8 bytecodeToQWord(U1 bytes[])
{
    U8 qword;
    U1 *buffer;

    buffer = (U1*)&qword;
    buffer[0] = bytes[7];
    buffer[1] = bytes[6];
    buffer[2] = bytes[5];
    buffer[3] = bytes[4];
    buffer[4] = bytes[3];
    buffer[5] = bytes[2];
    buffer[6] = bytes[1];
    buffer[7] = bytes[0];

    return(qword);

}/*end bytecodeToQWord*/

F4 bytecodeToFloat(U1 bytes[])
```

```c
{
    F4 flt;
    U1 *buffer;

    buffer = (U1*)&flt;
    buffer[0] = bytes[3];
    buffer[1] = bytes[2];
    buffer[2] = bytes[1];
    buffer[3] = bytes[0];

    return(flt);

}/*end bytecodeToFloat*/

F8 bytecodeToDouble(U1 bytes[])
{
    F8 dbl;
    U1 *buffer;

    buffer = (U1*)&dbl;
    buffer[0] = bytes[7];
    buffer[1] = bytes[6];
    buffer[2] = bytes[5];
    buffer[3] = bytes[4];
    buffer[4] = bytes[3];
    buffer[5] = bytes[2];
    buffer[6] = bytes[1];
    buffer[7] = bytes[0];

    return(dbl);

}/*end bytecodeToDouble*/

/*----------------------------------------------------------------*/

/*
Routines below convert Intel values to bytecode format
*/

void wordToBytecode(U2 word, U1 arr[])
{
    U1 *buffer;

    buffer = (U1*)&word;
    arr[0] = buffer[1];
    arr[1] = buffer[0];

    return;

}/*end wordToBytecode*/

void dwordToBytecode(U4 dword, U1 arr[])
{
```

```
    U1 *buffer;

    buffer = (U1*)&dword;
    arr[0] = buffer[3];
    arr[1] = buffer[2];
    arr[2] = buffer[1];
    arr[3] = buffer[0];

    return;

}/*end dwordToBytecode*/

void qwordToBytecode(U8 qword, U1 arr[])
{
    U1 *buffer;

    buffer = (U1*)&qword;
    arr[0] = buffer[7];
    arr[1] = buffer[6];
    arr[2] = buffer[5];
    arr[3] = buffer[4];
    arr[4] = buffer[3];
    arr[5] = buffer[2];
    arr[6] = buffer[1];
    arr[7] = buffer[0];

    return;

}/*end qwordToBytecode*/

void floatToBytecode(F4 flt, U1 arr[])
{
    U1 *buffer;

    buffer = (U1*)&flt;
    arr[0] = buffer[3];
    arr[1] = buffer[2];
    arr[2] = buffer[1];
    arr[3] = buffer[0];

    return;

}/*end floatToBytecode*/

void doubleToBytecode(F8 dbl, U1 arr[])
{
    U1 *buffer;

    buffer = (U1*)&dbl;
    arr[0] = buffer[7];
    arr[1] = buffer[6];
    arr[2] = buffer[5];
    arr[3] = buffer[4];
    arr[4] = buffer[3];
```

```
                arr[5] = buffer[2];
                arr[6] = buffer[1];
                arr[7] = buffer[0];

                return;

}/*end doubleToBytecode*/


/*------------------------------------------------------------------*/
/*
        this prints out the bytes of a datatype
*/

void printBytes(U1 bytes[], int nbytes)
{
        int i;
        for(i=0; i<nbytes; i++){ printf("byte[%u]=%X ",i,(U1)bytes[i]); }
        printf("\n");
        return;

}/*end printBytes*/


/*------------------------------------------------------------------*/

/*
        Returns the amount of free physical memory in bytes.
        Again, Linux didn't seem to provide anything outside of
        /proc/meminfo, free, etc.
        So, I simply return the max value
        (I apologize for this crude hack)
*/

U4 getAvailableMemory()
{
        return(0xFFFFFFFF);

}/*end getAvailableMemory*/

#include<sys/stat.h>

/*
        Returns size of file in bytes
*/

U4 getFileSize(char *name)
{
        U4 size;
        S1 ret;
        struct stat buffer;
        ret = lstat(name,&buffer);
        if(ret==0){ return((U4)buffer.st_size); }
        else{ return(0); }
```

```
}/*end getFileSize*/

/*-----------------------------------------------------------------*/

/*
    Linux distribution doesn't have string->64-bit conversion
*/

U8 stringToU8(char *str)
{
    return((U8)atol(str));

}/*end stringToU8*/
```

There were two major problems that I ran into during the port:

- Memory status calls
- String to 64-bit integer conversion

I searched and searched for a clean way to get memory status information (how much physical memory was free, how much memory was paged to disk, etc.). The closest I could come to a solution was to parse the /proc/meminfo file, and even this didn't seem like a palatable solution. So, I axed support completely. In particular, the getAvailableMemory() function, instead of returning the actual amount of free physical memory, returns a very large unsigned integer value.

This isn't as bad as it sounds; it only means that the HEC virtual machine is more likely to occupy paged memory.

Another barrier I encountered was the apparent lack of support for integer-string conversion functions with respect to integers in the 64-bit range. While Microsoft provided more than ample support for 64-bit integers, Linux fell flat on its face. Again, I was forced to compromise by using atol() with the hope that the string argument would only rarely cross outside of the 32-bit ceiling. This is how I tackled the implementation of the stringToU8() function.

intlinux.c

Most of the problems arose during the construction of intlinux.c. The intlinux.c file handles the interface to native OS services by implementing the HEC virtual machine's interrupts. This file was a real problem child, primarily because of what Linux was missing. As a result of certain limitations inherent in Caldera's Linux distribution, I had to omit (or completely reimplement) certain portions of the system interface. Specifically, the following functions needed re-engineering:

- handlefileIO()
- handleFileManagement()
- handleProcessManagement()
- handleMemoryStatus()

- `handleNativeCall()`
- `handleIPC()`

The `handlefileIO()` function lost a small portion of its functionality due to the lack of ANSI C support for wide characters. The `handleFileManagement()` function also required a certain amount of work to make it speak Linux.

The `handleMemoryStatus()` and `handleNativeCall()` functions were almost entirely dropped. This forced me to cut a large chunk of functionality out of the Linux port. As I have mentioned earlier, the system call interface to obtain memory status information was not very well documented, and I did not have time to start reading kernel source. Nor did I feel like parsing `/proc/meminfo`.

According to the dozen or so books I own on Linux, Linux programs that use shared libraries must mention those libraries on the command line when they are compiled. For example, let's say we have the following library code:

```
int returnOrder(char *str)
{
    if(strcmp(str,"Mark1")==0){ return(0); }
    else if(strcmp(str,"Multics")==0){ return(1); }
    else if(strcmp(str,"Unix")==0){ return(2); }
    else if(strcmp(str,"Linux")==0){ return(3);}
    else{ return(-1); }
}
```

Assume this is in a file named order.c . We would compile this into a shared library using the following two steps:

```
gcc -c -fPIC order.c
gcc -shared -o liborder.so order.o
```

The first command creates an object file (`order.o`) that we feed to the second command. The second command creates the shared library.

To ensure that Linux can find the shared library, the following two commands can be issued (assuming that `liborder.so` is in `/root/mylibs`):

```
LD_LIBRARY_PATH=/root/mylibs/
export LD_LIBRARY_PATH
```

Let's say we have a source file named `main.c` that uses the shared library by declaring it as an external entity.

```
extern int returnOrder(char *str);

int main(int argc,char *argv[])
{
    printf("%d\n",returnOrder("Linux"));
    return(0);
}
```

This application can be compiled using the following command line:

```
gcc  -L ./   -o main   main.c  -lorder
```

Note how the lib prefix and so suffix of liborder.so are excluded when we specify the name of the shared library using the -l switch. When we run the main program, the number 3 will be displayed on the screen.

The entire point of the previous demonstration was to show that Linux shared libraries have to be specified on the command line of the applications that use them.

This is nowhere near as flexible as Microsoft's approach. With Win32 DLLs, you can dynamically specify the name of a DLL and load it at run time. This allows the HEC virtual machine to use DLLs without having to mention them when the virtual machine is built. The alternative would be to recompile the virtual machine every time you wanted to access a new shared library. This is not an elegant solution.

To see what I'm talking about, take a gander at the body of the intwin32.c version of the handleNativeCall() function:

```c
case 0:
{
     HINSTANCE file_handle;
     file_handle = LoadLibrary(&RAM[R[$R2]]);
     R[$R3]= (U8)file_handle;
     if(file_handle==NULL){ R[$R4]=1; }
     else{ R[$R4]=0; }

}break;
case 1:
{
     address =
     (FunctionPtr)GetProcAddress((HINSTANCE)R[$R2],"gateway");
     if(address==NULL)
     {
          R[$R5]=1;
     }
     else
     {
          R[$R5]=0;
          (address)(&RAM[R[$R3]],&RAM[R[$R4]]);
     }

}break;
case 2:
{
     int unload;
     unload = (int)FreeLibrary((HINSTANCE)R[$R2]);
     if(unload==0)
     {
          R[$R3]=1;
     }
     else
     {
          R[$R3]=0;
     }

}break;
```

At no time is the name of the DLL file mentioned. It is completely a dynamic quantity. It can be anything. In other words, the name of the DLL file loaded is unknown at compile time. It does not have to be specified. Because of this, I find the Windows approach to be far more accommodating and appealing than Linux's. In fact, because I was unable to find a way to recreate this kind of run time-oriented functionality in Linux, I dropped native support completely.

Surprisingly, the `handleIPC()` function required only partial modification. In particular, I had to replace the mutex facilities that I had used on Microsoft with file locking. Using semaphores on Linux was truly a pain, and I crashed my system several times just trying to get a simple example to work. Richard Stevens (the renowned author of the three-volume TCP/IP series) recommends file locking for this very reason. I decided to follow his advice.

I was pleasantly surprised at how little I had to change the networking code. It seems that Microsoft stayed closer to the spirit of the original Unix implementation than I had expected.

```
#include<sys/socket.h>
#include<netdb.h>
#include<sys/types.h>
#include<sys/ipc.h>
#include<sys/sem.h>
#include<errno.h>
#include<netinet/in.h>

char fname[_POSIX_PATH_MAX];

void handleIPC()
{
    switch((U1)R[$R1])
    {
        /*use file locking instead of semaphores (RS p.463)*/

        case 0:
        {
            int fd;
            fd = open(&RAM[R[$R2]],O_WRONLY|O_CREAT|O_EXCL,0644);
            while(fd<0 && errno==EEXIST)
            {
                fd = open(&RAM[R[$R2]],O_WRONLY|O_CREAT|O_EXCL,0644);

            }
            if(fd<0){ R[$R3]=0; R[$R4]=1; }
            else
            {
                R[$R3]=fd; R[$R4]=1;
                strcpy(fname,&RAM[R[$R2]]);
            }

        }break;
        case 1:
        {
```

```
            int retval;
            retval = close((int)R[$R2]);
            if(retval==-1)
            {
                R[$R3]=1;
            }
            else
            {
                retval = unlink(fname);
                if(retval==-1){ R[$R3]=1; }
                else{ R[$R3]=0; }
            }

}break;
case 2:
{
    struct sockaddr_in address;
    int client;
    int err;

    address.sin_family=AF_INET;
    address.sin_port = htons((unsigned short)R[$R3]);
    address.sin_addr.s_addr = inet_addr(&RAM[R[$R2]]);

    client = socket(AF_INET,SOCK_STREAM,0);
    if(client<0)
    {
        R[$R5]=1;
    }
    else
    {
        err = connect(client,
                    &address,
                    sizeof(struct sockaddr_in));
        if(err==-1)
        {
            R[$R5]=1;
        }
        else
        {
            R[$R5]=0;
            R[$R4]=(U8)client;
        }
    }

}break;
case 3:
{
    if(close((int)R[$R2])==-1)
    {
        R[$R3]=1;
    }
    else
    {
```

```
                              R[$R3]=0;
                      }

          }break;
          case 4:
          {
                int nLeft;
                int index;
                char *buffer;

                nLeft=(int)R[$R4];
                index=0;
                R[$R5]=0;
                buffer = &RAM[R[$R3]];
                while(nLeft>0)
                {
                      int ret;
                      ret = send((int)R[$R2],
                                  &(buffer[index]),
                                  nLeft,
                                  0);
                      if(ret==-1)
                      {
                            R[$R5]=1;
                            break;
                      }
                      nLeft = nLeft - ret;
                      index = index + ret;
                }

          }break;
          case 5:
          {
                int nLeft;
                int index;
                char *buffer;

                nLeft=(int)R[$R4];
                index=0;
                R[$R5]=0;
                buffer = &RAM[R[$R3]];
                while(nLeft>0)
                {
                      int ret;
                      ret = recv((int)R[$R2],
                                  &(buffer[index]),
                                  nLeft,
                                  0);
                      if(ret==-1)
                      {
                            R[$R5]=1;
                            break;
                      }
                      nLeft = nLeft - ret;
```

```
                        index = index + ret;
                }

        }break;
        case 6:
        {
                if(gethostname(&RAM[R[$R2]],(int)R[$R3]))
                {
                        R[$R4]=1;
                }
                else
                {
                        R[$R4]=0;
                }

        }break;
        case 7:
        {
                struct hostent *hp;
                int i;

                hp = gethostbyname(&RAM[R[$R2]]);
                if(hp==NULL)
                {
                        R[$R4]=1;
                }
                else
                {
                        if((*hp).h_addr_list[0]!=0)
                        {
                                struct in_addr addr;
                                memcpy(&addr,
                                        (*hp).h_addr_list[0],
                                        sizeof(struct in_addr));
                                strcpy(&RAM[R[$R3]],inet_ntoa(addr));
                        }
                        for (i =1;(*hp).h_addr_list[i]!=0;++i)
                        {
                                struct in_addr addr;
                                memcpy(&addr,
                                        (*hp).h_addr_list[i],
                                        sizeof(struct in_addr));
                                strcat(&RAM[R[$R3]],":");
                                strcat(&RAM[R[$R3]],inet_ntoa(addr));
                        }

                        R[$R4]=0;
                }

        }break;
        case 8:
        {
                struct hostent *hp;
```

```
                        struct in_addr hostaddr;

                        hostaddr.s_addr = inet_addr(&RAM[R[$R2]]);

                        hp = gethostbyaddr((char *)&hostaddr,
                                           sizeof(struct in_addr),
                                           AF_INFT);
                        if(hp==NULL)
                        {
                            R[$R4]=1;
                        }
                        else
                        {
                            strcpy(&RAM[R[$R3]],(*hp).h_name);
                            R[$R4]=0;
                        }

                }break;
                case 9:
                {
                        struct sockaddr_in address;
                        int server;
                        int err;

                        address.sin_family=AF_INET;
                        address.sin_port = htons((unsigned short)R[$R3]);
                        address.sin_addr.s_addr = inet_addr(&RAM[R[$R2]]);

                        server = socket(AF_INET,SOCK_STREAM,0);
                        if(server==-1)
                        {
                            R[$R5]=1;
                        }
                        else
                        {
                            err = bind(server,
                                       &address,
                                       sizeof(address));
                            if(err==-1)
                            {
                                R[$R5]=1;
                            }
                            else
                            {
                                err = listen(server,5);
                                if(err==-1)
                                {
                                    R[$R5]=1;
                                }
                                else
                                {
                                    R[$R5]=0;
                                    R[$R4]=(U8)server;
                                }
```

```
                }
            }

        }break;
        case 10:
        {
            int connection;
            struct sockaddr_in client;
            int length;
            connection = accept((int)R[$R2],
                                &client,
                                &length);
            if(connection==-1)
            {
                /*printf("accept failed\n");*/
                R[$R5]=1;
            }
            else
            {
                R[$R5]=0;
                strcpy(&RAM[R[$R3]],inet_ntoa(client.sin_addr));
                R[$R4]=(U8)connection;
            }

        }break;
        case 11:
        {
            if(close((int)R[$R2]))
            {
                R[$R3]=1;
            }
            else
            {
                R[$R3]=0;
            }

        }break;
        case 12:
        {
            if(close((int)R[$R2]))
            {
                R[$R3]=1;
            }
            else
            {
                R[$R3]=0;
            }

        }break;
        default:
        {
            ERROR1_LVL2("INT 10 %lu function not handled",(U1)R[$R1]);
        }
    }
```

```
        return;

    }/*end handleIPC*/
```

Building HEC

I tried to make building HEC on Windows and Linux as easy as possible. To an extent, I think I succeeded. The source code trees for the Linux and Windows ports of the HEC virtual machine and their associated development tools are both located on the companion CD-ROM. An expanded view of these trees is supplied in Figure 8-9.

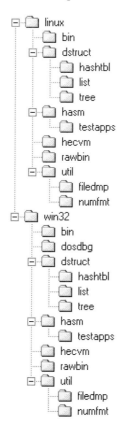

Figure 8-9

The source tree holds the source code to fundamental components, like the virtual machine (hecvm), the bytecode assembler (hasm), and binary utilities (filedmp and numfmt). However, I also included the source code to the data structures I discussed in Chapter 5 (hashtbl, list, and tree) and the code I used to build a bytecode executable from scratch (rawbin).

> **NOTE**   In the following discussion, I will be explaining how to build the Windows version of the HEC virtual machine. An equivalent version of this discussion applies to the Linux port and is available on the CD in the `\linux\linux.txt` file.

The first thing you need to do is copy the win32 branch from the CD-ROM to your hard drive. For the sake of this explanation, I will assume that everything is copied to `C:\hec\win32`.

```
C:\> copy D:\win32 C:\hec\win32
```

Next, you have to open a DOS window and execute Visual C++'s `vcvars32.bat` file (assuming that you have Visual Studio installed). This batch file is always located in the `bin` subdirectory of a Visual C++ installation.

```
C:\> C:\apps\devstudio\VC\bin\vcvars32.bat
```

This will allow the DOS session to find the necessary Visual Studio executables. Once this is done, you should change directories to where you copied the contents of the win32 source branch.

```
C:\> cd C:\hec\win32
```

From here you should execute the `bldall.bat` batch file, which will automatically build everything:

```
C:\hec\win32> bldall
```

> **NOTE**   When you run `mvbin.bat` or `bldapps.bat` for the first time, you may receive an `access denied` message. This is because the .exe and .RUN files you copied from the CD are read-only. You can correct the problem simply by either deleting the copied executables or changing their properties.

Once you have fresh executables, you should copy them to the `C:\hec\win32\bin` directory by executing the `mvbin.bat` batch file:

```
C:\hec\win32> mvbin
```

At this point, it might be a good idea to place `C:\hec\win32\bin>` into your PATH:

```
set PATH=C:\hec\win32\bin;%PATH%
```

Now you are ready to actually take HEC for a drive. Move to the testapps directory and execute the `bldapps.bat` batch file. This will invoke the HASM assembler so that all of the `.ASM` files are assembled.

```
C:\hec\win32\hasm\testapps\> bldapps
```

Once this batch file has completed, you can invoke the HEC virtual machine and execute some bytecode.

```
C:\hec\win32\hasm\testapps>..\..\bin\hecvm  timedate.RUN
allocating 132096 bytes
1000108253
53 50 7 10 8 101
53 50 0 10 8 101
Mon Sep 10 00:50:53 2001
```

```
Sat Sep 01 23:10:00 2001
-697253
```

If you want to make some modifications and rebuild, you might want to invoke the `wipe.bat` batch file to remove the old binaries.

To summarize, there are four basic batch files that you will deal with:

- `bldall.bat` — Builds all the win32 binaries

- `mvbin.bat` — Relocates the win32 binaries to the bin directory

- `bldapps.bat` — Assembles bytecode test suite

- `wipe.bat` — Removes old win32 executables

Rolling Your Own...Run-Time System

Creating and Following Trends

In the software game, you can follow someone else's lead or forge your own way. There are advantages and shortcomings to each alternative. I, however, am biased towards the latter.

Howard Bloom once made an interesting analogy between the evolution of our culture and a colony of bees. It seems that 95% of the time, most honey bees use the same well-known pastures that have a sufficient supply of pollen. There are, however, usually about 5% of the bees that go their own way and explore the uncharted territory farther away from the hive. These bees correspond to the visionaries in our society who have enough belief in their own ideas to take a chance with some new concept. Sometimes these bees discover valuable resources, and other times they just starve. Nevertheless, when the colony's normal pollen resources are exhausted, it is the pioneering of the small 5% contingent that allows the colony to survive.

 NOTE   As a scientist, what Howard Bloom is doing is attempting to elicit an aspect of a complex system (the human race) by examining a much simpler one (a bee colony). This is generally known in scientific circles as *constraining the problem*. By instituting limitations that focus attention on certain aspects of a problem, it's often easier to illuminate the underlying mechanics.

For the next few decades, we will witness the gradual demise of Moore's Law. Since the invention of the transistor, performance gains have been achieved by shrinking the dimensions of the transistors in a circuit. Eventually, this well-known path will no longer yield sufficient return. The colony will be in danger of stagnating. When this happens, like Howard says, it is that small group of 5% that will pave the way for the new approach.

Rather than follow someone else's virtual machine specification, I decided to create my own. Rather than follow the herd, I looked for a different route.

If you decide that my virtual machine is not to your liking, I would strongly encourage you to build your own. In order to help you do this, I've dedicated this section to showing you how you can build your own virtual machine.

In addition, constructing a virtual machine is a task that is very similar to building a hardware emulator. This happens to be one of the fundamental steps required to build an operating system. So, why not go the rest of the way and look at operating system construction? If you are curious about how operating systems are built, you are in luck because I decided to look at this topic also.

Project Management — Critical Paths

In the late 1950s, researchers began applying network theory to the planning, scheduling, and coordination of projects. Most approaches represented a project in terms of a graphical network called a *project network*, which is used to display *precedence relationships*. In other words, the project network displays which tasks must be performed before others. Project networks consist of *arcs* and *nodes*. An arc represents a particular activity and a node represents the moment in time when all activities leading to the node are completed. For example, Figure 8-10 displays the project network for compiling a C program.

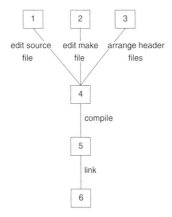

Figure 8-10

Figure 8-10 shows that different phases of a project can be completed in parallel. For example, during the editing phase the source file and make file can be modified in tandem. In addition, the figure also illustrates the precedence relationships between editing, compiling, and linking. You must edit before you compile, and compile before you link.

The basic goal of using a project network is to search for bottlenecks, evaluate scheduling changes, and identify critical paths. Without wading into the mathematical underpinnings of project management, a *critical path* is a path through a project network that cannot be altered without delaying the entire project. In the parlance of network theory, critical paths consist of activities that all have *zero slack*. This means that the activities cannot be delayed without affecting the entire project in a negative manner.

The previous definition is the (somewhat) formal description of a critical path. Typically, in the software industry, the term has a more general connotation. Informally, the term "critical path" defines a specific set of activities that must be performed in a particular sequence in order to complete a project. The critical path defines the collection of activities that will not tolerate being rearranged without making the project much more complicated (if not impossible). When this term is bandied around in a staff meeting, this is the intended meaning. This informal definition is the one I will use in the following two sections.

Run-Time System Critical Path

The best way to describe the critical path of the steps involved in building a run-time is with a network diagram. I begin by supplying such a diagram (see Figure 8-11) and then elaborate on the different steps.

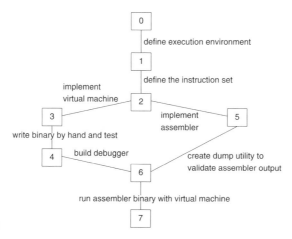

Figure 8-11

The first thing you have to do is establish the ground rules of the game. You have to decide on what kind of environment you want to execute in (i.e., stack based vs. register based) and what kind of address space the virtual machine will use. Once that is done, you will need to create an instruction set.

What happens next is a matter of personal preference. You can either construct an assembler first, or start with the virtual machine proper. Eventually you will have to merge them together so that you feel secure that the assembler is generating instructions that the virtual machine can process.

In terms of my own experience, building the virtual machine was more tedious than building the assembler. This is one reason I built the virtual machine first. In particular, I found that the only way to get a good look at the behavior of each instruction handler was to build a bytecode executable by hand, byte by agonizing byte. This way, I could institute subtle bitwise variations and test the results. I also felt more secure in terms of building the virtual machine first because I wanted to feel like I had a target ready for the assembler when it was complete. This is more of a psychological reason than anything else.

You may wonder why I build the debugger only after testing the virtual machine with a hand-built executable. Wouldn't it be easier to test the executable with a debugger? I decided that I would rather make sure that the virtual machine did what it was supposed to before I plugged in a debugger module. This may have been more tedious, but it helped me to sleep better at night.

If you have a team of developers, and you're able to nail down the ground rules with regard to the instruction set encoding, you could have one group of engineers build the assembler and another group of engineers build the virtual machine. The group with the most bugs has to answer the tech support lines.

Operating System Critical Path

The art of bootstrapping an operating system has always fascinated me. I can remember in 1985 when the next-door neighbor, who was an electrical engineer, told me that an operating system was just another kind of computer program. This caused me to think: "Well, if the operating system is a program, what is loading and executing the operating system?"

A lot of my questions were answered in 1987 when Andrew Tanenbaum presented Minix to the world. Finally, I had my hands on commercial-grade source code. However, the source code really only explained the operation of Minix. There was no HOWTO that gave me any idea on how I could go about building my own operating system.

My primary motivation behind presenting this mini-HOWTO is that it might be able to inspire the development of new, completely different operating systems. To be honest, the status of operating system design has become pretty stagnant. There's really about a handful of production-quality operating systems in the market. Someone needs to stir up the water a little and create something new. Remember, evolution favors change and permutation. If we're going to advance, we need to innovate, and I'm not talking about building application components into the operating system.

Part of the problem is due to the byzantine complexity that is inherent in operating system architecture. Hundreds of thousands of hardware-related details make it easy to become lost in the trees. The result is that software engineers tend to fixate on existing systems instead of playing with new ideas. To be honest, the last time I felt like I had encountered a revolutionary idea in operating system implementation was when Andrew Tanenbaum made key Minix kernel components, like the file system and memory manager, completely pluggable. Which is to say that they could be replaced without having to recompile the kernel. That was quite a while back.

In my opinion, the key to spurring evolution is to make new ideas accessible. In order for advances to benefit a civilization, they have to be effectively propagated. The more accessible software is, the easier it is for the general public to assimilate it. Accessibility is what largely accounts for the success of Windows and Linux. Anyone with enough money to get their hands on a PC can run these operating systems. It's no big surprise, then, that Windows now owns a hefty chunk of the server market. By locking their Unix implementations to hardware and keeping the price out of reach of the ordinary software engineer, the commercial Unix vendors, which prospered in the 1980s, may very well be dooming themselves to a shrinking niche market.

NOTE The critical path for operating system construction that I'm about to describe was passed down to me by a couple of old fogeys from Control Data named Mike Adler and George Matkovitz. Mike told me that this basic scheme was used by CDC to develop the Scope 76 operating system for the CDC 7600. George was able to supplement Mike's recollection with a few of his own experiences. Although the design strategies Mike and George described were used back in the 1960s and 1970s, you will see that they are still pertinent enough to be applied to modern system implementation.

As it turns out, building a functioning operating system involves just a few steps more than those required for building a virtual machine. In light of this, the network diagram for operating system construction is really just an extension of the virtual machine network diagram presented in the last section (see Figure 8-12).

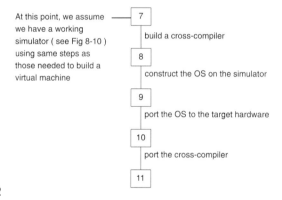

Figure 8-12

The idea is to begin by constructing a software-based simulator that can emulate the behavior of the target hardware platform. You can think of a simulator as a virtual machine that is highly focused on imitating a given processor. Performance and portability really aren't valued as much as the ability to serve as a believable replacement for the actual hardware.

Once you have an emulator in place, you need to build a cross-compiler. The cross-compiler will run on the same operating system you built the simulator on. However, the cross-compiler will generate executables that will be run by the simulator. This will allow you to build a new operating system from the safety and comfort of an existing platform. Indeed, some existing operating systems are like old reclining chairs to which we become accustomed. It's always better to fight from the high ground and work on a platform with which you are already familiar.

In the old days (i.e., the 1960s), sometimes a simulator was used because the hardware didn't exist yet. In this case, building a simulator could prove frustrating as hardware specifications tended to change frequently. This was back when a smoke test really meant that the hardware might start to smoke. Today, however, the simulator is the equivalent of the X-Men's danger room. It is a specially controlled environment that allows hazardous operations to be performed without having to worry about killing anything.

The advantage of this approach is that it allows you to get a better idea of what the operating system code is doing. If you ran the operating system code on the actual hardware, and the hardware crashed, you would have little or no way to find out why it crashed. The hardware would shut the machine down and you would be left with a blank screen. If you are lucky, the chip techies might be able to soup up your development machine to do something like store the crashed machine's state in flash RAM. The only other recourse would be to carefully scan the source code, which can really soak up a lot of time.

With a simulator, you can observe problems in what is basically an experimental laboratory. If a problem occurs, you can program the simulator to fail gracefully so as to allow you to perform a kind of digital autopsy. You can muck around with a lab coat on, like Agent Scully surveying the crime scene and making observations on the likely cause of death.

In terms of implementing the operating system proper, Richard Burgess (the architect of MMURTL) recommends that you implement the basic components in the following order:

- Process management and communication

- Memory management

- File system

- Device I/O

I would tend to agree with Richard's advice. You should try to start with the core, the kernel, and work your way outward.

One thing you might want to keep in mind is that it is a wise decision to insulate your operating system from the hardware it runs on. For example, interrupts on the Intel platform should be immediately wrapped by a much more abstract interface. This will allow you to port your creation later on. When Dave Cutler designed Windows NT, he made sure to include what is known as a Hardware Abstraction Layer (HAL). The HAL is what allowed Windows NT to be ported to other platforms besides Intel.

Note that insulating your operating system from hardware is not just a matter of keeping certain source files in different directories. It is also a matter of making careful design decisions so that the basic operation of the kernel does not rely upon the peculiarities of a given processor. The safest assumption you can make is that your hardware interface will change every couple of years.

If you want a really good example of an operating system that is portable, take a look at NetBSD. Portability is NetBSD's claim to fame. The online manuals that describe the process of porting NetBSD will probably be able to offer you a couple of ideas as to how you can keep your own operating system portable. The last time I visited the NetBSD Internet site, one engineer was in the process of porting NetBSD to a Playstation!

Once you have an operating system running on the simulator, you'll need to cross your fingers and move the operating system over to the target hardware. If there's a problem, it's probably due to a design flaw in your simulator, particularly if your operating system code functions normally on the simulator. Once the operating system has been successfully ported, you'll need to bootstrap the cross-compiler. This is performed by allowing the cross-compiler to build its own source code so that it effectively creates a compiler that runs on the new operating system. This is illustrated in Figure 8-13.

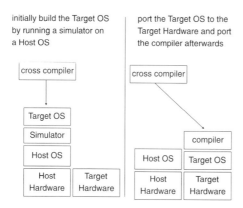

Figure 8-13

That's it. The simulator and cross-compiler are both major investments. Compared to the alternative, which is working in the dark, they are worthwhile undertakings.

References

Compiler Theory

There are a lot of books devoted to compiler and language design. However, just like any other field, there is an elite set of really good books. What follows is what I view as the best of the best.

Aho, Alfred, Ravi Sethi, and Jeffrey Ullman. *Compilers: Principles, Techniques, and Tools*. Addison-Wesley, 1988. ISBN: 0201100886.

> The celebrated "Dragon Book." For several years, this was the book on compilers. Its failure to address contemporary topics is one of this book's shortcomings. However, the example at the end of Chapter 2 is still a good introduction for beginners.

Grune, Dick, Henri Bal, Cerial Jacobs, and Koen Langendoen. *Modern Compiler Design*. John Wiley, 2001. ISBN: 0471976970.

> In my opinion, this is the book that will replace the Dragon Book. Its strong points are that it is current, covers a lot of object-oriented material, and is easy to understand. Those features place this book on deck to become the compiler text.

Leon, Steven. *Linear Algebra with Applications*. Macmillan, 1986. ISBN: 0023698101.

Levine, John. *Linkers and Loaders*. Morgan Kaufmann Publishers, 1999. ISBN: 1558604960.

> Building a linker or a loader is still somewhat of a hidden art. This is the only book that I know of on the topic. This book also explains the idiosyncrasies of several popular file formats.

Muchnick, Steven. *Advanced Compiler Design and Implementation*. Morgan Kaufmann Publishers, 1997. ISBN: 1558603204.

This book is just what it says: advanced. Its most notable feature is that it has several chapters devoted to back-end code generation. In particular, this book provides an exhaustive treatment of optimization.

Scott, Michael. *Programming Language Pragmatics*. Morgan Kaufmann Publishers, 2000. ISBN: 1558604421.

This is an introductory book on programming language and compiler theory. It's easy to read and understand. Given this text's recent publishing date, it also looks into contemporary subjects like exception handling. My only objection is that Scott does not spend enough time discussing implementation issues.

Crypto

There is not a lot of current, industrial-strength literature available on cryptography and cryptanalysis. These are the sources that I'm familiar with.

Menezes, Alfred, Paul Oorschot, and Scott Vanstone. *Handbook of Applied Cryptography*. CRC Press, 1997. ISBN: 0849385237.

Schneier, Bruce. *Applied Cryptography, Second Edition*. John Wiley, 1996. ISBN: 0471128457.

Of the three books listed in this section, this book is by far the most readable and engrossing. The afterword authored by Matt Blaze could be likened to Robert Brooks' "No Silver Bullet" essay with regard to cryptosystem security.

Stinson, Douglas. *Cryptography Theory and Practice*. CRC Press, 1995. ISBN: 0849385210.

Exceptions

There are almost no books that venture into exception handling with any sort of depth. Most of the rigorous treatments are online or can be purchased from journals.

Boling, Elie, and Peter Kukol. "Underneath Structured Exceptions & C++ Exceptions." http://www.borland.com.

This is an explanation of exception handling in terms of the Borland C++ exception interface to OS/2. It's a look under the hood at an exception handling approach that shifts a lot of record-keeping responsibility to the operating system.

Christensen, Morten. "Methods for Handling Exceptions in Object-oriented Programming Languages." Odense University, Denmark, Department of Mathematics and Computer Science, 1995.

This is a very readable and well-done master's thesis. It's absolutely free and available online.

Schilling, Jonathan. "Optimizing Away C++ Exception Handling." http://www.sco.com.

This paper focuses on optimizing the static, table-driven approach to exception handling as it is implemented in SCO C++.

Java

There are several places in this chapter that I use Java to illustrate a concept. If you are new to Java, I would recommend getting your hands on the following books.

Arnold, Ken, and James Gosling. *The Java Programming Language, Second Edition*. Addison-Wesley. ISBN: 0201310066.

In my opinion, James Gosling ranks right up there with Dennis Ritchie, Bjarne Stroustrup, and Kenneth Iverson. Java is the brainchild of James Gosling. Scott McNealy told James to go do something interesting, and Java was born.

Campione, Mary, and Kathy Walrath. *The Java Tutorial, Second Edition*. Addison-Wesley, 1998. ISBN: 0201310074.

This book allows you to familiarize yourself with the Java language by presenting a large number of bite-size examples. The tutorial is organized into a series of trials that allow you to focus on particular areas. This book is the most painless way to learn the ins and outs of Java.

Flanagan, David. *Java in a Nutshell*. O'Reilly, 1997. ISBN: 156592262.

This book is a good reference source for the bare essential parts of the language. The Java API has exploded in size and scope to the point that there are more packages not covered by this book than there are documented in the book.

Linux

As I mentioned earlier, the online Linux help is fragmented, disorganized, and incomplete. It is a good thing that I had the following two books on hand to help me perform the port. Without these books, I would not have been able to do it.

Johnson, Michael K., and Erik W. Troan. *Linux Application Development*. Addison-Wesley, 1998. ISBN: 0201308215.

Eureka! These guys covered most of the essential Linux API topics that I really needed (file I/O, time and dates, process management, sockets, etc.). The only shortcoming of this book is that it really doesn't cover semaphores.

Welsh, Matt, Matthias Kalle Dalheimer, and Lar Kaufman. *Running Linux*. O'Reilly, 1999. ISBN: 156592469X.

This book does an excellent job of managing to cover many different topics in sufficient detail. This is the book I would recommend to a beginner.

Appendix

numfmt Utility

The numfmt utility can be used to display the bytes that represent a given number. I used this program during the development of the assembler to verify that the assembler was generating the correct bytecode. The numfmt program has the following command line:

```
numfmt type  value
```

The type field can be one of the following values:

Table A-1

Type	Description
d	Value is assumed to be a double-precision float
f	Value is assumed to be a single-precision float
i	Value is assumed to be an integer
c	Value is assumed to be an ASCII character
w	Value is assumed to be a wide (16-bit) character

For example, entering the following command:

```
numfmt    i    -129
```

displays the output:

```
DEC [0]->[7]    [+127][+255][+255][+255][+255][+255][+255][+255]
DEC [7]->[0]    [+255][+255][+255][+255][+255][+255][+255][+127]
HEX [0]->[7]    [  7f][  ff][  ff][  ff][  ff][  ff][  ff][  ff]
BIN [0] [01111111]
BIN [1] [11111111]
BIN [2] [11111111]
BIN [3] [11111111]
BIN [4] [11111111]
BIN [5] [11111111]
BIN [6] [11111111]
BIN [7] [11111111]
```

The program begins by printing out the bytes that constitute the value in decimal format. The first row starts with the lowest address in memory (i.e., index 0 in the byte array). From this we can infer that we are running on a little-endian platform because the lowest order byte (0x7F) is the first. Decimal output is followed by hexadecimal and binary equivalents.

filedmp Utility

The filedmp command processes a bytecode executable and emits a summary of its contents. This includes the bytecode executable's header, debug information, and the bytecode section itself. As with numfmt, this program helped me check whether the HASM assembler was doing its job.

In general, I would usually test the HASM assembler by processing an assembly source file and examining the listing file the HASM assembler produced. Then I would validate the listing file using numfmt and by comparing the listing against the output produced by filedmp.

The filedmp program has a very simple command line:

```
filedmp    filename.RUN
```

Following is an example. We will invoke filedmp on the ipc1.RUN executable created in Chapter 6. The command:

```
filedmp    ipc1.RUN
```

produces the following output:

```
HEADER------------------------>
magic=DEED
bytes in symbol table 65
bytes in string table 18
bytes in bytecode 259

SYMBOL TABLE------------------>
PROC 0
     id=main
     address=0
     line=2
     LOCAL->0
          id=buffer
          fpOffset=-40
          line=3
     LOCAL->1
          id=mutex
          fpOffset=-64
          line=4

STRING TABLE------------------>
0)main(null)
1)buffer(null)
2)mutex(null)

BYTECODE---------------------->
address=0                        [ 23][  2][ 32][  2][  1][  3][ 14][  0]
address=8                        [  0][  0][  0][  0][  0][  0][ 64][ 54]
address=16                       [  1][  1][ 14][  7][ 17][  2][255][255]
address=24                       [255][255][255][255][255][192][ 32][ 21]
address=32                       [ 17][  0][  9][  1][  0][  8][109][ 14]
address=40                       [  8][ 17][ 53][ 17][ 17][  9][  0][  8]
address=48                       [105][ 14][  8][ 17][ 53][ 17][ 17][  9]
```

```
address=56     [  0][  8][110][ 14][  8][ 17][ 53][ 17]
address=64     [ 17][  9][  0][  8][101][ 14][  8][ 17]
address=72     [ 53][ 17][ 17][  9][  0][  8][  0][ 14]
address=80     [  8][ 17][ 32][  9][ 21][  3][  8][  0]
address=88     [  0][  0][  0][  0][  0][  0][  0][ 39]
address=96     [ 10][ 32][ 22][ 10][ 32][  9][ 21][  3]
address=104    [  8][  0][  0][  0][  0][  0][  0][  0]
address=112    [ 18][ 39][  0][  3][  9][  0][  0][  0]
address=120    [  0][  0][  0][  0][ 10][  3][  8][  0]
address=128    [  0][  0][  0][  0][  0][  0][ 16][ 39]
address=136    [  0][  3][  9][  0][  0][  0][  0][  0]
address=144    [  0][  0][ 13][  3][  8][  0][  0][  0]
address=152    [  0][  0][  0][  0][ 16][ 39][  0][  7]
address=160    [  9][  2][255][255][255][255][255][255]
address=168    [255][216][  3][  8][  0][  0][  0][  0]
address=176    [  0][  0][  0][ 22][ 39][  0][  3][  8]
address=184    [  0][  0][  0][  0][  0][  0][  0][ 18]
address=192    [ 39][  0][  3][  9][  0][  0][  0][  0]
address=200    [  0][  0][  0][ 10][  3][  8][  0][  0]
address=208    [  0][  0][  0][  0][  0][ 16][ 39][  0]
address=216    [  3][  9][  0][  0][  0][  0][  0][  0]
address=224    [  0][ 13][  3][  8][  0][  0][  0][  0]
address=232    [  0][  0][  0][ 16][ 39][  0][ 32][  9]
address=240    [ 22][  3][  8][  0][  0][  0][  0][  0]
address=248    [  0][  0][  1][ 39][ 10][ 32][  1][  2]
address=256    [ 29][  2][ 42]
```

As you can see, the symbol table information is displayed in a format that is very similar to the summary placed at the end of a HASM listing file. The bytecode section is decomposed into a series of eight-byte rows. The leftmost byte in each row corresponds to the lowest address in that row. The value of the leftmost byte's address is provided on the left-hand side of the row by an `address=xxx` field.

Index

About the CD

The CD-ROM included with this book contains the source code for both the Win32 and Linux ports of the HEC distribution. The HEC distribution includes the HEC virtual machine, assembler, debugger, and associated development utilities. I also included source code for some of the data structures discussed in Chapter 5. Building the HEC distribution is easy and quick, as described in detail in Chapter 8. I made a point of implementing simple build scripts, so that anybody who is remotely familiar with Windows or Linux should be able to perform a build.

Bill Blunden

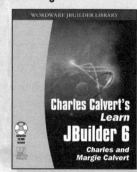

CD/Source Code Usage License Agreement

Please read the following CD/Source Code usage license agreement before opening the CD and using the contents therein:

1. By opening the accompanying software package, you are indicating that you have read and agree to be bound by all terms and conditions of this CD/Source Code usage license agreement.

2. The compilation of code and utilities contained on the CD and in the book are copyrighted and protected by both U.S. copyright law and international copyright treaties, and is owned by Wordware Publishing, Inc. Individual source code, example programs, help files, freeware, shareware, utilities, and evaluation packages, including their copyrights, are owned by the respective authors.

3. No part of the enclosed CD or this book, including all source code, help files, shareware, freeware, utilities, example programs, or evaluation programs, may be made available on a public forum (such as a World Wide Web page, FTP site, bulletin board, or Internet news group) without the express written permission of Wordware Publishing, Inc. or the author of the respective source code, help files, shareware, freeware, utilities, example programs, or evaluation programs.

4. You may not decompile, reverse engineer, disassemble, create a derivative work, or otherwise use the enclosed programs, help files, freeware, shareware, utilities, or evaluation programs except as stated in this agreement.

5. The software, contained on the CD and/or as source code in this book, is sold without warranty of any kind. Wordware Publishing, Inc. and the authors specifically disclaim all other warranties, express or implied, including but not limited to implied warranties of merchantability and fitness for a particular purpose with respect to defects in the disk, the program, source code, sample files, help files, freeware, shareware, utilities, and evaluation programs contained therein, and/or the techniques described in the book and implemented in the example programs. In no event shall Wordware Publishing, Inc., its dealers, its distributors, or the authors be liable or held responsible for any loss of profit or any other alleged or actual private or commercial damage, including but not limited to special, incidental, consequential, or other damages.

6. One (1) copy of the CD or any source code therein may be created for backup purposes. The CD and all accompanying source code, sample files, help files, freeware, shareware, utilities, and evaluation programs may be copied to your hard drive. With the exception of freeware and shareware programs, at no time can any part of the contents of this CD reside on more than one computer at one time. The contents of the CD can be copied to another computer, as long as the contents of the CD contained on the original computer are deleted.

7. You may not include any part of the CD contents, including all source code, example programs, shareware, freeware, help files, utilities, or evaluation programs in any compilation of source code, utilities, help files, example programs, freeware, shareware, or evaluation programs on any media, including but not limited to CD, disk, or Internet distribution, without the express written permission of Wordware Publishing, Inc. or the owner of the individual source code, utilities, help files, example programs, freeware, shareware, or evaluation programs.

8. You may use the source code, techniques, and example programs in your own commercial or private applications unless otherwise noted by additional usage agreements as found on the CD.

CAUTION   By opening the CD package, you accept the terms and conditions of the CD/Source Code Usage License Agreement.
   Additionally, opening the CD package makes this book nonreturnable.
